Carl Sagan

A Life

Keay Davidson

John Wiley & Sons, Inc.

New York • Chichester • Weinheim • Brisbane • Singapore • Toronto

Published by John Wiley & Sons, Inc.
Published simultaneously in Canada.

This publication is designed to provide accurate and authoritative information in
regard to the subject matter covered. It is sold with the understanding that the publisher is not engaged in rendering professional services. If professional advice or other
expert assistance is required, the services of a competent professional person should be
sought.

Library of Congress Cataloging-in-Publication Data

Davidson, Keay.
    Carl Sagan : a life / Keay Davidson.
        p.   cm.
    Includes bibliographical references and index.
    ISBN 0-471-25286-7 (alk. paper)
    1. Sagan, Carl, 1934–1996. 2. Astronomers—United States
Biography.   I. Sagan, Carl, 1934–1996.   II. Title.
QB36.S15D38   1999
520′.92—dc21
    [B]   99-36206

Printed in the United States of America
10 9 8 7 6 5 4 3 2 1

This book is dedicated to the memory of space scientist
James B. Pollack (1938–1994)
and to the work of the
National Organization of Gay and Lesbian Scientists
and Technical Professionals Inc. (NOGLSTP) in Pasadena, California.

The test of a first-rate intelligence is the ability to hold two opposed ideas in the mind at the same time, and still retain the ability to function.

—*F. Scott Fitzgerald*

Each psyche is really an ant-hill of opposing predispositions. Personality as something with fixed attributes is an illusion.

—*Lawrence Durrell*

Contents

Illustrations follow page 282

Preface

One autumn evening in 1969, when I was sixteen, I skipped my homework and instead sprawled on my bed, reading a wondrous book published a few years earlier: *Intelligent Life in the Universe*. The authors were two astronomers, a Russian named I. S. Shklovskii and an American, Carl Sagan. This book changed my life. I suspect that if I hadn't read it, I would not have spent much of the past three decades thinking, reading, and writing about many of the things about which I think, read, and write. Early in the book appears a black-and-white photo of a cloud of stars, somewhere near the center of our galaxy. "There are approximately a million stars in this photograph," the caption states. "According to the estimates of Chapter 29, a planet of one of these stars holds a technical civilization vastly in advance of our own." I stared at that photograph, entranced, for a long time.

By the late 1960s I had ceased to believe in God. Without God, the cosmos seemed drabber—just molecules and plasma—and quite pointless. But a new, more enchanting cosmos was offered by Sagan and Shklovskii. In their conception, the galaxies were like mammoth Petri dishes, brimming with life. On millions of worlds, microbes had probably evolved into intelligent beings. Perhaps these beings were curious about the rest of the cosmos and were seeking other beings by transmitting radio signals in all directions. Perhaps their centuries of accumulated learning, encoded in invisible electromagnetic waves, were passing through my bedroom at that very moment. Sagan and Shklovskii defended this view on grounds that seemed perfectly rational and perfectly "scientific," and that remain so today.

However, people can believe in rational things for irrational reasons. Indeed, as historians of science increasingly acknowledge, the history of science makes more sense if one takes into account the occasional importance of non-rational factors (social prejudices, political tendencies, religious influences, and so on). In retrospect, I realize that as a youth, I accepted the notion of alien life for a fundamentally psychological reason, namely to fill a spiritual void within. I *wanted* to believe in aliens, so I did, and I tacked on the scientific rationales (which are perfectly valid in their own right) after the fact.

And—truth be told—Sagan, the great "rationalist," did the same thing. He admitted as much in his 1985 novel, *Contact*, through the introspections of his alter ego, the fictional radioastronomer Ellie Arroway. This contradicts the accusations of those (especially on the political right) who accused him of being "scientistic" and hyper-logical. On the contrary, in his Pulitzer Prize–winning book, *The Dragons of Eden* (1977), Sagan affirmed the value of both rational and irrational ("intuitive," some prefer to call them) insights; they walk hand in hand down the great road to Truth.

Sagan and Shklovskii's book was enthralling for terrestrial reasons as well. It was published in 1966, not too many years after the United States and the Soviet Union had almost blown each other to smithereens over Cuba. To a generation of schoolchildren raised on cold war propaganda and trained in "duck and cover" exercises, the idea that Soviet and American scientists might coauthor a book (such collaborations are routine nowadays) seemed only slightly less fantastic than the notion that invisible alien messages were passing through my suburb. Shklovskii and Sagan's "remarkable collaboration" (as the *Washington Post* called it) presaged the other great activity of Sagan's life: helping to prevent our civilization from self-destructing. In time, he would become a feared foe of the military, the Reagan Administration, and the nuclear weapons establishment.

Sagan was different things to different people. To a generation of young Americans, his eloquence on television and the printed page was an irresistible summons to scientific careers. To his scientific colleagues, he was a sometimes stimulating, sometimes upsetting gadfly who proposed both brilliant and irresponsible ideas about the solar system. To NASA, he was its most valued—albeit unofficial and erratic—propagandist. To diehard cold warriors, he was a fuzzy-headed, left-leaning academic who meddled in the machinery of nuclear weapons policy. To some conservatives and cultural traditionalists, he was a suspicious symbol of atheism, secularism, and naively rationalistic "scientism."

But to the general public—which tends to resent science for undermining religious faith and New Age folklore—he offered an alluring compensation for all that science has destroyed. That compensation was a vast and fascinating cosmos, wherein exotic beings chatter by radiotelescope and explore via starship. Critics had accused science of robbing the cosmos of old enchantments—gods, angels, astrological forces. But Sagan re-enchanted the stars in new, scientific-sounding ways purged of medieval irrationalisms (but invested with new, modern, alluring ones, such as the idea of benevolent aliens who would transmit instructions for solving terrestrial problems).

He was a hero of my childhood and youth. But a childhood hero is a dangerous thing to have, because one eventually outgrows childhood. One summer evening at a poolside party in Santa Cruz, I was seated next to the physicist-author Freeman Dyson. I asked him if he ever had a hero. "Yes," he replied, "and I was unfortunate enough to meet him." (Dyson's hero was the brilliant but cantankerous geneticist J. B. S. Haldane.) In that regard, when I began this project, the writer Timothy Ferris warned me that some biographers end up hating the subjects of their biographies. Indeed, I was worried about what I might learn about Sagan; like all professional science writers, I had heard some less than flattering stories about him. (Not all proved to be true.) His most serious flaws involved interpersonal relations. Three marriages—that tells you something. And consider this: he dedicated three of his books to intimates (*The Dragons of Eden* to Linda Salzman, *Comet* to Shirley Arden, and *Shadows of Forgotten Ancestors* to Lester Grinspoon); he eventually had falling-outs with them all, one by one. One of his oldest associates, the distinguished planetary scientist Tobias Owen, declined to discuss Sagan with me because he felt uncomfortable talking about what he called Sagan's "Jekyll and Hyde" character. Yet after scrutinizing Sagan's life in detail, I must say that I not only still like him but respect him more than ever; his personal foibles are not atypical of ambitious males, and are far outweighed by his virtues. Because he lived, the world is a better place.

As a scientist, Sagan speculated freely, sometimes wildly, and outraged his more cautious colleagues. A few regarded him as a charlatan. Even some of his closer mentors, notably Gerard Kuiper and Harold Urey, nursed serious doubts about his sense of scientific responsibility. Yet he helped to pioneer much of modern space science, particularly the subject of planetary atmospheres. He also raised a crop of graduate students, who now launch robotic explorers to the planets.

Sagan was also something of a prophet. He anticipated some interesting scientific discoveries, although sometimes (and oddly) for the wrong reasons. A striking example has come to light since his death. In the mid-1960s he and his colleague Jim Pollack suggested that Mars once underwent horizontal crustal motion (partly akin to terrestrial plate tectonics). They based this suggestion on the belief that Mars was covered with linear geological ridges, which they thought might be the true nature of the legendary "canals." They argued that horizontal crustal motion had compressed the crust, raising the ridges. Sure enough, in May 1999, NASA scientists reported magnetic observations of Mars indicating that the planet might have undergone horizontal crustal motion some four billion years ago. Yet (as has been positively known since the 1970s) the "canals" do not exist; they are purely psychophysiological illusions! In other words, Sagan's crustal theory was on the right track, yet it was based on a completely erroneous assumption.

What are we to make of this? Should the Sagan-Pollack paper be dismissed as a "lucky guess"? Or do they deserve some credit for vaguely anticipating an important geological discovery about Mars? (The history of science is full of scientists who anticipated correct theories for at least partly incorrect reasons—for example, Nicolaus Copernicus, who argued that Earth orbits the Sun, and Alfred Wegener, the best-known pioneer of continental drift theory.) Sagan's career contains a number of other such "lucky guesses." Another example is a paper that Sagan and Richard Isaacman published in 1977 that suggested, based on computer modeling of planetary formation, that giant planets might form extremely close to alien stars. Is it just a coincidence, then, that astronomers have recently discovered many giant extrasolar planets, an amazing number of which are far closer to their parent stars than once thought possible?[1] Sagan may also have been prophetic in his and George Mullen's early work on the possible role of ammonia in warming Earth's early atmosphere. Long criticized, this notion was revived in a paper written by Sagan and Christopher Chyba and published in *Science* magazine after Sagan's death. As space scientist James P. Kasting observed in an editorial for *Science* several months after Sagan's death, "It seems likely that his excellent scientific intuition will once again be found to be correct."[2]

Even if such lucky guesses are nothing more than that—lucky guesses—they are instructive reminders of a little-appreciated fact: Science does *not* usually evolve in the simple, linear, logical ways still described in many high school textbooks (as well as many scientific papers). Rather, science often advances via lucky guesses, offbeat hunches, reckless speculation. This is especially true of "frontier" sciences such as space science, where little is known and the race often goes to the swift and the imaginative rather than to the plodding and the cautious. Appropriately, after Sagan's death in December 1996, *Nature* magazine called him "a pivotal figure in [the] exploration of the solar system."

He is best known, though, as a science popularizer—in particular, as the host of the 1980 television series *Cosmos*, which drew about a half-billion viewers around the world. Sagan was "the greatest popularizer of the 20th century," Stephen Jay Gould wrote in *Science* magazine after Sagan's death. The National Academy of Sciences, awarding him its Public Welfare Medal in 1994, noted that to the public, "Carl Sagan's name may be associated more with science than that of any other living U.S. scientist."

The price of fame is a big head, and Sagan's head grew mighty big; eyewitness testimony to this effect abounds. As much as I admired him, I was always bothered by his seeming imperturbability and omniscience. Nothing seemed to rattle him, at least in public, and he had an answer (sometimes a glib one) for almost everything. Most scientists, by contrast, are rarely so self-assured. To them Truth is like a blob of mercury—it's hard to pin down. Sagan's air of omniscience made him seem sometimes slightly inhuman, more like Mr. Spock than Mr. Wizard.

Now that I have explored his life for two years, I understand him better. Now his imperturbability strikes me less as arrogance than as a half-conscious pose—the "objective" pose that is part of the propagandistic and rhetorical style of elite scientists. This hyper-dignified, above-it-all, judgelike and priestlike demeanor inspires others to perceive these scientists as they wish to be perceived; that is, as objective, neutral, and able to assess data without prejudice. That public perception accounts (justifiably or not) for much of the prestige of science. If scientists were not any of these things, then why would they be any more trustworthy than poets, artists, preachers, or politicians?

Which raises a troubling point. In hands other than Sagan's, that rhetorical style—that priestlike self-assurance—has often led modern society to grief. Witness science and technology's recent debacles, from Bhopal and thalidomide to Chernobyl and the *Challenger* explosion. Such tragedies often stem from the entrenchment of scientific decision-making in too few hands. Witness, also, the scientific-sounding (and often near-demented) reasoning behind the construction of the two superpowers' nuclear weapons complexes, which for almost a half-century threatened all life on Earth. Incredible as it seems now, in the late 1960s the mayor of Libertyville, Illinois, proposed acquiescing to a nearby military nuclear weapons project because the "experts" knew what was best for the American people. (The "almost miraculous technology of our world today has far surpassed our meager ability to comprehend," the mayor explained. "Under these circumstances, it would certainly seem more prudent to place our confidence and security in the hands of those whose lives are dedicated to the profession of defending and protecting our lives, our loved ones, and our properties than to try to accumulate sufficient knowledge to make an independent decision.")

If "experts" could always be trusted to make the right moral decision, then public participation would not be necessary—but they cannot be, and so it is. Too often, the "expertise" of experts is a camouflage for special interests, prejudices, and bureaucratic priorities. No one should be required to have a Ph.D. in nuclear engineering to be entitled to an opinion on nuclear power, or in genetics to hold one on the genetic engineering of crops, any more than one should be required to have a doctorate in constitutional law to have an opinion on a candidate for the Supreme Court, or a degree in monetary policy to comment on an appointment to the Federal Reserve.

Still, a certain minimal knowledge is essential; otherwise, in a high-tech, knowledge-based society, democracy becomes meaningless. Hence the need (an ever-growing one) for popularizers. That was one reason Sagan worked so hard to educate the public about "nuclear winter" issues in the 1980s—to convince people that the technical issues of nuclear strategy and weaponry were *not* incomprehensible and that they were entitled to have opinions on them. Warfare is too important to be left to the generals, Clemenceau said; likewise, nuclear weapons are too important to be left to the weaponeers.

Unfortunately, Sagan leaves no obvious successor—no other scientist who shares his extraordinarily diverse interests, literary ability, show-manship, scientific prowess, and progressive politics. He was a Renaissance man. But sadly, the trend in science is away from Renaissance men (and women). As Big Science becomes Big Business—as universities clamor for software and biotechnology contracts, for example—it under-goes an increasing division of labor, akin to that in factories. Hence we see fewer and fewer multidisciplinarians like Sagan who are unafraid of breaching the walls between specialties. In turn, this decline of multidis-ciplinarity could have long-term political consequences. People who are afraid of transgressing intellectual boundaries are less likely to see the forest as well as the trees and, hence, to challenge societal misuses of sci-ence. "Now, we only rarely find the distinguished scientist or other type of public figure capable of exercising moral leadership," Paul Joseph laments in the socialist journal *New Politics*. "The Carl Sagans are few and far between."[3]

Sagan was part of the great tradition of knowledge popularization, a tradition with expressions as diverse as Will and Ariel Durant's histories, the popular science books of Isaac Asimov and Lancelot Hogben, and the television shows of "Mr. Wizard." This tradition has a core convic-tion: For democracy to continue working in an increasingly knowledge-dependent age, knowledge must be democratized. Knowledge is power.

Acknowledgments

Hundreds of people assisted me in this project. Here are some of the more important ones.

First thanks goes to Carl Sagan himself, who, through his writings, helped inspire me to become a science writer.

Emily Loose, my editor at Wiley, originally proposed this project. She then oversaw it from start to finish; her wisdom, patience, and good humor are a writer's dream. Also thanks to my copy editor, Nancy Tenney, to Marcia Samuels, who managed production, and to my agent, Russell Galen.

Other than Emily, my closest confidante in this project was my friend Barbara Gallagher. She carefully read the entire manuscript and made numerous shrewd suggestions, especially on psychological issues and the history and philosophy of science. She also brought to the project her great warmth, humor, and energy, which made the bad times easier.

I am especially indebted to the brilliant and endearing Annie Druyan, who persuaded other Sagan family members to talk to me; to Nick Sagan, whose affectionate but frank observations on his father's psyche influenced my own; to Dorion Sagan, whose erudite and irreverent critique of his dad's philosophy of science convinced me that mine was on the right track; and to Sagan's sister, Cari Greene, who offered irreplaceable insights into the lives of their parents, Rachel and Sam Sagan. Also thanks to the amazing Lynn Margulis, who for two days welcomed me into her home and treated me like a son.

Also much appreciation to Lucille Nahemow, for sharing her priceless oral history interview with her mother, a onetime intimate of the young Rachel Sagan.

I am profoundly grateful to Ronald E. Doel. A historian of science, he brilliantly critiqued the manuscript line by line. Sometimes we disagreed, and I did not always take his advice (probably to my misfortune), but I always learned from him. In the best spirit of scholarship, he selflessly shared unpublished documents from his research on the history of solar system astronomy, including his unpublished taped interview with Sagan in 1991. In this interview, Sagan's remarkably frank and self-critical remarks (quoted extensively herein, with permission from Doel and Annie Druyan) shed light on numerous otherwise puzzling aspects of his career.

I am also deeply thankful to the distinguished astronomers/planetary scientists who read virtually the entire manuscript and offered many important suggestions. They are Donald Goldsmith, David Morrison, and Dale Cruikshank. Sir Arthur C. Clarke corrected a few minor errors, and numerous people reviewed smaller parts of the manuscript; I am indebted to them all.

Special thanks are due to my assistants at university archives, who scoured them for crucial papers. Yeoman work was done by Jeremiah James at Harvard and Gavi Hanssen at the University of Arizona–Tucson. Also thanks to Steve Secker at the University of Chicago for searching records related to Sagan's college years. Thanks, too, to the librarians and archivists who recovered valuable papers at the University of California campuses at Berkeley and San Diego, Indiana University, Cornell University, the Truman Library, and Oregon State University, as well as the American Philosophical Society and the Neils Bohr Library at the American Institute of Physics. Also thanks to staffers at the beautiful University of California libraries at Santa Cruz and San Francisco, where much of this book was researched and written.

I am indebted to Lawrence Wittner for his advice and for generously sharing documents from his seminal research into the history of the peace movement. Also, Raymond Jeanloz and Kathryn Day-Huh of the Miller Institute at Berkeley granted me access to an invaluable document that radically altered my interpretation of Sagan's early relationship with the U.S. national security apparatus. And I cannot thank Tim Willard of the National Archives enough for recovering the seventeen-year-old Sagan's letter on UFOs to Secretary of State Dean Acheson.

Also much gratitude to the general historians who personally inspired me in the 1970s, notably Arnold M. Shankman and James Harvey Young at Emory University, and to the historians of science, including Robert Silliman of Emory and David Lindberg, Aaron J. Ihde, R. C. Stauffer, Ron Numbers, Victor Hilts, Gunter Risse, and Robert Siegfried of the University of Wisconsin. Also to former Emory president Sanford Atwood, who, after hearing my Stipe Society lecture on the history of the idea of extraterrestrial life, uttered one wonderful, encouraging word that kept me going for the next quarter of a century. And thanks to Joel Van Pelt, my editor at the Oxford University Press multi-volume *American National Biography*, from whom I learned much.

In early 1999 I lectured on early findings of this book at the University of California at Berkeley and Oregon State University in Corvallis, and benefited from suggestions and criticisms by certain audience members—particularly Gunther S. Stent at Berkeley and Doel and Mary Jo Nye at Oregon State.

Amelia K. (Amy) Smith, who was with this project almost from the beginning, transcribed mountains of taped interviews and dictations. She also offered many suggestions for the book itself, and was a delight to work with. Also much thanks to Tom Burdan for extensive additional transcriptions. Without Amy and Tom, I could not have finished this book.

Further thanks to my friends Dale Carter and Inger H. Dalsgaard, who independently proposed the idea for a Sagan book and offered valuable suggestions; Sir Martin Rees and Fred Whipple, for their encouragement and suggestions early in the project; Stanley Miller, for reminiscing at length about Sagan and hastening my access to Harold C. Urey's papers; Maria Goodavage and her family, who shared the late Joseph Goodavage's taped interview with Sagan in 1972, just before Sagan's early fame turned incandescent; Nanette Asimov, for guiding me to her uncle Isaac's letters; Rabbi Morrison Bial and Rabbi Valerie Lieber, for their guidance on religious issues and the former's charming memories of the young Sagan's training for his bar mitzvah; and Gail Foorman, who talked me through this project's darkest moment. Also thanks to the 3 A.M. gang at Kinko's, especially Natalie.

Also much gratitude to my *San Francisco Examiner* colleague Bob Stephens and to Frank M. Robinson and Vincent Di Fate, who enthusiastically shared their expertise on the literature and history of science fiction; to my bosses at the *Examiner*, Dick Rogers and Phil Bronstein, for their enthusiasm, generosity, and great patience; to Emily Gurnon, a great sounding board; and to Andy Pollack, for a reason he surely won't soon forget. Also to veteran science writer David Perlman of the *San Francisco Chronicle*, one of the first reporters to cover Sagan, who shared reminiscences and documents.

I also wish to thank the *New York Times Book Review* for quickly running my author's query, which requested interviews with anyone who had known Sagan as a child or youth. A small flood of responses ensued, almost all of them useful.

Special thanks to the filmmaker Lynda Obst, who interrupted her killer schedule while shooting Denzel Washington and Annette Bening to sip tea and share her fascinating reminiscences with me, then let me take over her office for two days while I read voluminous documents from the making of the movie *Contact*. Also thanks to Johnny Carson and his staff at Carson Productions in Santa Monica for providing documents and videotapes; and to Geoff Haines-Stiles of the *Cosmos* production team.

I also wish to thank the good folks at the Committee for the Scientific Investigation of Claims of the Paranormal (CSICOP) in Amherst, N.Y., whose work I have often written about, and usually admired, over two decades. Special gratitude to Tim Binga for providing abundant documents from the Center for Inquiry and CSICOP archives, especially on the prehistory of the 1969 AAAS debate on UFOs. One caveat: Sagan was a co-founder of CSICOP, but he was not totally uncritical of the organization. Nor am I. I hope that the organization's membership accept my gentle criticisms with good humor, while remembering this: we disagree on short-term tactics, not on long-term strategy. Also, a word of advice to readers in general—those who wonder why the main text doesn't cite their favorite Sagan anecdote (e.g., his comic run-in with Apple Corp.) should check the footnotes: that's where it is, along with many other gems that didn't make it into the narrative.

For inspiring me over the years, I wish to thank Timothy Ferris (although he doesn't like everything written herein, specifically my critique of the *Voyager* records), medical writer Andrew Skolnick (the bravest reporter I know), Andrew Fraknoi, John Wilkes, Deborah Blum, Tom Lucas, William J. Broad, Kimberly Shlain Brooks (the smartest blonde in Los Angeles), and the irreplaceable Martin Gardner (whose writings on skepticism had a lifelong impact on at least two adolescents—Sagan and me). Numerous other people who contributed to this project are listed in the notes at the back of the book.

I sincerely apologize to anyone whose name I have forgotten to include. There are two, though, whom I shall never forget, although they are now lost in America. Here's to ME and LK, wherever you are.

Obviously, all mistakes in this book are my responsibility alone.

1

Brooklyn

ALL HIS LIFE, Carl Sagan was troubled by grand dichotomies—between reason and irrationalism, between wonder and skepticism. The dichotomies clashed within him. He yearned to believe in marvelous things—in flying saucers, in Martians, in glistening civilizations across the Milky Way. Yet reason usually brought him back to Earth. Usually; not always. A visionary dreams of a better world than this one. He refuses to think that modern society and its trappings—money, marriage, children, a nine-to-five career, and obeisance to a waving flag and an inscrutable God—are all there is. Sagan was blinded, but not by these. He was blinded by the sheer glory of the new cosmos that was unveiled by science during the first two decades of his life. This cosmos was an ever-expanding, unbounded wonderland of billions of galaxies. And across the light-years, Sagan dreamed, random molecular jigglings had perhaps spawned creeping, crawling, thinking creatures on alien landscapes bathed in the glow of alien suns.

This vision blinded Sagan, sometimes, to the needs of the people around him. These included friends who worshiped him, although he hurt them; wives who were entranced by his passions, although they were enraged by his absenteeism and often illogical "logic"; sons who were enthralled by his example, even as they struggled to escape his shadow; and colleagues who envied and honored him, even while they scorned his wilder notions and mocked his pomposities. Hardly anyone who knew Carl Sagan intimately has an unmixed opinion of him. In the final analysis, *he* was the dichotomy: the prophet and the hard-boiled skeptic, the boyish fantasist and the ultrarigorous analyst, the warm companion and the brusque colleague, the oracle whose smooth exterior concealed inner fissures, which, in the end, only one woman could heal.

SAGAN'S INNER WAR stemmed, in part, from his childhood relations with his parents. Rachel and Sam's marriage epitomized a great philosophical principle: Opposites attract. Sagan later traced his analytical urges to Rachel, a cunning, acid-tongued neurotic who had known extreme poverty and been abandoned by her family. Her intellectual ambitions had been thwarted by the grand irrationalisms of her time—by societal bigotries against the poor, against Jews, against women (and wives in particular). She worshiped her only son, Carl. He would fulfill her unfulfilled dreams.

And Carl's sense of wonder came from Sam, a quiet, soft-hearted escapee from the czar. Sam gave apples to the poor and soothed labor-management tensions in New York's tumultuous garment industry. He was awed by the young Carl's brilliance, his boyish chatter about stars and dinosaurs—but not overawed. Sam would have adored his son had he been just another Jewish kid in wartime Brooklyn who played kickball in the streets while Nazi subs haunted the coastline.

Posterity's judgment of Rachel Molly Gruber Sagan (1907–1982) is wildly contradictory. "Vivacious," "a witch," "brilliant, very perky, very bright," "insane—very paranoid," "you knew she was coming from a mile away," "completely loving," "a waif . . . who needed all the affection she could get"—so say those who enjoyed or endured her.[1] Her education was meager, her looks unlovely. Neglected by her family, she grew up almost homeless in New York City during World War I and the 1920s. Yet she had flash and charisma, a feisty sense of fashion, and a rapid, eloquent tongue. She made (and dumped) friends fast, and boyfriends faster. She wrote well, too. Her first child, Carl, would inherit her literary skill.

Her prose style might be described as "Take no prisoners." Shortly before her death, unmellowed by age, she gleefully wrote to two married friends about Carl and his third wife Ann Druyan's new Ithaca mansion, describing it as

> a weirdo of a house, most of it underground (great protection from a nuclear blast) . . . the result of a lurid nightmare of the architect. Because I was aghast and against it, they don't speak to me. . . . [Carl] must and will have installed a sophisticated burglar alarm—there are threats against him by some crazy people who claim he appears in their dreams and keeps them from sleeping. One such was apprehended.[2]

Rachel's bilious prose camouflaged her pride. How far she had come from her rotten beginnings! Through the Depression and Hitler and Alger Hiss, she had raised to adulthood a boy who, by the century's twilight, had become the world's best-known living scientist, a multimillionaire TV star and Pulitzer Prize–winning author, and recently wed to a brainy, luminous brunette (a lady so desirable that a prior suitor had written a novel about her[3]). He was so famous, in fact, that he *haunted the minds of the mad*. My son, the specter!

Bragged Rachel, the onetime waif, at the end of her letter:

> We are not the run of the mill, are we, or the rank and file or the ordinary plebeian.
>   Aren't you glad you know us?
>
> Hysterically,
Rachel

Rachel's origins were vague; she preferred it that way. She and her family tended to be secretive about embarrassing family matters, Carl Sagan wrote in a November 28, 1994, letter to lifelong friend Lucille Nahemow, a professor of psychology at the University of Connecticut at Storrs, who specializes in family issues and who studied Rachel's life.[4]

Carl's sole sibling was his sister, Carol, nicknamed Cari. A social worker, she is married to a Union Carbide executive. In the living room of their handsome home in Houston, she showed this writer a faded black-and-white photo of a middle-aged couple standing on a boardwalk at the beach. The man in the photo is Leib Gruber, Rachel's father. Tall and unsmiling, he wears a dark suit and a big black hat. He looks like a movie mobster. "The rumor," Cari said as she served coffee and Passover muffins, "is that he was a murderer."[5]

Leib Gruber was born in the late nineteenth century in the village of Sassow, part of the Austro-Hungarian Empire—an empire "creaking in all its multi-national joints," as Arthur Koestler put it, "waiting to fall to pieces." Across the continent, the vipers of anti-Semitism stirred: the Dreyfus case in France, village slaughters in rural Russia. Conspiracy theorists touted the fraudulent *Protocols of Zion* as "proof" of a global Jewish conspiracy. In reality, few Jews outside an intellectual and artistic elite—Freud, for example—found influential careers within Emperor Francis Joseph's doomed empire. Leib's father sold fish. Young Leib was big-boned and strong, and raised cash in a medieval manner—carrying travelers on his back across the shallow stretches of a river. In the words of his grandson Carl Sagan, he was "a beast of burden."[6]

According to one version of a family legend, in 1904 Leib killed an anti-Semite.[7] He fled to the New World, leaving behind his young wife, Chaiya. (His loyal brother supposedly stayed in Austria to take the rap for the crime.) Leib got a job in the United States. He made enough money to transport Chaiya to New York on a Hamburg-based ship, the *Batavia*. She arrived with one dollar in her bag. The couple anglic their names, from Leib to Louis and from Chaiya to Clara. Then they settled down and bred two children. The first was Rachel, whose official birthdate was November 23, 1907. (The true birthdate is uncertain because Rachel was secretive about her age.)[8] Chaiya died during a second childbirth.

For whatever reason, Leib/Louis decided that he couldn't manage little Rachel. He sent her to Austria, where she lived with relatives. In the meantime, he remarried. Unfortunately, the Austrian relatives didn't want—or couldn't stand—the energetic little girl. After a few years, they shipped Rachel back to New York, to her father and her stepmother, Rose (the woman in the photo). Rose received her stepchild with less than open arms. "By the time she was eight," Professor Nahemow observes, "Rachel was rejected on two continents."[9]

Rachel's family was dysfunctional before "dysfunctional" was a cliché. Leib gave his children nasty nicknames. He called Rachel "hair lice" (she had returned from Austria with lice in her hair).[10] Rachel's stepbrother Abraham was institutionalized for mysterious reasons; his very existence was a family secret. (Carl Sagan first heard about his stepuncle at Rachel's funeral in 1982.)[11]

Leib had a good side. On one occasion, Rachel's schoolteacher reprimanded her for misbehavior. Leib protected Rachel from Rose's wrath by lying to his wife, claiming that the reprimand was actually a compliment. Still, Rachel avoided home as much as possible. She hated Rose. Rachel "never accepted Rose as her mother. She knew she wasn't her birth mother," Cari Sagan says. "She was a rather rebellious child and young adult . . . 'emancipated woman,' we'd call her now." Professor Nahemow obtained many details about Rachel's childhood from Nahemow's mother, Flora Bernstein, one of Rachel's closest childhood friends. Once Rose stormed into Flora's childhood home, accusing Rachel of being a "whore." Flora's mother "unceremoniously threw her out."[12]

Flora, a resident of Liberty Avenue in Brooklyn, met seven-year-old Rachel when she was skipping rope with friends. Rachel invited the shy, pretty new girl to play. Rachel, Flora learned, "was inventive and fun to be with." In turn, Flora offered Rachel access to her home. The Bernstein residence was much nicer than the Grubers' grubby digs. The Bernsteins threw many parties with interesting people (none of whom were wanted for murder in Austria). Ambitious, Rachel seized her opportunity: she became "outgoing and very affectionate" toward Flora's mother. In turn, Mrs. Bernstein adored Rachel—enough to make Flora jealous. Rachel, Flora now believes, "was a waif, an unfortunate child who needed all the affection she could get."

Rachel had a reputation for taking "chances." She "would come to [Mrs. Bernstein's] Hebrew school and pick up boys," Flora recalls. "She was always . . . very conscious of the opposite sex. She dressed well and had a good sense of fashion. Rachel was the first one in the crowd who bought a bathing suit. There was a law about the length of suits and Rachel's was too short. She was thrown off the boardwalk in Coney Island."[13]

Rachel was smart. She completed an equivalency test to receive a high school diploma. "Brilliant, a very perky little woman, smart, well read, very interesting to talk to," recalls one of her relatives, Beatrice Rubenstein.[14] Rachel explored New York's high culture with the guidance of a savvy relative, Sarah Cohen. They lacked money but managed to get into concerts, plays, and ballets via hook, crook, and subway. Sarah "learned to get through turnstiles without paying, and took Rachel along. Sometimes they entered [the show] at intermission and stood in the back."[15]

As the war-mad 1910s became the money-mad 1920s, Rachel and her female pals formed a club. They called themselves the "'It' Girls" after screen heartthrob Clara Bow. By that time Rachel was a brassy, bold, five-foot-two cyclone. She was hardly a beauty. But no one, male or female, could resist her allure as she blew into a room and leveled it with her street-smart mouth and radiant eyes. "Rachel was unpredictable," recalls Flora Bernstein. "She sometimes stole other girls' boyfriends just to show that she could do it. But at other times she was very protective of her friends. I once went in a car with a boy. Rachel wrote down the license number and said, 'You take good care of my friend. If anything happens to her, I have your number.'"[16]

At a party, "'It' Girl" Mary Brodsky introduced Rachel to a quiet young man. He was skinny, red-haired, and covered with freckles. When they went swimming, she gasped at the extent of his red-splotched flesh. "Are you freckled *everywhere*?" she demanded. "Everywhere!" he boasted. Samuel Sagan made Rachel's hormones race, and she his. "She saw dad's red hair and immediately fell in love," Cari Sagan says. "And he was swept off his feet by her, which is understandable because she was very, very charismatic and vivacious." They were married within weeks.[17]

In Carl Sagan's lakeside home in upstate New York, his widow, Ann Druyan, keeps a black-and-white photo of the young Sam and Rachel. They are kissing enthusiastically, Hollywood-style, on a boardwalk. They wed in the early 1930s, the bleakest days of the Great Depression. At that time, Sam was a poorly paid usher at a movie theater.[18] In Germany, Nazis were marching. American Jews feared an upsurge of local fascism. "The apprehensiveness of American Jews," *Fortune* magazine observed, "has become one of the important influences in the social life of our time."[19] No matter; Rachel and Sam were in love. They married, had two kids, survived it all. They lived long enough to retire to Florida, to play Scrabble and shoot pool, to watch their son grow famous on television. Sagan's secretary Shirley Arden recalls how playful the couple remained to the end: "Sam took the golfer's stance à la Johnny Carson, gave Rachel a lecherous look, and said, 'Just you and me, babe.' Rachel was a sensuous woman. Sam adored her and put up with her foibles."

Rachel, Cari Sagan Greene recalls, would fuss over Sam's hair and "make sure that the little dip in my father's hair was just so. . . . She wanted the man that she married to look the way she thought 'good' looked. . . . He was sort of indulgent; he knew it was inevitable; it didn't bother him a bit." In 1979, at age seventy-four, Sam lay in a hospital dying of lung cancer. Rachel slipped into the bed with him, to hug and comfort him.[20]

WHEN SAM SAGAN* was five years old, he left the Ukraine and joined the hungry, hopeful millions then streaming to America. As an adult, he would recall little about his Ukrainian hometown, save one detail: it was near a prison.[21] An appropriate memory. The entire Pale of Settlement, a vast expanse of farmland between the Baltic and the Black Seas, was effectively a prison where the Jews of the Russian Empire were forced to live, subjected to many governmental restrictions. Incorporating fragments of dismembered medieval states, the Pale seethed with ever-growing numbers of impoverished peoples, including former serfs.[22] Their lives were humdrum at best, nightmarish at worst—more like Bernard Malamud's *The Fixer* than *Fiddler on the Roof.*

Sam was born on March 2, 1905. It was a triumphant year in the history of science, and an ominous one in Russian history. Outside Russia, "the year 1905 was the turning point in several areas of science, heralding radical changes," says historian of science Stephen G. Brush.[23] That year brought pivotal accomplishments by many researchers, Sigmund Freud and Albert Einstein among them.

Freud and Einstein—two Jews, who overcame anti-Semitism and rose to fame by challenging our view of reality. In 1905, Freud published *Three Essays on the Theory of Sexuality,*[24] one of his classic explorations of the unconscious. As he explained, the mind is not merely a "reasoning" machine, as Victorian optimists had believed. Rather, the mind is

---

*Many immigrants' names were Americanized on their arrival at Ellis Island. Cari Sagan says that to her knowledge, "Sagan" is her father's original Ukrainian surname, not a shortened version of a longer name such as Sagansky.

haunted by ghosts, by irrational forces of desire and repression. Freud believed that these ghosts surface in symbolic forms. One form is the self-destructive group behavior called war.

Also in 1905, Einstein published three historic papers. The most radical was his theory of special relativity, which transformed concepts of time, space, mass, and energy.[25] Special relativity paved the way toward his later, even stranger work on *general* relativity. In general relativity theory, gravity is not a Newtonian "force" or action-at-distance; rather, it is the consequence of the "curvature" of space. General relativity implied a whole new cosmology, a cosmos that (as it turned out) expands over time. As astrophysicists later showed, the cosmos expands because it was born billions of years ago from the big bang, a kind of "explosion" whose ejecta cooled into innumerable galaxies.[26] And each galaxy is an ocean of stars, whose light may illumine countless planets, many of them perhaps inhabited.

The Freudian and Einsteinian revolutions posed big questions, questions that tormented Carl Sagan much of his adult life. Reason and irrationalism—polar opposites, yet uncomfortably united. Earth and the cosmos—different realms, yet part of each other. Sagan explored such dichotomies in many of his books, in cosmological ruminations such as *Cosmos* and *Contact*, and in his essay-poems on consciousness and evolution, *The Dragons of Eden* and *Shadows of Forgotten Ancestors*. Humanity, he believed, must reconcile its rational and irrational sides. Succeed, and empyrean vistas open before us; the cosmos is ours to explore, with all its strange and wonderful sights and (perhaps) peoples. Fail, and we won't make it out of the solar system alive. All our bright promise will be lost; all our long progress will end in a bright, noisy flash.

Freud's outlook grew dark as Europe tore itself to bits in one war, then rearmed for a worse one; and darker as the cancer attacked his mouth. By contrast, Sagan was an optimist—always was, even as the blood disease ravaged his body, even as he waited to be arrested at an atomic site, even as he gazed into the poker faces of nuclear weaponeers and realized that they really believe in their research, believe that instruments of annihilation will forever keep the peace. Sagan experienced all this yet still believed in the future, in humanity, in the eventual triumph of reason. At heart, he was a child.

He descended from a hopeful people. Pessimists stayed in the Ukraine, scratching their meager existences from the dark soil. Optimists said to hell with it and headed west, usually to America. The 1900s were a good time to leave: the Russian Empire quaked with revolts and pogroms, foreshocks of the greater revolution to come, in 1917. The czarist regime struck back with typically cloddish brutality. Six weeks before Sam Sagan's birth in 1905, troops killed more than a hundred peaceful protesters in St. Petersburg. In June, sailors mutinied aboard the battleship *Potemkin* in Odessa. The revolts triggered an anti-Semitic backlash. Thousands of Jews, including many women, were arrested on political grounds. According to Moses Rischin, "In 1904, of an estimated 30,000 organized Jewish workers, 4,476 were imprisoned or exiled to Siberia."[27] Young Leon Trotsky observed one of the 1905 pogroms. He noted how "the gang rushes through the town, drunk on vodka and the smell of blood."[28]

According to family legend, after Sam's mother died in childbirth, his Ukrainian relatives sent him to New York to join his father, who had already journeyed there. Five-year-old Sam and his uncle, George, first glimpsed the New York skyline in 1910, from a ship approaching Ellis Island.[29] Many immigrants' hearts raced as they read this passage in a guidebook: "Hold fast, this is most necessary in America. Forget your past, your customs, and your ideals. Select a goal and pursue it with all your might. . . . You will experience a bad time but sooner or later you will achieve your goal. . . . Do not take a moment's rest."[30]

"Do not take a moment's rest." This might have been George Sagan's credo, or his grandnephew Carl's. George was old enough to join the booming New York garment industry. In 1916 he founded his own firm, the New York Girl Coat Company. Eventually he became a wealthy man, a country-club type and a member of the board of educational and public-spirited institutions. When the firm celebrated its fiftieth anniversary in 1966, the *New York Times* ran a story on the front page of its business section. The story included a photo of a grinning George Sagan admiring a little girl modeling his wares.[31] As a joke, Carl Sagan mentioned the firm in his 1985 novel *Contact*.[32]

Sam had more intellectual ambitions. Like many immigrant Jews, he believed in the transformative power of education. He eventually enrolled at Columbia University, hoping to become a pharmacist. Then his father died. End of dream.[33] To support his family, Sam went to work for Uncle George as a garment cutter. "[H]is job," Carl Sagan later wrote, "was to use a very scary power saw to cut out patterns—backs, say, or sleeves for ladies' coats and suits—from an enormous stack of cloth. Then the patterns were conveyed to endless rows of women sitting at sewing machines."[34] Textile fibers wafted through the air; some, perhaps, found their way into Sam's lungs and hastened his ultimate end.[35] This proletarian fate did not embitter Sam. He was good with people, liked them; they adored him. By the late 1940s he was a factory manager. He made enough money to send his son to a great university, to be taught by noted scholars who would escort him to fame.

"You will experience a bad time but sooner or later you will achieve your goal." The guidebook had been right. This was America; optimism, it seemed, made sense.

CARL SAGAN WAS BORN in Brooklyn on November 9, 1934. His mother, Rachel, named him in honor of her biological mother, Chaiya/Clara, "the mother she never knew," in Sagan's words.[36]

As a science popularizer, Sagan sometimes drew on childhood memories to illustrate scientific points. "Most of us have a memory like this: you're lying in your crib, having awakened from your nap," he and his wife, Ann Druyan, wrote in *Shadows of Forgotten Ancestors*. "You cry for your mother, at first tentatively, but when no one comes, more emphatically. Panic mounts. Where is she? Why doesn't she come? you think, or something along those lines—although not in words, because your verbal consciousness is still almost wholly undeveloped. She enters the room smiling, she reaches in and picks you up, you hear her musical voice, you smell her perfume—and how your heart soars!"[37]

Rachel was madly in love with her little boy. She told him he was brilliant. He believed her. Throughout Sagan's life, Rachel's devotion to her son awed or amused or disgusted outsiders. "She worshiped the ground he floated above," joked Peter Pesch, the best man at Sagan's first wedding. "He could do no wrong. That's got to be a good start in life—a mother that thinks you are the Sun, the Moon, and the Earth."[38] Sagan's boyhood friend Robert Gritz recalls Rachel bragging to everyone about Carl—for example, gloating, "Oh, Carl got an A!"[39] The writer Timothy Ferris, who befriended Sagan in the 1970s, remembers the aged Rachel as "an *ur*-mother who'd made a kind of shrine to Carl in the spare bedroom with all his awards and everything, and to whom every accomplishment was just a step toward the next accomplishment."[40]

"There's no way of understanding him without understanding her very well," says Sagan's first wife, scientist-author Lynn Margulis. "His mother had made him so dependent on this one relationship—on *her*. He was worthy of every attention, all the time, every need [was] always filled."[41]

Despite this adoration, there were hidden fears in Sagan's life. He later wrote that starting at age two, he was "frightened . . . by real-seeming but wholly imaginary 'monsters,' especially at night or in the dark. I can still remember occasions when I was absolutely terrified, hiding under the bedclothes until I could stand it no longer, and then bolting for the safety of my parents' bedroom—if only I could get there before falling into the clutches of . . . The Presence."[42] Sometimes he awoke "drenched in sweat, my heart pounding." (A child is terrified of the dark, then grows up and becomes an astronomer. Psychoanalysts may make of this what they will.)

Rachel's devotion to Carl was double-edged. She had experienced life's darker side. She had little patience with those—even children—who fantasized about life. The slightest whimsical observation might irk or anger her. In his final years, Sagan recalled a "blustery fall day" when he was about age five, looking out the living room window at Lower New York Bay. The water was choppy and the sun was about to set. His mother came by the window and they gazed toward the Atlantic Ocean. On the other side of the sea, World War II was beginning. "There are people fighting out there, killing each other," she told him. Carl replied: "I know. I can see them." She fired back: "No, you can't. They're too far away."

This seemingly trivial incident gnawed at Sagan. His adoring mother had *contradicted* him! He later wrote: "How could she know whether I could see them or not? . . . Squinting, I had thought I'd made out a thin strip of land at the horizon on which tiny figures were pushing and shoving and dueling with swords as they did in my comic books."[43]

Rachel "could be utterly charming," Lynn Margulis recalls. Yet Rachel also could scan a newcomer, find her or his vulnerability, and "stick it in"—make a caustic remark that deeply hurt.[44] Sagan's sister, Cari, remembers how as a child, "I always had a deep voice and she would imitate it, not in a pleasant way, just in a way that wiped me out emotionally. . . . It was devastating." Cari's mother gave Carl more attention: "I can never remember her hugging me," Cari said.[45]

Sagan's son Nick, a television writer, recalls his grandmother as a delightful fireball. She was a great cook and loved to make him spicy spaghetti and meatballs. But "she was insane—in a sometimes wonderful, and sometimes not wonderful, way . . . very paranoid. She was convinced that restaurants weren't sanitary and that the waiters would always spit in the food." Rachel's eccentricities affected Sagan emotionally. Her dedication to logic, like his, sometimes bordered on the illogical. Once Carl, smelling her cooking, made an "Mmm!" sound. "What do you mean?" she snapped angrily. "You haven't even tasted it yet!" Over the long run, Nick believes, his father compensated for Rachel's wackiness: "She was irrational in certain ways, and that led to his very *ultra*-rational kind of way with things."[46]

Arrogance often hides insecurity; pretentiousness usually conceals ignorance. These are psychological truisms. Rachel was touchy about her limited education. Once she and some friends went to an Arthur Miller play and argued about it afterward. Feeling slighted, Rachel reportedly stormed off, declaring: "You'll hear from me when I get *my* degree."[47] She wanted to go to college, but Sam vetoed the idea. He also forbade her to get a job. Uncharacteristically, she complied; no other man could have said no to Rachel and lived. She was resentful, but she didn't let her mind rot. She "read a great deal . . . was very interesting . . . an intellectual person," Cari says. "When I was taking piano lessons, she would be resting on the couch, reading the *New York Times*."[48]

In the 1980s and 1990s, Sagan, Ann Druyan, and their intimate friend the movie producer Lynda Obst, met in southern California to plan the film *Contact*. Obst recalls how they sat around for hours, telling stories about their mothers: "*Hours!* . . . We were all really interested in psychology and figuring ourselves out." Sagan revered his mother's memory, but by that time he didn't have any illusions about her; he had seen how she treated his first two wives. He was also beginning to look into his own soul, to understand the kind of person *he* was—the kind of person Rachel had made him. "All the time we talked about Rachel . . . [Carl] wasn't angry with her . . . but he also knew how controlling she was, and how tough and mean she was to his other wives, and how selfish she made him in certain kinds of ways—how 'entitled' is a better word," Obst says. "Rachel had so many secrets and so many issues. . . . I think she had a lot of rage. And Carl was her production—Carl was a 'Rachel Production.' And she launched him into the world to stake her claim. In some sense he was shot out of a cannon."[49]

Indeed, little Carl was an impressive kid, sometimes too impressive. "I was thrown out of Sunday school," he recalled. Someone had asked, How did Pharaoh's daughter know that Moses was a Hebrew child? The answer was, "He was circumcised," but the teacher was too embarrassed to say it. Carl kept "pushing and pushing and pushing" the teacher to answer the question. "Did [the child] have a Hebrew letter on it? How could you know? . . . And the teacher couldn't give me the answer, even though he knew it, because he was embarrassed."[50]

Jews were a large fraction of the populace in Bensonhurst, a Brooklyn neighborhood. The Sagans lived in a modest apartment a short walk from the Atlantic Ocean. Nearby was Coney Island, a site of frequent Sagan family outings. Old photos show Carl lolling on the beach, with baby Cari on his back.

The 1930s. The Great Depression (which fascists blamed on Jews). Framed pictures of FDR (attacked by bigots for his "Jew Deal") on kitchen walls. Edward G. Robinson (born Emmanuel Goldenberg) movies at the Bijou. Father Coughlin on the radio, denouncing Jews. "My family never hid the fact that they were Jewish, [but] didn't shout it from the rooftops," Cari Sagan says.[51] The exact nature of the family's religious faith is unclear. In a 1991 interview, Sagan recalled that they were Reform Jews, the more liberal wing of Judaism's three main groups (Orthodox, Conservative, and Reform).[52] Cari, however, says they were Conservative

(that is, more conservative than Reform but more liberal than Orthodox).[53] In any case, both agree that their father, Sam, showed little religious interest. Cari says Rachel "definitely believed in God and was
active in the temple. . . . My mother only served kosher meat. . . . There
[were] never any pork products or shellfish in the family or household."
The couple occasionally quarreled, but not over religion.[54] Carl said:
"My mother and my father were deeply in love with each other, and so
my father went along for my mother's sake."[55] In turn, Cari noted,
Rachel was flexible: "My dad liked bacon and eggs. And so he would go
out on a weekend or some time and have it at a restaurant. And my mother
was okay with that because it wasn't brought into the house."[56] In this
Judaically fluid atmosphere, the teenage Carl would nurse primal doubts.

Secularization was in the air. The great rabbi Mordecai Kaplan, the
originator of Reconstructionist Judaism, a new, fourth branch of Judaism, urged Jews to abandon superstition, to rebuild their lives around
ethnic identification rather than ancient folk tales.[57] The Humanist
movement was well under way; its diverse band of intellectuals, leftists,
and religious skeptics urged Americans to concentrate not on a doubtful
hereafter but on the certain here and now.[58] Trotskyists passed out literature on street corners. One's aunt or uncle might be an active member of
the Communist party. "In the park right across from Carl's, on a Sunday
afternoon," his friend Gritz remembers, "it was like Hyde Park in London: guys would stand up and give speeches for or against Stalin."[59]

Sam was no intellectual, and as a factory boss he was certainly no
Marxist. But he gave his children a social conscience. Cari was awed by
his warm relationship with his workers at the factory—no mean feat in
the highly unionized and combative garment industry—and decided to
become a social worker.[60]

As for Carl, he was four or five years old when his parents took him
to the New York World's Fair of 1939–1940. Holding their lunches, they
walked by a man selling pencils. Sam took Carl's apple and gave it to the
man. Carl disliked apples; nonetheless, he started wailing. It was *his*
apple! To avoid embarrassing the man, Sam carried Carl away until their
voices were out of earshot. "We don't really need that apple," he
explained to his son gently. "That fellow was hungry."[61] Carl never forgot the lesson. Many decades later, his enemies would include the
nation's most virulent right-wingers.

At the nadir of the Depression, Sam Sagan had been a miserably paid
movie usher in New York City. Six decades later, his only son's name
would glisten on the movie screen. Sagan recalled his parents: "My relationship with them was really very good. I missed them often. Still miss
them. . . .

"Every now and then, when I am working or I am shaving or some-thing like that, I hear—as clear as a bell—one of them saying my name: 'Carl,' just like that. . . . It's unmistakable. I know whose voice it is. . . . I turn around before I can do any cerebration on it. . . . [Memory of their voices] has to be in many different parts of my brain. And it's not surpris-ing that my brain would sort of, you know, play it back . . . every now and then."[62]

When Sagan repeated this story publicly, parapsychology buffs mis-understood his meaning. They excitedly spread the rumor (in words to this effect): "Carl Sagan, the king of skeptics, is in psychic contact with his dead parents!" Pseudoscientists and occultists were always misunder-standing Sagan. He was the best-known scientist of his time, and they yearned to convert him to their various causes. And it is true that through-out his life, Sagan proposed many unusual ideas, some so unusual that his more conventional colleagues scorned him as a sensationalist, a head-line grabber. But for all his fancies, Sagan was too good a scientist to be fooled by his brain's neurological mirages; he was too confident an atheist to think he would ever see or hear his parents again, no matter how much he loved and missed them. The skeptic inside him—the "Rachel" inside him—knew better.

DURING THE DEPRESSION, Thomas Wolfe observed a new intellectual force afoot: thousands of bright young Jews, the children of immigrants. In *You Can't Go Home Again*, Wolfe described "the Jew boy" eagerly read-ing in a New York tenement building. "For what? Because, brother, he is burning in the night. He sees the class, the lecture room, the shining apparatus of gigantic laboratories, the open field of scholarship and pure research, certain knowledge and the world distinction of an Einstein name."[63]

New York City, 1939. The nation was still groggy from the Great Depression. Evil was afoot around the world—Hitler and Mussolini in Europe, militarists in Japan. Yet pessimism did not come easily to Amer-icans. They loved to talk about the future and the wonders it would bring. Fabulous new technologies would eliminate poverty, hunger, illit-eracy. Synthetic foods would feed the starving. Miracle drugs would heal the sick. Television would bring high culture—for free!—into every home. An ordinary Joe could afford his own small airplane. (And would keep it, one presumes, in a backyard hangar.) Aviation would make long-distance travel routine. Hence, national and international cultural barri-ers would dissolve; hence, different societies would better understand each other; hence, farewell to war![64]

The Depression had stirred radical juices. Socialists and Communists were on the march, radicalizing workers, threatening to redistribute wealth and topple the greedy few. But technology's propagandists promised to improve society without any need for class revolts or ideological bickering. How? Simple! Technology was the physical embodiment of Enlightenment rationalism. Rationalism or reason was the royal road to Truth, to optimal solutions for all problems, solutions that would satisfy everyone regardless of class or ethnicity or nationality. (Gender was not on the intelligentsia's radar screen at that time.) Therefore (the propagandists argued), technology, being reason's physical embodiment, was inherently nonideological. Its control could be entrusted to politically neutral "experts," professional Benthamites whose goal was the greatest good for the greatest number.[65]

Who could question such a noble agenda? As in the 1939 film *The Wizard of Oz*, where Emerald City looms miragelike beyond the poppy fields, the "City of Tomorrow" beckoned on the horizon of 1939. It would be a city of superhighways and robots and television—of everything, in fact, displayed at the 1939 New York World's Fair. While Hitler blitzkrieged into Poland and France, Americans fantasized about a coming techno-utopia that satisfied all needs while requiring a minimum of societal self-criticism or personal introspection. There was no need to question *who* would control the technology, or for what ends. Carl Sagan's generation was raised on this technological faith. It is little wonder that for decades afterward, Sagan collected Fair memorabilia—postcards, ashtrays, and the like.

At the Fair's Futurama exhibit, operated by General Motors, participants "flew" over a moving map of the America of Tomorrow. They passed futuristic cities with elevated highways and cloud-piercing skyscrapers. Fairgoers were informed about future wonders: weather control, robots, atomic energy. "It showed beautiful highways and clover leafs and little General Motors cars all carrying people to skyscrapers, buildings with lovely spires, flying buttresses—and it looked great!" Sagan remembered.[66]

In retrospect, Sagan acknowledged, he had accepted the Fair's "extremely technocratic" message in "an uncritical way." Young Carl thought: "That's what tomorrow is going to be like. Gee! And I'm going to live in it!" He gasped at a display in which a flashlight illuminated a photoelectric cell, creating a crackling sound. In another exhibit, a sound wave from a tuning fork registered as a sine wave on an oscilloscope. "Plainly," Sagan observed, "the world held wonders of a kind I had never guessed. How *could* a tone become a picture and light become a noise?" He also witnessed, for the first time, the technology that would make him famous: television.

One of the Fair's most publicized gimmicks was the burial of a time capsule at Flushing Meadows. It contained mementos of the 1930s to be recovered by our descendants millennia hence. The time capsule thrilled Carl. Imagine, relics of *our* day, unearthed and pored over by inhabitants of an epoch unimaginably more wonderful than ours! How they will smile as they examine the pop-culture artifacts of our century, or struggle to decipher the script of old documents, written in languages as obscure to them as Chaucerian English is to us.

As an adult, Sagan and his colleagues would create his own time capsules—capsules destined to survive not for millennia inside the Earth, but for millions of years in the galaxy. The *Pioneer* plaques and the *Voyager* records—all are long-term spinoffs of Sagan's wide-eyed scamper through the World's Fair. These metallic messages to the cosmos may drift through the Milky Way for billions of years, never to be found. And if they *are* found, it'll be by creatures not of this world. But space is terribly vast; there is only an infinitesimal chance that aliens will one day scrutinize these micrometeorite-scarred ambassadors of Earth, these relics of A.D. 1939, of the spirit of Flushing Meadows, of the high hopes that soon crashed and burned in the chaos of World War II.

A NEW YORK BOY, particularly a Jewish boy, could not fail to be aware of the Second World War. The headlines were full of strange words such as *Blitzkrieg* and *Anschluss*. Parents whispered about the fate of European relatives. In 1942, when Sagan was seven, the struggle between fascism and democracy took place literally within earshot. His friend Robert Gritz remembers lying in bed at night and listening to the far-off "boom!" of exploding merchant ships, more victims of Hitler's "wolf packs." Kids on Brooklyn beaches stumbled on the resulting debris— binoculars, jackets, body parts.[67]

"Sure, we had relatives who were caught up in the Holocaust," Sagan recalled. "Hitler was not a popular fellow in our household, even before the war. But on the other hand, I was fairly insulated from the horrors of the war. . . . I spent time drawing Grumman Avengers shooting down Stukas."[68] "Fairly insulated" is correct. Rachel, Cari says, "above all wanted to protect Carl from the horrors of war. . . . She had an extraordinarily difficult time dealing with World War II and the Holocaust. This was something that was never talked about, essentially, that I can recall. . . . We had relatives who were slaughtered."[69] By shielding Carl's eyes from the ongoing apocalypse, Rachel ensured that he would grow up an optimist. Emotionally, that optimism would be his greatest strength; intellectually, it would be his greatest liability. It was a mental blinder that kept him politically naive until he was in his fifties, when he finally opened his eyes and faced the dragon in his mental Eden: the nuclear age, the threat of global annihilation. Carl inherited this mixed legacy from Rachel.

"I wouldn't say she was ugly or plain," Gritz says of Rachel. "You wouldn't give her a second look, but you wouldn't say, 'Oooh, she's funny-looking.'" Rachel frequented a beauty salon run by Gritz's father. Sometimes she brought Carl. "She dressed nicely—a skirt, makeup, her hair coiffed. She took good care of herself." While Rachel submitted herself to Mr. Gritz's handiwork, Carl and Robert played outside. "Cops and robbers, Americans versus the Nazis, and so on." Young Carl was "well built—very athletic," in contrast to the exercise-averse, skinny adult he would become.

Sagan "kept his nose in the air" and had little to do with most children, Gritz recalled. "He was aloof—'standoffish' is the best description. Head in the clouds. . . . I think his mother inculcated in him an idea that they were somehow better than the riffraff in the street. . . . I could speak to him about things I couldn't speak [about] to my other friends. My relationship with my other friends was almost one-dimensional—there was no intellectual or cultural interaction. But with Carl, it was on different levels."[70]

Sagan's parents were liberal Democrats.[71] That was nothing unusual in the Brooklyn of that day, where FDR was second only to Moses and where many neighbors were farther left. (Gritz recalls assuming that Carl's parents weren't Communists simply because they didn't greet friends as "comrade.") This politically lively atmosphere nurtured Sagan's lifelong liberalism. Also, the culture tolerated oddballs (to quote Irving Howe: "Attitudes of tolerance, feelings that one had to put up with one's cranks, eccentrics, idealists, and extremists, pervaded the Jewish community").[72] This tolerance may explain Sagan's adult willingness to converse calmly with, rather than to eviscerate, his ideological opposites—from pseudoscientists to theologians to militarists.

Sagan's parents, too, knew the fine art of restraint: "I never saw his parents lay a hand on him," Gritz says. "He was an only child for a long time. He was the apple of their eye. He got a lot more from them than we did from our parents, materially speaking." The Sagans didn't have much money in the early days; Carl slept in his parents' bedroom. Yet Sam and Rachel managed to create a cultivated, upscale atmosphere. They even bought a small piano. Sagan recalled "a lively intellectual life. . . . Both my father and mother read, there were wonderful arguments about politics and other matters, friends and visitors that I got to listen to [while] sitting in the corner. We had Shakespeare in the house."[73] Other boys in the neighborhood built toy ray guns "out of old orange crates," Gritz says, but Carl "didn't have to do that; his parents would buy [toys] for him." A half-century later, Sagan wrote evocatively about the day that his parents bought him a pricey electric train with tracks and a headlight.

Yet Sagan was not spoiled. He was, in fact, unusually deferential to his parents. This amused his friends. "Carl called his father 'Father' and his mother 'Mother,'" Gritz says. "Nobody did that in those days! Your mother was 'Ma,' your father was 'Dad' or 'Pa.' People laughed at him because it was peculiar." Sagan also pronounced aunt "ahhnt"—more grounds for neighborhood merriment. When Carl told Gritz, "My mother said I have to be home by three o'clock," Carl left in time, Gritz recalls. "He was a very obedient person, a very conforming child to his parents' wishes, which we [other boys] were not."

Still, fires burned inside Sagan. He permitted a lucky few to feel their warmth. Gritz recalls how they cooed over a deck of "French postcards"—playing cards displaying naked women. They also shared more sophisticated interests. For one thing, they listened to classical records together; Sagan was a real aficionado of the musical masters. "My mother had classical records and an old wind-up phonograph," Gritz says. "We listened to classical music together; we enjoyed that very much. [The Sagans] had a record of Toscanini playing the Rossini overture to *William Tell* with the famous finale, the 'Lone Ranger' music." Decades later, Sagan's passion for the classics would be reflected in his choices of music to be included on the *Voyager* record, bound for the stars. "We also listened to the radio together—*Captain Midnight* and *Superman*. Sagan was *very* big into *Superman*." Gritz recalls that in one of their favorite shows (from his description, it was probably *Superstition*), mysteries, especially occult ones, prove to have simple, logical explanations. Did *Superstition* reinforce Sagan's fledgling skeptical tendencies?

The boys also experimented with lenses to make objects appear closer. Coincidentally, Sagan had begun to wonder about the stars: what were they? He recalled one winter in Brooklyn when he was five years old. The stars, he said,

> seemed to me different. They just weren't like everything else.
> And so I asked other kids what they were. . . . They said things like "they're lights in the sky, kid."
> I could tell they were lights in the sky, but what were they—little electric bulbs on long black wires? . . . I asked my parents, they didn't know. I asked friends of my parents, they didn't know.
> [His mother suggested:] "I've just gotten you your first library card. Take the streetcar to the New Utrecht branch of the New York Public Library and find a book. . . . [The answer] has to be in a book."
> I went to the library. I asked the librarian for a book on the stars. She came back and gave me a book. I opened it. It was filled with pictures of people like Jean Harlow and Clark Gable.

I was humiliated. I gave it back to her and said, "This wasn't the kind of stars I had in mind." She thought this was hilarious, which humiliated me further. She then went and got the right kind of book. I took it—a simple kid's book. I sat down on a little chair—a pint-sized chair—and turned the pages until I came to the answer.

And the answer was stunning. It was that the Sun was a star but really close. The stars were suns, but so far away they were just little points of light. . . . And while I didn't know the [inverse] square law of light propagation or anything like that, still, it was clear to me that you would have to move that Sun enormously far away, further away than Brooklyn [for the stars to appears as dots of light]. . . .

The scale of the universe suddenly opened up to me. [It was] kind of a religious experience. [There] was a magnificence to it, a grandeur, a scale which has never left me. Never ever left me.[74]

By the time Carl and Robert were six or seven, they found that by holding two lenses in the right positions, they "could see the craters on the Moon," Gritz recalls. They also studied "the red colors of Mars." The boys broadened their astronomical education by visiting the American Museum of Natural History in New York City, and its famous Hayden Planetarium. The displays included meteorites, rocks from space. One imagines them standing awestruck before these celestial oddities. Their very solidity proved what Sagan would later emphasize in lectures: space is a *place*.

Carl Sagan later wrote about his childhood trips to the museum. "I was transfixed by the dioramas—lifelike representations of animals and their habitats all over the world. Penguins on the dimly lit Antarctic ice; okapi in the bright African veldt; a family of gorillas, the male beating his chest, in a shaded forest glade; an American grizzly bear standing on his hind legs, ten or twelve feet tall, and staring me right in the eye."[75] Like many children, Sagan became fascinated by dinosaurs and read all he could about them.[76]

Popular culture reinforced Sagan's growing interest in science. His parents had taken him to see the 1939 New York World's Fair and Walt Disney's film *Fantasia*, both of which excited him about different aspects of science (the latter included a dinosaur sequence).

Sagan was also a sports buff. Contrary to stereotypes about Jewish intellectuals as Woody Allenish nebbishes, the New York Jewish community encouraged an interest in sports, especially basketball and baseball. Baseball players like Sandy Koufax (Brooklyn's own) and Moe Berg (Princeton grad, spied for the Allies during World War II) symbolized what Jews could achieve in America.[77] Carl "was really a fanatic Yankee fan," Gritz says. "We could recite the batting averages of all the guys on the team."

Indeed, numbers enthralled Sagan, especially big ones. At age eight, the future author of *Billions and Billions* had the "childish compulsion to write in sequence all the integers from 1 to 1,000. We had no pads of paper, but my father offered up the stack of gray cardboards he had been saving from when his shirts were sent to the laundry." His mother interrupted the project: Carl had to bathe. The boy protested. Supportive in ways unimagined by Dr. Spock, Sam offered to continue writing the numbers while his son washed. "By the time I emerged, he was approaching 900, and I was able to reach 1,000 only a little past my ordinary bedtime. The magnitude of large numbers has never ceased to impress me."[78]

The Sagans also subsidized Carl's growing interest in chemistry by buying him chemistry sets, with literally explosive results.[79]

HOW DID SAGAN become interested in the possibility of extraterrestrial life? It would be satisfying to report that he traced his interest to Orson Welles's notorious "War of the Worlds" radio broadcast of Halloween 1938. Welles and his radio actors depicted a Martian invasion of Grovers Mill, New Jersey, as if it were really happening—as if New Jersey were under assault by Martians, armed to their tentacles with ray guns and poison gas. Unfortunately for biographers, Sagan was four years old at that time. He never mentioned having heard it. It might even have been past his bedtime. Still, the resulting brouhaha—front-page press coverage, exaggerated reports of attempted suicides and riots—tells us something about the mood of the era.[80] While most astronomers scoffed at talk of Martians, the public assumed they might indeed exist.

Is it a coincidence that belief in Martians surged in the late nineteenth century, along with belief in ghosts and otherworldly "ectoplasm," while traditional religions waned?[81] Enter Percival Lowell, a member of a distinguished Boston family. He was a diplomat, experienced in the courts of the Far East, and an elegant, rather romantic writer. On the brink of age forty, Lowell abandoned the diplomatic corps to found an astronomical observatory in Flagstaff, Arizona, bankrolled by family money. There, from the early 1890s until his death in 1916, he used his refractor to sketch Mars and its "long, thin" lines—"a mesh of lines and dots like a lady's veil." He claimed the lines were "canals" built by a dying race of Martians. (He was inspired by Italian astronomer Giovanni Schiaparelli, who in 1877 first saw the lines and called them "canali" [channels], which was mistranslated into English as "canals.") Their goal: to channel water from the polar caps to famine-stricken farmlands. Lowell wrote several enjoyable books about his observations, gave rousing public speeches, chatted with reporters—there was a touch of the adult Carl Sagan about him.[82] After his demise, most astronomers dismissed the "canals" as optical illusions. Still, the mass media, especially science-fiction pulp magazines, kept alive the legend of the Martian canals. It was the UFO fad of its era, impermeable to scientific scorn. According to Sagan, by age ten he was steeped in the "romantic and wonderful" legends of the canals.[83]

Cultural historians and social psychologists might read all kinds of meanings into Lowell's vision of the ill-fated red planet. The late nineteenth century was, after all, the great age of terrestrial canal-building: the Suez, Panama, and other grand waterways were in planning or under construction. And throughout the millennia, humans have projected earthly images onto the stars, seeing human and animal shapes in the constellations, perceiving a "face" on the Moon.[84] So why shouldn't an age of great engineers imagine canals on Mars? Lowell might also have projected onto Mars the fear he perhaps shared with other fin de siècle, wealthy, New England–bred white Protestant males that their "genteel" breed would be swamped by the swelling tide of poor, illiterate, non-Protestant, Eastern European (often Jewish) immigrants (like Sam Sagan).[85] Perhaps that is why Lowell wrote so poignantly about the frantic inhabitants of the fourth planet. Modern SETI (Search for Extra-Terrestrial Intelligence) buffs claim that galactic aliens have super-technologies indistinguishable from magic. Likewise, Lowell assumed that the Martians were superior to us:

> A mind of no mean order would seem to have presided over the [canal] system we see,—a mind certainly of considerably more comprehensiveness than that which presides over the various departments of our own public works. Party politics, at all events, have had no part in them; for the system is planet wide. Quite possibly, such Martian folk are possessed of inventions of which we have not dreamed, and with them electrophones and kinetoscopes are things of a bygone past, preserved with veneration in museums as relics of the clumsy contrivances of the simple childhood of the race. Certainly, what we see hints at the existence of beings who are in advance of, not behind us, in the journey of life.

Yet the Martians were doomed.

> The drying-up of the planet is certain to proceed until its surface can support no life at all. Slowly but surely time will snuff it out. When the last ember is thus extinguished, the planet will roll a dead world through space, its evolutionary career forever ended.[86]

Carl Sagan was eight when he decided that extraterrestrials exist. Since stars are other suns (he reasoned), then they might have planets— perhaps inhabited ones. He might have been nudged toward this conclusion by a news story in early 1943. That January, news media publicized an article in the *Astrophysical Journal* reporting a possible discovery of an extrasolar planet (a planet that orbits another star). Astronomers Dirk Reuyl and Erik Holmberg of the University of Virginia said they had detected an unusual wobble in the absolute motion of a star, 70 Ophiuchi. They attributed the wobbling to the back-and-forth gravitational tug of a huge object, ten times the mass of Jupiter, as it orbited the star. Was it a planet?[87]

In the early twentieth century, extrasolar planets were thought to be extremely rare. The leading concept of planetary formation was various "tidal" hypotheses. According to these, long ago the Sun almost collided with another star. During the close encounter, the Sun ejected hot gases. The gases condensed into Earth and other planets. Space is so vast that stellar near collisions are very rare; therefore, according to the astronomer James Jeans, extrasolar planets must also be very rare. And if there are no extrasolar planets, then there can be no aliens outside the solar system.[88] In June 1934, just before Sagan's birth, the astronomer Henry Norris Russell of Princeton University wrote an article for *Scientific American* entitled "Fading Belief in Life on Other Planets." In Olaf Stapledon's visionary tale *Star Maker*, written in the 1930s, a traveler journeys through a James Jeans–like cosmos and laments: "The appalling desert of darkness and barren fire, the huge emptiness so sparsely prickled with scintillations, the colossal futility of the whole universe, hideously oppressed me."[89]

But tidal hypotheses soon fell out of favor. Russell's graduate student, Lyman Spitzer Jr., showed that the solar ejecta would be too unstable to condense into planets. In the 1940s, astronomers returned to a modified version of a much older theory of planetary formation, the nebular hypothesis. This hypothesis held that the Sun, Earth, other planets, and their moons coalesced from a primordial cloud of dust and gases. Such clouds pervade the galaxy; presumably, they are continually collapsing into new planetary systems. Hence extrasolar planets should be common. And aliens, too? In 1943, Reuyl and Holmberg's "discovery" of an extrasolar planet (later disproven) received a fair amount of press coverage. It might have been a factor in Sagan's decision that aliens exist.

Another factor was Edgar Rice Burroughs. When Sagan was ten, a friend introduced him to Burroughs's writings. Nowadays, Burroughs is mainly remembered as the creator of Tarzan, the ape-man. But Burroughs was also the George Lucas of his day, a prolific author of fabulous outer-space romances set on Mars, Venus, the Moon, and other worlds. Sagan found these tales of exotic extraterrestrial worlds teeming with otherworldly creatures fascinating.

Burroughs was born in 1875, the son of a Union soldier who became a Chicago businessman. The boy yearned for a life of adventure. At age twenty-one, he served with the 7th U.S. Cavalry at Fort Grant, Arizona.

While in Arizona, he might have learned about Lowell's Mars research at his Flagstaff observatory. Burroughs chased Apaches; otherwise, his dreams of glory came to nothing. By 1911, at age thirty-six, he was back in Chicago, a financial failure, selling pencil sharpeners and pawning his wife's jewelry. On a whim, he began writing a fantasy story, "Under the Moons of Mars." It told about a soldier-cowboy who traveled to the red planet. In 1912 he sold the tale to *All-Story* magazine for $400, a lot of money in those days. Many more stories followed. Then books—stacks of them. He was a writing machine. He became wealthy. He settled in southern California, where his Tarzan stories were made into films with Johnny Weissmuller and other actors. The town of Tarzana is named after Burroughs's most famous creation.

Burroughs's Mars novels are not science fiction per se. Rather, they mingle elements of Wild West tales and "sword and sorcery" literature. The hero is John Carter, a Virginia gentleman who became a Confederate soldier. After Appomattox, he heads west to become a cowboy. While in the Arizona Territory, he hides in a cave to escape Apache attackers. For some reason, he undergoes a psychic experience in which "there was a momentary feeling of nausea, a sharp click as of the snapping of a steel wire. . . ." He looked down and saw his body on the cave floor. His soul left the cave, looked skyward, and was "drawn with the suddenness of thought through the trackless immensity of space." After "an instant of extreme cold and utter darkness . . . I opened my eyes upon a strange and weird landscape." He was standing on the surface of Mars. Various adventures followed—encounters with many-armed aliens, rescuing the beautiful Martian princess, and so on.

Young Carl was captivated. He even tried to repeat Carter's spiritual voyage to Mars. As he recalled: "[Carter] was able to transport himself to the planet Mars by standing in an open field and sort of spreading out his arms and wishing. At least that's as close as I could get to the method. And at an early age, eight or nine, I tried very hard to put the Carter method to the experimental test. But no matter how hard I tried, it failed—perhaps not entirely to my surprise, but I thought there was always a chance."[90]

THE WORLD OF SCIENCE FICTION became science reality in August 1945. The United States dropped two atomic bombs on Japan. Hundreds of thousands of people died; countless more suffered long-term illness. One of Sagan's friends explained to him why the bombs exploded: because they were made of atoms. For all its horrific potential, an incredible new source of power was now available for once-unthinkable feats—perhaps even spaceflight? Science-fiction magazines began depicting astronauts cruising the cosmos, borne by atom-powered rockets. Sagan quit fantasizing about soul travel to Mars and began thinking about rockets.[91]

"He was tall and gangly as a boy," recalls Rabbi Morrison Bial, now in his eighties, who trained Sagan for his bar mitzvah ceremony. "He was relatively quiet. But once you began talking to him, these things came out of him, [whereas] most of the boys had nothing particular to say. . . . At age twelve he knew more about stars and constellations and dinosaurs than I did." The ceremony was held at Beth Sholom–Peoples Temple (now Temple Beth Ahavath Sholom) at Bay Parkway and Benson Avenue in Bensonhurst. Bial has instructed countless bar mitzvah pupils over the decades; Sagan is one of the few he vividly remembers. (Another one, by coincidence, is radioastronomer Paul Horowitz, a leading figure in the search for extraterrestrial intelligence.)[92]

The Second World War had boosted the Sagan family's fortunes. The garment industry boomed (soldiers needed uniforms). Thanks to cousin George, Sam became manager of the New York Girl Coat Company's factory in Perth Amboy, New Jersey; the family bought a house at 576 Bryant Street in the nearby town of Rahway. Carl transferred from David A. Boody Junior High School in Brooklyn to Rahway High School, which he entered in September 1948.[93] Compared to Brooklyn, Rahway had few Jews. It was an industrial town—smoky, dirty, smelly, not particularly cultivated. (Nowadays it is best known as the site of a major prison and of Merck Pharmaceuticals.) Carl often rode around town on his Schwinn bicycle.

Rahway High was a "tan brick, nondescript building built around a courtyard, three stories high," recalls Sagan's fellow student Deborah M. Shillaber. "We were in the same math class. I was the only girl. He was impressed (a) that there was a girl in the class and (b) that there was someone that could get the same grades he could get." She laughed. "We were both straight-A students in everything.

"He was so bright! All of us immediately sensed that. He made comments in class that would have let us know he was bright—which would have turned off some children who were afraid of him or awed by him. 'Arrogant' is a good way [to describe him]. I was almost going to say 'pompous.' "[94]

School frustrated Sagan in part because of his intelligence. As an adult he recalled being bored in high school because he wasn't challenged by the work and his teachers' lectures were uninspiring. His teachers, however, were alert enough to appreciate Sagan's brains. He was a mythology buff; once, he "covered every [black]board in the entire classroom, of which there were many, in detail about the histories of the Greek and Roman gods," his sister, Cari, remembers. "Right then and there, the administration of the high school said to my parents, 'This kid ought go to a school for gifted children, he has something really remarkable.' My parents chose not to do that. He went to Rahway High School. They thought he'd get the education he needed there." Money might have been an obstacle: the school for the gifted was expensive, perhaps costlier than Sam and Rachel could afford.[95]

Shillaber says Carl "was our basketball scorekeeper and 'statistician' for the boys' basketball [games]. We traveled on the boys' basketball bus because I was a cheerleader." The other cheerleaders, perky and voluptuous in their red, black, and white uniforms, were more interested in the basketball players, and huddled beside them on the bus. So Shillaber and Carl sat together. She remembers him as being physically well-built, "a rather imposing presence," but "a bit awkward, a bit of a loner.

"When we went to out-of-town games, we sat together and argued over a book [we had] read or what had gone on in a class that day. There was no sexual interest [between us] whatsoever. At the time, I was going with a guy at Harvard, so I was not interested in anybody in the high school." She "didn't find [Carl] particularly attractive. [He was] almost nerdy! He was not unattractive physically, [but] I don't recall he ever made any overtures to any girls."

He told her about astronomy. "He was so gung-ho about his desire to learn astronomy. His eyes lit up when he would start to talk about this. It went over like a lead balloon with me. {But} it was something to let him talk about when [we were] on a bus for a long ride." There weren't many bright males at Rahway High, Shillaber notes; few students went on to college, and most of them to a state school.

Shillaber is now a widow and a volunteer middle-school librarian. "I was not born in the era when women had to have a career," she sighs. "I could never settle on what to do with my life." Carl Sagan—male, driven, and insatiably curious—would never have that problem.[96]

SAGAN WAS PRESIDENT of the Rahway High chemistry club, which met on the first and third Thursdays of each month. Meanwhile, at home on Bryant Street, he maintained his own basement laboratory. "My prize piece of equipment was a Leibig condenser." He used dangerous chemicals such as hydrofluoric acid, and conducted research in a "completely unsystematic" way. He used cardboard cutouts of atoms to teach himself about atomic valence states. Thanks to the cutouts, "you could actually build up 'molecules' in two dimensions. . . . I found that about as interesting as doing [chemical] experiments." This was an early hint that he would incline toward theoretical work, not lab experimentation.

Another hint was his failed attempt, at age twelve or thirteen, while still in Brooklyn, to impress a slightly older girl and her sister. He showed the girls his basement lab. His chemical equipment glistened. During their visit, he "succeeded in blowing up a test tube." The girl's sister ran out in horror, "holding her eyes. I thought I'd done something terrible. But I didn't." The worst consequence was a black stain on the ceiling. A theoretician in the making.[97]

But would he actually become a scientist? He was taunted by the memory of an encounter with his maternal grandfather, Louis Gruber. Mr. Gruber was a very practical man. He had survived poverty and oppression; talk of stars made no sense to him. Through a translator, grandpa asked Carl what he wanted to do for a living. Carl said he hoped to become an astronomer. The grandfather replied impatiently: "Yes, but how will you make a living?"

A shadow of doubt arose in Sagan's mind. Were people actually paid to be astronomers? He dreaded going into some dull workaday job. "Some summers I stayed at home, resolutely refusing to go and work in my father's factory, which was proposed to me—that seemed like death."[98]

A high school teacher set him straight. His sophomore biology instructor, Lee Yothers, said he was pretty sure that Harvard paid astronomer Harlow Shapley a salary, Sagan recalled. "That was a splendid day—when I began to suspect that if I tried hard I could do astronomy full-time, not just part-time."[99]

Yothers's good news came at an ideal time. In the late 1940s a new age was dawning. Scientists in New Mexico were launching surplus Nazi V-2 rockets to the fringe of space.[100] The RAND Corporation in California was investigating the feasibility of space satellites. In January 1946, radar engineers with the Signal Corps near Belmar, New Jersey— about twenty miles from Brooklyn—bounced a radar signal off the Moon.[101] A front-page story in the New York Times speculated that the technique might be used to communicate with other worlds.[102]

But would humanity survive long enough to realize such wonders? Other headlines were ominous: Winston Churchill warned that an "iron curtain" was descending over Eastern Europe; the Soviets developed their own atomic bomb; "Mr. X," writing in Foreign Affairs, called for "containing" the USSR; China went Communist; war began in Korea. Many adults despaired. The former utopian H. G. Wells announced that the end of the world was nigh and penned his grim farewell book, Mind at the End of Its Tether.[103] But Sagan was young and eager to see tomorrow. Amid the clanking of swords, he heard only the roar of distant rockets.

By that time, he had graduated from Burroughs's Mars novels to more sophisticated forms of science fiction. In 1947, while passing through a candy store, he discovered a magazine called *Astounding Science Fiction*.[104] The cover depicted a futuristic atomic power plant. He paid twenty-five cents for it, then sat down on an outdoor bench and began reading a short story—"Pete Can Fix It" by Raymond F. Jones.

The story stars a boy almost exactly Sagan's age at the time, thirteen-year-old Jack, the son of a nuclear physicist named Professor Grandin. The story opens as the Grandin family is driving on vacation across the American Southwest toward Los Angeles. Jack is a clever boy, the narrator notes: "The boy's intuition for mechanical and electrical tinkering was little short of genius. He . . . spoke of [subatomic particles] . . . with the same familiarity that others of his generation spoke of baseballs and Boy Scout hikes."

En route to L.A., the family sees a succession of road signs that declare: "Pete Can Fix It." They finally reach a filling station, "Pete's." Pete emerges. He is a gaunt, spooky-looking young man with strangely discolored skin who "moved stiffly as if from painfully arthritic joints." Unbeknownst to them, he is a visitor from a parallel Earth in an alternate universe. On that alternate Earth, a nuclear war had ravaged civilization. Using a mysterious gizmo, Pete stimulates the Grandins' brains so that they imagine they are seeing the ruins of his former planet, a devastated "parallel" Los Angeles. "As far as their eyes could see there were only skeletons of buildings, vast heaps of rubble and debris—and nowhere any life." Pete shows his customers these dreadful sights in hopes of preventing a similar nuclear holocaust on the Grandin family's Earth.

To educate people about nuclear war, Pete declares, one must scare them nearly to death. For "reasoning, argument, pleading will never keep man from pulling down the world about his own head. Only fear, terrible shattering fear of the consequences can persuade him to turn aside from self-destruction." He urges young Jack to follow his example: "Fear—fill the whole Earth with fear—fear of man's own evil."[105] The plot is eerily significant, considering Sagan's later career as an antinuclear activist. As Sagan's friend Ronald Blum characterized it, Sagan's goal with the "nuclear winter" campaign was "his greatest gift to mankind—to scare the shit out of everybody. He should have gotten the Nobel Prize for it."[106]

Sagan later wrote that as a boy in the late 1940s, "Pete Can Fix It" introduced him to "the social implications of nuclear weapons. It got you thinking."[107] He became a science-fiction fanatic.

Sagan had literary ambitions of his own. His mother was a skilled writer and an articulate exponent; so was Carl. He read extensively on the subject of extraterrestrial life and memorized all the arguments in its favor. About age sixteen, he wrote (in pencil) a long essay on extraterrestrial life in a school notebook. Portions are reproduced below with spelling and grammatical errors intact.

Sagan began by emphasizing the sheer immensity of the cosmos:

> Let us pause a moment to observe our universe. The group of stars, of which our sun is one, our galaxy, is known as the Milky Way. A conservative estimate places the number of stars in it at 300,000 million. Probably, it is at least 400,000,000,000 considering the multitude of undiscovered "dwarfs," "dark stars," and the like.
>
> Within the range of the Hale telescope at Palomar are over a hundred million extragalactic nebulae which are galaxies similar to our own. Astronomers are convinced that our galaxy is little better than average in respect to total number of stars. Taking the conservative estimate of the previous paragraph, we arrive at the stupendous total of 30 quintillion (30,000,000,000,000,000,000) stars or another way, thirty million million million stars photographicable by man. And if this total is a bit overwhelming, to you, dear reader, [do you] know the estimated number of stars in the universe? No? Then sit down and loosen your collar button. The number in very round figures is somewhat more than one hundred seventy octillion (170,000,000,000,000,000,000,000,000,000) stars. This number is about 170 trillion times more than all the men, women, and children ever born on this planet since the first *Homo Heidelbergensis* evolved over a million years ago. Take every grain of sand on every beach on the Earth. Multiply it by ten. That number is now one-one hundredth the number of stars in the universe.
>
> The reader now, perhaps, has some idea as to the immensity of the universe.

He alluded to the old tidal hypotheses of planetary formation, according to which planets had condensed from solar ejecta ("chunks," in Sagan's term). The tidal hypotheses implied that extrasolar planets were rare. Carl would have none of that. He assured his readers that

> the Tidal Theory simply was incorrect. There are at least half a dozen glaring errors, probably more. Our knowledge of gravity and atomic physics reveals that if two stars travelling at several miles per second in different directions proximate close enough for a gravitational clash either (1) the larger would attract the smaller to it, resulting in a collossal cosmic explosion (i.e., a nova); (2) the smaller would become a satellite of the larger (i.e., a double star); (3) their respective orbits would be alterred, resulting in no immediate damage. . . . However, chunks would certainly *not* be extracted. Princeton's Dr. Henry Norris Russell has stated that if the alien sun did proximate close enough for tidal disruption to occur, it could hardly have provided the angular momentum the [solar] system now possesses. . . . Dr. [Lyman] Spitzer, at Yale Observatory has deduced that if extremely hot gas is extracted from a

sun, it would not condense into planets and satellites, but, rather, diffuse explosively.[108]

Might extrasolar planets be inhabited? This question got him interested in biology. He read a popular work, *Life on Other Worlds* (1940) by Sir Harold Spencer Jones, the British Astronomer Royal. The book included a detailed discussion of organic molecules and environments conducive to life. Jones emphasized the crucial link between the chemical origin of life and the possibility of extraterrestrial life. "What is certain is that if suitable conditions exist, if there is an adequate supply of energy and if there is a suitable transformer for that energy, which can turn it into the chemical energy of carbon compounds, then the complex organic substances which form the basis of living cells not only can arise but will arise. . . . It seems reasonable to suppose that wherever in the Universe the proper conditions arise, *life must inevitably come into existence*" (emphasis added). Sagan's heart surely soared when he read that.

Sagan was even willing to allow for the possibility of life on a seemingly hostile, frigid, giant gas planet—Jupiter. Jones had written of the outer planets: "These dreary, remote, frozen wastes of the solar system are not worlds where we can hope to find life of any sort."[109] But in his essay the young Sagan countered:

> Today, human vanity, although not so much the Church, is again retarding scientific progress. For a reason which the author cannot fathom, few scientific journals will accept a paper for publication which bases its body upon, for example, a discussion that it is conceivable for a totally alien form of life to exist on a planet such as Jupiter. To the average reader, the preceding statement seems somewhat absurd if he is aware that a human being transported to Jupiter would be simultaneously asphyxiated, poisoned, frozen solid and crushed by his own weight. Nevertheless, it is entirely feasible for a form of life to exist on Jupiter as I will prove below.

What was Sagan's "proof"? Unfortunately, his unfinished essay never returns to this issue. That's a shame, for Sagan, as an adult, would spend much time investigating the feasibility of Jovian life.

The essay is obviously the work of a budding popular writer. Sagan favors short, direct, subject-predicate sentences. He employs down-to-earth analogies that would tantalize lay readers. For example, he discusses how natural selection "selects" favorable mutations:

> Picture a Devonian Period fish. He lived about 350 million years ago. He is gigantic, grotesque, and carnivorous. He has a number of baby fish. One, upon birth, can extract oxygen from air. Other fishes cannot.

Therefore, this newborn fish is a mutation. However, other fish can extract oxygen from sea water. The newborn fish can only extract oxygen from air. He is born in sea water. Hence, he is asphxiated [*sic*].

. . . Now picture another Devonian Period fish. He has a number of baby fish. One, upon birth, can extract oxygen from air. Other fishes cannot. Therefore, this newborn fish is a mutation. If he were to be born underwater, he would die at birth. However, his egg rises to the surface. He is born above water. He experiments with his fins. Soon he swims away. He reaches land and drags himself upon the beach. . . . These . . . are no longer fish; they are amphibians. The Carboniferous Period has begun.

Which brings him back to his key point: aliens surely exist.

Non-injurious mutations have occurred on this planet [Earth]. They are occurring on this planet. They will keep on occurring on this planet. Now why in the name of logic can't they occur on another planet?

"In the name of logic." As his later life would show, this could have been his credo.

What would the extraterrestrials look like? In science-fiction magazines of the 1940s, they either looked absurdly human (like crew-cut bankers in silver suits) or incredibly weird (multi-tentacled, multi-eyed, and the like).[110] This question forced Sagan to confront the concept of biological evolution. Evolutionary biologists had long debated whether evolution "converges" or "diverges." By the former, they meant a tendency to generate similar-looking life forms in like environments. By the latter, they meant a tendency to generate a wide diversity of life forms, rarely if ever repeating the same models. The history of life offers examples of both convergence and divergence. For example, nature has (many biologists believe) "re-invented" the eye numerous times; hence it is an example of convergence. But kangaroos imply divergence: they are found only in Australia.[111]

Perhaps inspired by the bizarre alien menageries of science fiction, Sagan opted for divergence—with one crucial caveat. On the one hand, he believed that physically speaking, extraterrestrials would hardly resemble us at all. They might not even have similar biochemistry (organic molecules based on carbon). Quoting again from his notebook essay:

"Life as we know it" is principally any organism with a carbon-hydrogen-oxygen-nitrogen metabolism. That is to say, without oxygen, hydrogen, nitrogen, and carbon, life as we know it is impossible.

> . . . [But:] Almost beyond the shadow of a doubt, there is life as we
> *don't* know it. Yes, the author is speaking of a life-form that does *not* pos-
> sess a C-O-H-N metabolism; that does *not* demand Terran [terrestrial]
> standards of maxima and minima in regard to atmospheric pressure and
> constituents, gravity, temperature and 'toxics'; and that does not look,
> smell, or feel like anything we know of . . . [that is] utterly alien.

On the other hand (as Sagan argued later, as an adult), he believed
that life ultimately advances toward the biological function that humans
call "intelligence." Intelligence enhances survival (he believed); hence
evolution favors it. Hence aliens not only exist, they are "intelligent" in
a human or neohuman sense of the word. Therefore we might be
able to communicate with them (for example, through mathematical
code), even if they are physically as different from us as bananas or
coffeepots.

This is as good a time as any to raise an important point, one that
will be significant later in this book. The modern search for extraterrestrial intelligence (SETI) is based on the assumption that intelligence is a
convergent biological trait—that is, a trait generated over and over again
on many worlds. If it isn't, then there's no one out there intelligent
enough to "talk" to! Indeed, anti-SETI scientists might accuse SETI
advocates (like Sagan) of trying to have their evolutionary cake and eat it
too; that is, of accepting the randomness and infrequent repeatability of
all kinds of biological traits, *save one:* intelligence. As if the medieval
"great chain of being"[112] were still in business, SETI enthusiasts treat
intelligence as the ultimate goal of all evolution, as the apex toward
which life converges on all worlds.

Yet on Earth, only one of Earth's billions of estimated species, *Homo
sapiens*, has ever developed anything like the intelligence of humans.
(Chimps playing with colored chips and counting up to nine won't cut
it.) And why (critics ask) should the universe be any different? The cosmos might be crawling with life, yet none of it might care to, or be able
to, "communicate" with us, any more than we can, or wish to, "communicate" with tapeworms, aardvarks, or dung beetles.[113]

As we shall see, the adult Sagan's insistence on the inevitability of
cosmic intelligence is important partly because it undergirded his quasi-
religious belief in alien super-beings. He believed that these creatures,
perhaps dwelling in other galaxies, were benevolent and might help us to
solve our terrestrial problems. Viewed from a psychological perspective,
they were secular versions of the gods and angels he had long since abandoned. His secular "faith" stemmed from the choice he made when he
reached the two paths diverging in the evolutionary yellow wood—the
paths of divergence and convergence. Assuming intelligence to be a uni-

versal phenomenon, he chose the latter path, and that would make all the difference.

Sagan's notebook concludes with a few scattered, intriguing inserts—for example, a long calculation that concludes: "A point on the equator of a globe ten feet in diameter must make 31,293,864 revolutions per/second to attain a speed equivalent to the speed of light." At the end of the notebook, the teenager recorded this quote from Albert Einstein: "Common sense is actually nothing more than a deposit of prejudices laid down in the mind prior to the age of 18."

A WOULD-BE CAREERIST must be not merely smart and hardworking. He or she must also make the right contacts—must befriend influential people. Sagan learned this fact early. When he became interested in space travel, he sought information from top experts. Another child might have settled for a trip to the school library. Not Sagan. He wanted to talk to the Ph.D.'s, the engineers—the rocket-builders themselves.

For example, he suspected (as many did after the invention of nuclear weapons) that the first space rockets would be atomic-powered. The Fairchild Engine and Airplane Company was working on nuclear-powered aircraft in Oak Ridge, Tennessee. He wondered: Were these aircraft the ancestors of atomic rockets? So Sagan wrote to the company. An official wrote back, stating that the project was "highly classified" and no further information was available. Meanwhile, a fledgling military think tank called RAND Corporation in Santa Monica, California, had recently designed a model for a space satellite. Sagan wrote to RAND, too, seeking literature, but RAND turned him down perfunctorily.[114] Sagan was sixteen, restless to escape New Jersey, to punch a hole in the sky. Didn't anyone care?

He struck gold, though, when he wrote to astronomers. One was Robert S. Richardson, who worked at the brand-new Palomar Observatory in faraway southern California. There, under skies not yet obscured by smog and the electrical glow of shopping malls, observers used the world's biggest telescope to survey the cosmos. Richardson also wrote science fiction, which pleased Sagan: it "suggested to me an open mind." More decisive, perhaps, was Sagan's correspondence with another sometime science-fiction writer, the famed astronomer Donald Menzel of Harvard.[115] Their correspondence paid off: slightly more than a decade later, Menzel would invite Sagan to join the Harvard faculty.

STAGE PRESENCE—Carl Sagan had it. He was tall, and oddly attractive, with dark hair, piercing eyes, and an easy grin; well-spoken, with a deep voice, and erudite; and capable of charm and warmth. Briefly, he caught the acting bug. He appeared in both the junior and senior class plays. The latter performance, held November 17, 1950, was of James Thurber's comedy *The Goose Hangs High*. According to the 1951 yearbook, "A complicated plot concerning the financial troubles of the Ingals family held the suspense until the very end."[116] After the play, Rachel threw a party for Carl and the cast. With typical cleverness, she made a cake in the shape of a goose. The goose's neck broke, so Rachel supported it with a ribbon attached to the ceiling.[117]

Across the nation, wiry antennae were sprouting from rooftops. The age of television had arrived, and Sagan wanted to be a part of it. According to his 1951 yearbook, he participated in a "Television Quiz Team" on WCBS-TV in New York. The yearbook ran a photo of Sagan beside this caption:

WAAT RADIO FORUM

On April 25, Carl Sagan, representing Rahway High School, participated in the Junior Town Meeting of the Air. Sponsored by the Kresge-Newark Department Store, and broadcast on station WAAT, the topic of the forum was "Is it socially desirable to televise investigations?" Charles Brown was alternate.

Sagan belonged to the high school debate club. In his junior year, he was the "American Education Week Essay Contest Winner." In his senior year, he placed second in the American Legion oratorical contest.[118] He was not averse to controversy. According to his third wife, Ann Druyan, he told her that in high school he had been denied victory in a Columbus Day speech contest because he dared to say the then-unsayable: Columbus's exploration of the New World wasn't necessarily a good thing.[119] It opened the door to European exploitation of the New World, with disastrous consequences for the natives.[120]

In Sagan's 1951 high school yearbook, his class photo appears on the same page as those of seven other males. His list of activities is more than twice as long as any of the rest. In his senior year he was sports editor for the largely female journalism club, which every two weeks published its newspaper, the *Wawawhack*, a small broadsheet. He was also president of both the French club and the chemistry club, and a member of the National Honor Society, the literary club, the debating club, the senior play, the chorus, and the Key club. Earlier in high school he had belonged to the photography club and the biology club. At his Brooklyn junior high school, he had been president of the science club. Although his Rahway classmate Deborah Shillaber recalls Sagan as a loner, he appears to have been well known: the senior class voted him both the male Class Brain and the male Most Likely to Succeed.

Clearly, he was a workaholic in the making. Of the seven other boys on that page in the yearbook, only two list career ambitions—one to be a carpenter, the other a mechanic. Under Sagan's photo are these words:

> Astronomy research is Carl's main aim,
> An excellent student, he should achieve fame.

CARL SAGAN WAS PART of a vanguard generation. Previously, anti-Semitic bigotry had blocked Jews from many careers, including academia and science. As historian David Hollinger has pointed out, in the 1930s it was considered amazing when Lionel Trilling won an assistant professorship at Columbia University.[121] In the year of Sagan's birth, no less a figure than T. S. Eliot wrote that for Christianity to thrive, "Any large number of free-thinking Jews" is "undesirable."[122] Then came World War II and the Holocaust, which shook the conscience of the Western world. American anti-Semitism waned. Sagan's generation of Jews, the children of impoverished immigrants, surged into the professions, into academia and science. Just as today's immigrant Asian-American parents push their young to study hard, to succeed, to make the family proud—in short, to prove they are "good Americans"—so did the immigrant Jewish parents of the Progressive era. Their pushing paid off: their young would soon constitute much of the American intelligentsia. In one of Sagan's college classes, as his friend Peter Pesch laughingly recalls, "the instructor was assigning lab partners and he'd be reading out these names—'Blum, Goldberg, Goldstein, Finklestein,' and then, all of a sudden, 'Cecil, Nanny,'—and somebody would shout out, 'Hey kid, don't you know we have a quota here?'"[123]

To choose a college, many young people consult with a high school guidance counselor. Not Sagan; he traveled to Princeton and spoke with one of the nation's leading astrophysicists, Lyman Spitzer Jr. (Spitzer helped to pioneer much "Big Science," including thermonuclear fusion research and the Hubble Space Telescope.) As Spitzer listened, Sagan explained that he wanted to be an astronomer who used space rockets. Did that mean he should take college engineering classes, as well as astronomy? "Up until then, I had thought this was necessary—another holdover from the fiction I'd been reading, in which the rich amateur built his own spaceship," Sagan recalled. Spitzer assured him that there was no reason an astronomer had to know "every nut and bolt of a spacecraft" in order to use it.[124] Leave the engineering to the engineers.

Sagan was intrigued by the catalog from the University of Chicago. "Inside was a picture of football players fighting on a field, and under it the caption 'If you want a school with good football, don't come to the University of Chicago.'

"Then there was a picture of some drunken kids, and the caption 'If you want a school with a good fraternity life, don't come to the University of Chicago.' It sounded like the place for me."[125] He applied and was accepted. (The school offered him a scholarship, which "made the decision extremely easy.")[126]

Sagan graduated from Rahway High School on June 5, 1951. That autumn he entered the University of Chicago. Less than a decade earlier on that campus, Prof. Enrico Fermi and his colleagues had secretly built the first nuclear reactor beneath the stands of a squash court.[127] Thus began the nuclear age, with all its dark prospects. Sagan entered college in the middle of the Korean War, the first major, if indirect, clash of the superpowers. The United States and the Soviet Union faced off over alternate visions of the ideal society. To many, compromise was unthinkable. Soon, some warned, the skies would rain atomic-tipped missiles. To remain an optimist, it helped to be very foolish or very young.

2

Chicago

IN THE LATE 1950s, C. P. Snow attracted attention for his theorizing on what he called the Two Cultures—the sciences and the humanities. Between them, Snow feared, yawned a chasm preventing those who staked their careers on poetry (say) from appreciating those who staked them on thermodynamics.[1] Carl Sagan did not directly address the Two Cultures issue, but he was clearly aware of it. His career as a science popularizer was a struggle to bridge that chasm, to show poets and thermodynamicists (and painters and astrophysicists, musicians and mathematicians) that they had something to say to each other.

To bridge this gap required special men and women. They had to have open minds, open hearts, and uncommonly broad educations in both sciences and humanities. They needed to know history—in particular, each culture's centuries-old debts to the other. Sagan fulfilled these requirements, thanks to all he learned at the University of Chicago.

"The Athens of the Midwest," admirers called it.[2] Sagan was one of the last beneficiaries of its controversial "Hutchins program" of classically oriented education. The program was named for Chancellor Robert M. Hutchins, who left the year Sagan enrolled. While too "dead white male" for today's tastes, the program in its heyday was an intellectual feast, and it transformed many students' lives. They could not pick and choose classes as they pleased, like the hors d'oeuvres of today's college catalogs (Foucaultian architecture here, Postmodern basketweaving there). Rather, they were required to study a fourteen-part curriculum built around classical works. The teaching was implicitly historical. If one was to study, say, Newtonian physics, then one began by reading Newton's original writings. Science was presented not as a separate discipline—as a royal road to truth, independent of other disciplines—but as part of the larger culture; in Sagan's words, "as an integral part of the gorgeous tapestry of human knowledge. It was considered unthinkable for an aspiring [Chicago] physicist not to know Plato, Aristotle, Bach, Shakespeare, Gibbon, Malinowski, and Freud—among many others."[3]

The program conveyed a crucial wisdom: The long saga of science is not the steady, dramatic march to truth depicted in high school classes and television documentaries. Rather, that saga includes many episodes when researchers wandered down blind alleys, utterly befuddled or, worse, dangerously confident as they neared disaster. Our ancestors were not idiots; they had perfectly good reason to believe what we now recognize as nonsense. "In an introductory science class," Sagan said, "Ptolemy's view that the Sun revolved around the Earth was presented so compellingly that some students found themselves reevaluating their commitment to Copernicus." Likewise, while studying chemistry at Chicago, Sagan's future wife Lynn (Alexander) Margulis temporarily accepted the eighteenth-century phlogiston theory. Another Chicago student, Sagan's friend Peter Pesch, an astronomer, observes that many of his scientific colleagues today are intellectually "very, very narrow." By contrast, "the kind of education that we got at Chicago made it possible for Sagan to do things like *Cosmos.*"

Anyone who studies Sagan's life long enough recognizes its seeming contradictions: its scientistic tendencies tempered by philosophical hunger, its ruthless skepticism crossed with a love of mythology, dreams, and theology camouflaged as science fiction. Within Sagan wrestled two worldviews: on the one hand, his liberal, secular, scientific-technocratic, future-oriented, anti-metaphysical values; on the other hand, the classical, historically based, and anti-scientistic culture of the Hutchins program. "Anti-scientistic" is not an overstatement. Some of the program's builders had warned of the "cult of science." Hutchins's intellectual sidekick, the unstoppable Mortimer Adler, had attacked academics for atheistic and scientistic leanings.[4] (In response, science- and secular-minded Humanists of the 1930s attacked the Hutchins curriculum as reactionary.) To the dialectically minded, though, Sagan's "contradictions" are not failings but signs of intellectual vigor. His inner theses and antitheses ended in synthesis in *Cosmos,* a hybrid of Snow's Two Cultures, whose heroes included the thoroughly contradictory Johannes Kepler (who cast horoscopes yet pioneered pre-Newtonian astrophysics).

Despite his classical leanings, Hutchins was "one of the best friends science could have at Chicago," geology professor F. J. Pettijohn later wrote. He cited Hutchins's stellar scientific appointments, among them Willard Libby, Harrison Brown, Clair Patterson and—decisively for Sagan—Harold Urey.[5] Urey inspired the experiment that changed Sagan's career. Urey also, ultimately, played a part in derailing Sagan's career. As long as Urey was on board, Chicago was perhaps the best training ground (except possibly for Caltech) for any young person interested in exploring the solar system. It remained so until about 1960, when West Coast campuses and the dawning space age began to lure the boffins (including Urey and Sagan) away.

CARL SAGAN ENTERED the University of Chicago in the autumn of 1951. He was sixteen years old, almost seventeen. He brought to Chicago all his high school enthusiasms—science fiction, space travel, astronomy. His dorm room was jammed with science-fiction magazines. "He had this enormous interest in science fiction—he turned me on to science fiction," Pesch says. Sagan was "very self-confident . . . a fascinating person. Wonderful smile. Very warm, very open. Completely unpretentious and genuinely enthusiastic about ideas and concepts. Broadly interested in the world."[6] Yet Sagan reserved his talkativeness for a chosen group, an intellectual elite. Some students regarded him as quiet, aloof, the kind of youth who always seemed to be at the edge of photos, in shadow. If you were interested in what he was interested in, then he would converse eloquently for hours. If not, then he was nowhere to be found. In his terms, his behavior made complete sense: he had vast ambition and limited time—a likely male lifespan of seventy-odd years—in which to fulfill it. Why should he waste time with people with lesser things on their minds? By the time of his death, he had generated a résumé more than one inch thick.

During his freshman year, Sagan lived at 141 Burton-Judson Courts, off the 1000 block of East 60th Street. Later he moved to Hitchcock House, and after that to 5317 South University Avenue.[7] Jerome Luks recalls Sagan as "a good neighbor, a good buddy, very outgoing. [He was] a Ray Bradbury freak. He couldn't get enough of him. . . . He convinced me to read a Bradbury book, *Fahrenheit 451*, which I did." The story depicts firefighters of the future whose job is to burn books rather than stop fires. Luks read it and was unimpressed: "It was far-fetched." Sagan, a future ACLU member, civil libertarian, and defender of pseudoscientists' right to speak their minds, replied: "Not necessarily."[8] Meanwhile, in Washington, D.C., Joseph McCarthy performed for the television cameras.

During this time, Sagan's favorite topic was space travel. He talked about it all the time. He was enthralled, for example, by the book *The Conquest of Space* by the famous German-born science writer Willy Ley. The book contained spectacular illustrations of future spaceships, space stations, and bases on Mars, painted by legendary "space artist" Chesley Bonestell.[9] Sagan bet his friends that humans would land on the Moon by 1970, an uncannily accurate prediction. He also worked at WUCB, the student radio station, to produce a show about spaceflight and extra-terrestrial life. And atop Ryerson Hall, he and a band of future astronomers learned (with the guidance of the astronomy club adviser, Guy C. Omer Jr.) how to operate equipment in the campus observatory.[10] Other club members included Tobias Owen, who, like Sagan, would go on to a distinguished astronomical career. Sagan ran the astronomy club's "theoretical" section, and arranged speeches by famous professors such as Subrahmanyan Chandrasekhar.

Omer "taught me how to make the right ascension and declination drives go, [and] gave me a key to the observatory . . . and so there I was: I could go and look at the stars if ever there was a clear night in Chicago," Sagan later recalled. Yet he wasn't much of a stargazer. The club's logbooks show that Owen and several other members showed up night after night, for years, to meticulously record their observations. But Sagan observed only seven nights between October 1952 and November 1953; and when he observed, he left only terse notes. One searches the logbooks in vain for early fragments of Saganish eloquence. His most vivid entry dates from 2:15 to 3 A.M. on November 25, 1952, during his sophomore year: "Some [cloud] openings; then clouded over. Also COLD!"[11]

There are different types of scientists: observers (e.g., many astronomers), experimenters (e.g., most chemists), field researchers (e.g., most geologists and anthropologists). Then there are theoreticians. (Of course, many scientists are more than one of these things.) Theoreticians' main tools are their brains, plus pencils and paper (and, increasingly, supercomputers). Carl Sagan was a theoretician. He liked the *ideas* of astronomy—the equations, the computer models, the grand hypotheses. In college, he preferred the pleasures of book learning, blackboard debates, and back-of-the-envelope calculations to the sore elbows of mirror-grinding, the frustration of broken sidereal drives, and the meteorological frustrations ("Clouds again!") of amateur astronomy. Likewise, as a teenager he had meddled with chemicals in his basement lab, but he found the cardboard cutouts of atoms just as pleasing. As an adult, he rarely conducted hands-on research with chemicals or instruments. When he needed experimental work done, he established alliances with scientists like Stanley Miller, Cyril Ponnamperuma, and Bishun Khare, who mixed all the chemicals, who fixed all the cranky equipment, who (Khare) enjoyed glass-blowing their own flasks, who preferred the odors and gurglings of a chemistry lab to abstract theories and cold equations.

One of Sagan's students, David Morrison, recalls how he and a colleague laughingly gave Sagan a tour of an observatory "to show him what it was really like to be in an observatory. . . . He was *not* an observer, that's all there is to it."[12] Occasionally, Sagan broke down and played astronomer for a while: at McDonald Observatory in 1956, where he tried to watch Mars (with little success, thanks to lousy weather); at Arecibo, Puerto Rico, in 1975, where he listened for alien radio messages (but they weren't talking). His Arecibo colleague Frank Drake still recalls how bored Sagan looked, gazing out the window at the subtropical greenery, like a schoolboy trapped in detention hall.[13] To Sagan, this wasn't astronomy; it was data collection. The wrigglings of oscilloscopes, the printouts from mass spectrometers were mere sense-data, only tips of epistemological icebergs. They barely hinted at the bigger, grander truths for which he lusted.

Besides, Sagan's hormones were kicking in. "Much more important" than stargazing, he later joked, was that at Ryerson Observatory, "I could bring young women to a place where we could be undisturbed—which was far and away more important than being able to look through the six-inch telescope!" He was Hollywood handsome, like a young James Mason, but in a raffish, Brooklynish way; and polished, even graceful, but forcefully so, with none of Mason's Humbert Humbertish tentativeness. He knew who he liked. There is no sign that he felt the standard teen fear of being "unpopular." Sagan either regaled you with his enthusiasms or ignored you. All that mattered was whether you interested him. If you were a dull person bent on slipping quietly into the vast fifties main-stream of white-bread conformity, he looked through you as if looking through glass. He apparently did not show special favors to women—did not talk down to them, as if they were children—which, one surmises, at least some of them found strange but alluring, like being seduced by someone eager to ravage a previously unravaged part of their bodies: their brains.

Whether he ravaged anything else is unclear; Sagan left virtually no reminiscences about his college dating habits, and what he did recall was typically self-centered, concerned less with the girl than with how he thought she perceived him. His female friends included a woman named Sandra. She invited him to dine at home with her family. During the meal, he rattled on about the coming age of space exploration. Astro-nauts on the Moon. Rockets to Mars. Life on other worlds. Sandra's re-action is unrecorded, but according to Sagan's account her family's star-tled looks revealed what they were thinking: "This boy is really crazy."[14]

ENTHUSIASM AND RAW INTELLIGENCE were not enough, though; Sagan had to *study*. The Hutchins curriculum was grueling. Sagan had been "Class Brain" at Rahway High School, but at Chicago he was just another bright kid amid hundreds. Four decades later, secure in his fame, he admitted having entered Chicago "with profound gaps in my edu-cation." He knew very little about the arts, had not read much world literature, and had little knowledge of the different world cultures. In a program with so much emphasis on the humanities, he had serious catching up to do.

His major was physics, a logical choice for a would-be astronomer. Physics and astronomy have been intimately linked since Isaac Newton. Astronomy's subjects are planets and stars, neutron stars and galaxies. Their structures and behaviors are cosmic-scale demonstrations of abstract principles of physics. For example, one can use Newton's gravitational equations to explain both the fall of an apple and the orbit of the Moon.[15]

Even for a future astronomer, the physics curriculum was challenging. One physics class was so intellectually daunting that Sagan's friend Ronald Blum hung over the entrance a sign that read: "Relinquish hope all ye who enter here." "Me and Peter and Carl and some other guys used to sit in the first two rows," Blum says. "The first two rows were almost solidly Jewish. Peter [Pesch] was sort of our adopted Gentile." The teacher administered a tough exam every Friday. "It punched my guts out every week. We would listen to lectures like three times a week, then have separate problem-solving classes every Friday, then have this horrible, gut-wrenching examination. It was like boot camp."[16]

Philosophy class was rough, too, Sagan recalled. Philosophy professor Joseph Jackson Schwab "used to throw erasers at me every time I said something he thought was stupid. Some days I was covered with chalk dust. And once or twice, I threw the eraser back."

The stress of class work was severe for many students. "There were a lot of suicides," Sagan's first wife, Lynn Margulis (then Lynn Alexander), recalls.[17] Pesch agrees: "Some people couldn't adjust; some hung themselves. When you've built your ego strength around being a 'brain,' and then discover you're not as big a brain as you thought, it's tough to take."[18] Indications are that Sagan too felt this stress, and that he had to work hard. "To the best of my knowledge, Carl studied mostly by himself," says Blum. "I think he did an awful lot of reading. Occasionally he would get together with the rest of us to work on problems. My impression is that as a physics intellect, he was not the top rung. He was about like me—that is, getting A's but always with difficulty and occasional B's. He had to work really hard. There's no question he was uncommonly gifted. But as far as being a physicist, he was not front rank." Pesch, however, recalls Sagan as less reclusive: "He wasn't a genius, you know. He wasn't the highest grade-point average. We met every night for homework sessions before tests; we'd study together. Our 'socializing' was around meals and studying." The university had a minimal social life; when the kids took a break, they played Ping-Pong, at which Sagan excelled. He also served as captain of a campus basketball team.[19]

To some degree, Sagan set his own educational agenda, and sometimes that agenda interfered with his formal education. Peter Vandervoort, a fellow student (later associate chair of the university astronomy department), recalls how in the spring of 1955, Sagan's senior year, "we were taking a course in electrodynamics from Peter Meyer. And Meyer was upset with Carl because he wasn't turning in his homework." The reason was that Sagan was too busy with courses in other subjects, such as evolution, which he must have enjoyed more. He was majoring in astrophysics, but there he was, putting evolutionary biology ahead of the basic training of an astrophysics career. Sagan was "this very brash, articulate young man," Vandervoort says, "riding off in different directions, who doesn't attend to details of his studies in the physics department."

Vandervoort also recalls a professor who occasionally filled out recommendations for students seeking fellowship grants from the National Science Foundation. Sagan was an NSF grantee. The professor laughed and told how, when he filled out recommendations for other applicants, he always wrote: "Better than Sagan."[20]

To SAGAN, the rationale for his broader interests was simple: he refused to pigeonhole himself. He apparently sensed that the coming space age would be radically interdisciplinary: astronomers would have to talk to biologists and chemists and geologists and atmospheric physicists and many other experts whom they normally ignored. Hence he trained himself in subjects unrelated to astrophysics—in particular, biology, which was the topic closest to his first love, extraterrestrial life.

Rare is the scientist with world-class understanding of two broad disciplines, say, astronomy and biology. Sagan was one of the rare ones. The Hutchins program gave him the confidence to straddle disciplines. He traced this confidence to a biology course in which, he recalled, "there were only three topics. The first was enzyme chemistry; the second was diabetes; and the third was the physiological concomitants of the expression of emotions." True, this selection of biological science was unrepresentative—no Darwin, no genetics! Yet the class explored those three topics so deeply—he read diabetes papers published that very year[21]— that he evidently concluded that he could understand any topic he wished if he worked hard enough. Millions of readers would later enjoy the results: prose from a hyper-polymath conversant with astrophysics, biology, neuroscience, primate communication, atmospheric physics, geopolitics, nuclear strategy . . . Sagan was the multidisciplinary scholar par excellence, the Renaissance man so uncommon in the age of specialization, of industrialized academia, where the divisions of labor are as real as in Henry Ford's factories.

THE STRESS of Sagan's college years may have affected his health. At age eighteen, midway through college, he developed achalasia, a strange and frightening ailment that causes the esophagus to constrict uncontrollably. Sufferers have trouble swallowing food. Sometimes the constriction is so severe that they struggle to breathe. Was his achalasia stress-related? "It was definitely a physical problem," his sister, Cari, recalls; even so, "we thought that it might have had something to do with"—she pauses—"Rachel. And [his] intenseness."

Gastroenterologists do not fully understand the etiology of achalasia. Stress is partly implicated in some cases; judging from a review of recent medical literature, however, little research on psychosomatic factors is being done. Far more ink is devoted to surgical solutions. Whatever caused Sagan's achalasia, the condition would haunt him well into adulthood. When he was an adult, it necessitated surgery that almost killed him. He feared choking so much that he nibbled at his food, slicing it into minuscule pieces. Sometimes he stood and literally hopped up and down, struggling to make the food go down his throat.[22] He once confessed to his friend Timothy Ferris that being able to finally swallow a mouthful of food gave him an absurd sensation of pleasure and relief.[23]

Apparently because he was unable to eat heartily after he developed achalasia, Sagan lost weight. As a teenager he had been tall and skinny; by young adulthood, he was a genuine beanpole. Once he stayed overnight at Ronald Blum's house and awoke in the middle of the night, gasping for breath. Blum rushed him to a medical facility. There, Blum saw Sagan with his shirt off and was surprised by how thin he was— "almost delicate," Blum recalls. "He had narrow shoulders, no chest to speak of. I thought he really needed to work out."[24]

Some people respond to an insidious illness by slowing down. Not Sagan. He had titanic goals, and he fully intended to achieve them. The achalasia seemed to be a useful reminder to him that his time in the sun might be limited. To fulfill his dreams, he could not dawdle. The heavens called; soon, the first spaceships would crisscross the sky. He intended, somehow, to be a part of it all. Every minute counted, and he was often curt toward people he believed were wasting his time. "I had my trajectory and I knew where I wanted to go," he recalled. "I was always deferring gratification in order to do what I wanted to do."[25] When Blum earned extra money by working as an orderly at a hospital, he offered to find Sagan a job there, and Sagan replied: "My time is too valuable." Blum remembers thinking, in response, that Sagan was a "supercilious asshole."[26]

Blum still wrestles with his memories of Sagan, toward whom he had strongly mixed feelings. There were "contradictions in his nature," Blum reflects. He was "a brilliant, far-ranging intellect with uncommon literary gifts who often seemed curiously immature and totally self-centered." Sagan "generally was not what I would call 'effusive.' I would almost say his personality seemed a shade 'dark.' . . . He had off-putting mannerisms; he was arrogant. I liked him, but I couldn't love him. [He was] slightly detached—more like a Cambridge don. He was autonomous, self-sufficient. . . ."

"But if you got onto a topic that engaged him—philosophical or scientific or literary—he would talk a lot, very forcefully. He had strong opinions. He was someone whose persona came across as cold and arrogant and distant. But he felt this was a requirement of his intellectual commitment—to be rigidly honest, very intolerant of anything irrational."

Sagan was poised in print as well as in person. By the late 1960s, his prose would win a loyal following among people who had no clue what he looked like, or how he declaimed serenely on cosmic ideas like a scholar thrice his age. He wrote like an adult who already had a Ph.D., dozens of scientific publications to his credit, an honorary degree or two, and numerous lab assistants and graduate students slaving under his whip. The juvenile pomposities of his teenage essay were replaced by a dry wit—H. G. Wells crossed with Noël Coward. "In this Humanities 2 class," Blum recalls, "I would write papers and I would always get a B. Sagan would always get an A.

"I said, 'Carl, how do you do it?' And he said, 'Want to look at one of my papers?'

"I did, and I thought, 'I can write like that.'" To Blum, Sagan's literary style was "phony . . . colorful prose and mythical images. I read a couple of his papers and I absorbed the essence of what I thought was the way to get an A.

"I was supposed to write a report on Conrad's *Heart of Darkness*. Instead of writing what I *really* thought, I dressed it up with colorful prose and mythical images—and sure enough, I got an A."[27]

MODERN SCIENCE is Big Science—bureaucratized, industrialized, corporatized. As in any bureaucracy, success requires more than brains and diligence. It also helps to know the right people. The right people can open doors, pull strings, arrange grants, schedule rendezvous with other powerful figures, and champion one's nomination to high posts. With friends like these, many otherwise unpromising scientists end up doing important research and concluding their careers with Festschrifts and three-column obits in the *New York Times*.

Shrewd beyond his years, Sagan recognized early the value of glad-handing. But his glad-handing was not insincere, not the practiced amiability of Willy Loman; he glad-handed only those people whose work or ideas interested him. Since he was interested in virtually everything scientific, this meant that he accosted a lot of notable people. The high school brain who had written to RAND as casually as he chatted with cheerleaders, who sought college advice from Lyman Spitzer—Lyman Spitzer!—readily befriended, in college, scientific giants his shyer classmates tiptoed around. By the end of his graduate student years, he would be on a first-name basis with at least three Nobel laureates (H. J. Muller, Joshua Lederberg, and Harold Urey) and one future Nobelist (Melvin Calvin). Rather than waste his summers relaxing and partying, he spent them working for top scholars. He would spend the summer of 1952 working with Muller; of 1956, with the nation's preeminent planetary astronomer, Gerard Kuiper; of 1957, with the famed physicist-polymath George Gamow; and of 1959, with Calvin. These men were titans of the predawn hours of the space age. Their work and writings schooled the generation that would launch robots to the planets and humans to the Moon. Having worked for them, Sagan's ascent was almost assured. How did he manage to meet such powerful people? "Chutzpah!" his friend Pesch asserts. "He liked people and he would just go up and talk to them."[28]

But first, one person had to provide the right prod at the right moment. That person was his number-one fan, his mother, Rachel. At the end of the first quarter of his freshman year, Sagan returned home. One day as he was heading out to shoot some hoops, his mother yelled out to him that he should go to visit the nephew of a friend of hers who was a graduate student and fellow science major. Typical of Sagan's obedience to his mother, he changed his plans and went to see the student, Seymour Abrahamson. Abrahamson was studying at Indiana University under the Nobel Prize–winning biologist H. J. Muller.[29] As Sagan discovered, he and Abrahamson shared an interest in the fledgling subject of the origin of life. How had the first molecules of life formed on the early Earth? And did they form easily, or with some struggle? If the former, then those molecules might form readily on other planets; Darwinian evolution might be under way at this very moment, in countless points of light across the galaxy.

When Sagan returned to school, he wrote a letter to Abrahamson in which he expressed some of his thoughts about the origin of life, and Abrahamson, who must have been impressed, showed the letter to Muller. Sagan's enthusiasm appealed to Muller, and he invited Sagan to come out to Indiana for a few days to talk about their ideas. Delighted, Sagan took "some Toonerville-trolley kind of train from Chicago to Bloomington" late in the second quarter of 1952.

They quickly hit it off. Sagan appreciated Muller because he didn't dismiss the possibility that there might be life on other planets. This was not at all a fashionable position among scientists at the time. He also found Muller's intellectual energy exciting and was impressed by his rigor as a scientist. When, to his surprise, Muller asked him to come work with him that summer, Sagan immediately accepted the offer.

Herman Joseph Muller was something of an iconoclast in the world of science, and he had taken unpopular positions—both scientifically and politically—in his career. Born in New York City in 1890, he got his doctorate in zoology from Columbia University in 1915, and within a few years was the chair of the biology department of the University of Texas at Austin. The age of "classical" genetics was in full swing; Thomas Hunt Morgan used fruit flies (*Drosophila*) to show how genes on chromosomes transmit certain traits from generation to generation. For his part, Muller did pioneering work showing how X rays greatly increased the mutation rate in *Drosophila*.

Some mentors try to suppress their young charges' dreams and redirect them in more "productive" directions. But Muller listened happily as Sagan pontificated about extraterrestrial life and space travel. Both enjoyed science fiction. They even attended a Chicago science-fiction convention.[30] Two of Sagan's wives offer interesting comments on their warm friendship. "I love Muller," recalls Lynn Margulis. He "was very worth revering . . . remarkably educated . . . an absentminded-professor type."[31] Muller, says Ann Druyan, treated Carl "with such kindness when he was the most naive and gawky and dorky of young grad students." Naturally, Sagan "adored" him.[32]

Muller's moral support had a downside, however: it bolstered Sagan's confidence beyond reason, encouraging him to pursue intellectual will-o'-the-wisps. Still, a supportive mentor is usually preferable to a repressive one. Besides, Muller was not one to crush unorthodox ideas: he had had many of his own.

In the 1920s, while capitalism ran wild and paved the way to the Great Depression, Muller had edited a newsletter titled *Iskra* (Russian for "spark"), after one of Lenin's publications. After Muller's political activities drew unfriendly attention from the Texas authorities, he moved to Germany's Kaiser Wilhelm Institute. His stint there ended when the Nazis raided and closed it. From there, he headed to Moscow—"the workers' paradise"—and accepted a job as a senior geneticist at the Institute of Genetics in Moscow. When the "paradise" turned into a hell, he barely escaped with his life and returned to America, to teach at Indiana.

Muller was also a eugenicist, not the easiest thing to be in the aftermath of Nazism. His vision of eugenics was immeasurably more humane and democratic than Hitler's, though. Muller advocated "improving" the human gene pool by voluntary means—by artificial insemination of women with sperm from distinguished men (although there is serious doubt that their "distinction" is genetically transmissible)—and only after society had been made more democratic and egalitarian, to prevent eugenic abuses. In this way, Muller foresaw our present dilemma: how to use biotechnology and genetic engineering to better human life, not to control and exploit it. In that sense, he was always a socialist. In 1963, the American Humanist Association named him its Humanist of the Year.[33]

In short, Sagan and Muller were two iconoclasts, basking in each other's enthusiasms. Hence, Muller listened patiently as seventeen-year-old Sagan confided one of his new interests: flying saucers.

SINCE ANCIENT TIMES, people have observed mysterious objects in the sky. The first modern mass sightings of UFO-like objects began on November 17, 1896, when a fireball-like object passed over San Francisco.[34] The object might have been a disintegrating meteor: November 17–18 is the annual peak of the impressive Leonid meteor shower. Nonetheless, word spread that it was an airship secretly built by inventors (like the secretive Captain Nemo of Jules Verne's fiction).

The story triggered copycat sightings across the American West in the late 1890s. Some people reported seeing pilots aboard the airships. A few wondered: Were the airships Martian vehicles? A Texas newspaper published a story about an airship crash.[35] The purported alien pilot was buried in a local cemetery. The story—the Roswell fable of its day—was later exposed as a hoax.

The first true "flying saucer" sighting occurred on the afternoon of June 24, 1947. A Boise, Idaho, business executive named Kenneth Arnold was flying his private plane near Mount Rainier in Washington State when he observed nine silvery objects flying at high speed along the horizon. Suspecting they were secret Soviet vehicles, he informed news media. Reporters noted Arnold's comment that the objects had a skipping motion—like saucers tossed across the surface of water—and coined the term "flying saucers." (In fact, Arnold did not claim that the objects were saucer-shaped.) Recent research by this writer and others hints that Arnold, too, was fooled by a disintegrating meteor.[36]

Even President Harry Truman was intrigued. He summoned an aide, Gen. Robert B. Landry, who later recalled his meeting with the Chief Executive: "We talked about UFO reports and what might be the meaning for all these rather way-out reports of sightings, and the subject in general. The president said he hadn't [given] much serious thought to all these reports; but at the same time, he said, if there was any evidence of a strategic threat to the national security, the collection and evaluation of UFO data by Central Intelligence warranted more intense study and attention at the highest government level."[37]

The UFO craze began when Carl Sagan was twelve years old, an impressionable age. Years of exposure to science fiction had prepared his imagination for this—real alien visitors. "It seemed pretty believable to me," he reflected in the 1990s. After all, the first two-stage rocket had just been successfully launched by the Jet Propulsion Laboratory, and that seemed a sure sign that before long we'd be sending rockets to the Moon and beyond. If we had developed the technology for spaceflight, "why shouldn't other, older, wiser beings be able to travel from their star to ours?" Sagan reasoned. He noted that the flurry of UFO sightings had commenced soon after the U.S. nuclear attacks on Japan. Maybe, he conjectured, the aliens were alarmed by the explosions and had come to see if they could be of help to us, or, more worrisome, maybe they were on reconnaissance missions for the purpose of ensuring that our nuclear weapons weren't turned on them.

Sagan was so concerned about the sightings that he recalled being perturbed that his parents and all the adults he knew seemed totally uninterested, preoccupied as they were at the time with issues like the threats of "Communist China, nuclear weapons, McCarthyism, and the rent. I wondered if they had their priorities straight."[38]

Sagan was not, however, alone in his concern. Besieged by saucer reports, the Air Force started a small UFO-investigating arm, Project Blue Book, at Wright-Patterson Air Force Base in Dayton, Ohio. Its adviser on astronomy was J. Allen Hynek, then of Ohio State University. In 1952, Sagan's freshman year at the University of Chicago and several years after the craze began, Blue Book received a record number of saucer reports. Blue Book director Capt. E. J. Ruppelt later wrote in his memoirs that 1952 was "just one big swirl of UFO reports, hurried trips, midnight telephone calls, reports to the Pentagon, press interviews, and very little sleep." Air Force pilots had filed numerous reports of silver disks flying by, and what appeared to be saucers had even been picked up on radar in Japan and Korea.[39]

This news agitated Sagan, who had been working on a script about space travel for the student radio station, WUCB. The show promised interviews about spaceflight with noted scientists, including astronomer Gerard Kuiper, anthropologist Margaret Mead, and geoscientist Harrison Brown (more examples of Sagan's desire to schmooze with the high and mighty). Sagan decided to work saucers into the script.[40]

Marilyn Monroe graced the cover of *Life* magazine for April 7, 1952. In the upper right-hand corner of the cover, a headline stated "There Is a Case for Interplanetary Saucers." A few days earlier, Sagan had felt confident enough of Muller's friendship to mail him an advance copy of the radio script. It was titled "Ad Astra . . ." ("To the Stars . . ."). He

requested Muller's advice on the show's discussion of the possibility of
life on other worlds. Sagan's accompanying letter is typical of a bright
youngster with big ideas: it is verbose, disorganized, and slightly pompous. He states bluntly that the show is "propaganda," designed to raise
the consciousness of students at Chicago about the "incalculably great
consequence" of the subject of space travel. He also promises that the
show will provide evidence that the UFOs really do come from space.

The script of this show offers a fascinating glimpse of the dramatic
flair and showmanship that would fully emerge in *Cosmos*. Sagan wrote:

/Fade in *loud* the Allegro con Fuoco of Dvorak's "New World"
Symphony through the first presentation of the theme. Then fade
down/
Announcer 1: "Ad Astra . . . ," the dramatic documented story of
the conquest of space, the last frontier. WUCB-Chicago, with a technical background laid by noted scientists, brings you a factual preview of
the greatest adventure awaiting Mankind, an event you will see in *your*
lifetime—interplanetary flight.

The show promised to discuss how the coming space age "will affect
you, your children, and your planet." Another topic would be

the intriguing problem of life on other worlds. You will be told the
remarkable theory of the origin of life on earth, *with the chemical equations*, that, although virtually unknown to the layman, is accepted as a
working hypothesis in scientific circles.
We will interpret the mystery of the flying saucers in the light of
significant new evidence and its correlation with space flight and extraterrestrial life. Also, you will hear the startling report of the United
States Air Force's "Preliminary Studies on the Flying Saucers" which
suggests that the saucers *are* extraterrestrial in origin.

Future interplanetary rockets would have nuclear-powered engines,
Sagan wrote. He cited the U.S. government's effort to develop nuclear-
powered aircraft. If nuclear aviation were achieved, then "atomic-powered
spacecraft would be but a step" away. In a conspiratorial mood, he suggested that the U.S. government was running a secret rocket program
that had progressed further than publicly revealed. He wrote:

Think it's a wild dream? On the evening of December 29 [1948] . . .
Secretary of Defense James Forrestal announced the formation of the
(quote) "Earth Satellite Vehicle Program." (unquote) Nothing more has
been heard in over three years. . . . Once a manned artificial satellite,
or, as it is better known, a space station is constructed, flight to the

moon, Mars, and Venus would come relatively soon and as a matter of course.[41]

The Russians, Sagan added ominously, also had a secret rocket program. Its goal: the Moon.

The program ended:

> /Fade in of the Scherzo from Dvorak's "New World" Symphony not too loud . . .
>
> You have just heard the first in a series of programs entitled "Ad Astra . . ." and presented as a student service by station WUCB-Chicago. . . . Your announcers were Richard Connor, Roger Kelley, and Mike Reedy. This program has been written and produced by Carl Sagan and engineered by Ferben Simons.

In the script, the seventeen-year-old Sagan typed, then crossed out, this sentence: "This has been a Carl Sagan Production."[42]

On April 16, Muller wrote to Sagan and thanked him for the "fascinating" script. Muller was a busy scientist, supervising graduate students, attending conferences, writing papers. Yet he took the time to include a two-and-a-half page, single-spaced, typewritten summary of his views on the origin of life and extraterrestrials, for quotation on the show. Among the statements he offered was his expectation that life "almost certainly does exist on Mars." Sagan had found an extraordinarily supportive, as well as speculative, mentor in Muller, who not only encouraged Sagan's unconventional thinking, but also responded to requests with enthusiasm.

That summer, Sagan worked in Muller's lab in Bloomington, doing "routine things," such as checking fruit flies for mutations. He later recalled that his work with Muller was his first taste of real scientific research. Sagan did not, however, demonstrate a flair for this kind of science. One time he examined a fruit fly specimen and was convinced he had discovered a new species based on an odd feature of its eyes. Muller kindly explained that the oddity was a not uncommon mutation.

Not only did Muller support Sagan's enthusiasms and offer him his first chance to see real science in the works, he also strongly influenced the showmanship in Sagan that would later make him so famous. Muller was himself something of a showman in his lectures. Later in life, Sagan credited one lecture of Muller's in particular with having made a strong impression on him. He even considered dramatizing a lecture of the kind in his film, *Contact*. The topic of this lecture was extraterrestrial life. Muller opened the talk by announcing that he had just returned from a trip to some other planets, on which he had found life forms, and that he wanted to show some slides of those alien beings. There followed, Sagan recalled, slides "of the most astonishing creatures . . . much more bizarre than you can ever think about, much more bizarre than anything in science fiction." After stunning his audience with this array of exotic beings, Muller delightedly announced that he had made a terrible mistake; he had shown them the wrong slides and what they'd been looking at were the microscopic organisms found in a drop of normal Earth pond water. Muller's intent, Sagan recalled, was to impress on his audience just how amazing life right here on Earth is, and he definitely made his point.[43] Sagan would later show a talent for just such dramatic, engaging stunts with which to make science fascinating.

As much as he enjoyed spending time with Muller that summer, however, Sagan did not really enjoy the work at Muller's lab. Years later, Sagan recalled one telling anecdote. At one point in the summer Muller went on a trip for two weeks and let Sagan use his office while he was away. As Sagan recalled, "The walls were covered with acoustic material. . . . I found that you could whirl and hurl a dissecting needle at the walls covered by this material and they would stick!" Alone in that room, whenever looking at bugs through a microscope was "more than I could bear, I would whirl and throw a few dissecting needles." After Muller's two-week trip, he returned to the lab and noticed the holes in the wall. "He couldn't figure out how they had come about. And I, to my eternal shame, didn't come forward and tell him. I was a terrible, callow youth."[44]

SAGAN DID SOMETHING ELSE that summer that, by all indications, he never revealed to a soul.

Several years ago, Tim Willard, a sharp-eyed employee of the National Archives, was declassifying stacks of old State Department documents. He stumbled across an August 1952 letter from Sagan to then Secretary of State Dean Acheson.[45] The letter, which offers a fascinating view of Sagan's thinking at that time, concerned flying saucers.

Sagan's concerns in the letter were apparently provoked by recent news. By the midsummer of 1952, the latest UFO wave had hit newspaper front pages all over the country. On July 10, the crew on an airplane near Quantico, Virginia, reported a light "too bright to be a lighted balloon and too slow to be a big meteor," as described by Project Blue Book director E. J. Ruppelt in his 1956 memoir. At 11:40 P.M. on July 19, at National Airport, radar operators "picked up eight unidentified targets east and south of Andrews A.F.B." The targets weren't airplanes, because they would "loaf along at 100 to 130 miles an hour," then accelerate to "fantastically high speeds" and escape the area. That night, airline crews witnessed eerie lights in the same locations scanned by the radar operators. Airport "tower operators also saw lights, and jet fighters were brought in," Ruppelt recorded. Newspaper headlines screamed "INTERCEPTORS CHASE FLYING SAUCERS OVER WASHINGTON, D.C."[46]

Captain Ruppelt later wrote that "the president's air aide, Brigadier General Landry, called intelligence at President Truman's request to find out what was going on. Somehow I got the call. I told General Landry that the radar target could have been caused by weather but that we had no proof."[47] (By "weather," Ruppelt meant "anomalous propagation," a then poorly understood phenomenon in which temperature layers of the atmosphere distort radar reflections. This causes radar to "see" nonexistent objects, sometimes moving at inconceivably high speeds.)

Such sensational stories might have made Sagan wonder about the aliens' intentions. A recent popular science-fiction film, *The Thing* (1951), had depicted a murderous alien. A subtler alien menace appeared in the 1951 movie *The Day the Earth Stood Still*, in which the otherwise benevolent extraterrestrial threatens the destruction of humanity if it extends its warlike ways into space. Sagan raised the question of alien intentions in his letter to Secretary Acheson on August 3, 1952. No doubt hoping to add credibility to his query, Sagan sent the letter on Indiana University stationery, and typed "Dr. H. J. Muller's Laboratory" at the top. (Actually, that might have sent entirely the wrong signal. Muller was a former Soviet sympathizer, and had likely been watched by intelligence agencies.) Sagan asked the Secretary if he would please describe what steps the U.S. government would take in the event that the UFOs turned out to be alien craft on reconnaissance missions for the purpose of monitoring the progress of the people of Earth in designing spacecraft and nuclear weaponry. What would we do to try to communicate with the aliens, Sagan wanted to know, and also what measures of defense would we take, particularly in joining together with the other countries of the world to meet the threat. Sagan closed the letter by acknowledging that such a threat was "extremely remote," but that nonetheless he would like to hear from the Secretary. The letter is remarkable both for Sagan's hubris in expecting the Secretary to pay any attention to such an inquiry, and also in revealing that Carl Sagan, the future scourge of UFOlogists, at this time was so much a believer that he wanted to know if the nation was prepared to defend itself against attack by extraterrestrials.

Unfortunately for Sagan, Acheson had his hands full with the Korean War, Stalin, Sen. Joseph McCarthy's hearings, and Communist China. Sagan received a prompt but perfunctory letter of response:

My dear Mr. Sagan:

In response to your letter of August 3, 1952, the Department of the Air Force, which is investigating the flying saucer reports, has indicated that there is no evidence to date substantiating the speculation that these objects are of inter-planetary origin. Under the circumstances of a purely hypothetical situation, the Department had no comment to make on the questions you asked.

> Sincerely yours,
> For the Secretary of State:
> Grace B. Ruckh
> Assistant to the Chief
> Division of Public Liaison[48]

WHY DID AN ESTABLISHED SCIENTIST like H. J. Muller spend time with this impatient New Jersey teenager who had a short attention span for tedious research and was obsessed with UFOs and aliens? Muller was a generous man. For all the disappointments of his life—betrayed by a political ideology, revolted by Hitlerian perversion of the eugenic ideal— Muller clung to his socialist ethics, which cherished "ordinary" people, however unschooled and immature.

His kindness rubbed off on Sagan. Though later in life, after he had become famous, Sagan struck many colleagues as arrogant, he almost always displayed patience and good humor when addressing laypeople. After Sagan's death, his friend Paul West published a novel, *Life with Swan* (1999), that featured a blatantly Saganish character, one Prof. Raoul Bunsen, who, West wrote, was "as willing to answer stupid elementary questions as to formulate, almost as masochistic exercise, questions nobody could answer."[49] A true science popularizer must have a democratic soul; he cannot afford to feel contempt for his audience. Otherwise, why bother popularizing? As Sagan's fame grew, he became accustomed to standing at a podium and listening as an audience member stood and asked him a question about UFOs or astrology or other silliness. Then, typically, Sagan responded firmly but politely, trying to make the questioner feel intelligent, not like an ignoramus. Any other speaker might have snapped, "That's the dumbest thing I ever heard." But Muller wouldn't have said that; nor did Sagan.

3

The Dungeon

As HUMANITY ENTERS the twenty-first century, two great questions of the twentieth century remain unanswered: How did life begin? And does life inhabit other worlds? The questions are related; as Carl Sagan knew from his teenage years on, the answer to one offers clues to the other. In the optimistic decades after World War II, many scientists (Sagan included) expected both questions to be answered quickly. To date, both remain intractable, reminders of how often the high hopes of youth gray into pessimism, and how selfishly Mother Nature guards her secrets.[1]

How did life begin? The Earth is a blue-green-brown oasis of life in a cosmic void. But it was not always so. Billions of years ago, Earth was as lifeless as the Moon is today. How did our world evolve from a rock pile of planetesimals into the garden of the solar system? How did mere molecules assemble into the chemical building blocks of life—nucleic acids, amino acids, proteins—and thence evolve into microbes and mollusks, fish and fowl, humans and hippopotami?

The biblical book of Genesis offers a wonderfully poetic account of the steps in the creation of life:

> In the beginning God created the heaven and the earth.
> . . . God said, Let the earth bring forth grass, the herb yielding seed, and the fruit tree yielding fruit after his kind, whose seed is in itself, upon the earth; and it was so.

But religious explanations of life and the cosmos lost intellectual appeal in the eighteenth and nineteenth centuries for many reasons. One is the rise of modern science, especially the geological concept of a world far older than implied by Genesis, and the Darwinian theory of evolution by natural selection. A second important reason is political revolutions, the industrial revolution, and new social philosophies—Marxism, for instance. These challenged the authority and intellectual credibility of the Christian church, which was an ideological buttress of both aristocratic and bourgeois societies.[2] The American Revolution of 1776 was relatively conservative as revolutions go; its leaders, however, included many deists, who believed that God remained aloof from terrestrial affairs. According to them, all God had done was to create the universe and set its wheels in motion, like a great watchmaker winding a watch. Then God left it to run by its own rules—for example, by the Newtonian laws of gravity and motion.[3]

Deism is but a short step from atheism. The French scientist Pierre Simon, Marquis de Laplace, proposed that the solar system had formed not by divine fiat but, rather, all by itself, from the gravitational collapse of a primordial cloud of dust and gas. When Napoleon asked Laplace what role his theory left for God, the cheeky astrophysicist replied that God was "an unnecessary hypothesis."[4] One consequence of Laplace's idea (previously anticipated by the philosopher Immanuel Kant) is that planetary formation is a routine consequence of Newtonian physics.[5] Through telescopes, astronomers could see what appeared to be interstellar clouds; perhaps these were new solar systems in formation. And if so, perhaps they would eventually have inhabitants of their own.[6]

Ironically, the latter idea drew support from an unexpected quarter: Christian writers and preachers. As far back as the seventeenth century, some divines had pondered the religious implications of the new cosmos unveiled by telescopes. The Milky Way appeared to contain thousands and thousands of stars (how naive they were!). Why would God create myriad planets in space, then fail to populate them? They *must* be inhabited: what could better demonstrate God's omniscience and infinite creativity? In the nineteenth century, this theme was hammered home by the great Scottish orator Rev. Thomas Chalmers.[7] The astronomy writer Rev. Thomas Dick also frequently speculated about alien life.[8] So tight was the presumed link between extraterrestrial life and Christian revelation that in the 1850s when the famed scholar William Whewell argued against the existence of aliens, he was accused of encouraging atheists.[9]

That is why Charles Darwin's theory of evolution by natural selection (1859) marked a turning point in the history of the idea of aliens.[10] Darwin was not interested in the possibility of extraterrestrials. But his theory undermined theological arguments about life on Earth and, by inference, on other worlds as well. The diversity of terrestrial life could be explained by a materialistic mechanism, natural selection. No divine intervention was required. Hence, the Christian argument that life *must* pervade the cosmos because it reflected divine goodness and might was moot. If life exists elsewhere, it must be for scientific reasons—for reasons based on physics, chemistry, biochemistry, and so forth—and nothing else.

And that was a depressing revelation, for as telescopes improved, other planets looked less and less suitable for life, at least life as we know it.

Darwin suggested that all terrestrial life has evolved from simple microorganisms, born from chance interactions of chemicals eons ago in a "warm little pond."[11] Thus we reach the single most important question of Carl Sagan's life: How prevalent, cosmically speaking, are these "warm little ponds"? Has the same physical process that spawned terrestrial life occurred on other worlds? Does this process occur readily, so that organic molecules and living creatures fill our galaxy and the galaxies beyond? Or does life, especially intelligent life, emerge so reluctantly, so sluggishly that the heavens are essentially lifeless—a magnificent, meaningless wasteland?

The question was impossible to answer in Darwin's time, and remains close to impossible in ours. One reason is that no one, to this day, has satisfactorily explained how the earliest life forms arose on *this* planet. Research on the subject has been under way for decades. In numerous laboratories, scientists have tried to simulate how on the early Earth, nonliving molecules could randomly come together, forming complex systems that copy themselves, mutate, and evolve—in other words, "live." Despite much progress, final answers remain elusive.

The idea of nonliving matter transmuting into living matter is an old one. For centuries, the advocates of "spontaneous generation" argued that life emerged routinely from nonliving matter. Anyone could see that rotting meat "transformed" into maggots. Experiments revealed the true explanation: the maggots grew from eggs dropped by flies. Later, some scientists claimed to show that laboratory chemicals "spontaneously generated" microbes. But the great chemist Louis Pasteur performed a classic experiment proving the true source of the microbes: they had fallen from the air. Pasteur claimed that his experiment ended all hope of explaining life in mechanistic terms—and a good thing, too. He was a religious man, and had no desire to see God's highest creation explained in terms of physics and chemistry. If spontaneous generation of life were possible, then what need was there for God?

CARL SAGAN REJECTED RELIGION from an early age. As noted earlier, in the early twentieth century powerful forces of secularization were sweeping through American Judaism (as through all Western culture). The Holocaust caused some Jews to reject God altogether: what deity would have permitted such a horror?[12]

Sagan celebrated his bar mitzvah at age thirteen. "But in exactly that period when I was sort of seriously reading the Bible," he recalled, "I found all sorts of obvious contradictions with reality . . . [for example],

two different, contradictory accounts of the origin of the world in Genesis. That propelled me away"[13] from religion. Previously, he had soured
on Edgar Rice Burroughs's Mars novels because they contained inconsistencies in logic.[14] Now he started looking for similar inconsistencies in
the ancient texts that had given hope to billions. Were they just old
wives' tales? He learned the Bible well. As an adult, debating preachers
about religion, Sagan often startled them with his ability to cite passages
by chapter and verse.

How Jewish was Carl Sagan? As with so many aspects of his life, the
answers are contradictory. On the one hand, through most of Sagan's
life, he said virtually nothing about his Jewish background. This might
have been at least partly for practical reasons; he was extremely ambitious and no doubt preferred to evade the anti-Semitism that (while fading) persisted in American society, including academia, for decades after
World War II. "We were born in an age when you kept a low profile,"
recalls Blum, Sagan's Chicago schoolmate. In their college days, "you
wouldn't think [Sagan] had a drop of Jewish interest in his body. . . . I
had the feeling the word 'Jewish' was so excluded from his conversation."

Interestingly, Sagan's failure to come to grips with his Judaism may
account for one of his cardinal traits: his optimism. The central tragedy
of twentieth-century Judaism is, of course, the Holocaust. The Holocaust not only destroyed millions of lives, but it also (in the view of
many) destroyed any remaining illusions about the inner decency and
rationality of human beings. The nineteenth-century dream of "Progress," many concluded, was a fantasy. How could one continue to believe
in Progress after Germany, once the citadel of European culture and
science, had stooped so low? If Carl Sagan had confronted—truly confronted—the meaning of the Holocaust, could he have remained so boyishly optimistic, so sure of the virtues of Reason and the inevitability of
Progress? Without that self-assurance, his subsequent career might have
been quite different—still brilliant, no doubt, but surely less messianic.

His evasions are worth at least a moment's scrutiny; they reveal so
much. Even in the 1980s, when he briefly touched on Nazism in his
popular writings, he did so in highly indirect ways—so indirect that they
bordered on the banal. For example, in his 1985 book, *Comet* (coauthored with his third wife, Ann Druyan), he proposed an astronomical
explanation for the origin of the swastika (which long predated Nazism).
About the same time, in his novel, *Contact*, the fictional aliens send to
Earth a signal that includes a replay of an early television broadcast of
Hitler at the 1936 Olympics. In both books, Sagan dealt not with the
central horror of Nazism (its high-tech, rationally planned genocide, the
ultimate perversion of the Enlightenment ideal); rather, he dealt merely
with its symbols—the swastika, the Olympics image—as if Nazism was

merely a puzzle in semiotics. Perhaps he could not bring himself to stare into that real-life hell; to do so might have shaken his core beliefs, those bright hopes nursed by a more upbeat source of symbology—the New York World's Fair.

On the other hand, Sagan apparently felt an inward pride in his Jewishness. Well into adulthood, he retained a deep affection for his bar mitzvah teacher, Rabbi Morrison Bial (whom Sagan asked to attend a ceremony in his honor a few decades after he had left Rahway). Sagan's wives were all Jewish. The first and last of his four sons, Dorion Solomon (his child by Lynn Margulis) and Samuel Democritus (his child by Ann Druyan), have traditional Jewish names; and his daughter, Alexandra, has the Jewish middle name Rachel (in honor of Sagan's mother).

Regarding Israel, Sagan was more skeptical about Israeli politics (at least in the 1970s) than was his fiercely pro-Israel second wife, Linda Salzman, according to their son, Nick (whom they sent to a Hebrew teacher as a child). In Sagan's last years, as we shall see later, he reached a kind of political rapprochement with religion in general: he allied himself with progressive religious leaders eager to save the planet from destruction. His religious skepticism, which troubled so many Christians, evidently caused little trouble among American Jews, whose community has traditionally been far more tolerant of skeptical intellectuals, including atheists. In the mid-1980s Sagan accepted awards including the Nahum Goldmann Medal from the World Jewish Congress at a ceremony in Jerusalem; the Brit HaDorot (Covenant of the Generations) Award from the Shalom Center, an American Jewish peace group, in New York; and the Maurice Eisendrath Award for Social Justice from the Central Conference of American Rabbis and Union of American Hebrew Congregations, in Washington. In 1996, a few months before his death, while he was undergoing medical treatment in Seattle, he addressed the international convention of B'nai B'rith in Washington by telephone. The convention gave him its Dor L'Dor (Generation to Generation) Award. During Sagan's telephone talk, he noted that his father, Sam, had been the president of a B'nai B'rith lodge in New Jersey. The Judaic tradition of questioning dogma, Sagan added, had encouraged him "to ask questions early"; hence his religion was at least partly "responsible for the kind of science that I do." It was an impressive acknowledgment coming from the man who, more than four decades earlier, had seemingly lacked (in Blum's view) "a drop of Jewish interest in his body."

WHICH BRINGS US BACK to the late 1940s, to the young Sagan's religious doubts. These upset his mother, Rachel. Despite her flinty skepticism about most matters, she trusted in the unseen world. Her faith gave her a sense of stability. Now her only son—her future genius—was rejecting the faith of his fathers? Their religious quarrels, Sagan later admitted, were "traumatic" because for Rachel "there were a lot of emotional, traditional connections" at stake. "There was a time," he recalled, "when my mother and I would have—'fights,' I guess is the word, on this issue. I think it only lasted about a year." Then Rachel realized that it was "hopeless" for her to try to change Sagan's mind, and they stopped fighting.[15]

Sagan's loss of faith intersected neatly with his growing fascination with extraterrestrial life. He had rejected a supernatural explanation of the origin of life (and everything else); therefore he needed to find a scientific one. A great deal was at stake: if life emerged easily by mechanistic means on Earth, then it might be very common in the heavens; if it emerged with difficulty, then very rare. This stirred his interest in the scientific study of the origin of life. Until the early 1950s, such study was almost nonexistent; there had been theoretical papers published here and there, and a book or two, but not much else.[16] While his teenage peers read Mickey Spillane and J. D. Salinger, Sagan turned to physicist Erwin Schrödinger's *What Is Life?* (1946) and chemist A. I. Oparin's *Origin of Life* (written in the 1920s and published in English in 1938).

A titan of physics, Schrödinger developed key insights into wave mechanics in the 1920s. Emboldened by his triumphs, he tried to fertilize ideas in an unfamiliar terrain: biology. He encouraged physical scientists to try to explain life in purely physical terms, at the atomic and molecular scales. Biologists alone would not unlock life's mystery; they should welcome, not dismiss, advice from physicists and chemists. True, he was poaching on a discipline beyond his training. But he had no choice, as he explained in the book's charming introduction:

> [T]he spread, both in width and depth, of the multifarious branches of knowledge during the last hundred-odd years has confronted us with a queer dilemma. We feel clearly that we are only now beginning to acquire reliable material for welding together the sum-total of all that is known into a whole; but, on the other hand, it has become next to impossible for a single mind fully to command more than a small specialized portion of it.
>
> I can see no other escape from this dilemma (lest our true aim be lost for ever) than that some of us should venture to embark upon a synthesis of facts and theories, albeit with second-hand and incomplete knowledge of some of them—and at the risk of making fools of ourselves.[17]

Carl Sagan, the paragon of the multidisciplinary scientist, couldn't have said it better.

Sagan also read Oparin's *Origin of Life*. Oparin rose to distinction and controversy in the early days of Bolshevik Russia. With Marx, the Bolsheviks agreed that religion was "the opiate of the masses"; it prevented the people from recognizing their true oppressors, the capitalists. Thus Marxist scientists had a responsibility to seek nonsuperstitious explanations for biological phenomena. Historians contest exactly how decisive Marxism was in spawning the modern science of life's origin.[18] Nonetheless, it is striking that during the first, hopeful decade of Bolshevik socialism, three historic proposals on the origin of life came from Marxists—Oparin in Russia, J. B. S. Haldane in England, and H. J. Muller in the United States.

While Muller was working in Moscow, he came into conflict with Oparin, who by that time was a skilled political operator as well as an imaginative scientist. Muller and Oparin strongly disagreed over a key issue: Did life begin as a gene or as a cell? In 1926, Muller had proposed that the earliest life forms were large molecules able to replicate themselves, similar to the viruses then being discovered by microbiologists. Muller called the primordial entities "naked genes" because they lacked cell-like shelters, which they acquired later.

Oparin, however, thought that cells came first. He pointed to lab experiments involving cell-like objects called coacervates, which could easily be generated with the right mix of chemicals. In Oparin's view, these "protocells" were the first life forms. They acquired genes later. Oparin's cells-first hypothesis is of a piece with his later hostility to the idea that life can be explained purely in terms of physics and chemistry; that is, in terms of large molecules like the nucleic acids DNA and RNA. As a Soviet Marxist, he argued that the ultimate guide to biology should be the "laws" of dialectical materialism, not those of physics and chemistry. Caustically, Muller countered that the idea of cells evolving without genes was "like a science of organic chemistry which omits carbon."[19]

What really split Muller from Oparin, though, was the rise of a Stalinist lackey, Trofim Lysenko. This crank agronomist promoted a bastardized version of Lamarckism, an outmoded, pre-Darwinian doctrine of evolution according to which organisms pass nongenetic characteristics on to their offspring. (A fabled example is the giraffe's long neck, the result, Lamarckians said, of its stretching to reach high leaves.) Lysenko claimed that his radical agricultural theories could boost the Soviet harvest. The USSR was hungry, so Stalin backed Lysenko. The cowardly Oparin escaped persecution by siding with Lysenko, even praising him. Anti-Lysenko biologists were imprisoned. The Soviet genetics community was destroyed and has never fully recovered.[20]

During the Lysenko nightmare, Muller courageously attacked Oparin by name.[21] Oparin denounced him and called "for my expulsion from the Soviet Academy after I had already resigned," Muller later wrote to Sagan.[22] Muller's friends feared for his safety, and they persuaded him to flee to the West. After some hesitation, he escaped to Edinburgh (by way of a stint on the Loyalist side of the Spanish Civil War). During World War II he returned to the United States, and by 1945 he was a professor of zoology at Bloomington. The next year, he won the Nobel Prize in physiology and medicine for his *Drosophila* research.

Years later, when Muller responded to Sagan with critiques of his radio script for WUCB, he raised only one strong objection, specifically, to Sagan's reference to all concepts of the origin of life as "Oparin's theory."[23] There were other important theorists, Muller noted (J. B. S. Haldane, J. D. Bernal, Muller himself). Sagan recalled years later that Muller had been quick to point out to him the crucial problem with Oparin's theory. This flaw was that if a cell couldn't reliably reproduce its hereditary material, then it couldn't pass on its features to offspring or undergo mutations that would drive evolution.[24] Sagan then became an enthusiast for Muller's "naked gene" theory, which would, in fact, be the basis of Sagan's first published scientific paper.

ONE MAY SAY unpleasant things about Oparin as a human being. Still, he deserves credit for pioneering an important idea regarding the origin of life. In the 1920s, he first argued that the earliest chemical building blocks of life, complex organic molecules, were likeliest to emerge in a hydrogen-rich (reducing) atmosphere. (A similar theory was independently proposed by Haldane.[25]) This idea is the basis of Stanley Miller and Harold Urey's historic 1952 experiment on the origin of life at the University of Chicago. Sagan was a student there at the time and witnessed the resulting excitement. The Miller-Urey experiment had a major impact on his thinking and career. "The Miller-Urey experiment is now recognized as the single most significant step in convincing many scientists that life is likely to be abundant in the cosmos," Sagan later said.[26]

The theory of a hydrogen-rich early atmosphere came to be accepted thanks in part to a woman unconnected to the study of life's origins. In the 1920s Cecilia Payne-Gaposchkin taught astronomy at Harvard. Sagan's friend Frank Drake knew her decades later, when he was a student there, and recalls the oddball atmosphere of her classroom. She was six feet tall, probably weighed two hundred pounds, and was "a very businesslike person, she was not warm, she was not friendly. . . . A chain-smoker, . . . [a] giant woman, who very often was lecturing with a cigarette in her mouth." Her husband was a Russian-born astronomer and reputedly an enthusiastic nudist, while her son, who was six foot four, "used to scare people. . . . He walked around, sort of like Frankenstein, and grunted." He'd walk up behind her while she was on stage and start doodling on the blackboard. "A very strange family," says Drake.[27]

In the 1920s she found evidence that the Sun consists primarily of hydrogen, not (as was generally believed) elements similar to those on Earth. Researchers were initially skeptical. Eventually, though, Henry Norris Russell verified her thesis. Then in the 1930s, the astronomer Rupert Wildt found that the giant gas planets Jupiter and Saturn had dense, hydrogen-rich atmospheres.[28] These discoveries implied that the Sun had been born from an immense cloud rich in hydrogen gas, which gravitationally collapsed into our solar system. The interstellar gas bathed early Earth in an atmosphere rich in hydrogen. This early atmosphere eventually escaped into space, but not before triggering the formation of organic molecules. Those "organics" were the starting points of biological evolution. That was the theory, anyway. But was it true?

HAROLD CLAYTON UREY (1893–1981) was a leader in pre- and postwar American science. He was a tough, gruff native of Indiana, a Nobel Prize winner in chemistry (he discovered deuterium), and a key figure in the World War II Manhattan Project, which developed the atomic bomb. After the war he became a critic of national nuclear policy. He sought ways to beat atomic swords into plowshares—to find peacetime applications for nuclear science, which had ended so many Japanese lives and threatened to end humanity in general. He found such applications in the field of geochemistry. By studying ratios of isotopes in geological sediments, he was able to determine how ocean temperatures had varied in the past, information important for studying climatic change, among other matters.[29]

Like some scientists of the late 1940s, Urey grew interested in the origin of the solar system. This was an old issue going back to Laplace, and earlier. Laplace's nebular hypothesis had been popular in the nineteenth century, then fell out of favor from the 1900s to the 1930s, when "tidal" hypotheses (stellar near-collisions) reigned. Then, during World War II, the German researcher C. F. von Weizsacker proposed a modified version of the nebular hypothesis, which partly overcame old technical objections.[30] Urey believed that the study of the planets and their origins was no longer a matter just for astronomers and physicists; now chemists like himself could get involved. A new science emerged: cosmochemistry.[31] In fact, the 1950s and 1960s hybridized a number of once-unrelated fields, as scientists began talking about "astrobiology" (or "exobiology"), "astrogeology," "astrochemistry," and the like. David Fisher, one of Urey's students, later wrote that Urey "fathered a generation of cosmochemists in Chicago and grandfathered another generation in California. . . . He was a gruff man, impatient and demanding, and somehow—for his honesty, perhaps, or his genuine passion for knowledge and understanding, or perhaps simply his interest in us—we all loved him."[32]

In late 1951, when Sagan entered the University of Chicago, another entrant was Stanley Miller, a twenty-one-year-old first-year graduate student fresh from the University of California at Berkeley.[33] That autumn, Miller attended one of Urey's lectures. The chemist explained his theory that early Earth had a hydrogen-rich atmosphere, in which the chemical building blocks of life could have easily formed. Perhaps (Urey noted) lightning bolts provided the energy that caused the early hydrogen-rich molecules methane and ammonia to assemble into organics. It'd be interesting, Urey added, if someone would demonstrate this experimentally—that is, by simulating the atmosphere of the primitive Earth in a flask. (Melvin Calvin of Berkeley had tried to, but used the wrong atmosphere, one too rich in carbon dioxide and water vapor.)[34]

Miller was intrigued. He had been looking for a subject for his doctoral thesis, and this one sounded exciting. He approached Urey and asked for permission to do the experiment. Urey reacted cautiously, warning Miller that this was a risky project for a dissertation. But Miller persisted, and Urey finally went along—on one condition. If Miller failed to obtain interesting results within a year, then he had to find a different thesis topic. Miller agreed.[35]

Imagine the early Earth: a lifeless terrain, scarred by impacts from meteor and comets. The ground regularly shakes and the sky briefly glows as another mountainous impactor slams into the crust. Overhead is the primordial sun, dimmer than it is now, and orbited by pinpoints of light—the other planets. On Earth, the original blanket of hydrogen gas still hovers above the surface, not yet having escaped into space. Much of the hydrogen is locked within molecules—methane, ammonia, and water.

If Urey was right, then all Miller needed to do was to expose a mixture of those same chemicals to the right energy source (such as electricity or ultraviolet light). Then they should rearrange their atomic components and form *organic* molecules. That is what chemistry is, after all: the reshuffling of atoms into different groupings.

In Miller's experiment, carbon (C) was available from methane (CH_4), nitrogen (N) from ammonia (NH_3), oxygen (O) from water (H_2O), and hydrogen (H) from all three. An electrical discharge would break the molecules apart, possibly causing them to rearrange into organics.

About this time, H. J. Muller had written a letter to Urey, his fellow Nobelist, and urged him to meet Sagan.[36] They did meet, and during their chat Urey mentioned Miller's experiment. Intrigued, Sagan visited Miller in his "dungeon"-like basement lab, as Sagan recalled it. In the dungeon, Miller filled a flask with methane, ammonia, and water. He then switched on the "sparking" device and left for the night. The next morning he examined the flask: the water within had turned "noticeably pink." Inside were hydrocarbons, chains of carbon and hydrogen atoms. He let the sparking device run for another two days. The result: a scummy layer that, upon analysis, proved to contain an amino acid called glycine. Finally Miller let the experiment spark for a week, after which he found many more types of amino acids, including unknown types. This was a startling result.[37] Previously, skeptics had argued that the building blocks of life could no more self-assemble into complex organics than a windstorm could turn a forest into wooden homes.[38] Yet that is exactly what Miller appeared to have done, in an experiment mimicking presumed conditions on the primordial Earth.

News media jumped on the story. The experiment delighted that tough old Marxist, Haldane, who reportedly said that he could "die happy now."[39] Some reporters interpreted the experiment as a latter-day version of the creation of the Frankenstein monster. Of course, Miller hadn't created life, only its molecular building blocks. Still, a 1953 Gallup poll asked Americans if they thought scientists would eventually create living creatures in the laboratory. Seventy-nine percent replied "No."

Miller described his results in a seminar at the University of Chicago, with Urey present. Carl Sagan sat in the audience. During the question period, Sagan later recalled, other professors didn't seem to appreciate the importance of Miller's experiment, and his results were "roundly condemned by nearly every faculty member who made a comment." As he watched Urey try to defend Miller, and saw how nervous Miller was and how heated the discussion got, Sagan realized for the first time just how emotionally intense research could be.[40]

Miller recalls the scene differently. Now in his late sixties, bustling, bespectacled, and ebullient, he remains active in origin-of-life work at the University of California at San Diego. "What Carl didn't realize," Miller says, "was, it wasn't that they didn't *understand* the importance. It's that they just couldn't believe the *results!*"[41] All those amino acids! Thick coats of them! It seemed almost too easy. Almost a century after Pasteur claimed to shut the door for good on mechanistic explanations of life's origin, young Stanley Miller had reopened it.

THE MILLER-UREY EXPERIMENT thrilled Sagan. Take a reducing atmosphere and inject electricity, and what do you get? The assembly parts for life! Gobs of them! Anyone could see where this led. Hydrogen gas pervades the cosmos; therefore Miller-Urey–type chemical processes might be under way in the atmospheres of countless other planets. Miller-Urey processes generated organics so easily that life could no longer be considered a miracle or an improbable fluke. On the contrary; it was an *inevitability*. It seemed so simple, so obvious.

Sagan was enraptured. Miller's achievement would surely rank among the great moments in the history of efforts to explain the "miracle" of life in nonmiraculous terms. Past examples included Galvani's demonstration that the frog's nervous system responds to electrical impulses, and Wohler's synthesis of the organic substance urea from ordinary chemicals.[42] Meanwhile, in England, two young scientists, James Watson and Francis Crick, were close to explaining heredity in purely physico-chemical terms.[43] "What is life?" Schrödinger had asked. Increasingly, it appeared to be what nonbelievers like Sagan had always said it was: a complex, delicate, fascinating machine, but a machine nonetheless. Who needed "souls" or "spirits" or "vital forces"?[44] Physics would explain it all, using atoms and molecules.

Sagan took one of Urey's undergraduate classes and wrote an honors essay on the origin of life. "It was very naive," he later admitted. "I had the idea that in one fell swoop I could understand the origins of life, though I had not had much [training in] chemistry or biology." Urey read the paper and remarked that it showed the signs of naive youth.[45] Sagan later acknowledged that the paper "was riddled with misconceptions."[46]

Urey's style of advising students was much different from Muller's patient instruction. Urey was somewhat blunt, and he talked to students the same direct way that he talked to scientific colleagues. Sagan later recalled struggling to follow Urey and hesitating to interrupt him to ask any questions. He also recalled that Urey often criticized other scientists in harsh terms.[47] Urey's treatment of these scientific rivals was an omen. Eventually Urey would direct his assaults at Sagan himself—with serious consequences for the young man's career.

Undaunted by Urey's scorn for his undergraduate paper, however, Sagan kept rewriting it for years. He frequently consulted Muller about it and Muller also directed him toward other experts, such as origin-of-life expert Sidney Fox and Sewall Wright, a famous population geneticist at the University of Wisconsin.

Sagan was so eager to talk to whatever scientists he thought could advise him that on a car trip to California with a friend, the nineteen-year-old Sagan stopped at the California Institute of Technology in Pasadena and "just showed up unannounced" in Linus Pauling's office. The legendary chemist was tall and rail-thin, with bright blue eyes and a crinkly grin, and very hospitable. He listened amiably as Sagan explained his ideas on the origin of life. At one point Pauling leaned back and closed his eyes. Sagan grew worried: was Pauling falling asleep? Gradually Sagan realized "that was his way of clearing distractions" from his mind. Pauling opened his eyes, made some useful suggestions, and Sagan went on his way.[48] This kind of chutzpah, and this unabashed enthusiasm, were to become hallmarks of Sagan's career.

SAGAN'S PERSISTENT INTEREST in life's origins was matched only by his persistent interest in UFOs. At least as late as 1954, when he was a college junior, he suspected that they might be extraterrestrial vehicles, and he tried to persuade Muller of this. The Nobelist countered (perhaps tongue in cheek) by citing one "saucer" report that suggested UFOs were Soviet-built. Sagan replied, in a letter dated January 27, 1954, that there was no reason to believe that all UFOs were of Soviet making. In defense of his position, he pointed out that legitimate sightings had occurred well before the Soviets came to power. He also argued that the Soviets would not take the risk of flying their saucers over U.S. territory, where many sightings had occurred, because if one crashed or was shot down and its origin was discovered, that might start a war. In addition, some of the saucers had been observed making flying maneuvers that would require materials much stronger than anything on Earth and that a human being would not be able to survive.[49]

That is Sagan's last known defense of UFOs. Thereafter, his faith was shaken by two books—*Fads and Fallacies in the Name of Science* (1951) by Martin Gardner[50] (another University of Chicago graduate, and later the mathematics editor of *Scientific American*) and *Extraordinary Popular Delusions and the Madness of Crowds* (1841) by Charles Mackay.

Fads and Fallacies was a founding tract of the modern "skeptics" movement. Breezily and wittily, Gardner details the pseudoscientific beliefs of anti-Einstein theorists, pyramidologists, medical quacks, psychic researchers, orgone therapists, L. Ron Hubbard (founder of Dianetics and its far more profitable descendant, Scientology), and crank cosmologist Immanuel Velikovsky, among others. While enjoying Gardner's account, Sagan was startled to find that it included a chapter that demolished the UFO fad.

Mackay's book didn't deal with UFOs—it was written a century before the saucer craze. Still, Sagan drew major lessons from Mackay's accounts of the repeated instances in which humans have been gulled by false notions, ranging from get-rich-quick schemes to fortune-telling. Gradually, Sagan began to recognize what flying saucers really are: not a physical phenomenon, but a psychological and a sociological one. "It was stunning," Sagan later reflected, "how many passionately argued and defended claims to knowledge had amounted to nothing. It slowly dawned on me that, human fallibility being what it is, there might be other explanations for flying saucers."[51]

In time, Sagan would become a devastatingly effective critic of the UFO cult—indeed, of the flood of pseudoscience and superstition engulfing America in the second half of the twentieth century.

A SIGN OF HOW FAR Sagan's skepticism evolved during his undergraduate years is that in 1955, only one year after he had written his defense of UFOs to Muller, he began to doubt one of his most cherished hopes: that life exists on Mars. As a boy, he had thrilled to read about the "canals" of Mars and John Carter's adventures on the red planet. But now he began to suspect that Mars was lifeless. One reason is that he realized, probably while working on his paper about the origin of life, that the atmosphere of Mars is so thin that it provides little barrier to solar ultraviolet radiation. The radiation would bake any Martian life forms from sunrise to sunset. How could they endure?

Another reason was his growing doubts about the chief argument for Mars life: the so-called wave of darkening. A dark coloration periodically spread and retreated across the Martian surface. Some attributed the wave to seasonal changes in vegetation. But in late 1955, Sagan stumbled across a new—and nonbiological—explanation for the wave of darkening. The *Proceedings* of the Astronomical Society of the Pacific ran an article by Prof. Dean B. McLaughlin of the University of Michigan. McLaughlin suggested that Mars had active volcanoes, as violent as Krakatoa. The waves of darkening occurred when the volcanoes erupted, spewing ash over the planet.[52]

The thesis didn't seem totally unreasonable; in recent years, a Japanese astronomer had reported seeing bright glows—volcanic eruptions?—on Mars.[53] In December 1955, Sagan wrote to Muller to express his growing pessimism about the possibility of Martian life. In the meantime, his heart—usually lost in the stars—had suddenly turned earthward: he had met a girl.

LYNN ALEXANDER (later Margulis) and Carl Sagan dated for more than two years before they married. As Margulis remembers it, she met Sagan on a staircase. He was coming up the stairs of Eckhart Hall, the math building, on the main university campus, and there they chatted. She was about sixteen years old at the time, one of the campus's many bright and very young minds who had left the inanities of high school early for the intellectual feast of the Hutchins program. He was twenty and very talkative: "Tall, handsome, with a shock of brown-black hair, and exceedingly articulate, even then he was full of ideas," Margulis recalls. "I was a scientific ignoramus. Carl, and especially his gift of gab, fascinated me. Already he seemed to be a polished professional. From our first meeting he shared with me, and with anyone else who would listen, his keen understanding of the vastness of time and space. His love for science was contagious."[54] She had the impression that he was "famous" on campus.

Sagan's feelings about Lynn are unclear. He left no known account of their first encounter. Indeed, a shallow biographer would be tempted to conclude that as a young man he had no deep personal feelings about anyone—that he lived in an abstract world of ideas and ideas alone. On the surface, though, he was all ebullience and charm; and it was the surface that stirred Lynn's heart. From the mid-1950s to the early 1960s, their relationship followed its tragic arc—from the Eckhart Hall staircase to mutual affection to marriage to children to the Alameda County divorce court. After it was all over, after five years of marriage, she would wonder whether he had cared for her at all. As we shall see, he had. His seeming inner coldness was, in fact, just another surface, beneath which raged yearnings and anxieties and a certain self-loathing. But he kept this inner self under lock and key. In this sense, he was very much a man—a *man*, mind you—of his time.

Sagan's friends from the time speak of Margulis with real warmth. "We loved her," recalls Sagan's friend Peter Pesch. "She was marvelous—interested in ideas, concepts, completely open-minded, tolerant, excited, loved to talk. She was so *intense;* she still is. Very perceptive and very warm and with an absolutely first-rate mind, which makes a terrific combination. A huge heart and a terrific intelligence."[55] Margulis was attractive; she could have landed many other men besides Sagan. "She knocked the socks off a lot of guys," says her college friend Rachel Patinkin Grainer. "She was a very experienced young lady before she met Sagan."[56]

Like Sagan's, Margulis's origins were modest. She grew up in a tough Chicago neighborhood where schoolgirls carried razor blades. Her father was a lawyer involved with road development.[57] Her mother "barely ran a household. . . . She was interested in men, marriage. . . . She was beautiful." In other words, Margulis says, "I didn't have an intellectual background to rebel against."[58]

But she was exceptionally smart, and gained early entrance—at age fourteen—to the university. The Hutchins program transformed her life, as it had Sagan's. She read the original genetics papers of Gregor Mendel. She was fascinated by heredity: How do life forms grow and develop? Why are some plants white, others red, and others pink? "How does the flower *know* to come out that way?" A biologist in the making.

Her budding interest in the life sciences pleased Sagan, who was also fascinated by living organisms, particularly those that didn't dwell on Earth. He already knew a great deal about the science of biology, and described for her his vision of its future. Life, he said, would be explained (as Schrödinger had prophesied) in the language of physics and chemistry.

Undoubtedly, this trend toward a physicochemical explanation seemed especially exciting because it felt close to home. Watson, one of the two men in England who had recently decoded the double-helical structure of DNA (the agent of heredity), was one of Muller's former students.[59] The DNA discovery reinforced hopes of explaining the origin of life in terms of "naked genes," Muller's hypothesis, which influenced Sagan's slowly fermenting first scientific paper. And Sagan's friend Stanley Miller had recently demonstrated—on their own campus—how easily organic molecules could have formed in the reducing atmosphere of the early Earth.

Watson's associate, Crick, trained as a physicist, once said he went into molecular biology in hopes of expunging from it the last traces of "vitalism," a quasimystical belief that living organisms contain nonphysical properties not reducible to physics or chemistry.[60] Sagan, an assertive young atheist, could have shared Crick's sentiment. Cleanse the laboratories of superstition. Let the light of reason flood in the windows.

Both Sagan and Margulis were biological visionaries, holistic thinkers on the grand scale. He regarded life and intelligence as universal phenomena, while she viewed terrestrial life as a unity. Yet like prophets offering different prophecies, neither found the other's vision appealing. She regarded the quest for extraterrestrial life as uninteresting, even silly, while he was deeply suspicious of her (and James Lovelock's) "Gaia" hypothesis (developed years later), according to which the terrestrial ecosystem is a single, self-sustaining life form. One wonders: If Sagan and Margulis had shared a common vision, would it have compensated for everything else that their marriage lacked? Would they have become one of those luminous scientific couples—like the Curies—whose love of knowledge is a cement stronger than love itself?

One of Lynn Margulis's relatives, the witty Nobel Prize–winning physicist Sheldon Glashow, observed after Sagan became a TV celebrity that Sagan's youthful persuasiveness had "convinced [Lynn] to study biology rather than English." Slyly, Glashow added: "Lynn is possibly Sagan's greatest contribution to science."[61] Indeed, in strictly scientific terms, she would become more distinguished than he. She would win admittance to the National Academy of Sciences, which, having a number of members who shared Glashow's attitude but less of his subtlety, would somewhat awkwardly reject Sagan's candidacy. And ironically, she would evolve in a scientific direction—toward "Gaia"—very different from the one that Sagan had championed, one far more holistic, less reductionistic, than his; one that (he would later grumble) emitted the whiff of metaphysics.[62]

AFTER THREE YEARS of study, Sagan received his first bachelor's degree, with general and specific honors, in 1954. He obtained a second bachelor's degree in physics in 1955, and his master's degree in physics the following year.[63] Although poorly prepared for college, he had worked hard and performed well. "So I was not delayed in my trajectory by anything," he recalled.[64]

With such undergraduate success under his belt, he proceeded to the doctorate. He applied for, and was accepted into, the University of Chicago's graduate astronomy program, which was based at Yerkes Observatory in Williams Bay, Wisconsin. His classes there were scheduled to start in the autumn of 1956.

College love affairs sometimes break apart as one or both lovers depart for graduate school or postdoctoral positions elsewhere. Sagan and Margulis were lucky in this regard, however, because Yerkes was only a few hours' drive northwest of Chicago, and it was easy for them to see each other regularly.

A nice bonus about the position at Yerkes was that the director, Gerard Kuiper, invited Sagan to spend the summer before working at McDonald Observatory in Fort Davis, Texas. Sagan had originally been considering a trip to Europe, but changed his plans and accepted the post. He wrote lightheartedly to Kuiper that, after all, Europe would forever be at a constant distance from him, whereas Mars would not.[65] The reference was to the fact that Mars was scheduled to reach "opposition" late that summer—that is, it would be in a position relative to the Earth and Sun guaranteeing that it would be unusually close and bright. If the weather cooperated, the dry, clear Texas skies would be ideal for observing the opposition.

Reflecting later on his experience in Texas, Sagan commented that the Lone Star state "was my real introduction to big telescopes, planets." Unfortunately, the opposition he had come to observe wasn't much fun. The weather was lousy, both in Texas and on Mars. "That was . . . a time of great dust storms both on Mars and in Texas!" Sagan recalled, and he couldn't see much of anything. The miserable viewing conditions, he later said, "stiffened my resolve that the way to learn about the planets is not by peering through this ocean of air but to *go* there"—that is, in spaceships.

While hoping for the dust to clear, Sagan and the fifty-year-old Kuiper had little to do. So they "just sat around and talked. . . . I remember Gerard urging me to do an experiment with flypaper to catch the dust particles and see what I could deduce of the [dust's] geology," Sagan recalled. They enjoyed each other's company, and talked about "absolutely everything."[66] The Dutch-born Kuiper had a distinguished scientific record; among other things, he had discovered the atmosphere of Titan (the first moon known to have a non-negligible atmosphere). He also predicted the existence of a dense cloud of icy bodies in the outer solar system. It is now named for him (the "Kuiper belt"), and so was a NASA aircraft once used for high-altitude infrared astronomy. He was also full of war stories. During World War II, he had worked with U.S. military forces to capture or rescue German scientists. His most celebrated exploits were with "Alsos," a team of experts sent to investigate Germany's atomic-bomb project. He obtained military infrared sensors (used for night fighting). He brought them back to the United States and put them to use in astronomy.[67]

Kuiper introduced Sagan to order-of-magnitude calculations. For someone like Sagan, who relished big numbers, these types of calculations were a revelation. Sometimes referred to as back-of-the-envelope calculations, this rough "guesstimating" method allows for fast checks on ideas and for fairly free-wheeling experimentation to see what numbers might work. "It cut through nonsense like a knife through butter," Sagan wrote. He thrilled to this new power, almost a "secret rite": "Wow! What power! What an amazing leverage on the universe. . . . That was a really important experience for me."[68] It would later get him into trouble, though.[69]

Sitting in the dark observatory, waiting for Mars to finally peek through the dust storm, Kuiper and Sagan talked about the possibility of extraterrestrial life. Kuiper had first attracted press attention in the 1940s with his speculations about possible Martian vegetation. Back then, talk of aliens—even miserable lichen—made most astronomers uncomfortable. Their discomfort grew worse when Kuiper's speculations were reported by *Time* magazine. Famed astronomer Otto Struve, who still ran Yerkes in 1949, wrote an angry memo to Chancellor Robert Hutchins that referred to the "Mars affair," with its "*Sensational and Grossly Exaggerated Publicity*" (his emphasis). Struve harshly criticized what he saw as Kuiper's pursuit of fame.[70] In this sense, Kuiper's career—one unusually close to the spotlight, for an astronomer—anticipated Sagan's.

On those warm Texas nights in the summer of 1956, as the red planet glowered through the thick gusts of dust, they talked happily about everything from Hitler's failed atomic-bomb effort to the Martian canals.

(Kuiper was "open-minded" about the canals, Sagan later recorded.)[71] They had no way of knowing that a golden age was ending. For a short time longer, humans would be earthbound, and would continue viewing the planets as they always had, as small, blurry images seen through telescopes. As long as that short time lasted, the human imagination could continue to run free throughout the solar system, envisioning any wonders it wished: planet-girdling oceans or carboniferous jungles on Venus; ruined Martian civilizations, crisscrossed with dried canals; peculiar microbes squirming within warm, moist crevasses of the lunar crust; and heaven only knew what alien menageries in the hypothesized eternal twilight of the Mercurian terminator, where the Sun supposedly always hung low in the sky. Such myths had entertained generations of science-fiction lovers, just as ancient youths had listened, hushed, to tales of Jason and the Medusa. But soon the space age would dawn. Swarms of robotic argonauts would begin scouting the inner solar system, exposing its true nature and expelling its imagined aliens as surely as the industrial revolution drove fairies and werewolves from the Celtic moors.

LIKE SAGAN, Lynn Margulis was ambitious. She got a plum summer assignment working in Mexico, on an anthropological project with famed University of Illinois professor Oscar Lewis (noted for his studies of poverty—among others, the classic *The Children of Sanchez*). While Sagan was working at McDonald Observatory in Texas, he drove south of the border to see her. While he was there, Margulis recalls, he was astonishingly rude to her Mexican colleagues, acting like a prince disdainful of the serfs. She was so upset that she decided to end their relationship.

How can we reconcile Sagan's solidly liberal politics with his treatment of Margulis's Mexican colleagues? Many people have political convictions that do not jibe with their personal behavior, of course. And the young Sagan's liberalism, while sincere, had an abstract aspect; it was the clever, witty, after-dinner-speaker liberalism of Adlai Stevenson, not the passionate, heart-wrenching, take-to-the-streets liberalism of Martin Luther King Jr. Like so many aloof intellectuals, the young Sagan seemed to think in terms of People rather than people, of Humanity rather than humans.

Consider his writings. He rarely wrote about living human beings, and when he did, he did not write well. His prose lacks the affectionate personal anecdotes about living people that make Richard Feynman's writing so enthralling. Strangely, Sagan wrote most warmly about beings who were farthest removed from him—specifically, by death or biology. His biographical essays of famous but dead scientists are

near-masterpieces, triumphs of characterization and psychological insight. Likewise, he wrote affectionately, even sensuously, about John Lilly's
dolphins (with whom Sagan played in pools), and with touching concern
about animals who suffer through laboratory experiments. And he wrote
almost reverently of hypothetical extraterrestrials who, he thought, would
be morally superior beings, godlike yet doting: witness his characterization of the sweet-tempered alien (who simulated Ellie Arroway's father)
in his novel, *Contact*. To put it bluntly, the young Carl Sagan was a strange
mix of the boyishly enthusiastic and the aridly intellectual—a man who
bubbled excitedly over ideas, while feeling most comfortable with the
non-living, the non-human. He would remain that way until middle age,
when Ann Druyan would transform his soul.

Until then, to the living, he remained an enigma—a man who was
both enormously appealing and enormously vexing. His girlfriend, Lynn
Margulis, found his personal contradictions too stark to tolerate. She
called it quits. Startled, he devoted all his persuasive powers to winning
her back, and he barely succeeded.

JOHN C. (JACK) BRANDT recalls his first arrival at Yerkes Observatory.
You drive through the rolling cornfields of southern Wisconsin, with
their silos and little schoolhouses and inert cows. Then suddenly, it
looms out of the mist: the telescope dome. It is attached to a building
creepily out of place with its surroundings, an aged Gothic structure that
bristles with gargoyles and parapets. Inside, the building is dark, with
creaky floors and funny little corridors and passageways. There is an elegant, old-world library, with ladders ascending to the highest volumes.
Inside the dome is the ancient forty-inch telescope, which, oddly, is
hardly ever used, because of frequent adverse weather.[72] Within the
medieval-looking structure, aging men with strange accents mumble
about plots and conspiracies against them. Among them saunters Carl
Sagan, a skinny, bright-eyed, talkative young Brooklyn native with the
profundity of a rabbi and a voice of gold, who talks about spaceships and
about extraterrestrial life.

Dale Cruikshank, son of an Iowa grocer, felt as though he was entering "a new world" as he drove up to Yerkes in his 1950s Studebaker.
He found the observatory full of "foreigners. An Iowa boy doesn't have a
lot of contact with foreigners! Here's Van Biesbroeck the Belgian, and
Strömgren the Dane, and Chandrasekhar the Indian, and Kuiper the
Dutchman, and on and on."[73] In the 1950s, these were among the most
distinguished surnames in world astronomy. The *Astrophysical Journal*,
astronomy's leading technical publication, was based at Yerkes in those

days. The observatory atmosphere was formal, old-world: everyone called everybody else "Mr."

The local town was Williams Bay, which was very dull. "We'd go down and watch the stoplight change from one color to another," Brandt recalls.[74] Helene Thorson, whose family rented a room to Carl Sagan, worked at the observatory for one of the astronomers; her family lived in town. "The townsfolk mostly found the astronomers strange," she recalls. In her youth, in the 1940s, Williams Bay was the kind of place where renters posted signs advising "Gentiles Only."[75] Sagan recalled his one-year residence there as "awful. [I faced] the only anti-Semitic incidents I've had in my adult life."[76] (He did not give specifics.) A leading Yerkes astronomer was Subrahmanyan Chandrasekhar, a native of India. Helene Thorson recounts that "my mother recalled to me times where Chandrasekhar's wife, whom my mother befriended, would have trouble getting served in the drugstore because the stupid proprietor thought she was black."

Sagan's rented room was on the second floor of the Thorson family home at 92 Geneva Street. He was "a well-mannered man who kept to himself . . . a serious chap," Thorson recalls. But he could let loose, too. She remembers him coming into Prof. Joseph Chamberlain's office "and talking excitedly about the solar wind. . . . One sensed even then that Sagan would turn out to be a great communicator! . . . Sagan was always warm and friendly, just like one of the guys!"[77]

Well, not all of the guys; much of the Yerkes atmosphere was a dark carnival of bickering and backstage scheming. It had been that way for a long time. In the late 1940s, for example, director Otto Struve had described the observatory in a private memo as "a mass of intrigue and petty domination."[78] Remote scientific facilities have a history of generating infighting and personality disorders. (Radioastronomer Frank Drake recalls how at one observatory he had to remove a gun from the hand of a crazed staffer.)[79] Likewise, polar outposts have generated a disturbing number of psychiatric episodes.[80] And heaven knows how tempers may flare aboard the cramped International Space Station when it is completed and fully staffed sometime early in the twenty-first century.[81]

The working atmosphere at Yerkes was strongly influenced by the man in charge, Gerard Kuiper. Dale Cruikshank, an undergraduate summer assistant, recalls that Kuiper "was very rational. Extremely rational. . . . He was very, very focused. Nothing would get in the way of him achieving his goal, whatever that might be. . . . He was overbearing and he projected an arrogance, sometimes to the point of rudeness."[82] Sagan and Kuiper had enjoyed themselves in Texas, but at Yerkes Kuiper was a different man.[83] There he was surrounded by his peers, all clever, some conniving; many intensely disliked him. To some degree, Kuiper, like many creative people who develop their brains rather than their social skills, brought it on himself. Cruikshank was one of Kuiper's doctoral students and, later, had the honor of writing his mentor's official obituary-memoir for the National Academy of Sciences. Kuiper, he remembers, was a peculiar man with almost no friends. Peter Pesch says that behind Kuiper's back, staffers made fun of his oddities—for example, wearing three pairs of eyeglasses at once (one atop his head, one hanging from his neck, and one over his eyes). He baffled and embarrassed students he barely knew by inviting them to his office (decorated with his wartime souvenirs, including a German jet engine and a Nazi whip) and pathetically pouring out his anxieties and insecurities and complaints. One irreverent staffer named his pet squirrel Gerard.

Kuiper carried on a particularly absurd squabble with Geoffrey Burbidge, a huge, brilliant, gossipy, and rather scary-looking Britisher. (He has been called "Jabba the Astronomer.") Once, Mrs. Kuiper left groceries in the McDonald Observatory refrigerator with a note stating, "These are Kuiper groceries. When borrowing, please replace in kind." Burbidge retaliated by inserting his own package with a note announcing, "These are Burbidge groceries. When borrowing, please repay in kind." On one occasion, Kuiper and Burbidge were at McDonald Observatory at the same time. According to Cruikshank, Kuiper made a student sit in the observatory dome "all day long to guard the spectrometer, to make sure that Burbidge didn't come up and sabotage it."

"He sent the FBI after us," Burbidge now says, chortling ominously. In those days the Air Force was hoping to control space exploration and had hired Kuiper as a planetary observer. For this purpose, Kuiper had received some government-owned astronomical equipment, which ended up being mysteriously damaged. Kuiper told the FBI to interview two staff astronomers, including Burbidge. This was all nonsense, Burbidge now harrumphs—he wasn't even around when the damage occurred. Scientifically speaking, he now says, Kuiper "was a great man." But "if he was blinking rapidly, you could tell he was lying."[84]

To some degree, such disputes are typical of remote observatories, where staffers, as Sagan later commented, "don't have anything else to do except to engage in the primate dominance hierarchy. Those who were not the alpha male *wanted* be the alpha male." At Yerkes, the struggles tended to be subterranean—knives flashing in the dark, so to speak—because, as Sagan recalled, "the openness about 'feelings' that came about in the sixties [was] *unheard* of in the fifties. People were *fantastically* repressed."[85] The power struggles that Sagan witnessed at Yerkes influenced his later views on hierarchies within human and primate societies,[86] which he would detail in his books *The Dragons of Eden* (1977) and *Shadows of Forgotten Ancestors* (1992, co-authored with his third wife, Ann Druyan).

However, nothing that Kuiper or Burbidge did to each other could match what Harold Urey—who wasn't at Yerkes at all, but ensconced on the Chicago campus—did to Kuiper. Originally they were friends. They shared ideas and data concerning a common interest, the origins of the solar system. Kuiper believed that the planets had condensed from "giant gaseous protoplanets," whereas Urey thought they slowly accreted from cold, solid, asteroidlike "planetesimals." In time, Urey accused Kuiper of failing to properly credit his research. They also split bitterly over the issue of whether the early Moon had been molten or was always a cold, solid body. According to historian Ronald Doel, Urey tried "to end all [National Science Foundation] subsidies for Kuiper's editorial projects" and to remove Kuiper as president of the International Astronomical Union's Planets and Satellites Commission.[87]

Sagan later recalled, "There was a time when I believe I was the only person on speaking terms with both Urey and Kuiper, which was a great strain on a still-very-young undergraduate or graduate student."[88] The crux of the argument between Urey and Kuiper was that Urey thought Kuiper had plagiarized him, failing to cite Urey at a crucial point in a scientific paper. Though the viciousness of their dispute upset Sagan, he apparently did a good job of negotiating his way between them. "Walking that fine line between the two clashing giants" was good preparation for Sagan's subsequent career, which would generate controversies grander than anything between Kuiper and Urey.

ALTHOUGH KUIPER WAS the director of Yerkes, some suspected that the real power behind the throne was Subrahmanyan Chandrasekhar, a stern native of India, a man whose genius was matched only by his aloofness. In 1949, then-director Struve had written in a private letter that Chandra was "the chief squeezer . . . with Kuiper a ready tool. . . ."[89]

Chandra (as he was always called) intimidated students. They avoided his office when he was inside.[90] Sagan, who apparently did well in Chandra's courses, recalled one of the astrophysicist's classes:

> Chandra was giving a colloquium. Three walls of the lecture room had blackboards on them, all spotlessly clean when Chandra began his lecture. During the course of his lecture, he filled all the blackboards with equations, neatly written in his fine hand, the important ones boxed and numbered as though they had been written in a paper for publication. As his lecture came to an end, Chandra leaned against a table, facing the audience. When the chairman invited questions, someone in the audience said: "Professor Chandrasekhar, on blackboard . . .

let's see . . . 8, line 11, I believe you've made an error in sign." Chandra was absolutely impassive, without comment, and did not even turn around to look at the equation in question. After a few moments of embarrassing silence, the chairman said, "Professor Chandrasekhar, do you have an answer to this question?" Chandra responded, "It was not a question; it was a statement, and it is mistaken," without turning around.[91]

An astronomy student rebuked by Chandra felt like a priest rebuked by the Pope. Lynn Margulis recalls that once Sagan arranged for Chandra to address the campus astronomy club. "He gave a fantastic talk. I didn't understand a lot of it, but I loved it."

"And after the talk," she recalls, "Chandrasekhar said [sternly to Sagan], 'Thank you very much for inviting me—but young man, when you introduce a professor to a formal event, you wear *a suit and tie.*'" She grins at her ex-husband's comeuppance: "Carl was mortified!"[92]

Chandrasekhar wasn't really so humorless; the Yerkes janitor informed students that Chandra kept a desk drawer full of Mickey Mouse comic books.[93] But as with many aloof people, his chilly exterior concealed hidden hurts. Born in 1910, a native of India who studied in England, then migrated to the United States, Chandra was "scarred" by "ugly incidents of harassment and humiliation because of the color of his skin," his biographer records.[94] Chandra was one of the grand figures of astrophysics (he later won the Nobel Prize) at a time when it was beginning to digest the cosmic implications of Einsteinian relativity and quantum physics. He demonstrated how stars called white dwarfs—tiny, near-dead stars that have crushed their atoms together—could exist. This was an important step toward concepts of even more compressed states of matter, leading to the notions of neutron stars and (ultimately) black holes. Chandra remained intellectually active well into his eighties. One of his last works, a formidably dense collection of equations, advised those seeking further information to consult the original notebooks (hundreds of pages of even more detailed equations) archived at the University of Chicago.

Chandra's past humiliations made him a confirmed political liberal. When he moved to Wisconsin, he became an outspoken Democrat who wore an Adlai Stevenson button. He roped students, including Sagan, into raising funds for Democratic candidates. This may not have been the safest thing to do in rural Wisconsin; one of the state's latest U.S. senators had been Joseph McCarthy. Sagan recalled how in 1956, on "Dollars for Democrats Day," "Peter Pesch and I went door to door. I think I got one dollar all day." A cop arrested Sagan, charging him with "peddling without a license." Later the charge was dropped and he was remanded to the custody of one of the astronomers, the gentle Bengt Strömgren. In his soft Danish accent, the bemused Strömgren scolded Sagan: "Be a *good* boy."[95]

In these years, Sagan's encounters with scientists such as Chandra, Muller, Urey, and Linus Pauling clearly taught him a valuable lesson: Scientists cannot live in ivory towers; they must participate in politics. Sagan took their example to heart. As a result, the Williams Bay hassle was not his last run-in with law enforcement.

RARE IS THE GRADUATE STUDENT whose work earns a mention in the *New York Times*. On page 6 of the December 29, 1956, edition, several paragraphs into a story about Kuiper addressing the American Association for the Advancement of Science meeting in New York, we read: "Another University of Chicago scientist, Carl Sagan, suggested that organisms on the order of rock-lichen could exist in the Martian environment."

"Both Mars and the Earth," he was paraphrased, "probably were formed about the same time in the Solar System and had similar seas and oxygen atmospheres until the Martian ones were lost to interplanetary space because of a weak gravity." (Sagan later told author Rae Goodell that the newspaper had credited some of his comments to Kuiper, and vice versa.)

For Gerard Kuiper, an accomplished, Ph.D.-holding astronomer, to receive such press was one thing. But a mere grad student! The news item "scandalized" other faculty, Sagan recalled. "The mere fact that a graduate student paper on such a speculative topic had made the *New York Times* made faculty members angry."[96]

Sagan was, however, no ordinary first-year grad student. One month after the *Times* item appeared, Sagan's first scientific article, written when he was an undergraduate, was published in the prestigious journal *Evolution*. The sixteen-page article, entitled "Radiation and the Origin of the Gene,"[97] proposed ways to explain how the earliest living organisms might have emerged from organic molecules. He noted Oparin's opinion that once amino acids formed, they would "spontaneously" link together, forming long-chain protein molecules, key building blocks of living organisms. Sharing Muller's low opinion of Oparin, Sagan added dryly: "The statistical likelihood of this happening is, of course, very small." However, this did not require scientists to quit seeking a scientific explanation for life and to revert to a supernatural one (as advocated by the scientist-mystic LeComte du Nouy). Sagan suggested that a possible solution lay in an organic molecule called adenosine triphosphate, or ATP, an essential energy source within cells. He believed that somehow ATP formed on the early Earth, providing the energy necessary for long-chain proteins to form. (Sagan got this idea from H. F. Blum's classic of theoretical biology, *Time's Arrow and Evolution*, published in 1951 shortly before the Miller-Urey experiment.) Within a few years, Sagan would test this theory experimentally.

While eloquent beyond his years, this article lacks the skillful organization and, hence, the persuasiveness of Sagan's later technical writings. He reminded *Homo sapiens* of their humble evolutionary roots:

> If there is one generalization we can make from the picture presented by paleontology and evolution, it is this: that organisms die but their genes pass on—often mutated and redistributed, it is true, but genes nevertheless; and it is difficult, therefore, to escape the conclusion that the design of the organism is merely to provide for gene multiplication and survival. . . . [W]e should note the work of Macallum and his successors, which shows significant similarities between the chemistry of protoplasm [e.g., in humans] and of the waters of the present seas. This is suggestive that in time the naked gene found it of greater adaptive value to control the immediate environment by becoming no longer naked, and incorporating some of the sea around it into a new biological entity. All the evolution beyond this point, up to and including ourselves, has been the story of greater gene control of the environment, in order to ensure gene reproduction and gene survival.[98]

That, then, is all we humans are: carrying vessels for genes, which call all the shots.[99] "Radiation and the Origin of the Gene" offers something rare in scientific reports: a cosmic context.

Astronomer-historian Donald Osterbrock, author of a historical study of Yerkes, recalls, "Carl was a very brilliant guy—I admired him, liked him a lot."[100] Sagan knew that he was bright, too, Osterbrock notes, and that self-awareness "sometimes didn't make him too popular with other people."[101]

Why should he hide his light under a bushel? He had the talent; why not flaunt it? Sagan's show-biz leanings had been obvious early on—in high school plays, in his teenage appearances on television and radio, and in his college work with WUCB. He did not simply want to inform readers and audiences; he wanted to enchant them. He explained this yearning years later by saying that, after all, someone who's in love wants to let the world know about it. True; but is that the sole explanation why he sought the limelight? According to one cliché of pop psychology, those who fail to connect intimately with others sometimes compensate by doing so indirectly—by, say, becoming entertainers, who make people laugh, or by creating fine art or literature, which moves their souls. How many bad Hollywood movies have depicted the hapless starlet who craves the love of anonymous millions in place of one true, intimate relationship? "He was always nervous, except if he had ten thousand people [admiring him]," Lynn Margulis declares. "He was terrible on a personal basis."

At Yerkes, staffers gave public astronomy lectures on Saturday afternoons in the observatory. Sometimes a few dozen listeners showed up—usually vacationers passing through Williams Bay. In keeping with his strong early interest in performance, Sagan requested permission to deliver lectures, and permission was granted. The forty-inch telescope made an impressive backdrop for the sleek young twenty-two-year-old Brooklyn native with the startlingly deep, resonant voice. We can surmise that audiences hung on his every word and laughed with unanticipated delight at his dry humor—this was a *science* lecture? Sagan's Saturday lectures struck Cruikshank as "very smooth . . . very much in control. [He was] a real presence. *Definitely* a presence." To edify his audience about the telescope's "clock drive," for example, Sagan propped a chair against the telescope, and then began his speech. As the minutes passed, the telescope imperceptibly shifted, keeping pace with the stars. Finally the chair tipped forward and fell with a crash.

In a cerebral environment such as Yerkes, any showman is apt to be scrutinized skeptically. His first screw-up is eagerly awaited. For Sagan, sure enough, that moment came. As Cruikshank tells the story, at some point the forty-inch telescope suffered a mechanical problem. The rumor (ill-founded or not) spread that it might break down, or even fall over. Some observatory official issued a warning: Don't *ever* let the forty-inch shift into such-and-such a position.

Unfortunately, after one of his lectures Sagan forgot to switch off the clock drive. Hours afterward, Cruikshank entered the observatory and discovered the telescope tipped at a perilous angle. "I had this terrible, terrible sinking feeling that if I go over and even *touch* that thing, over she goes.

"Of course, I had to report it." He recalls an enraged official snapping, "That damn Sagan!"[102]

But Sagan's showmanship only kept evolving. For the 1957 to 1958 academic year, he organized an entire science lecture series on the Chicago campus. It was titled "something like 'The Creation of Life in the Universe,'" Sagan recalled. Among the distinguished speakers were Kuiper, Urey, Muller, Strömgren, George Gamow, and the anthropologist Sherwood Washburn. Decades later, Sagan said that the series had "very much the kind of breadth that I've tried to [achieve] in [the television series] *Cosmos* and lots of other places. . . . It was a wild success" and had to "be moved from the Oriental Institute to Mandel Hall, the biggest place on campus." Before each talk, Sagan dined with the speaker, then introduced him before his speech. Yerkes faculty fumed. "Sagan's circus," Chandra called it.[103]

Sagan's chutzpah peaked when he picked a speaker to describe recent trends in biology: himself. "It was audacity for a young grad student to organize such a program. It was chutzpah for him to put *himself* on there," especially considering the fame of the other speakers, says then-student Peter O. Vandervoort. "And he was absolutely correct, because he gave a magnificent lecture!"

His peers watched his ascent with awe. They were so shy, so inarticulate, while he seemed so comfortable and knowing on stage. And he seemed to have such fun doing it! "Those of us with much more conventional tastes and standards were somewhat offended by the extent to which he was pushing himself forward. I include myself," Vandervoort says. "I liked Carl, personally. But at the same time . . ." He thought for a moment. "I suppose I was envious. I suppose I was jealous.

"I'll make no fine point on it: I was a better student on matters of technical detail than Carl was. [But] Carl had the vision. And the vision wins."[104]

SAGAN AND MARGULIS continued to see each other throughout Sagan's first year at Yerkes. Their similarities drew them together. For one thing, both could radiate great warmth (Margulis more consistently than Sagan). They were also both fiercely secular. Over a winter holiday, they visited Sagan's colleague and friend at Yerkes Peter Pesch and his wife at their apartment and were stunned to see their Christmas tree. "Carl and Lynn jumped on us for it and accused us of trying to pass ourselves off as Christians." Pesch, a nonreligious Gentile, nevertheless enjoyed ordinary holiday customs. "I said," he recalls, " 'This is an *old custom!*' It was literally jarring to them."[105] Decades later, Sagan would establish friendly diplomatic relations with religious leaders as part of a joint effort to save Earth's environment. But he would never lose his distaste for what he viewed as superstition.[106]

During that first year at Yerkes, Sagan and Margulis began discussing marriage. She took the possibility seriously but was uneasy about certain things, such as his relationship with his mother. She felt he was too dependent. One time Sagan drove Margulis all the way from Chicago to New York, then dropped her off a few blocks from his house so Rachel Sagan wouldn't see her.[107]

When Margulis finally met Rachel . . . well! "She was a witch," Margulis recalls, "the worst person you'd ever seen. She was *so* smart, and she

[had] only her smartness to defend herself. She had all this incredible intelligence for nothing else.

"I have a sister who's very charming and very overweight, and [Rachel] would say—this is typical of Rachel—'Oh, Diane, you're such a beautiful girl, it's such a shame you're so *fat*.'" Or she would say to someone with crooked teeth who didn't want to open their mouth: "Were your teeth straightened?" There was "just something so vulnerable about her. Her vulnerability made her attack other people."

Eager to win her potential mother-in-law's affection, Margulis made the innocent mistake of confiding to Rachel that her own mother had a history of emotional troubles. Throughout her life, Rachel evidently kept careful mental note of such confidences—they might be useful ammunition later.[108]

According to Pesch, Margulis also worried about Sagan's attitude toward his father, Sam. She feared he didn't love his father enough because he was poorly educated. She asked herself, would Carl be the kind of father who doesn't love his children because they aren't smart?[109] "I actually made a tape [recording] about why I should not marry him," she recalls. "My father never could stand him." So why did she marry him? "My biggest passion in life," she admits with a sigh, "was to get out of the South Side of Chicago." Back in the 1950s, "you did not go with a man and live with him or sleep with him in some public way—[and] you *certainly* did not leave the South Side of Chicago and go west because he got a fellowship [as Sagan would] unless he married you first."

True, she had many doubts about Sagan—in particular, his tendency to belittle her, and his unhealthy emotional dependence on his mother. "There was no doubt about his brilliance, interest, fascination," she said. "But from the time I was sixteen to the time I was nineteen, I broke that relationship many times, maybe three or four times." But Sagan was a persistent suitor. "He was very strong-minded," she comments. Besides, "He was handsome, attractive, very educated, very interested in what he was doing, he was clearly on a way to making a living. He was Jewish. . . . Everything your mother would want!" Sagan was twenty-two, Margulis was nineteen; they scheduled the wedding for June 1957.

So informed, Rachel Sagan burst into tears. Lynn Margulis would eventually be profiled in a book of the world's one hundred most influential scientists, but she recalls how Rachel "was for twelve hours crying in her room that I wasn't 'good enough' for her son." Desperately, Rachel blurted out Margulis's little secret about her mother. What (Rachel demanded) if this "nutsiness" was genetic? What if Lynn transmitted it to their kids—to Rachel's grandchildren! Sagan's sister, Cari, observes dryly: "Rachel would never have thought *any* woman was good enough to be Carl's wife."[110]

THE WEDDING WAS HELD in a Chicago hotel on June 16, 1957. Rabbi Jacob Weinstein presided. "It was hotter than hell," Margulis recalls. Sam and Rachel Sagan attended, and Rachel tried to smile. In Carl and Lynn's wedding picture, Lynn looks pretty and seductive, and Carl grins awkwardly, looking for all the world like a high school basketball player on prom night.[111] The next day, the happy couple motored to Colorado. There, Sagan would spend the summer working in the University of Colorado physics department with the legendary physicist and science popularizer George Gamow.[112] From Boulder, Sagan wrote to H. J. Muller that they had rented a beautiful house from a cousin who was traveling in Europe. The house had a patio that looked out on a stunning mountain view.[113] Throughout his life, Sagan would choose homes with similarly breathtaking views. As he built his career, they enabled him to keep one eye on the universe.

A key theme of Lynn Margulis's career would be "symbiosis"—the cooperation of life forms for mutual benefit. This insight would spur her to revive an old idea that modern cells are assemblages of formerly independent cells. For example, the little mitochondrion that energizes your bodily cells was once an independent cell itself, but it discovered a life of greater safety and leisure within bigger cells than in the liquid jungle outside them. Likewise, the bigger cell benefited from its acquisition of mitochondria, which greatly enhanced its energy reserves. You scratch my back, I'll scratch yours: this is an emerging theme of evolutionary theory, a far cry from the "nature red in tooth and claw" mythology that haunted the Victorian imagination. Sagan and Margulis's relationship was symbiotic, too. He introduced her to biology, explained its basic genetic concepts to her, and had biological contacts (via his relationship with Muller) that might have eased her entry into a biology program in the University of Wisconsin graduate school. In turn, her presence at Wisconsin might have been the main reason he encountered Joshua Lederberg, who altered Sagan's career more decisively than anyone save Muller himself. Margulis also gave Sagan a comfortable home where she cooked and cleaned and, in general, created a little emotional kingdom like his childhood home. By the standards of the fifties, they were the ideal couple. But the fifties were ending, and for Sagan the sky was calling.

4

High Ground

LONG THE OBJECT of lovers' gazes and poets' ruminations, the Moon became a target of cold war intrigue in the late 1950s. Carl Sagan was briefly sucked into the world of classified research. While there, he explored a bizarre question: Do simple life forms inhabit the Moon? His investigation of possible lunar life is a forgotten cautionary tale of science; it epitomizes the perils of overextrapolation, of romance disguised as science, of wishful thinking camouflaged by equations. Decades later, during an interview at his Ithaca mansion, he relaxed and good-humoredly dismissed his youthful lunar speculations: "*Completely* wrong! *Absolutely* incorrect!"[1] By then he could afford to laugh; he was famous and rich. But in the 1950s, had he been less brilliant, eloquent, and well connected, his far-out lunar hypotheses might have detonated his career before it left the launch pad.

MANY STILL BREATHING recall precisely where they were and what they were doing on December 7, 1941. Many more will never forget November 22, 1963. And the dates August 1914, October 1929, and September 1939 still chill the spine. A thousand years from now, only historians will grasp their meaning. To them, surveying the dusty records of the twentieth century, one date will stand out from all others—a date that is a watershed not only in history but in human evolution.

That date is October 4, 1957. Sagan was entering his second academic year at Yerkes when the Soviet Union launched the first space satellite, *Sputnik*. People turned on their radios and heard the little satellite's ominous "beep-beep-beep" as it orbited Earth every ninety-odd minutes. To their shock, Americans had been beaten into space by their primary ideological foe. Centuries of technological advance had brought humanity to this point: it could now hurl atomic weapons anywhere in the world—and, hence, annihilate the world—as fast as it took to get up, shower, and drive to work in the morning.

But optimists, including Sagan, nursed brighter hopes. To them, the cold war was a blip on the historical radar screen. Once it settled down, the real space age would begin. Humans (perhaps Americans and Russians together) would go to the Moon, then the planets, then the stars. This was one "age of exploration" that would never end. For all intents and purposes, the cosmos was infinite. Just as the invention of lungs opened the atmosphere to the first brave amphibia, the invention of space rockets could make the universe humanity's backyard—if humanity didn't blow itself up first.

Which seemed quite possible in the 1950s, the high noon of the American century. The issue of nuclear fallout was in the news. Nuclear bombs were routinely test-exploded above ground in Nevada and the Soviet Union. The bombs injected into the atmosphere mountains of radionuclides, which circled the globe for months, then rained back to Earth. In Nevil Shute's novel *On the Beach*, the last survivors of a nuclear holocaust hole up in Australia, awaiting the arrival of radioactive mists, which they know will kill them.[2]

In real life, scientists debated the dangers of fallout. Muller warned that fallout could damage the human gene pool, and Linus Pauling that it would boost the incidence of leukemia; antinuclear activists called for an outright ban on nuclear tests.[3] H-bomb pioneer Edward Teller vehemently disagreed. He claimed that the dangers were exaggerated—and besides, the tests were essential to ensure the credibility of the U.S. nuclear deterrent. Perhaps partly to deflate enthusiasm for a nuclear test ban, the military began to test nuclear weapons underground and (a few times) in outer space.[4] Down there and up there, they produced little or no atmospheric fallout. (Space tests showed how blasts might affect the ionosphere and military communications.) The United States first tested an atomic weapon on the edge of outer space in 1958. At one point Teller speculated about the feasibility of detonating nuclear weapons on the Moon, ostensibly for scientific purposes—for example, to create seismic waves that would allow lunar geologists to map the lunar interior. In retrospect, such suggestions sound suspiciously like attempts to continue testing nuclear weapons for military purposes, under the cover of "science."

Fallout also worried Joshua Lederberg. A month after the *Sputnik* launch, the University of Wisconsin professor traveled to Calcutta, India, to confer with the legendary British geneticist J. B. S. Haldane.[5] A colorful old leftist, Haldane had recently retreated to India "as a refugee from the U.S. occupation of Britain." He had also been one of the first experts to take seriously Lederberg's work on the genetics of microbes (for which Lederberg would soon win the Nobel Prize). On November 6, Lederberg arrived in Calcutta, and in his memoir he recalls that "it was over-whelming. . . . There were cows roaming around, free and unencum-bered, and there were people dragging very heavy carts. . . . Half the population seemed to be living and sleeping out on the street." That evening the two savants dined in a "rather large" palace with servants. Outside, a lunar eclipse occurred. Earth's shadow passed over the Moon, which turned amber red, then dark. The event awed local inhabitants, who celebrated in the streets.

During dinner, Haldane noted that this was the fortieth anniversary of the Russian Revolution. He wondered, out loud, if the Soviets might try to top *Sputnik* by launching a nuclear bomb into space and detonat-ing it on the Moon. During the eclipse, as the Moon's bright surface dis-appeared, the nuclear blast might be visible from Earth—a "red star," akin to the symbol of the Soviet revolution, no less. The two men made mental calculations: given that a certain number of grams of explosive emits a flash of intensity x, then a nuclear bomb seen from 240,000 miles away should generate a flash of . . . yes, the blast might be "barely visi-ble" from Earth! This troubled them. Unlike the average person in the street, they were biologists aware of the possible value of other worlds for resolving age-old mysteries of the origin of life. Nuclear blasts on the Moon could shower fallout over that alien world, damaging lunar organic molecules or microorganisms (if any). It would be the biological equivalent of detonating Tutankhamen's tomb before entering it.

Lederberg decided to take action. The following month, back in Madison, he wrote memos (including one titled "Lunar Biology") about the scientific dangers of human contamination of the Moon. Nuclear tests were not the sole threat; so were any future crash landings on the Moon of space probes powered by radioisotopic electric generators. Also, Moon-bound rockets might carry stowaways—spores and microbes—that could proliferate on the Moon, making it difficult to distinguish between local organic molecules or life forms and terrestrial intruders. Lederberg sent his memos to "scientific notables," asking "what steps might be taken to avert what I saw as a potential cosmic catastrophe."[6] Time was of the essence: the "space race" between the United States and the USSR was under way. Irrevocable decisions might soon be made.

On January 31, 1958, the U.S. Army launched the first successful American satellite into orbit. Factions in the military hoped to invade space and make it U.S. territory. Biological considerations were the least of their concerns. President Eisenhower's science adviser, James Killian, later recalled "the fantasies that *Sputnik* inspired in the minds of many able military officers. . . . the world was going to be controlled from the high ground of space."[7] On February 25, Air Force Lt. Gen. Donald L. Putt assured a congressional committee that the Moon would be a fine place to base U.S. missiles. Nuclear bombs, he explained, could be launched to Earth from missile silos dug deep into the Moon's surface. And the Moon might only serve as the first step toward establishing bases on other planets. Such talk raised the hackles of leftist journalist I. F. Stone, who suggested renaming the military "the Department of Lunacy." He blamed the brass's celestial ambitions on rivalries among the military branches, and he quipped, in reference to the Navy's planned launch of a manned balloon eighty thousand feet up to take a close look at Mars, that "if there is enough water on Mars to float a boat, the Navy will claim jurisdiction."[8] Despite such criticism, the military moved ahead with some of these plans, and the Air Force gave Kuiper a lot of money to develop a "lunar atlas," an updated map of the Moon, crater by crater. Kuiper invited Sagan to participate in the project. Sagan, however, preferred theory to observation (and years later, offended lunar scientists by calling the Moon "dull"), and he declined.[9]

To become an astronomer, Sagan needed a doctorate. Initially, he decided that he wanted to write a doctoral thesis requiring "mathematical rigor." Bravely, he entered the inner sanctum of the paragon of analytical elegance—Subrahmanyan Chandrasekhar. Seated before the great man, Sagan proposed that Chandra serve as his doctoral adviser for a thesis on the origin of the solar system. Chandra was unimpressed. "He rapidly convinced me that he wasn't interested—nor was I," Sagan later recalled, laughing.[10]

According to Geoffrey Burbidge, the professional staff at Yerkes "had meetings trying to decide what to do with Sagan. Nobody really wanted to work with him because—well, the good side is that he was independent. But people knew he would do his *own thing*." An iconoclast himself, the caustic Burbidge (one of the last defenders of the steady state theory of cosmology) regards Sagan as "a real manipulator"—"a very bright, very intelligent guy" whose demeanor as a graduate student convinced outsiders he was higher-ranking than he was. "Nearly all his mail that came to Yerkes was addressed to 'Dr.' or 'Professor' Sagan," Burbidge recalls.[11] Frank Drake, who adored Sagan, recalls the first letter he received from him, an inquiry regarding the use of radiotelescopes for analyzing Venus. The letter sounded as if it was "from a very senior staff member at Yerkes. Only later did I discover it was from a graduate student!"[12] (But what would one expect from a young man who, at age seventeen, had used the word "sobriqueted" in a letter to the secretary of state?)

After Chandra's rebuff and some rumination, Sagan decided to go with his first love for his dissertation topic: extraterrestrial life. True, no one knew whether extraterrestrial life existed. But it might be studied indirectly, by using one of the revolutionary inventions of nineteenth-century astronomy, the spectroscope. A spectroscope breaks starlight into its rainbowlike spectrum of wavelengths. Dark and bright spectral lines reveal the presence or absence of elements. Spectroscopes, Sagan believed, might detect organic molecules, the building blocks of life, in the atmospheres of other worlds. He might have been inspired by a recent development, which he later recalled had excited him: in 1957, the astronomer William Sinton used infrared spectroscopy to detect possible organic molecules—chlorophyll, perhaps?—on Mars.[13] He discovered a banded pattern in the atmosphere, which led to the name "Sinton bands." These bands were widely regarded as strong evidence for life on the red planet.[14]

Sagan hoped to use spectroscopy to detect life on even more distant worlds, particularly Jupiter. Jupiter might be a gigantic version of Stanley Miller's lab experiment: a world brimming with hydrogen; sparkling with lightning, caused by convective storms; and containing (according to theory) a considerable amount of water. Ammonia, methane, water, and electricity were the key ingredients for the Miller-Urey "primordial soup" of organic molecules. Suppose biomolecules once formed on Jupiter. Might they, over eons, have evolved into living creatures? Years later, Sagan would speculate about a hypothetical Jovian ecosystem. Amid the multicolored clouds, immense herds of "balloon animals" might float, propelling themselves with the anatomical version of "jet engines" and grazing, like cows, upon mists of organic molecules.

In 1952, Harold Urey had suggested that organic molecules might explain the distinctive hues of Jupiter's atmosphere, including its famous Great Red Spot.[15] In Sagan's initial outline for his doctoral thesis,[16] he speculated further: perhaps organic molecules could explain "unidentified spectral features" in the atmospheres of Uranus and Neptune, and in comets and interstellar clouds. This proposal was far ahead of its time. In those days, only a few scientists took seriously the possibility of complex organic molecules floating in the atmospheres of worlds such as Jupiter, much less filling the interiors of comets (like so much pond scum) or drifting, miasmalike, on interstellar grains far from the Sun. Nowadays, astronomers have increasingly accepted the pervasiveness of cosmic organics, a veritable alphabet soup of small molecules in the outer solar system and throughout the Milky Way.[17] Hence, Sagan justly deserves the label "unrecognized prophet."

To be accepted to the doctoral candidacy, Sagan had to pass a preliminary exam. "He passed," Margulis recalls, yet "they called him in and they said, 'Sagan, this answer is unbelievable!' He said, 'Why?' . . . 'Because you've forgotten, and simply did not mention at all, the most important instrument for the entire field!'

"And he said, 'Oh my God! Spectroscopy!'"

Sagan's failure to cite one of astronomy's main tools reminded Margulis—who would soon be pregnant—of a mother who forgets to pick up her baby.[18] Of course, Sagan knew plenty about spectroscopy; he had taken two courses on it. It would be a major topic of his doctoral thesis. The trouble is, he was an intellectual omnivore; he wanted to know everything; and he had not yet learned how to manage it all.

Sagan's lack of focus was not a pressing matter to Margulis at that time. Her marriage was still young, and very happy. She and Sagan had moved to Madison, more than fifty miles from Yerkes, because she had entered the biology graduate program at the University of Wisconsin there. Sagan was happy enough to move so far from his work because he could escape from the squabbles and backstabbing, which had become increasingly unpleasant.

Fellow graduate student Peter Pesch recalls, "all the faculty resented the fact that he lived at Madison and wasn't day-in and day-out at the observatory, studying and taking classes."[19] At the same time, Sagan's out-of-town status and his popular Saturday speeches gave him a certain aura. Among students, Cruikshank says, "the main thing I remember was the attitude toward him [as being] somebody who sort of sweeps in with some grand gestures and flamboyance, and then is gone." Some made "snide remarks," Cruikshank recalls, but "very few of them, really."[20]

The Sagans lived at 116 Craig Avenue in the politically progressive, bookstore-packed college town,[21] home to intellectual leaders such as geneticist Joshua Lederberg, who would soon win the Nobel Prize, and radical historian William Appleman Williams, teacher of future New Leftists. Their marriage, she recalls, was "as happy as it could be . . . until the kids were born." Then Sagan would change.

IF ANYONE can be called the godfather of exobiology, it is Joshua Lederberg. Exactly how Sagan and Lederberg met is unclear. Lederberg himself doesn't remember for sure. He suspects that he met Sagan through Lynn Margulis, given that she was a student at Wisconsin.[22] In a February 27, 1976, letter to Lederberg, Sagan recalled that they had been brought together by Prof. Jim Crow, who was well known to Muller and was teaching in the department where Lynn was studying at Madison. However fate brought them together, it launched the most high-profile dynamic duo of the early days of exobiology, the science of extraterrestrial life.

On campus, the thirty-three-year-old, Yale-educated Lederberg, the son of an Orthodox rabbi, was an intimidating presence. Graduate biology students worried that he might show up when they were presenting a paper and tear their conclusions apart in just a few words. But when he and Sagan met, they got along fine. Lederberg had begun to question the Miller-Urey experiment's key premise—that the building blocks of life necessarily formed on Earth. Why couldn't organic matter have formed on other worlds, he wondered, perhaps even in outer space, and migrated to Earth?[23] This idea tallied neatly with Sagan's emerging thoughts on space organics. Nineteenth-century scientists had developed the "panspermia" hypothesis, according to which terrestrial life had evolved from space-faring alien microbes. In 1954, Lederberg's friend Haldane had revived the idea, referring to such cosmic biota as "astro-plankton."[24] In a June 1958 paper for *Science* titled "Moondust," Lederberg and Dean B. Cowie suggested that extraterrestrial organic molecules might have rained onto the lunar surface over billions of years. There, in the sub-Antarctic cold, they might steadily accumulate in the crust, many feet deep. On Earth, the celestial micro-visitors would be destroyed by the atmosphere or devoured by subsequent life forms. But on the airless, lifeless, almost unchanging Moon, these primordial organics might survive, waiting for the first lunar astronauts to uncover them. By studying them, lunar biologists might figure out how life started on Earth. Early in the space age, critics questioned the value of going to the Moon; Lederberg's proposal suggested a scientific reason for doing so.

Sagan and Lederberg probably met in early 1958. Sagan listened, entranced, to Lederberg's speculations. Thus began an informal scientific collaboration that would endure for two decades. As Lynn Margulis, later a microbiologist, might have remarked, Sagan and Lederberg's relationship was symbiotic.[25] "He wanted to learn some planetary astronomy," Sagan recalled, "and there I was wanting to learn some biology, so we metaphorically speaking fell into each other's arms. I lent him books, he lent me books. A wonderful experience. [He was] a very quick thinker; we would cover a lot of ground in very short conversations."[26] As Sagan wrote to Lederberg in 1976, "if not for the encouragement by H. J. Muller and yourself, I might not have had the courage to seriously pursue what later has come to be called exobiology."

The older scientist did more than talk; he escorted Sagan into the corridors of power. By then, Lederberg's concerns about lunar despoliation had inspired the governing council of the National Academy of Sciences (NAS), on February 8, 1958, to express "its concern about planetary contamination."[27] Afterward, Lederberg helped to start two groups to discuss ways to prevent contamination by future rockets and spaceships. These groups were WESTEX (Western Group on Planetary Biology) and EASTEX (its East Coast counterpart), both operating under the NAS Space Sciences Board.[28] WESTEX and EASTEX spawned much of the early modern science of exobiology. (Wags said that, as it concerned extraterrestrials, exobiology had no subject.) Early members included distinguished researchers such as Melvin Calvin, Tommy Gold, Norman Horowitz, Harold Urey, Stanley Miller, and Harold Weaver (all of whom would have important ties to Carl Sagan). Lederberg picked Sagan as an adviser to WESTEX and praised his subsequent "excellent service." As for Sagan, he never forgot his "fantastically good discussions" with these Olympians of science who had welcomed him, a mere graduate student, into their midst.

Sagan encountered Calvin (a future Nobelist in chemistry) at a WESTEX meeting at Stanford in 1958. Calvin's interests included the origin of life and extraterrestrial life, including the possibility of organics in meteorites. He was so impressed with Sagan that he invited him to spend the following summer working at his Berkeley lab. The Berkeley summer job would prove important for Sagan, partly because there he learned how to use an infrared spectrometer and developed research related to his doctoral thesis.[29] Subsequently, the Berkeley job would help him to win an important fellowship.

As one of Sagan's mentors, Lederberg served a function that Muller couldn't and Urey wouldn't. All three mentors were Nobelists, but Muller and Urey had their limitations, Sagan-wise. Muller liked and respected Sagan, but was controversial because of his Marxist past and eugenicist views; Urey had enormous influence but didn't think much of Sagan's work (and would think even less of it as the years passed). But Lederberg offered the best of both—total respectability and a real affection for Sagan. Lederberg asked Sagan to serve on the newly established NAS committee on exobiology. "I sort of glided effortlessly from attending late-night bull sessions at Lederberg's house to advising the government on the issue," Sagan later said.[30]

Now white-haired and rotund, an international scientific celebrity, Lederberg recalls that he thought Sagan was a "very bright young guy, full of ideas. . . . Some of them [were] kooky, but they were well worth listening to." He thinks he related to Sagan so easily because Lederberg had been perceived as a wunderkind just as Sagan was. But he was also paternal toward Sagan. "I was often his protector and defender from folks who thought he was wild," he recalls. "He had a lot of offbeat ideas. They were always at some level not illogical, and some of them could prove to be right; and I would point out [to others] the value of listening closely to someone who has that degree of rigor and imagination at the same time. [On] any topic he got into, he certainly did his homework— very, very thoroughly."

Unfortunately, Sagan's attention span was short, Lederberg recalls: "He didn't stick to things very long. I think part of his reputation for not being 'solid' has less to do with lack of rigor on any one item than that he didn't build a body of work on one particular topic. His interests were so catholic."[31]

Through the years, Lederberg's name was frequently allied with Sagan's. Together they fought to protect planets from terrestrial contaminants; to advocate a quest for Martian life in oasislike "microenvironments"; and to speculate, at a dangerously late date, about Martians as big as polar bears. Sagan told Ann Druyan, his third wife, that until he met her, the best conversations he had ever had were with Joshua Lederberg.[32]

After the 1970s, however, the two men rarely saw each other. Sagan became a limousine-riding celebrity, swamped by commitments and causes, and difficult to reach. Even so, Lederberg's imagination would continue to influence Sagan, as, for example, in his twilight achievement, the film *Contact*.[33] Lederberg also still fondly recalls the tight bond they shared. "It's very hard for me to think of him in the past tense," he said. "He's a present image to me. . . . In his earlier days, he was as close to me as anybody."[34]

EVEN AS SAGAN EXPANDED his horizons through his relationship with Lederberg, he maintained close ties with his first true mentor, H. J. Muller. As a fellow science-fiction fan, Sagan wrote to Muller, on June 18, 1958, recommending that he read Fred Hoyle's astrobiological romance *The Black Cloud*. A minor classic of science fiction, *The Black Cloud* depicted an encounter between Earth and an interstellar cloud that turned out to be alive—and intelligent.[35]

In the same letter, Sagan cryptically referred to a project in which he had become involved that was sponsored by an organization with an interest in lunar probes. The organization had commissioned a study from Sagan, and Sagan was enclosing his summary paper for Muller's review. Sagan did not identify the organization, but it was probably one of a number of groups that he advised in the post-*Sputnik* era—the Armour Research Foundation, Caltech's Jet Propulsion Laboratory, NASA, the Air Force, or the RAND Corporation. Desperate to catch up with the Russians, U.S. space planners were struggling to assemble teams of interplanetary experts. "Where are the people who know what they are doing?" one space official, Albert R. Hibbs, asked in March 1959.[36] Sagan became one of those people.

The summary in Sagan's letter to Muller is missing. Its subject, though, is revealed in Muller's reply on June 21, which refers to the topics of lunar organics and biosynthesis. Muller praised the paper and, supportive as ever, advised Sagan to submit it for publication in no less prestigious a journal than *Science*.

What exactly was Sagan up to? He was developing his own hypothesis about the possible biological significance of the Moon. Whereas Lederberg thought lunar organics might have fallen from space onto the primordial Moon, Sagan suspected they formed on the Moon in the same way that they supposedly formed on early Earth—via Miller-Urey–type processes. He also suspected that those organics had not merely lain there for billions of years, buried in the lunar crust; rather, they might have evolved into something more complex. Something *alive*.

The idea of lunar life was an old one, going back to the ancients. In 1835, the *New York Sun* had fooled millions of readers into thinking that the astronomer John Herschel had seen, through his telescope, winged creatures on the Moon.[37] As late as the 1920s, Percival Lowell's onetime associate, astronomer W. H. Pickering, "saw" Old Testament–style swarms of insects on our sister orb.[38]

But by the 1950s, the scientific consensus was clear: the Moon was lifeless. It had no air to speak of; early reports of snow and ice were optical illusions. The crater-scarred surface had apparently changed little over millions of years.[39]

Undaunted by consensus opinion, Sagan speculated as follows: Billions of years ago, the Moon might have had an atmosphere, enhanced by gaseous emissions from lunar volcanism. If the atmosphere included substantial amounts of hydrogen, then Miller-Urey–type processes could have commenced. Solar ultraviolet light (in place of lightning) could have triggered chemical reactions that generated organic molecules, such as amino acids. True, the same solar ultraviolet light would normally destroy the same organics; but many organics might have escaped and survived, perhaps to this day. How? Suppose the organics formed high in the primeval lunar atmosphere. As they grew more complex, they grew heavier; gradually they sank toward the surface. There, the atmosphere was denser and they were safer from solar UV rays. Over millions of years, the organics might have accumulated in deep layers on the lunar surface. The steady drizzle of space dust would cover them up—added protection from UV. In short, the lunar crust might be rich in pre-biological molecules.

More fantastic, the molecules might have evolved, like their terrestrial counterparts, into microorganisms. They might have survived for eons, nourished by residual crustal gases, melted permafrost, and volcanic warmth. They might—unlikely as it seemed—survive to the present.[40]

This scenario raised a major environmental concern. Suppose that robotic probes or future astronauts inadvertently transport terrestrial "bugs" to the Moon and leave them there. On Earth, some microbes have demonstrated an astonishing hardiness, surviving in the most inhospitable conditions—say, within nuclear reactors or vacuum chambers. These super-bugs might find the Moon to their liking. They might devour the local organic molecules like army ants descending upon a picnic. The result would be, in Sagan's words, "an unparalleled scientific disaster," destroying evidence that could answer questions about "the early history of the solar system, the chemical composition of matter in the remote past, the origin of life on Earth, and the possibility of extraterrestrial life." Sagan thought that the Moon offered a marvelous opportunity for investigating these questions.[41]

Hence (Sagan urged) future space missions should be planned with great caution. His warning anticipated the spirit of the modern environmental movement—in particular, of efforts to protect fragile ecosystems such as Antarctica. Indeed, Sagan's push to protect the Moon saw print two years before the bible of the postwar environmental movement, Rachel Carson's *Silent Spring*.[42]

Then a science-fictionish fear arose: What if lunar microbes hitch a ride back to Earth? What if those microbes find Earth to their liking? Might they proliferate madly, annihilating much of the terrestrial ecosystem?[43] Even on Earth, exotic organisms sometimes invade and overwhelm local plant and animal forms: the kudzu plants that ruined much of agriculture in the southern United States are but one example. Sagan urged that "space suits must be designed to eliminate cracks and joints in which [lunar] microorganisms might lodge."[44] Such warnings laid the groundwork for one of the odder sideshows of the future Apollo Moon program: the lunar "quarantine."

CARL SAGAN'S FASCINATION with space organics, among other interests, led him into the hush-hush world of classified military research. Later in life, Sagan was a celebrated peace activist. Many a scientific activist's past, however (Urey's, for example), includes a fat Pentagon grant or two. Nonmilitary funding for pure scientific research was scarce in the pre-*Sputnik* era, when scientists and intellectuals were derided as "eggheads." For many researchers, the military was the only source of cash. Sagan had sought classified work at least as early as 1955. That summer, he landed a job as a physicist in the Nuclear Analysis Division of the General Electric Company in Cleveland. Its goal: to develop a nuclear-powered airplane. But Sagan's job fell through "due to delay in security processing."[45] (The plane was never built.)

At Yerkes, Kuiper received substantial amounts of Air Force money.[46] He received so much, in fact, that it irritated his colleagues. Geoffrey Burbidge claims that Kuiper affixed the names of other staffers to funding applications, although those staffers had no connection to Kuiper's research. "Kuiper did a lot of things that upset the younger faculty—

really upset us," recalls Burbidge. "The young people agreed we would not reappoint Gerard [as director]. We were so upset that we went down and talked to the dean of sciences. . . . I was certainly one of the ringleaders. . . . We came back from Chicago to Yerkes, and Chandra called me into his office." Chandra said the dean had just called him and wanted to know if the delegation—Burbidge et al.—was to be trusted. Chandra vouched for them. "I told Gerard to his face what we'd done. At first, he didn't want to believe me. Chandra convinced him we did mean it. He never forgave me."[47] Such was the Yerkes atmosphere—a Medician realm of "putsches and counterputsches," in Sagan's words.[48]

Sagan, by contrast, was happy to go along when Kuiper enlisted him in an Air Force–related project at an organization called the Armour Research Foundation in Illinois (now part of Illinois Institute of Technology).[49] All his life, Sagan kept the exact nature of his work at Armour under wraps. Only once, it seems, did he confide the information to anyone—when he used it to improve his chances of winning a fellowship.[50] When Sagan was asked later in life what he had done at Armour, he gave a cagey reply: "I'm not sure Armour got their money's worth, but I loved it. . . . They let me do an extended development of the theory of the escape of planetary atmospheres. How this was connected with their Air Force–sponsored mission, I have not the foggiest idea, but as long as I was able to present reports . . . they were happy." Among other things, he studied whether an unidentified spectral line in the near-infrared spectrum of Jupiter might be caused by an organic molecule, methylamine. At one point—"a big crisis"—Armour officials rebuked him for generating "an enormous bill" for outside research.[51]

As it turns out, however, Sagan actually did more at Armour than he admitted. He belonged to something called Project A119. One of his jobs, a classified one, was to investigate this question: Might scientists gather scientifically useful information by detonating nuclear weapons on the Moon? He wrote a paper whose title cites the "possible contribution" nuclear blasts on the Moon might make to "the solution of some problems in planetary astronomy." In a separate paper, he considered the impact of such blasts' radioactive fallout on the Moon.[52]

Lederberg and Haldane were not being paranoid after all. The military *was* thinking, at least on paper, about the possibility of detonating nuclear weapons on the Moon. Why? At this late date, when so many crucial cold war documents remain classified, we can only guess. Perhaps some officials within the Pentagon hoped to evade the growing political pressure against terrestrial nuclear tests by shifting blasts to the Moon. Who (they probably figured) would care about *lunar* fallout, except a few eggheads?

Space historian William E. Burrows mentions in his 1998 book, *This New Ocean*, how, in 1956, W. W. Kellogg of RAND Corporation considered the possibility of launching an atomic bomb to the Moon.[53] Also in 1959, Burrows reports, a secret Air Force document warned that the Soviets could gain "immense propaganda advantages" by detonating a bomb on the Moon. A twenty-kiloton blast (about as powerful as the bomb that hit Hiroshima) would be easily visible on Earth, "[f]rom the penthouses of metropolitan areas to the nomadic shepherds of Afghanistan."[54] The cold war was in full swing, not only on Earth but in the sky. And Carl Sagan—the future anti–cold warrior, the scourge of nuclear weaponeers—was a part of it. A very small part, but a part nonetheless.

As it turns out, Kuiper was directly involved with a related Armour project, as revealed by two documents from the Kuiper archive. One is a memo dated April 8, 1958 (a few months after the first successful launch of a U.S. satellite), written by Kuiper and Thornton Page, that suggests that a nuclear explosion on the Moon might reveal some key properties of the lunar crust as well as the chemicals found there. The memo discusses the likely effects of the detonation of a hydrogen bomb, including the creation of a new crater that would be visible from Earth. But because of contamination effects, they suggest that a TNT bomb would be preferable in some ways. The other memo is a request for a security clearance for Kuiper from the Office of Naval Research, which states that he had been retained as a consultant to the Air Force Special Weapons Center. (Thanks to Ron Doel for sharing these memos.)

In retrospect, peace activists might wonder, how could Sagan, who later campaigned so eloquently against militarism, have accepted Pentagon cash so blithely, have been an adviser in a quixotic and (short-lived) quest to militarize the Moon? Sagan was young; his thesis adviser was neck-deep in military research; and the cash was there for the taking, at a time when pure science still lacked decent support. Besides, back then, before the civilian space effort was fully operational, the U.S. space program *was* a military operation. Anyone who wished to be a part of the space program had to rub elbows with the brass. Without revealing the true nature of his work at Armour, Sagan later acknowledged that in his graduate school days, he was "happy" to get military support. That would end, though, come the Vietnam War.

MOST DOCTORAL DISSERTATIONS are narrowly focused. "Don't let me catch anyone talking about the Universe in my laboratory," the early-twentieth-century physicist Ernest Rutherford harrumphed,[55] and most graduate students take his dictate to heart. But Sagan's doctoral dissertation had three subjects, all speculative, particularly the first two: (1) possible lunar organics and life; (2) possible organic molecules in the atmosphere of Jupiter; and (3) the possible cause of unexpectedly intense microwave radiation from Venus.[56]

The second topic reflected Sagan's long fascination with the planet Jupiter. This fascination lasted to his death; one of his final tasks was to serve as a team scientist for the *Galileo* space probe, part of which plunged into the Jovian atmosphere in December 1995. Jupiter is enormous beyond imagining, so big that one thousand Earths could fit within it. At least sixteen moons orbit Jupiter. They are like a miniature solar system, offering both fire and ice: Io, with its active volcanoes, and Europa, with its polar crust, thought to conceal a watery (perhaps inhabited?) ocean. The robotic reconnaissance of this realm has barely begun. It offers us a place to rehearse for grander missions of the far future, missions to extrasolar planetary systems.

As a teenager, Sagan had written in his private notebook that he thought it was feasible that some form of life might be found on Jupiter. He did not explain why he thought this. Certainly Jupiter—colder than Antarctica, swept by a deep and poisonous atmosphere, possessed of a crushing gravitational field and dangerous radiation belts—is inhospitable to earthly life.[57]

In keeping with this long-standing interest, on March 18, 1959, while developing his doctoral thesis, Sagan wrote Muller that Jupiter might be less inhospitable than it appears. Despite its reputation for extreme cold, Jupiter has "great internal sources of heat" generated by the planet's "slow gravitational contraction," he wrote. The highly reducing Jovian atmosphere might have mimicked Stanley Miller's experiment on a grand scale, brewing organic molecules. Sagan calculated that over billions of years, Jupiter would have generated the equivalent of 10 to 100 grams of organic matter per square centimeter. (Sagan made similar order-of-magnitude calculations for the Moon and other worlds. The calculations tended to be one-dimensional and overoptimistic, because they paid too little attention to how much organic matter the same environment might destroy over time.) Sagan's letter to Muller anticipated the *Galileo* probe to Jupiter thirty-six years before it entered its giant atmosphere but seriously underestimated how long it would take to become reality. Sagan's estimate was that we would be able to send probes to Jupiter within only a few years.

In the same letter to Muller, Sagan referred to two exciting new developments. One was that Joshua Lederberg, who had just recently won the Nobel Prize and moved from Madison to a big new position at Stanford, had invited him to come spend some time with him in California to work on planetary biology. The other big news was that his wife,

Lynn, had just given birth to their first child, an eight-pound two-ounce boy named Dorion Solomon Sagan. Sagan wrote eloquently in the letter about the effect the birth had on him, making him more aware than ever of being a "transitional creature" caught between "the primeval mud and the stars."[58]

CARL SAGAN LOVED CHILDREN, and naturally, he adored his newborn son. But according to Lynn Margulis, Sagan soon realized what every new father realizes: he is no longer number one. She recalls that Sagan quickly began to resent Dorion; he was getting all too much of Lynn's attention. Sagan's demands for attention added to Lynn's burdens. For her, it was bad enough having to do all the housework (Sagan, she says, considered himself too good for domestic chores). And now, she had to satisfy two babies: Dorion and Carl! What about *her* needs, her ambitions? She watched, with growing anger, as he flew off to scientific meetings, leaving the diapers and laundry to her.[59] This was, of course, a time when this was a fairly typical division of labor between husband and wife, but the burden on Margulis, who was striving at the same time to launch her own impressive scientific career, was a serious strain on their marriage.

SAGAN'S FIRST SIGNIFICANT scientific collaboration was with Stanley Miller, several years his elder, whose famous experiment had strongly reinforced Sagan's vision of pervasive cosmic life. By the late 1950s, Miller had moved to the department of biochemistry at Columbia University. One day, while visiting the New York area, Sagan dropped by Columbia and visited Miller. "In his typical manner," Miller recalls with amusement, "he wanted me to do some experiments for him. He wanted me to take a Jupiter atmosphere, put a spark to [electrify] it, and see what you got. . . . He wanted me to do the whole damned thing; he gave the grand ideas."

Well, not quite: Sagan was planning to spend the summer of 1959 working in Melvin Calvin's laboratory at Berkeley and, while there, learning how to use an infrared spectrometer. Using this instrument, Sagan would determine the spectral signatures of organic molecules in Miller's samples, in hopes of learning if any matched the spectral signatures of other planets. In other words, he wanted to learn if organic molecules, the building blocks of life, are floating in the atmospheres of alien worlds. This work was the beginning of a quest that would fascinate him to his last days. About their work together, Miller says, "I didn't realize how smart he was, [although] I had a pretty good idea."[60] Sagan was nothing if not persuasive; the mild-mannered Miller agreed to run the experiments.

In his lab at Columbia, Miller mixed and spark-discharged various chemicals to Sagan's specifications. Then Miller shipped the products to Sagan at Berkeley. Using an infrared spectrometer, Sagan analyzed the samples' chemical composition. Later, he mailed Miller a speculation about what might be going on in the Jovian atmosphere. Jupiter was an intense source of radio noise; perhaps the Great Red Spot was the site of electrical activity, as in thunderstorms. If so, then the Jovian atmosphere might be continually "sparking" its methane, ammonia, and water content with lightning bolts. The possible result: an atmosphere rich in organic molecules. Sagan speculated that the Jovian atmosphere might contain the explosive chemical acetylene. Thus continuous "chemical explosions" on Jupiter might provide energy to generate "a variety of compounds of high molecular weight, many of them brightly colored," thereby explaining "the coloration of the Jovian cloud layer." Later, writing in the *Astronomical Journal*, Sagan and Miller reported that their simulations of reducing atmospheres had produced many organic molecules.[61] Jupiter, it appeared, was a potential witches' brew of organics. Had it evolved living creatures, floating in the atmosphere?

Their work attracted press attention. A brief, muddled *New York Times* account ran on August 20, 1961. It began:

LIFE ON JUPITER?

Jupiter appears to be a better possibility than Venus for life outside the earth, according to a recent study by Dr. Carl Sagan of the University of California's Space Sciences Laboratory and Department of Astronomy.

AMID THIS RESEARCH, history intervened.

On September 12, 1959, after two failed attempts, the Soviets succeeded in crash-landing their space probe *Lunik II* on the Moon. The possibility of terrestrial contamination of other worlds was no longer an academic issue. Now it was a practical one.

By coincidence, Muller was hosting a meeting of the National Academy of Sciences (NAS) at Bloomington that was scheduled for November 16. Nine days after *Lunik II* hit the Moon, Muller invited Sagan to give a paper at the NAS meeting.[62] In a sense, the NAS meeting was Sagan's debutante ball—his coming-out to the nation's most prestigious scientific society.

At the meeting, Sagan presented two talks on his research about life on the Moon. An abstract of that speech, published in the November 20 issue of *Science*, cited how solar UV radiation might drive the synthesis "of indigenous lunar organic matter."[63] Perhaps encouraged by his brief entree to the Valhalla of science, Sagan sent Muller on December 9 a new draft paper about the possibility of life on Venus.

Several months later, Sagan's NAS papers were published in the NAS *Proceedings*.[64] In them he further discussed possible lunar life forms—subjects for a science of "parabiology," in his phrasing. Organisms might survive beneath the lunar surface in warm, moist crevasses, shielded from intense solar ultraviolet rays by a deep dust layer. The possibility of lunar life "must not be dismissed in as cavalier a manner as it has been in the past," he wrote. Future lunar paleontologists might find fossils of primeval lunar creatures. Muller praised the *PNAS* papers as "fine accomplishments" that he read with "great joy."[65]

Harold Urey, however, was dismayed. He wrote to Sagan saying that one of the papers was "enormously wordy" and implied that it was essentially a waste of time. At the same time, he invited Sagan to come and spend some time with him the following year at his new lab, at the University of California at San Diego. Stanley Miller was expected to be there as well, and Urey was looking forward to putting together a good new research group.[66]

Urey's philosophy of science was very different from Sagan's. To Sagan, the twenty-five-year-old optimist, the universe was full of thrilling possibilities. What's the harm of speculating? But to Urey, the grouchy sixty-six-year-old veteran of scientific and political wars, truth was best approached modestly. Theories should be built one fact at a time, and upon facts alone. Why waste years of a scientific career imagining castles in the air when almost all prove (as history shows) to be illusions? Urey had never lost the soul of the Indiana country boy, suspicious of slick talk, who was six when his father, a farmer-preacher, died[67]—existential proof that life was hard, no affair for fools. Nor had he lost the spirit of every acid-stained chemist who, accustomed to the maddening vagaries of laboratory experiments, struggles to distinguish one hydrogen isotope from its nearly indistinguishable cousins and is distrustful of the abstract babblings of theorists.[68]

Urey's letter foretold trouble between the two men. Their relationship would never quite gel—with fateful consequences for Sagan's career.

IN EARLY 1961, John F. Kennedy became president of the United States. His administration began badly: the Bay of Pigs debacle, trouble with Castro and Khrushchev, and the Soviet launching of the first human in space, Yuri Gagarin. Kennedy—handsome, eloquent, cultivated—was a master of symbolism, and sought a new banner for his tarnished administration. "The New Frontier" is what he offered. It appealed to

Americans' belief in themselves as a people on the move, always seeking new experiences. The New Frontier, he declared, was outer space. He called on the nation to launch an American to the Moon and safely return him to Earth by the end of the decade.

Was it worthwhile sending humans, when robots could do the same job? The robots vs. humans debate split the space community in the 1960s and persists to this day. Scientists have tended to favor robots; they are cheap, and they generate abundant data. Grassroots space buffs, however, believe that humans will and should eventually live in space, initially in small research stations similar to those scattered across Antarctica. (The roomy, futuristic-looking U.S. base at the South Pole is inhabited year-round and offers many of the comforts of home, including excellent cuisine.)[69]

Throughout his life, Carl Sagan vacillated on the robots vs. humans issue. Initially, he cared little for astronautics. He and other scientists felt, correctly, that the human space program is so expensive that it tends to swallow funds badly needed for robotic missions. "Guys in a tin can in low Earth orbit are where the excitement isn't," he once said.[70] He argued (overoptimistically) that continued improvements in robotic "intelligence" would allow robots to fulfill scientific tasks at which humans, with their quick creative judgment, are at present superior. He scorned the space shuttle.

Yet Sagan knew that the human exploration of space is inevitable. He had read too much science fiction not to think so. Otherwise, why would he bother speculating about "terraforming" Venus and Mars, or advocating interstellar flight as a reasonable goal for humanity? He rationalized human space travel on political grounds: it was a way to prevent war. In the 1960s, he had an extremely uncomplicated understanding of why wars begin. He thought they constituted a way for humanity, in effect, to blow off steam. So why not blow off the same steam in a more peaceful manner, by touring the planets? Spaceflight is a "good thing. More effort up there, less chance of fighting down here," he told the Harvard-Smithsonian newsletter in 1963,[71] only a few months after the Cuban missile crisis almost sparked nuclear war.

In the 1960s, on a visit to the Kennedy White House, Sagan would propose the same notion to his old college acquaintance Marcus Raskin, by then an adviser to National Security Council chief McGeorge Bundy. Raskin now recalls how Sagan talked about "how to get funds to do research on trips to the Moon, on whether there was life in outer space. [Sagan argued] that looking for life outside Earth was very important." Lynn Margulis says Raskin dismissed Sagan's notion of space as an alternative to war as "puerile."[72] (Raskin can no longer recall exactly what he said, but adds that it is "more than conceivable" that he said "puerile.") Still, such puerile thinking has a distinguished ancestry. The erudite

Raskin notes that "William James wrote an essay—in 1903, I believe—about alternatives to war [and said] what you had to do was find alternatives to war which were 'manly.' 'Manly' was a very, very big phrase throughout the nineteenth century in American thought and politics."

Raskin thought the idea of space collaborations with the Soviets was "terrific." But it was hard for him to believe (as Sagan argued) that space exploration alone would make the world a more peaceful place, knowing "what the linkages were between the space agency budgets and military contracts, and the use of space for [military] surveillance. The idea that it was going to *take the place* of the cold war and change the stranglehold that the military had on scientific collaboration at that time was puerile—it wasn't going to happen."[73] Sagan's naïveté is particularly baffling considering his own ties to the military-industrial complex—Armour, RAND, and an Air Force scientific advisory panel, not to mention the Air Force's favorite planetary astronomer, Kuiper.

Carl Sagan was that rare hybrid, a left-leaning space activist. One of his friends, a 1960s leftist, snapped at him: "We can't be looking up at the stars with the mess at our feet!"[74] But Sagan believed we could do both—believed, in fact, that the "stars" could benefit us here on Earth. He did not think (as many had come to believe by the 1960s) that science was invariably the handmaiden of power, the instrument of oppression. Rather, he believed that science could serve liberal ideals. This faith was so strong and foolish that it is almost touching. Consider one proposal he suggested in a public lecture for a technological solution to racism. Scientists could invent "semi-intelligent" robots, "unquestionably inferior to almost all human beings on Earth. Those with a burning need to hate can hate such simulacrums of life."[75] Surely he did not think the solution was as simple as that? By that time, he had experienced anti-Semitism in Wisconsin and (as we shall see) worked for civil rights in the Deep South. Having experienced such confrontations with irrational bigotry, how could he imagine they required only a technological fix? "Puerile"? Undoubtedly.

However naive, young Carl Sagan was "a person of nobility and moral purpose," Raskin says. "In all this, he had a notion of how science was to serve humankind. He was going to stick with that idea." Meanwhile, his future nemesis Edward Teller and the military were "building more and more and more nuclear and hydrogen weapons, making it harder and harder and harder for humanity to escape this noose around its neck. Sagan understood this, and wanted to stop it."[76]

FOR ALL HIS NAÏVETÉ in politics, Sagan was nonetheless becoming a shrewd scientist. At Yerkes he made what remains one of his most important contributions to science, his "greenhouse" model for the atmosphere of Venus. Long before the present public concern about terrestrial "global warming," Sagan showed how a similar effect turned Venus into a planetary hell. His model was flawed, as pioneering scientific papers often are. In later years, after he had mostly moved on to other interests, other people modified his work and corrected his misconceptions. Still, any historical account of this subject must cite a small number of pioneers, and Sagan is among them.

When Sagan was a college senior in 1955, it was still possible for an intelligent science-fiction fan to believe in a romantic Venus. True, growing evidence indicated that Venus was uncomfortably warm, perhaps even a desert world. But a few distinguished scientists thought otherwise. That year, the Harvard astronomers Donald H. Menzel and Fred L. Whipple published an article in the *Proceedings* of the Astronomical Society of the Pacific arguing that Venus was entirely covered by an ocean. A watery world, from horizon to horizon and pole to pole! The ocean would be carbonated, like a soft drink. A global ocean would explain why Venus had so much carbon dioxide in its atmosphere: the water blocked the gas from being absorbed by silicates in crustal rocks.[77] Perhaps by coincidence, the year before the Menzel-Whipple article appeared, Isaac Asimov (under the pen name Paul French) had published his story "Lucky Starr and the Oceans of Venus."[78]

This pleasant vision of a wave-washed Venus was shaken the following year. In May and June 1956, Cornell H. Mayer, T. P. McCullough, and R. M. Sloanaker of the Naval Research Laboratory (NRL) in Washington, D.C., scrutinized Venus with a radiotelescope some fifty feet wide. To their surprise, they realized that Venus emits extremely intense microwave radiation. The most logical explanation was that Venus was exceptionally hot, about 600 degrees Kelvin, hundreds of degrees above the boiling point of water on Earth, much higher than predicted.[79] Their report raised immediate doubts about Menzel and Whipple's watery Venus. Surely such great heat would vaporize all the water. But was Venus really that hot?

Venus is some thirty million miles closer to the Sun than Earth is. Thus, scientists had long assumed it was warmer than Earth, although not nearly as scalding as Mayer et al. inferred. "Most other people I talked to said that [Mayer et al.] was absurd—you could not have so high a surface temperature," Sagan later recalled.[80] The intense microwave signal must have some other explanation, a nonthermal one—that is, the signal must be generated by something other than great heat. But what?

Several possibilities arose. Perhaps the radiation came from far above Venus, not from its surface or atmosphere. To be specific, perhaps the radiation was emitted by an extremely energetic ionosphere, a region of electrically charged particles between Venus's upper atmosphere and outer space. Or consider this: astronomers had recently discovered strong radiation from Jupiter. It was explained as "synchrotron radiation," caused by electrons spiraling around magnetic fields in the Jovian magnetosphere. Might a similar phenomenon exist in the vicinity of Venus? If so, then it might generate the microwave radiation.[81]

These nonthermal explanations appealed to people who might be called the Venus romanticists. They wished to see Venus remain a potentially habitable world, not be transformed into a scalding-hot, uninhabitable desert. Perhaps they had grown up on the same science fiction that Sagan had, and found it hard (as he did) to part with childhood dreams.

Sagan added the Venusian microwave mystery to his multipart doctoral thesis. His goal was to figure out how the Venusian atmosphere might grow hot enough to emit Mayer et al.'s observed signal. Previously, he had learned about something called the greenhouse effect, possibly during an optics class at the University of Chicago. He learned that Earth is tens of degrees warmer than it would be otherwise because its atmosphere naturally contains carbon dioxide gas, which traps infrared radiation, like a blanket. "I remember finding that interesting," Sagan recalled. "No greenhouse effect and the mean temperature of the Earth is below the freezing point of water—and we're all dead! That I found a very compelling fact. It gave me great respect for the greenhouse effect!"[82]

The terrestrial greenhouse effect had been studied in 1895 by Svante Arrhenius, the great Swedish chemist. He calculated that the planet's average temperature would rise by 10 degrees Centigrade if the atmospheric carbon dioxide content doubled. Later, experts began to wonder if the burning of fossil fuels could generate enough carbon dioxide to substantially warm Earth's average temperature, perhaps with disastrous climatic, agricultural, and environmental results. In the 1950s, Roger Revelle of the Scripps Institution of Oceanography in San Diego began studying this question. He arranged for carbon dioxide–measuring instruments to be installed on Mauna Loa in Hawaii in 1957. The massive modern campaign to study global warming and other climatic change can be traced, at least in part, to Revelle's work.[83]

Sagan, however, was interested in a possible greenhouse effect on Venus. The idea was not a new one. In 1940, the astronomer Rupert Wildt cited spectroscopic analysis of Venus indicating that its atmosphere contained a considerable amount of carbon dioxide.[84] Sagan came across this paper while developing his thesis work. As he read it, he recalled, "two things astonished me. One is that [Wildt] said . . . there's a lot of carbon dioxide here, and if you have really a lot of carbon dioxide, you're going to have a bigger greenhouse effect than we have on the Earth."[85] Second, Wildt had cleverly checked how different gases trap radiation by consulting literature not typically consulted by astronomers, technical journals published by the boiler and furnace industry.[86] Wildt calculated that Venusian carbon dioxide must boost the planet's surface temperature to over 400 degrees Kelvin.

Later, though, Mayer et al.'s radioastronomical analysis of Venus indicated a far higher temperature. What could account for the huge discrepancy between Wildt and others' temperature estimates and the NRL team's? Some atmospheric ingredient besides the carbon dioxide must be trapping the escaping infrared radiation and maintaining Venus's almost unbelievably high temperature.

Sagan suspected that the extra ingredient was water vapor. His calculations showed that water vapor would trap infrared wavelengths that slipped past the carbon dioxide. This didn't seem like an unreasonable idea at the time. After all, only a few years earlier, Menzel and Whipple (both far more distinguished than Sagan, a mere graduate student) had suggested that the entire planet was bathed by a watery ocean! Astronomers tried to detect Venusian water vapor directly, using spectroscopes, but this was difficult. Water vapor in Earth's atmosphere got in the way, making it difficult to tell whether the water vapor they were seeing was on Venus or on Earth.

According to Sagan, he did his Venus greenhouse work almost entirely on his own, with little or no supervision. At the time, "absolutely nobody on the planet, as far as I could find, was interested in the *Venus* greenhouse effect. . . . So I sort of stumbled through myself." Isolated in cold, windswept Wisconsin, he huddled in the library and taught himself the science of the greenhouse effect by studying research papers from as far back as the nineteenth century, by scientists such as British meteorologist Sir George C. Simpson (1878–1965). In retrospect, Sagan said, people have praised his analysis of the Venusian greenhouse as "classic and pioneering." He acknowledges modestly that "it was right and all that, but it's *embarrassingly* crude. . . . I had essentially *no* supervision. [That] is what it came down to, on at least that part of the thesis."[87]

Sagan's water-vapor hypothesis drew partial support from research by John Strong of Johns Hopkins University. He ascended in a balloon to take spectroscopic pictures of Venus. The balloon rose above most of Earth's water vapor, making it easier to take accurate spectral images of Venus. Strong brought back "a thin strip of wax paper [on which] were spectroscopic readings of the light from Venus," according to the December 14, 1959, issue of *Time* magazine. The spectra indicated water vapor in the Venusian atmosphere.

Different people read Strong's finding in different ways. To Sagan, it partly supported his theory that the Venusian atmosphere contained water vapor, which could plug the holes in the greenhouse and keep the planet hot enough to boil Menzel and Whipple's hypothetical ocean into vapor. Even so, Strong's data indicated that "there is probably not enough [water vapor] to support fully the greenhouse explanation."[88] But science is like a gestalt diagram: where one scientist sees rabbits, another sees ladies with hats.[89] To Whipple, Strong's data supported their oceanic idea, a "beautiful vindication," Whipple wrote to Urey on December 14, 1959. *Life* magazine ran a seven-page photo spread on Strong's flight, headlined: "TARGET: VENUS—THERE MAY BE LIFE THERE." The Strong expedition, *Life* said, "has just discovered an exciting and highly significant fact about Venus: its atmosphere contains water vapor. This means that life—even as we know it on earth—may exist on Venus."[90] *Time* agreed, saying: "The traces on Dr. Strong's chart did not reveal whether Venus has oceans of water or only whiffs of vapors. But they did leave room for hope that when the first earthling explorers feel their blind and perilous way under the cloud deck of Venus, they may find a kind of life not wholly different from life on earth."[91]

Later, Strong launched a balloon carrying more refined instruments. His new data indicated that the Venusian clouds were made of water-ice particles.[92] Sagan was delighted. These particles, about 0.0006 inch in diameter, would "block nearly all the infrared rays that manage to struggle up from the surface through the carbon dioxide and water vapor in the lower atmosphere. The clouds, in effect, repair all remaining holes in the greenhouse roof." To a viewer near Venus, Sagan said, the clouds would resemble the dense veils of cirrostratus in terrestrial skies. "Here was a startling picture: a red-hot planet wrapped in clouds of ice!"[93]

A PECULIAR POSTSCRIPT: Sagan came close to reaching a totally different conclusion about Venus. We know this because Harold Urey's archive at the University of California at San Diego contains the "corrections and additions" to one of Sagan's papers, which has the arresting title "Venus as a Planet of Possible Biological Interest." The paper itself is missing from the archive, but the corrections and additions allow us to infer what it said. In this paper Sagan suggested, among other things, that the surface air pressure on Venus is "somewhat smaller" than on Earth. He believed this because Venus "has lower gravity and probably higher exosphere temperature than Earth, [hence] the rate of escape of molecules from the Cytherean [Venusian] atmosphere should be slightly greater than from the terrestrial atmosphere." (In fact, the surface pressure later proved to be 93 times that of Earth. In his final dissertation, Sagan argued that it is several times the pressure of Earth's atmosphere.)

But the real surprise in the "Biological Interest" paper is this: Sagan cited ultraviolet observations of Venus that reveal banded clouds, implying high-speed planetary rotation. On this basis, he suggested that Venus rotates so quickly—shifting between daylight and nighttime, when it cools—that its surface is cooler than Mayer et al. suspected (just as one avoids overcooking a barbecue by rotating it on the spit). Sagan offered "the highly tentative conclusion . . . that the surface temperatures of Venus are within the adaptive capabilities of at least some terrestrial organisms. The probability of indigenous Cytherean life would also be increased. Even if the noontime equatorial temperatures [are too high for life] . . . , more moderate temperatures must exist near the poles."[94]

Life on Venus! Internal evidence from the Urey archive indicates that Sagan was working on this paper in 1959, possibly as late as January 1960. Hence his ultimate, opposite conclusion—that Venus was far too hot for life—was probably reached sometime between then and June 1960, when he presented his doctoral dissertation.

What changed his mind about Venus? Urey had previously scolded Sagan for his lunar speculations. Perhaps the Nobelist raked him over the coals for the "Biological Interest" paper, too. Many a shrewd professor has saved many a reckless graduate student from a hare-brained, potentially career-damaging notion. Luckily for Sagan, "Venus as a Planet of Possible Biological Interest" was quickly forgotten. Still, the possibility of Venusian life would continue to haunt him for years.

Unfortunately, Sagan did not follow up on the apparent high-speed motion of Venusian clouds. Had he done so, he might have anticipated the sensational discovery that the Venusian atmosphere rotates far faster than the planet itself. (This phenomenon is now known as "superrotation," and it remains one of the outstanding puzzles of the inner solar system.) Indeed, in the 1960s, when amateur astronomer Charles Boyer reported evidence of the high-speed cloud motion, Sagan scornfully dismissed his claim as a speculation by an "inexperienced amateur." This was one of the few instances when Sagan's imagination utterly failed him.

IN APRIL 1960, Carl Sagan described his greenhouse hypothesis of Venus at a meeting of the American Astronomical Society in Pittsburgh. One of the attendees, Fred Haddock, a radio astronomer at the University of Michigan, strongly objected to the premise of Sagan's argument. Haddock argued that Venus's microwave spectrum isn't shaped like the spectral curve of a hot body at all. Rather, he claimed, it resembles the curve from a synchrotron-radiation source in space. Haddock and Sagan argued over the true shape of the Venusian spectrum. His battles over Venus were just beginning.[95]

As SAGAN WAS STILL wrapping up his doctoral work at Yerkes, his mentor there suffered a comeuppance. Kuiper's days at Yerkes were numbered. All his tussles with other staffers climaxed in late 1959, when they voted not to reappoint him as director. Then, in January 1960, they terminated his leadership.[96] He remained on staff for several months, then moved to the University of Arizona and a new and far more gratifying life.

For Sagan, the timing was terrible. He was still working on his doctoral dissertation, with its controversial elements—among them, his notions about lunar and Jovian organics, and his contested model for the Venusian atmosphere. Kuiper had been Sagan's chief defender. Now Kuiper had fallen. Much of the Yerkes staff felt uneasy about Sagan, about his ambitions, his arrogance, his offbeat interests, his media savvy. Would his dissertation survive the new regime? Just barely. In a letter to Sagan almost a decade later, Kuiper recalled that he was the sole faculty member at Chicago who had lobbied for approval of Sagan's dissertation.[97] In the late 1960s Kuiper wrote to a professor at MIT that despite "some faculty opposition," he had "pushed [Sagan's Ph.D.] through" because he believed that Sagan was highly intelligent and would go on to do important research work. He also commented that Sagan had performed admirably on his oral examination.[98]

Sagan's eighty-five-page, four-part dissertation is dated June 2, 1960, and titled "Physical Studies of Planets."[99] Former Yerkes professor Joseph Chamberlain, now retired and living in Texas, recalls that he had "serious concerns" about details of Sagan's work on Venus. He feels that Sagan did not adequately explain how the Venusian atmosphere trapped all the necessary heat to explain Mayer et al.'s observations. Still, compared to other astronomy students, Sagan was "probably superior," Chamberlain acknowledges. "He certainly had a sound background in physics. He did very well in coursework. He came across as being very enthusiastic with whatever he was doing." Chamberlain respected Sagan enough to coauthor a paper with him (about the ionization of nitrogen gas in the upper atmosphere of Earth). Most important, Sagan's greenhouse theory, Chamberlain says, "basically turned out to be right."[100]

Kuiper picked a somewhat novel dissertation committee. Besides Kuiper and Yerkes astronomer D. Nelson Limber, it included Leonard Reiffel (Sagan's boss from the Armour Research Foundation) and Kimball C. Atwood, a professor of gynecology and obstetrics. "I believe I am the only astronomer ever to have a professor of gynecology and obstetrics on his four- or five-person thesis committee," Sagan laughingly recalled. "The reason was he was the only molecular biologist at University of Chicago at the time," and hence relevant to Sagan's papers on lunar and planetary organics.[101]

Chamberlain says he was supposed to be on the dissertation panel. But Kuiper scheduled Sagan's oral examination for a time "while I was on sabbatical leave in Boulder. So by the time I got back that quarter it was a fait accompli."[102] No doubt Kuiper, the lame duck, was racing to wrap up his business at Yerkes (including Sagan's dissertation) before he left for Arizona. Perhaps Kuiper feared that Chamberlain would make trouble at Sagan's oral exam and decided to keep him out. After all, Chamberlain was the man who once said to Sagan: "I've been following your career in *Time* magazine."[103] (Chamberlain says he was joking.) Or perhaps Kuiper figured it wasn't worth the hassle of bringing Chamberlain all the way back from Boulder. Kuiper has passed away, so we'll probably never know the truth. But one thing is certain: against the odds, Kuiper pushed Sagan's dissertation to acceptance, thereby launching one of the most colorful careers in modern science.

The space age was dawning. Many of its brightest minds were headed to the Sunbelt—to launch sites in Florida and to NASA facilities, the aerospace industry, and academia in the South and West. Urey and Miller were moving to a campus in San Diego; Kuiper, to one in Tucson; and Sagan, to Berkeley. Where the sun sets, his real career would begin.

5

California

MANY SCIENTISTS' most creative years come after they win their Ph.D.'s and enter a postdoctoral fellowship. The trick is to choose the right fellowship. At Harvard or Stanford? Chicago or Caltech? Brandeis or Seattle? Amherst or Iowa? A "prestige" campus isn't always the best choice; some fish fare best in small ponds.

Chosen wisely, a good fellowship leads to academic Shangri-la: friendships with the "right" people, intriguing research, lucrative grants, brainy collaborators, competent lab technicians, worshipful graduate assistants, sabbaticals at Aspen, guest lectureships in Prague—all in all an impressive career, one that climaxes, perhaps, with the fabled flight to Stockholm, where one shakes the hand of the king of Sweden and joins the ghostly dynasty of Nobelists.

But some choose unwisely. They accept a fellowship that looks attractive (a nice stipend, plenty of free parking on campus, good local coffeehouses, the spouse's mom lives nearby) at a university with a less than lustrous faculty, cramped laboratories, a second-rate library, and graduate assistants who fret about whether it's worth sacrificing all happiness in order to discover a new subatomic particle. Those who enter the wrong fellowship may find their careers diverted into backwaters far from the great ocean of research. They may end up scrounging for grants, strip-mining their Ph.D. theses for ideas, and writing for obscure Hungarian journals. Ultimately they end up arguing over intellectual minutiae with bitter fellow burnouts, hosting gossipy luncheons with the dean, and teaching bored sophomores at eight A.M. How often has a once-promising professor (to quote B. F. Skinner's *Walden Two*) recognized "the dance of death in which he has been caught"?[1]

Carl Sagan chose wisely. A turning point in his career came when he won the two-year Miller Fellowship at the University of California at Berkeley, starting September 1, 1960. Berkeley was perfect. It had many

109

distinguished departments, especially Astronomy. It thronged with the right people,[2] especially Nobelists and future Nobelists: Melvin Calvin, E. O. Lawrence, Glenn Seaborg, Emilio Segre, Edwin McMillan, Luis Alvarez, Owen Chamberlain. Even better, California was becoming a center of space science and space-probe development. Also, it was far from the bone-chilling winter winds of Chicago, Williams Bay, and Madison. For a young space scientist, it was a terrific place to start a career.

How did Sagan win so prestigious a fellowship? For one thing, he obtained recommendations from highly prominent scientists (including two Nobel laureates, Lederberg and Muller, and a future Nobelist, Calvin). A fourth recommendation letter was written by Prof. Harold Weaver, chair of the Berkeley astronomy department, who met Sagan while he was working in Calvin's lab in the summer of 1959.[3]

Sagan was originally nominated for the fellowship by Lederberg, who by that time had moved from Wisconsin to Stanford. In his recommendation letter, Lederberg praised Sagan's "excellent service" as a consultant to WESTEX. The Nobelist, then pioneering the science of exobiology, also admitted to "a selfish motive" for nominating Sagan to the Berkeley post: being at nearby Stanford, Lederberg would benefit from being able to discuss ideas for experiments with the younger man.[4]

Melvin Calvin's recommendation described Sagan as "an extremely competent young man," who had an "aggressive" scientific mind.[5] But H. J. Muller is the one who really praised him, saying he "stood head and shoulders above" any other students his age that Muller had met.[6]

Sagan knew how important the California fellowship would be to his career, and he was determined to win it. He was that rare hybrid, a head-in-the-clouds visionary who is also a cunning careerist. He filled out the fellowship application form in January 1959 in Madison, where he, Lynn, and ten-month-old Dorion were living. The form asked: "Have you any constitutional disorder or physical disability?" Sagan answered (perhaps not entirely accurately, considering his achalasia) "No." He asserted an ability to read "French, German, some Spanish." He listed memberships in seven scientific societies devoted to topics as diverse as genetics and rocketry. He also cited his membership, unusual for a twenty-four-year-old, on two committees of the National Academy of Sciences.

These were impressive testimonials, but probably not good enough to ensure his victory. In the fierce competition for the Miller Fellowship, Sagan needed an ace, something truly distinctive, something that would make the Miller judges sit up and take notice. So he decided to confide to them information that he was required by federal law to keep secret. He revealed his research at the Armour Research Foundation on the remote detection of lunar nuclear explosions.[7] He must have known the risk he was taking. The information was classified; he had previously cautioned Muller not to discuss it with others. After all, the cold war was still "hot," and Washington did not look kindly on the leaking of nuclear information. But the risk was worth taking if it would get him to California.

The risk paid off. On March 7, 1960, William R. Dennes, chair of the executive committee for the Miller Institute for Basic Research in Science, informed Sagan that he had won the two-year fellowship starting in September 1960. The stipend was a substantial sum in those days—$7,500 per year, plus a $500-a-year "contingency fund" for travel, supplies, and equipment.[8]

The Miller Fellowship would change Sagan's life. His California idyll of the early 1960s lasted less than three years, yet from that time on, he was—metaphorically, at least—a permanent Californian. He would repeatedly return to the Golden State for the rest of his life, sometimes for years at a time, to work on science or television or movie projects, sporting sunglasses and cruising the freeways in his Porsche with the license plate PHOBOS (after a moon of Mars). He would experience fundamental life dramas in the West—his two divorces, in Oakland and Los Angeles; his death, in Seattle. The land where the sun sets had always welcomed visionaries, iconoclasts, eccentrics, hustlers, and showmen. It became Sagan's home away from home.

AMBITION DEFINED young Carl Sagan. After arriving in California, he and Margulis moved to a handsome residence at 6000 Skyline Boulevard in the Berkeley Hills overlooking San Francisco Bay. "They had this gorgeous view of the Golden Gate Bridge," recalled his friend Ronald Blum, who by that time had moved to a doctoral program at Stanford. "I wondered, 'How could these people afford this place?' I had the impression that Carl thought he should never deny himself *anything*."[9]

Blum was also puzzled by "how totally Lynn seemed to accept her role as wife and mother. Everything was about Carl and Carl's career. Carl expected everything to be done for him" by Margulis, he recalls. In Yiddish, Blum says, Sagan would have been called a yeshiva *bocher*, "an impractical guy who sits in the synagogue all day, talking about fine points of law and the Bible, and he comes home and his wife is doing all the work. Sagan was literally an otherworldly person. He lived with his life in the clouds, in the galaxy. His time was too valuable for ordinary human concerns."[10]

Sagan seemed to feel free to spend his time the way he wanted, with little concern for the burden on Margulis. Blum enjoyed a board game called Tactics II, which concerned strategy and combat. He recalls that one day he brought it to Sagan's house and they played it avidly all day long. "His very first move was to completely outflank me," Blum recalls, "by landing his paratrooopers on a little island off the coast of my capital city." The move was illegal, but Blum didn't stop the game. When Sagan finally won, however, Blum lightheartedly pointed out that the first move was against the rules, and he recalls that Sagan got enraged. "He got so upset . . . I was astonished by his total involvement in the game . . . so many hours. This was a guy whose time was 'too valuable' to spend earning money [in college]. And yet he spent this whole day playing this game. We never played it again, of course."[11]

Careerwise, the move to California was a good one for both Sagan and Margulis. She was admitted to the graduate program at Berkeley, where her professors included the philosophically minded biologist Gunther Stent. The Bay Area was hipper, more open-minded than the Midwest. Across the water in San Francisco, poets were protesting alienation, conformism, and militarism; marijuana was the recreational drug of choice. Sagan and Margulis made many friends, among them two former University of Wisconsin students, Nina Landau (later Serrano) and her husband, Saul. At the time Saul Landau was a taxi driver, one of the many budding New Leftists who had been inspired by William Appleman Williams's history classes at Madison. (In time, Landau would become a leading U.S. leftist, author, and commentator for progressive radio stations.)

The Landaus dined with the Sagans, and "as I recall, we smoked a little weed and danced to the proper music," Landau says. "It was just getting into the sixties. Carl was a little 'tighter' than everybody else—more uptight. We all thought he was sort of crazy, thinking about life in outer space. He was presenting this as science but to me, this was science fiction."[12]

Nina remembers being "very impressed" that Margulis was a scientist. Few women, much less mothers, were scientists at that time. Lynn was "small and slender, wiry, highly ambitious, high energy . . . and nice. I liked her," Nina recalls. But Nina's deepest memories are of Sagan: "You don't meet people like Carl except maybe once every two generations," she says with a laugh. "My memory of him is a guy in a suit, whereas all the other men in our lives wore jeans. He was totally consumed with the idea that there was probably life on other planets, in outer space. He was on *fire* with his ideas. He would go on and on."[13]

Sagan flew off to places such as Green Bank, West Virginia, where he and older, more distinguished scientists discussed ways to contact extraterrestrials (about which more shortly). They discussed epochal topics such as: Do advanced technical civilizations last long enough to establish interstellar contact? Or do they blow themselves up first? (The question seemed especially topical in those days, as the United States and the Soviet Union faced off over Cuba and Berlin.) The scientists even played with a formula for estimating the number of alien civilizations. It included a variable, L, which represented the average lifespan of a technical civilization.[14]

To Nina, Sagan's space speculations were "weirdo." She was more interested in the arts, and viewed space exploration "as very reactionary, as an expansion of the cold war, to expand military advantages, to have more wars and more killings." She thought that at a time of global crisis, he should be focusing on Earth, not the heavens. "I felt he was missing the boat," she says; "that while he was looking up at the stars, life on Earth was going to hell. [I insisted that] we've got make sure all the children are fed! We've got to stop wars! We've got to do something about the strontium-90 in mothers' milk!"

But Sagan had a way of winning over doubters. Nina recalls how he treated her son, Greg, then six or seven years old, who was a big space buff. "The two of them would sit there and go on and on about space." Greg would draw pictures of "space" and show them to Sagan, who would react with delight. "This charmed me and warmed me, to see his interest in my child. They had a special relationship." Some time later, Sagan told her that Greg had just taken him aside and informed him: "Carl, I have to tell you something. I'm not into space any more. I'm into baseball now." Sagan assured Greg that was fine and that the boy should follow his heart. "And I just melted at that," Nina recalls.[15]

To HIS OWN CHILD, Sagan was less doting. After Dorion was born, in 1959, Sagan's "real character came out," Margulis remembers. "He was totally jealous of Dorion . . . If I picked Dorion up, he would take it as a personal insult." It was rough on her, doing all the work. Sagan "never changed a diaper in his life, he never cleared the table of his dishes, he never washed the dishes." If he got home late, she snapped: "You had another press conference, didn't you?"[16] Life grew tense on Skyline Boulevard.

Sagan felt he simply didn't have the time for domesticity. His work was too important. Conquering the solar system, communicating with aliens—how could domestic needs rival such an agenda? Like many "futurists," he focused on the forest and sometimes badly neglected the trees. In California, his tendency to take on whatever projects interested him caught up with him. He seriously overcommitted himself, getting involved with three big projects—the *Mariner 2* space probe to Venus, the Stratoscope balloon project, and origin-of-life experiments at a NASA facility. Meanwhile, he began to write articles for science journals, to give speeches, and to be quoted in news media.[17] His endeavors kept him away from home for long periods. His child was growing up, and his wife was wising up, without him. "It's no trick to make an awful lot of money," a character in *Citizen Kane* cautions, "if all you want is to make a lot of money."[18] Likewise, Sagan wanted to be famous, which isn't that hard—if all you want is to be famous.

Yet who can blame him? Here he was, present at the creation of the space age, a unique transition in history—in evolution—that would not be matched again. Why settle for the banalities of domesticity, for diapers and backyard barbecues? In many ways he was a deeply private man who kept his innermost feelings to himself; perhaps he realized he had made a mistake in marrying so young. But should he be expected to pay for that mistake by abandoning his glistening future? Would he have achieved as many great things if he had stayed home more and basked in togetherness? Perhaps, given his ambition, he would have ended up old, frustrated, and bitter, blaming his wife and children and grousing about what he might have been. It is currently unfashionable to sympathize with the white male careerists of the 1950s who neglected wife and children to chase glory, and certainly their behavior wrought much pain and suffering. But these men deserve some sympathy, too. They achieved much, and many, like Sagan, would pay for it in spades.

FAR OFF, the horns of battle called. The cold war had shifted to the frontier of space, and the United States was losing. With dizzying speed, the Soviet Union seized one cosmic "first" after another: the first animals in space; the first probe to contact another world (*Lunik II*, which slammed into the Moon); the first astronaut (Yuri Gagarin); the first photos from the far side of the Moon; the first female astronaut (Valentina Tereshkova).[19] Many Americans feared that Soviet space conquests were omens of future terrestrial conquests, of Soviet tanks rolling into Western Europe, of communist puppet states in Asia and Latin America, perhaps even of a Soviet first-strike nuclear attack on the United States. Anxiety turned to hysteria. If the Soviets were first to the Moon, Arthur C. Clarke warned, "they will have won the solar system, and theirs will be the voice of the future. . . . As it will deserve to be."[20] *Life* magazine quoted one scientist as saying that "unless we depart utterly from our present behavior, it is reasonable to expect that by no later than 1975 the United States will be a member of the Union of Soviet Socialist Republics."[21]

Naturally, NASA was desperate to achieve a first—*any* first. All eyes turned toward the planet Venus. It was a brilliant world but a shy one, noticed usually in the wee hours by paperboys and milkmen who saw it hovering above the red ribbon of dawn or in the early evening by tired commuters who glimpsed it above the sunset and wondered if it was a UFO. Its brilliance owed to its perpetual cloud cover, beneath which—what? A humid jungle? A global ocean? A planet-wide Sahara raked by dust storms? More than a hundred times farther away (in a straight line) than the Moon, Venus came closer to Earth than any other planet. It was the logical target for the first interplanetary space probe.

"For me, it was just a dream come true," Sagan recalled. "We were actually going to go to the *planets!*" He was summoned to Caltech's Jet Propulsion Laboratory (JPL) in Pasadena to advise engineers designing the *Mariner* interplanetary probes about the kinds of observational instruments the probes needed and the key scientific questions the probes should be trying to answer.[22] Meanwhile, the Soviets prepared to launch their own rockets toward Venus.

Sagan's first major article for a "mainstream" scientific journal appeared in March 1961, in *Science* magazine. "The Planet Venus" was a writing tour de force.[23] Sagan's prose soared, and he unleashed his sense of humor (which somehow survived the magazine editors' blue pencils). He cited the numerous competing hypotheses about Venus: that it was a humid jungle; that it was swept by a carbonated ocean or a petroleum sea; that it was a desert with vast dust storms, or that it was some other form of wasteland. Thus, "those planning eventual manned expeditions to Venus must be exceedingly perplexed over whether to send along a paleo-botanist, a mineralogist, a petroleum geologist, or a deep-sea diver." Even one of Sagan's critics, the famed astronomer E. J. Öpik, called it a "very stimulating and imaginative article."[24]

The article presents Sagan's greenhouse model for the atmosphere of Venus. It also contains fragments of his earlier, arm-waving speculations about life there. Native life was "unlikely," he wrote, but still, "conditions are much more favorable at higher altitudes, especially just beneath the cloud layer," where aerial microorganisms might drift on wind currents. He argued that space probes fired into the Venusian atmosphere must be sterilized in advance, to make sure they wouldn't contaminate any life forms there.

His most dazzling proposal was that humans remake Venus into a habitable world through a process called "terraforming." Once again, he was reflecting his science-fiction background. The term terraforming had been invented in short stories of the 1940s written by the legendary Jack Williamson (under the pseudonym Will Stewart).[25] The concept of planetary transformation was even older than this, however. In the 1930s, Olaf Stapledon suggested electrolyzing Venus's supposed oceans to generate oxygen for its atmosphere.[26] Arthur C. Clarke's *The Sands of Mars* (1951) described the terraforming of the red planet.

Sagan's terraforming proposal mirrored the technocratic self-confidence of the mid-twentieth century. At that time, some visionaries (including many U.S. government officials, such as Interior Secretary Stewart Udall) were talking about terrestrial "weather control."[27] Clouds would be seeded, bringing rainfall to deserts. Military brass considered enlisting weather as a weapon of war. Perhaps tornadoes could be dissipated, and hurricanes redirected. Meanwhile, engineers envisioned technical solutions to the world's biggest problems—poverty, hunger, economic underdevelopment. Rather than confront radical questions about class barriers and the distribution of wealth, they advocated mega-engineering "fixes" for societal woes—for example, the construction of monstrous hydroelectric dams, which would turn "wastelands" into suburbs and croplands. Nuclear weapons could be used to dig canals in Central America and harbors in Alaska.[28] Human-triggered rainstorms would wash smog from Los Angeles skies.[29] The Bering Strait would be dammed and cold Arctic water pumped south into the Pacific. The departing Arctic water would be replaced by warm Atlantic water, thereby making the polar climate more temperate.[30] Given their optimism about remaking Earth, it isn't surprising that some visionaries proposed doing the same for Mars and Venus.

But how? If Sagan was right, Venus was hellishly hot; how could its atmosphere be made cooler and habitable? In his 1961 article, he proposed seeding the upper atmosphere of Venus with microorganisms from Earth. He believed Venus's atmosphere contained clouds of water vapor and crystallized water. The windblown microbes would feed on these and proliferate. Basking in the intense sunlight some thirty million miles closer to the Sun than Earth is, the "bugs" would undergo photosynthesis and convert atmospheric carbon dioxide and water vapor to CH_2O and oxygen (O_2). Finally, the organisms would sink into the lower atmosphere and decompose, yielding carbon and water. The result: the carbon dioxide concentration of the atmosphere would drop, weakening the greenhouse effect and cooling the planet; and the oxygen level would rise, enabling humans to breathe there. In time, Venus would become "a much less forbidding environment." Sagan called this project "microbiological planetary engineering."[31]

His idea made the March 27, 1961, *New York Times:*

HABITABLE VENUS SCIENTIST'S GOAL

Astrophysicist Would Seed Atmosphere
With Algae to Release the Oxygen
Surface Believed Arid

"Greenhouse Effect" Is Seen As Producing Very High
Temperature on Planet.[32]

Many other periodicals picked up the story. John F. Allen of the *San
Francisco Examiner* wrote: "It is entirely possible to change the surface of
the planet Venus from a lifeless inferno of whirling dust storms to a cool
and pleasant place habitable by human colonizers."[33] The April 10, 1961,
issue of *Newsweek* reported how "a brilliant, 26-year-old University of
California astronomer named Carl Sagan described a bold new way to
reclaim Venus for Earthmen." The project's roots in terrestrial mega-
engineering schemes is implied by *Newsweek*'s use of the word "reclaim";
on Earth, the Bureau of Reclamation championed the construction of
hydroelectric dams.[34] Likewise, Arthur C. Clarke wrote approvingly in
his book *The Promise of Space* that Sagan's scheme "is certainly a grandiose idea, but it differs only in scale from the projects that have brought
life to the barren places of this planet."[35] Sagan was beginning to make
his distinctive mark as an exceptionally imaginative and eloquent propo-
nent of the human future in space. "Carl's mind was the most restless
I've ever encountered," recalls David Perlman of the *San Francisco Chronicle*, who was one of the first distinguished science writers to cover
Sagan's activities. "He got me excited about the Big Bang [theory] when
I was still thinking Steady State [theory], and even though some of his
Berkeley seniors felt he was Peck's Bad Boy—brash and argumenta-
tive—they had to concede his brilliance."

MEANWHILE, BACK IN PASADENA, Sagan became embroiled in heated
debates about the *Mariner 2* probe, which would fly to Venus. One key
question was whether *Mariner 2* should carry a camera. Sagan and his
colleagues argued long and hard about this. Nowadays, it is difficult to
imagine a time when scientists didn't naturally place cameras aboard
robotic spacecraft. We are accustomed to the spectacular images from,
say, the Hubble Space Telescope, and from the Mars Pathfinder probe
on the surface of Mars. These spacecraft are to space what Ansel Adams
was to the American West.

But decades ago, few astronomers anticipated this breathtaking
bumper crop of space imagery. Back then, telescopes offered only murky
images of the planets. According to traditional accounts of modern
astronomy (recently challenged by historian Ronald E. Doel), many
astronomers regarded planetary astronomy as somewhat *déclassé*, a holdover from the Percival Lowell era.[36] The real action was in studying
galaxies, red shifts, stellar evolution, and the expanding universe. They

half-consciously thought of planets as physical abstractions, as minor gravity wells in celestial mechanics calculations, rather than as places like, say, Yosemite or Yellowstone.

Besides, planetary probes were a nascent technology, with limited space and power resources. Cameras (it was thought) took up space needed for "real" instruments. In retrospect, space scientist David Morrison suggests dividing the debate into two camps, "the scientists" and "the explorers." The scientists preferred to make predictions about what would be found in the vicinity of a planet (say, a magnetic field of a certain intensity) and then send instruments designed to test those specific predictions. By contrast, the explorers—like Sagan—expected to discover the unexpected.[37]

"There was a prevailing view that cameras were a complete waste of time," Sagan recalled. But he felt they were important "precisely because they could answer questions we were too stupid to ask."[38]

The "scientists," one might surmise, were numerocentric; they preferred highly *quantitative* data—numbers—to visual modes of interpretation. Many of them were physicists or engineers, which are number-hungry professions. They liked data they could feed into the increasingly popular electronic computers. To them, perhaps, pictures did not constitute real data. In contrast, Sagan, unconsciously struggling to unite Snow's Two Cultures, had a certain aesthetic sensibility; he recognized pictures as both scientifically meaningful and worth having in their own right. In the decades to come, his stance would be repeatedly vindicated. Time and again, space probes with cameras have exposed the unexpected. As a result, the solar system has proven to be far more complex than ever anticipated.[39] With few exceptions, each new world seems unique unto itself, like a hitherto unknown epoch in the history of abstract art. Mere numbers cannot convey such richness. In space, a picture is worth a billion bytes.

Still, Sagan's colleagues had some justification for scoffing at his photo fervor. His definition of "unexpected" included things likelier to be proposed in *Astounding Science Fiction* than in *Astrophysical Journal*. For example, he thought there might be occasional clearings in the Venusian clouds, through which a *Mariner 2* camera could peer and see—what?[40] Perhaps the cloud-brushing mountains reported (erroneously, we now know) by earlier observers? Mountains atop which temperatures might be cool enough to support life?[41] Likewise, he suggested that aliens once visited our solar system, stopped off at the Moon, and left artifacts that might be visible to cameras.[42] And in a 1963 speech, he advocated placing cameras aboard probes to Mars, partly because they might spot "many artifacts of advanced life forms"—that is, Martians.[43] Caltech's JPL officials overruled Sagan, and the *Mariner 2* carried no camera to Venus.

Determined to beat the Soviets to Venus, NASA rushed to assemble the 447-pound *Mariner 2* in less than a year. Space robots were relatively new things under the sun, and journalists struggled to describe this one. *National Geographic* called it a "dragonfly in space" and an "ungainly, skeletal spacecraft."[44]

The different scientific teams had to move fast in developing their instruments. One of Sagan's *Mariner 2* associates, Stillman Chase, recalls that the program manager had a block of lead on his desk, and said: "This represents your instrument, and we're going to fly this instead if you don't finish on time."[45] Sagan was, by his own account, "deeply involved"[46] in developing one of *Mariner 2*'s instruments, the infrared radiometer.[47]

Much was at stake with *Mariner 2* for Sagan. His credibility as a scientist rested, to a great extent, on his doctoral work predicting a greenhouse effect on Venus. That work could be instantly shot down if one of the *Mariner 2* instruments, a microwave radiometer, flew by Venus and observed a phenomenon called "limb brightening."

To be specific: As we have seen, some scientists disagreed with Sagan's belief that the intense microwave signal that had been picked up coming from Venus came from the planet's surface. Rather, they suggested that it came from a strongly ionized region far above the planetary surface. If this were so, then as *Mariner 2* flew by Venus, the microwave signal should appear brighter toward the edge (limb) of the Venusian disc than toward its center. This is called limb brightening.

Sagan's entire greenhouse theory would be ruined if *Mariner 2* observed limb brightening, and his model of the Venusian atmosphere would be irrelevant. But what if, by contrast, the probe observed "limb darkening," a *weaker* microwave signal toward the limb? This would support one of Sagan's crucial assumptions—that the signal came from the planet's surface. But darkening would not in itself prove his greenhouse model. There were other possible explanations at that time for Venus's apparent heat, including a suggestion by a Russian scientist that the heat came from radioactivity left over from a Venusian nuclear war![48]

Such are the trials of doing science—it is often much easier to disprove a theory than to prove it. Theories are easily shot down, while truths are gruelingly difficult to establish. Suppose, for example, that I observe hundreds of white swans. Does that mean I am justified in stating "All swans are white"? No, a black swan might show up tomorrow, and the sighting of a single black swan would disprove the all-swans-are-white hypothesis.

The observation of limb brightening would be Sagan's version of a black-swan sighting, the single, crucial blow that would undermine much of his doctoral toil (and with it, perhaps, much of his subsequent fame). He was nervously aware of this. To a great degree, his personal hopes for the future rode with *Mariner 2* all the way to Venus. His anxiety at this time may explain why, for the rest of his life, he emphasized so eloquently the point, championed by the controversial philosopher of science Karl Popper, that no theory can be considered "scientific" unless one can conceive of a way, *in principle*, to disprove it. Pseudosciences and the occult, Sagan argued, fall far short of this standard. Often their hypotheses are too vague and slippery to generate predictions that can conceivably be tested. Obeying no firm rules of logic or research, pseudoscientists and occultists can always invent facile explanations for negative results (as when an astrologer, for example, attributes a failed prediction to "bad vibes"). As Sagan believed, a theory that cannot conceivably be disproved may make one feel warm and cozy inside; it may soothe much of life's pain and irrationality. However, it is not science.

Sagan's Popperian ethic extended in later life to, of all things, television advertising. His son Nick recalls how in the 1980s, after Sagan's television series, *Cosmos*, made him internationally famous, "people wanted him to do TV commercials. . . . My dad's response was always like this: 'I tell you what I'll do: why don't you just . . . book time for me to be on television and I will do an independent test of your product versus all the other products. And . . . I will give you a completely independent, objective view—on the air, live.' Of course, no one took him up on it."[49]

IN THE EARLY 1960S, as Tom Wolfe observed in *The Right Stuff*, the average American believed the following about U.S. space launches: "*Our rockets always blow up.*"[50] Actually, they didn't, not always; but many of them did. To cover its bets, NASA liked to launch two identical probes every time an interesting planet came within range. And sure enough, with almost amusing regularity, one of the twin probes would end up literally in the drink—say, blown up over the Atlantic Ocean after a wobbly takeoff from Cape Canaveral. Others traveled far into space, then stopped sending telemetry signals and were never heard from again. NASA's first probe to Venus, *Mariner 1*, was launched on July 22, 1962; true to form, within seconds it veered off course, and a range safety officer ordered its destruction. Technicians later discovered the cause of the accident: they had accidentally omitted a single hyphen from the computer launch code. Naturally, everyone at the Cape was nervous on August 27, when the surviving Venus probe, *Mariner 2*, stood on its launch pad.[51]

At 1:53 A.M. the Atlas D booster fired and ascended smoothly into space. The probe was scheduled to reach Venus before the Christmas holidays. In coming months, during its journey over more than 100 million miles—more than 400 times the distance from the Earth to the Moon—*Mariner 2* endured as many perils as Pauline. Its instruments seriously overheated, its solar panels went haywire, it was reportedly struck by a small meteor.

As 1962 waned into autumn, though, a greater threat emerged: that come Christmastime, when *Mariner 2* sailed by Venus and transmitted its findings home, no inhabitant of Earth would be alive to hear them. In October, U-2 overflights revealed that the Soviets were secretly installing nuclear-tipped missiles in Cuba. President Kennedy ordered Soviet premier Khrushchev to remove the weapons. Former secretary of state Dean Acheson urged Kennedy to attack Cuba.[52] Nuclear war appeared imminent. Some SETI scientists wondered if technical civilizations in general tend to self-destruct. If so, then the value of L (the average life span of a technical civilization in the galaxy) must be low, and SETI is a waste of time: few if any advanced civilizations will survive long enough for us to chat with them across the light years. Neither will our own civilization, it seemed in late 1962, as schoolchildren rehearsed "duck and cover" exercises and families dug backyard bomb shelters. Never before in human history had the value of L appeared so low.

Things were also getting more grim at home on Skyline Boulevard. As Sagan was off at JPL consulting about *Mariner 2* and making headlines with his imaginative ideas, Margulis was increasingly stressed with the burdens of running the household, even while struggling to continue her own graduate work. Further complicating the pressures on her, she became pregnant with a second child, another son, Jeremy, who was born in 1960.

Margulis recalls that she "was happy in the marriage until the kids were born. And when the kids were born, every small act became a conflict. . . . If I paid attention to them, [Carl felt] it was taking away from him. He needed ten thousand people to be raving about him all the time. I was just one young woman, trying to go to school and take care of kids and run a household. Every distraction he considered personal."

Rachel's child "was the embodiment of everything she wanted. He couldn't basically have anything but these very superficial intellectual relations. . . . *He* was a baby."[53]

By the time Jeremy was born, Sagan felt so neglected by Margulis that at home he turned sullen, even paranoid. Meanwhile, she felt that he belittled her—and that he had done so for years. She was not the only one to feel the icy edge of his arrogance; so had colleagues, even many who liked him.

Theoretical physicists, like surgeons, are noted for their arrogance. Nobelist Wolfgang Pauli once said that every theoretical physicist's first word is "Nonsense!"[54] But Sagan was subtler than the bumptious Pauli. Like his mother, Rachel, Sagan communicated disdain for others indirectly, not so much by what he said as by how he said it. Sagan's cool, urbane manner and his rapid, clever repartee gave him an inherent advantage in debate with less articulate, less self-assured colleagues. Sagan wielded logic like a swordsman, swiftly and precisely, and spoke with a self-confidence not always justified by the data. They, by contrast, tended to dwell on the uncertainties and ambiguities, on the details wherein the devil resides. Sagan seemed decisive, able to recall the precise page on which he had read an obscure fact;[55] they, by contrast, seemed slow-witted.

Decades later, after two divorces, not a few career disappointments, and at least a few frayed relationships, Sagan acknowledged his past abrasiveness. He recalled how in the early 1960s he had met the distinguished geophysicist Harry Hess. Hess asked his opinion of the National Academy of Sciences Space Science Board, which had considerably enhanced Sagan's career by welcoming him onto its various committees. Sagan's ingratitude was acidic: "I was very dismissive [of this] organization which, after all, had been *very* kind to me," he recalled. Hess asked Sagan if he would like to serve on the full board. With the thoughtlessness of a true smartass, Sagan replied: "No, I'll leave that to my dotage." Later, Sagan discovered that Hess had been named to head the board. Embarrassed, Sagan realized he had acted like a cocky punk. "I had rejected [the board] on really very clumsy and inept grounds. That was one of the many imperfections of my youth. . . . It was just not nice of me."[56]

At the time, though, Sagan was too young, too full of himself, too excited about the future to realize how frequently he offended other people. Only a great shock would show him how badly he was behaving. That shock would soon come, courtesy of Lynn.

LEGEND HOLDS that Thales walked at night, gazing at the stars, until he fell into a well. Likewise, Sagan's head remained in the clouds, even as his marriage careered toward ruin, and even as some scientists began to suspect that he was irresponsible.

His scheme for transforming Venus into a habitable planet, which had attracted so much press attention, was the most far-out idea he had proposed thus far. Yet it was mild compared with some lurid schemes kicking around the bohemias of the astrophysical community. How about rebuilding entire stars? or galaxies? The scientists Freeman Dyson and Nikolai Kardashev speculated that super-advanced civilizations could keep themselves warm and energized by pulverizing entire planets and wrapping the resulting dust cloud around their local star (like a blanket).[57] The idea intrigued Sagan. Are such cosmic civil engineering projects really under way, elsewhere in the universe? If so, might we be able to see them? Through telescopes, Sagan and others suggested, we might perceive the infrared glow of construction projects bigger than stars, directed by beings with brains unimaginably mightier than our own. What would these aliens look like? Would they seem like gods to us? Would they deign to communicate with us? Or would they ignore us, as we ignore the ants at our feet?

The idea of aliens is a very old one. The ancients (for example, the atomist philosopher Democritus and the poet Lucretius) speculated about the inhabitants of other worlds.[58] In 1749, Ben Franklin assured the readers of *Poor Richard's Almanac* that "it is the opinion of all the modern philosophers and mathematicians that the planets are habitable worlds."[59]

The possibility of radio communication with aliens was discussed from the earliest years of radio, circa 1900. While testing primitive radio equipment atop Pike's Peak in Colorado, Nikola Tesla, an eccentric pioneer of electrical engineering, reported receiving mysterious radio signals. He proposed publicly that the signals came from Martians. In August 1924, the U.S. Navy maintained a brief radio silence in hopes of hearing Martian messages.[60]

In May 1933, eighteen months before Sagan was born in Brooklyn, the front page of the *New York Times* ran this startling headline: "New Radio Waves Traced to Centre of the Milky Way. . . . Only Delicate Receiver Is Able to Register—No Evidence of Interstellar Signaling."[61] The story reported a speech by Karl G. Jansky of Bell Telephone Laboratories in Holmdel, New Jersey, to the International Scientific Radio Union in Washington. Jansky, the *Times* said, had used a special antenna to discover "mysterious radio waves which appear to come from the centre of the Milky Way galaxy." On a radio speaker, the signals were a "steady hiss type static of unknown origin." The emissions varied with the seasons, evidence that they came from space, not from terrestrial radio sources. The last paragraph of the article adds (as if by afterthought): "There is no indication of any kind, Mr. Jansky replied to a question, that these galactic radio waves constitute some kind of interstellar signalling, or that they are the result of some form of intelligence striving for intra-galactic communication."

Jansky's antenna was the first radiotelescope.[62] The "signals" he detected were only natural radio noise coming from the interstellar matter and the billions of stars in the Milky Way.

Suppose aliens tried to communicate with us, or we with them; how could we understand each other's messages? Via mathematics, according to standard SETI doctrine. If one assumes—just for the moment, for argument's sake—that terrestrial mathematics reflects universal properties of the cosmos, then that same mathematics should be valid on every planet with intelligent beings. We could distinguish an "intelligent" alien signal from cosmic background noise by examining it for mathematical regularities—a sequence of prime numbers, for example.[63]

Modern SETI dates from September 19, 1959, when *Nature* ran a paper by the scientists Giuseppe Cocconi and Philip Morrison. Terrestrial radiotelescopes, they pointed out, were sensitive enough to detect radio signals from other stars. Aliens might be trying to contact Earth right now. Humans should consider using radiotelescopes to detect their signals. There was just one problem: what radio frequency should we listen to? There are millions of possible electromagnetic frequencies; trying to locate a narrow-band alien signal seemed much tougher than finding a needle in a haystack. Morrison and Cocconi suggested easing the search by concentrating on a band of the radio spectrum that stands out against the natural radio cacophony of the galaxy. Because this band is so "obvious" to us, it might also be obvious to aliens. Similarly, if someone says "Meet me in San Francisco" but doesn't say where, you might first look at well-known locales—the Golden Gate Bridge, for example. What, then, is a possible cosmic equivalent of the Golden Gate? Cocconi and Morrison suggested that it was the frequency of 1420 megacycles per second, also known as the 21-centimeter line. This is the natural frequency of vibrating atoms of hydrogen gas, then thought to be the commonest element in the cosmos. The frequency of 1420 megacycles per second might be the equivalent of a cosmic "chat room" where all the worlds gather to converse. It was worth checking out, anyway.[64]

By coincidence, radioastronomer Frank Drake had also started thinking about extraterrestrial communication. In the late 1950s, while working at a radiotelescope in Massachusetts, he had briefly detected a mysterious signal from the Pleiades, a powdery star cluster also known as the Seven Sisters. That night, "I was 26 years old. . . . I'm past 60 now, and I still can't adequately describe my emotions at that moment," he wrote in his memoirs.[65] Sadly, he realized that the signal was just a fluke, one of the countless odd radio "noises" (ranging from auto spark plugs to secret military projects) that annoy radioastronomers.

Still, the incident whetted Drake's imagination. Soon afterward, he transferred to a job at the National Radio Astronomy Observatory radiotelescope in the radio-"quiet" valley of Green Bank, West Virginia. Drive through there and turn the dial on your car radio; all you hear is crackling. The place is a radioastronomer's dream. While lunching at a local cafe with acting observatory director Lloyd V. Berkner, Drake suggested (again, independently of Cocconi and Morrison) that they search for alien signals at 1420 megacycles per second. Fine, Berkner said. Drake named his alien hunt Project Ozma, "for the princess of the imaginary land of Oz—a place very far away, difficult to reach, and populated by exotic beings." Later Otto Struve, the former Yerkes director and a world-famous astronomer, took over Green Bank and gave Ozma his blessing.[66] In fact, it is remarkable how many famous scientists blessed SETI early on. Their enthusiasm belies popular myths (reinforced by television shows and Hollywood movies) that a scientific "priesthood" invariably stonewalls progress. On the contrary; the "priests" are sometimes the shock troops of change.

About four A.M. on April 8, 1960, Drake pointed the Green Bank telescope at a star called Tau Ceti. He observed the star all day and heard nothing unusual. The radio waves, natural background noise from the heavens, were etched by a pen on a moving sheet of paper. Then Drake moved the radiotelescope to the second target, a star called Epsilon Eridani. Suddenly the needle wobbled wildly. He turned on the loudspeaker and heard pulses, neatly spaced in time. The result was "a moderate amount of pandemonium" in the radiotelescope observatory.

Again he was disappointed. As it turned out, the signal came from a secret military project. Drake continued observing the two stars for the next few months, then shut down Project Ozma.[67] But he had in no sense failed. He had examined only two stars, while there are 300-odd billion of them in the Milky Way galaxy. And beyond the Milky Way are hundreds of billions of other galaxies.

The first SETI "conference" occurred at Green Bank in November 1961. A small, elite group of experts were invited to discuss ways to improve on Ozma—to hasten the discovery of an alien signal. "I don't remember which of us mentioned Carl Sagan's name first," Drake recalled, "but we both wanted him." Drake was familiar with Sagan, who had sought his aid two years earlier regarding microwave emissions from Venus. "He knew more about biology than any astronomer I'd ever met, and was fast making a never-before-heard name for himself as an 'exobiologist.'"[68]

Among the other guests were Calvin (Sagan's Berkeley colleague), Cocconi, Morrison, Struve, J. Peter Pearman, S. S. Huang, John C. Lilly, D. W. Atchley, and Bernard M. Oliver (vice president for research and development of Hewlett-Packard). Decades later, Sagan recalled the gathering as "wonderful, these good scientists all saying that it wasn't nonsense to think about the subject. . . . [T]he fact that they came showed that they didn't think it was beyond the pale. . . . There was such a heady sense in the air that finally we've penetrated the ridicule barrier."[69]

Sagan was the youngest attendee, "dark, brash, and brilliant," Drake remembers. He was struck by how Sagan, despite his age, was "extremely confident—was not humble. He thought he knew as much as anybody there, even people very senior to himself. That was the way he was his whole life. . . . He tried to present an image of being very sophisticated. . . . He did not hesitate to challenge prominent figures like the Morrisons and Struves. That's what I mean by 'brash.'"[70] During the conference, news arrived: Calvin had won the Nobel Prize for his work on the chemistry of photosynthesis. Champagne flowed.[71]

A key point of discussion was: What is the most rational way to go about seeking radio signals from aliens? The Milky Way galaxy has perhaps 300 billion stars (about 50 stars for every person on Earth). To search the galaxy randomly, star by star, would take practically forever. So one must concentrate, at least initially, on the most promising targets—stars similar to our Sun.

How long might the search take? That depends partly on the abundance of alien civilizations. If they are abundant, we might find one quickly; if rare, the search might take decades or centuries. In the late 1940s, the teenage Carl Sagan had estimated the number of galactic planetary systems in his school notebook. He cited several reports (later disproved) of the detection of extrasolar planets, and then tried to estimate how many solar-like systems exist in the Milky Way. He came up with the remarkable figure of 200 million.

For SETI scientists, estimating the number of civilizations capable of radio communication is no mere amusement. The greater the number of planetary civilizations, the shorter the average distance between them. By determining their average distance, the scientists can estimate whether civilizations might be close enough to Earth for two-way conversation over reasonable periods of time. For example, the nearest star to Earth, Proxima Centauri, is slightly more than four light-years away. If we transmit a signal to the Proxima Centaurians in, say, the year 2000, they would receive it in 2004. We could listen to their reply in 2008. Such communication would be slow, but not unimaginably so. But suppose that alien civilizations are extremely rare, only a tiny percentage of the stars in the galaxy. Then civilizations might be an average of thousands of light-years apart, making true conversation almost impossible. By the time we received their signal, they might have gone extinct. Or vice versa.

At the Green Bank conference, Drake wrote this equation on a blackboard:[72]

$$N = R_* f_p n_e f_l f_i f_c L$$

The variables represent:

> N —the number of civilizations in the Milky Way galaxy *able* and *willing* to engage in interstellar communication
>
> R_* —the rate of star formation in the galaxy (that is, the number of newborn stars that arise per year)
>
> f_p —the fraction of stars with planets
>
> n_e —the fraction of habitable planets in an average planetary system
>
> f_l —the fraction of habitable planets on which *any* form of life arises (microbes, mollusks, etc.)
>
> f_i —the fraction of inhabited planets on which life evolves into "intelligent" beings
>
> f_c —the fraction of alien societies that develop the technical ability to communicate with outside planetary systems, as well as the will to do so

The last, most ominous variable was L:

> L —the average lifespan of a technologically advanced civilization (that is, how long a typical advanced civilization survives before it dies off or self-destructs)

The values of most of these variables were poorly known in 1961, and they are little better known today. At the Green Bank conference, Sagan and Calvin discussed the fifth variable (the fraction of habitable planets on which any form of life arises). Clearly still inspired by the Miller-Urey experiment, Sagan argued that alien life was inevitable—a "forced process,"[73] in his words—wherever the environmental conditions are right (as in a reducing atmosphere, for example).

Sagan also argued that the range of planets suitable for life might be broader than generally assumed. Historically, scientists assumed that Earth is favored for life because its average temperature is just right[74] (like the bears' porridge in "Goldilocks"). Traditionally, astronomers expected habitable planets to occupy "habitable zones" a certain distance from their stars (Earth is an average of 93 million miles from the Sun). If the planets are much closer to their star, they are too hot for life; any farther out, too cold. So astronomers reasoned, anyway. But Sagan knew from his research on Venus that a planet's temperature is not strictly dictated by its distance from the Sun. Conceivably, a planet far from its parent star could be warm enough for life thanks to a strong atmospheric greenhouse effect.[75] So the total number of habitable planets might be far more than assumed.

To Sagan, the most troubling part of the Drake equation was the variable L, the longevity of an average technical civilization. In the early 1960s, as the superpowers braced for conflict over Berlin and Cuba, some feared that the value of L—for Earth, at least—might be revealed at any moment to be distressingly small, as swarms of bombers began dropping their nuclear cargoes.

But perhaps not; perhaps global tensions would ease, the superpowers would resolve their ideological tensions, and humanity would march united into a glorious future on Earth and in space. Perhaps the average galactic civilization tends to survive because most develop worldwide governments before nuclear war wipes them out.

Sagan estimated that one million "advanced technical civilizations" exist in the galaxy at any given moment. Thus "approximately 0.001 percent of the stars in the sky will have a planet upon which an advanced civilization resides." On this basis, he calculated an average distance of several hundred light-years between advanced civilizations. If aliens sent us a signal during, say, Galileo's trial in the seventeenth century, we should receive it soon.

The Miller-Urey experiment implies that organic molecules are common in the cosmos. However, this does not guarantee the cosmic pervasiveness of life, much less intelligence. The Green Bank conferees confronted the question: On how many planets have biomolecules evolved into intelligent creatures who are able and willing to build radios for interstellar signaling? This question was hard to answer in 1961 and is not much easier to answer today, because we have few good answers for another question: How did intelligence emerge on Earth? And was its emergence inevitable, or a fluke unlikely to be repeated again elsewhere? If terrestrial life ended tomorrow, then reemerged and evolved over billions of years, would a new form of intelligence emerge? Or are we simply evolutionary accidents, from now-broken molds? Evolutionary biologists tend to favor the "fluke" argument. Hence some of them (Ernst Mayr, G. G. Simpson, and others) have publicly opposed SETI as a waste of time.[76] An argument in their favor is that only one intelligent species, *Homo sapiens*, has ever inhabited Earth.

Really? Not everyone agrees. The "hit of the conference," Drake recalls, was a speech by John C. Lilly.[77] He argued that Earth has at least one other intelligent species—dolphins.

A neuroscientist by training, Lilly is one of the strangest characters in modern American science. His offbeat career has inspired at least two major films about unorthodox scientists (*The Day of the Dolphin*, starring George C. Scott, and *Altered States*, with William Hurt). In the 1950s, Lilly conducted news-making research on brainwashing to simulate how North Koreans psychologically abused American soldiers. He described how he experienced hallucinations when he placed himself inside watery "isolation tanks."[78] More celebrated was his research on dolphins at a Virgin Islands laboratory bankrolled by the U.S. Navy (which was interested in using the creatures for military purposes—hauling underwater bombs, for example[79]). Lilly maintained that dolphins were intelligent beings with brain structures similar to those of humans. They had a "language"—clicks, squeaks, grunts; he "talked" to them. At the time of the Green Bank conference, Lilly's book *Man and Dolphin* (1961) was drawing international attention, and *Life* magazine profiled him.

Dolphin intelligence, if real, would contradict the assumption of many anthropologists and paleontologists that humans acquired intelligence via toolmaking. Dolphins lack the limbs to make and manipulate tools; nor do they need them in their watery paradises. If Lilly was right, then the emergence of intelligence might be more common, less context-specific, than generally assumed. Just as the Miller-Urey experiment implied that building blocks of life form easily, Lilly's work hinted that intelligence is more than a one-time miracle. If it arose twice—in radically different environments—on Earth, then the evolutionary "fluke" argument fell apart. Intelligence might be a routine galactic phenomenon, after all.

At Green Bank, the other conferees were so impressed by Lilly that they dubbed their little group the "Order of the Dolphin." Each attendee received a little pin sporting an image of a dolphin.[80]

In the 1960s or early 1970s (the exact date is unclear), Sagan visited Lilly's lab and swam with the dolphins. He also tried out one of Lilly's isolation tanks. (So did the physicist Richard Feynman, who, Lilly recalls, "gave me one of his books and wrote in it: 'Thank you, Dr. Lilly, for the hallucinations.'"[81]) In his best-selling book *The Cosmic Connection* (1973), Sagan included a chapter about his experiences with the dolphins, in which he was not entirely uncritical of Lilly's research.[82] The chapter is one of Sagan's most relaxed, self-revealing essays; he describes these endearing creatures in almost sensuous terms. (Throughout Sagan's life, he wrote about animals more affectionately, less ham-handedly, than he wrote about living people.) Lilly now recalls how Sagan visited the Caribbean lab "two, three times. I liked him very much. He had a good sense of humor."[83]

Lilly's admirers were less charmed by his subsequent career. He began taking mind-altering drugs and wrote strange, sometimes incomprehensible books about his experiences. His dolphin research, once so acclaimed, fell into disfavor and is now largely ignored. "We've come to realize [dolphins] are *not* intelligent,"[84] Drake now says.

Now in his mid-eighties and living in Hawaii, Lilly claims that he has psychically communicated with extraterrestrials via drugs. The extraterrestrials—"transcendent beyond-humans," he calls them—inhabit "other dimensions." When asked to describe these mental communications with aliens, he amicably declined, explaining that they are impossible to express in words. "It's like trying to experience what happens in orgasm. Try to put *that* in language!"

He recalled that when Sagan visited the Caribbean laboratory, he declined to take drugs. "I was into LSD at the time and he didn't want to take that. LSD is pretty powerful stuff." Nor would Sagan try ketamine, an anesthetic that is Lilly's drug of choice for his flotation-tank "experiments." Lilly attributes Sagan's refusal to take drugs to his careerist personality: he was one of those people who is "still on the executive ladder,[85] trying to climb it. And they don't want to get off the ladder!" As we shall see, Sagan was less straitlaced than Lilly thought.

By the late 1970s, Sagan stopped referring to Lilly in his writings. He repeatedly mentions dolphins in his 1977 best-seller about the brain, *The Dragons of Eden*, but Lilly's name is absent.

Lilly's strange decline epitomized that of a not terribly uncommon personality type of the late twentieth century, the once-capable scientist who, tired of the rigors of cold, hard reason, begins to dip into pseudoscience and mysticism. Some, like J. Allen Hynek, apparently enjoyed their late-life ventures into the irrational and were little the worse for it. Others ended up going off the deep end, philosophically speaking—Lilly, Timothy Leary, Brian O'Leary, James McDonald (about whom more later). Sagan knew this last set of people—fairly well, in the cases of Lilly and O'Leary. Their disappearance into uncharted waters may have reinforced Sagan's anxiety about the future of science and reason, an anxiety that he expressed in one of his last books, *The Demon-Haunted World*.[86] He might have wondered: If capable scientists could drift so far from common sense, what hope was there for civilization?

Still, Lilly's work also encouraged Sagan to ponder a less gloomy question: Are any animals "conscious"? And "intelligent"? If so, do they deserve legal "rights" akin to ours? He never forgot the dolphins' happy-sounding chatter as they cavorted in Lilly's sunlit pools. When Nick Sagan was a little boy, his father took him to Sea World and showed him the dolphin tank. Nick recalls how his father grinned like a child and expertly imitated their sounds—the eeks, the grunts, the squeaks. Embarrassed, Nick slapped his forehead and said, "Oh, Dad!"

"He didn't mind doing that at all," says Nick, now approaching thirty. "It was very sweet, in a way. . . . He never lost a very, very strong connection with himself as a kid."[87]

BUT SUPPOSE LILLY'S DOLPHINS are intelligent: So what? Even if they're intelligent, they lack the manipulative skills to make tools; they probably lack the will, too. Perhaps almost all civilizations in the heavens are pre-, non-, or anti-technological. Maybe technological civilizations, like ours, are the exception to the rule; everyone else in the galaxy has the common sense to skip the industrial revolution, the communications revolution, and the computer revolution. Maybe most aliens live in extra-terrestrial caves, subsist off the fruits of the land, and are as happy as chipmunks. Their cultures might be an astro-anthropologist's thrill: artistic, philosophical, fascinating—but nontechnological. No technology, hence no radio. Therefore we'll never discover them and they'll never discover us.[88]

Except, perhaps, by one means—by what Sagan called "direct contact." By starship.

Around 1960, almost all scientists regarded flight to the stars as effectively impossible, period. The stars were simply too far away to be reached in tolerable periods of time.[89] The major problem was Einstein's cosmic speed limit.[90] No physical object can reach or exceed the speed of light, 186,000 miles per second. Do the math: In a year, a beam of light travels one light-year (six trillion miles). The nearest star is four light-years away. Hence the fastest conceivable spaceship could not reach that star, Proxima Centauri, for at least four years. Galactic civilizations are probably an average of hundreds or thousands of light-years apart; therefore face-to-face contact with aliens would entail centuries of travel. And that's assuming humans could build a rocket able to fly almost as fast as light, hardly a safe assumption! As the Nobel Prize–winning physicist Edward Purcell said in the 1960s: "All this stuff about traveling around the universe in space suits . . . belongs back where it came from, on the cereal box."[91]

By contrast, Sagan was the first distinguished American scientist to defend publicly, and in detail, the possibility of interstellar travel. He did so in an article, "Direct Contact among Galactic Civilizations by Relativistic Interstellar Spaceflight," in 1963. Radio communication, he wrote, was far inferior to the goal of interstellar travel, because only with the latter would we be able to communicate with any technically unsophisticated cultures or be able to gather biological specimens. In other writings, he discussed possible types of starships—among others, Robert W. Bussard's interstellar "ramjet," which would fuel its thermonuclear engines by sucking in hydrogen gas from space.[92] Starships traveling close to the speed of light would benefit from Einstein's principle of time dilation: on-board time would slow down. A crew bound for the Andromeda galaxy would age only three decades before arriving there.[93]

"I believe that interstellar spaceflight at relativistic velocities to the farthest reaches of our Galaxy is a feasible objective for humanity," Sagan wrote. "And if this is the case, other civilizations, aeons more advanced

than ours, must today be plying the spaces between the stars." He estimated (based on various questionable assumptions) that each star in the
galaxy is visited an average of once every 100,000 years. And each star
with intelligent life receives alien visitors every 10,000 years, which
raises the question: Have aliens visited Earth during the last 10,000
years? And if so, did they leave evidence of their arrival? Ancient legends
might contain clues of past alien visits, he said. He also proposed that
aliens might have left "some kind of base" in our solar system, possibly
on the Moon. "Forthcoming high resolution photographic reconnaissance of the Moon from space vehicles—particularly of the back side—
might bear these possibilities in mind."[94]

Sagan no longer took seriously the possibility that UFOs were alien
vessels. However, he was intrigued by suggestions (made by Russian
writers in the late 1950s) that extraterrestrials might have visited Earth
in the distant past. Perhaps an alien probe's arrival is recorded in untrans-
lated inscriptions on the walls of ancient temples. Long fascinated by
mythology, Sagan wondered if ancient myths contain hints of alien
encounters with humans.

Such speculation "appalled" Sagan's friend and colleague Stanley
Miller. "It raises the question of whether he is a serious guy,"[95] he said
decades later. Even the gentle Frank Drake looks back on Sagan's speculation about ancient astronauts and acknowledges that it "was not good
science."[96] A few Sagan-watchers apparently wondered if he had truly
abandoned his youthful fascination with UFOs. Did he still harbor secret
hopes that the aliens are overhead in their silver ships, awaiting an oppor-
tune time to land?[97]

SAGAN'S SPECULATIONS about prehistoric alien visitors, the terraforming of Venus, and interstellar flight seriously threatened to mar his
already somewhat exotic reputation. One way to avoid being perceived as
a crank is to attack those whose views are even more outlandish. This
may explain why, in 1962, he decided to go public with his skepticism
about UFOs. At age twenty-seven, he testified as an expert witness in the
trial of a UFO hoaxer charged with defrauding elderly women.

For legal reasons, Sagan's published account of the trial does not use
the real name (Reinhold Schmidt) of the defendant. Instead, Sagan
referred to him by a pseudonym, "Helmut Winckler." The account displays Sagan's literary traits—his playfulness, his clear prose, his ability to
interweave speculation and solid science. At times the essay is too cute;
he sounds a little too pleased with his own puckish erudition, like Henry
Higgins commenting wittily on the ill-spoken unwashed. Still, the article
(published in a 1966 book) gives an early sense of his engaging personal-

ity, a combination of the professorial and the boyish.[98]

Sagan became involved in the trial in the spring of 1962, when the Alameda County district attorney's office phoned the Berkeley astronomy department. The caller was seeking an "expert witness," Sagan recalled, to testify in the criminal trial of Schmidt, "who claimed repeated contact with inhabitants of the planet Saturn. . . . With considerable wry amusement, and professional asides, the message was conveyed to me." Sagan agreed to testify.

The stocky, soft-spoken, sixty-four-year-old Schmidt ("Winckler") had once sold agricultural implements in Nebraska. (He had since moved to Bakersfield, California, where he was a grain buyer.) On the stand, he described how he had driven through Nebraska in 1957 and encountered "a parked flying saucer." From it emerged "several men and women—of exceedingly human appearance—dressed in flowing robes and speaking mellifluously." Their purpose: to help humanity and save it from atomic destruction.

The aliens later let Schmidt board their saucer, then flew him over the Arctic Circle and to the bottom of the ocean. There, he saw Soviet missiles poised for firing. The aliens mentioned that they had recently done Earthlings a great favor. The planetary axis had begun to tilt, threatening to mess up seasons; so the UFOnauts straightened it out. "You don't know what a sigh of relief I breathed," Schmidt told the court.

The latter claim intrigued Sagan. During a break, he asked Schmidt how the terrestrial axis could tilt without astronomers noticing that the stars were out of position. Schmidt replied "that he could hardly be held responsible for statements made by the inhabitants of Saturn."

Schmidt also described a saucer flight to the Egyptian pyramids. The aliens mentioned that one of their colleagues, presumed by Schmidt to be Jesus Christ, had come to Earth millennia before. They also took Schmidt to visit a southern California mine containing a very special kind of quartz: it cured cancer. "Soon after landing," Sagan wrote, Schmidt "was selling quartz stock. I have the distinct impression that he sold half interests in the mine—many, many half interests." Schmidt's investors included "elderly, wealthy widows," some of whom he romanced.

The assistant district attorney called Sagan to the stand. The purpose: to provide scientific evidence against the thesis that Saturnian beings would (like Schmidt's purported aliens) resemble *Homo sapiens*. Sagan described how astronomers used spectroscopes and thermocouples to ascertain the chemical composition and temperatures of celestial objects. Saturn's atmosphere has no oxygen and a great deal of methane and ammonia, gases that can kill humans. The Saturnian temperature is hundreds of degrees below zero Fahrenheit, obviously too cold for humans. Furthermore, Saturn's gravity is 17 percent greater than Earth's. (Sagan explained how physicists know this, based on Saturn's radius and mass.) Hence: "Any beings which evolved there would probably be much squatter than we." Besides, it was hard to believe that after four billion years of evolution, humans and Saturnians would have evolved in the same direction. (As mentioned earlier, Sagan regarded evolution as mainly divergent, not convergent.)

Cross-examination followed. The defense attorney began by asking Sagan if it wasn't true (which, in fact, it is not) that centuries ago, "university scientists like yourself" thought Earth was flat. The assistant district attorney objected to the question—it sought "hearsay evidence." Sustained. The defense lawyer then asked Sagan how he knew that the same physical laws work on Saturn as on Earth. "Suddenly," Sagan observed, "in a proceeding for fraud in a California criminal court, we had plunged into one of the basic questions in the philosophy of science." He tried to explain why the spectral lines were trustworthy and why it was reasonable to think that Newton's laws applied to Saturn as they do to Earth. "Glancing over to the jury, however, I had the distinct impression that the seed of doubt had been planted. I could imagine them thinking: After all, maybe the physical laws *are* different on Saturn. How does anyone know?" The defense attorney also cleverly got Sagan to admit that the temperatures measured for Saturn were of its *outer* atmosphere. The interior atmosphere might be warmer, and have a more hospitable chemical composition.

Sagan disagreed; based "on various chemical equilibrium grounds," he doubted that the chemical composition was substantially different. "I said that there is such an overabundance of hydrogen in the upper atmosphere of Saturn that it would instantly react with any of the oxygen around; that some estimate could be made of the abundance of hydrogen in the lower atmosphere; that oxygen was expected to be absent on theoretical grounds; and that the body of Saturn was believed to be at least in part metallic hydrogen. I thought it was highly unlikely that free molecular oxygen existed at the surface of Saturn.

"The defense attorney replied, 'but these are indirect arguments, aren't they? You don't really *know* there's no oxygen on Saturn.' I could only agree that the evidence was indirect.

"I felt, however, that science often proceeds on indirect evidence and that the conclusions still had substantial reliability."

A San Francisco paper alluded to Schmidt's romantic liaisons with his victims, and paraphrased Sagan as saying that Saturn "is too cold for warm sentiment by any measurement."[99] The Oakland newspaper, which reported the case in detail, buried at the end of one story the note that "The state produced Dr. Carl C. [*sic*] Sagan, University of California astronomer and National Academy of Science[s] consultant, to testify on the composition of multi-ringed Saturn. That planet, the savant said, contained noxious gases in such quantity that a human being could survive for only a brief period."[100]

After three hours and fifteen minutes of deliberation, the jury reached its judgment: Guilty. On November 17, 1961, Schmidt was sentenced to one to ten years in state prison for grand theft.[101] A decade earlier, Sagan had been a young UFO enthusiast. Now he was a UFO basher. Just in time, too. When Schmidt's attorney compared scientists to flat-earthers, he was anticipating the future. In years to come, both the sophisticated and the unsophisticated would begin to question science's claim to omniscience, to superiority over other modes of understanding. When that time came, Sagan would return to the front line, to defend scientific reason as the royal road to Truth.

6

Harvard

BEFORE THE OPERA, an unsteady rumble emanates from the orchestra. The musicians are warming up. How they pluck, tinkle, and groan at their instruments, with vigor or with melancholy, may foreshadow the show itself, its arc and outcome. Likewise, transient episodes in a man's life may tell us everything vital about him, good and bad; and they may foreshadow the days that remain. In Carl Sagan's life, that period fell between 1962 and 1968. It began with his welcome to Harvard, the Mount Olympus of academia. It ended with his effective expulsion six years later.

Prior to 1962, he was a fast-ascending minor star of the space age. He was almost Kennedyesque—witty, handsome, engaging company. A stellar teacher, too: students could not take their eyes off him. He wrote like an angel. True, he proposed exotic ideas—about interstellar travel, radio chats with extraterrestrials, even possible alien visits recorded in ancient myths and crypts. And he could be abrasive, almost disrespectful. But (colleagues reasoned) he was very young. Surely he would mature, mellow with age. One could imagine him becoming an elder statesman of science—a Vannevar Bush, a James Conant.

He had no plans, however, to become a Bush or a Conant, an Ivy Leaguish, pipe-smoking insider whose goals jibed snugly with those of the postwar power elite. Sagan was an outsider—a dreamer, a Jew, a leftist, an unashamed careerist and showman. He talked to the people, not to elites. He belonged on stage, not in smoke-filled congressional hearings on the science budget. Many years later, Sagan's enemies would mistake him for a technocrat, a guru of "scientism"; but that was his camouflage. Underneath, he was a scientific messiah. He saw space exploration as an evolutionary leap forward, not merely as the latest feint in the chess game of superpowers. Despite his business-suit demeanor, Sagan was

136

more like an artist or a rabbi or a hippie. His concerns were transcendental. Aliens like gods! Relativistic travel to Andromeda, and beyond! Sagan was one of those rare people who measure time in centuries, millennia, and geological layers, not in fiscal years, obsessing on futuristic possibilities they surely won't live to see. How could such a man settle for a life that offered merely power and respectability?

THE INVITATION FROM MOUNT OLYMPUS came while Sagan was still in California, entangled in pet projects and a failing marriage. He had his hands full. Margulis felt he was insensitive and self-absorbed, and she complained about his neglect of household duties. Meanwhile, he struggled to become a great scientist. He simultaneously tried to design an instrument for an astronomical balloon, to resolve a key puzzle in the origin of life, to work with the *Mariner 2* team, to reassess the possibility of life on Mars, to advise RAND Corporation, and to propound way-out notions ranging from interstellar flight to the search for alien intelligence. He also wrote articles, talked to reporters, ventured into the science-publishing business, simulated microbial life on Mars, lectured at Berkeley, and brainstormed with Joshua Lederberg. Also, he defended his embattled "greenhouse" theory of Venus, which was at this point "embarrassingly crude," he later admitted.

Sagan's Venus work attracted his first major scientific adversary: E. J. Öpik. A cantankerous stutterer and native of Estonia, Öpik had spent much of his career on the run, first from the Bolsheviks, then from the Nazis. He finally settled at Armagh Observatory in Ireland and published his *Irish Astronomical Journal*.[1] It included Öpik's articles on popular astronomy, whose fans included future popularizer Sagan, who later recalled how eagerly he waited for each new issue. Sagan greatly admired Öpik, partly for anticipating findings about stellar evolution twenty years before they were widely confirmed, and partly for what Sagan saw as Öpik's courage. At a Berkeley meeting of the International Astronomical Union in 1961, Sagan was impressed by the way Öpik stood up to the Soviet delegates. "[H]e felt he had to condemn them for being Stalinist lackeys! It was amazing," he later recalled.[2]

Naturally, Sagan was distressed to discover that Öpik disliked Sagan's greenhouse theory of Venus. Venus didn't have enough carbon dioxide and water vapor to explain the great heat, Öpik insisted. His alternative was the "aeolosphere" hypothesis. In this "dust bowl" model of the Venusian atmosphere, nonstop dust storms scour the planet. The particles (supposedly calcium and magnesium carbonates) rub together; their friction generates the high temperature. Nonetheless, with elderly noblesse oblige, Öpik praised Sagan's "very stimulating and imaginative article" on Venus, which appeared in the March 1961 issue of *Science*.[3]

Sagan's Venus writings also impressed two of the nation's leading astronomers, Donald Menzel and Fred Whipple, both at Harvard. This is especially striking because Sagan's work threatened to undermine an alluring theory they had first championed in 1955—that Venus is covered by a global ocean.[4] Sagan, on the contrary, maintained that Venus was too hot for an ocean; any water would boil into the atmosphere.

According to an oft-quoted dictum of the physicist Max Born (one that dimly anticipated the modern debate between scientists and Postmodernist scholars), science progresses only when old scientists die out and the young whippersnappers take over. If one takes Born literally, then power (in particular, the ultimate form of power—the power of the living over the dead), not reason, decides scientific debates. This is sometimes true, but not always. Menzel and Whipple, for example, reacted to Sagan's theory in a highly un-Bornian manner. Not only did they not take Sagan's disagreement personally, but they asked him to come to Harvard to give a colloquium on planetary research. He did, and then they offered him joint posts at Harvard and at Smithsonian Astrophysical Observatory.

Most scholars would have fallen on their knees in gratitude. Not Sagan. He was cooler. To him, every opportunity offered another opportunity. He told Menzel and Whipple that he "wouldn't accept anything less than assistant professor. I don't know why I said that, but I did." They were startled, and assured him that "lecturer" was a very distinguished title at Harvard. After all, it was *Harvard!* Even the great geophysicist Harold Jeffreys had been a Harvard lecturer! *Harold Jeffreys!* But Sagan stuck to his guns, and they gave in. Fine, they would make him an assistant professor.[5] First, though, Whipple sought approval from Harvard president Nathan Pusey. He wrote to Pusey that Sagan was "an extraordinarily able young man." Despite Sagan's youth (he had completed his Ph.D. only a year and a half earlier), Sagan would "add substantially to the scientific strength" of the department.

Pusey approved the appointment,[6] and Menzel relayed the good news to Sagan in California. On February 26, 1962, Sagan formally accepted the Harvard job with one understanding: he would not start work in Cambridge until early 1963. In the meantime, he would take a leave of absence from Harvard to extend his stay in California. With luck, this would give him extra time to finish his scientific research, perhaps even to save his marriage. Fate took a different turn, however. In the late afternoon of his California idyll, he would face the first major humiliations of his adult life, the first hints that he was not all he appeared or wished to be.

ASTRONOMERS HAVE LONG YEARNED to escape Earth's atmosphere. Its turbulence and smog obscure celestial bodies, mess up spectra, and block important wavelengths of light; that is why stars twinkle, and why Percival Lowell built his observatory in the hills near Flagstaff. After World War II, Lyman Spitzer Jr. envisioned launching telescopes into orbit; there, they could observe the cosmos unhindered.[7] Before that great day came, though, astronomers such as John Strong would use balloons and airplanes to ferry telescopes above most of the atmosphere. One such project was Stratoscope, a balloon carrying a robotic telescope. The project had been managed since 1957 by Martin Schwarzschild and other astronomers at Princeton.

During Sagan's Miller Fellowship at Chicago, he traveled east for his first winter holiday and visited Princeton. There, he persuaded the Schwarzschild team to fly an infrared detector on the flight of Stratoscope II. Sagan pointed out that the first robotic space probes were scheduled to fly by Mars about 1963. Conceivably, the balloon-borne instrument might detect Martian organic molecules akin to those reported by William Sinton from his ground-based observations. The Princeton scientists were enthusiastic, and Sagan agreed to develop the spectrograph.

Seeking the right infrared detector, Sagan and Frank Drake visited Frank Low's lab at Texas Instruments near Dallas. Low was developing a new infrared detector using germanium and published details of his work in a late-1961 issue of the *Journal of the Optical Society of America.* "Frank Drake and Carl Sagan, who was just a young whippersnapper at the time, were very interested," Low later recalled. "Carl's thing at the moment was that if we had a good enough infrared detector we could probably beat the Russians to the discovery of life on Mars."[8]

But Sagan dropped the ball. For whatever reason—his failing marriage, a crushing workload—"he just would not follow through and see that the instrument got designed and built," recalls Peter Vandervoort, later associate chair of the astronomy department at the University of Chicago. "I know the people at Princeton were very unhappy with the working relationship. [They felt] that Carl had let them down."[9]

Fortunately, Sagan's colleagues at the University of California stepped in and developed the spectrograph. In 1963 it was launched into the stratosphere aboard Stratoscope II. At 78,000 feet the infrared telescope acquired a "crude spectrum of Mars," Low said, but it saw no organic molecules.[10]

"This," Vandervoort concludes, "is an example of Carl at his very best and worst." At his best, Sagan had the ability to make connections, to identify good goals, to recognize opportunities. And at his worst—well, in Vandervoort's words, Sagan's failure to follow through "made him unpopular with his associates." He paused and corrected himself: "'Unpopular' is too strong a word. But he was not as well regarded as he might have been, because he did not look after details."[11] His personality was revealing yet another contradiction—a tendency to let details slip, while he insisted (in certain cases) on near-tyrannical control of everything.

Later, Sagan wrote to Kuiper to explain what had gone wrong in California, confessing that he had tried to do too much.[12] He did not, however, mention one crucial development: his marriage was disintegrating.

Margulis had reached the end of her rope. Early in the marriage, she recalls, "what I learned very quickly was that if I didn't want to have fights, [then] don't criticize him . . . and I learned to do *everything*—to do the bills, to do the laundry, to clean the house, to take the children to preschool . . . the dog . . . the garden . . . to do *all* the cooking—he never cooked anything—[and] to do all the cleaning up *after* the cooking." Still, life wasn't all bad at their handsome East Bay home, with its spectacular view of San Francisco Bay—the kind of view that Sagan loved. Some Russian guests who visited were so impressed that they asked the young Sagans: "You can live in this house? *You* people?!" And Sagan wanted to save the marriage, Margulis recalls. Toward the end—she thinks it was in Palo Alto—"he took me out when I told him I was leaving him. . . . We were walking on the street and he told me how I was crazy because he was such an important person, and he was going to be much *more* important, and that I was really married to a fantastic guy and I was crazy to even think about leaving."[13] It was a very Saganish sales pitch—big on career, tongue-tied on love.

But his mood darkened as he juggled more and more responsibilities. During one particularly paranoid moment, Margulis recalls, he questioned the paternity of their second child, Jeremy. (The accusation seems even more ludicrous now than it did then: Jeremy bears a startling resemblance to Sagan.) The accusation enraged Margulis: "He has *questioned* the paternity of that child!" she exclaimed almost four decades later when recalling the insult. "Does he *look* like Carl? . . . He's a hundred percent Carl, right? And only *Carl* could question the paternity of that kid." She says Sagan "was jealous of his children from the time they were born."

It got worse. "He hit me a few times," Margulis recalls. "My sister got furious when she found out. But I used to protect him—I would never tell. I wouldn't! I was a good person; I [didn't] believe a good person [would] tell things like that. And he did it out of his own total frustration—emotional ambivalence and frustration and lack of control and stuff like that. It was bad."[14] In late 1962, Margulis left, when Jeremy was two and Dorion was three and a half. For a few months they stayed with

Sagan's cousins Eugene and Arlene Sagan, who lived in Berkeley. Margulis filed for divorce at the Alameda County courthouse.

Margulis recalls her mother's reaction: "Oh Lynnie, how can you do it? He's finally making a living, he's finally not a student anymore, you've got these gorgeous children, you have a nice house. How can you leave him? How can you think about leaving him?" Margulis was clearly hurt— "I felt so betrayed by that," she recalls.

To this day, Margulis has violently mixed feelings about her first husband. On the one hand, after his death she and Dorion dedicated their book *Slanted Truths* (1997) to Sagan. She happily showed me numerous color photos of her visiting him in the early 1990s—looking affectionately toward him—at his sickbed in Seattle.

And she partly credits him for the start of her brilliant scientific career. "I learned about the four bases of DNA and all that from him." In her 1998 book, *Symbiotic Planet*, she writes: "Convinced, in part by Carl, that inheritance phenomena would ultimately succumb to a unique chemical explanation, I thought the science of genetics would give us the best clue to how evolution works."[15] She had only a "liberal arts no-major" from the University of Chicago and so was "shocked" to be accepted by the biology department at Madison in 1958. There, while Sagan slaved on his doctoral dissertation at Yerkes, she studied cell biology and genetics. From there she would go on to one of the most dazzling and controversial careers in modern biology.

On the other hand, she recalls many dissatisfactions with Sagan as a husband. He had "limited capacity for any kind of personal relationship. . . . What we have as personal relationships, he had to have with a television audience. He had to have ten thousand people all adulating him to make up for that fear that his mother was going to leave him. . . . He was a better speaker than he was a listener. And he never listened to anything on any kind of emotional level, at all. . . . He was just noticeably untouched—untouched and untouchable—about anything like that."[16]

His crowded career made him tense, and Margulis didn't always soothe him. She spoke her mind, which Sagan—proud, prim—didn't always appreciate. The noted astrophysicist A. G. W. Cameron says colleagues told him that Sagan would speak at a conference, "and Lynn would stand up and criticize the hell out of it in the meeting. That could not help but be a cause of friction."[17] Sagan was chronically late for appointments (he disliked wearing a watch). Frank Drake recalls one meeting where Sagan was scheduled to speak; naturally, he was late. This was after the divorce, and Margulis was in the audience. Finally Sagan rushed in and Margulis announced, loudly: "Hey! *There's* the father of my children!"[18]

She also dismissed his deepest interest: extraterrestrial life. When they married, she told him "there's nothing to be said about it because you don't have any data one way or another. . . . I guess I thought it was silly." Her present view is that communication with aliens is probably hopeless. Of the tens of millions of species on Earth, she says, "almost none of them communicate with each other . . . and we have *a hundred percent* of our chemistry in common." So how likely are we to communicate with aliens who don't share our biochemistry? She also speculates that Sagan's desire to believe in aliens was partly psychological, linked in some vague way to his relationship with his mother. "This desperate need, this mother/extraterrestrial need," she called it.[19]

After the divorce, she discovered Sagan's teenage notebook, in which he had waxed so excitedly about evolution and extraterrestrial life. About a year after the divorce, in 1963, she wrote sarcastically in the same notebook about her postmarital attitude toward the teenager Sagan (the spelling and punctuation have been left intact):

> It almost seems blasphemous, sacreligious to contaminate that purity of [teenage Carl's] logical thought with mundane, modern chatter. . . . It is remarkably revealing to see how fundamentally imperturbable he has been in these [approximately] 13 years since then, and how refined! His most recent papers, emanating from the authority of his Harvard title of Assist. Prof are on production of adenosine triphosphate under primitive earth conditions and intelligent extraterrestrial life. What has compelled him to travel the unbroken path in a search for 'ultramundane' [extraterrestrial] life? I wonder.

Margulis's written remarks also describe the teenage boy's "pomposity": "how easy it is to spot the insecurity, the groping and the pseudoness of that poor young author. The handwriting may have been slightly more open then, the mind also?" She also cites a quality that would later enrage Sagan's second wife (and some colleagues)—his relentless logic.

> How naive I was so few years later to hang on [Carl's] each expertly delivered phrase and mistake my curiosity and open eagerness for the ignorance that he accussed [*sic*] me of in so many bitter nightly scenes. Did I ever really love such a man? He seems to suffer that enormous defensive burden—like our present [United States military] "defense posture" [which,] although miserably troublesome[,] we are unable to abandon . . . for economic and historical reason. From the vantage point of so many years and improved education (not wit or intelligence) it is so clear how emotionally based his "logic" or erudition was—and how desperately needed. The fascinating thing was then, and is now, how extraordinary [is] the single mindedness of [his] purpose. In all these years he has picked up nearly no new interest; caution has been

superimposed by the repercussions of critical colleagues—not by intrinsic direct observations. Poor Carl. How easily deluded we are. . . .

. . . Is it true, as it so seems, that no love (as I've [heard?] it subsequently from so many) flowed from Carl Sagan to me? Surely I felt it for him—in my state of mental imprisonment I must have even showed it toward him, not unbegrudgingly. As I look back . . . I think . . . our marriage was as sophomoric as Carls little essay.

So there she was, a young woman with two children, no husband, and a career barely beginning. What would become of her? She wrote in the notebook:

My Jeremy lies here restless, picking at his eyes. He has a cold, & perhaps pink eye. I see his attractive face & body and my whole self cries out with protective love. He is so incredibly bright and healthy now too. The thought of any suffering, the fantasies of losing these dear boys fills me with gushes of anguish. . . . Dorion is restlessly awake.[20]

THE DIVORCE WAS ALSO very difficult for Sagan. A striking testament to the distress it caused him is a memo he wrote to himself after Margulis had filed for divorce. The memo is titled "Lynn's present difficulties." (An arrow pointed at her name adds: "and mine, and mine.") This memo shows that Sagan was deeply troubled by Margulis's decision to leave him, aware that he was at least partly to blame, and hopeful that he might be able to salvage the marriage if he took certain steps. In his characteristic logical fashion, he first lists what he sees as the main reasons that Margulis has decided to leave him. Then he lists positive steps he can take to convince her to change her mind. Among the reasons he cites for her decision to leave is his "authoritarian belittlement" of her during their eight-year relationship. The memo expresses a striking degree of self-criticism and anger at himself for his behavior during the marriage. At one point, he refers to himself as "you asshole." He also engages in a certain amount of self-psychoanalysis, speculating, for example, that he has the ability to project onto another person in his life some of his own "odious" traits. He is upset with himself for not being able to express to Margulis how much he loves her. One factor in the breakup, he notes, is what she perceived as their son Dorion's "abandonment anxieties" (an apparent allusion to her belief that Sagan had not been an attentive enough father).

The memo indicates that Margulis's friends and some family members were advising her to leave. It also illustrates the difficulty of competing career demands in a two-career academic family: Sagan cites his imminent departure for Harvard and the pressure that he was putting on

Margulis to finish her own Ph.D. degree in an unreasonably short period of time as additional sources of stress.

Sagan was an inveterate optimist all his life, though, and the memo expresses his determination to make things work out. He tells himself not to force the issue right away by taking any immediate legal action. He points out that his move to Harvard might actually be a good thing, because life on the Cambridge campus would help stabilize their lives. He also notes that Margulis might get a position at nearby Brandeis University, where research related to her interests was under way.

The most revealing aspect of the memo, however, is this: his admission that as much as he wants to save their marriage, he is still unable to tell Margulis how much he loves her. He admits to himself that this may be due to his fear that she will reject him and leave anyway. Of all Carl Sagan's writings, this agonizing private memo best conveys the contradictory warring forces within him, the troubling mix of intense emotion and stark rationalism.

DECADES LATER, Sagan blamed the divorce for his having worked only "fitfully" on *Mariner 2*.[21] Here he was, a lifelong space fanatic, privileged to work on the first successful interplanetary mission—and yet he puts in only limited energy. As his stress level increased, he dreaded the occurrence of episodes of his achalasia, which he was all too aware might one day choke him to death.

He confided his feelings to his old friend Ronald Blum. "Carl was really prostrate. He was shattered; he promised to change," Blum recalls. "I remember driving in a car around Berkeley with Carl, and him talking about how desperate he was to keep his family together. I became convinced he really, really loved her." Blum tried to mediate; he spoke at length to Margulis, assuring her, "Carl really loves you." She reacted "noncommittally."[22]

Saul Landau did not consider Sagan an intimate friend. But after the marriage dissolved, Sagan called him up and they saw each other a few times. Landau felt he was "hand-holding" the distraught Sagan. "We had a couple of dinners together. He was having some problem swallowing, he took forever to chew. He took very tiny bites. Whether this was 'in his head,' I don't know. He was also very upset about the breakup. What was he going to do with his life?"[23]

WORK. WHEN ALL ELSE FAILS, there is work. And for Sagan, there was no lack of work in the early 1960s, as *Mariner 2* slid toward Venus. In those otherwise miserable years, he enjoyed more "big breaks" than most scientists enjoy in a lifetime. The biggest break led him, via the RAND Corporation, to the publishing post that would make him one of the most influential figures in planetary science.

It need not have happened. Life is so chancy: might his have been radically different if he hadn't encountered Lynn Alexander, his future wife, on that staircase in the mid-1950s? Consider this chain of events: Lynn's subsequent study at the University of Wisconsin might, conceivably, have triggered his encounter with Lederberg; who, in turn, made Sagan an adviser to the Space Science Board, nominated him for the all-important Miller Fellowship, and introduced him to the man who would publish Sagan's historic book (with I. S. Shklovskii) on extraterrestrial life. In June 1960, the same board held a "Conference on Planetary Atmospheres" in Arcadia, California, where Sagan met W. W. Kellogg. Kellogg was a pioneer in the use of satellites for space science and a researcher at RAND Corporation in Santa Monica; together they wrote a seminal report on the atmospheres of Venus and Mars. In turn, while Sagan was at RAND, he met A. G. Wilson, who was starting a new space science journal, *Icarus*. Wilson invited Sagan on board as an associate editor. Six years later, Sagan would become editor in chief of that same publication, the preeminent journal of American planetary science. Much of Sagan's subsequent scientific prestige stemmed from his editorship of *Icarus* until the late 1970s (when he quit to become a TV star).

A glorious fate. Would it have happened if Sagan hadn't encountered Lynn Alexander on that staircase? Perhaps; perhaps not. Given his chutz-pah, he probably would have met Lederberg sooner or later. But soon enough? Timing is everything. Shortly after their encounter, Lederberg won the Nobel and took off for California. Had they not met when they did, perhaps they wouldn't have met at all. Or perhaps they would have met, but not until years later, by which time the national hysteria over *Sputnik* had faded. Having missed Lederberg, perhaps Sagan would have remained in Madison, fallen in love with its cultural riches and book-stores, and become planetarium director at some Midwestern science museum, there to remain for decades, never to become an international celebrity. Who knows?

But enough speculation. In real life, during the time he was in Cali-fornia, Sagan did end up working at RAND, meeting Kellogg and Wil-son, and becoming an associate editor of *Icarus*. Sagan's work with RAND (which stands for Research ANd Development) is another example of his youthful willingness to rub elbows with the military. Funded by the U.S. Air Force, RAND was the brains behind U.S. nuclear weapons strategy. (In Stanley Kubrick's antiwar film *Dr. Strangelove*, RAND was parodied as the "BLAND Corporation."[24]) RAND helped pick Soviet "targets"—industries, ports, train depots, bridges, bomber bases, perhaps cities—for hypothetical nuclear wars. Also, RAND luminaries such as Bernard Brodie and Herman Kahn speculated about ways to fight "limited" nuclear wars, wars in which each superpower would launch only a few nukes at a time, hoping to negotiate a truce before unleashing an all-out, planet-destroying holocaust.[25] Officially, the United States never committed itself to fighting limited nuclear wars; but behind closed doors, our leaders and generals tried to develop the capacity to do so. Many of them believed that a war might be fought rationally, even scientifically, like a chess game, with a single "winner." This dream of the "winnable" nuclear war haunted strategic thought through the 1980s, when Sagan, by then a leading antinuclear activist, suggested that there was no such thing: even a limited nuclear exchange might trigger an all-annihilating global climate change, a "nuclear winter."

At RAND Sagan's main pursuit was space science. His title was "Consultant, Planetary Sciences." He studied the atmospheres of Venus and Mars. Why did RAND care about extraterrestrial atmospheres? At that time, RAND officials were interested in Earth's upper air, where (Air Force generals thought) the next war would be fought. Come doomsday, nuclear-armed bombers and intercontinental missiles would arc through the stratosphere, hauling nuclear weapons toward targets in the USSR. En route, they might be blown off course by high-altitude winds; also, ionospheric and auroral activity might upset communications and navigation. To prepare for such eventualities, Pentagon officials needed to learn more about the upper atmosphere and its vagaries.[26] Planetary astronomers persuaded them that changes in the atmospheres of Venus and Mars might shed light on changes in our own; hence they asked the Pentagon to fund ground-based telescopic studies of those worlds. (They didn't stress that ground-based telescopes yield such murky images of the planets that the results would be almost worthless.) Brave but gullible, the brass has rarely hesitated to waste good money on dumb ideas— "psychic" spying, bomb-toting dolphins, anti-ICBM systems, and the like. Likewise, it happily bankrolled the proposal by the planetary astronomers (who probably chuckled all the way back to their observatories). Hence, Sagan's work at RAND.[27]

Now in his eighties, Kellogg recalls the twenty-six-year-old Sagan as "very impressive . . . very much to the point . . . very persuasive in presenting his ideas." Their collaboration on the planetary atmospheres report was "delightful. He was charming, always full of ideas, great fun to work with."[28] Their report, published in 1961, was titled *The Atmospheres of Mars and Venus: A Report by the Ad Hoc Panel on Planetary Atmospheres of the Space Science Board* (Publication 944, NAS-NRC). It was Sagan's first important scientific publication on space science, other than his doctoral thesis and the *Science* article about Venus. Based on two workshops with E. J. Öpik and other scientists, the report included different theories about the causes of Venus's great heat. Sagan and Kellogg hoped their report would establish a consensus on the nature of the Venusian atmosphere, though "as it turned out, we couldn't," Sagan later observed.

As previously mentioned, Sagan was at RAND when he met A. G. Wilson. Wilson and the noted astronomer Zdenek Kopal were starting a new journal, *Icarus*. Its subject: our solar system. Wilson asked Sagan to serve as an associate editor, beginning in 1962. Cocky as ever, Sagan "immediately objected" to the name *Icarus*. He was a mythology buff, and he remembered how Icarus had plunged in flames from the sky. But Kopal "won me over on the spot" by stressing that the magazine would be open to far-out ideas, the kind of ideas that Sagan loved most.[29]

In 1962–1963, the first year of publication, *Icarus* published articles shepherded by Sagan from three scientists. He knew at least two of them personally from his University of Chicago days: John C. (Jack) Brandt (who contributed the article "A Model of the Interplanetary Medium") and Ronald Blum ("The Interaction between the Geomagnetic Field and the Solar Corpuscular Radiation"). Sagan himself wrote two articles that year: "Is the Martian Blue Haze Produced by Solar Protons?" and "Structure of the Lower Atmosphere of Venus."

Sagan loved jazzy ideas, but he was no sucker; he could be a tough editor. During his associate editorship at *Icarus*, he had a revealing exchange of letters with two former Yerkes colleagues, Dale Cruikshank and Alan Binder. Both men were at the University of Arizona at the time; both were destined for distinguished careers. Cruikshank recalls how he and Binder, while graduate students, submitted to Sagan an article on a possible atmosphere of the Jovian moon Io. Sagan responded "with some very cogent scientific arguments that were really quite subtle, that we had not thought of," Cruikshank recalls. Nonetheless, with the feistiness of the young, they resubmitted their article with a letter boasting that no less an authority than Gerard Kuiper agreed with them. ("Calling in the big gun!" Cruikshank now calls this, jokingly.) Sagan was unfazed. He fired back a letter citing his detailed objections and listing references to other scientific literature. Sagan's willingness to stand his ground, while being so helpful, impressed Cruikshank. "Of course, we were only students. But it impressed me from the very outset that this was a man who is a scientist of considerable substance—and I never lost that view."[30]

On the opposite side of the world, at least one distinguished scientist agreed. As it happened, RAND monitored and translated Russian scientific and technological reports. While Sagan was a RAND consultant, someone on staff called his attention to a paper by a Soviet radioastronomer,

I. S. Shklovskii. Shklovskii's paper described a thermal model for the atmosphere of Venus that was, "as far as I could tell, identical to my own," Sagan later recalled. He was relieved; Shklovskii was a distinguished scientist, and "I thought: 'Finally, someone else has done this calculation and gotten the *same* results!' . . . I remember breathing a real sigh of relief." Later Sagan discovered that Shklovskii was describing *his* (Sagan's) work. (The RAND translator had neglected to translate the Russian's reference to Sagan.)[31] Shklovskii probably learned about Sagan's work from the Kellogg-Sagan monograph on the atmospheres of Venus and Mars, which had been translated into Russian.

Sagan and Shklovskii had much in common. Both were brilliant controversialists whose wilder ideas scandalized their colleagues. Born in 1916, Shklovskii was Jewish, the son of an Orthodox rabbi, in a nation notorious for its anti-Semitism. He was also something of a political maverick, whose friends included Soviet H-bomb pioneer-turned-dissident Andrei Sakharov. Shklovskii had forecast the existence of the 21-centimeter line (the natural radio frequency emitted by interstellar hydrogen) before astronomers discovered it in space. He also successfully predicted the discovery of stellar "synchrotron" radiation (emitted by charged particles spiraling through magnetic fields of stars).[32]

What excited the news media, though, was Shklovskii's hypothesis about the moons of Mars. In 1877, an American observer had discovered that Mars is orbited by two tiny moons, Deimos and Phobos. Each appeared to be several miles in diameter, as big as a fair-sized city. In the 1940s, an American astronomer reported a puzzling anomaly in the orbit of Phobos. In the late 1950s, Shklovskii proposed a possible solution: the moons were hollow. No natural satellite can be hollow; hence they might be gigantic Martian space stations. Perhaps they were launched long ago, by a now-vanished Martian society.

As for Sagan—well, Shklovskii was clearly his kind of Russian. Sagan mailed a preprint of his controversial paper on interstellar spaceflight to Shklovskii. The Russian happily responded: "The prey runs to the hunter." He said he was writing a book about topics including extraterrestrial life, to be titled *Vselennaia, Zhizn, Razum* (Universe, Life, Mind). It was published in Russian in early 1963, and included Sagan's ideas about interstellar flight. "When I received a copy of the book," Sagan wrote, "I was struck by its broad scope and novel insights." And then he got an idea.[33]

SOMETIME IN THE EARLY 1960S, Ronald Blum was in a car with Sagan when Sagan mentioned that he had been named to the advisory board of a publishing house. "I didn't want to probe," Blum now admits, "because I was so jealous."[34]

The publisher was a new one, Holden-Day Inc. of San Francisco. Its owner, Fred Murphy, hoped to cash in on the booming market in science publishing. The Russians' *Sputnik* launch had terrified Americans; politicians and pundits began reassessing the quality of U.S. schools and science teaching. Journalists stopped deriding intellectuals as "eggheads," and popular science books flooded bookstores. "*Sputnik* was like throwing a match on high-octane gasoline," Murphy says. The son of a Boston brewery owner, he was in his early thirties, an enthusiastic raconteur who enjoyed textbook publishing's intellectual stimulation—the opportunity to talk to college professors. (He fondly recalls meeting "the world's expert on the rectal temperatures of hibernating bears.") When Joshua Lederberg was still at Madison, Murphy, then working for the science publisher Addison Wesley, visited him in hopes of persuading him to write a textbook on molecular biology. Lederberg "threw me out of his office. [He said,] 'I've [gotten visits from] people from publishing companies all over the country.'

"People told me, 'You've *got* to see Lederberg.' So I went back again —and he threw me out again! I had to go down to the hotel and get a couple of Scotches. I was depressed."[35]

Eager to branch out on his own, Murphy started his own publishing company, Holden-Day, in San Francisco. (He got the company's name from the maiden names of his mother and his father's mother.) Meanwhile, Lederberg moved from Wisconsin to Stanford University in nearby Palo Alto. A true go-getter, Murphy "went back to see Lederberg for the third time. And he says: 'Didn't I throw you out of my office in Madison?' I said, 'It's different now—I've started my own company, it's called Holden-Day.' And he said, 'That's different—sit down.'" Murphy persuaded the Nobelist to join Holden-Day's editorial board.

At some point during their conversations, Lederberg mentioned Sagan's name. Sagan, Lederberg told Murphy, had given "spellbinding" guest lectures to faculty at Madison. "This guy is something special," Lederberg assured Murphy. "I think you should make him an adviser."

Murphy visited Sagan; he recalls, "my first impression of Sagan was this: 'This guy is very bright and his knowledge is very broad. He's highly egotistical and very impatient.' The guy was brilliant. I thought, 'Wow, this guy really has an ability [to communicate] that other people don't have. Lederberg is smarter than Sagan, but he can't express himself like Sagan."

Murphy appointed Sagan to the Holden-Day board in 1961. Sagan was at this time still a young married professor, hardly a moneybag. As Murphy recalls, Sagan "was married to Lynn. I think they had a Volvo station wagon, and I wondered, 'How could *this* guy have a Volvo?'" Once when they took a drive together, Murphy didn't walk to the car as fast as Sagan wanted. "Sagan said something very quick, a little nasty—

something like, 'Hurry up, Fred, get your ass in the car,' or words to that effect. Lynn corrected him and said, 'Carl, you can't act like that. This is your *publisher*.' "[36]

Which brings us back to Shklovskii. Sagan was dazzled by the Russian's book, *Universe, Life, Mind*, and urged Murphy to reprint it in English. Murphy agreed. Sagan contacted Shklovskii, who was glad to agree to the translation. Sagan recalled that Shklovskii also "invited me to add additional material as I saw fit."[37] Fateful words. Sagan seized his chance. He took Shklovskii's offer literally and wrote extensive new passages for the text, adding (according to Murphy) "more than a hundred percent to the book." (Shklovskii also made "a large number of changes and additions" for the English text.) When the book finally appeared in 1966 under the title *Intelligent Life in the Universe*, "by I. S. Shklovskii and Carl Sagan," it would mark the young American's first acclaimed literary effort—his first, tentative brush with fame.[38]

Now retired to Boca Raton, Murphy acknowledges that he was helping himself by appointing Sagan to the Holden-Day board. "Lederberg was really touting Sagan. And I wanted to impress Lederberg, after getting thrown out of his office twice!"

SAGAN HOPED TO MEET Shklovskii in person, and made efforts to try to bring him to the United States. But the cold war got in the way. The probability of their meeting was likely to be "smaller than the probability of a visit to the Earth by an extraterrestrial cosmonaut," Shklovskii wrote to Sagan.[39] Shklovskii was a top scientist who knew many Soviet official secrets; his government rarely let such people venture abroad. According to Fred Murphy, Shklovskii told Sagan, "The bastards won't let me out because they know I won't come back."[40]

During the same years that Sagan and Shklovskii developed *Intelligent Life* by mail, Sagan stayed busy opening yet another front in his complex career: biological research. In the early 1960s, Sagan pursued at least five interdisciplinary topics related to biology: possible "microenvironments" on Mars; "Mars jar" experiments; the synthesis of adenosine triphosphate (ATP); supposed organic matter in a meteorite; and the feasibility of interstellar migration of microbes.

The first of these topics was, to the public, the most exciting. At an aerospace conference in Boulder, Sagan urged that the first robotic probe to Mars include a telescope for scanning the planetary surface. The telescope should be powerful enough to discern objects smaller than 100 feet wide. One reason: to "permit detection and close observation of many artifacts of advanced life forms or, alternatively, the exclusion of many categories of advanced life forms." He noted that no one had ruled out the possibility that the Martians—if any—might be sending us radio signals. He didn't mean that they *were*, mind you, just that no one had absolutely disproved it.[41]

(This was Popperianism with a vengeance. Throughout his career, Sagan expressed a similar philosophy: even extraordinarily remote possibilities are worth checking out. That is why Sagan, as late as the 1990s, advocated having the Mars *Global Surveyor* satellite check out the so-called face on Mars, although he knew it was almost certainly a geological fluke. His attitude was: Sure, it is almost certainly a fluke—but what if it isn't? To his colleagues, such a question bordered on the preposterous. It was like asking someone, "Do goblins exist?" and receiving the pompous reply: "I refuse to rule out the possibility pending the collection of further data." With that attitude, a scientist could waste his whole career chasing will-o'-the-wisps. It's no wonder that some scientists began to suspect Sagan's motives. He made such statements, they grumbled, not because he was admirably open-minded but, rather, because he enjoyed seeing his name in the newspaper.)

As noted earlier, in the mid-1950s Sagan had doubted the habitability of Mars, based on the intense ultraviolet flux and Prof. Dean B. McLaughlin's nonbiological explanation for the "wave of darkening." But observations by William M. Sinton revived Sagan's hopes. Sinton, of the Lowell Observatory, made infrared spectral measurements of Mars. The resulting spectral signatures resembled those of a common terrestrial life form, algae. Lederberg praised Sinton's observation as perhaps "the most pertinent evidence" for Martian life.[42] N. B. Colthup suggested that the "Sinton bands" came from acetaldehyde, a simple, common organic molecule.[43]

Colthup's proposal excited Sagan, who began speculating about acetaldehyde deposits on Mars. Stanley Miller was skeptical and warned Sagan in a letter that he thought the idea was totally off base. Acetaldehyde, he explained, strongly absorbs solar radiation. Thus sunlight would continually degrade any Martian acetaldehyde deposits. To keep the supply constant, the planet would have to generate acetaldehyde "at an enormous rate." But, according to Miller, Sagan disregarded his advice.[44] Sagan might have liked Colthup's idea because it resembled his own hypothesis about an organics-covered Moon. Even so, Sagan admitted that the odds for Mars life were only "fair to middling." (The chances were "somewhat better" on Jupiter, he added.)[45]

While at Stanford in the early 1960s, Sagan and Lederberg speculated about a Mars ecosystem they called a "microenvironment." (At the time, Sagan was officially a "Visiting Assistant Professor of Genetics" in the Stanford medical school.) Life, they reasoned, might endure the hostile conditions of Mars by restricting itself to tiny, habitable oases—the microenvironments. Perhaps Mars's water existed primarily just beneath the surface, frozen in permafrost. They wrote an article on "microenvironments" for the *Proceedings* of the National Academy of Sciences.[46]

Decades in advance, Sagan and Lederberg's microenvironments paper pioneered NASA's present approach to Mars exobiology. Nowadays, space scientists no longer hope to find microorganisms scattered willy-nilly across the Martian surface. The microorganisms, if any, probably live underground, beneath ice-covered lakes or in hot springs, sustained by water melted from volcanically warmed permafrost. Future astronauts may use drilling equipment to unearth the micro-creatures, or their fossils.[47]

In a second area of biological research, Sagan simulated living "Martian" ecosystems, using what were called "Mars jars." (Similar experiments had been conducted earlier by scientists such as Hubertus Strughold of the U.S. Air Force's School of Aviation Medicine in San Antonio.[48]) Sagan and his colleagues Stanley Scher and E. Packer placed terrestrial organisms inside the "jars." Sagan reported the results at a June 1963 conference in Denver titled "Symposium on the Exploration of Mars." "In every sample of soil tested," his report read, "there is a small population of microorganisms which are able to survive, and possibly reproduce, on Mars. . . . The present evidence strongly suggests, but does not conclusively prove, that life exists on Mars."[49]

In the 1960s, scientists—Lederberg, Wolf Vishniac, Norman Horowitz, Gilbert Levin, and others—developed life-detection devices for Mars robotic landers. Lederberg recalls that one of Sagan's jobs was to help him provide a "sanity check" for such schemes.[50] As usual, Sagan urged his colleagues to place cameras aboard Mars robots. Who knew what they might see? Sagan wasn't alone in thinking they might see something exciting. Plant physiologist Frank Salisbury wrote in a lead research article for *Science* in 1962:

> The remote possibility that Mars is the abode of intelligent beings should make us think very carefully before we drop elaborate robots on Mars to look for signs of life—machines that reach out, suck in, pulverize, and analyze samples from the Martian surface. If there is *intelligent* life, the telemetered data received from the robot might be difficult to interpret! At least I can imagine how I might react if such an apparatus landed in my back yard and started grabbing for my apple tree, the cat, and maybe me!

Salisbury also thought the Martian canals might be intelligent artifacts, and seconded Shklovskii's hypothesis that the Martian "moons" could be space stations. Perhaps (Salisbury added) the moons weren't discovered until 1877 because the Martians didn't launch them until then. Salisbury also mentioned reported flashes on Mars: "Was this volcanic activity, or are the Martians now engaged in debates about long-term effects of nuclear fallout?"[51] That so prestigious a journal would publish so exotic an idea as recently as the Kennedy Administration should give us pause; it suggests how tenaciously humans cling to extraterrestrial fantasies. Imaginatively speaking, Sagan was a loner; but he was by no means alone.

SUPPOSE, FOR ARGUMENT'S SAKE, that nearby planets are inhabited. How did the life arise? In the study of the origin of life, there are two distinct camps: those who believe that life began on Earth, and those who believe it formed elsewhere, then migrated here. The former espouses what could be called the "endogenous" theory; the latter, the "exogenous" theory. According to the latter camp, terrestrial life is related to life on other worlds; microorganisms migrate between worlds, perhaps aboard meteorites or comets. The best-known version of this idea is the nineteenth-century notion of "panspermia." Perhaps the whole galaxy is a common garden, a kind of cosmic archipelago where the microbes, plants, and animals vary morphologically from star system to star system, yet all share a common ancestry.

Or perhaps not. Perhaps terrestrial life is no more related to the biologies of Alpha Centauri or Upsilon Andromedae than turkeys are related to diamonds. Even so, if Stanley Miller's experiment is universally relevant, then life on *all* worlds might have begun by similar means—by Miller-Urey chemical processes that spawned the first organic molecules. In that sense, at least, we and extraterrestrials might have something in common.

A decade had passed since Miller's famous experiment, and a puzzle lingered: How did early organics acquire enough energy to assemble themselves into large organic molecules such as proteins? Miller had already demonstrated how amino acids, the building blocks of proteins, could have formed on the early Earth. However, none of his laboratory amino acids spontaneously united into proteins, which are basic ingredients of living creatures. What was the "missing link" between amino acids and proteins?

In *Time's Arrow and Evolution* (1951), a classic of theoretical biology, Harold F. Blum had stressed the possible importance of adenosine triphosphate (ATP) in the origin of life. In modern cells, ATP is a "universal" source of energy, and it is a major product of plant photosynthesis. Conceivably, primordial ATP might have provided the energy for early amino acids to assemble into even more complex structures—into proteins. That could have bridged much of the gap between "nonliving" amino acids and "living" organisms. Sagan recognized this, too, in his 1957 paper "Radiation and the Origin of the Gene."

There was one catch: how did ATP *itself* form? Sagan hoped to find out, while in California, in an experiment with Cyril Ponnamperuma and Ruth Mariner. Cyril Andrew Ponnamperuma (1923–1994) was born in Galle, Ceylon (now Sri Lanka). A chemist, he studied in London under legendary scientist-speculator J. D. Bernal, the X-ray crystallographer who helped to pioneer our understanding of the atomic structure of bio-molecules. As a graduate student at Berkeley, Ponnamperuma partici-pated in some of Melvin Calvin's experiments simulating the origin of life. Ponnamperuma received his doctorate in 1962, at age thirty-nine. Then he moved to NASA's Ames Research Center off Highway 101 south of San Francisco. Ames was a center for NASA's brand-new exo-biology program.[52]

In those days there was "incredible optimism" about solving the mysteries of the origin of life, recalls Mariner, then one of Ponnampe-ruma's lab technicians. At the time she was in her late twenties, a Mas-sachusetts native who had studied zoology in Illinois, then followed the sun to California. Sagan and Ponnamperuma "were really an amazing pair," she said. "They really supported each other in this excitement. As far as I can recall, Sagan had absolutely the same boyish enthusiasm and curiosity that he had publicly later."[53] They conducted a series of experi-ments partly at Ames and partly at Calvin's Berkeley lab. First, they mixed various gases, including phosphorus; then they transported them to Berkeley and exposed them to radiation from a cyclotron. Next, they mixed one of the products—adenine—in water with other ingredients (a sugar and a phosphorus compound) and irradiated it with ultraviolet light. This supposedly simulated the early Earth (the gases mimicked the early atmosphere, the solution mimicked a small pond, and the cyclotron and the UV light mimicked the intense ultraviolet radiation of the early Sun). With any luck, the experiment would generate organic products including ATP.

At that time, Mariner says, laboratory safety rules were looser. Unpleasant fumes wafted around. She analyzed the organic products of the experiment using the traditional technique of paper chromatography. Chemicals were poured onto a special filter paper, inside a small cham-ber. The chemicals bled through the paper, and different molecular types separated into different spots and streaks. By comparing the locations of the streaks with known substances, technicians could identify some chemical components from the original sample. "The whole atmosphere of the [chamber] became saturated with these horrendous solvent and acid mixtures," she says. "When the solvent had migrated down the paper, we would wheel these [chambers] into the courtyard and open the top so it could evaporate. This horrible stench came out, and we would hear windows everywhere going *slam! slam! slam!*"

Being the "theoretician" side of the experiment, Sagan didn't mess around with the instruments or chemicals. Still, Mariner recalls, he "was often in the laboratory, peering over my shoulder, making me nervous." Perhaps nostalgic for his boyhood chemistry lab, he peppered her with questions: How do you do this? How do you do that?[54]

The results were paper chromatography sheets covered with smears. They published their findings, and photos of the smears, in the July 20, 1963, issue of *Nature*. The smears are identified by name, for example, "adenine" and "adenosine." Amid these big smears is a tiny one labeled: "ATP." They had (they thought) recreated the formation of ATP on the primitive Earth—repeated the chemical process that energized the assembly of amino acids into proteins. Ponnamperuma was ecstatic. He had been "very convinced" that the experiment would generate ATP, Mariner recalls, and "when it appeared to do that, he jumped for joy."[55] It was a sensational achievement.

Or was it? The dramatic moment came when they exposed the alleged ATP to—of all things—the ground-up tails of fireflies. Firefly tails glow because of energy from ATP. And sure enough, according to science writer Walter Sullivan, the firefly tails "glowed happily."[56] Apparently, they really had synthesized ATP. That part of the experiment was "a lot of fun," Mariner recalls. (Their *Nature* paper notes: "Firefly tails were supplied by Schwarz Bioresearch, Inc., Mount Vernon, New York."[57]) Later, Sagan used a biblical metaphor to speculate what early Earth looked like: "In primitive times, ATP may have been made 'free,' produced abiologically and raining down on primitive organisms like manna from heaven."[58]

The 1960s was the golden age of origin of life research, when victory appeared imminent. Soon, it appeared, scientists would learn the ultimate secret—how life emerged from the dust. Ponnamperuma, who had studied philosophy in college, reflected on his work's philosophical implications. Life "is only a special and complicated property of matter . . . basically there may be no difference between a living organism and lifeless matter."[59]

Reading such words, the religious surely shuddered. Orthodox faith was already in trouble by the mid-1960s. Theologians increasingly spoke of God in metaphorical, rather than literal, terms. In 1966, *Time* magazine ran a famous cover story asking "Is God Dead?" The question seemed all the more relevant following the apparent breakthroughs in origin-of-life research. As Pasteur had asked, a century earlier: If life emerged on its own, then what need was there for God? While evading the religion question, Ponnamperuma was "quite optimistic" that science would solve the mystery of life's origin, and "the time needed to solve our problem may not be long."[60]

Ultimately, many thought, scientists might create life itself—say, a Muller-like "naked gene" capable of replication, mutation, and evolution. Fittingly, Ponnamperuma's division at Ames was called "Life Synthesis."[61] The creation of life, Sagan wrote a few years later, "may be proved in a decade. . . . Once the problem of the interaction between primitive nucleic acids and primitive polypeptides is solved, it will be possible to state fairly that life has been synthesized in the laboratory. Not, of course, anything familiar, like an aardvark or an axolotl; merely a molecular system capable of self-replication, mutation, replication of its mutations, and some degree of environmental control."[62]

Shortly before the *Nature* paper appeared, Sagan remarked in an address to the Harvard Club of New York that it looked as if the synthesis of life in a laboratory was "only a short time away from realization." He also stated that "we may have some confidence that similar events occurred in the early history of Mars, and that life may have come into being on that planet several billions of years ago."[63]

He must have felt on top of the world professionally. How fortunate he was to live at a time of such grand discoveries—and to share in them. His marriage had collapsed, his work on *Mariner 2* and Stratoscope was in trouble, yet there he was: on the cutting edge, alive and alert, bound for Harvard, his future apparently assured. It is "our immense good fortune," he boasted to the Harvard Club, "to be alive at the first moment in history when the tantalizing problems of the beginning of life on earth and the possibility of life on other worlds can be approached with rigor and in detail. To hold in our hands the keys to these ancient riddles is a triumph of the highest order; it heralds an age of exploration and discovery unsurpassed in the history of mankind."[64]

Back then, reasonable people could still talk about the possibility of microscopic life on the Moon, in the upper atmosphere of Venus, all over Mars, and perhaps in other worlds of the solar system. And beyond our star system were billions of others, no doubt brimming with civilizations—a million? ten million? a hundred million? Estimates varied wildly, but most were optimistic. Imaginations took flight. Sagan wondered whether aliens might differ from us not only morphologically but biochemically. Perhaps the principles of cellular metabolism and transmission of heredity vary from world to world. "[F]or all we know," he wrote at this time, "[Earthly] biology is literally mundane and provincial. . . . it is quite premature to conclude that ours is the only, or even the best of all possible biochemistries."

His optimism was almost boundless. Consider his opinion of the planet Mercury: It was the tiniest planet, and the one nearest the Sun—unbearably hot, no doubt. But lifeless? Not necessarily. He cited astronomical observations indicating that Mercury had "a definite, although very thin, atmosphere." At the time, astronomers believed that Mercury always maintained the same face toward the Sun. Sagan reasoned that the Mercurian atmosphere might conduct heat from the Sun-facing side to the dark side. Hence the dark side may have "equable" temperatures. (A similar notion was a staple of old pulp science-fiction stories.) "Liquid water," he wrote, "may be present there temporarily, and we may therefore begin thinking about the possibility of life on the night side of Mercury." In the eternal darkness of the Mercurian far side, life processes might be driven by unknown "energy sources" that take the place of terrestrial photosynthesis. In short, "in any inventory of biologically interesting planets Mercury must be included."[65]

He was wrong, of course. As it turned out, there is no Mercurian atmosphere; and as radar measurements proved in the mid-1960s, the little planet does not always keep the same face to the Sun (because it does not orbit the Sun in the same time it takes to rotate once). Still, Sagan's errors sometimes contained important grains of truth. In the 1970s and 1980s, scientists realized that not all terrestrial ecosystems depend on sunlight or its byproducts. On the dark ocean bottom, creatures nourished by volcanic gases cluster around thermal vents. And deep underground, crustal gases nourish "thermophilic" microbes. Hence, despite Sagan's erroneous ideas about life on Mercury (and, as time would show, on the Moon and Mars), his speculation about unknown "energy sources" that support life in strange realms was vaguely prophetic.

To THIS DAY, popular accounts rank the ATP experiments among Sagan's notable scientific achievements. In Paul West's novel *Life with Swan*, the character based on Sagan is erroneously credited with "seizing God's microphone" by "discovering a chemical called ATP, the prime energy-store for tissue."[66] In reality, "there was difficulty in reproducing some of these experiments" later, Ruth Mariner says. "We lab technicians were embarrassed by the sight of those chromatograms in prominent journals because they are just so messy." She believes the experiment probably did generate a "trace" of real ATP, "but the majority [of product] was certainly not [ATP]," contrary to claims in the original paper.

Any flaws in the experiment were "totally Cyril's responsibility," Mariner stresses. "I don't think Carl had anything to do with actually

planning the experiment. His involvement was in the theoretical model."
After subsequent experiments failed to generate ATP, Mariner didn't feel
it was her place to make a fuss about the contradictory findings. "I was a
lowly technician doing the work that was outlined for me." Ponnamperuma never published the subsequent contradictory findings. That was
typical of Cyril, Mariner remarked. "I don't think he ever looked back.
He was always looking forward."[67]

Stanley Miller dismisses the ATP experiment as "unfortunate" because
there's no reason to believe that adequate sources of phosphorus were
available on the early Earth. He recalls writing a response, published in
Nature, that treated the experiment "with scorn." While Miller suspects
that they probably did generate ATP, the finding was meaningless
because the necessary reagent (phosphorus pentoxide) didn't exist on the
early Earth. Regarding Ponnamperuma, Miller claims: "Not many people in the field have much use for him. He was good at press agentry.
What he did basically was to repeat other experiments and issue press
releases."[68]

Nonetheless, Ponnamperuma continued to make news. He would
eventually become one of the best-publicized figures in the search for
the origin of life and extraterrestrial life. In 1967, he electrified a mixture
of methane and ammonia thought to mimic conditions in the atmosphere of Jupiter. As a result, he generated nineteen chemical "precursors"
of amino acids; when water was added, complete amino acids formed.
Also, he and colleagues discovered that yeast and bacteria could survive
in an atmosphere similar to that of Jupiter. In 1969, Ponnamperuma's
photo made the front page of the *New York Times* when he reported finding organic materials inside a carbonaceous chondrite meteorite from
Murchison, Australia. The materials included numerous amino acids,
including some not found in terrestrial organisms.

In 1971 Ponnamperuma moved to the University of Maryland in
College Park, where he remained a prominent researcher in the field
until his death in 1994.

By that time, the early optimism of origin-of-life scientists had faded.
Growing evidence undermined the key premise of the Miller-Urey
experiment—that Earth's early atmosphere was reducing. According to
geological theory, the early atmosphere was not nearly as hydrogen-rich
as Miller and Urey assumed. Rather, it was likely only mildly reducing.
If so, then how could life have emerged on the early Earth?

For these and other reasons, two notable figures, Francis Crick and
Leslie Orgel, suggested a literally far-out alternative: a return to panspermia theory. They speculated that terrestrial life came from space—
specifically, from microorganisms deliberately launched to Earth by
extraterrestrials.[69] This was the sad impasse facing the field a generation

after Miller's inspiring experiment. Nor had anyone fulfilled Sagan's prophecy by creating "life" in a test tube. By that time, though, NASA management had given the Life Synthesis lab a new, humbler name: "Chemical Evolution."[70]

DO WE DESCEND FROM THE STARS? Crick and Orgel's hypothesis is an "exogenous" conjecture of the origin of life; that is, it holds that life came here from space. There have been many similar theories, as far back as the nineteenth century. The first major exogenous hypothesis, "panspermia" (from the Greek for "mixture of all seeds"), was proposed in late Victorian times. Its advocates included the physicist William Thomson (Lord Kelvin) and the chemist Svante Arrhenius. They argued that long ago, meteorites brought alien microorganisms to Earth. We are their descendants.[71] In his 1908 book *Worlds in the Making*, Arrhenius wrote: "It is . . . very probable that there are organisms so small that the radiation pressure of a sun would push them out into space . . . a small number of spores will fall on some other world, and may there be able to spread life if the conditions are suitable. [Hence] all organic beings in the whole universe should be related to one another."[72]

Some panspermia advocates offer the theory as a solution to supposed problems with the theory of evolution. In modern times, for example, astronomer Fred Hoyle has attacked evolutionary theory, arguing that it cannot explain the complexity of terrestrial life. The only way that life could be so complex, he says, is if it developed over an essentially infinite amount of time and traveled from world to world, thereby avoiding the problem of re-creating itself on world after world. This idea fits neatly with Hoyle's steady state theory, according to which the universe is eternal—it has always existed and always will. Likewise, early in the twentieth century, Arrhenius claimed that the cosmos is eternal, and rejected claims (based on nineteenth-century thermodynamics) that it would end in "heat death." Naturally, such arguments do not carry much weight with either cosmologists (who have largely rejected steady state theory) or evolutionary biologists. In the nineteenth century, panspermia defender Lord Kelvin was also a leading critic of Darwinian theory. In retaliation, Darwin's leading champion or "bulldog," Thomas Huxley, ridiculed Kelvin's panspermia hypothesis as "creation by cockshy," with "God Almighty sitting like an idle boy at the seaside and shying aerolites [at Earth], mostly missing, but sometimes hitting a planet!"

Later, panspermia theory fell out of favor. One reason is that critics argued persuasively that microorganisms couldn't survive the rigorous conditions—the deadly radiation, for example—of an interplanetary or interstellar voyage. Also, by the mid-twentieth century, many problems facing evolutionary theory were largely resolved, climaxing in the "neo-Darwinian synthesis."[73] So the panspermia hypothesis seemed irrelevant by the 1950s, when its rival, the endogenous concept, received its biggest boost: the Miller-Urey experiment.

Still, in the decades since, a small number of scientists have defended exogenous hypotheses of the origin of life. Some, like Hoyle and N. C. Wickramasinghe, argue that viruses and microbes live on comets, then fall to Earth—sometimes triggering epidemics.[74] In 1996, David McKay of NASA and his colleagues claimed to find evidence of fossil microbes in a meteorite from Mars, sparking the speculation that humans are descended from Martian microbes.[75] At present, McKay et al.'s claims have been rejected by most experts. And almost all of them dismiss Hoyle and Wickramsinghe's bizarre hypothesis.

A substantial number of space scientists, however, are friendly to a halfway solution to the mystery of the origin of life, a solution that blends the endogenous and exogenous hypotheses. According to this idea, space gave Earth the chemical building blocks of life, not life itself. Joshua Lederberg and Dean Cowie advocated this idea in 1958 in their "Moon-dust" paper for *Science* magazine.

Throughout his career, Sagan tended to side with the endogenous hypothesis. This is understandable; he had been present at the University of Chicago when Miller conducted his class experiment, the sine qua non of the endogenous outlook. Yet Sagan retained a fascination with exogenous hypotheses, although he insisted they were not essential to explain the appearance of life on Earth. In the 1980s and 1990s, he and his colleague Christopher Chyba would investigate ways that comets might have dumped organic molecules on the early Earth.[76]

There have been periodic bursts of enthusiasm for exogenous theories over the past half-century, and Sagan played a small part in one of them. In the late 1950s and early 1960s, researchers claimed to have found evidence of organic materials in a class of carbon-rich meteorites known as carbonaceous chondrites. Sagan's associate Melvin Calvin made such a claim in 1959. Then in March 1961, the scientist Bartholomew Nagy of Fordham University and a number of his colleagues reported finding possible fossilized organic materials within a carbonaceous chondrite. They told the press: "We believe that wherever this meteorite originated, something lived." They were profiled in a four-page article for *Life* magazine. "Are there traces of life from other planets now present on earth?" *Life* asked. "This is a strange, unnerving possibility, unacceptable to many scientists and incredible to most other people, but it may be true."[77]

Debate ensued. Critics argued that the Nagy team's "plant" fossils were contaminants that entered the meteorite after it landed on Earth.

The leading critic was Edward Anders of the University of Chicago, who insisted that the meteoritic organics were merely ragweed pollen. But surprisingly, Harold Urey, who had been so critical of Sagan's work on extraterrestrial organics, was excited by the Nagy team's claims. Urey even suggested a three-step explanation for the supposed fossils: (1) They originally came from a terrestrial ocean. (He thought the fossils resembled a type of algae that grows in water.) (2) Then an impact event knocked the fossil algae and part of the ocean to the Moon. (3) Then another impact event on the Moon knocked the fossils back to Earth. About that time, a few experts seriously proposed that the Moon once had surface running water. The Princeton-educated scientist John J. Gilvarry argued that the lunar *maria* (Latin for "seas") were literally sediment from now-vanished lunar oceans. The maria are dark, Gilvarry proposed, because "a primitive form of life" once inhabited them.[78]

Initially, Sagan thought the "fossils" resembled pollen from a terrestrial plant, the evening primrose. He and H. G. Baker sought advice from a leading pollen expert, Gunnar Erdtman, director of the Palynological Laboratory of the Swedish Natural Science Research Council in Stockholm. Sagan later informed Urey in a memo that Erdtman had determined that the apparently organic remnants "did not resemble any recent or fossil terrestrial pollen or sporelike bodies of which he was aware." Erdtman also concluded that no Earth processes he knew of could have created the "fossils" out of any known type of pollen grain. This contradicted Anders's claim that the mystery materials were "contaminants." Erdtman also rejected Sagan's "evening primrose" suggestion as "untenable." Sagan assured Urey that Erdtman knew what he was talking about and that his conclusions should be respected. On this basis, Sagan, like Urey, apparently leaned toward the Nagy hypothesis: the mystery "fossils" came from outer space.

Urey grew excited. He wrote to Sagan that he was impressed by Erdtman's conclusions and that he suspected this was a convincing refutation of Anders's ragweed pollen idea. Sagan, however, didn't want to irritate the highly respected Anders. Despite his reputation for brashness, Sagan was a pro when it came to walking verbal tightropes; he could have been a professional diplomat. (In fact, his writings might interest scholars who specialize in the analysis of scientific rhetoric.) Sagan wrote to Anders saying that while it was his impression that the fossils were probably not remnants of primrose pollen, he also didn't think that Nagy could convincingly claim that they were extraterrestrial. Sagan was notorious for his penchant for double negatives, statements that allowed him to suggest outlandish things without actually *asserting* them. Via a string of multiple negatives, Sagan appeared to take both sides in the Nagy debate—the pro-contaminant (anti-space) view and the anti-contaminant (pro-space) one—simultaneously. A real charmer when he wanted to be, Sagan added that if evidence did eventually show that the fossils were from Earth sources, that proof would be due "in no small part to your [Anders's] own critical efforts." Hence, whatever the outcome of the Nagy debate, Sagan's reputation would be safe.[79]

In the June 7, 1963, issue of *Science*, sure enough, Anders and Frank Fitch published powerful evidence that the meteorite samples were indistinguishable from terrestrial ragweed pollen. Although the debate dragged on for a few more years, it became the received wisdom among most scientists that Nagy had been fooled by an ordinary form of pollen that plagues millions of allergy sufferers.

The brouhaha inspired Sagan to examine a broader question: Was panspermia a feasible way to distribute life across space? In his paper "Interstellar Panspermia," he calculated the odds that microbes traveling between star systems would reach Earth or other worlds. First, he made the assumption (as Arrhenius had, long ago) that the "bugs" might be pushed across space by radiation pressure from stars. He calculated that a microbe expelled from Earth into space "would reach the orbit of Mars in weeks, the orbit of Jupiter in months, the orbit of Neptune in years, and the distance to the nearest star in a few tens of thousands of years. The transit time across the galaxy is a few times [one hundred million] years. Compared with the age of the solar system, these are all relatively short transit times."

However, Sagan noted, the little microbes would be in constant danger. Radiation from stars (including our Sun) was a serious threat. But, he reasoned, interstellar microbes might safely penetrate our solar system as far inward as the "gas giant" planets (Jupiter, Saturn, Uranus, and Neptune). Hence, he argued that the best places to look for evidence of interstellar panspermia in our solar system are the moons orbiting these planets, especially Triton, the largest satellite of Neptune.[80]

The scientific community's rejection of Nagy's claims hurt his reputation. The usually gruff Urey showed a kinder side when he urged Sagan in a letter that Nagy should not be forced out of this area of research (there was pressure to do so).[81] Nagy died in the late 1970s, almost two decades before the whole controversy repeated itself in a new form: the "Mars rock" debate. (At that time, the media went wild about "space bugs" all over again. It was as if no one had learned any lessons from the Nagy debate, lessons about the dangers of handling and misinterpreting meteorites.)

Nagy's fate demonstrates the wisdom of Sagan's diplomatic maneuvers during the controversy. By 1962, Sagan had to step lightly. He was developing a dangerous reputation for wacky thinking (lunar organics, terraforming, interstellar flight). He was also starting to annoy would-be collaborators, who discovered that he didn't always deliver on his promises. Other researchers were starting to grumble: Who *is* this guy? Science is not merely ideas; it is politics, too. Sagan could not build a career solely on speculations; nor could he risk offending powerful people as carelessly as he had offended, say, Harry Hess or the Stratoscope II team. Scientific reputations are easily shattered. Hence Sagan had to start choosing his words—and his alliances—carefully.

FEW SCIENTIFIC DISPUTES are uglier than "priority" disputes. Most scientists don't go into science for the money; all they ask is to receive fair credit for their discoveries. After Carl Sagan became famous, a few critics griped that he occasionally received credit for other people's work. This undoubtedly happened. In his book *The Cosmic Connection*, for example, Sagan failed to credit the science writer Eric Burgess for proposing the initial idea for the *Pioneer* plaque. Sagan heard about the idea from other people and may not even have been aware of Burgess's priority. Or perhaps Sagan figured that he and his wife at that time, Linda Salzman, did all the work designing the plaque, so why credit anyone else? Or perhaps he simply forgot.[82]

Most of the time, though, Sagan disseminated credit with scrupulous care. His public actions and private words attest to this. In their first collaboration, graduate student Chris Chyba asked Sagan's permission to list him as coauthor of the resulting paper. "He declined. He said that it had been my idea and I had done virtually all the work and he shouldn't be a coauthor."[83] Sagan's colleague Brian Toon recalls: "Sagan and I wrote a paper and sent it to *Playboy*. They loved it. But Carl didn't feel that it was fair to put his name on it since I had actually written the paper. *Playboy* quickly lost interest, being more interested in Carl than in the content of this paper."[84]

If anyone gave Sagan credit where credit wasn't due, it was the American news media. The mainstream media are not known for their scholarly refinement; they tend to oversimplify stories by seeking heroes. And by the 1970s, when it came to science coverage, Sagan—charismatic, articulate, witty, handsome—was the hero of choice. It is no surprise, then, that in the 1980s reporters referred to "Carl Sagan's theory of nuclear winter," although the idea was largely developed (as Sagan emphasized) by others. Sagan sometimes tried to make up for the lapses of the press. For example, he and Rich Turco partly dedicated their book on the nuclear winter hypothesis to Paul J. Crutzen and John Birks, whose work helped to inspire the idea.[85] Otherwise, Sagan seemed too disheartened by media inaccuracies to waste time correcting them. When

Donald Menzel told Sagan how pro-UFO writers attributed sensational statements to him, Sagan lamented that he could not stop others from misquoting him.[86]

Perhaps he should have tried harder; he might have avoided one of the saddest blows of his life. Over the years, some news stories implied that Sagan "discovered" the greenhouse effect of Venus (to the neglect of poor old Rupert Wildt). When this happened, a few scientists, perhaps those already angered by Sagan's arrogance, popularity, and wealth, blamed Sagan, not the press. A noted scientist who played a part in depriving Sagan of admission to the National Academy of Sciences in 1992 claimed (obviously based on his reading of popular articles) that Sagan had not given Wildt fair credit.[87] The charge is false. Not only did Wildt greatly respect Sagan, but in Sagan's 1960 doctoral thesis, the very first sentence in the Venus "Introduction" states:

> The radiation balance of Venus was first discussed by Wildt (1940), who showed that the amount of carbon dioxide then thought to exist above the cloud layer could cause a moderately efficient greenhouse effect. For a slowly rotating Venus, Wildt calculated that the topical noontime surface temperature would exceed 400 degrees K.[88]

Indeed, many who knew Sagan attest to his strong moral sensibility. In general, he said and did what he believed to be the right thing, even if it offended others (it sometimes did). His honesty about his work is illustrated nicely by comments he made to historian Ronald Doel about his role in the *Mariner 2* probe to Venus. While he had been "deeply involved" in developing the probe's infrared radiometer, he said, "I don't want to overstate my contribution—it was minimal—to the *Mariner 2* design. . . . I was going through a divorce. I was not as engaged in the flight phase after launch.

"I did not go to watch the launch, which I so much wanted to do. I came in for a day for mission operations. And only afterwards did I work in any significant way on trying to understand, on the one hand, the infrared data, and on the other hand, the microwave data."[89]

Divorce may not have been the sole cause of his problems. Sagan didn't enjoy the unreserved confidence of the infrared radiometer team leader, Gerry Neugebauer, who was only two years older. By the time *Mariner 2* was Venus-bound, Sagan had developed a reputation as a scientific speculator. In those days, to many scientists, speculation violated an unspoken professional code. Stillman Chase, a member of the infrared radiometer team, remembers those hectic days. "Even then [Carl] was quite a charismatic figure, and he had quite a standing in the scientific community. [But] he was viewed somewhat askance by other scientists, like Gerry.

"Gerry and I talked about this a lot. Gerry Neugebauer is a very straight [shooter]. His integrity is so unimpeachable that it's almost painful. And he was a little bit put off by Carl's popularization of the science. The thing is, people like Gerry would not speculate. They were very loath to speculate about things. And Carl never had that problem. [Neugebauer had] very fundamental beliefs about how a scientist should conduct himself. And Carl wasn't living up to that standard. Carl had a larger view of his role, and Gerry just didn't have the dynamic range to figure that out."[90] (Neugebauer declined to be interviewed for this book. Sagan "was a good friend of mine," Neugebauer said, but he was too "old and sick" to recall details of Sagan's work on *Mariner 2*.[91])

On December 13, 1962, the day before *Mariner 2* reached Venus, Sagan was far from the excitement at Caltech's Jet Propulsion Laboratory in Pasadena. He was an hour or so's drive away, holed up at RAND in Santa Monica, getting ready for his post-California life—for his return East, to Harvard and chilly winters. He wrote a letter, seeking money, on RAND stationery to the Alfred P. Sloan Foundation in which he requested the funds to support work by himself and a team of post-doctoral fellows on the atmospheres and surfaces of the planets. The money would give him a "very welcome sense of freedom" in his research. He was, in effect, asking for a blank check to study whatever he wished.[92] A very Saganish request.

The *Mariner 2* flyby was a success, a huge boost to America's beleaguered space program. Slowly, the cold war seemed to be turning in favor of the United States. Only weeks earlier, President Kennedy had cajoled the Soviets into withdrawing their missiles from Cuba. In a span of two months, the United States had showed that it would not be intimidated, on Earth or in the solar system. The Soviets' Venus probe had stopped transmitting and disappeared, but NASA's technical prowess awed reporters. When, after a journey of 182 million miles, *Mariner 2* flew tantalizingly close to Venus, one observer compared the feat to "sitting on a merry-go-round and shooting a bullet to hit a fast-flying sparrow over the horizon."[93]

During the thirty-five-minute flyby, the infrared radiometer observed Venus at wavelengths of 8.4 and 10.4 microns. It measured the temperature of Venus's upper atmosphere at −30 degrees Fahrenheit. The instrument detected no breaks in the cloud cover (hence Sagan's wished-for camera wouldn't have seen much). Meanwhile, the microwave radiometer scanned the face and limb of Venus at wavelengths of 13.5 and 19 microns. It detected limb darkening, as Sagan's greenhouse model had predicted; the intense radiation really did come from the planetary surface. In fact, Venus's surface was even hotter than anyone had thought—about 800 degrees K. For all practical purposes, Venus was as hot as hell.

Neugebauer, Kaplan, and Chase reported their results in the March 8, 1963, issue of *Science* magazine. Sagan, embroiled in his divorce at that time, is not listed as a coauthor. A footnote adds, however, "We acknowledge the help of Carl Sagan, who was an active participant during the conception and initial planning of this experiment."[94]

For the rest of the 1960s, a few scientific diehards refused to believe the *Mariner 2* observations. They insisted that Venus wasn't as hot as the space probe reported. The planet might be cool enough for life—even for glaciers. Battles over the true nature of Venus would continue for years.

Still, in early 1963, as Sagan returned to Harvard, the handwriting was on the wall. The *Mariner 2* mission didn't simply inaugurate the age of interplanetary flight. Something was ending, too, something closer to the human heart than the human mind. A *New York Times* editorial recalled the old question of "whether or not life in some form existed on Venus and hence elsewhere in our solar system and possibly also beyond it. . . . The answer is a disheartening, disillusioning 'No! Not on Venus!' . . . The message from Venus may mark the beginning of the end of mankind's grand romantic dreams."[95]

7

Mars and Manna

IN FEBRUARY 1963, Sagan returned from California to Cambridge—a new home, a clean slate, a chance to start over. He had attained the peak of academia, and he was only twenty-eight. Despite his California troubles, Harvard had high expectations of him. In seconding Sagan's grant application, Donald Menzel informed the Sloan Foundation that Harvard thought Sagan was one of the best young astronomers of his time. He also complimented Sagan's personality, and commented that he had impressive ambition and breadth of knowledge.[1]

Later that year, in April, Sagan wrote to Gerard Kuiper that he "made the mistake of overcommitting myself" in California. Even so, he had some accomplishments to show from that time, and as evidence he enclosed a preprint of a paper. He also told Kuiper that he was already "deeply immersed in research" at Harvard.[2]

Donald Goldsmith was a Harvard undergraduate at the time Sagan arrived. "Everybody was talking about Sagan, what a bright, smart guy he was." And young—physically, he resembled an undergraduate. Goldsmith took a course Sagan was teaching on planetary astronomy, which was "the most enjoyable course, perhaps, I took at Harvard. . . . He told marvelous anecdotes." Goldsmith tried, unsuccessfully, to get Sagan as his faculty adviser. But a graduate student, James Pollack, fresh out of Princeton, succeeded in getting Sagan as his thesis adviser. Goldsmith recalls that one day he, Pollack, and Sagan drove in Sagan's "battered Ford," perhaps to hear Lew Kaplan of JPL talk about planetary atmospheres at MIT. On the way back—a lovely spring day—they had a flat. Goldsmith was proud to show his knowledge of cars, so he changed the flat. Pollack said, "So that's how you get your 'A' in astronomy, eh, Don?" On a final exam, Goldsmith "made jokes in several languages and Sagan much appreciated it. And we became sort of friends." The Sagan entourage was taking shape.[3]

At Harvard, Sagan would become a nationally known scientific figure—not famous, exactly, but getting there. With Pollack, who received his Ph.D. in 1965, he would study the atmosphere and terrain of Mars and propose an important new hypothesis of their nature. They would also elaborate and defend Sagan's embattled theory of the Venusian greenhouse effect. In time, these two men, with remarkably similar backgrounds yet remarkably different personalities, would be one of the great duos of modern space science.

Also in the mid-1960s, the mass media would begin exploiting Sagan. He was not a complete unknown to journalists; his name had appeared in national newspapers and magazines at least as far back as 1956, late in the first term of the Eisenhower Administration. He had even appeared on a television broadcast about Venus.[4] But his real publicity breakthrough came in 1966, with the publication of his book *Intelligent Life in the Universe* (coauthored with Shklovskii). About this time, Sagan served briefly as an adviser on the film *2001: A Space Odyssey*. Dining with the film's creators, he acquired his first taste of Hollywood.

Simultaneously, he would rediscover an old love: UFOs. In 1965 and 1966, a wave of UFO sightings swept the nation. The resulting media hoopla sparked congressional and scientific investigations. Reporters called Sagan for the scoop on saucers. A Walter Cronkite television special on UFOs included a clip of Sagan, a dulcet-toned oracle of scientific wisdom. He offered journalists an amiably skeptical stance on UFOs, which was an engaging alternative to the harrumphy finger-wagging of Menzel, the era's only other well-known saucer skeptic.

In those days, few U.S. newspapers had full-time science reporters, partly because editors and publishers assumed that there were few interesting scientists.[5] Hence Sagan would be a revelation. He talked clearly, bracingly, about "fun" ideas: life on Mars, extraterrestrial cultures, interstellar flight, the UFO controversy, "balloon animals" in the upper atmosphere of Venus, the need to quarantine lunar rocks lest they contain killer microbes, and so forth. By the time Sagan left Harvard, science reporters knew him on sight. They gravitated toward him at NASA press conferences, while his neglected colleagues were left staring at their microphones.

For all this, he would pay a price. His interests were dizzyingly diverse—too diverse. Most professors spend their lives establishing expertise in narrow subjects. Few see their work trumpeted in newspapers or on television. Naturally, they resent young go-getters who stake claim in a dozen different specialties, commenting suavely to media on topics far from their training. Sagan might have gotten away with this had he established stronger alliances at Harvard. He had always been good at making connections, but, strangely, he made few at Harvard.

The problem is not simply that his Harvard colleagues were jealous of him, although that is part of it. The truth is that some sincerely did not respect him.

Also during Sagan's Harvard years, he would become more overtly political. During those years, the larger world fell apart. The patriotism and "New Frontierism" of the early 1960s ended in the rage and disillusionment of the middle and late 1960s. Young and old clashed over Vietnam, over drugs, over the meaning of life and work. Students seized campus buildings. Sagan's political maturation started slowly, when he began traveling to the South to lecture to black students about the new age of space. About this time he also recognized that the war was an atrocity, a repudiation of everything noble in the American soul, and he said so.

After four years at Harvard, campus officials would deny his bid for tenure. A key reason is a furious letter, written by someone out of Sagan's past, someone to whom Sagan had demonstrated inadequate obeisance. Of course, Harvard rarely grants tenure to anyone, even a potential superstar like Carl Sagan. What is telling, though, is this: hardly anyone lifted a finger to keep him.

ON THE SECOND ANNIVERSARY of Carl Sagan's death, in 1998, William J. Broad wrote an article in the *New York Times* pointing out one of Sagan's legacies: a large generation of space scientists, educated by him at Harvard and Cornell.[6] One of Sagan's most successful students was David Morrison, now chief scientist at NASA's Ames Research Center in California. Originally an amateur astronomer from Danville, Illinois, Morrison entered Harvard's graduate astronomy program in the autumn of 1962. That spring, he took Sagan's course on the planets. "I was fascinated by the subject matter—*and* the person," Morrison recalls with his puckish grin, "as were two other students there, [including] Jim Pollack. . . . Carl, as you know, is a charismatic teacher; and he was then, also. So he *naturally* inspired interest in the subject. . . . He gave a regular lecture course . . . a very polished, charismatic lecture every time the course met, two or three times a week." Their relationship was fairly formal by 1990s standards, though; the students called him "Dr. Sagan." "I never called him 'Carl' until the day I got my Ph.D.," Morrison said.

Sagan also became a highly popular speaker on "open nights" at Harvard College Observatory. "People would come to hear a speaker, and if, as occasionally happened, the sky was clear, they could then go look through one of the telescopes," Morrison says. "The talk that Carl gave frequently was called 'Planets are Places.' . . . That was an innovative, perhaps a radical idea—that planets are not points of light that an amateur astronomer would look up and identify against the constellations . . .

they were actually worlds in their own right." Those are commonplace ideas now, "but frankly, those were not commonplace in 1963."

"Other-worldly Sagan" was the caption of a picture in an April 1963 article in the Smithsonian Astrophysical Observatory's in-house newsletter. It included a pencil sketch of the grinning young scientist. It began:

> At 60 Garden Street there has recently appeared a neat young man no more unworldly-looking than a banker. But what is he? One of SAO's and the world's foremost students of planetary environments—including the possibility of life beyond the Earth.
>
> The recent "Mariner" probe carried an instrument suggested by him and two others to measure the infrared emission from Venus. Mariner's close-up report indicated that Venus supports no life, just as he had publicly theorized since 1959.
>
> He is one of a very few experimenters presently trying to reconstruct that greatest of mysteries, the origin of life. By applying to a hydrogen-methane-ammonia-water atmosphere, similar to the infant earth's some 4 billion years ago, energies such as ultra-violet light which abounded then, complex organic molecules are formed. This whole process has not yet been completed in a single laboratory experiment—but soon? Says he, "It will not be surprising if, within the next 10 years, a living system, able to reproduce itself, will be synthesized. . . ."
>
> Carl Sagan works in such interesting fields that to listen to him is more imagination-stirring than to read science fiction. (Which, says he, used to entertain him but "is getting poorer because science itself is moving so fast—reality is far more exciting than most fiction.")

The author asked Sagan all the usual questions: Was he interested in flying to the Moon? No, it was "too dull." He would like to go to Mars, "but not to live, only for a visit." Would beings on other worlds resemble humans?

> "Pretty surely not [Sagan replied]. Evolution is opportunistic, not foresighted. We humans are minimally efficient, stuck with every ancestral adaptation. For instance, our optic nerve passes through the light path—bad engineering; the squid's eye is better designed."

He defended space exploration as "a good thing. More effort up there, less chance of fighting down here."

"So that," the article concluded, "is Carl Edward Sagan. . . . One of our typical 'average' researchers who from their quiet offices are reaching far out into space and time."[7]

On the surface, Sagan was all energy and optimism. Fred Whipple tried to make him feel at home. He reminded Sagan that besides earning an annual Harvard Observatory salary of $12,210, he would have many privileges as an Assistant Professor, such as the use of the Faculty Club. The only privilege he wouldn't have, Whipple joked, "is the professor's right to tether his cow in Harvard Yard."[8]

Initially, Menzel was accommodating to Sagan's private idiosyncrasies. Since childhood, Sagan had been an enthusiastic stamp collector. Shortly after Sagan's arrival, Menzel sent his secretary a memo telling her that Sagan had requested some of the stamps that came on letters (some from faraway lands) to the department. She sent Sagan 215 stamps.[9]

Though he had been warmly welcomed, however, he felt insecure. The young man who was so engaging when he was at the podium—the center of attention—was less comfortable in the elite, competitive environment of Harvard. Elsewhere, he had been a fireball amid firecrackers; now he was in Cambridge, surrounded by fireballs. Decades later, he blamed his unease during this period partly on the environment and partly on himself. On the one hand, "there was something about the Harvard community which reminded me of Williams Bay. There was a kind of inhibited, self-confident, dismissive-of-non-standard-points-of-view point of view."

On the other hand, he admitted, "I was very uncomfortable with a lot of the social aspects at Harvard. I'm sure a significant part of it was due to my own social clumsiness. That was not one of the best parts of the Harvard experience. Faculty parties, faculty meetings, that sort of thing—I didn't have a great time at [those]."[10]

He did not, however, reveal his anxieties. To others, he came off as a young man thoroughly in command of the situation. "Carl just dominated a room," recalls Jim Cornell, a veteran public affairs officer at the Smithsonian Astrophysical Observatory. Sagan was hard to get to know personally, Cornell remarked; he displayed a certain "arrogance" and seemed to address you not as an individual, but, rather, "as a member of the public."[11] The astronomer-author Jay Pasachoff, a student at Harvard in the 1960s, once saw Sagan at a party. "Someone started a party game, where people were supposed to describe something, and Carl was asked to describe a room. He started by saying it was ten feet by fifteen feet. Then he said it was thirty feet tall. He was not thinking on the plane that other people were. He was thinking on another dimension."[12]

Sagan was "a very flamboyant personality . . . he radiated a lot of energy," says Valerie Sorenson, who was his Harvard secretary for a year. "When he came into a room or when you talked to him, with his deep voice, he just had—I don't know whether I should use the word 'charisma,' but he had a lot of energy and was a rather dramatic persona.

"He was friendly and he was aloof—both! He was thinking about himself almost all the time—[about] how things could benefit him. Very self-absorbed; he was an amazingly self-absorbed person. I don't mean that he was mean and selfish; that isn't the way he came across. But he did have Carl Sagan on his mind all the time."[13]

No MAN IS AN ISLAND, even at Harvard. Sagan needed allies; they might make all the difference several years hence, when he came up for tenure. Yet he had trouble finding faculty eager to work with him. One reason is that the Harvard astronomy department was somewhat balkanized, partly because different geniuses liked to do their own things and perhaps partly because departmental titans had squabbled so badly during the 1950s.[14]

Still, Sagan managed to scrape together some associates, the most important being his student Jim Pollack. There was also A. T. Young. Another was the theoretical physicist Sidney Coleman, with whom he performed a "statistical analysis" demonstrating the need to sterilize spaceships bound for other worlds.[15] A longer-lasting collaboration began when the chemist Bishun Khare arrived on campus. Khare was a native of India, previously employed at the Ontario Research Institute in Toronto. One day, he recalled, he saw an ad in *Physics Today* from someone at Harvard who was seeking "somebody who had the background in organic chemistry and physical chemistry and physics, spectroscopy, some interdisciplinary type of thing. And just for the fun of it, on a plain sheet of paper, I just wrote that I was interested to know about this position. And then within a week or so, I got a call in my lab from [someone asking] 'would you take this much salary?'" He said yes, and spent the next thirty years working with Sagan.

Khare would replace Stanley Miller as Sagan's primary chemist, the man who would simulate the atmospheres of other worlds, determining what strange organic molecules they might breed. He was exactly what Sagan needed, everything that Sagan wasn't: a hands-on lab man, one who did his own glass-blowing and enjoyed shopping for equipment in the campus chemistry store. Harvard was, of course, an intellectual hothouse, a workaholic's dream, and Khare loved it. "You could go to the chemistry library any time of the night, Xerox whatever you wanted to," he recalls.[16]

Some other potential collaborations fizzled. Richard Goody, a leading figure in atmospheric studies and planetary science, was over in the engineering department. He and Sagan jointly organized seminars, but their relations "were uniformly tense," Sagan said later. "He conveyed from the beginning a distaste for both the subject matter and content of my work. I didn't have the same feeling about his [work]; I thought he did very good work. But that, needless to say, was a barrier to a more intimate relationship. What was it he hated about my work? . . . I never asked him. I should, after all these years. I've always wondered." (Goody, however, now says that while he regarded the young Sagan's papers as "good but not otherwise outstanding," and while "his personality and mine were at opposite poles," Sagan "certainly had a great talent for expressing ideas. I remember him with respect.")

In short, Sagan recalled, "I was not working much with other faculty members in astronomy. There were very few problems that I could go talk to anybody [about at Harvard]." This is true of much of his early career, he later admitted, for "in a lot of periods, it just seems like I'm there mulling away and struggling on my own."[17]

Sagan's eccentricities could be grating. A longtime mythology buff, he was intrigued by words with mythological roots and insisted on their proper use. For some reason, he launched a one-man campaign to convince space scientists to replace the term "Venusian" with "Cytherean." This annoyed Donald Menzel. He wrote a memo to Sagan saying that words are meant for communicating and "not one person in fifty" would understand the word "Cytherean." He also told Sagan that he "should get back on the beam" by doing "some more productive science."[18]

Sagan tended "to rub people the wrong way," reflects Don Goldsmith, his former student. Sagan was "pushy, aggressive, intelligent, energetic, far-seeing, fond of a joke, fond of a good story, and so on. . . . I think what really rubbed people the wrong way about Carl was that in no time, he could outdo you, at least superficially. . . .

"As time went on, people tended to put around the gossip that Carl wasn't much of a scientist. But the fact is, as far as I could tell, he was a very good scientist; but he was *only* very good, just as Stephen Hawking is merely *extremely* good—which is a long way from being Isaac Newton or Albert Einstein."[19]

"Very good," of course, is not good enough for Harvard. Socially uneasy and unable to make the right ties, Sagan was a somewhat shadowy figure on campus. Except, that is, to his students. As a teacher, he was first rate. His knowledge, humor, and enthusiasm enthralled many of his students. His first Harvard graduate student was Jim Pollack, who loved working with him (and would do so for three decades).

Sagan and Pollack's first great accomplishment was to revolutionize astronomers' view of the ever-changing sphere of Mars, the red planet. At the other end of the telescope, its orange-red face glowered, splotched with dark blurs and streaks. Its appearance altered from week to week and month to month, like an evolving Rorschach blot. What was going on up there?

MANY SPACE BUFFS in the 1960s had no doubt that we would eventually launch humans to Mars, probably in the 1970s—the early 1980s at the latest. Popular magazines included "artists' conceptions" of future Mars bases. One episode of the television show *Outer Limits* showed dragonlike creatures that snaked through Martian sands, then popped up and ate astronauts. Who knew, after all, what space creatures might look like?

In mid-1963 in Boulder, Sagan addressed an aerospace conference on future exploration of Mars. He argued that, due to the vast territory on Mars, exploration would take considerable time. He also asserted that Martian organisms might be "advanced" and of substantially different biology from those of Earth life.[20] In light of this, he advocated sending "creative and thoughtful" biologists to Mars, as they might spot unusual life forms that robots would miss.

As usual, Sagan's main concern was that Mars-bound probes be sterilized. Otherwise they might haul terrestrial microbes to the red planet. Those microbes might devour any local Martian biota, ruining a golden opportunity for future biologists. Sagan and Lederberg eventually got into a big argument with Bruce Murray, Norman Horowitz, and other space scientists who doubted that Mars was inhabited and wanted to loosen the requirements for costly, time-consuming sterilizations.

But was Mars worth the visit? Through the 1960s, many liberals and social activists expressed doubts over the morality of pouring billions into space while malnourished Americans lived in shacks in Appalachia and black Americans couldn't get served at Southern lunch counters. Why seek extraterrestrial life while terrestrial life was in such a sorry state? The critics included many scientists. Some—space scientist James Van Allen, for example—supported robotic missions to the planets but opposed human spaceflight. Robots, he and others argued, were cheap and generated floods of useful scientific data, whereas astronauts were just playing Buck Rogers. The critics included the editor of *Science*, Philip Abelson. He told a meeting of the American Psychological Association: "The half of the world that is undernourished could scarcely be expected to place a higher value on landing on the moon than on filling their stomachs."[21] Barry Commoner, the noted biologist-environmentalist, told the Senate Astronautical and Space Science Committee that the search for extraterrestrials was likely to fail because they probably don't exist. To claim that they do is "a weak prop for the serious decision [to seek them,] given its profound economic and social consequences."[22]

Moralistic arguments were one thing; scientific ones were quite another. Mars would remain a scientifically attractive target as long as NASA publicists could describe it as a potentially inhabited world without their consciences hurting them. And in the early 1960s, the evidence for Mars life, while indirect, appeared tantalizing enough to outweigh moral objections. One key piece of evidence was William Sinton's spectral observations, the "Sinton bands." These implied the presence of Martian organic matter, such as acetaldehyde.

Another clue was the "wave of darkening." What could explain this, save seasonal changes of vegetation? True, in the mid-1950s Dean McLaughlin had proposed that the "waves" shifted as Martian winds blew volcanic ash hither and yon. But it was difficult to imagine that Mars—a tiny planet that, being tiny, probably cooled early in its history—was still undergoing such massive volcanism. So for the time being, the vegetation thesis held sway.

NASA prepared to launch *Mariner 4*, a space probe, which would pass Mars in mid-1965.[23] (The *Mariner 3* launch had failed.) Unlike *Mariner 2*, *Mariner 4* would carry a camera. With luck, the camera might solve age-old Martian mysteries. Even the most sophisticated space buffs couldn't help hoping, deep in their hearts, that the pictures would reveal a Mars worthy of Edgar Rice Burroughs. Or, if not Burroughs, then Chesley Bonestell, the space artist whose renderings defined the solar system for a generation of Americans. Bonestell depicted needle-nosed spaceships descending onto a pastel-orange Mars, crisscrossed by algae-green waterways that might or might not have been canals. Daydreaming over Bonestell's paintings in books and magazines, many adolescents thought: Why not? They imagined a rust-colored wasteland, not unlike Monument Valley, sprinkled with odd-looking plants and shy, scurrying creatures. Overhead, even in daytime, stars glistened in the thin Martian atmosphere.

How thin? In the early twentieth century, Percival Lowell had estimated the surface air pressure as being less than 10 percent of that of Earth. That was very low, by terrestrial standards. Still, one could easily imagine lower forms of life surviving in those conditions. Lowell's pressure estimate endured into the early 1960s. Then came shocking news, based on ground-based observations with sensitive sensors: the true pressure was only about 1 percent of that of Earth. (Later measurements revealed that the pressure is even lower, about three fourths of one percent.[24]) Not only is air essential to life, but such low pressure essentially precluded the existence of surface bodies of water—the essential elixir of known biology.

For the pro-Mars lobby, this was bad news indeed. Worse, new observations of Mars revealed that the Sinton bands had nothing to do with Mars. They were caused by deuterated water in the atmosphere of Earth, which had contaminated Sinton's spectral analysis of Mars.[25] So much for Sagan's excitement about possible Martian acetaldehydes! Sinton had made his mistake by conducting his Mars and "control" observations (comparing Mars spectra with lunar spectra) on different nights. "If you did that in an analytical chemistry course," Stanley Miller says with a cackle, "you can kiss your grade goodbye." Years afterward, when Sagan was, in Miller's words, "carrying on about Mars," Miller would tease him by asking: "Carl, would you tell us the acetaldehyde story?"[26]

Evolutionary biologists have tended to doubt the existence of intelligent extraterrestrials. In the 1960s, the top doubter was the famed paleontologist George Gaylord Simpson, who wrote an anti-SETI essay titled "The Nonprevalence of Humanoids." Simpson argued against looking for life on Mars, citing research by C. C. Kiess et al. indicating that the Martian atmosphere was thick with poisonous nitrogen oxides. Sagan investigated the Kiess team's claim and concluded, to the contrary, that any nitrogen oxides would be negligible. Wittily, he wrote that the amount of oxides in the Martian atmosphere is at most one-tenth the amount of oxides in the air above Los Angeles and that "life in Los Angeles may be difficult, but it is not yet impossible."[27]

Sagan reported this happy finding in a letter to Harold Urey. Blunt as ever, Urey wrote back to Sagan that Kiess's work on Martian nitrogen oxides was obviously wrong anyway, and that Sagan was wasting his time by paying attention to it. Dismayed to be accused of proving the obvious, Sagan responded with a peremptory "many thanks."[28]

THE TOPIC "POSSIBLE MARTIAN ECOLOGIES" appeared on the agenda of a Mars conference at the Charter House Hotel in Cambridge, Massachusetts, in January 1964. Sagan chaired the meeting. Another topic was "the rectilinear markings," otherwise known as the "canals." Prior to the conference, Sagan stressed its importance, noting that the attendees would make a "critical evaluation of existing evidence relevant to life on Mars," and that he wanted them to consider all the possible methods for detecting life. Speeches from subsequent Mars conferences in 1964 and 1965 were reprinted in a 516-page book, *Biology and the Exploration of Mars*, published by the National Academy of Sciences in 1966. The book has twenty-nine articles, nine of them authored or coauthored by Sagan.

In one article, "Higher Organisms on Mars," Sagan asked a startling question: "Is it possible that there is an indigenous civilization on Mars?" He continued:

> Statistically, the likelihood seems very small. The lifetimes of both Earth and Mars are about 5 billion years. If the putative Martians are behind us, it is most likely that they are far behind us, and have not yet achieved a technical civilization. If they are even slightly more advanced

than we, their presence should be discernible. The telescope reveals no obvious signs of a reworking of the Martian environment by intelligent beings; although in the inverse situation, the detection of life on Earth with an optical telescope on Mars would be marginal. . . . A radio observatory of contemporary terrestrial manufacture on Mars could detect local television broadcasting on Earth. No formal searches have been made from Earth with narrow-bandpass receivers for comparable transmissions on Mars. . . . Finally, again extrapolating from terrestrial technology, an advanced Martian civilization might be expected, by this time, to have arrived on Earth. There is no evidence for such visits.

He resorted to one of his favorite arguments, an order-of-magnitude or "back-of-the-envelope" calculation: "If we uncritically apply terrestrial analogy, we find that if the Martians were 5000 years behind us, they would not yet have a civilization; if they were 50 years ahead of us, we should, by now, have deduced their existence." On this basis, he calculated the odds of a Martian society more advanced than ours as one in 100 million, adding dryly: "These probabilities are very low."[29]

In NASA's 1964 "summer study" about Mars at Stanford, the participants concluded that it was "entirely reasonable that Mars is inhabited with living organisms."[30] On November 28, NASA launched *Mariner 4* toward Mars. On Earth, a new UFO wave soon began. Saucer buffs speculated that saucers came from Mars; perhaps *Mariner 4* would spot their civilizations.

CARL SAGAN HAD SOME highly unusual ideas. How deeply did he believe them, though? He wore his Optimist hat in public, when he talked blithely about the possibility (however remote) of "advanced life forms" on Mars. But in conversations with colleagues, he often donned his Skeptic hat. He could be a stern opponent. In February 1965, as *Mariner 4* arced across the solar system, Sagan responded to a letter from Frank Salisbury, who had sent him a manuscript for possible publication in *Icarus*. Salisbury's manuscript argued that intelligent life might exist elsewhere in the solar system. In his response, Sagan assured Salisbury that he had carefully considered the article, but that it was not appropriate for *Icarus* because much of the evidence for extraterrestrial life that Salisbury cited "may be psychological rather than astronomical in origin." By this Sagan was referring to such evidence as the so-called canals and UFO sightings. He pointed out, for example, that the astronomer E. M. Antoniadi had argued in the 1930s that the "canals" "break up into disconnected fine detail when the seeing becomes superb." Sagan was also skeptical about Salisbury's references to the possible artificiality of the Martian moons, and Martian "flashes" (nuclear blasts?).[31]

THE GRAY PAGES of *Icarus* required one standard of evidence; the silver screen required another.

Arthur C. Clarke was arguably the world's greatest living science-fiction writer. As a young man in the 1930s and 1940s, he and his British chums had run the British Interplanetary Society. They designed hypothetical spaceships, and garnered members such as George Bernard Shaw. Once they persuaded C. S. Lewis, who wrote science fiction but dismissed spaceflight as poppycock, to go to a pub with them. (Lewis's amicable parting words were: "I'm sure you're all very wicked people, but how dull it would be if everyone was good!")[32] At one point Clarke invented the concept for communications satellites but didn't bother to patent the idea. His subsequent essay about this feat is titled "A Short Prehistory of Comsats, or: How I Lost a Billion Dollars in My Spare Time."[33]

Sagan probably drew inspiration from Clarke's writings, such as the novel *The Sands of Mars* (about terraforming Mars) and the short story "The Sentinel" (about the discovery of an intelligent artifact on the Moon). Likewise, Clarke followed Sagan's work on the terraforming of Venus. In the mid-1960s, Clarke and filmmaker Stanley Kubrick began turning "The Sentinel" into a film tentatively titled *Journey beyond the Stars* (later *2001: A Space Odyssey*). One of Kubrick's bigger headaches was how he should depict the aliens in the film. Hollywood aliens usually looked like actors in cheap rubber suits, or like giant insects wearing drag-queen makeup. What would real aliens look like? At one point Kubrick considered depicting an extraterrestrial wearing an "all-black suit with white polka dots," according to one account.[34] Wisely, Clarke advised Kubrick to seek Sagan's advice.

Sagan first glimpsed movie glamour in Kubrick's New York penthouse, where the three men dined and talked. Kubrick explained that he wanted the aliens to look human. Clarke was opposed; aliens almost certainly wouldn't look like humans. Sagan urged them not to show the aliens at all. "I said it would be a disaster to portray the extraterrestrials," he later told the writer Neil McAleer. "I argued that the number of individually unlikely events in the evolutionary history of man was so great that nothing like us is ever likely to evolve again anywhere else in the universe. I suggested that any explicit representation of an advanced extraterrestrial being was bound to have at least an element of falseness about it and that the best solution would be to suggest rather than explicitly to display the extraterrestrials."[35] Sagan's insight revealed a hitherto unseen aesthetic subtlety.

Kubrick followed Sagan's advice. When *2001* premiered, stunning audiences with its breathtaking special effects and neo-Nietzschean symbolism, they never glimpsed the aliens, super-beings who transformed astronaut David Bowman into one of their own. Unseen, the aliens acquired an otherwise unimaginable emotional power. To this day, the film retains a quasimystical allure. Young people of the late 1960s loved watching it stoned. So do their children.

There is an addendum to Sagan's encounter with Kubrick, which Clarke revealed after Kubrick died in early 1999. As mentioned earlier, Sagan's brashness sometimes irked others. "The first—and only!—time I took Carl to meet Stanley Kubrick, we arranged for a longer meeting the next day," Clarke says. "However, Stanley took me aside and said, 'I can't stand the fellow—make some excuse—say I'm busy tomorrow!'" So Clarke took Sagan to the World's Fair instead.

A CLASSIC DICHOTOMY: Hollywood dreams and everyday disillusionment. July 14, 1965, was the Bastille Day of exobiology. It revolutionized the young science in the hardest way possible, by humbling it in front of the world.

On that day, the *Mariner 4* space probe flew within ten thousand kilometers of Mars. The probe transmitted to Earth twenty-one close-up photos of Mars. They showed a shocking scene, a planet covered with craters, like the Moon. The lunar analogy was so unexpected that people overreacted to it. They concluded that Mars *was* like the Moon: namely, lifeless. Headlines announced the grim news: humans are alone in the solar system. Science-fiction writers were heartbroken; they had spent their careers populating the solar system with fictional beings and could no longer do so with a clear conscience. Sure, they could write about aliens in other star systems instead. But the stars are so far away, so abstract, and so lacking in individual personalities like the planets of pulp lore: Mars, the "angry red planet," crisscrossed with canals fed by melting polar caps; Venus, the dinosaur-haunted jungle world . . . "No, no, the stars are not enough," Isaac Asimov lamented. "It's the solar system we want. . . . The solar system we can never have again."[36]

Sagan was upset by a *New York Times* editorial titled "The Dead Planet," which said *Mariner 4* had shown that Mars was lifeless. A quarter of a century later, he was still angry about that editorial. "Specious arguments, completely wrong! In fact, Mars is much more earthlike than anyone was saying in 1965," he remarked in 1991. "So I took it as my responsibility, maybe a quixotic mission, to point out the possibilities [of Martian life], which were being excluded on inadequate evidence."[37] He emphasized that *Mariner 4* had recorded its images thousands of miles from Mars. If aliens flew thousands of miles past Earth, how easily could they perceive intelligent life here? Not easily at all, he argued. To prove his point, he obtained satellite photos of Earth and scrutinized them for any signs of terrestrial intelligence. He found virtually none.

One exception was a crisscross pattern of harvested trees in a snow-covered forest. If it is so hard to spot terrestrial life from space, then why should *Mariner 4* be expected to detect Martian life?[38]

This was an old argument, by the way. The ancient writer Plutarch proposed that lunarians look down at Earth, "lying like the sediments and dregs of the universe amidst damps, mists, and clouds," and wonder how anything could inhabit such a horrid place. In the nineteenth century, the flamboyant astronomer-popularizer Camille Flammarion, the Carl Sagan of his day, argued for the existence of lunar beings. He took a balloon flight and observed, far above Earth, how still and lifeless it appeared. So, he concluded, if Earth was so full of life and yet appeared lifeless from afar, why might not the moon also harbor life?

Only Mars landers could determine whether Mars was inhabited, Sagan reasoned. At that time, NASA was planning to launch a huge Mars lander (so big that it would be sent aboard a Saturn rocket) called Voyager (not to be confused with the star-bound *Voyager* probes of later years). However, *Mariner 4*'s grim images of Mars helped undermine support for the Mars Voyager mission, which was canceled in 1967.

In retrospect, Sagan's plea to launch interplanetary cameras had backfired. The black-and-white, low-resolution pictures contained too little detail to make Mars look very interesting, but just enough detail to reveal the dispiriting craters. The images were so bleak, in fact, that they invigorated opponents of Mars missions. *Science* editor Philip Abelson sent Sagan a draft of a paper arguing against the probability of Martian life. Mars, Abelson said, has such weak gravity that it probably lost any reducing atmosphere early on. Hence it never generated organic molecules. Also, Abelson said, the *Mariner 4* photos showed no hot springs—possible abodes of microbial life—like those envisioned by Sagan and Lederberg in their microenvironments paper. Sagan fired back that he thought Abelson's conclusion was "very dubious" because the photographs were of such poor quality that they were inconclusive. Also, he argued, a Martian reducing atmosphere might have lasted longer than Abelson thought, despite Mars's lower gravity. Being farther from the Sun than Earth is, Mars was colder, so its hydrogen gas would be less energetic and, thus, less able to escape Martian gravity.[39]

Private letters would not save the Mars program, though. To spare NASA's future Mars missions from the congressional budget ax, space scientists needed to sell Mars to the public. In particular, they needed to exploit the ultimate propaganda tool: television. But television wasn't interested. The three networks (which *were* television, in those pre-cable days) were too busy covering the manned Gemini and Apollo programs to spend much time on the Mars program. Television was about imagery, which the astronaut program generated in bulk: spectacular launches, nervous wives watching the rockets ascend, handsome American heroes pointing their thumbs straight up. In contrast, *Mariner 4* offered . . . what? Drab pictures of a dead planet? Besides, robotic missions were too small to carry political clout; their very cost-effectiveness worked against them. They required comparatively tiny budgets and limited staff, so who would miss them if they were slashed from the next fiscal year? No one, except (legislators reasoned) a bunch of eggheads and slide-rule users. Nor were there major pro-space groups—like The Planetary Society, the National Space Society, and the L-5 Society of future decades— that could drum up grassroots support for robotic missions.

Who, then, could save future Mars flights? In the 1950s, Wernher von Braun had gone on Walt Disney's television show to talk about the future age of solar system exploration.[40] In the 1960s, Carl Sagan started doing the same thing. Once he was invited on Dave Garroway's television show along with Gilbert Levin, who was developing life-detection instruments for Mars robot landers. Levin was a tall, easy-smiling Baltimore resident in his thirties, who got his Ph.D. in sanitary engineering at Johns Hopkins. Under a NASA contract, he developed a life-detection device called Gulliver. Sagan, Levin recalls, was "very dynamic, enthusiastic, and had a wonderful way with the English language—despite the trace of the New York accent."

During the program, Garroway first interviewed Levin. The engineer explained how Gulliver worked by placing a prototype on the ground, then "getting down on my hands and knees. I exhaustively described all the mechanisms—how the string was shot out—I bored everybody with the details." Gulliver would fire a long, sticky string into the Martian terrain. Martian soil would stick to the string. Then Gulliver would reel the string back for automated microbiological analysis.

"After I had finished, Dave turned to Carl and said to Carl, 'What do you think of this experiment going to Mars?' Carl just went off on a completely different level. He waxed philosophic—he talked about the implications for our religion, our society, our politics. And I realized: we were very different."[41]

Levin had explained the science, the *how* of Mars research. But Sagan had explained the *why*. That evening, one imagines, countless wives told their husbands who had appeared on Garroway's show: a handsome young man, "Carl somebody," who had explained so charmingly and convincingly why taxpayers should send string-squirting robots to Mars. A TV evangelist was born.

Decades later, Sagan reminisced about his private Mars campaign of the 1960s. "People would say, 'Sagan is off again doing his speculative thing.' *Of course* I was doing my speculative thing, that was my intention! I didn't pretend that it wasn't speculative. I was saying, 'Look, here is a niche in which you can imagine life. And don't you have to know more about the niche, or look directly for life, before you exclude it?' And this was at a critical time when we were designing [robotic] missions, so I wanted to be sure to have these issues considered in the choice of instrumentation and so on. It was a conscious effort. I certainly knew there was some career risk, because everybody told me that at the drop of a hat. . . . I figured I'd take my chances. . . . I didn't expect that there wouldn't be a penalty."[42]

In 1966, he wrote (with Jonathan Norton Leonard) his first truly "mainstream" book, *The Planets*, which was part of Time-Life's series of popular science books. Time-Life sold these well-illustrated volumes through its big-selling magazines *Time* and *Life;* that guaranteed a large readership. Kuiper wrote the foreword for *Planets*. Inside, Sagan took the reader on a tour of the whole solar system, and explained why it was worth visiting. About Mars, he cited I. S. Shklovskii's theory that Phobos contains relics of a vanished Martian civilization, including "libraries and museums . . . the glorious history and achievements of their doomed civilization." While few scientists expected to find such wonders on Mars, Sagan added, "explorers . . . will certainly look for archeological evidence of long-dead civilizations. . . . Life may have started early on Mars and evolved faster, reaching its civilized climax hundreds of millions of years ago."[43]

Sagan also promoted Mars in the pages of *National Geographic*. In those days, the magazine was a staple of middle-class homes. It was always there, lying on the coffee table, or packed in bookshelves, its yellow binding an unmistakable invitation to visit the ocean bottom or the inside of a volcano or the grinning, bare-breasted inhabitants of a Pacific isle. Sagan's paean to Mars exploration appeared in the December 1967 issue.

Mariner 4's photos (Sagan assured *Geographic* readers) were no cause for disillusionment. Mars might still be inhabited—by humble life forms, true, but life nonetheless. And true, Mars had little air and virtually no oxygen or water. But was oxygen really that indispensable for life? The early Earth lacked oxygen, too; certain microbes survive without oxygen; and "some, like the bacteria that cause tetanus, are actually poisoned by it." The article included a color painting of a hypothetical Martian plant, protected from ultraviolet radiation by a translucent, flying saucer–shaped shell. Even if no life survives today, the Martian crust might contain fossils of a vanished carboniferous era. Imagine the Mars of eons past: perhaps its climate was more pleasant, and "oceans of a sort lapped Martian shores." No preacher whose projected date for the Second Coming had come and gone argued more eloquently for sticking to the old-time faith, to the goal of Mars exploration—first with robots, then with humans.

Sagan ended the article on a messianic note. He had already advocated space exploration as an alternative to war. Now he made a broader claim: spaceflight might ease the worsening tensions of modern life. In fact, space exploration might be "a prerequisite for our continued survival as a species. . . . Our planet is in danger of becoming a vast closed society, with its tensions and enormous energies turned inward upon itself." He did not explain exactly how space technology could alleviate global problems that were primarily political, sociological, economic, ideological, spiritual, and psychological in nature. A clue, though, lies in his remark about the energies of our society becoming "turned inward" upon the society itself. For all his liberalism, Sagan apparently viewed social conflict in the same way he viewed war: as a kind of thermodynamic phenomenon. Society accumulates pressure like an overheating pot; so take the lid off and let the steam out—or in human terms, head skyward.

Sagan's article included a quote from Arthur C. Clarke: "Though men and civilizations may yearn for rest, for the Elysian dream of the Lotus Eaters, that is a desire that merges imperceptibly into death. The challenge of the great spaces between the worlds is a stupendous one, but if we fail to meet it, the story of our race will be drawing to its close. Humanity will have turned its back upon the still untrodden heights and will be descending again the long slope that stretches, across a thousand million years of time, down to the shores of the primeval sea." On this apocalyptic note, Sagan concluded: "Mars moves through our skies in its stately dance, distant and enigmatic, a world awaiting exploration. If we but choose, it waits for us."[44]

How many readers scanned those last lines and thought: "Right on!"? And how many thought: "What a lot of bunk!"? In the late 1960s the nation split apart, and with it much of the world. One month after Sagan's words graced coffee tables everywhere, the Tet offensive shocked Americans who had assumed we were slowly "winning" the Vietnam War. President Johnson announced he wouldn't run again; Martin Luther King and Robert Kennedy were assassinated; police busted war protesters' heads in Chicago. Meanwhile, students rioted in France and Soviet tanks rolled into Czechoslovakia. For some, spaceflight offered a welcome distraction from this terrestrial mayhem. Is it surprising that so many sighed with relief the following December, when *Apollo* astronauts orbited the Moon and read a Bible passage to the world? But for others, the space program was immorally wasteful and irresponsible. The heavens could wait; first, humanity had to clean up its act on Earth. For the rest of his life, Carl Sagan would argue that it was possible to do both—to have Mars and manna too.

MEANWHILE, SAGAN HAD NOT FORGOTTEN about Venus. He and Lederberg had suggested that Martian life might survive in isolated microenvironments. Might Venus have habitable microenvironments, too?

The Venusian surface was horribly hot; of that Sagan was sure. Not everyone agreed, though. In 1967 John Strong and William Plummer proposed that the intense Venusian microwave radiation came not from the surface but rather from intense atmospheric electrical activity. Thus Venus might still have "large areas of habitable surface," they wrote in *Astrophysical Journal*.[45] The Nobel Prize–winning chemist Willard F. Libby of UCLA (who invented carbon-14 dating) proposed that ice sheets, lakes, and "small oceans" might exist near the Venusian poles. "Life seems to be distinctly possible at the edges of the ice sheets," he wrote in the March 1968 issue of *Science*.[46] In Britain, the iconoclastic astronomer V. Axel Firsoff studied Venus through his telescope. He claimed to see icy polar caps and bright points—snow-clad mountains?—poking above the Venusian haze. "The south cap was exceptionally clear. . . . My wife saw it without any previous experience of observing Venus."

Firsoff scorned Sagan's greenhouse theory: "The worst feature of this extravagant conception is that it appears to be unsound in physics, being based on a straight extrapolation from data applicable to modern atmospheric pressures." If Venus were extremely hot, its oceans would evaporate, forming dense clouds that would block sunlight and cool the surface. Consequently, he argued, "it is wrong to jump to the conclusion that Venus is totally unsuited for life, even of a near-terrestrial type." Firsoff envisioned a Venus with "a barren rocky desert in the tropics . . . followed by a zone of torrential, boiling hot rains, giving rise to circumpolar seas, which grow colder and colder, eventually to yield to mild winter conditions and caps of real snow, as visual observation suggests."[47]

Sagan ignored such fantasies. Still, he and others suspected that biologically speaking, Venus might not be a totally lost cause. Most exobiologists were turning their sights toward Mars, but, recalls biophysicist Harold Morowitz, then at Yale, "there was a group of us who thought that decision was being made all too quickly because in many ways Venus was a more interesting planet." They were impressed by Strong's spectral data, which implied that "there might be a lot more water on Venus than has subsequently emerged to be the case.

"One night," Morowitz reminisces, "at least four members of the group were eating dinner—myself, Sagan, Kim Atwood, and [Wolf] Vishniac. We decided that since we were the four people who were interested in Venus, we should form a society." What to name it? "Society of Venusian Biologists" was considered, but "Venusian" struck Morowitz as "an ugly word. Carl suggested 'Society of Cytherean Biologists,' but that sounded too snobbish. Then—I cannot tell you who this came from, it might have been me—we picked 'Society of Venereal Biologists.' We elected officers!" The society lasted exactly one evening.

Ask people who knew the young Carl Sagan to describe him, and one word keeps popping up: "brash." He was "a brash young junior faculty member," Morowitz says. "When I say 'brash,' I mean he didn't have a lot of unexpressed opinions! He would say what was on his mind. It was often controversial. These were fields where there were many unanswered questions, and he always generated excitement." Sagan and Morowitz discussed whether Venus's microenvironment might be its upper atmosphere. Floating creatures might thrive at great heights, far above the searing surface.[48] In a joint letter to *Nature*, they described this hypothetical Venusian ecosystem. A typical Venusian might resemble a balloon or a "float bladder," which varies its altitude by changing its air pressure. (It needs to regulate its altitude, lest it be sucked fatally into the boiling-hot lower atmosphere.) One of these "gas bags" might be "about the size of a ping pong ball. Much larger organisms would also be possible." Capable of photosynthesis, they could ingest life-supporting minerals blown aloft by winds.[49]

Sagan described a similar ecosystem for the Jovian atmosphere in his book *The Planets*. This book included an arresting, slightly comical artist's rendering of the creatures—weird, watermelon-shaped balloons floating through the clouds of an alien world. They have huge mouths, through which they suck floating organic particles. To propel themselves hither and yon, they exhale gases in one direction or another.[50]

Sagan fell in love with this idea of "balloon animals." A decade later, he and E. E. Salpeter developed a far more detailed account of floating Jovian creatures and published it in the normally staid *Astrophysical Journal Supplements*.[51] In Sagan's television series, *Cosmos*, one of the most spectacular images showed these strange entities, drifting amid the storm clouds of the Jovian atmosphere and grazing like cows on aerial organic mists.[52]

The "ping pong ball" reference in the 1967 letter to *Nature* inspired a cartoon in the *Saturday Evening Post*. According to Sagan, it showed "a ping pong player (dressed in Florida sports shirt and Bermuda shorts) about to serve, and interrupted by the cry from his ping pong ball, 'Stop! I am a friendly visitor from another planet!' "[53]

WHEN IT CAME TO extraterrestrial life, Sagan didn't follow a dogmatic party line. Sometimes he argued that it was possible (as when he espoused lunar life, balloon animals in the skies of Venus and Jupiter, and polar bear–sized creatures on Mars). Other times he shot down arguments for exobiology (as when he showed that the surface of Venus is too hot for life). An example of the latter is his explanation for the Martian "wave of darkening." Until the mid-1960s, many astronomers regarded the wave of darkening as evidence of Martian vegetation change. Yet Sagan and Pollack discovered its true nature, which was *non*biological. It's ironic: Sagan blew away the last indirect evidence for Martian life even as he struggled to convince Americans to support Mars missions. He was a complicated man.

The Sagan-Pollack theory of Mars brightness changes should also interest scholars who study how scientific ideas evolve. In recent decades, many historians and philosophers of science have claimed that scientific objectivity is a myth. They argue that scientists—like most of us—follow their hearts, not their minds; their desires, not the data. And this is certainly true, much of the time.[54] Still, when it came to the nature of Martian brightness changes, Carl Sagan followed his mind, not his heart.

The Sagan-Pollack Mars theory is intriguing for another reason, too: it's based on a mistake. The history of science is full of seeming blind alleys that led to historic breakthroughs. Roentgen discovered X rays because he accidentally exposed photographic plates to electric discharges from a vacuum tube; Fleming accidentally discovered penicillin when he left a Petri dish exposed to aerial microbes. And Feynman had one of his best insights when someone was clowning around—when a man tossed a plate and the physicist observed its curiously wobbling descent.[55]

Sagan and Pollack's mistake came when they proposed a new explanation for the "canals" of Mars. *Mariner 4* saw no long, linear features that clearly matched Percival Lowell's description of "a mesh of lines and dots like a lady's veil." This raised (once again) the issue of scientific objectivity. Had past astronomers completely hallucinated the lines? Or were they real physical features of the planet that astronomers had misinterpreted due to the limitations of human visual acuity? Long ago, skeptics such as E. M. Antoniadi had argued that the canals were "a psychophysiological rather than an astronomical problem," Sagan and Pollack noted in the October 8, 1966, issue of *Nature*. But if this were so— if the canals were simply illusions caused by the human eye's struggle to make sense of "disconnected fine detail near the limit of resolution"— then why didn't astronomers report canals on other worlds? For example, on "Mercury or the Moon or Jupiter"?[56]

In the early twentieth century, a few scholars suggested that the canals were natural, not artificial, objects. One theory held that they were giant crustal wrinkles that formed after Mars cooled and contracted from a primordial molten state. This theory tallied with the then-popular theory of contractionism, which explained the topography of all rocky planets, like Earth and Mars, on the assumption that they cooled from a molten state.

By the 1960s, though, contractionist theory was dead. Replacing it was an exciting new hypothesis: plate tectonics (a greatly modified version of the old continental drift concept). It explained Earth's mountain ranges, ocean basins, and other large-scale features on the assumption that the crust consists of numerous thick slabs. These drift about, carrying continents atop them like logs stuck in ice. New crust emerges volcanically at the mid-ocean ridges. On maps, for example, a long, thin, mid-ocean ridge arcs like a zipper for thousands of miles through the north and south Atlantic; it reveals where the Americas and Europe-Africa split apart, many millions of years ago. One day, either Sagan or Pollack (Sagan couldn't remember who) glanced at a map showing the mid-ocean ridges. He noticed their vague similarity—in their great length and relative linearity —to the Martian canals. Might plate tectonics also have occurred on Mars? Were the canals the Martian equivalent of terrestrial undersea ridges?[57]

Traditionally, Sagan noted later, astronomers assumed that Mars was as smooth "as a bowling ball." But if Sagan and Pollack's hypothesis was correct, then Mars had undergone substantial crustal change. Its surface elevations must be more extreme; it must have high-altitude "continents" and low-lying "ocean" basins—minus water, of course (its air pressure was so low that bodies of water would readily evaporate). Astronomers could not distinguish these elevation extremes through telescopes. Radar could, though. By bouncing high-frequency radar pulses off the Moon, Venus, and Mars, astronomers mapped topographical variations on those worlds. They discerned mountains and craters beneath the overcast of Venus. As for Mars, Sagan wrote in his *National Geographic* article:

> Formerly scientists thought the dark areas were lowland basins, but we have analyzed radar signals bounced off Mars, as well as other evidence, and have found indications that many dark areas are gentle slopes reaching heights of as much as ten miles.
>
> We think the bright areas tend to be lowlands, similar to our ocean basins, but filled with dust rather than water. And the canals that cross these dusty seas, and at least some of the finer lines found by Mariner IV—as we interpret the evidence—turn out to be ridges comparable to the oceanic ridges and seamounts that lace ocean bottoms on earth.[58]

In short, he maintained, the canals were real physical features—but natural ridges, not artificial structures. Old-time astronomers had not hallucinated the lines; they had seen genuine objects, although they misinterpreted their nature. Sagan probably found this explanation emotionally as well as intellectually satisfying, because he believed passionately in science. Science led to truth, whereas religion, mysticism, and metaphysics he viewed as mental murkiness that only led down blind alleys. But scientific objectivity was cast in doubt by the canal dispute of the late nineteenth and early twentieth centuries. Noted astronomers of that time had reported seeing the lines, and convinced the public they were real. If the canals were pure or near hallucinations, then perhaps science was less a royal road to truth than an overgrown, unmapped, meandering, pitmarked path through a dark thicket, leading nowhere in particular. For reasons unrelated to the old canal debate, by the 1960s historians and philosophers of science (notably Thomas Kuhn) were already beginning to suspect that that was the case.

Sagan and Pollack's proposed explanation for the "canals" was not merely a novel theory in astrogeology. It was also an unconscious defense of science's superiority to other belief systems. In coming years, as increasing numbers of scholars doubted scientific omniscience, Sagan would find new occasions to defend it.

YEARS LATER, as we shall see, Sagan and Pollack's explanation for the canals was disproven. They were not long, thin ridges; rather, they were illusions, largely unrelated to the true terrain of Mars.[59]

Yet this incorrect hypothesis steered Sagan and Pollack toward two important insights, first, that the wave of darkening is caused by windblown dust, not by vegetation changes, and second, that Mars has dramatic mountains and valleys. Thus, well before future space probes mapped Mars in detail, these two young Harvard scientists correctly anticipated broad features of the red planet (while erring in some details). Far from being as smooth as a bowling ball, Mars has dramatic topographical variations—immense peaks and abyssal gorges far more spectacular than anything in the Himalayas or the American West. It is, in fact, an astrogeologist's delight. Someday space-suit-wearing graduate students in astrogeology with sledgehammers and magnifying glasses will clamber about its surface.

During the Martian springtime, Sagan and Pollack said, winds blew small, bright particles (which, being lightweight, were easier to loft) off hillsides. Because the particles were bright, their departure made the terrain (as seen from space) appear to darken. This, and not seasonal vegetation change, accounted for the long-mystifying wave of darkening. Come wintertime, the winds grew fiercer. They blew the little particles back onto the hillsides, brightening them again and ending the wave cycle. "Thus," Sagan wrote in *National Geographic*, "Wind-blown dust and not living plants may explain these intriguing changes on Mars."[60] Echoing an earlier proposal by space scientist D. G. Rea, Sagan believed that the reddish surface consisted substantially of an iron-rich mineral called limonite.[61]

No scientific idea is completely original. Every thinker stands (to paraphrase Newton) on the shoulders of giants—or at least on the shoulders of countless pipsqueaks. Had anyone anticipated Sagan and Pollack's explanation for the wave of darkening? If anyone did, it was Dean B. McLaughlin of the University of Michigan. In the 1950s, as we have seen, he attributed the surface changes to windblown ash from erupting volcanoes. McLaughlin's theory was incorrect; there is no evidence of present-day volcanism on Mars (although there are enormous shield-type volcanoes, the biggest in the solar system). Still, Sagan had known about McLaughlin's theory in 1955. Might it have unconsciously influenced his later theory about windblown *dust*? Sagan contemplated the question many years later: "I don't know. Maybe something about McLaughlin was in my head. It sometimes happens that a thing is in your head and you don't know if you read it or thought of it yourself. . . . I was not *consciously* aware of McLaughlin's priority." Obviously he had forgotten the letter he wrote to Muller in 1955 reporting the publication of McLaughlin's hypothesis in the *Proceedings* of the Astronomical Society of the Pacific.[62]

In any case, McLaughlin's work had been qualitative, not quantitative. "Nobody had actually done the dust transport physics . . . [so] it doesn't take away from the contribution we made," Sagan said. Still, as noted earlier, Sagan was sensitive to possible "priority" questions. In his writings of the 1970s, he went out of his way to praise McLaughlin's work, thus guaranteeing the little-known Michigan astronomer a footnote in scientific history.

Every good story has a lesson, and this one has several. Unhappily, the lessons are contradictory. On the one hand, Sagan and Pollack's astrogeological theory of the canals ultimately fell flat, reinforcing the modern suspicion that scientists aren't as objective as they like to think. On the other hand, Sagan promoted the nonbiological explanation for the wave of darkening, although it undermined the last indirect evidence for life on Mars—his passion since childhood. There is something noble, even heroic, about Sagan's determination—in this case, anyway—to follow the data, not his desires.

JIM POLLACK DID NOT TRY to cover up his public shyness; he wore it
on his sleeve. Sagan was comfortable in front of television cameras; Pollack was not. He spoke slowly and dispassionately; he didn't even *like*
publicity. By the summer of 1976, when the Viking landers landed on
Mars, Pollack was a distinguished space scientist himself. Once he served
on a panel at a televised press conference—and fell asleep. "That shows
you how interested *he* was in publicity," observes his sister, Ginny Pollack Breslauer. She joined him in California for the *Viking 1* landing.
The media buzzed with anticipation: would the *Viking 1* find life on
Mars? Sagan was going off half-cocked, speculating in the *New York
Times* and elsewhere about large creatures that might hop past the *Viking
1* camera. Pollack and his sister took a break from the tension by heading
to a southern California resort. The clerk said there were no available
rooms. A no-nonsense New York businesswoman, Ginny whipped out
a newspaper, showed its reference to the brilliant Dr. Pollack, then
pointed to her red-faced brother: "*This* is Dr. Pollack!"

"We got a suite!" she recalls gleefully. "And my brother was ready to
kill me."[63]

Sagan and Pollack—Batman and Robin, one scientist called them.[64]
The mystery was: which one was Batman? Both men were recognized
experts on the Venus atmosphere. But by the early 1970s, Sagan had
moved on to many other topics; he still coauthored papers on the subject
with Pollack, but Pollack did most of the work. David Layzer of Harvard
expresses a common view: "The general feeling was that Carl's scientific
reputation in [Venusian studies] was due largely to Jim's work and to
their papers. [Jim] was an incredibly hard worker. And very, very smart.
And very pleasant."[65]

At Harvard, Sagan later remarked, "Jim Pollack was my first graduate student. [With him], I had someone I could talk to about every aspect
of planetary science. And if I don't get to say it later, let me say it now: I
learned at least as much from Jim as he learned from me."[66]

Their childhoods were eerily similar; their adult personalities, utterly
different. Sagan was brash, aggressive, colorful, sometimes chilly, and
sometimes a glad-hander; he loved way-out ideas and leaped from interest to interest. Pollack was quiet, careful, cautious, meticulous; he loved
to plow and replow the same field, steadily perfecting his calculations.
Born on July 9, 1938, James Barney Pollack, like Sagan, came from a
New York–area Jewish family in the women's garment business. Like
Sagan's parents, Pollack's parents had (Ginny says) "the most wonderful
marriage." As in Sagan's family, there were two kids—an older boy, a
younger girl. Like Sagan's parents, Pollack's were smarter than their
occupations—and were determined that their children would do better.

And like Sagan, Pollack had no hankering to enter the garment trade. "Ginny can have the business!" he declared.

Pollack grew up in Woodmere, Long Island, described by his sister as "a very affluent and successful Jewish community." He was a class brain: he scored 800 (the top score) on his college math boards. His English score was in the 700s, which worried him. To improve it, he memorized the dictionary and taped lists of words around the house. In the basement, he managed a "rocket science laboratory" (shades of the young Sagan's basement chemistry lab). There, "he would mix chemicals and do experiments. Then he would come upstairs to the third floor, where we still have a big deck, and he would look through his telescope at the sky."

"Early on," Ginny says, "he almost stuttered because I think his mind was going much faster than his mouth." At Lawrence High School, he wrote a science column called "Mental Pablum." He loved baseball, ranked first on his track team, and was high school valedictorian.[67] Pollack graduated from Princeton in 1960 and earned a master's at Berkeley in 1962. Then he entered Harvard's graduate program in astronomy, became Sagan's student, and received his astronomy Ph.D. in 1965. He "was certainly a private person and somewhat ethereal in his thinking about the world," recalls Jay Pasachoff, a fellow graduate student at Harvard. "He was mainly concerned with science.

"I went with [Jim and] one other fellow to Quebec for the total eclipse. We drove together, bringing some apparatus that we had borrowed from Donald Menzel. After chasing around, looking for a hole in the clouds, we did observe the eclipse, observing from a riverbank.

"On the way home, we came through the border, and the border agent asked me who I was, where I was born, and he asked the same questions of Jim, who couldn't quite remember his address, which part of the dorm he lived in. He couldn't remember his dorm number! I was getting nervous about whether he would be able to re-enter the United States." Finally, the customs officer noticed the crates in the back of Pasachoff's car—"Property of U.S. Air Force"—and waved them by.[68]

When Jim concentrated, Ginny says, "he was like a laser; there were blinders on him. He had such a form of concentration, it was incredible. I remember a party in the backyard when they landed on the moon. He had a portable TV outside and all he wanted to do was watch the landing on the moon."[69] Pollack's reticence may have been partly a form of self-protection. While Sagan had much to tell the world, Pollack had one big secret that few would ever know.

As different as night and day, the two men would stick together for three decades. When Sagan became a celebrity, his scientific reputation suffered; but Pollack's kept rising, all the way to his tragically early end. Scientists had mixed opinions of Sagan. But they revered Pollack; an oil portrait of him hangs at NASA's Ames Research Center. In 1989, Ginny accompanied Pollack to a ceremony at which his colleagues gave him a lifetime achievement award. Sagan was there, smiling and applauding. One guest confided to Ginny: "Now *Jim* is Batman."[70]

EVEN THE BRIGHTEST researcher, though, is almost helpless without research grants. Sagan knew how to rake them in. By late 1965, he held a $198,000, three-year NASA grant to study "Biochemical Activities of Terrestrial Microorganisms in Simulated Planetary Environments" (the "Mars jar" research with his sometime colleague Stanley Scher) and a $134,684, two-year NASA grant to study general exobiology. Meanwhile, he served on Working Group V of the Committee on Space Research (COSPAR, a branch of the International Council for Science), plus the Bioscience Subcommittee of NASA's Space Sciences Steering Committee, the American Geophysical Union's Committee on Planetary Atmospheres, the organizing committee of the International Astronomical Union's (IAU) Commission 16 (Physical Study of Planets), IAU Commission 17 (the Moon), the NAS Panel on the Origins of Life, the International Academy of Astronautics organizing committee regarding communication with extraterrestrial intelligence, and the NAS Space Science Board's exobiology committee and planetary atmospheres study panel. Also, he was secretary of the Space Science Board's Subgroup on Scientific Undertakings for Man in Space, and chaired a Mars conference at Cambridge and the Mars and Mercury sections of the Gordon Research Conferences.

He was a busy consultant—to the U.S. Air Force Scientific Advisory Board's Geophysics Panel, to the same board's Committee to Review Project Blue Book (the Air Force UFO office), to MIT's Instrumentation Laboratory, to Cornell University's Arecibo Ionospheric Observatory, and to the TYCHO Study Group at NASA's Office of Manned Space Flight.

And, of course, to RAND, the Air Force think tank. Sagan's Harvard resume shows he had a "Top Secret" clearance with the Air Force and a "Secret" clearance with NASA.[71] He was not alone: "I once saw a CIA file on some Soviets," he recalled. "And I recognized who had given the information to them—which of my colleagues—from [their] characteristic phrases."[72]

For a few years, Sagan felt comfortable in this shadowy world. In 1963 he traveled to a COSPAR meeting in Warsaw, Poland. There he had, he recalled, "a six-hour ideological debate with the Chinese delegation." He also conveyed a message from Pugwash, the antinuclear group, to a local notable, Leopold Infeld, the famous physicist and friend of Einstein. "I was invited to his home, and had dinner there, and met his children." As a distinguished physicist living in the Eastern bloc, Infeld was likely to hear intriguing tips from time to time. He told Sagan that China was about to test its first atomic weapon, and urged him to get the information back to the United States, to alert others. For the first time, a Third World nation would own nuclear weapons—and it was a nation on the doorstep of Vietnam, where American troops were fighting.

Sagan returned to the United States and spoke to a contact linked to the CIA. For some reason, Sagan recalled, the contact "was wholly disinterested [in the Chinese atomic bomb]. I could tell, because he didn't make notes. It wasn't on his list of questions." In 1964, almost thirty years old, Sagan was starting to question his government's competence and morality.[73] Soon, so would many other Americans. On October 16, 1964, China detonated an atomic bomb equivalent to twenty thousand tons of TNT.

SAGAN'S ARREST for political fundraising in Williams Bay in 1956 had been a fluke. He wasn't overtly political again until the early 1960s. At Madison, he had missed being present at the birth of a section of the New Left, in William Appleman Williams's history classes. He missed history's tide again in Berkeley, which he left before the free speech movement. But he got to Harvard just in time to join the civil rights movement.

In the early 1960s, countless Northern youth caught buses south to Alabama, Georgia, and Mississippi, where they marched with Martin Luther King Jr., Medgar Evers, Ralph Abernathy, and others. Their number included many young Jews from liberal and leftist families. Sagan traveled to Alabama in 1963 to engage in what he recalled as "lots of marches and rallies, lots of work that I did on a very . . . journeyman level." In 1965 he lectured about astronomy at Tuskegee Institute, a historically black college. "I read about Carl Sagan at Harvard and I invited him to come talk to high school teachers, and he did," recalls Tuskegee professor James Henderson, now retired. "And from then on, he came back about six or eight times." The men became lifetime friends. At Tuskegee, Sagan's science speeches were a hit. He was also "a great mixer," and helped to pay one student's tuition.[74]

About that time, the Vietnam War reached a bloody impasse. The U.S. government seemed unable and unwilling to extricate itself from the quagmire, and it ignored sage advice from its own experts. Sagan's college acquaintance Marcus Raskin was a leftist intellectual who, somehow, landed a job in the Kennedy White House, ostensibly to serve as the "conscience" of National Security Advisor McGeorge Bundy. But Raskin's conscience was too genuine for Bundy, who fired him.[75] In November 1963, Kennedy was assassinated. Lyndon Johnson became president. Thereafter, the bloody impasse became a bloody nightmare. "My realization of what a horror the American involvement in the Vietnam War was," Sagan later observed, "didn't really hit me until '64–'65 —earlier than many, but later than I should have.

"I can remember a party at Harvard, where there must have been fifty faculty members. . . . One other guy and me were the only ones who were opposing the Vietnam War. There were two of us that thought there was anything wrong with it, and dozens who thought it was just great." That "guy" was Dr. Lester Grinspoon, a faculty professor of psychiatry and, subsequently, a fateful figure in Sagan's life. Grinspoon recalls that in 1966, at the soiree at the home of surgery professor Jacob Fines, "I found that there were two of us taking on this room full of people who were defending the United States position in Vietnam." The other one was Sagan, who was "quite passionate" in his opposition to the war. "We were so concerned about our country doing something stupid, immoral," Grinspoon says. "He struck me as very bright, brilliant, very personable, with a great sense of humor—a man whose brilliance was linked to an extraordinary imagination." That soiree kicked off a three-decade friendship "where we considered ourselves each other's best friends," says Grinspoon. Sagan's political open-mindedness impressed Grinspoon, who noted that, among other things, Sagan was "open to students who were very much involved with SDS [Students for a Democratic Society, a 1960s radical group]. I know he was involved with SDS at some level."[76]

At some point, Sagan realized that he was part of the vast machine that made the war possible. He had advised the military, accepted military research money, accepted its security clearances, and engaged with its allies in the intelligence service. This was the machine that he now saw devoting its immense might to crushing impoverished peoples of Southeast Asia.

In 1966, as U.S. bombers napalmed the tropical jungles and hundreds of thousands of American youths were sent to fight, Sagan took a stand. It was not a particularly daring stand, compared to that of those who burned their draft cards in front of television cameras or refused to enlist or headed for Canada. But for Sagan, it was a big step, a rejection of the shadowy military world he had first encountered at Yerkes, through Kuiper, and had known ever since. He informed the U.S. Air Force Scientific Advisory Board's Geophysics Panel that he was resigning. "I just had had it up to here with the Vietnam War, and the attitudes I encountered with general officers in the Pentagon appalled me," he later remarked. "They tried to dissuade me, saying that I could recuse myself on issues connected with the Vietnam War and just worry about nuclear strategic issues, and other things like that. [But] I was just too uncomfortable to do it. And again, a number of senior people who were friendly to me in the scientific community told me that was really dumb and I shouldn't do it—the contacts were invaluable and all that—but I just couldn't bear it."

He had reached a moral crossroad. "Before that, I was happy to get some military support. I certainly was a consultant for many years to the RAND Corp.; that was military money that was supporting me.

"But once I got a serious look at Vietnam, I couldn't do it, and I haven't since. I've given talks at [military] service academies and the National War College and the CIA and the NSA and all that, but I've not accepted any [military] money for research since then. [Some colleagues thought this was] a really stupid move; [they were] concerned for my career. There were those who said 'If they don't spend it on me, they'll spend it on something terrible! I'm helping [end] the war by draining money from the military.' There were all kinds of specious arguments."[77]

Sagan also turned in his security clearance. In later years he told his third wife, Ann Druyan, what he had told the brass: "I don't want to know anything more secret than what the head of the Bureau of Indian Affairs knows. . . . I certainly don't want to be a party to this crime."[78]

DURING THIS PERIOD Sagan encountered another occasional war protester, Linda Salzman, who became his second wife. A student at Tufts (she graduated in 1968) and an aspiring artist, Salzman met Sagan at a dinner party (according to one of Sagan's later secretaries, Shirley Arden, to whom Salzman told the story). The moment (Salzman recalled) that she saw this tall, dark, handsome fellow with the dazzling smile, she said to herself, "That's for me!" She was a pretty brunette, with doe-like eyes and a warm smile. Sagan was enchanted by her beauty, soft-hearted sexiness, and fun-loving ways, so much lighter-hearted than his own. They began dating; in time they became intimate.

During Sagan's Harvard years, Salzman "lived right down the street in Cambridge," recalls Valerie Sorenson, Sagan's secretary. "She was very nice—very innocent, I thought. And she was crazy about [Carl]. She really wanted to get married. She was a Jewish girl and she tried to explain to me how that was—all the pressures on a Jewish girl to get married."[79]

Linda Salzman was born in 1940 to Phil and Rae Salzman of New York. According to Linda and Carl's only child, Nick Sagan, Phil Salzman ran a store and came from a family that represented "a really colorful side of New York—Jewish intellectual, but also sort of grifterly." One relative married a mobster. Linda's parents died when she was a teenager, a blow that haunted her for decades.[80]

Sagan's friends regarded Sagan and Salzman as an unlikely match. "My mother was a rebel and something of an iconoclast," says Nick Sagan, now a television writer in California. "She wanted to be an artist, . . . to make her own way." Salzman had artistic yearnings, but she was not a firebrand intellectual like Lynn Margulis. Still, under Salzman's early influence, Sagan would begin to develop his own nonscientific sides, and to explore more seriously the unnerving appeal of irrational belief systems.

EVEN AS THE VIETNAM WAR RAGED, U.S. and Soviet officials began paving the path to détente. They wished to avoid future confrontations like the one with Cuba in 1962, which had almost ended in nuclear war. President Lyndon Johnson and Soviet premier Aleksey Kosygin conferred at Glassboro, New Jersey. Arms negotiators began discussing ways to limit both sides' antimissile projects. "Massive retaliation" was out; "peaceful coexistence" was in. In Carl Reiner's 1966 film *The Russians Are Coming, the Russians Are Coming* (a comedy), frightened New Englanders arm themselves against the equally frightened crew of a stranded Russian submarine. But they ultimately band together in a crisis, and the curtain falls on a thawing cold war.

With his usual good timing, Sagan's book *Intelligent Life in the Universe* (coauthored with Shklovskii) appeared in 1966. What a novel concept it seemed: an American scientist and a Soviet scientist actually talking to each other about a thrilling topic. The book was a triumph of popular science writing. Its arresting front cover included a black-and-white composite photo of the Earth with a galaxy in the background. Its 509 pages covered everything from the origin of life to interstellar travel, from the possibility of Martians to UFOs.

Sagan loved clever epigraphs, and opened each chapter with fitting literary quotes. (His Hutchins education had not gone for naught.) The text consists of alternating remarks by Sagan and Shklovskii but reads smoothly, like one voice. (A subtle notational system allows the reader to tell who wrote which passage. Sometimes, though, it is obvious—for example, when Shklovskii comments on dialectical materialism.)

The book alternates between cosmic sobriety and down-to-earth whimsy. It opens with an epigraph from Pindar's *Sixth Nemean Ode*, then shifts to a Walt Kelly "Pogo" cartoon. Then we see a photo of countless stars at the galactic center. The caption reads: "According to the estimates of Chapter 29, a planet of one of these stars holds a technical civilization vastly in advance of our own." The best books convey a sense of their authors' personalities; anyone reading *Intelligent Life* could tell that Carl Sagan was an erudite man with a sense of fun.

Perhaps no modern writer has matched Sagan's ability to make space seem so enormous, creation so prolific, and time so vast, as a sampling of his remarks will attest:

> Interstellar space is as empty as a cubical building, 60 miles long, 60 miles wide, and 60 miles high, containing a single grain of sand.[81]

> On the average, a million solar systems are formed in the universe each hour.[82]

> The light producing the image of a very remote galaxy on the photographic plate may have left the galaxy when the first cells were forming in the primitive oceans of the Earth.[83]

He discussed SETI lightheartedly, noting that aliens might transmit coded signals for assembling "material goods":

> We might receive, for example, detailed instructions for the construction of . . . a scale model of the capital of Delta Pavonis 3, a household appliance of Beta Hydri 4, or perhaps a novel scientific device developed on 82 Eridani 2.[84]

(This sentence anticipated the plot of his novel, *Contact*.)

He added a moral spin to an account of stellar nucleosynthesis:

> The existence of the elements gold and uranium on the Earth provides strong evidence that the material from which the Earth was formed once passed through a supernova. The influence of these two supernova products, gold and uranium, on the recent history of mankind is striking. Possibly, there are other planets in the galaxy, formed in regions of the Galaxy where supernova explosions are few. Are their inhabitants happier for having no gold and uranium?[85]

The back cover of the book included blurbs from H. J. Muller, Isaac Asimov, Frank Drake, and Fred Whipple. The *Christian Science Monitor* called it "fascinating . . . a smoothly flowing style. [Sagan] is particularly adept at explaining scientific concepts for laymen . . . transcendent." *Newsweek* cited it as "a unique collaboration-by-mail between two distinguished astronomers." "A remarkable collaboration," said the *Washington Post*. Muller's blurb put the co-authorship in a historical context: "It is high time . . . for serious theoretical collaboration between the U.S.A. and the U.S.S.R. . . . . That two people who have been so constructive in their complementary works should now succeed in joining forces is cause for international rejoicing."

AS USUAL, HAROLD UREY was less enthusiastic. Prior to publication, Sagan had sent Urey galley proofs of the book and requested a promotional blurb. Urey replied coldly that he didn't think a book on the subject of extraterrestrial life could really have any value, given how little was known about the subject. He also noted, ominously, that the section about the origin of the solar system gave short shrift to his own work on that topic.[86]

Still, *Intelligent Life in the Universe* established Sagan as a young scientist to watch. It also identified him as an important advocate of improved U.S.-Soviet relations. (That status would prove useful decades later, when he befriended Mikhail Gorbachev, led the "nuclear winter" debate, and pushed for joint U.S.-Soviet Mars missions.) The lay liberal intelligentsia began to notice Sagan. An extract of the book appeared in *Saturday Review*.[87] Sagan's discussion of UFOs was reprinted in the antimilitarist *Bulletin of the Atomic Scientists*.[88] Intrigued by Sagan's eloquence, science writers began to phone him for quotes. They found him approachable and articulate—and clever, and eloquent, and amusing. "Boyish," many thought. His voice was handsome, very bass but soft, an alluring mix of the stereotypically hypermasculine and hyperfeminine— authoritative yet reassuring. He spoke melodiously, with an arresting habit of "punching" certain vowels and consonants ("*BILL*-yunnns").

In the words of exobiology historian Stephen J. Dick, *Intelligent Life* became "the bible of the SETI movement."[89] The book sold well— about twenty-five thousand copies, publisher Fred Murphy says—but not as well as it deserved. "We were young people and pretty amateurish at this," recalls Murphy, now retired and living in Boca Raton. "The bottom line is [that we promoted it] very inadequately." Even in San Francisco, he had trouble persuading a local bookstore to carry *Intelligent Life*. Holden-Day was "a small company, geared to textbooks. I didn't know anything about trade books. If Random House had had this book, it would have sold hundreds of thousands of copies."[90]

It also might have propelled Sagan to global fame far earlier. As it happened, *Intelligent Life* brought him to the attention of scientists and some intellectuals, but its initial success was transient. Not until the early 1970s (when he participated in the *Mariner 9* mission, co-designed the *Pioneer* plaque, wrote *The Cosmic Connection*, and began appearing on Johnny Carson's television show) would Sagan taste real fame. At that time, Dell would issue a paperback edition of *Intelligent Life*. The paperback was obviously designed for the "counterculture" generation: the black-and-white galaxy was gone, replaced with a psychedelic image of Saturn.

When the *Pioneer* plaque made news, Sagan was discovered by another young writer with a great future, Cynthia Ozick. In a somewhat stream-of-consciousness essay for *Esquire*, she called *Intelligent Life in the Universe* "a kind of speculative Miltonic epic, thronged with epigraphs from poets, philosophers, early physicists, the Bhagavad Gita." A self-professed "scientific illiterate," she described her slightly contentious interview with Sagan in a New York hotel room. He removed his shoes— "a monarchal gesture. Star-scientists are, after all, the emperors of our pygmy intelligences. . . . His manner toward scientific illiterates?— *noblesse oblige*, instructional grace.

"He denies that the [*Pioneer 10* and *11*] undertaking—a Message to Super Beings on a plate of gold!—partakes of hubris, Tower-of-Babelism, Pharaonic solar boats, messianic faith." She compared his assumption that aliens would be benevolent to religious faith. "What you postulate is Angels," she scolded him. "Faith, the same old faith."

"Not faith," Sagan replied. "Calculation. Extrapolation."

"But you don't *know*. You might as well confess to a belief in seraphim."[91]

YEARS LATER, Shklovskii and Sagan would finally meet, at a SETI conference in Soviet Armenia. The Russian's warmth and bawdy humor endeared him to the visiting Americans. Later Soviet authorities permitted Shklovskii to travel to the West. According to Frank Drake, Shklovskii was tired of fourth-rate Soviet shoes, so in England he spent much time in shoe stores. In Berkeley, Shklovskii bought "playing cards with dirty pictures on them and a campaign button that said 'Pray for Sex.'" He pointed to the button and joked: "In your country, this slogan is offensive for one reason. In my country, two reasons."[92] In the 1980s, Sagan's novel, *Contact*, includes a Russian scientist, Vaygay, who is a thinly disguised version of Shklovskii. (We know this because Vaygay tells the same playing-card joke.)[93]

Sagan's professional relationships tended to be transient. For every Jim Pollack or Bishun Khare, who stood by Sagan's side for decades, many more worked with Sagan just once or twice. His interests were broad and his attention span short. After a collaboration, Sagan typically moved on—nothing personal, no hard feelings. Sagan and Shklovskii never collaborated on another book, either. Shklovskii died in 1985; several years later, as the cold war faded into history, his memoirs were published in English. He mentions Sagan briefly: "With his American business sense, Sagan effectively used the 'Soviet-American book' as the springboard to a dynamic pop-science career. . . . Now he's a very progressive millionaire, an active fighter against the threat of nuclear conflagration, and a scientist on the rosily optimistic flank of the spectrum on the question of extraterrestrial civilizations. I have no grievance against this businesslike, cheerful, and congenial American: at my request he did all he could to help my brother when he fell sick in Paris."[94]

Intelligent Life in the Universe was Sagan's only book for Fred Murphy's publishing house, Holden-Day. After attracting such favorable reviews, Sagan couldn't be expected to stick with a small San Francisco textbook house with an inadequate marketing arm.

Technically, Holden-Day did not owe Shklovskii any royalties. There was no U.S.-Soviet copyright convention at that time. Still, Sagan felt that Holden-Day should pay Shklovskii a token fee as a gesture of gratitude. Sagan "didn't want to give anything to Shklovskii out of his royalties," Murphy says. "He sort of put the burden on me." At the time, "Holden-Day was being held together with airplane glue and paper clips, and we were not obligated to pay Shklovskii a thing. [But] we made out a check to Shklovskii for $1,000, which was not very much."[95]

Sagan's friend Ronald Blum also sold two books to Holden-Day, and is now a close friend of Murphy's. Murphy, Blum observes, has "mixed feelings about Carl. He feels that Carl deserted him after he gave him his first big break."[96] At one point, Murphy says, Sagan sued him to recover unpaid royalties. "He got this big-time law firm. He got very litigious." Murphy maintains that he wanted to pay Sagan the royalties, but Holden-Day was in financial trouble and its spare cash was "a matter of survival." Sure enough, the firm eventually folded in the 1980s.[97]

SAGAN'S HARVARD COLLEAGUES watched him rise toward fame. David Morrison, one of Sagan's graduate students, recalls how "in 1967 or 1968," he had a meeting with Prof. David Layzer, who was on a campus committee that monitored graduate students' progress. "I was right in the middle of my thesis . . . and [he] told me privately that 'obviously' Carl Sagan was 'not competent' to be a thesis adviser. . . . He advised me to drop Carl and drop my thesis and start all over with a new subject with a new adviser. It was a terrible position to put a graduate student in." (Morrison refused and finished his Ph.D. under Sagan.[98] Layzer denies that the incident occurred.)

Even Kuiper nursed doubts about his old student. On March 3, 1967, Prof. Bruno Rossi of MIT wrote to Kuiper and told him that the university was considering offering Sagan a post in astrophysics. Rossi sought Kuiper's opinion of Sagan. (Kuiper, it should be recalled, had only recently written the foreword to Sagan's book *The Planets*.) On March 3, 1967, Kuiper responded with a letter that concluded by enthusiastically recommending Sagan for the position. But he weakened the force of his recommendation by expressing concerns about Sagan's responsibility as a scientist. While he complimented Sagan's intelligence and the originality of his ideas, he cautioned about what he perceived as Sagan's tendency to reach premature scientific conclusions and noted that Sagan's grasp of data could be "a bit shallow." The field of space sciences in general was, Kuiper warned, in the midst of a heady period of excitement, and many scientists in the field had displayed what he called an "excessive aggressiveness" about their ideas. He said that Sagan was not necessarily guilty of this, but that given Sagan's enthusiasm for such a broad range of subjects and for interesting ideas, he would benefit from an academic environment where, "amidst competent colleagues," his more irresponsible tendencies could be disciplined. In such an environment, he argued, Sagan could be expected to make significant contributions.[99]

It was one thing for Sagan's critics to call him "a bit shallow" or to question the responsibility of his scientific conclusions. But for his former thesis adviser to do so . . . ! MIT is a top institution that hires only the best. It doesn't seek young upstarts who require training in restraint about decision-making. Rossi could not have missed Kuiper's underlying message: the man who had single-handedly fought for acceptance of Sagan's doctoral thesis at Chicago had less than total confidence in his judgment.

In 1967, Sagan was up for tenure at Harvard. Harvard rarely awards tenure to anyone, yet, according to his later recollections, Sagan was confident that he would get it. He could, after all, claim some real achievements at Cambridge. His Mars and Venus research with Pollack was clearly important. Meanwhile, Sagan was advising NASA, the National Academy of Sciences, RAND Corporation, the Air Force, and other agencies; surely *that* would impress the tenure committee. He was widely regarded as a superb instructor. Perhaps he also thought that Harvard would be impressed by his science popularization—in particular, by *Intelligent Life in the Universe*. Just look at those blurbs on the back cover! Perhaps he was in the same situation as at Yerkes in the late 1950s, when he assumed that his colleagues would be delighted by his popularization efforts.

Sagan was, however, naive in his assessment of his situation. Perhaps his ascent had been too easy. A number of times before Harvard, he could have self-destructed. Yet people had always stepped in to rescue him. He might have missed getting his doctorate, but Kuiper pushed it through; he broke his promises to the Stratoscope II team, but Berkeley scientists did his job for him; he largely withdrew from *Mariner 2*, leaving others to fill the gap; and Lord knows what angel prevented "Venus as a Planet of Possible Biological Interest" from seeing the light of day.

But there was no one to save him from the wrath of Harold Urey. Sagan and three colleagues wrote a paper, "Thermodynamic Equilibria in Planetary Atmospheres," which they submitted to *Astrophysical Journal*. The coauthors were Ellis R. Lippincott of the University of Maryland department of chemistry and Richard V. Eck and Margaret O. Dayhoff of the National Biomedical Research Foundation in Silver Spring, Maryland. The paper described how astronomers might remotely detect life on other planets by scanning their atmospheres for organic molecules "far in excess of their thermodynamic equilibrium proportions." Sagan had previously sent a draft of the paper to Urey for comment, who fired back some criticisms.

Astrophysical Journal published the paper in February 1967.[100] Urey read it and, apparently, hit the roof; it contained few or none of his suggested changes. About the same time, Urey (like Kuiper) heard from Dr. Rossi of MIT. Rossi told Urey that MIT was thinking of hiring Sagan, and would he mind commenting on the young man? For almost a decade, Urey had been irritated by the young astronomer's shenanigans; here was a chance to blow off steam. Urey stuck a copy of Sagan's *Astrophysical Journal* article in an envelope to Rossi, along with a letter that can only be described as an all-out blast.

Urey complained that Sagan and his coauthors had made no substantive changes in the article in response to Urey's criticisms. He also said that the article was typical of Sagan's academic papers, which he said were far too wordy and lacking in intellectual meat. Much of what Sagan wrote, Urey said, was unnecessary rehashing of already well-established findings made by other people. He specifically cited Sagan's work on the amount of nitrogen oxides in the atmosphere of Mars, which, Urey complained, was totally unnecessary work because Urey had himself established as far back as 1961 that there was no nitrogen on Mars. Urey further criticized Sagan for having "dashed all over the field of the planets," studying so many different subjects, from the origin of life to the characteristics of atmospheres. Though he concluded that Sagan was intelligent and interesting, and might well make a contribution to the MIT department, he ended on a strongly negative note, saying that he had lacked confidence in Sagan's work "right from the beginning."[101]

Though this letter was sent to MIT, another letter that Urey wrote to Harvard may have killed Sagan's hope for tenure there. Fred Whipple, now in his early nineties, says he was "very fond" of Sagan, "and I tried to keep him here. The reason I couldn't keep him was because of Harvard's ad hoc committee." When a teacher is up for tenure, the school seeks the opinion of a committee of outside academics. "There happened to be a Nobel Prize winner on that committee who didn't like the amount of publicity Carl was getting and blackballed him. It was Harold Urey. The story is that he wrote a letter to the ad hoc committee and in it was a damnation"—Whipple paused and corrected himself—"a very negative response to Carl Sagan. I did see the letter later." Especially because Urey was a Nobel Prize winner, the committee would have weighed his advice heavily. Sure enough, the committee denied Sagan's bid for tenure.

Why exactly was Urey so upset? "I think it had to do with the large amount of publicity Carl's writing got," Whipple says. Urey "considered that *infra dig*—not dignified—for a Harvard professor. It was the way he felt. Quite a few scientists in those days didn't feel it was right to have that sort of publicity."[102] Another possible reason for Urey's rage (as historian Ronald Doel told me) is that Sagan was a former student of Urey's old nemesis, Gerard Kuiper. Urey's 1950s battles with Kuiper over solar system astronomy were long and bitter; they left scars. Furthermore, Urey as a chemist was contemptuous of the casual manner with which astronomers treated questions of astrochemistry—as casual as the manner in which (he believed) Sagan had theorized about other planetary atmospheres. Urey was fighting not merely for what he regarded as integrity in chemical theorizing but also for chemistry to be accepted as a legitimate player in debates over astronomical and astrophysical phenomena. For many decades, chemists have deeply resented what they perceive as physicists' tendency to treat chemistry as a topic of "secondary" epistemological value (that is, as one that can ultimately be reduced to physics). Urey's anger may, in part, reflect this resentment.

Urey might not, however, have been the sole engineer of Sagan's downfall. As mentioned earlier, Sagan didn't have many allies on the Harvard faculty. His Harvard friend Lester Grinspoon—himself a controversial figure, a pioneering advocate of the decriminalization of marijuana—suspects that people on campus also brought Sagan down: "I know Harvard well enough to know there are people there who certainly do not like people" who are outspoken.[103] Also, Urey probably wasn't the only scientist who wrote a hostile letter to the ad hoc committee. A leading astronomer who requests anonymity says that in the late 1960s he was visited by a scientist, the director of a "large research group," who proudly showed a letter he was sending to Harvard—a letter assailing Sagan. "It was clear he took pleasure in this. [Carl] was much resented for his notoriety and celebrity."

Other astronomers envied Sagan all his life, Grinspoon adds. "Wherever you turned, there was one astronomer being quoted on everything, one astronomer whose face you were seeing on TV, and one astronomer whose books had the preferred display slot at the local bookstore."[104]

Like Thales—who, as mentioned, walked with his head in the clouds until he fell into a well—Sagan was surprised to be denied tenure. After five years as an assistant professor, he recalled, "there was a standard review, and at the end of that I was, to my surprise, and to the surprise of at least some others, denied tenure." At the time, Sagan didn't realize that Urey had opposed his tenure bid. Sagan remembered that "Fred Whipple and others said, 'Wait another year and we'll send it through again.' . . . I had tenure at Smithsonian so I could stay at the Smithsonian side forever. But this was the Harvard side [that rejected me]. So I was open to offers [at other colleges] as a result."[105]

Years later, Whipple told Sagan what Urey had done to him. By that time Sagan knew; Urey had recently sent him a letter that Sagan interpreted as a *mea culpa*. In 1991, long after Urey's death, Sagan was still wondering what he had done to upset him. "The only thing I can think of in that period is that I did send him a copy of my book with Shklovskii and he [Urey] said 'Your description of my work is unrecognizable.'*

"Then I went back and discovered that there were a number of references to Urey's work which the indexer [of *Intelligent Life in the Universe*] had not included under 'Urey.' That's the only thing I can think of [that might have upset Urey]. But I don't think it was that bad a sin to result in [being denied tenure]."[107]

In fact, Urey's name doesn't appear at all in the index of the hardcover edition of *Intelligent Life in the Universe*. By contrast, Muller, Lederberg, and Kuiper have entries. The omission was obviously accidental and was corrected later: the index to the subsequent Dell paperback edition includes extensive references to Urey. Might Urey's omission from the original index have been the real source of his rage against Sagan? Surely he wouldn't enjoy being omitted while his nemesis, Kuiper, got such prominent play. Urey might also have been upset by this remark in the book regarding solar system accretion: "The second mechanism, suggested by the American cosmochemist Harold C. Urey of the University of California and others, is based on weak chemical bonds between colliding bits of matter. In effect, the condensates in the primitive nebula are imagined to be sticky. The view is not so very different from that of Lucretius."[108] Urey might not have appreciated his rigorous research being likened to the musings of an ancient poet.

Still, Urey probably would have opposed Sagan's tenure bid in any case. From the late 1950s on, he and Sagan had expressed fundamentally different philosophies of science. Urey was the tough, old-time empiricist, reluctant to speculate about things remote and unseen. Sagan, by contrast, thought those things were especially worthy of speculation.

As we have seen, different people had radically different opinions of Sagan. To some critics, he was a near charlatan and an egomaniac. But

---

*Urey's actual charge in the June 29, 1966, letter to Sagan is that the book "mentions my views slightly and quite incorrectly, I think."[106]

to Fred Whipple, he was "a good scientist and a wonderful popular writer, and I was just sorry that we couldn't keep him . . . a sweet, kindly person."[109]

STILL, SAGAN'S HARVARD YEARS didn't end on an entirely sour note. Before leaving Cambridge, he ascended to a powerful post in planetary science. And he remarried.

Since 1962, he had been an associate editor of *Icarus*. When the journal's publisher, Academic Press, sought a new editor, Sagan was a logical candidate. His literary skill was obvious—witness his books *Intelligent Life in the Universe* and *The Planets*, and his many technical and popular articles. Kuiper advocated giving Sagan the job. So did Joseph C. Chamberlain, the Yerkes professor who had once questioned Sagan's work on the Venus greenhouse effect. Chamberlain met with an Academic Press representative and stressed Sagan's "breadth of . . . understanding" of science. Also, perhaps surprisingly (given Sagan's reputation for brashness), Chamberlain praised the young man's "tact."[110] Tact is a valuable quality for a journal editor, who sometimes mediates between flustered authors and invisible, often imperious referees.

In July 1968, Sagan's name first appeared on the cover of *Icarus*, along with those of co-editors A. G. Wilson and Zdenek Kopal. The following January, Sagan became editor in chief. Until the end of the next decade, the cover displayed his name alone, a form of self-advertising rare in the self-effacing world of science.

He took over *Icarus* just in time for the Golden Age of planetary exploration. The first Moon landing was only months away; the Soviets were launching probe after probe into the atmosphere of Venus; and the next few years would bring numerous planetary missions to Mercury, Mars, and the outer planets. "I hope to make this journal a true reflection of the excitement and high standards of recent studies of the moon and planets," Sagan wrote to Kuiper. Changes were due: "In the past, *Icarus* has had the policy of permitting associate editors to submit their own contributions without further review. Such a policy can potentially lead to certain abuses, and I intend to see that all future papers be subject to competent review." Sagan also planned to significantly expand *Icarus*'s coverage of space news, conferences, and books, and to report the results of space missions.[111]

Icarus was known for publishing unusual articles, and Sagan was happy to continue doing so.[112] In his first year of editorship, he published one scientist's piece claiming that Earth is orbited by at least ten small "moonlets" besides the Moon. Another article suggested that "polywater," a then-hypothesized exotic form of water, exists on Venus. (As it turned out, neither polywater nor the moonlets exist.) "I tried to publish on a regular basis papers that were to differing degrees outrageous, in an attempt to stir up the community to disprove this or that," Sagan later recalled.[113] Sagan's appreciation for "outrageous" ideas recalls Karl Popper's praise for "bold conjectures." The philosopher Deborah A. Redman paraphrases Popper's view as follows: "Not only should science proliferate theories as much as possible, subjecting them to crucial tests so that science grows, it should propose 'bold conjectures,' that is, conjectures that run a great risk of being false. Highly falsifiable theories (those that rule out more) are preferred to less falsifiable ones. . . . [S]cientists should not be cautious."[114] And certainly no one would ever accuse Sagan of caution.

MARTIN LUTHER KING WAS ASSASSINATED in Memphis on April 4, 1968. Two days later, while race riots ripped U.S. cities, Sagan and Linda Salzman were married in Boston. She was twenty-eight; he was thirty-four. He had been single for five years and was ready to give love another try. Salzman later reminisced that for her, meeting Sagan was love at first sight. She usually called Sagan "Carlo." Sagan and she had moved in together and had been living together for some time when she gave him an ultimatum: he had to decide by December 31, 1967, whether to marry her or to move out. The ultimatum apparently did the trick.

Sagan's friend Lester Grinspoon, who was Sagan's best man at both this wedding and his third wedding, to Ann Druyan, had doubts about the marriage from the start. He thought that Sagan and Salzman might be too different to make for a good marriage. "Carl had an enormous curiosity," he says, "a towering intellect, and linked to those two things was his staggering imagination. And Linda just wasn't in the same ballpark." Still, Grinspoon recalls how appealing Salzman was—a "weekend hippie," in his words—and thinks that her more carefree, lighthearted approach to life was good for Sagan. He recalls that she had "a voluptuous quality to her—in fact, she was flirtatious, coquettish. . . . She was very attentive to how she looked, loved to shop." She "taught Carl a lot. She taught him how to have more fun. He tended at that time to be a little stiff, both in relations with people and in how much he'd let himself go. Even his great sense of humor was a little bit reined in. Linda taught him more about popular music, how to just enjoy himself and relax; she was a fun person. She opened him up to people he wouldn't have had anything to do with otherwise—more casual, nonacademic people."

Sagan's friend Isaac Asimov, the prolific science and science-fiction writer, attended the wedding. Asimov met Salzman and was charmed by her—"an extraordinarily attractive young artist, rather shy and soft-spoken, and quite obviously deeply in love with Carl. I took to her at once."

Asimov was the formal witness for the signing of the marriage cer-
tificate. An atheist, Asimov noted that a rabbi presided over the wedding
ceremony, "a little, I think, to Carl's irritation, as it had been to mine
under similar circumstances twenty-five years before." Sagan's parents
attended, and Rachel was at her vexing best. Asimov later wrote in his
diary:

> In his little sermon, the rabbi spoke of the beginning of the universe,
> but put a religious cast upon it. Carl told me afterward that he had been
> hoping to get some mention of the big bang, and was disappointed that
> he had not.
>
> At the reception afterward, I was happy indeed, for the *hors d'oeuvres*
> and cake were excellent. What I remember best, however, did not make
> me happy. I met Carl's parents, and his mother said to me, calmly, "And
> how are your grandchildren, Dr. Asimov?"
>
> What did she *mean*, my grandchildren? I knew perfectly well that I
> was old enough to have grandchildren. At forty-eight, I could easily
> have had a twenty-five-year-old daughter who might just as easily have
> had a five-year-old child. Just the same, I *didn't* have any grandchildren,
> and she might just as easily have sneaked up upon it by first asking if I
> had children, then how old they were, and *then*, if it seemed likely,
> whether I had grandchildren.
>
> I said, freezingly, "I am *not* a grandfather."
>
> Mrs. Sagan said, "There's nothing wrong with being a grand-
> father."
>
> "Undoubtedly. I just happen not to be one."
>
> "Mr. Sagan and I have never been so happy as since we've had
> grandchildren."
>
> "Look, be delirious with happiness for all I care, but I am not a
> grandfather."
>
> Despairing of the effects of pure logic, I was looking about for
> something hard and heavy to reinforce the point I was making, but [my
> wife] Gertrude pulled me away.[115]

Someone once asked Mamie Eisenhower why she had married Ike,
and she replied: "Because we had nothing in common." Neither did
Sagan and Linda Salzman. "Part of the attraction [between them] was
she was so free-spirited and so artistic," their son Nick recalls. "The way
her mind worked was very different from the way his mind worked."[116]
That they married was an important sign: new yearnings were stirring
in Sagan's mind and heart. By training he was a scientist, a scorner of
illogic and metaphysics. He was the sort of man one expects to scoff at
art, intuition, irrationalism. Yet he married Salzman, an aspiring artist, a
hippie type. During their marriage, he would begin to express a hitherto
unseen side of himself, the side that resists logical classification and easy
explanation, that hides like a ghost within the neurological machinery.

8

Mr. X

CAREERWISE, THE BEST THING that ever happened to Carl Sagan was joining the faculty of Harvard University. The second-best thing was being denied tenure by Harvard. It's paradoxical: had he remained at Harvard, surrounded by colleagues who viewed him with indifference or disdain, he might never have become an important science popularizer.

Harvard shared the "proper," no-nonsense air of New England culture. By contrast, Cornell, in upstate New York, was in farm country where hippies were beginning to settle and where conscientious objectors stopped by to protest the war and share a toke before fleeing to Canada. Cornell was an excellent university—Ivy League—but the best American students didn't necessarily include it on their Top Ten lists. Some perceived it as an "ag" school (it had a large agricultural education program) in a hick town with little night life. Sagan's secretary, Valerie Sorenson, helped him move to Ithaca. But when he asked her to stay, Sorenson, a divorcée, refused: "It was a one-horse town, an insular community, and for someone who was single and trying to make her way, it was not a good place to stay."[1] The move was a comfortable one for Sagan's new wife, Linda Salzman, however. She had a "beatnik, bohemian kind of quality to her," recalls her son Nick. "It fit in really well with Ithaca, [with its] hippies trying to escape the culture."[2]

If Chicago, Yerkes, Berkeley, Stanford, and Harvard created Sagan the scientist, then Cornell created Sagan the celebrity. "It's clear that many people at Harvard thought that Carl was flaky, they thought that he was not a serious scientist, and that he was far too interested in personal aggrandizement through public speaking and the press. . . . He was much more accepted and honored at Cornell," observes his former student David Morrison.[3] Lester Grinspoon agrees: "Harvard doesn't need superstars—it's got so many of them. At Cornell, he *was* superstar."[4]

208

Indeed, Cornell regarded Sagan with awe. His presence made the school "cool" as it never had been before. His youthfulness, charisma, and optimism (during the grim Vietnam era) appealed to the "TV generation," who were taking their SATs and choosing a college, and wondering: Why not go to Cornell, home of that cool astronomer?

During Sagan's first decade at Cornell, he would show up all the snobs and green-eyed detractors at Harvard. He became the preeminent voice of American space science, a national (later international) celebrity visible enough to attract his first *non*scientific critics. Meanwhile, he continued doing science as he liked to do it: by flitting, butterflylike, from flower to flower. Not for him was the life of the pigeonholed academic who becomes a world-class expert on T-Tauri stars but knows nothing about the big bang. Nor for him was the stoic seclusion of the scholar, who takes bitter pride in refusing to popularize his life's toil on the reproductive strategies of carp. Sagan liked talking to reporters. He had liked being on stage, in the spotlight, ever since high school, when he delivered Thurber's bons mots to an audience of proud parents.

True, Sagan worked too hard. He did too much. His scientific accomplishments might have been less arguable had he restricted himself to one or two main fields and diligently plowed them until it was time to abandon all hope and become chair of the department. He bit off more than he could chew—and thus enjoyed one wonderful banquet after another, while most of his colleagues picked at their beets and parsley. In the process, Sagan befriended many fascinating fellow diners. His scientific lone-wolf days (for example, when he taught himself greenhouse theory) were over. Increasingly, as Cornell's David Duncan Professor of Astronomy and Space Sciences and director of its Laboratory for Planetary Studies, he relied on collaborations, usually transient ones. The results were sometimes scientifically significant, or at least headline-grabbing. They ranged from his work with George Mullen on the role of ammonia in the early atmosphere of Earth to his *Astrophysical Journal* article with E. E. Salpeter on the hypothetical "balloon animals" of Jupiter. He maintained close collaborations with a chosen few, particularly Jim Pollack and Bishun Khare. With Pollack, Sagan would erect an impressive edifice of research on the Venusian atmosphere. And with Khare, he would develop an iconoclastic view of cosmic organic chemistry, one centered on inexplicable brownish smears that he dubbed "tholins"—substances he thought might be important clues to the origin of life.

Also in the 1968–78 decade, Sagan cultivated his nonscientific side. He had just married an artist; she helped him tap his inner feelings, instincts, intuitions. Though he had felt awkward in social situations at Harvard, his social skills blossomed after he moved to Cornell. Perhaps in this less stuffy setting, he felt free to let his idiosyncratic conversational style out of the box. Eventually, he would become a Noel Coward of science, a man for whom fine conversation was an art, for whom bold articulation and quickness of wit were absolute virtues. He would dominate a conversation, and deservedly so, for he typically knew more about the topic at hand—and discussed it more suavely—than anyone else present. But he listened as well as he talked. During intense conversation, his dark eyes gazed at you as if you were the sole other sentient being in the cosmos. If you anxiously described the sorry state of your own research, he generously offered tips and suggestions—often crazy ones, but occasionally brilliant ones, too. Dale Cruikshank recalls that Sagan often sent an encouraging letter to an author of an interesting scientific paper—including Cruikshank's future wife, astronomer Yvonne Pendleton, in an era when most female scientists struggled to be taken seriously—and frequently added "a very cogent and penetrating comment or two. . . . Yvonne considers Carl to be one of the senior scientists most influential on her work and her career."

History does not record how many intellectual Gordian knots were cut by Sagan's razor-sharp tongue at wine-and-cheese faculty gatherings; there were more than a few. And he remembered what you said with astonishing precision; months later, he recalled your statements as accurately as if he had tape-recorded them. When he entered a room, the conversational level noticeably improved, as it must have in Oscar Wilde's day when he sauntered into a salon. Through conferences jammed with colleagues Sagan floated, beaming and chatting and joking; he was a six-foot gravity well toward whom everyone naturally gravitated. He was fun. "Hey, Carl is here!" It would be an overstatement to say that everyone loved him, for his bluntness upset many and his talent many more; in any case, he rarely failed to cause excitement.

At Cornell, Sagan flexed his new-found artistic muscles in his breakthrough bestseller, *The Cosmic Connection*. He became a television star, the upbeat educator of sleepy-eyed millions viewing *The Tonight Show*. During the Viking mission, he was the television networks' favorite talking head, whose playful speculations about an inhabited Mars maddened his colleagues but titillated viewers. And like a performance artist with a NASA-sized budget, he engaged in grand forms of self-expression: he sent "messages" to aliens aboard star-bound space probes, the *Pioneers 10* and *11* and the *Voyagers 1* and *2*. But aliens are highly unlikely to recover these probes, these infinitesimal specks now leaving our solar system for the galactic wilds. Their messages (two plaques and two records encoded with the sounds and imagery of Earth) are best thought of as glorious, useless gestures—as shouts in the dark, assertions of hope in an indifferent universe. And, of course, as splendid publicity stunts for Carl Sagan.

At the same time, he fought to maintain a public image of scientific sobriety and hardheadedness. He retained credibility with his orthodox colleagues partly by attacking their antithesis, the airhead purveyors of pseudoscience and occultism then storming the cultural marketplace. Of course, crank ideas were nothing new. Historically, they tend to come in waves, sometimes stirred by larger societal tensions such as wars and economic dislocations. And right on schedule, the 1970s—the era of economic stagnation, of long gasoline lines, of American humiliation in Southeast Asia—brought a crank renaissance. Books on psychic phenomena, pyramid power, and the Bermuda Triangle flew off shelves, while UFO "abductions" soared and New Age cults enlisted legions.[5]

Meanwhile, within ivory towers, a growing number of academics began questioning the reliability of science itself. Was it truly the royal road to truth? Or was it just another belief system, no more trustworthy than religion, art, or other routes to awareness?[6] Such talk scared the culturati's Nervous Nellies, to whom another Dark Age is always just around the corner. Science and reason (they warned) were in danger—and with them, Western civilization. Carl Sagan became their hero. But he was discomfited by their zeal. Not content to be their attack dog, he developed a more complex view of the tension between rationalism and irrationalism, one prefigured by the structure of the human brain. He expressed this view in his first truly literary work, the book that climaxed his 1968–78 decade: *The Dragons of Eden*. A crazy salad of ideas about myths, dreams, and evolution, *Dragons* won the Pulitzer Prize.

Thereafter, the intelligentsia realized that Sagan was no longer merely a scientist or a late-night TV show guest. He was a luminary. The 1968–78 decade set the stage for his life's climax, when he became the reigning king of science popularization. In that long twilight, amid personal chaos and physical pain, he deployed those troublesome, unscientific traits—feelings, instincts, intuitions—to paint his alluring visions on the television and movie screens; to express, in short, what it meant to be what he called "a collection of water, calcium and organic molecules called Carl Sagan."[7]

THOMAS ("TOMMY") GOLD BROUGHT SAGAN to Cornell.[8] Gold epitomized Cornell's openness to offbeat geniuses. Over the years, he had proposed at least as many unusual ideas as Sagan had. Working with Gold "was very stimulating, because he was always tossing off original ideas," recalls one of his former doctoral students, Steven Soter. "He would have several a day. And some fraction of them would turn out to be right."[9] Scientists find inspiration in the oddest places: in the 1940s in

England, Gold and his fellow scientists Fred Hoyle and Hermann Bondi left a movie, one whose ending was the same as the beginning. Gold asked: What if the universe is like that? Constantly recreating itself, generating new atoms from the vacuum, never dissipating as it expands through infinity? Thus was born the steady state theory, the prime rival to the big bang theory of the birth of the universe.[10]

In the late 1960s Gold suggested, correctly, that pulsars were neutron stars, stars that have nearly collapsed, crushing their atomic nuclei into neutrons. Nowadays astronomers have identified hundreds of neutron stars, which emit whirling beams of radiation, like lighthouses scattered across the galactic shoals. The recognition of neutron stars is one of several watersheds separating the old vision of the cosmos—a comparatively placid realm, which expands gracefully into the night and occasionally pops with supernovae—from the present one: an Einsteinian fever dream of galaxy-gobbling black holes, gamma-ray bursters, spooky gravitational lenses, and superinflation, plus (perhaps) a countergravitational force called the cosmological constant and innumerable outlaw universes with unique physical constants of their own.

Some of Gold's spectacular ideas fared less well. In the 1980s, the *Atlantic Monthly* published a cover story about his theory that Earth's crust contains vast reservoirs of methane gas, suitable for mining (for use as fuel—in future gas-powered automobiles, for example).[11] Drillers have found no persuasive evidence of these reservoirs, although interest persists (witness the front-page story in the April 16, 1999, *Wall Street Journal*). In the 1960s, Gold forecast that astronauts might sink into dust-covered crevasses on the Moon. They should "wear snowshoes and be equipped with avalanche cords," he advised NASA.[12] As it turned out, the lunar surface was firm; no snowshoes were needed. To this day, the "dust" forecast is a sore point with Gold. He doesn't exactly deny having made it, but he accuses the media of exaggerating his warning.[13] Years later, Sagan repeated Gold's gaffe by warning that the *Viking* probes might sink into Martian quicksand. Clearly, the dry Gold and the effusive Brooklynite were brothers under the skin.

In the 1960s Gold ran the Center for Space Sciences and Radiophysics at Cornell. The school's leaders, he recalls, sought "to build up a world-class astronomy department." He had tried to hire Sagan even before Harvard denied him tenure. Gold remembered that Sagan "was interested in big things, major things, asked very good questions, [and] made a good impression on me."[14] Besides their penchant for science-fictionish speculation, both men believed that the universe is, to use a Hollywood term, life-affirming: it generates complex organic molecules more readily than commonly thought. Geologists traditionally explained petroleum as a residue of decayed prehistoric biota, but Gold argued that it formed by astrochemical processes; there is more oil in Jupiter than beneath all the Earth's Arabian sands and North Seas.[15] Likewise, Sagan believed that organic molecules might exist on the Moon. Sagan was wrong, and Gold almost certainly wrong. Yet both were thinking along the right lines. As it turned out later, complex organic molecules pervade much of the outer solar system and beyond.

True, Sagan had shortcomings. "He was a little pushy, concentrating the conversation on work that he had done, on opinions he had, brushing other comments out of the way," Gold remembers. "He was not arrogant, but just kept insisting on advancing himself [to] anybody to whom he was speaking at the time. [He] always had to turn the conversation around to himself.

"Quite frankly, his reputation as an astronomer was not all that high at that time. He tended to suggest things that he didn't have all that much proof for." Then Gold laughed. "Anybody could accuse me of that even more!"

Gold visited Cornell provost (and later president) Dale Corson and urged him to hire Sagan. Gold assured Corson: "Dale, you will not regret this."[16]

According to Sagan, Gold offered him the job "shortly after we appeared on a panel together on Mars. . . . I came to Cornell to look it over. I liked, very much, their physics and chemistry departments. The astronomy department was small but very good," with notables including physicists Ed Salpeter and Hans Bethe, the latter a pioneer of the modern theory of stellar nuclear fusion. Then Gold drove Sagan to a nearby state park, which Sagan thought rivaled the beauty of Zion National Park. That clinched it. Sagan accepted the job.[17] Eventually he and Salzman would settle in a handsome lakeside home surrounded by forest, where the night sky was unsullied by city lights.

With permission from Harvard-Smithsonian, Sagan transferred his Cambridge laboratory equipment to Cornell.[18] His Harvard colleague Bishun Khare moved to Ithaca, too. There, in Sagan's Laboratory for Planetary Studies, they would spend many years simulating what, according to some theories, is the womb of the galactic ecosystem—mists of interstellar organic molecules that veil the bright urban coastline of the Milky Way. Sagan was sometimes prophetic for the wrong reasons, and an example is his work on space biochemistry. Although he erred in expecting to find organic molecules on the Moon and Mars, they have since turned up elsewhere in the solar system and cosmos. In the opinion of Dale Cruikshank, a leading authority on the search for space organic molecules, "There are two people in astronomy who made it okay to use the word 'organic' in astronomy. Carl is one of them, and Mayo Greenberg the other."

IN THE LATE 1960s and early 1970s, the nation's campuses were in an uproar. The Vietnam War was in full swing, and students were burning their draft cards in protest. Cornell students seized the engineering building for several days. Carl Sagan marched and wore antiwar buttons. He attended "one or two" mass protests in Washington during the late 1960s, Steve Soter says. And in 1972, Sagan would join other professors in coauthoring a protest against the bombing of Cambodia.

His Astronomy 101 class enthralled at least one graduate student of literature, Deane Rink. The long-haired Rink, who had helped to found the local chapter of the radical Students for a Democratic Society, noticed when Soter—Gold's associate, who occasionally worked with Sagan—started attending SDS meetings. Unlike hirsute, jeans-wearing SDS members, Soter was short-haired and conservatively dressed, "and had therefore come under suspicion of being an infiltrator, provocateur, or FBI plant," Rink recalls. His suspicions faded when he met and befriended Soter. One day, Soter mentioned that Sagan wanted to meet an "articulate student radical." Rink agreed to serve as the anthropological specimen, and that evening drove to Sagan's home. Salzman welcomed him at the door. A "perfunctory meal" was served. Then Rink and Sagan sat down in the living room to discuss politics.

"My ultimate litmus test for the good Dr. Sagan was to offer him a joint," Rink says. Sagan took a puff. They talked "until the wee hours of the morning." In retrospect, Rink suspects that Sagan "tolerated my bombast and saw through my false bravado." In time, Rink and Soter would join Sagan in bringing *Cosmos* to the television screen.

FOR YOUNG PEOPLE of the 1960s and 1970s, marijuana use was a rite of passage. To the very youngest, smoking the illegal drug was the boldest way to rebel against parental and governmental authority. But many young adults used "weed" too. The term "groves of academe" took on a new meaning in universities, where the spiky-leaved plants grew vigorously and covertly under ultraviolet lamps in dormitory closets.

Sagan had been a regular marijuana user from the early 1960s on.[19] He believed the drug enhanced his creativity and insights. His closest friend of three decades, Harvard psychiatry professor Dr. Lester Grinspoon, a leading advocate of the decriminalization of marijuana, recalls an incident in the 1980s when one of his California admirers mailed him, unsolicited, some unusually high-quality pot. Grinspoon shared the joints with Sagan and his wife, Ann Druyan. Afterward Sagan said, "Lester, I know you've only got one left, but could I have it? I've got serious work to do tomorrow and I could really use it."[20]

Grinspoon's 1971 book *Marihuana Reconsidered* included a long essay by an unidentified "Mr. X," who described his happy experiences with the drug. The essay identified Mr. X as "a professor at one of the top-ranking American universities" but disguised his identity by saying he was "in his early forties." In my 1999 interview with Grinspoon, he revealed that Mr. X was Sagan (who turned thirty-seven the year the book was published by Harvard University Press).[21] To Grinspoon, Sagan's use of the drug is dramatic disproof of the popular wisdom that pot diminishes motivation: "He was certainly highly motivated to work, to contribute."

Mr. X's essay is of interest not merely because it reveals Sagan's use of an illegal drug but also because it offers a glimpse of feelings he rarely shared. Portions of the account follow, beginning with Sagan's drug-induced version of Plato's myth of the cave.

It all began about ten years ago. I had reached a considerably more relaxed period in my life—a time when I had come to feel that there was more to living than science, a time of awakening of my social consciousness and amiability, a time when I was open to new experiences. I had become friendly with a group of people who occasionally smoked cannabis, irregularly, but with evident pleasure. Initially I was unwilling to partake, but the apparent euphoria that cannabis produced and the fact that there was no physiological addiction to the plant eventually persuaded me to try. My initial experiences were entirely disappointing; there was no effect at all, and I began to entertain a variety of hypotheses about cannabis being a placebo which worked by expectation and hyperventilation rather than by chemistry. After about five or six unsuccessful attempts, however, it happened. I was lying on my back in a friend's living room idly examining the pattern of shadows on the ceiling cast by a potted plant (not cannabis!). I suddenly realized that I was examining an intricately detailed miniature Volkswagen, distinctly outlined by the shadows. I was very skeptical at this perception, and tried to find inconsistencies between Volkswagens and what I viewed on the ceiling. But it was all there, down to hubcaps, license plate, chrome, and even the small handle used for opening the trunk. When I closed my eyes, I was stunned to find that there was a movie going on on the inside of my eyelids. Flash . . . a simple country scene with red farmhouse, blue sky, white clouds, yellow path meandering over green hills to the horizon. Flash . . . same scene, orange house, brown sky, red clouds, yellow path, violet fields . . . Flash . . . Flash . . . Flash. The flashes came about once a heartbeat. Each flash brought the same simple scene into view, but each time with a different set of colors . . . exquisitely deep hues, and astonishingly harmonious in their juxtaposition. Since then I have smoked occasionally and enjoyed it thoroughly. . . .

I can remember another early visual experience with cannabis, in which I viewed a candle flame and discovered in the heart of the flame, standing with magnificent indifference, the black-hatted and -coated Spanish gentleman who appears on the label of the Sandeman sherry bottle. Looking at fires when high, by the way, especially through one of those prism kaleidoscopes which image their surroundings, is an extraordinarily moving and beautiful experience.[22]

"I smile, or sometimes even laugh out loud at the pictures on the insides of my eyelids," Mr. X/Sagan wrote. Even so, he remained the astute scientific observer:

While my early perceptions were all visual, and curiously lacking in images of human beings, both of these items have changed over the intervening years. . . . I test whether I'm high by closing my eyes and looking for the flashes. They come long before there are any alterations in my visual or other perceptions. I would guess this is a signal-to-noise problem, the visual noise level being very low with my eyes closed. . . . [Flashed images resemble] cartoons: just the outlines of figures, caricatures, not photographs. I think this is simply a matter of information compression: it would be impossible to grasp the total content of an image with the information content of an ordinary photograph, say 10^8 [100 million] bits, in the fraction of a second which a flash occupies.[23]

"I find that today a single joint is enough to get me high. . . . in one movie theater recently I found I could get high just by inhaling the cannabis smoke which permeated the theater." Pot enhanced his pleasure in music and food. ("A potato will have a texture, body, and taste like that of other potatoes, but much more so.") In sex, too: marijuana "gives an exquisite sensitivity, but on the other hand it postpones orgasm: in part by distracting me with the profusion of images passing before my eyes."[24]

The drug also "greatly improved my appreciation for art, a subject which I had never much appreciated before." The following reminiscence suggests the origin of the pivotal beach scene in Sagan's novel and film *Contact*:

I have spent some time high looking at the work of the Belgian surrealist Yves Tanguy. Some years later, I emerged from a long swim in the Caribbean and sank exhausted onto a beach formed from the erosion of a nearby coral reef. In idly examining the arcuate pastel-colored coral fragments which made up the beach, I saw before me a vast Tanguy painting. Perhaps Tanguy visited such a beach in his childhood.[25]

During a high, he said,

> Sometimes a kind of existential perception of the absurd comes over me
> and I see with awful certainty the hypocrisies and posturing of myself
> and my fellow men. . . . There is a myth about such highs: the user has
> an illusion of great insight, but it does not survive scrutiny in the morn-
> ing. I am convinced that this is an error, and that the devastating
> insights achieved when high are real insights; the main problem is put-
> ting these insights in a form acceptable to the quite different self that
> we are when we're down the next day. Some of the hardest work I've
> ever done has been to put such insights down on tape or in writing.
> The problem is that ten even more interesting ideas or images have to
> be lost in the effort of recording one.

From such insights, he drew political inspiration:

> I find that most of the insights I achieve when high are into social issues.
> . . . I can remember one occasion, taking a shower with my wife while
> high, in which I had an idea on the origins and invalidities of racism in
> terms of gaussian distribution curves. It was a point obvious in a way,
> but rarely talked about. I drew the curves in soap on the shower wall,
> and went to write the idea down. One idea led to another, and at the
> end of about an hour of extremely hard work I found I had written
> eleven short essays on a wide range of social, political, philosophical,
> and human biological topics. . . . I have used them in university com-
> mencement addresses, public lectures, and in my books. . . .
>   . . . If I find in the morning a message from myself the night before
> informing me that there is a world around us which we barely sense, or
> that we can become one with the universe, or even that certain politi-
> cians are desperately frightened men, I may tend to disbelieve; but
> when I'm high I know about this disbelief. And so I have a tape in
> which I exhort myself to take such remarks seriously. I say "Listen
> closely, you sonofabitch of the morning! This stuff is real!"[26]

Sagan added: "I have on a few occasions been forced to drive in heavy
traffic when high. I've negotiated it with no difficulty at all, although I
did have some thoughts about the marvelous cherry-red color of traffic
lights."[27]

Did pot enhance Sagan's scientific work? "I have made a conscious
effort to think of a few particularly difficult current problems in my field
when high," wrote Mr. X. "It works, at least to a degree." While stoned,
he thought of a "very bizarre possibility" that might reconcile certain
disparate facts, "one that I'm sure I would never have thought of [while]
down. I've written a paper which mentions this idea in passing. I think

it's very unlikely to be true, but it has consequences which are experimentally testable, which is the hallmark of an acceptable theory."[28] A pothead Popper!

INTELLECTUALLY, SAGAN MADE an instant impression on his new associates at Cornell. Steve Soter recalls meeting him at Tommy Gold's house. Soter had just "published a paper in *Nature* on the rotation and heating of the planet Mercury, which was a neat little problem and solution. I think Carl was interested in that. We became friends in a very short time." Conversations with Sagan were "intense"—not relaxed affairs. When he was excited by an idea, he focused on it like a laser beam. "He wanted to see where ideas would lead."[29]

For some, Sagan's intellectual intensity bordered on abrasiveness. As we have seen, he insisted that the clouds of Venus were water ice crystals. But a number of astronomers, such as Kuiper and Öpik, believed that the clouds were some sort of dust.[30] If the clouds were dust, they threatened Sagan's greenhouse hypothesis. Dense dust clouds would block sunlight, preventing it from reaching the surface. Conceivably, the Venusian surface might be pitch-black, contradicting Sagan's premise that the intense heat came from the Venusian surface.

But Sagan perhaps also had psychological reasons for clinging to his water-ice clouds theory. Decades later, he would claim that he evaluated Venus and Mars based solely on the data and was unswayed by his yearnings for extraterrestrial life.[31] This is a half-truth. In fact, he tried to have his cake and eat it too: to follow the data *and* keep open the possibility of a romantic, old-fashioned, habitable Venus. As we have seen, he argued that balloon animals might inhabit the Venusian upper atmosphere, far above the searing surface; and that future astronauts might terraform Venus into a pleasant, habitable realm.

These twin fancies would stand or fall on one assumption: that the Venusian atmosphere was rich in water vapor. "If the clouds are composed of water, we should not exclude the Venus clouds as a possible biological habitat," Sagan wrote.[32] He had not forgotten the science-fiction dreams of his childhood, the kind acquired in long, happy hours reading *Astounding Science Fiction* or Ray Bradbury. Many a lover of science fiction regretfully puts away such dreams, as adulthood, career, and sexuality call one to duty. But not Sagan. He envisioned the future exploration of the Venusian atmosphere by aeronauts in balloons:

> The probability that the clouds of Venus are such a pleasant environment—the most earthlike extraterrestrial environment in the solar system, so far as we know—opens up the perhaps amusing prospect of astronauts floating in somewhat larger balloons, ballasted and valved

for the pressures of the lower Venus clouds, and clad in shirtsleeves and 19th century oxygen masks. We can imagine them peering wistfully down at the inaccessible surface of Venus below.[33]

This is not the kind of prose one expects from the cold, unbiased scientific analyst of popular myth.

Ironically, Sagan was quick to accuse his critics of having psychological motives. Previously, he had acknowledged to himself his tendency to see his own faults in other people. He committed similar "projection" in the scientific debate about Venus. He claimed that evidence for its extreme heat was

> greeted by considerable skepticism—some of which, I believe, has psychological rather than scientific roots. If Venus really had a thermometric temperature in excess of 600 K, then a variety of pleasant possibilities—a habitable, ocean-covered Venus, for example—would be removed from the field of reasonable discourse. . . . These examples illustrate an understandable and very human tendency towards the selective rejection of disquieting data, and the lengths to which a sufficiently desperate theoretician may be driven.[34]

The pot was calling the kettle black, to use a politically incorrect but effective metaphor. Sagan projected onto his critics the "desperation" he increasingly felt, as space exploration slowly exposed the bleak reality of the inner solar system: wastelands of baking rocks, not nurseries for exotic biota. When push came to shove, he was scarcely more neutral than Percival Lowell. Nor (as will be argued later) is any scientist; nor should they always be. Objectivity is often not only unattainable, it can be undesirable.

Years later, Sagan's onetime student Clark Chapman analyzed his former professor's behavior. Sagan, Chapman wrote,

> has been the most dynamic and influential planetary scientist since the early 1960s. A man of vivid imagination, he keeps alive a wide variety of conceptions of planetary environments. By suggesting often outlandish alternatives and challenging traditionalists to disprove them, he has inspired doubts about many accepted theories. Sagan's role is essential for a healthy science because a bandwagon effect frequently leads to premature consensus among scientists before equally plausible alternatives have even been thought of, let alone rationally rejected. . . .
>
> But Sagan has not always taken a detached view of the Venusian clouds, which have been a major part of his serious research since his days as a graduate student. Long after most of his colleagues agreed that his once-accepted water-ice model for the clouds of Venus was incompatible with radio and polarimetric data, the loquacious Sagan continued to press his case. Sagan watchers were forced to conclude

that he actually believed in water-ice clouds (as most scientists believe in their own theories). Some even began to wonder if he believed also in his whimsical gas-bag creatures on Jupiter or polar bears on Mars![35]

No one can blame Sagan for fiercely defending his Venus theory. He had much at stake. The theory was, at that time, his sole strong claim to scientific fame. (The *Mariner 9* space mission, which would verify his and Pollack's theory of Martian dust, was several years away.) Besides, Sagan was almost thirty-five, which for American males is the halfway moment between the cradle and the grave, a moment tense with symbolism, especially for fanatical careerists. If the Venus work fell through, then what would happen to his already shaky reputation?

Sagan knew what down-and-dirty scientific combat is like; he had learned from masters. As a graduate student, he had shuddered through Kuiper's dogfights with Urey. These and other scientific battles implied that scientific debate has no etiquette, that (to paraphrase Barry Goldwater) rudeness in the defense of truth is no vice. Now it was Sagan's turn to tussle with Kuiper. At a conference they both attended in April of 1969, they argued about the clouds of Venus. At some point during the quarrel, Sagan depicted his own position as a "minority view," which seems to have particularly irked Kuiper. Why is unclear. (Perhaps he thought Sagan was depicting himself as a latter-day Galileo, defending Truth against a senile Inquisition.) The next day, Kuiper sat down and wrote Sagan a highly critical letter.

Kuiper begins the letter by saying he is "saddened" by Sagan's comments and is writing out of both friendship and professional concern. He notes that he was the only one in the department at the University of Chicago who pushed for Sagan's dissertation. Then he cautions Sagan that he is on "dangerous grounds" because he seems to be overly attached to certain scientific thinking—specifically on the clouds of Venus. New astronomical findings clearly contradict Sagan's view, Kuiper warns. He also takes special umbrage at Sagan's use of the term "minority view," objecting that science is not like politics, in which minority views are genuinely important. Almost paternalistically, he recommends that Sagan read the book *Reason and Nature: Essay on the Meaning of the Scientific Method*, by philosopher Morris Cohen, which Kuiper thinks makes valuable points about the need for scientific objectivity.[36]

Sagan responded with a letter that is striking for its equanimity, though perhaps a bit forced in thanking Kuiper for his "kind letter." Sagan says he is well aware of Morris Cohen's book and is likewise a fan of it, and that he concurs fully with Kuiper's view of how science should be done. The only real difference between their views (Sagan asserts) is in the way they are interpreting data. The jury is still out, and given the rapid rate at which new data were arriving, the matter would probably soon be resolved one way or the other. Sagan comes across in this letter as entirely unfazed by Kuiper's warning.[37]

SAGAN'S GREENHOUSE MODEL for Venus wasn't the only endangered part of his doctoral thesis. So was his hypothesis about life on the Moon. It would be tested soon, in July 1969, when the first astronauts were scheduled to set foot there.

Throughout the 1960s, Sagan continued to take seriously the possibility of lunar life. He cited the Soviet astronomer Nikolai A. Kozyrev's spectral observations of alleged carbon emissions on the Moon (in the late 1950s) as possible evidence for "lunar subsurface organic matter."[38] Some thought the Moon had reserves of underground water, which might support life forms. A few suggested that long, sinuous channels, or rilles, on the Moon were dried lunar riverbeds. Another prominent researcher, John J. Gilvarry, proposed that the *maria* were appropriately named— that they were vanished oceans, which might have been inhabited.[39] "Meandering marks have been found [on the Moon] that look so much like dried-up river beds that it is hard to think of anything else they could possibly be," Isaac Asimov wrote in the *New York Times Sunday Magazine* a week before the lunar landing. "In the moon-crust samples biologists may find organic molecules representing a point part of the way toward life." In a burst of neo-Saganish optimism, Asimov suggested that the research might reveal cellular processes so primitive, yet so relevant to terrestrial life, that "by taking the long trip to the moon we will be taking the shortest route to unmasking the riddle of disease on earth."[40]

Sagan believed that humans could do useful research on the Moon, but he opposed sending them there as early as NASA planned. Still, driven by cold war pressures, NASA planned to land humans on the Moon by 1969. Sagan and others feared that astronauts might inadvertently bring lunar microbes back to Earth, and that these might trigger a terrestrial epidemic.

To protect Earth, NASA developed its controversial "quarantine" program. The astronauts Neil Armstrong and Buzz Aldrin were scheduled to land on the lunar surface in the Lunar Excursion Module (LEM). (Their companion Michael Collins would remain behind in the *Apollo* capsule, in lunar orbit.) On the Moon, Armstrong and Aldrin would collect rocks. To ensure that they didn't trek lunar microbes into the LEM (like a child tracking mud into the house), they would leave their gloves and boots on the Moon. Then they would rocket off the lunar surface, rendezvous with Collins, and fly home, landing in the Pacific. After landing, they would use a vacuum cleaner to sweep up dust inside the capsule, just in case it contained any lunar life forms. When a frog-man opened the capsule door, he would give them isolation garments to don. Then, when the astronauts were leaving the craft, the frog-man would spray them with disinfectant. From there, the astronauts would be flown to the main quarantine facility, the $16 million Lunar Receiving Laboratory in Houston. They would remain sequestered inside the facility for three weeks. If they showed no ill effects, then they could leave.[41]

To some, the quarantine was a joke. Skeptics feared that as soon as the frogman opened the capsule door, lunar microbes would escape into the atmosphere and the ocean. *Time* magazine quoted one official of the Apollo Moon program as saying: "Of course, it's a sham, but what else could we do?"[42] Some space scientists were nevertheless angered when in May 1969 NASA announced that it would relax the quarantine rules. But Edward Anders of the University of Chicago was as skeptical about lunar pathogens as he had been about the Nagy team's meteoritic "organics." Anders informed reporters that he would gladly *eat* a sample of lunar rock.

Sagan was a lecturer in the Apollo astronaut training program from 1968 to 1972, at the Manned Space Flight Center in Houston.[43] He was not, however, a major figure in NASA's quarantine project, so one imag-ines that some of his colleagues grimaced when *Time* magazine ran his photo in a June 1969 story about the quarantine project, one month before the *Apollo 11* landing. The article asked: "Is the Earth Safe from Lunar Contamination?" In the photo, Sagan looked tall, skinny, and seri-ous, wearing a dark coat and tie; he leaned, with one foot on a table, before a Stanley Miller–style experiment. The quarantine was worth-while, he assured *Time*: "Maybe it's sure to 99 percent that *Apollo 11* will not bring back lunar organisms, but even that one percent of uncertainty is too large to be complacent about."[44] This was not the last time Sagan received star billing for a project managed by others.

IN JUNE 1969, just before the *Apollo 11* landing, Sagan's achalasia almost cost him his life. He had undergone esophageal surgery in hopes of correcting the condition. Sagan's friend Isaac Asimov recalled in his diary that "it didn't seem as though he were in any particular danger at first, and when I visited him [in the hospital] on June 18, we joked easily and made arrangements to have dinner, all four of us, when he got out." But later he suffered a pneumothorax, a condition in which his lung cav-ity filled with blood from the surgical incisions. Sagan's friend Dr. Lester Grinspoon saved his life by lifting him by the shoulders a half-dozen times every twenty minutes, over and over, for forty-eight hours straight, so that he could breathe more deeply; the ward nurses at Massachusetts General Hospital were not strong enough to do so. "I saw his color deteriorating—he was getting bluer and bluer," recalls Grinspoon, who managed to sneak very brief catnaps during the ordeal. "They put drains in and gave him nine units of blood. He had lost an awful lot of blood." Sagan came "very close" to dying. Afterward, the exhausted Grinspoon left, and Sagan then "became paranoid psychotic in the hospital. I was getting calls from Mass General Hospital because he wouldn't let them as much change a drain without talking with me first. That's not unusual—it's called 'ICU psychosis.' "[45] Asimov noted in his diary that he "visited periodically and sat with a rather distraught Linda and did my best to keep her calm."[46]

Sagan recovered and was back on his feet by July. But the operation was unsuccessful, and the achalasia continued to trouble him for years. "He would be at dinner and he would become quite uncomfortable because when he swallowed food, it wouldn't go all the way down," his friend the writer Timothy Ferris recalls.[47] After meals, Sagan's son Nick says, Sagan sometimes had to stand and hop up and down, lest the food "come back up and choke him."[48]

JULY 16, 1969. The historian David Nye would later observe that tourists came to Cape Canaveral like pilgrims to Mecca; they worshiped the *Apollo 11* launch vehicle as if it were "a sacred object." Among the celebrity observers was novelist Norman Mailer, fresh from the antiwar protests. Like so many political radicals, he was skeptical about the space program. Perhaps as a Jew, he was particularly sensitive to the rocket's roots in Nazi technology. Cynically, he observed that the searchlight-bathed *Saturn V* rocket "glowed for all the world like some white stone Madonna in the mountains, welcoming footsore travelers at dusk. Perhaps it was an unforeseen game of the lighting, but America had not had its movie premieres for nothing."[49] The rocket launch was, however, an indisputably awe-inspiring experience. The eeriest thing was that for the first few seconds, one heard no sound; a fireball ascended skyward in perfect silence, applauded solely by the clapping Atlantic waves. Then suddenly the sound wave hit: an immense growl, from all directions, like a biblical Revelation. Even Mailer was overwhelmed and gasped, dumb-struck: "Oh, my God! oh, my God! oh, my God! oh, my God!"

On July 20, 1969, Armstrong, the commander of *Apollo 11*, set foot on the Sea of Tranquility. He and his colleague, Aldrin, collected many pounds of rocks. When they returned to Earth, they spent a few weeks in the quarantine chamber. President Nixon waved at them through the chamber's window. Geologists were itching to get their hands on the

rocks right away. Instead, thanks to Sagan and other quarantine advocates, the geologists had to wear special gloves (to prevent contamination)
and to examine the rock samples in enclosed chambers. "A lot of people,
especially geologists, were furious at me for the difficulty I made [for]
them," Sagan later admitted.[50] One unnamed geologist compared Sagan
to the Black Plague.[51]

Tommy Gold was one of the scientists scheduled to receive a lunar
sample from *Apollo 11*. To analyze the sample, he made arrangements to
use a "very good scanning electron microscope" at a Corning Glass plant
a few hours' drive from Cornell. "Sagan was extremely keen to come
along and did so, evidently because he thought he might find the remains
of living creatures in the dust." At the plant, they stared at a TV image of
microscopic features on the lunar sample. There were no fossils.[52]

Sagan was disappointed, Gold recalls. But there was plenty of humble pie to be eaten. The Moon proved to be very different from what
other top brains had expected, as well. Gold, for example, had suspected
that its surface was covered with deep dust and crevasses, which might
swallow astronauts. It wasn't, and didn't. The Moon surprised Harold
Urey, too. For years he had been the Moon program's leading scientific
champion, arguing that the Moon was a primordial pile of planetesimal
rubble left over from the early days of the solar system. Its crust had
never melted, he insisted during his furious debate with Kuiper. Having
never melted, its rocks must (Urey said) hold clues to the processes by
which the solar system formed. The rocks would be the Rosetta stone of
the solar system, he prophesied in a widely publicized phrase. But analysis of the lunar rocks revealed that they *had* melted billions of years ago.
In fact, as we now know, at one point the entire crust may have been a
"magma ocean." So the Moon, while very old, was certainly no Rosetta
stone of solar system origins. Urey readily admitted he had been wrong.[53]

Sagan summarized the negative results of his lunar rock analysis in a
paper, "The Search for Indigenous Lunar Organic Matter," which he
submitted to the journal *Space Life Sciences*. An editor sent the paper to
Urey for comment. Urey criticized it harshly, calling it "superficial."[54]

CARL SAGAN WAS A CONTRADICTION. To critics like Urey, the young
astronomer was a reckless speculator. But to laypeople absorbed by pseudosciences and occultism, Sagan was the Dark Prince of skepticism, the
party pooper who coldly shot down their ideas about UFOs, psychic
phenomena, and other fringe ideas.

By the 1960s, Sagan had long since rejected his adolescent notion
that UFOs are extraterrestrial spaceships. Yet he could not quite put the
subject out of his mind. Like a disappointed lover, he continued to hang

around the subject, as if missing its exhilarating air of mystery. He discussed it with reporters, testified about saucers before Congress, served on an Air Force UFO panel, personally investigated lurid UFO reports, and starred in the first scientific "debate" on the subject. Sentimental journeys, all.

By the mid-1960s, the saucer fad had almost disappeared. "Are UFOs Still Being Seen?" a pro-UFO publication asked sadly.[55] Perhaps the elusive discs had gone the way of phrenology, spiritualism, sea monsters, and other denizens of "silly seasons" past. But in the summer and autumn of 1965, as *Mariner 4* flew by Mars and the Vietnam War escalated, Americans started seeing strange things in the sky. Eerie reddish lights drifted through the Midwestern night. Residents of Exeter, New Hampshire, watched bright discs flit overhead. In early 1966 in Michigan, rural residents freaked out as spooky glows hovered in nearby swamps.[56] The Michiganites were not happy when the Air Force's astronomy adviser, J. Allen Hynek, suggested they had seen marsh gas, naturally combusting methane gas from decaying vegetation. "It wasn't no hullabillusion," one backwoodsman assured *Life* magazine.[57] Michigan Congressman Gerald Ford (the future U.S. president) called for a federal investigation.[58]

From his office at Harvard, Sagan probably watched the latest saucer wave with nostalgia. By that time, he was a saucer skeptic, as he assured reporters who called him for quotes about the UFO wave. "There's not the slightest bit of evidence to convince us that the earth has been visited by creatures from other planets," he told *U.S. News and World Report.*[59] He also appeared on a *CBS Reports* show, hosted by Walter Cronkite, that took a skeptical view of the phenomenon.[60]

Sagan served on an Air Force UFO advisory panel, the O'Brien committee. The committee (named for its chief, scientist Brian O'Brien) evaluated the Air Force's official saucer project, Blue Book. Although depicted in a subsequent television series as an expensive, computerized outfit,[61] Blue Book was in fact a backwater operation, with a few staffers and filing cabinets crammed into an office at Wright-Patterson Air Force Base. Blue Book was primarily for show. The Air Force had not taken UFOs seriously for years but felt it had to keep up appearances to deal with inquiries from UFO-titillated members of Congress and their constituents. If UFOs represented an unknown physical phenomenon, Blue Book would never figure it out. So Sagan and the rest of the O'Brien committee advised the Air Force to commission a independent, full-scale scientific study. The result was the controversial Condon Commission, chaired by noted physicist E. U. Condon.[62]

Meanwhile, Sagan conducted private investigations of the UFO mania. In 1966, the first UFO "abduction" was described in journalist

John G. Fuller's book *The Interrupted Journey*. Fuller (who also wrote about "ghosts" seen on airplanes) said that one night in the early 1960s, when Betty and Barney Hill were driving through New Hampshire, they noticed a distant UFO. The next thing they knew, several hours had passed and they couldn't recall what had happened. They consulted a Boston psychiatrist, Dr. Benjamin Simon, who hypnotized them. Under hypnosis, they claimed that UFOnauts had stopped their car and taken them aboard a saucer, then subjected them to medical examinations.[63] The Hills appeared to be sincere people; still, sincere people can have hallucinations. The history of psychiatry includes an interesting parallel case—a *folie à deux*, it is called—of two women who fantasized traveling in time to eighteenth-century France.[64]

Sagan spent a "fair amount of time" with the Hills and Simon. The psychiatrist suspected that the Hills' story was an innocent dual hallucination, perhaps related to the stresses of their marriage, which was interracial—an extreme novelty at that time.[65] (Decades later, Sagan was baffled to watch as his Harvard friend Dr. John Mack, a noted psychiatrist and author, became a leading defender of the validity of UFO abduction claims.)[66] In the mid-1960s, at least one respectable American scientist, James McDonald, a professor of atmospheric physics at the University of Arizona, claimed that UFOs were alien spaceships. McDonald met with Sagan and his fellow member of the Order of the Dolphin, MIT physicist Phil Morrison. In Lester Grinspoon's home, they listened to a tape recording of Simon's psychiatric interview with the Hills. As Sagan later wrote to UFO investigator Walter N. Webb, he "spent many hours with Jim McDonald" and saw no evidence that there were any sightings that were credible evidence of extraterrestrial visits.[67]

McDonald's data was "pitiful," Morrison recalls. McDonald showed them "pounds and pounds" of data, including news clippings and tape recordings, about a UFO sighting on Long Island. The witness, a naval architect, drew a sketch of the "saucer." One thing puzzled Sagan and Morrison: the saucer had rivets on its side. "Are we really to believe this?" they asked McDonald. "Look at the rivets that cross the plates here. Do you suppose [aliens] use rivets? Don't you think [the witness] is drawing on his long experience in the Navy yard?" In retrospect, Morrison says of McDonald, "it was distressing that a serious scientist, a good man, would get involved in such research."[68] Like Brian O'Leary, John Lilly, Timothy Leary, J. Allen Hynek and a few other renegade scientists of the 1960s and 1970s, McDonald had heard the siren call of the Unknown and would pursue it to the end—in his case, to suicide.

Would Sagan join their wayward ranks? Donald Menzel appears to have feared so. Menzel was by then nearing retirement, and apparently felt real affection for Sagan, who had corresponded with him since high school. For almost two decades, Menzel had been the nation's pre-eminent scientific skeptic about UFOs. He had written two books arguing that most saucers were misidentified natural phenomena, such as mirages, meteors, sundogs, and the like. Naturally, Menzel's books enraged UFOdom's true believers. They resented his skepticism just as a backwoods evangelical resents being told that his cherished sliver of the true cross is ordinary plywood.

Why Menzel doubted Sagan's skepticism is unclear. A possible reason is Sagan's 1963 article speculating about interstellar travel. Although Sagan was a UFO skeptic, that article implicitly challenged a leading theoretical argument against UFOs—that the stars are too distant for spaceships to reach. The same article speculated about alien visits to Earth thousands of years ago, visits possibly recorded in ancient myths. To Menzel types, that speculation sounded dangerously like a UFO buff's goofiest daydreams. In early 1966, Menzel sent Sagan a memo asking to know his present opinion of UFOs. Sagan responded that his only statements on the subject were his 1963 article and a piece on flying saucers in the *Encyclopedia Americana*. He added that he had sometimes been misquoted by saucer believers, which was frustrating to him.[69]

Menzel was not satisfied. The latest UFO wave was breaking fast: *Life* magazine had just run a gaudy eight-page spread of so-called UFO photos. Most looked pretty phony. One "UFO" was an obvious lens flare within the camera, an effect familiar to any amateur photographer. Another photo showed what appeared to be a flying fruit bowl. In early 1967, about the time that Sagan's bid for tenure at Harvard was coming up, Menzel wrote to Sagan again and told him that he had heard a rumor that Sagan had expressed some thoughts that supported the existence of UFOs. Menzel said he would appreciate hearing Sagan's latest views on the subject.[70]

Sagan replied that he had not changed his skeptical assessment of UFOs, but that he had been following McDonald's work and would like to know Menzel's thoughts on that.[71] This was the wrong thing to say to Menzel, who despised McDonald. In a letter to Sagan, Menzel said that McDonald was an "absolute nut."[72]

In 1968 and 1969, Sagan struggled to persuade Menzel to participate in a public confrontation with pro-UFO scientists. Their tug-of-war dramatized a 1960s-style generation gap in science, a gap between younger scientists who were eager to fight pseudoscience on a democratic field of battle and older, elitist scientists too proud for such a brawl.

Sagan believed in the value of confronting crank ideas in public. His inspiration here came, like so much else, from H. J. Muller. In a draft memo written in the late 1960s, Sagan recalled how several years earlier, Muller had asked scientists to take part in a debate about evolution with creationists. Out of two hundred scientists Muller wrote to, Sagan was one of the few who agreed to participate.

The UFO debate was engineered largely by astronomer Thornton Page (who had worked with Kuiper on the nuclear-weapons-on-the-Moon paper). Formerly of Yerkes, Page served on the CIA's short-lived UFO advisory panel in the early 1950s. Originally, Sagan and Page tried to set up the UFO debate for the December 1968 meeting of the American Association for the Advancement of Science (AAAS) in Boston. They planned to pit scientists sympathetic to saucers (McDonald, J. Allen Hynek, etc.) against skeptics (Sagan, Menzel, and others). They hoped to time the debate for the release of the Condon Commission's long-awaited report on UFOs in late 1968. They were eager to enlist Menzel for the panel, and understandably so: as the nation's leading saucer skeptic and a top astrophysicist to boot, his presence would enhance the panel's newsworthiness.

Initially, though, Menzel refused to appear. Then he wavered. Maybe he should participate, just to keep the young folks straight-headed and the hucksters honest.[73] At that point, Sagan shot himself in the foot. During the Nagy debate, he had demonstrated his gift for uttering convoluted sentences packed with double negatives. He demonstrated the same prowess on July 29, 1968, when he testified on UFOs before the U.S. House of Representatives Committee on Science and Astronautics, chaired by Rep. J. Edward Roush of Indiana. The majority of speakers, who included McDonald and Hynek, were sympathetic to UFOs. Surprisingly, Sagan—the sole skeptic present—appeared to waffle on the UFO question.

"I'm delighted to tell about contemporary scientific thinking along these lines," Sagan began, "but let me begin by saying that I do not think the evidence is at all persuasive, that UFOs are of intelligent extraterrestrial origin, nor do I think the evidence is convincing that no UFOs are of intelligent extraterrestrial origin. . . . [T]he question is very much an open one, and it is certainly too soon to harden attitudes and to make any permanent contentions on the subject."

At the same time, he cautioned, the "capability of human populations to self-delusion has not been accorded appropriate weight" by the other speakers. He cited one of the books that had helped to make him a skeptic, Mackay's *Extraordinary Popular Delusions and the Madness of Crowds*. While "a moderate support of investigations of UFOs might very well have some scientific paydirt in it," Sagan maintained that "if Congress is interested in a pursuit of the question of extraterrestrial life, I believe it would be much better advised to support the biology, the

Mariner, and Voyager programs of NASA, and the radio astronomy programs of the National Science Foundation, than to pour very much
money into this study of UFOs."

Perplexed, Representative Roush pressed Sagan for more specifics:
"I'm not real sure, Dr. Sagan, whether you stated whether there is or
whether there is not extraterrestrial life. I was watching for that, and I
don't believe I heard you say it."

Sagan responded: "Congressman Roush, I have enough difficulty
trying to determine if there is intelligent life on Earth, to be sure if there
is intelligent life anywhere else." (General laughter.) "If we knew there
was life on other planets, then we would be able to save ourselves a lot of
agony finding out. It is just because the problem is so significant, and we
don't have the answers at hand, we need to pursue the subject. I don't
know. It beats me.

"There are individuals who very strongly want to believe that UFOs
are of intelligent extraterrestrial origin . . . [e]ssentially . . . for religious
motives; that is, things are so bad down here, maybe somebody from
up there will come and save us from ourselves." Likewise, some people
"very much want to believe UFOs are *not* of intelligent extraterrestrial
origins, because that would be threatening to our conception of us as
being the pinnacle of creation. We would find it very upsetting to discover that we are not, that we are just a sort of two-bit civilization. . . .

"I might mention that, on this symposium, *there are no individuals
who strongly disbelieve in the extraterrestrial origin of UFOs and therefore
there is a certain view, not necessarily one I strongly agree with—but there is a
certain view this committee is not hearing today, along those lines.*" (Emphasis added.)[74]

This clumsy last sentence, cluttered with Sagan's beloved double
negatives, led to misunderstandings later. Was Sagan saying he felt more
sympathy for UFO buffs than he had admitted? So saucer fans suspected.
They began whispering that Sagan was secretly one of them. The myth
that Sagan was a closeted UFOlogist would persist past his death: in
1997, the short-lived television series *Dark Skies* depicted Sagan as one
of its characters. This fictional Sagan secretly advised the military how to
handle the alien menace, liked to use the word "billions," and in general
resembled a bad parody on *Saturday Night Live*.[75]

Sagan's remarks before Congress infuriated Menzel. Sagan had been
the sole skeptic to testify in person at the congressional hearing, yet his
remarks had been mealy-mouthed. Menzel wrote a stern letter to Sagan
expressing his irritation that Sagan had been so apparently ambivalent.[76]

By now, Menzel was eager to ax the whole UFO symposium, and he
wrote to an associate that he would work to stop it. Shaken by the opposition of Menzel and other astronomers, Sagan and Page lost hope of

holding the symposium when they had planned. The next year, however, they tried again, campaigning to schedule the debate for the December 1969 AAAS gathering in Boston. In early 1969, when Sagan wasn't teaching classes or worrying about the lunar quarantine or fighting achalasia, he wrote a series of letters and memos arguing for the UFO symposium. At stake, he said, was the public's perception of science. He argued that only by taking on the pseudosciences directly and revealing their weaknesses would the scientific community cure the public's growing infatuation with them. Rather than cloister themselves in their ivory towers, scientists, he argued, should help the public see the differences between real science and pseudoscience, opening their eyes to the amazing power and beauty of real science.

Sagan's argument contains a powerful political message, although he did not recognize it at the time. For better and for worse, ours is a scientific age, and no society can be truly democratic if the public is ignorant of the basis for—and thus unable to comment or vote intelligently on—technical matters. Consider, for example, nuclear weapons and commercial nuclear energy. These technologies grew up in the 1940s and 1950s, behind wartime, cold war, and corporate barriers. The American public had little more say over their development than the Soviet people had over like technologies in their own nation. By the 1960s, many Americans were revolting against what they perceived as the smug tyranny of "experts." Not only did the experts disagree, but, the public had discovered, their professed "rationality" often camouflaged special interests and prejudices. In light of this growing distrust, even disdain, Sagan warned that scientists must be willing to show themselves as open-minded, thoughtful people with good reasons for their views.

Menzel wasn't buying the argument. Neither was E. U. Condon, who had recently issued his committee's highly skeptical report on the UFO phenomenon. Condon was a distinguished physicist, and no stranger to controversy. (He had a background in leftist politics, and in the 1940s Senator Richard Nixon had questioned his loyalty to the United States.) In Condon's view, Sagan's talk about democratizing the UFOlogical debate was hot air. The UFOlogists were not capable of rational discourse, he felt.[77] During his two-year saucer investigation, Condon had witnessed a good deal of the feverish irrationality of the UFOlogists' world. He concluded that the movement was packed with well-meaning fools, crude hoaxers, and scientific illiterates. The worst were propelled by a near-religious passion, and brooked no criticism. They were not amenable to reason—and certainly not to formal seminars like Sagan and Page's proposed symposium. Condon called the symposium "silly nonsense," and fought hard to stop it. At one point, Condon got so angry that he wrote letters of protest to Vice President Spiro

Agnew and presidential science adviser Dr. Lee A. DuBridge, both underlings of President Richard Nixon, the man who had questioned Condon's loyalty to the United States.

DESPITE ALL OF THE DISSENT, Sagan and Page managed to hold the symposium that December. They even managed to persuade poor old Menzel to appear. (He later canceled for health reasons.)[78] One key participant was the amiable J. Allen Hynek. Over almost two decades as the Air Force's astronomy adviser, he had met numerous laypeople who sincerely could not distinguish between the planet Mars and a landing UFO, or between windblown debris and a reconnaissance force from Coma Berenices. "You'd be surprised how many times we give Venus permission to land," an air traffic controller once told him. By the late 1960s, however, Hynek appeared dangerously close to following McDonald's lead, to jumping off the deep end. Hynek wrote a letter to *Science* magazine urging his colleagues to take UFOs more seriously; they might represent some unknown physical forces at least, and at best . . . aliens? He would not rule it out. In later years, he would speculate about UFOs coming from other "dimensions" and the like.[79]

In retrospect, Hynek had never been much of a skeptic. After his death, his longtime ally and fellow UFO buff Jacques Vallee, a computer scientist-astronomer, wrote that Hynek had "been interested in astrology since his early student days," studied Rosicrucianism, and was "fascinated with psychic surgery" and "psychic photography."[80]

Hynek was a scientist like certain other researchers in Sagan's life—John Lilly, James McDonald, Brian O'Leary, Timothy Leary, John Mack—who regarded "hard" science as too hard-headed. There must be something more to the cosmos, they argued, something unseen and wondrous. Apostles in search of a messiah, they were the late twentieth century's secular versions of the Victorian scholars (A. R. Wallace, Henry Sidgwick, William Crookes, and many others) who never recovered from Darwin's blow to their simple childhood faith, and spent the rest of their lives anxiously seeking "scientific" evidence—shimmering ectoplasms in seances, for example—that would restore that faith. Scientists have hearts, too. They can be just as foolish and desperate as the housewife who plunks down ten dollars for a visit to the palmist, or the starving actor who turns down a role because the director's planet is in the wrong house.

At the UFO symposium, Hynek and McDonald argued for taking saucers seriously. Hynek cautioned the audience against prejudging the future; tomorrow's science will seem as strange to us as our science would have seemed to an ancient. McDonald railed against the long history of supposedly shoddy government investigations into UFOs. Menzel's talk (read in his absence by AAAS president Walter Orr Roberts) called UFOs "the modern myth." Scientists of the next century, he wrote, would look back on the idea of UFOs as the "greatest nonsense" of our time.[81]

By contrast, Sagan's talk was relaxed. He was neither accusatory like McDonald nor sarcastic like Menzel. Sagan did not sympathize with the UFO devotees, but he empathized with them; he knew what they were feeling, because he had once felt the same devotion. Like them, he had felt the gravitational tug of fantastic ideas. But he had (he believed) outgrown them. And "precisely because these ideas have charm, exactly because they are of deep emotional significance to us, they are the ideas we must examine most critically. . . . Where we have an emotional stake in an idea, we are most likely to deceive ourselves."

Sagan suggested that at the root of the UFO craze was a cultural problem—boredom. He offered a personal anecdote:

> Once when I was on the faculty at Harvard, I gave a popular lecture on something-or-other, and in the question period at the end there were some questions about UFOs. I said that I felt at least a great fraction of them were misapprehended natural phenomena. For some reason that I don't understand, policemen are present at all such public gatherings, and as I walked out after the last question, two policemen outside the lecture hall were pointing up at the sky. I looked up and observed a strange brilliant light moving slowly overhead. Of course, I got out of there fast, before the crowd came out to ask me what it was. I joined some friends at a restaurant and said, "There's something terrific outside." Everyone went outside. They really liked it—it was great fun. There it was. It wasn't going away. It was clearly visible, slowly moving, fading and brightening, no sound attached to it.
>
> Well, I went home, got my binoculars, and returned. Through the binoculars I was able to resolve the lights; the bright white light was really two closely-spaced lights, and there were two lights on either side, blinking. When the thing got brighter we could hear a mild drone; when the thing got dimmer, we couldn't hear a thing. In fact it turned out to be a NASA weather airplane. When I showed my friends at the restaurant that what we were seeing was in fact an airplane, the uniform response was disappointment. I mean, it's no fun to go home and say, "You'll never guess what happened. I was in this restaurant, there was a bright light outside, it was an airplane." That's not a memorable story.

"But," Sagan added, "Suppose no one had a pair of binoculars. Then the story goes, 'There was this great light out there and it was circling the city and we don't know anything about it. Maybe it's visitors from somewhere else.' That's a story worth talking about," he concluded. "Despite all the novelties of our times, there is a kind of drudgery to everyday life that cries out for profound novelties; and the idea of extra-terrestrial visitation is a culturally acceptable novelty."[82]

Almost as comic relief, Sagan's friend Lester Grinspoon gave a talk suggesting psychological explanations for UFOs. (Carl Jung had engaged in similar theorizing in his last book, *Flying Saucers*, published in 1959.) Grinspoon—to his subsequent regret—proposed that cigar-shaped UFOs were phallic symbols, while round ones revealed memories of mothers' breasts.[83]

Prior to the meeting, Menzel warned that the symposium would do little good. The media, he said, would cover the juicy parts and ignore the rest. He may have had a point: in a Houston newspaper's account of the UFO lectures, the first words were: "Flying saucers may be sex symbols . . .".[84]

DESPITE HIS UNEASE about Sagan's stranger enthusiasms, Menzel joined in nominating him for membership in the prestigious Cosmos Club in Washington, D.C. It was an uphill fight, and even though Thornton Page lobbied for him and Menzel wrote a letter of endorse-ment, Sagan was rejected. Several years later, Page tried again to get Sagan admitted, and explained to Sagan that the original reason for re-jection was probably his association with the UFO issue.

Sagan did finally gain admittance to the Cosmos Club, thanks to sup-port from distinguished scholars including his old friend Will Kellogg of RAND Corporation.[85] The club's delay in accepting him, however, fore-shadowed his future troubles with an even more exclusive Washington institution—the National Academy of Sciences.

SAGAN'S WILLINGNESS TO JOIN in the UFO show sent a clear signal: he might be a new boy at Cornell, but he wasn't toning down his act to avoid offending any local versions of Urey, Menzel, and Condon. The life of the cloistered scholar was not for him. Within a few years, he would become an even more overt celebrity, one who rubbed elbows with TV and movie stars in Johnny Carson's greenroom. And he would become more outspoken politically, particularly on the war and on feminism.

In 1971, Sagan was one of eighteen authors of a book critical of the Nixon Administration's bombing raids on Vietnam.[86] A year later, in his book *The Cosmic Connection*, he unleashed his harshest antimilitary prose to date. He also made subtle digs—by noting, for example, the comparative cheapness of a SETI search, which "costs about the same as the replacement costs of U.S. aircraft shot down over Vietnam in Christmas week, 1972."

The Cosmic Connection also described a seriocomic incident in which Air Force intelligence had assigned a "translator" to accompany Sagan on a meeting with a Soviet scientist who was developing instruments to search for extraterrestrial life. Later when they were alone, the translator asked Sagan "in a style of vocalization that went out with James Cagney and Humphrey Bogart, 'Hey, kid, what'd ya find out?' . . . [His] occupation, if not his identity, gradually dawned on me. With a rising fury I explained to him that it was possible to have a conversation with a Soviet scientist that was intended for the benefit of science rather than for the benefit of the American military intelligence services."[87]

Still, Sagan was not yet the firebrand he would become during the "nuclear winter" controversy of the 1980s. During the late 1960s, Cornell nuclear physicist Hans Bethe and many other scientists attacked the plans of the Johnson and the Nixon Administrations for the proposed antiballistic missile (ABM) system. Advocates claimed ABM would shoot down Soviet ICBMs; opponents said it would accelerate the arms race.[88] Sagan's former Yerkes acquaintance Dale Cruikshank considered getting involved in the debate, but Sagan suggested that it might be unwise. Cruikshank sensed that Sagan feared Cruikshank would hurt his career, "or maybe even worse—a mysterious shadow could appear out of the night."[89] Sagan wasn't totally paranoid; the cold war had injured many promising scientific careers, including that of Cornell chemist Franklin Asbury Long. The Nixon Administration planned to nominate Long to head the National Science Foundation, then withdrew the nomination when he criticized the ABM system. (After other scientists protested, the Administration reinstated the nomination, but Long declined it.)[90] The safest scientific foes of militarism were those who, like Bethe, Linus Pauling, and others, were already famous. Sagan probably didn't feel famous enough to take the risks they did. Not yet.

AND AFTER A HARD DAY of science, popularizing, and politicking, Sagan headed home to his second family. Nick was born in 1970, and Linda "made her own baby food. She didn't trust the store's," Nick Sagan says. In keeping with current campus politics, the Sagans named their only child Nicholas Julian Zapata Sagan. Zapata refers to the Mexican revolutionary, and Julian to Julian Bond, the Georgia legislator, civil rights activist, and war protester.[91]

The Sagans' Ithaca home "resonated with the vibes of the Sixties," recalls one of his young friends, the artist Jon Lomberg, who later illustrated many of Sagan's books. "True, the odd Humanities professor had embraced the counterculture, but it was very rare for an academic in the sciences to be comfortable inviting hippies to fix their vans in his garage, which is what one of them was doing when I arrived at Carl's home [for the] first time," Lomberg writes in an unpublished memoir.

As mentioned earlier, the light-hearted Salzman helped Sagan to loosen up. Indeed, "Carl was not stuffy about whom he talked to," Lomberg recalls, "and included among his friends artists, poets, science-fiction writers and even an alumnus of Barnum and Bailey's Clown School, whose graduation picture was used by Carl for years in a lecture about detecting life on Earth."

During the winters, Carl and Linda flew to the Caribbean for a vacation of snorkeling and scuba diving. "The last few years I've been doing a lot more snorkeling than diving, just because my wife snorkels but doesn't dive," Sagan noted at the time. "There's something about the self-contained aspect of scuba diving that I like very much. . . . I have a little . . . camera and go down chasing the indigenous life forms. I don't hurt anybody—I just take a picture back. . . . There's the sense of a sort of another biology down there which I like very much, probably connected to my interest in finding life elsewhere. And there's another aspect: there's the sense of a third dimension."[92]

The couple's happiness would not last. They were "such opposite people in so many ways," Nick says. "He was the scientist, she was the artist. . . . Their styles of arguing tell a lot about them. My mother is fire: explosive, passionate, a sort of hot-tempered arguer. My dad would be very logical and very much like ice.

"I would always see myself as lukewarm water, with elements of each. . . . I did have the problem, growing up, of [thinking]: 'God, these people are so *different*—what drew them together and how the hell, *why* would they create me?' That sense of existential horror." It was a hint of things to come.[93]

9

Gods Like Men

THE CARIBBEAN, SOUTHERN CALIFORNIA, Soviet Armenia—Sagan's flight schedules marked him as a jetsetter. In 1970, while in southern California on other business, he paid a visit to an imprisoned man whose drug experiences made Sagan's look adolescent.

Timothy Leary was a former Harvard professor who experimented with LSD and other drugs. In the late 1960s he was arrested for drug possession and locked up in the California Medical Facility in Vacaville, near Sacramento. Behind bars, he wrote to Sagan and Frank Drake, "inviting us to meet with him about a special project he was contemplating," Drake later wrote in his autobiography. While in California, the two astronomers visited Leary in prison. Leary was "dressed in jeans and sneakers," Drake recalls. "He looked extremely lean and fit. . . . Then Leary, without a word of explanation, began to jog around the table in the middle of the room." During their hour-long conversation, Leary explained he wanted to build a starship "big enough to hold the three hundred most important people in the world . . . to establish a new civilization on an Earth-like planet of some nearby star." Then Leary asked them: "Which of the stars is my best bet?"

Drake and Sagan explained to Leary that interstellar travel would be extraordinarily difficult and far beyond present technology. Besides, a ship as big as Leary's would travel so slowly that everyone on board would die before reaching another star. "By the end of our talk," Drake recalled, "his look was veiled, preoccupied, crestfallen."[1]

A foolish consistency, it is said, is the hobgoblin of little minds. The next year, Sagan was on the other side of the globe, advocating the feasibility of technologies far more fantastic than Leary's starship—technologies deployed not by humans but by alien super-beings.

MOST CULTURES ACCEPT some form of religious hierarchy, cosmic divisions of power that dimly mirror societal and familial power structures. Jove was the "king" of the Roman gods. The Christian god is "our father in heaven." In the space age, when "mankind doesn't need gods" (to quote Captain Kirk), science-fiction writers, speculative scientists, and UFO buffs have in fact replaced the old cosmic power structures with scientific ones. For example, UFOs are "angels" or "devils" made of nuts and bolts. The former bring good tidings from our "superiors" in space (who urge us to behave and stop playing around with atomic bombs), while the latter bring anal probes into our bedrooms, where they examine our orifices (*that's* why they crossed the galaxy?). A century ago, Nietzsche fretted about what would happen when humans realized that God doesn't exist. How could he have foreseen the epoch of Roswell and Area 51?

Carl Sagan, too, believed in superior beings in space, creatures so intelligent, so powerful as to resemble gods. They are superior partly because their civilizations are millions of years old and have developed technologies unimaginable to us. They have evolved far enough to outgrow their warlike ways. And they are benevolent; they will even share the secrets of the cosmos with us, if we'll simply tune in to their radio transmissions. In short, they are all-powerful, all-knowing, all-loving. Is it any wonder that Sagan's first son, science writer Dorion Sagan, scoffs that "the search for extraterrestrial intelligence is a replacement for religion in a secular age"?[2]

Sagan believed in superior civilizations because he believed in Progress, in the most Victorian sense of that word. As a child, he had strolled with his parents past the sights of the New York World's Fair. He imbibed its "extremely technocratic"[3] message about a wondrous tomorrow long after humanity outgrows its adolescent fumblings such as depressions and world wars. As he grew, he reasoned that many star systems are older than ours; their inhabitants must have evolved further than we. If these superior beings visited us, they'd smile at our technologies, "relics of the clumsy contrivances of the simple childhood of the race. Certainly, what we see hints at the existence of beings who are in advance of, not behind us, in the journey of life."[4] So Percival Lowell spoke of the Martians, circa 1895. To smile at these beliefs is not to say that alien super-civilizations do not exist; perhaps they do. The point is that people would believe in them regardless, for the same reason that our ancestors believed in gods and that Lowell believed in superior Martians—because the belief fulfills some inexplicable need within the human heart. To modify Voltaire: "If aliens did not exist, it would be necessary to invent them."[5]

Which brings us to Soviet Armenia in September 1971. Sagan chaired the U.S. delegation to the first major international SETI conference, held at the Byurakan Astrophysical Observatory. "It picked up where the Green Bank meeting ten years earlier had left off, but lasted a whole week, with many more participants and some strong new blood," Frank Drake says. Sagan and Soviet scientist Nikolai Kardashev (a Shklovskii associate) had "cooked up" the idea for the meeting.[6] The attendees included Sagan, Drake, Phil Morrison, DNA researcher (and Nobelist) Francis Crick, the owlish-looking physicist Freeman Dyson, future Nobelist (for vision research) David Hubel, artificial-intelligence expert Marvin Minsky, laser pioneer Charles Townes (a Nobelist who wanted to use lasers for SETI), and origin-of-life researcher Leslie Orgel. The Soviet chairperson was famed astrophysicist V. A. Ambartsumian. Shklovskii and Kardashev were there, along with about thirty other Soviets. Sagan also invited two social scientists, the University of Toronto anthropologist Richard Lee and the University of Chicago historian William McNeill (author of *The Rise of the West*). McNeill brought to the conference something that early SETI theorists badly lacked: historical perspective on—and, hence, skepticism about—their grandiose plans.

At Byurakan, far-out ideas were discussed from "early morning to quite late at night."[7] Among them: the feasibility of life on frigid planets *without* stars; Bernard Oliver's plans for Project Cyclops, a proposed giant array of radiotelescopes that could act as a single huge SETI receiver; and the possibility of using nuclear bomb bursts to signal aliens.

Sagan suggested that certain "astronomical" phenomena might be gigantic beacons built by extraterrestrials, possibly beings within our own solar system. Aliens might communicate over interstellar distances, he said, by manipulating "a very small movable shield" above the surface of a local pulsar, in order to regulate its pulses (just as people once communicated by moving blankets in front of fires). In that regard, Sagan suggested looking for intelligent signals within pulsar emissions. Also, "fluctuating x-ray sources" from interstellar space might not be natural. Might they actually be huge lasers used to push starships across the galaxy? The stellar gods may "astroengineer" the galaxy as easily as we build a bridge or an overpass. (Later, in Sagan's novel, *Contact*, he described how extraterrestrials rearrange the matter of the universe to delay its eventual gravitational collapse back into a "big crunch.")

Given the relative youth of our technical civilization, Sagan argued, there could be no intelligent life out there that would be "as dumb as we." He estimated that there "are a million technical civilizations in the galaxy. This corresponds roughly to one out of every hundred thousand stars. Assuming these civilizations are distributed randomly, it follows that the distance to the nearest one is a few hundred light-years." Hence (he reasoned), it would take a while to start a two-way conversation with aliens, so let's start *now*.

Why the rush? Because they might share their secrets of success with us! "With an extremely advanced technology . . . problems which beset emerging societies such as ours will be solved."[8] In his subsequent book *Broca's Brain* (1979), Sagan said, "it is possible that among the first contents of such a [alien] message may be detailed prescriptions for the avoidance of technological disaster. . . . It is difficult to think of another enterprise [besides SETI] within our capability and at a relatively modest cost that holds as much promise for the future of humanity."[9] (Never mind that our terrestrial problems have deep historical, social, and economic roots; they are amenable to technical "quick fixes" from the stars. It's the New York World's Fair vision all over again—social change via wonder toys, not via redistributions of power and wealth; social change that discomfits no one, especially the powerful and wealthy.)

As mentioned before, Sagan sometimes criticized others for advocating far-out ideas similar to his own. This trait resembles his self-admitted tendency to "project" his personal flaws onto another person and, as a result, to resent that person. Likewise, Sagan's hope for extraterrestrial salvation via SETI blatantly contradicted his charge, at the 1969 UFO symposium, that it was "politically dangerous" for saucer buffs to nurse "the expectation that we are going to be saved from ourselves by some miraculous interstellar intervention." Such a delusion discourages us from trying "to solve our own problems."

Sagan was not alone in his optimism about the benefits of communication with extraterrestrials. Harvard astrophysicist A. G. W. Cameron wrote in his book *Interstellar Communication* that through SETI "we can expect to obtain an enormous enrichment of all phases of our sciences and arts. Perhaps we shall also receive valuable lessons in the techniques of stable world government."[10]

Can one imagine a sadder symbol of American society, circa 1970, than this? The United States was passing through one of its dark nights of the soul, an era of self-doubt and despair. The Vietnam War dragged on, endlessly, brutally, pointlessly. Cities turned into abysses of crime and drug abuse. Soon the oil crisis would strike, along with Watergate, Abscam, and other shocks to national pride. In short, society was going to hell—and some of its finest minds were praying for celestial salvation.

Humans have always projected terrestrial concerns onto the skies. Living in the great age of canal-building, when some scholars feared that Earth's seas were drying up, Percival Lowell looked to Mars—and what did he imagine seeing? A society building giant canals to prevent desertification. Likewise, the SETI scientists lived when Western nations were offering massive "technical assistance" to Third World nations to discourage them from going Communist. These scientists looked to the stars—and what did they imagine seeing? Super-societies eager to extend "technical assistance" to the rubes on Earth. It hardly occurred to these scientists that alien technology would be irrelevant to earthly needs. Technologies are not universally useful; they serve specific needs of specific cultures at given times. That is probably one reason the Romans never developed labor-saving machinery—because it would have undermined slavery, the foundation of their social structure. That is why the Chinese never made much use of gunpowder, clocks, or printing, although they invented them—because these inventions didn't fit their contemporary needs. And if aliens ever send us blueprints for their technologies, they are likely to be as useless to us as an eggbeater is to an aardvark.[11]

Sagan's real worry wasn't whether alien gadgets would sell at Sears. His real worry was that the aliens would ignore us, that extremely advanced societies might regard us as indifferently as we regard the ants at our feet. And even if they were open to interstellar conversation, we might not be able to detect their signals: their communications technologies might be radically different from ours. "It may be," he speculated, "that we are very much like the inhabitants of, let's say, isolated valleys in New Guinea, who communicate with their neighbors by runner and drum, and who are completely unaware of a vast international radio and cable traffic over them, around them, and through them."[12] In other words, we might be stuck in the galactic sticks.

Undaunted, the conferees issued an optimistic joint statement: "If extraterrestrial civilizations are ever discovered the effect on human scientific and technological capabilities will be immense, and the discovery can positively influence the whole future of man." They recommended searching for:

> . . . civilizations at a technological level greatly surpassing our own.
> . . . signals and for evidence of astroengineering activities in the radiation of a few hundred chosen nearby stars and of a limited number of other selected objects, covering the wavelength range from visible to decimeter waves, using the largest existing astronomical instruments.
> . . . signals from powerful sources within galaxies of the local group [i.e., near the Milky Way], including searches for strong impulsive signals.[13]

Amid this cheerful speculation, one observer voiced doubts. William McNeill was, as has been noted, a historian. Historians have a strong sense of the transience of societies and ideas, of the tragic or ironic fates that await most utopian visions. He tried to convey this perspective to the Byurakan conferees: "I must say that in listening to the discussion these last days, I feel I detect what might be called a pseudo or scientific religion." He doubted that we would even be able to understand the aliens' messages, or they ours: "Our intelligence, unless I misunderstand, is very much a prisoner of words, a prisoner of language, and I don't see how we can assume that the language of another intelligent community would have very many points of contact with our own. The differences in biochemistry, in the sensory span of intelligent beings, sensibility, in such things as size of body and neuron pattern, all seem to me to add up to a high improbability of mutual intelligibility."[14]

Three decades later, McNeill's pessimism seems prophetic. We have not managed to detect a single alien civilization, much less wrestle with decoding its versions of Linear B. The SETI search is still worthwhile, and may succeed one day. But it has taken far longer than many SETI enthusiasts expected, in part because they, like Sagan, believed uncritically in Progress, both on Earth and in the stars.

YET, LACKING SUCH OPTIMISM, would they have tried at all? Certainly they would not have undertaken what some might view as one of the more quixotic enterprises of the twentieth century: the design and launch of greeting cards to the stars. Over a six-year period, Carl Sagan and a little Bloomsbury group of like-minded friends and lovers sent messages to aliens. They sent these not by radio but by interstellar spaceship. They affixed plaques to two probes, and records to two more. All were successfully launched. At this moment they are racing out of our solar system, bound for the cosmic sea. In the low-erosion environment of deep space, they will survive hundreds of millions of years, longer than the Pyramids or the Rocky Mountains.

The messages are the famous plaques on the *Pioneer 10* and *Pioneer 11* spacecraft, which contain basic information about Earth and display a man and a woman, and the *Voyager 1* and *Voyager 2* records. Each of the latter is a metallic phonograph record. Encoded in its grooves are images and sounds from Earth, photos of cities and seas, music from Beethoven and Chuck Berry, and spoken greetings in numerous languages (including one from Sagan's son Nick). (Sagan also placed a plaque on the *LAGEOS* satellite, which is now high in Earth orbit and will remain there for millions of years. This plaque displays the long-term shifting of terrestrial tectonic plates. Should humanity become extinct, the plaque will inform future alien visitors of the time when Earth was inhabited, just as Shklovskii's mythical Martian "space stations" preserved relics of Martian culture.)

Space is vast, so the tiny spaceships are extremely unlikely to be found by anyone—whoever "anyone" might be. In Harold Urey's words, their probability of recovery is "exceedingly small . . . the smallest of any of the probabilities which I have considered."[15]

Why launch them, then? They are best viewed as a big-budget form of performance art, an expression of humanitarian sentiments that are "impractical" yet essential. Via these messages to the stars, Sagan began flexing the artistic and spiritual sides of his nature.

It was the science writer Eric Burgess who originally proposed launching a plaque on the *Pioneer 10*. At that time, NASA planned to launch the probe to Jupiter in early 1972. To reach the outer planets, it had to travel extremely fast, so fast that, by coincidence, it would exceed solar escape velocity. After a few decades it would pass the heliopause, the region that separates the solar environment and interstellar space. The *Pioneer* and its three fellow space probes would become humanity's first emissaries to the stars.

Sagan and Frank Drake discussed how to design the plaque in December 1971 at a meeting of the American Astronomical Society in San Juan, Puerto Rico. They decided the plaque should reveal the location of Earth by showing its position relative to known pulsars, plus their rotation rates. Thus, any sufficiently advanced aliens who recover a *Pioneer* could estimate when it was launched by comparing the listed rotation rates with the aliens' ancient records of rotation rates for the same pulsars.[16]

Sagan's wife Linda Salzman, with her artist's sensibility, suggested adding human figures to the plaque. NASA said okay. She drew the figures: a male and a female, both adult—and naked. As drawn, the man has his right hand raised, as if in greeting (like a movie Indian saying "How!"). The woman stands by, leaning slightly on one leg.

Newspapers reprinted the plaque, offending some readers. Feminists complained that the woman was too passive, just standing there while the man says "Hi" to the galaxy. The woman doesn't have genitalia, either, while the man's member is obvious. One woman was so upset she wanted "to cut off the man's . . . right arm!" she wrote to the *New York Times*.[17]

Some readers thought the plaque was pornographic. Newspaper bluenoses went to work: the *Philadelphia Inquirer* removed the woman's nipples and the man's genitalia from the published image. "A family newspaper must uphold community standards," an editor explained. According to Sagan, "the *Chicago Sun Times* . . . published three versions of the plaque in different editions all on the same day: in the first the man was represented whole; in the second, suffering from an awkward and botched airbrush castration; and in the final version—intended no doubt to reassure the family man dashing home—with no sexual apparatus at all." A reader wrote to the *Los Angeles Times*: "I was shocked by the blatant display of both male and female sex organs on the front page. . . . Isn't it enough that we must tolerate the bombardment of pornography through the media of film and smut magazines? Isn't it bad enough that our own space agency officials have found it necessary to spread this filth even beyond our own solar system?" Amused, another *Times* reader suggested that the plaque should show "a stork carrying a little bundle from heaven."

Then there was the racial issue. The drawings were line drawings, so on the white newsprint of newspapers the man and woman looked distinctly—well, white. And blond. In Berkeley, the radical *Berkeley Barb* reprinted the plaque on its cover above the caption: "Hello. We're from Orange County."[18]

Sagan was embarrassed, and his responses were almost comically glib. The "man and woman are not shown in precisely the same position or carriage so that the suppleness of the limbs could be communicated," he insisted in his 1973 book *The Cosmic Connection*. The female genitalia were omitted "partly because conventional representation in Greek statuary omits it.

"But," he admitted, "there was another reason: our desire to see the message successfully launched on *Pioneer 10*. In retrospect, we may have judged NASA's scientific-political hierarchy as more puritanical than it is."

The sexual issue received more press than the racial one, but "I personally feel much worse about" the latter, Sagan admitted later. Far from being Aryan stereotypes, the man and woman were based on "the classical models of Greek sculpture and the drawings of Leonardo da Vinci." Initially, he and Salzman tried to make the figures "panracial." But "somewhere in the transcription from the original sketch drawing to the final engraving the Afro was transmuted into a very non-African Mediterranean-curly haircut.[19]

Flaws and all, the plaque was affixed to *Pioneer 10*, and soared skyward on a late-winter day in March 1972. (A copy was later launched aboard *Pioneer 11*.) Disturbed by the racial and sexual controversies, Sagan—a well-meaning liberal with feminist leanings and a small but proud civil rights record—determined to do better next time. The chance would soon come.

MEANWHILE, SAGAN HAD NOT FORGOTTEN about his own solar system. In the early 1970s, he and colleagues indulged in imaginative speculation about the evolution of the atmospheres of Venus, Earth, Mars, and Jupiter.

By the early 1970s the Soviets had dropped numerous space probes into the Venusian atmosphere. The *Venera 9* landing probe sent back

surface photos that showed a rocky, dimly lit terrain. The images vindicated Sagan's belief—an essential component of his greenhouse theory—
that sunlight penetrates all the way to the surface. (The Soviets had
feared that the surface would be dark, so they placed floodlights on the
probe.)

But Sagan and Kuiper's heated quarrel over the Venusian clouds had
been for nothing: both were wrong. At Kuiper's lab in Tucson, Godfrey
Sill showed that the ground-based astronomical spectra of Venus's clouds
nicely matched that of sulfuric acid. This discovery solidified Venus's
reputation as the hellhole of the solar system.[20] As Owen Brian Toon
writes, a visitor approaching the real Venus would see "pale yellow
clouds as a soft, welcoming haze." But as one enters the atmosphere, the
clouds of concentrated sulfuric acid "would badly burn your skin if you
were exposed to it." Above the clouds, the view would resemble "a
smoggy day in Los Angeles"; farther down, a dense fog and a sulfuric
acid drizzle. Standing on the surface, beneath a rosy-peach sky, an astronaut would face horrific heat and crushing air pressure, greater than at
the ocean bottom.[21]

Sagan's original greenhouse model of Venus's atmosphere contained
some significant errors. These weren't his fault; they were common misconceptions in the late 1950s and early 1960s. One error was Sagan's
belief that the air pressure was two or three times that of Earth. In fact,
it is 93 times as high. Also, Sagan believed (as experts generally did until
the mid-to-late 1960s) that the primary gas in the Venusian atmosphere
was nitrogen, but it turned out to be carbon dioxide. And the surface
temperature of Venus is around 750 degrees K, some 150 degrees higher
than Sagan had originally believed.

Jim Pollack moved to Cornell in 1970. With the discovery of Venus's
extremely high pressure, he and Sagan recalculated their original models
of the Venus greenhouse effect. They developed what became known as
the "two-stream" theoretical model for calculating radiative transfer
(that is, heat flow) inside the Venusian atmosphere. That model ended
up influencing atmospheric physics in general, Toon notes: "That, to me,
is one of the seminal papers in that business. It led directly or indirectly
to a whole bunch of us using this, the two-stream model, to look at
atmospheric radiative transfer. I could cite you, probably without any
trouble at all, ten to twenty papers in the 1970s that . . . flowed one way
or another from what Carl and Jim did."[22]

Sagan's most important mistake was his belief that water vapor is an
important factor in the Venusian atmosphere. In fact, Venus has virtually
no water vapor, and Sagan's water-ice clouds were imaginary. "There's
almost no water there. It was the right theory but the wrong gas and the
wrong actual numerical parameters," says Sagan's former student David

Morrison, now chief scientist at NASA-Ames.[23] In addition, the near absence of water vapor undermined Sagan's proposal for terraforming Venus. Any algae seeded into the clouds would be simultaneously starved for liquid and menaced by sulfuric acid. Nonetheless, Sagan's greenhouse explanation remains basically sound.

By the early 1970s, then, scientists universally recognized Venus for what it is: a Dantesque wasteland. There are no glaciers, no lakes, no habitable mountaintops where strange creatures frolic in the cool alpine air. Menzel and Whipple's Venusian ocean is a forgotten fantasy, a cautionary tale of the early space age that we would do well to recall nowadays, when speculation runs wild about "vanished seas" on Mars and bizarre life forms in the dark ocean depths of Europa.

Menzel died in 1974. In 1997 I interviewed Fred Whipple, a cheerful ninety-one-year-old who remains active in astronomy. He regaled me with anecdotes from his long and distinguished career, including his encounters with many titans (for example, Edwin Hubble, who blew smoke rings down the length of a dinner table). Only once did Whipple grow reticent—when I asked him about the Venusian "ocean." "You don't always write perfect papers," he admitted with a sigh. "I'd like to forget about it."[24]

THIS NEW VISION OF VENUS—the planetary system's version of the ninth circle of hell—stems to a considerable extent from work by Sagan's colleague Jim Pollack. Space scientists tend to view Pollack as the real genius behind Sagan's Venus papers of the 1970s. "I always liked Jim, a very smart guy, a kind of low-keyed, very thoughtful and bright guy," recalls Brian O'Leary, then a young space scientist at Cornell. "I'd say in many ways he was brighter than Carl."[25]

By that time, a once-concealed issue in Pollack's life was emerging from the closet: homosexuality. In June 1969, the Stonewall riot in New York City had forced the issue of gay rights onto front pages. Jim Pollack was gay. At Cornell, he "roomed with a fellow and they were obviously a gay couple; we'd see them at gatherings," O'Leary says. While generally taciturn about being gay, Pollack didn't conceal it from the gentle, easygoing O'Leary or his wife, both of whom were anti-homophobic before anti-homophobia was cool. "He saw that I was a warm and accepting person. And vice versa."[26]

Later, Pollack would move to San Francisco, where the climate for gays in the 1970s was dramatically better than in almost any other place in the nation. Working at NASA-Ames, Pollack "kept his personal life sort of separate," David Morrison recalls. "He was gay. He lived with a couple of different guys for long-term relationships. He kept that separate from his work environment. I don't think most people here even knew he was gay. . . . I don't think he was actually hiding anything. . . . He just chose not to make a big deal of it."[27]

Sometimes, though, Pollack unwittingly or subtly let slip his sexual orientation. Dale Cruikshank recalls visiting "Jim and his then-partner at their apartment. So it was not a secret that these two men were partners, but it was certainly never openly discussed on the street or in the office, as far as I know.

"And then later, as I say, starting around ten years ago when I came here, it was clear that Jim had a different partner. My wife and I were entertained one night at their home for dinner, and I was actually slightly taken aback because Jim gave us a tour of the house, which included the one-bed bedroom. I was a bit surprised that he had gone to the point of taking us on the tour of the apartment. Both my wife and I have liberal attitudes toward these things. I have a son who is gay, as a matter of fact, so I've gotten a bit of an education on this subject myself."[28]

Toon worked with Pollack "for a really long time" and recalls that some of his "boyfriends would throw temper tantrums and go storming into his office." While many scientists relax and kick back with colleagues, Pollack was "just totally devoted to science. He was homosexual, for one thing, and I think that caused him political uneasiness. It wasn't like he disguised this, but it made him awkward. He didn't feel like he 'fit in' all the time. He was socially awkward."[29] He was dedicated to the gay rights cause, however, and at one point in the 1970s persuaded Sagan to find a job in the space agency for a man, Franklin Kameny, whose sexual orientation had caused another federal agency to fire him. Although Sagan's mother, Rachel, had been loudly homophobic, Sagan himself had no trouble with Pollack's private life.

On the whole, though, American society of the 1970s remained wary of gays. Isolated from mainstream culture, Jim Pollack poured his heart into his work, work that lent luster to the career of his colorful Cornell ally. Pollack "would keep Carl grounded in reality," Toon observes. When Pollack wrestled with cancer in the 1990s, "he was bedridden and unable to move—and he was still publishing papers."[30]

SAGAN AND POLLACK COLLABORATED over three decades. But, as mentioned earlier, most of Sagan's collaborations were transient, sometimes one-shot, affairs. Sagan's interests were so broad and his attention span was so short that he tended to hop from collaborator to collaborator.

One of his most important transient collaborations was with the physicist George Mullen. In the early 1970s, they tried to explain an old puzzle known as the faint early sun paradox. According to this paradox, the primal sun was some 30 percent dimmer than it is today; hence the primordial Earth must have been frozen. Yet geological evidence indicates that it wasn't frozen. In fact, it was warm enough for life to emerge. So what warmed early Earth?

Sagan and Mullen proposed that Earth's early atmosphere contained ammonia, which acted like a greenhouse gas, trapping infrared radiation. This kept the surface temperate and prevented the oceans from freezing.[31] The Sagan-Mullen paper is one of the seminal papers cited by Stanley Miller in 1992 when he nominated Sagan for membership in the National Academy of Sciences.

Nowadays scientists collaborate more by e-mail than face-to-face. Back then, though, when the Net was still a Defense Department plaything and scientists struggled to raise funds for trips to scientific meetings, they often met via "snail mail" or mutual relationships. Mullen had gone to graduate school at Syracuse University with Bishun Khare, Sagan's longtime lab associate. By 1969, Mullen was at Mansfield University, a liberal arts college some seventy-five miles from Cornell. Bishun invited him to Cornell. There Mullen met Sagan, and they began chatting. Around poor conversationalists, Sagan quickly became bored, but Mullen was a good one. They began discussing the possibility of developing a general theory of planetary atmospheres. Sagan mentioned the faint early sun paradox and suggested ammonia as the key to the puzzle. As Mullen recalls it, Sagan had laughingly mentioned that certain microorganisms live in urinals, which are ammonia-rich. He pointed out that the same reducing gas might trap infrared radiation, keeping early Earth warm for primordial microbes.

Sagan put Mullen and Khare to work investigating the infrared-trapping potential of ammonia. Mullen did computer calculations, while Khare shone radiation through flasks containing the gas. Mullen: "Even if we were just sitting around, talking, he was always moving his arms, gesticulating, saying, 'Think about this, think about that . . .' When I would bring my kids up, he was always interested in what they were doing." Mullen's daughter, Siobhan, then nine or ten years old, was particularly taken by the effusive, charming Sagan.[32]

Sagan and Mullen published their findings in the July 7, 1972, issue of *Science*. They concluded that, sure enough, "a few parts per million" of ammonia in the Precambrian atmosphere was enough to prevent the early Earth from freezing.

As we have seen, Sagan didn't hesitate to inject science-fictionish speculations into highly technical papers. He had concluded his 1961 "Venus" article in *Science* with a riff on terraforming. In 1976, he would enliven an otherwise dull article for *Astrophysical Journal* by envisioning "balloon animals" there. And in his 1972 paper with Mullen, Sagan speculated that greenhouse gases kept early Mars warm, too, with biological results:

> Earlier conditions on Mars may have been much more clement . . . the origin of life may have occurred, as it did on primitive Earth in the same period. . . . Over geologic time, Mars could have lost meters to tens of meters of liquid water by photodissociation, escape of hydrogen, and oxidation of surface material. . . . It is a debatable but hardly quixotic contention that martian organisms may have been able to adapt to the increasingly rigorous martian environment and may still be present.

In the future, the Sun will grow hotter after it consumes all its hydrogen gas, then begins devouring its heavier elements. The intensified sunlight will warm Earth, boiling and vaporizing the oceans until they form a dense layer of atmospheric vapor. This layer will trap heat, triggering a "runaway" greenhouse effect. Thus Earth will become too hot for life, as Venus is today. The same solar brightening will cause Mars, which is much farther from the Sun than Earth, and currently frigid, to warm, too. It might even regain its old, equable climate. "If there are any organisms left on our planet in that remote epoch," Sagan added slyly, "they may wish to take advantage of this coincidence."[33]

Sagan's dreams of space travel, to Mars and elsewhere, inspired a generation of young people. One of them was Mullen's little daughter, Siobhan. She later created her own company, Spaceport Canada, to develop launch sites for commercial satellites.[34]

DESPITE THE NEGATIVE FINDINGS of *Apollo 11*, Sagan continued to hope that life might be discovered by astronauts on future Moon missions. He clung to this hope because of his near-mystical certitude that "physics and chemistry are so constructed as to make the origin of life easy."

At Cornell, Sagan and various colleagues studied how different energy sources, from solar ultraviolet radiation to shock waves from thunder, could have generated the building blocks of life in a reducing atmosphere.[35] In a July 30, 1971, paper for *Science*, Sagan and Bishun Khare suggested that a key component of the early atmosphere might have been hydrogen sulfide that absorbed long-wavelength solar UV. A key component of hydrogen sulfide, sulfur, is abundant in the cosmos and is "a pervasive constituent of volcanic effluvia even today." In their experiments on a simulated hydrogen sulfide–rich atmosphere, amino acids resulted. Over a billion years, solar ultraviolet and shock processes could have bequeathed Earth 200 kilograms of amino acids per square centimeter—"a huge number suggesting congenial conditions for the origin of life."[36]

The Moon continued to disappoint Sagan, though. More lunar rocks were brought to Earth by astronauts on *Apollo* missions *12, 14, 15*, and *16* (*Apollo 13* aborted, as moviegoers everywhere know). No rocks contained organics. Yet Sagan had not abandoned hope for lunar organics even as *Apollo 17*, the last lunar mission, roared into the Florida night, bathing the stars and the coastline in orange.

At that moment, just before Christmas 1972, it was hard to believe that an era was ending; that the glamorous dreams of the early 1960s of permanent bases on the Moon and Mars were being abandoned for generations to come, as mistakenly as Portugal, having reconnoitered the New World, abandoned it to bolder powers. We would leave our tools and plaques on the Moon, then come home (it seemed) for good. The cold war appeared to be thawing; the United States had beaten the Reds to the Moon; Nixon went to China, and toasted Brezhnev in the Kremlin; and the whole point of the space age suddenly seemed lost on the average American. If we had discovered Sagan's wished-for lunar microbes, would we have abandoned the Moon so perfunctorily?

On the Moon, *Apollo 17* astronaut Jack Schmitt picked up samples of a peculiar orangeish soil. Sagan, barely suppressing his excitement, wrote to Noel Hinners at NASA headquarters suggesting that the material was similar to organics that Sagan, his colleagues, and others had produced in the laboratory.[37] As it turned out, he was grasping at straws. As space scientist Paul D. Spudis records in his 1996 book, *The Once and Future Moon*, the "beautiful orange soil" turned out to be very *un*biological— "an unusual black-and-orange glass . . . volcanic ash, the product of a huge fountain of liquid rock sprayed out onto the surface . . . about 3.6 billion years ago."[38]

Later in life Sagan acknowledged that his early idea that "there are massive amounts of organic matter in the Moon, and that you could contaminate it, is completely wrong, just absolutely mistaken."[39] Still, he didn't regret promoting the lunar quarantine, which would have protected the Moon from terrestrial contaminants and the Earth from lunar ones. "I'm not embarrassed by it, if that makes any sense," he said.[40] Sagan, who as a boy was inspired by the apocalyptic moralizing of "Pete Can Fix It," argued that it is worth raising an alarm about an unlikely danger, if the danger is potentially devastating. He added (in an observation that explains much of his subsequent environmental activism): "'Small chance of large danger' has influenced my thinking on greenhouse warming, ozone-sphere depletion, nuclear war and nuclear winter. . . . A small chance of a major catastrophe is worth taking note of."[41]

BY THE EARLY 1970S, space scientists assumed that Earth was the only inhabited planet in our solar system. The *Apollo* astronauts had found no life on the Moon; *Mariners 4, 6,* and *7* sent back pictures of an inhospitable-looking Mars; and Venus was clearly too hot and poisonous for life.

Mariner 9, by contrast, revived hopes for Martian life because its images revealed an almost completely unexpected sight: dried riverbeds, or something tantalizingly like them. Liquid water could not exist on the surface of Mars today, of course. Its air pressure is too low, so liquid water would rapidly evaporate. If water cut the channels, it must have done so in the past, presumably when Mars had a denser atmosphere. The water might still exist on Mars, trapped, perhaps, in the whitish polar caps or frozen in permafrost within the crust.

Intriguingly, some "riverbeds" appeared far more eroded than others. Also, riverbeds appeared in terrains of different ages (as revealed by their varying densities of impact craters). This implied that Mars had undergone more than one "watery" epoch. Perhaps its climate had flipped back and forth between warm, wet epochs and cold, dry ones, as Earth switches between ice ages and equable climates like that of the last ten thousand or so years.

Sagan had previously anticipated the possibility of a watery past for Mars. He based this speculation on his "crater counts" for Mars. In late 1969, he, Jim Pollack, and Clark R. Chapman wrote a paper concluding that the surface of Mars has about fifty times as many craters as expected based on the estimated rate of impact events in its vicinity. The intense cratering had generated a vast number of small particles, which buried much of the planet under a thick layer of dust. The dust, they suspected, had concealed any ancient evidence of river valleys on Mars. So perhaps evidence of life might still be found.[42]

Did life inhabit those ancient waters? In 1971, Sagan wrote a paper for *Icarus* in which he speculated that the large northern ice cap on Mars might vary in size over time. The planet's axis slightly "wobbles," which causes varying amounts of sunlight to illuminate the poles. During "sunnier" periods, the pole would evaporate, increasing the air pressure, which in turn would trap heat via a greenhouse effect. Thus there would be periods of warmer climate that were very favorable to life.[43] In short, he argued, modern Mars may only *appear* inhospitable because we are viewing it at "an unpropitious moment" during a colder climate period. If this were the case, then when the Viking probes landed there in 1976, he joked, they "will have arrived ten thousand years early."[44] Sagan romantically envisioned Mars's Pleistocene past—recurrent golden ages of warmth, water, lakes, and running streams, crawling with unimaginable bio-exotica. Such fancies did not impress his friend and frequent

critic, Caltech space scientist Bruce Murray. "I think we can say that
Mars has never had any oceans and no atmosphere for most of its life,"
Murray assured the *New York Times*. Murray was a geologist, one of those
people who dealt with the gritty, hard-to-systematize realities of Earth;
he had little patience with the intricate, abstract theorizing of Sagan
types. He implied that Sagan's Mars fantasies were linked to his childhood, to the pulp literature he had never fully outgrown. Just before
Mariner 9 slid into Mars orbit, Sagan, Murray, the writer Ray Bradbury,
Arthur C. Clarke, and Walter Sullivan participated in a panel discussion
about Mars in Pasadena. "I really don't think there is any life on Mars,"
Murray said. "Lowell's legacy is still plaguing us when it shouldn't."[45]
Then *Mariner 9* flew to Mars and revived hopes for Martian life—micro-
scopic life, at least.

That wasn't the only exciting news from *Mariner 9*. Its thousands of
astonishing, high-resolution pictures[46] revealed the solar system's biggest
volcano—two and a half times as high as Mount Everest. It also bore
the largest known scar in the solar system, an immense canyon 4,000
kilometers long, 200 kilometers wide, and three times as deep as the
Grand Canyon. These discoveries indirectly supported Sagan and Pollack's theory that Mars, far from being "as smooth as a billiard ball," has
great extremes of elevation. The *Mariner 9* images also upheld their
explanation for the "wave of darkening": variations in surface brightness
caused by windblown dust, not by seasonal vegetation changes.

Mariner 9 also, however, killed one old fantasy, Shklovskii's theory
about the Martian moons. During its orbit of Mars, the space probe
passed near both these little worlds and photographed them. "Freud says
somewhere that the only happy men are those whose boyhood dreams
are realized," Sagan later wrote. "I cannot say that it has made my life
carefree. But I will never forget those early-morning hours in a chilly
California November when Joe Veverka, a JPL technician, and I were
the first human beings ever to see the face of Phobos." Later he told
journalist Joseph Goodavage: "I've looked at every single photograph of
Phobos and Deimos. One of the reasons why I was interested in taking
those pictures was just to check out this exciting, speculative idea of
Shklovskii's." His conclusion: they were just "old, battered-up rocks."[47]

ON A MORE DOWNBEAT NOTE, the *Mariner 9* photos forced Sagan to
give up one childhood fascination: the Martian "canals." As we have seen,
after *Mariner 4*, he and Pollack had speculated that the "long, thin lines"
were real features, albeit geological ones—ridges akin to the mid-ocean
ridges of Earth. But *Mariner 9*'s detailed imagery showed nothing even
remotely resembling such ridges. Hence the ridge theory was "com-

pletely erroneous . . . 100 percent wrong," Sagan observed later. The canals were complete illusions, phantasms bred by wish fulfillment.[48] To this day, the "canals" myth remains one of the most vivid examples of the ability of some scientists to fool themselves—of the limitations of scientific "objectivity." Another vivid example, of course, is the career of Carl Sagan.

WHILE THE NEWS FROM MARS overall was exciting, Sagan's favorite candidate for extraterrestrial life remained Jupiter. His speculations about that giant world led to a blowout with his old thesis adviser, Gerard Kuiper.

Jupiter is enwrapped by colorful bands. Sagan suspected that these colors indicated organic molecules similar to organics that he and Bishun Khare had simulated in laboratory flasks. But other scientists were skeptical. They argued that any organics formed in the Jovian sky would rapidly break down again into methane, ammonia, and water. Another doubter was Kuiper. In an article for the February 1972 issue of *Sky & Telescope*, Kuiper referred obliquely to Sagan and Khare's work, saying that they had indeed generated "colored polymers," but "under conditions quite different from those in the Jovian atmosphere."[49]

Sagan detonated. He fired off a letter to Kuiper blasting his criticisms as "dead wrong." With the certitude that so often infuriated his foes, Sagan declared that the existence of large amounts of organic molecules in Jupiter's environment was "inevitable." He also took the opportunity to express his surprise that Kuiper had not referenced a recent paper Sagan had written about the Great Red Spot. The tone of Sagan's letter was cold and angry.[50]

One can imagine the reaction of the sensitive, slightly paranoid Kuiper to this missive. Sagan's final insinuation—that Kuiper had failed to properly credit Sagan's work—must have particularly stung: Kuiper was probably still sore from Harold Urey's "plagiarism" accusations of the 1950s.[51]

It was a sour twilight to their old relationship. Kuiper died in December 1973. Several weeks later, by coincidence, *Time* magazine ran a detailed profile of Sagan. The article included this quote from Kuiper: "Carl doesn't want to be confused by the facts."[52]

BY THE EARLY 1970s, the news media had soured on NASA. The television networks no longer carried nonstop coverage of Moon missions. The lunar quarantine had generated no exciting "bugs" threatening Earth's environment. Venus was a dreary oven. Even *Mariner 9*'s pictures drew little press attention, despite their close-ups of dried riverbeds and other hints of a more clement past. The media's indifference baffled Sagan. How could people care so little about historic exploration? Polls showed that double-digit percentages of Americans believed in UFOs, ghosts, and other fanciful notions, yet when real-life wonders came along, they yawned and changed channels.

The solution, Sagan believed, was better science popularization, and he knew he was the man for the job. He liked reporters, could explain things clearly and entertainingly, was moderately handsome, and had a superb, TV-friendly voice. Even better, he had vision: he could sell the public science as advertisers sold them soap, as evangelists sold them religion. And salesmanship was needed. The nation did not lack for science writers and popularizers. There were many fine ones. But a succession of "Mr. Wizards"—popularizers who explained the mechanics of science—was not enough. The nation needed someone who could make science seem like a cause, a calling, an ideal; someone whose description of the rings of Saturn or the icy clouds of Venus or the organic mists of Jupiter was so poetic, so stylishly delivered, that it sent a shudder down the spine. Nothing less would do.

And time was short: the 1970s was a disillusioned age. Many people, especially members of Theodore Roszak's "counterculture,"[53] were beginning to blame science for many of the world's ills. They viewed it (not altogether unfairly) as a juggernaut that filled the sea and sky with toxins, automated workers out of jobs, napalmed and cluster-bombed Vietnam, turned individuals into numbers, replaced ethical issues with game theory, and built foreign policy around the "logic" of nuclear annihilation. How could Sagan combat the counterculture's hostility?

Enter Jerome Agel. In the 1960s and 1970s, Agel was one of the New York publishing industry's lovable characters—"a man who always seems to be in motion, walking fast, talking fast, thinking fast," the *Newsday* columnist Dennis Duggan once observed.[54] Agel "produced" books as impresarios produced plays. First, he found a celebrity, usually a scholar, who had something interesting to say—Marshall McLuhan, Herman Kahn, Buckminster Fuller, Carl Sagan, whoever. Then Agel helped the scholar express his thoughts in book form. These books were perfect reading matter for the TV generation: short, easy to read, entertaining, full of pictures, and small enough to slip into the back pocket of your jeans. "Produced by Jerome Agel" appeared on the cover, beside the author's name.

As a child Agel had "dreamed about the planets, especially about Mars." He worked as a sports reporter and a newspaper editor and writer, then struck gold by producing McLuhan's highly popular *The Medium Is the Massage*. Afterward, still in his early forties, Agel decided to create "a book about the cosmos, the universe, the planets, and about the possibility of extraterrestrial life."[55] What he needed was a big-name scientist for the task.

While reading the *New York Post Magazine*, he came across a profile of Sagan by the writer Lee Dembart. "I wrote Carl in California, where the *Post* article reported he was working, and he replied that he would be delighted to visit with me on his next visit to Manhattan. He did. On a sunny spring day we met at my penthouse office on East 55th Street."[56]

Sagan was four years Agel's junior. They hit it off right away. The astronomer "had star quality," Agel recalls. "He was the Leonard Bernstein of science. He was the best thing to happen to American science since Sputnik."[57]

Among Agel's other interests, he is a Kennedy assassination buff. He wrote his own book proposing a novel explanation for the Kennedy assassination, to wit: Lee Harvey Oswald was a woman-hater who intended to kill Jackie Kennedy but shot Jack by accident.[58] Agel's fascination with the killing may have inspired Sagan's own, very private interest in the subject. The noted science writer Frederic Golden profiled Sagan for a 1980 cover story in *Time*. After Sagan's death, Golden reminisced:

> At times he . . . seemed oddly gullible. While I was having dinner with him in a Manhattan bistro many years ago, he suddenly pulled out a photograph of the crowd in Dallas's Dealey Plaza after President John F. Kennedy's assassination in 1963. He pointed to a tiny figure in the throng that he insisted resembled Lee Harvey Oswald. If it was Oswald, he said, in whispered tones, he couldn't have been the assassin.[59]

On the day they met, Sagan and Agel agreed to prepare a book proposal. They did, and seventeen publishers rejected it. The eighteenth—Velikovsky's publisher, Doubleday—said yes. Sagan's advance was $18,000, not too shabby for the time. The manuscript was due in January 1973. Its title: *The Cosmic Connection: An Extraterrestrial Perspective*.

IN 1969, THEODORE ROSZAK's book *The Making of a Counter Culture* profiled new value systems, particularly among the young, that opposed the materialistic, technology-obsessed, seemingly antihuman dominant culture. The counterculture was diverse, and elements of it were as sophisticated as the "New York intellectuals" were in their heyday.[60] Yet nowadays, "nostalgic" television shows and films (many with reactionary subtexts) depict the counterculture's goals as simplistic in the extreme: tune in, drop out, take drugs, play music, make love not war, and the like. A particularly common cliché is that the counterculture loathed technology in any and all forms.

However, a *sub*-counterculture sympathized with certain types of technology. Amory Lovins and others championed "appropriate" energy sources such as solar and wind power, especially for Third World nations seeking an alternative future to the mega-industrialization of the West and the Communist bloc.[61] LSD guru Timothy Leary proselytized for the personal liberation offered by a new gadget: the personal computer.[62] Stewart Brand and California politician Jerry ("Governor Moonbeam") Brown talked up physicist Gerard K. O'Neill's proposals for orbital space colonies big enough to hold thousands or millions of people. (Brand promoted space colonies—along with solar ovens and organic gardening tips—in his phenomenally popular *Whole Earth Catalogue*.)[63] And as shown by the title of Robert Pirsig's classic *Zen and the Art of Motorcycle Maintenance*, not everyone assumed that spiritual longings and technical prowess were antithetical.[64]

One expression of this pro-technology sub-counterculture was Sagan's *The Cosmic Connection*. It is a book about science and technology almost anyone—hippies and housewives, potheads and professors—could love. Unlike prior books about space exploration and SETI, *The Cosmic Connection* was intensely personal, almost intimate.

Sagan opened the book by recalling his childhood encounter with his grandfather, who greeted the boy's professed interest in astronomy by asking, "But how will you make a living?" It is hard to imagine an opening that could have appealed more to Sagan's young readers, the disaffected teens of the post-1960s era for whom revolution was no longer an option but for whom one question seemed urgent: not "How do I make a living?" but rather, "How do I make a life *worth* living?" Sagan seemed to be coming from the same place as he went on:

> Even today, there are moments when what I do seems to me like an improbable, if unusually pleasant, dream: to be involved in the exploration of Venus, Mars, Jupiter, and Saturn; to try to duplicate the steps that led to the origin of life four billion years ago on an Earth very different from the one we know; to land instruments on Mars to search there for life; and perhaps to be engaged in a serious effort to communicate with other intelligent beings, if such there be, out there in the dark of the night sky.[65]

If they all lived to be a hundred years old, none of NASA's paid publicists could write a more alluring sales pitch. Isaac Asimov wrote to Sagan that he had just finished *The Cosmic Connection* and "loved every word of it."[66] He also commented, flatteringly, that the only thing that disconcerted him about the book was that it showed that Sagan was smarter than he was.

Actually, Sagan did not write *The Cosmic Connection;* he dictated it, in part "during a very long transcontinental trip in a very short automobile."[67] He dictated practically everything, using a hand-held recorder. Recalls Lester Grinspoon: "I can't tell you how many times when we were smoking pot and he'd say, 'Oh, let me get that [insight recorded],' and he'd excuse himself to dictate outside the room."[68]

He prepared much of *The Cosmic Connection* with Agel's assistance. "Towards the end of December, 1972," Agel recalls, "we met for several days in Ithaca [to work on the book]. I am a morning person; Carl was a night person. We worked around the clock to meet the January deadline looming.

"Our last work session was on a Saturday night. We took a half-hour time-out to listen to the radio broadcast of the last quarter of a New York Knicks basketball game. We worked into the wee, wee hours (until 4:30 A.M. Sunday). Driving me back to my motel in his Porsche, Sagan enthusiastically declared: 'Now you know everything I know, Jerry.' "[69]

The opening chapter had a very sixties theme: the unity of terrestrial life, which it defended on evolutionary grounds. The chapter began by describing the general theory of the origin of life on Earth, from the self-assembly of simple molecules that evolved over time into more sophisticated organisms. "The secret of evolution is time and death," Sagan noted, pointing out how most species fail to adapt to changing environmental circumstances and, hence, disappear. "We care for a small fraction of the organisms on Earth—dogs, cats, and cows, for example—because they are useful or because they flatter us. But spiders and salamanders, salmon and sunflowers are equally our brothers and sisters." In Sagan's view, "the time has come for a respect, a reverence, not just for all human beings, but for all life forms—as we would have respect for a masterpiece of sculpture or an exquisitely tooled machine."

Eventually, we may detect aliens. "It is important that we extend our identification horizons, not just down to the simplest and most humble forms of life on our own planet, but also up to the exotic and advanced forms of life that may inhabit, with us, our vast galaxy of stars." Sagan's imagination worked overtime as he imagined the possible diversity of creatures on Mars—say, "organisms walking around with small ultraviolet-opaque shields on their backs: Martian turtles. Or perhaps Martian organisms carry about ultraviolet parasols." As for Venus, he was once again considering the possibility of its habitability: "It is conceivable that much stronger [molecular] bonds on Venus and much weaker bonds in the outer Solar System play the same role [in living creatures] that hydrogen bonds play on Earth. We may have been much too quick to reject life at temperatures very different from those on our planet." Life might even exist in the void between stars and planets, he hinted: "There are tiny grains between the stars, with the size and atomic composition of bacteria."[70] (The size similarity had been pointed out to Sagan years earlier by Joshua Lederberg in his effort to revive a form of panspermia theory.)

Chapters 7, 8, and 9 of *The Cosmic Connection* are an eloquent reverie on the value of space exploration. They describe cosmic realities so vast, so spectacular, that the prose approaches the ecstatic. In those pages was born what we might call Sagan the prophet. His written reveries would lead to the television series *Cosmos* and to *Saturday Night Live* parodies. According to the magazine *Changes*, Sagan was "the spokesman for hip astrophysics."[71]

The reviews were generally enthusiastic. *Time* magazine's favorable review included a photo of the handsome Sagan, grinning brightly.[72] *The Cosmic Connection* is "a book that is very nearly perfect," science writer Edward Edelson wrote in the *Washington Post*. Sagan's literary style is not easily paraphrased, Edelson observed, because he "builds to his effects with care; his paragraphs, not his sentences, are the basic unit."[73] *Sky & Telescope*, the astronomy magazine, ranked *The Cosmic Connection* "among the best of recent popular science books . . . a mind stretching experience."[74] "A *delightful* series of essays," declared Patrick Moore, the legendary British astronomy popularizer.[75]

In *Science* magazine, William Hartmann described the book as "thirty-nine genuine, vintage Sagan dinner conversations. . . . Ought to be read by high school and college kids, college dropouts, your nephews and nieces, everybody who ever uttered a word against science and technology, and by Richard Nixon and Gerald Ford."[76] The *Los Angeles Free Press* said: "A must for everyone curious about life in outer space and survival on earth. . . . As you read on, bells rings, lights flash, and you know that Sagan is right on target. . . . His warmth and wit come across, making it possible for the most uninformed reader to enjoy and learn."[77] According to the *Denver Post*, "it is remarkable how deftly Sagan can sugar-coat his serious thesis with close-to-us-all material and anecdotes. . . . His chapter on [UFOs] is probably the most devastating bit of debunking American folklore ever took."[78]

Not everyone was charmed. A nasty-spirited attack on Sagan appeared in the October 1974 issue of the *Atlantic Monthly*. The author, mathematician Alfred Adler, had attended the September 1971 conference on SETI in Soviet Armenia. Adler wrote that "the major substantive purpose of the conference, a determination of estimates for the number *N*, is quite clearly a total fraud. . . . [It was] a conference which exhibited the emperor's nakedness for even the most obtuse to see." In *The Cosmic Connection*, Sagan "has disclosed much more of himself and of his peers than perhaps even he or the reader would like. . . . It is part autobiography, part personal philosophy and speculation, part self-aggrandizement, direct and indirect."[79]

To Adler, Sagan epitomized "the modern technologist," who "is first of all a promoter. . . . His wit is arch and flat (chapter headings such as 'Hello, Central Casting? Send Me 20 Extraterrestrials,' or 'Some of My Best Friends Are Dolphins,' or 'The Cosmic Cheshire Cats,' are a numskull's delight). He believes himself to be Renaissance Man, with a profound understanding of man's creative sources . . . [and] he apparently regards himself as a master of politics and economics. . . . The modern technologist is a gifted, highly trained, opportunistic, humorless, and unimaginative ass."[80] Adler's piece upset some readers. "The self-righteousness and puerile, insulting tone of his remarks caused me more sadness than anger," wrote a Los Angeles man.[81]

Adler was in a minority. The English journal *New Scientist* profiled Sagan worshipfully: "If the aliens come tomorrow, and ask us for our leader, we shall take them to this man. He will be tall, dark, and swarthy, with a tendency to wrinkle his nose. He will come from a place called Ithaca, the legendary home for which Odysseus longed. . . . His name excites a growing band of followers around the world: Carl Edward Sagan. Mark the name well. . . . By every test, in the public eye and in response from the scientific community, the ideas of Carl Sagan . . . are ideas whose time has come."[82]

His fan mail swelled. In *The Cosmic Connection*, Sagan acquaints the reader with his mail—

some of it from schoolchildren who wish me to write their weekly assignments for them; some from strangers who want to borrow money; some from individuals who wish me to check out their detailed plans for ray guns, time warps, spaceships, or perpetual motion machines; and some from advocates of various arcane disciplines such as astrology, ESP, UFO-contact stories, the speculative fiction of von Danniken [*sic*], witchcraft, palmistry, phrenology, tea-leaf reading, Tarot cards, the I-Ching, transcendental meditation, and the psychedelic drug experience. Occasionally, also, there are sadder stories, such as from a woman who was talked to from her shower head by inhabitants of the planet Venus.[83]

The hardcover edition of *The Cosmic Connection* came out in the autumn of 1973. It sold so well that Dell bought the mass paperback rights from Doubleday for $350,000. As an adult, Sagan had always preferred a high standard of living—and now he had the money to back it up.

Sagan also made television appearances to promote the book. Although he had appeared on television before (he even narrated a BBC science show in England in 1968), his editor Walter Glanze claims that

Sagan initially "trembled at the thought of going on TV. He was in my office and Jerry [Agel] told him, 'Carl, you look too professorial. You have to change your hairdo.' He looked like an absent-minded professor." Glanze's "clear recollection was that Jerry had the idea for Sagan to have that ear-muff-type hairstyle."[84] (Agel denies influencing Sagan's hairstyle.)

To publicize the book, Sagan made a thirty-minute appearance on a CBS-TV show, *Camera 3*, where he was interviewed by students. He also appeared on Dick Cavett's talk show. His biggest break came in the autumn of 1973, when he was invited on Johnny Carson's late-night *Tonight* show. Thus commenced Sagan's real fame, as fame is defined in a democratic, mass-market society: the state of being known to a substantial percentage of the population regardless of class, sex, race, or education. The would-be popularizer was about to meet the *populi*.

10

The Shadow Line

GORE VIDAL ONCE SAID that age forty is a shadow line in American life, which "must be crossed in style—or else." As Carl Sagan approached this line, he took the fateful step that would catapult him to national fame. Ironically, fame came when his deepest convictions were challenged by events—by the failure of space probes to find life or organic molecules on other worlds, and by the increasingly ominous silence of stars scanned for SETI signals. Such challenges might have dispirited a less ebullient visionary. They certainly would have dispirited one less skilled at harboring contradictory views.

They did not dispirit Sagan, though, because he believed in himself, supremely so. Sobering experience was irrelevant to his destiny because that destiny, dreamed of since childhood, was ultimately all that mattered; the spotlight was waiting whether or not he still believed every word of his scheduled soliloquy.

Besides, it was early days yet, too soon for disillusionment. Space was vast, and the quest for life could always be redirected to new worlds. If life did not exist on the Moon, then perhaps it dwelled on Mars or Venus; if not these, then perhaps Jupiter; if not there, perhaps on its moon Europa; if not there . . . ; and so forth, across the galaxy and to galaxies beyond. In this sense, the hypothesis of extraterrestrial life was unfalsifiable; it could never be disproved, no matter how many worlds were explored and found barren. Future historians will probably regard exobiology as one of the most important new sciences of the twentieth century; yet in narrowly Popperian terms, it is unfalsifiable and, therefore, not scientific. Some critics even claim it is indistinguishable from religion. Christians await the Second Coming; SETI scientists await the first message from the stars. They are brothers under the skin.

This worked to Sagan's advantage, though. His audience—the American public, watching their flickering TVs in the bedroom darkness—remained deeply religious; in the United States, a known atheist was as likely to win public office as a Satanist. Thus Sagan's messianic style compensated (in the eyes of much of the public) for his discomfitingly icy logic and blunt secularism. His success also illustrated the allure of entangled opposites: he was an intellectual hermaphrodite, a walking contradiction who combined rabbinical sobriety with evangelical fervor. As he entered middle age, these opposed qualities coalesced into a seemingly seamless persona with enormous public appeal.

On November 30, 1973, a year shy of forty, Sagan won his first truly mass audience by stepping onto the stage of Johnny Carson's *Tonight* show. To some scientists, Sagan's appearance on the Carson show forever marked him as a fallen angel. He was no longer a scholar; he had sold out to the celebrity machine. How dare he stand on the same podium as Charo, Buddy Hackett, and Zsa Zsa Gabor? Tommy Gold at Cornell scorned Carson as "that night-time clown."

Sagan and Carson were an odd mix, the Jewish scholar from Brooklyn and the Methodist-raised amateur magician from corn country. Nine years older than Sagan, John William Carson grew up in Depression-era Nebraska. He was shy and aloof, a Midwestern boy wary of big-city vipers. But his ascent to the urban limelight began at age twelve when he discovered a book on magic; soon he was urging anyone within reach to "take a card." After graduating from the University of Nebraska, he traveled to Los Angeles and became an announcer on KNXT-TV, then ran a comedy show, *Carson's Cellar*, which flopped. He moved to New York City and hosted a top-rated quiz show. He became the permanent host of *The Tonight Show* in 1962.[1] He was pleasant and intelligent but unpretentious. His predecessor on *Tonight*, Jack Paar, had launched into polysyllabic, self-righteous rants, but that wasn't Carson's style. For the nervous middle class of the Vietnam era, Carson was the perfect late-night relaxant.

Unlike his TV competitor Dick Cavett, Carson showed no deep intellectual ambitions; but unlike his successors Jay Leno and David Letterman, he did not treat every bright remark by a guest as a setup for a joke or a sneer. Carson was an amateur astronomer with a sincere interest in science, and he was respectful of intellectuals and activists. In his show's early years, his guests included Margaret Mead, Saul Alinsky, Ayn Rand, Paul Ehrlich, and astronomer Robert Jastrow.

If Carl Sagan was the Hertz Rent-A-Car of science popularization, then Jastrow was Avis, the No. 2 who had to "try harder." Their careers shadowed each other's, sometimes unpleasantly. The founder of NASA's

Goddard Institute for Space Studies in New York City, Jastrow was an excellent science writer whose works include the acclaimed *Red Giants, White Dwarfs* (1968). He appeared on Carson's show and handled himself professionally, looking very much the academic: bespectacled, modest, not given to visionary orations. Sagan, of course, was none of these things. By the early 1970s, when Sagan's book *The Cosmic Connection* hit the best-seller lists, Carson—who had spotted Sagan on the Cavett program—invited the astronomer on the show, and he knocked the audience's socks off. While Jastrow had been professorial, Sagan struck an entirely different tone. He was darkly handsome, casual and utterly self-confident, full of energy, even funny. His unique manner of speech—the punched consonants, the deliberate emphasis on certain vowels, the sudden accelerations and equally sudden slowdowns that made his bass pitch melodious rather than monotonous—fascinated and entertained viewers. He described Mars and Saturn and Neptune vividly, as if he had just returned from them, as if he were Odysseus, home from the war and full of stories. This was a new kind of scientific public figure—hip, humorous, even sexy. He was so impressive, in fact, that Carson invited him back several weeks later. Thereafter, Carson bumped Jastrow and made Sagan *The Tonight Show*'s house astronomer, a post he held for two decades.

Perhaps Jastrow felt jilted. Who would not? Over the next two decades, he and Sagan repeatedly locked horns. The nastiest moment came in the late 1970s, when Jastrow wrote an obituary essay in the *New York Times* about one of Sagan's foes, the recently departed pseudo-cosmologist Immanuel Velikovsky, whose wild claims Sagan had worked hard to refute. While himself skeptical about Velikovsky's wacky ideas of solar system evolution, Jastrow questioned the soundness of one of Sagan's criticisms of Velikovsky (one that involved probability estimates). In a rare burst of pique, Sagan wrote a letter to the *Times* in which he called Jastrow's article a case of "scientific incompetence." In later years, they differed over politics; Jastrow was conservative, Sagan vaguely leftist. They disagreed over President Reagan's "Star Wars" antimissile project, nuclear winter, and greenhouse warming. They also split over religion: while Jastrow called himself an agnostic, he wrote a book suggesting that the Bible had foreseen the big bang theory. By contrast, Sagan's novel, *Contact*, depicted religious leaders as backwoods buffoons. Jastrow and Sagan were in many ways polar opposites, highly talented symbols of a growing cultural divide, not only in science but in the broader American culture of the post-Vietnam era.

Although Jastrow was only nine years Sagan's senior, a generation gap separated them personally and ideologically. While the ten-year-old Sagan played stickball in Brooklyn streets and yammered excitedly about

Edgar Rice Burroughs's fictional wars on other worlds, over in Queens the nineteen-year-old Jastrow prepared to fight in a real world war on Earth; only flat feet and poor vision kept him out of the conflict. As an adult Jastrow was muscular, an enthusiastic jogger who played squash and hardball; Sagan, by contrast, was skinny and frequently ill, a man who after college preferred smoking pot to all forms of exercise (except occasional snorkeling or scuba diving). Jastrow's outlook on the world was typical of the generation that kicked the hell out of Hitler and Tojo, a generation that had no doubt of America's might and its duty to exercise it. When Nikita Khrushchev accused the United States of holding onto Soviet rocket fragments that had fallen on the western U.S. coast, Jastrow humbled the Red dictator and made headlines by proving that the rocket had most likely dropped on Outer Mongolia. In contrast, Sagan despised the military that he had once innocently served; he advocated sending soldiers into space mainly to get them off the Earth. Jastrow was a respected administrator within the NASA bureaucracy, an official who speculated with discretion and skillfully managed giant, quarreling teams of egotistical scientists, whereas Sagan was a brash loner, a visionary on a mountaintop who struggled with recalcitrant lab equipment and at times seemed incapable of managing his own checking account. They were like many a father and son of the Vietnam era, gazing uncomprehendingly at each other across an emotional and political chasm. And, by 1974, while the "father" still held most of the power and prestige, the "son"—thanks to television—was clearly the Star.

Despite their differences, Jastrow did not underrate his younger competitor. He recognized what all of America realized in the wee hours as Doc Severinsen's band played its closing tune: Carl Sagan was a near-magical figure. Now in his seventies, Jastrow good-humoredly declines to rehash his old battles with Sagan. "All that is so far in the past I can't even remember—it's funny, but true!" he says with a laugh. And with the grace of a seasoned administrator, he adds this assessment of his departed rival: "I thought he was a great scientist and a great writer and a superb popularizer—a real triple-threat astronomer. And I think the world of science is much poorer without him."[2]

THERE ARE CELEBRITIES and then there are Celebrities. Before *The Tonight Show*, Sagan was slightly known to a small percentage of Americans who had caught his sound bites on television or read *Intelligent Life in the Universe*. After *The Tonight Show*, he became America's best-known scientist. Sitting in bed at 12:45 A.M., insomniacs watched Sagan with growing excitement. This was no tweedy Mr. Science, filling beakers with smelly chemicals in a black-and-white television image from the

1950s. This was a Mr. Science for the hip, disillusioned early 1970s, a boy-man with a startling basso profundo voice, one who kept his cool yet laughed merrily (sometimes at a startling high pitch). Sagan was, simply speaking, sexy, in a sense that transcends mere sexuality.

The young went on alert. Until that moment, the space program offered no convincing heroes for disaffected, anti-establishment, long-haired, pot-smoking college students. To them, astronauts were cornball patriots in crewcuts, blood brothers of the militarists then napalming Vietnam. But Sagan was different: he was youthful-looking (like the class president, but in a fun way). Perhaps he was a secret hipster, the kind of guy who, if handed a joint, might accept it with a laugh and actually inhale. In college dorms from coast to coast, students (like this writer) didn't stay up until 1 A.M. to watch Dinah Shore plug her golf tournament. They stayed up to see Carl Sagan.

On Sagan's first appearance—November 30, 1973—he and Carson discussed what we might want to say to an alien civilization and the pseudoscientific theories of writer Erich Von Däniken, who had been on the show the previous night. Carson and Sagan were perfect together: Carson bubbled with enthusiastic questions, and Sagan had all the answers. He was an oasis of intellect in an otherwise routine show (the other guests on that occasion were singer Helen Reddy, dog trainer Matthew Margolis, and impressionist Rich Little, who did an impression of Watergate-embattled Richard Nixon reading " 'Twas the Night before Christmas").[3]

Carson invited Sagan back for the January 9, 1974, show. On that night, Sagan discussed the "nonappearance" of comet Kohoutek, explained what comets are, talked about science and religion, and discussed the exploration of Mars. On February 26 and April 4, he returned to discuss the possibility of life on Mars and the *Mariner 10* mission to the planet Mercury. He also showed a picture of a giant "storm" on the planet Jupiter. Many Americans got their first close-up glimpses of other worlds from Sagan's photographic show-and-tells on *The Tonight Show*.

Over the next thirteen years, Sagan appeared on the Carson show twenty-six times—an average of twice a year. He once explained that he made every effort to fulfill an invitation to appear on the show because it gave him the biggest classroom in the country.[4]

The celebrity machine went into overdrive. On January 21, 1974, in a story about two of Sagan's books, *Time* magazine said that Sagan "has long been the prime advocate and perennial gadfly for planetary exploration." A "prime advocate" is just what NASA needed; after reaching the Moon, it seemed to lose its way and struggled to find a new mission. In accordance with Parkinson's Law, it sought a new mission that could justify the survival of its colossal budget—ideally, a piloted mission to Mars. But Congress, desperate to quench inflation fueled by the Vietnam War, said "No!" and reluctantly funded a drabber goal: the development of a piloted space shuttle fleet, a sort of trucking service to low Earth orbit. Sagan scorned the shuttle program. It would, he feared, devour funds desperately needed by the far cheaper, and scientifically much more worthwhile, planetary program, which launched robotic probes to other worlds.

He saw it as his mission, then, to get the public interested in those other planets—those subtly colored, untwinkling points of light in the sky that most people assumed were stars. He and Carson constituted a two-man conspiracy of the celestially minded—the professional astronomer and the serious amateur, both determined to get the public as excited about the heavens as they were. While Carson held up a spectacular blowup of the Great Red Spot or some other celestial wonder, Sagan explained to unseen millions across midnight America how planets are, indeed, Places. Like Marco Polo, who returned from his journeys to regale all listeners with tales of faraway China, Sagan used television and the print media to tell of faraway worlds—of Mars, a rust-red Wild West of dust storms and perhaps alien creatures; of Venus, an overcast oven where the poisonous air is so dense that it plays weird optical tricks; of Jupiter, a planet so massive that it almost collapsed and became a star. He used no technical jargon. He skipped the equations. He wielded analogies so clear and persuasive that they suddenly made clear what had been opaque, made viewers gasp as they recognized new truths. Sagan was cool as ice as he described cosmic sights that, by all reason, deserved the purplest of prose. His cool was cunning: he knew that the best way to sell the Future is casually, without hysterics or wild promises—to sell it as if it were not merely desirable but inevitable, as if it were a destination toward which all humanity is logically bound, one whose marvels will compensate for the disillusionments and miseries of the present, for the utopias that have failed on Earth and the gods who have vanished from the sky.

Sagan's success on *The Tonight Show* also brought him to the attention of *TV Guide*, which had more than ten million readers. The March 23, 1974, issue ran Sagan's article "Seeking the Cosmic Jackpot," which was timed to appear with the *Nova* television episode "The Search for Life" (on which he appeared). Space agency publicists must have hugged themselves with pleasure to read Sagan's last words:

> If we do find life on Mars, we will have hit the cosmic jackpot. The bio-
> logical perspectives we will gain promise significant practical benefits

for mankind. The sense of wonder and spirit of adventure that have gone out of much of modern life will be rekindled.

Such evangelical talk, like the feverish speculations at the Byurakan conference, are best understood in the context of their time, a time of perceived American decline, of Watergate corruption and defeat in Vietnam, of long gasoline lines and fears that Earth was running out of food, resources, and living space. The July 15, 1974, issue of *Time* picked Sagan as one of the two hundred "rising leaders" among young adults of the era.

CARL SAGAN MYSTIFIED CYNTHIA OZICK and enraged Alfred Adler. But kids who followed science, the stereotypical teenage outcasts with their Sears Roebuck telescopes who religiously watched *Star Trek* reruns, adored him. They began to imitate him, as follows: Stand ramrod-erect, chin in, voice low, and say, "This is Carr-uhhhl *Say*-gunnnn."

To the baby boomers, Carson's show wasn't exactly hip—too much Buddy Hackett. But Sagan became officially hip when he was profiled by *Rolling Stone*. At that time, *Rolling Stone* was the Bible of disaffected, affluent college kids who repudiated the establishment not by seizing campus buildings but by retreating to their dorms and playing Alice Cooper full blast. The magazine's stable of authors, notably gonzo journalist and drughead extraordinaire Hunter S. Thompson, epitomized the wildness of that era, an era when many Americans cheered as their president resigned, vice president Spiro Agnew admitted taking payoffs in paper bags, and U.S. choppers fled Nam like scared bats.

One young writer for *Rolling Stone* was Timothy Ferris. Then in his twenties, he had been an astronomy buff since his childhood in Key Biscayne, Florida, where his father had once been publicity director for the City of Miami Beach. Ferris mentioned Sagan's name to *Rolling Stone* editor Jann Wenner. "This guy sounds like he's got an interesting life," Wenner said, or words to that effect. "He's running around sticking plaques on spaceships and everything."[5]

Ferris interviewed Sagan for the magazine, and in the process they became close friends. Sagan loved intelligent conversation—to him it was the essence of good living—and Ferris provided it. Sometimes, though, they just sat quietly and listened to music—a true sign of mutual affection. "He stayed in my apartment when he would come to New York," Ferris recalls. "He loved to talk—we had long talks on the phone." Sagan "had a style of argument that was strictly rational," Ferris recalls. "He adhered to all of the rules."

Sagan was also "extraordinarily stimulating toward one's work." Ferris recalls people struggling to write books and no one would read them—except Sagan, who "sent them back a three-page, detailed critique."

Ferris seems to have brought out qualities of warmth and friendship in Sagan that some others rarely experienced. With time, Ferris would recognize the contradictions in Sagan's character; yet they clicked early on. "Carl was an interesting combination of rationality and emotion," Ferris says. "He was personally quite warm and emotionally involved. He used to sign his letters to me 'Love.' There wasn't anything constricted about him emotionally."[6]

AT THE SAME TIME, Sagan's growing fame spurred a reconciliation with his most famous detractor. Harold Urey had chided Sagan repeatedly about his scientific irresponsibility. Now the old Nobelist watched in astonishment as his wayward former student rose to fame. Urey was particularly impressed by Sagan's paper with George Mullen on the faint early Sun paradox. Urey wondered: had he misjudged Carl? A few years earlier he had helped to scuttle Sagan's bid for tenure at Harvard; so now, in late 1973, as Sagan began to become the nation's best-known astronomer, Urey's conscience was hurting him. He wrote an unusually warm, almost sentimental, letter to Sagan. Sagan had recently commented at a conference in Sydney about how nice Urey had been to him, but Urey said in the letter that in fact "I have not always been nice to you." Urey said that at various times he had tried to take Sagan aside and confess his past unkindnesses, adding that he now felt that he had been "completely wrong" for criticizing him. (Urey showed here the same nobility that he showed earlier, when admitting that lunar rocks contradicted his cherished theory of lunar history.) He closed by asking for Sagan's forgiveness and saying that he hoped Sagan would accept him again as a good friend.[7]

Sagan's reply was the epitome of graciousness. He said he could not think of "a single instance" in which Urey had been unkind to him. He also assured Urey that if Urey's remarks referred to a critique of a paper of his, or had to do with his not getting a promotion, he was sure Urey's comments had been made in the "best interest of science."[8]

Perhaps Urey was mellowing as he faced the anxieties of old age. He lived for seven more years, during which time he occasionally complimented Sagan on his latest achievements—for example, Sagan's 1977 book, *The Dragons of Eden*. Even so, Urey's doubts lingered. In 1976, a woman at the University of Chicago Alumnae Association wrote to Urey to ask whether Sagan deserved the Association's Professional Achievement

Award. Urey demurred in his reply, saying that he had a hard time knowing exactly how to comment about Sagan and evaluate his scientific work. He praised Sagan's talents as an adviser to NASA, and he expressed affection for Sagan as a friend, but said that Sagan's research was in areas that he wasn't keeping up with, so he really couldn't assess it. This was absurd, of course; Urey had spent much of his later career toiling in just the same vineyards as Sagan. He did make one criticism, which was to say that he didn't find Sagan's arguments about possible life on Mars and in Jupiter's atmosphere at all compelling. Urey's response is fascinating for the care he takes to neither praise Sagan nor damn him. In the end, it appears, Urey, like so many people, was of two minds about Sagan: he was simultaneously dazzled and dismayed by him.[9]

SAGAN BELIEVED he had to do more than champion science; he also had to attack its antithesis, pseudoscience. He was an especially effective opponent of pseudoscience because he was not an "establishment" figure like, say, Donald Menzel, the white-haired Harvard boffin long bankrolled by the Air Force. Sagan was too young, light-hearted, and prolific a speculator to be dismissed by pseudoscientists as just another academic party pooper. Hence, in the mid-1970s, as his writing and television career took off, he came to be perceived as the most effective critic of the pseudoscientific wave in pop culture. His book *The Cosmic Connection* was the intellectual equivalent of sugarcoated medicine. It delivered skeptical messages (about UFOs, Velikovsky, and like foolishness) within an otherwise wide-eyed paean to galactic wonders. By contrast, some professional skeptics struck the public as elitist nags, wagging their fingers like stern dietitians and saying "No! No! No!" but offering no compensatory sweets.

In light of the acclaim and success of *The Cosmic Connection*, as well as Sagan's new fame, his next book drew a far bigger advance: $50,000, three times that for the hardcover of *The Cosmic Connection*.[10] Yet *Other Worlds* (another Agel "production") was a much skinnier work, a wafer-thin, picture-packed collection of mini-essays on topics ranging from aliens to terraforming to pseudoscience. *Other Worlds* was the perfect introduction to Saganism for those who had discovered him on *The Tonight Show* but lacked the energy to finish all 274 pages of *The Cosmic Connection*.

Sagan's picture appeared on the back cover of *Other Worlds*. He looked dark-maned, dark-eyed, and almost sensuously handsome, with an adolescent litheness. In response he "got this fan mail—gushing letters by young women sending pictures of themselves," recalls his editor at Bantam, Walter Glanze. "One of them sent him a nude picture."[11]

In *Other Worlds*, Sagan lit into pseudoscientists such as Erich Von Däniken and Immanuel Velikovsky. Von Däniken wanted to rewrite the history of humanity: he claimed that aliens were responsible for the Pyramids and other historic artifacts. Velikovsky was more ambitious: he wanted to rewrite the history of the whole solar system.

In 1950, Velikovsky had published a sensationalistic book, *Worlds in Collision*. It argued that thousands of years ago, Venus was a comet. This comet was somehow ejected from Jupiter, as a tennis ball is shot from an ejector. Venus then barreled around the inner solar system and careered past Earth, triggering apocalyptic events and inspiring scary legends of doom, disaster, and locusts. While Moses was leading his people out of Egypt (Velikovsky asserted), the comet flew by and exerted mysterious forces on Earth, with the result that the Red Sea parted. Eventually, like teenage hoodlums in the B movies of that era, Venus calmed down and settled into its present middle-class, predictable orbit. Velikovsky said that humanity forgot these disasters because of a kind of "collective amnesia."

Velikovsky based his hypothesis on ancient manuscripts and legends that, he said, recorded these apocalyptic events. He claimed that very old astronomical records did not mention the planet Venus—and naturally not, because it had not yet settled into its present orbit. He also insisted that his hypothesis predicted certain celestial phenomena, including the great heat of Venus (a result of its violent ejection from Jupiter), which had been observed by *Mariner 2*. Velikovsky's claims led to his showdown with Sagan, who, of course, had his own ideas about the Venusian hothouse.[12]

Worlds in Collision blatantly violated the laws of physics. Although Velikovsky had certain scholarly credentials (he was a Russian-born psychoanalyst and M.D.), he "had only the vaguest understanding of such basic physical principles as conservation of angular momentum, gravity, and entropy," wrote the physicist Lloyd Motz, who was on friendly terms with him. Velikovsky described celestial objects behaving in ways in which they simply cannot behave—unless something is terribly wrong with modern physics textbooks. For example, Motz noted, to expel Venus, Jupiter would have had to "release or expend in a matter of seconds or minutes as much energy as our Sun emits in more than a year." Such an eruption would have expelled enough energy in those few seconds to have vaporized nearby planets, including Earth.[13]

When physicists cited these huge discrepancies between Velikovsky's hypothesis and physics doctrine, he shrugged and replied that his historical research showed that celestial objects behave in previously unknown ways, and that therefore physics must change to accommodate his findings. Throughout history, of course, scientists have proposed radical new theories that violated the commonsense physics of their time, yet proved (on the whole, despite some technical errors) to be correct. Copernicus's heliocentric hypothesis is one example; another is Alfred Wegener's concept of continental drift. In both cases, physics was modified to accommodate the heretical idea.

Velikovsky's theories, however, do not even fall into the category of science. Archeologists and ancient historians totally repudiated his interpretations of ancient records. Even if the records backed him, his predictions and calculations lack the rigor that true science requires.

How does one distinguish a bona fide scientific hypothesis from a pseudoscientific one? The classic response is that of philosopher Karl Popper, that no hypothesis can be considered "scientific" (which is not necessarily the same thing as saying it is "true") unless it generates predictions that are *conceivably* disprovable ("falsifiable," in Popper's term).[14]

Velikovsky's work, then, raises two key questions: Were his original hypotheses conceivably falsifiable? And have they subsequently been falsified or verified by astronomical observations? If falsifiable but verified, then our knowledge of astrophysics must be seriously incomplete. If not falsifiable, we can confidently toss his notions into the historical wastebin along with dusty tracts on phrenology, spiritualism, sea monsters, and other flummery.

A hallmark of pseudoscientific hypotheses is their vagueness and malleability: their proponents always manage to think up ad hoc ideas to explain away discrepant data (for example, the "Mars face" enthusiast who claims that NASA hides photos of the "face," the parapsychologist who blames negative results on the presence of skeptical observers, and so forth). Occasionally ad hoc explanations turn out to be correct, but the burden of proving them must rest on their proponents. Orthodox scientists are simply too busy wrestling with acknowledged mysteries to waste time chasing will-o'-the-wisps (especially those that are proposed by scientific ignoramuses and that brazenly transgress well-established scientific principles). Yet Velikovsky, despite his obvious ignorance of physics, angrily insisted that the burden of proof lay on his critics. It was not his job to prove his theory; it was their job to disprove him.

Velikovsky and his reverential fans presented Sagan with a challenge that, in his newly emerging role as defender of the scientific faith, he simply could not refuse. He was asked to combat Velikovsky in something of a scientific duel—a public debate in which Velikovsky could make his case, while a panel of scientists, Sagan included, could critique them.

This was a radically different way to confront pseudoscience. True, the UFO symposium at the AAAS symposium of 1969 had pitted UFO advocates against detractors, but all were bona fide physical scientists.

Velikovsky, by contrast, had no significant training in the physical sciences; his books implied that the "expertise" of his critics was a sham, that his historical scholarship was just as valid a source of knowledge about the natural world as their professional training in physics and astronomy. In short, the Sagan versus Velikovsky debate promised to be a particularly extreme form of turf battle—a fight over who deserves recognition as an authority in a given subject. The history of science is full of such turf battles; they often decide the fate of fundamental ideas.

The Velikovsky debate certainly differed from the usual old-fashioned scientific responses to pseudoscience: ignore it or suppress it. In the 1950s, Harvard astronomer Harlow Shapley had threatened to lead an academic boycott of the Macmillan publishing house if it published Velikovsky's book *Worlds in Collision*. Macmillan caved in and transferred publishing rights to Doubleday.[15] The historian James Gilbert has paraphrased Shapley as saying in regard to his campaign against Velikovsky that science "by its very nature should never be molested by popular belief; it is the sole purview of those who understand it." This view can be contrasted with a prior argument in American politics, espoused by the famous populist William Jennings Bryan, that it is (again, in Gilbert's words) "the democratic community's right to decide the validity of scientific theory," as, for example, in the Scopes "evolution" trial of 1925.[16]

Sagan, a fierce devotee of free speech, believed that Shapley's boycott had been unjustified. The AAAS public debate would constitute, in effect, an apology to Velikovsky, giving him the opportunity to submit his ideas to direct scientific scrutiny. The debate's ultimate goal was not to reassess Velikovsky's ideas (hardly any scientist took these seriously) but, rather, to reassure the public of science's basic fair-mindedness, at a time when a growing number of leftists and academics were depicting it as intellectual camouflage for ideological and social prejudices.

Some AAAS members, of course, opposed holding the debate. "Certain powers in the AAAS didn't want the symposium to happen," recalls Sagan's friend Don Goldsmith, an astronomer who helped organize the debate. "They felt, 'We've had enough bullshit from [Velikovsky]. AAAS is for science; this is non-science.'"[17]

The AAAS president at the time, however, was Margaret Mead, who thought the symposium would be worthwhile. She was an anthropologist famous for her affectionate studies of non-Western culture, and she apparently viewed the pseudosciences as many social scientists do—as being generally harmless alternative perceptions of reality, which should be tolerated (if not accepted) as one might tolerate, say, Azande cosmology or Eskimo marriage rituals. Besides, Mead was quietly interested in fringe science. In 1969 she had pushed the AAAS to accept the

Parapsychological Association as an institutional member; late in life, she served on the board of J. Allen Hynek's Center for UFO Studies. Says Goldsmith: "Whereas physical scientists thought, 'Why should we give this bullshit a hearing?' Margaret Mead was of the anthropological bent. She felt this might be interesting whether it's true or not."[18]

The symposium was held on February 25, 1974, in the Grand Ballroom of San Francisco's St. Francis Hotel. There were seven speakers, two of them pro-Velikovsky—Velikovsky himself and the Illinois scientist Irving Michelson. (No other pro-Velikovsky scientists could be found.) The room was packed. As Don Goldsmith recalls, "It is hard to outdo the spectacle of a seventy-eight-year-old gentleman rising to confront the critics who had rejected him for scores of years, with his supporters in the audience cheering his wit and hissing at his opponents, while his detractors sat applauding and protesting in opposite phase."[19]

The astronomer Dale Cruikshank attended the debate to see what he calls the "clash of the titans"—Sagan vs. Velikovsky. Indeed, Sagan dominated the anti-Velikovsky side. "I'm not sure who won on the arrogance side, but they were both in top form," Cruikshank recalls wryly. Velikovsky "was an elderly man, tall and slender, big head of gray hair, and he sort of swept in with two or three people in his entourage, each of them carrying a big bundle of papers. And whenever he would snap his fingers somebody would run up with another document to support the point he had just made."[20] During his address, Velikovsky insisted that since the publication of *Worlds in Collision*, astronomers and space scientists had repeatedly verified his "predictions" (for example, the great heat of Venus) but failed to credit him for them. He declared defiantly that "Nobody can change a single sentence in my books." His supporters in the audience stood and applauded.

Sagan was coolly composed by comparison. In the view of many present, his talk was a blend of intense analysis and amiable wit, with imaginative arguments so compelling that they seemed unanswerable. One of his key points was that Velikovsky's most heralded "prediction," that Venus was hot, was not a prediction in any meaningful sense of the word. Velikovsky claimed that he had anticipated Venus's great heat long before the *Mariner 2* space probe flew by the planet in 1962. The trouble with this claim is multifold. First, Sagan pointed out, Velikovsky had never defined precisely what he meant by "heat." To say Venus is hot is like saying the Sun is big. *How* hot? A specific temperature is not needed, just a range will do: say, 600 to 800 degrees K? Yet Velikovsky never provided this. Second, Sagan observed, Velikovsky never provided a convincing explanation of why Venus would be hot. He implied it was because of the frictional heat experienced by Venus on being ejected from Jupiter, although in fact (as Motz previously explained) this would

have vaporized it instead. Finally, people before Velikovsky had suspected that Venus is hot, based partly on its closeness to the Sun and
partly on its atmosphere (Wildt's 1940 suggestion of a greenhouse-
driven high surface temperature). So Velikovsky's prediction was not a
true scientific prediction—not even a lucky guess. His overall theory, in
fact, was so maddeningly vague, Sagan concluded, that it could not be
used to make meaningful predictions. To recall Popper, Velikovskian
doctrine cannot be falsified, even in principle. Hence Velikovsky's theory
was classic pseudoscience. (In all fairness, it must be added that most historians of science reject Popperian models for the evolution of strictly
scientific ideas. However, Popperianism still provides a useful, albeit ide-
alized, way to distinguish between science and pseudoscience.)

Opinions of Sagan's performance vary. Staff writer Robert Gillette of
Science magazine described Sagan as "Velikovsky's bête noire . . . an articulate man with a switchblade wit."[21] By the time the seven-hour symposium (split into two parts) ended, "most of the reporters present . . .
seemed to regard Velikovsky as the loser," Gillette said. A reporter from
Science News, however, observed: "Sagan's 56 pages of criticism would
ordinarily be sufficient to lay to rest for all time such a picked-apart theory, but Velikovsky's supporters are not easily dissuaded, and the controversy is sure to continue."[22] In fact, Sagan's speech trounced Velikovsky.
Nowadays, the pseudoscientific psychoanalyst is largely forgotten, save
by a handful of devotees who haunt the World Wide Web. Sagan
remains their leading bête noire.

Was Sagan's campaign against pseudoscience really worth his time?
After all, Von Däniken and Velikovsky were just the latest variations
on old themes. Pseudoscientific and occult ideas are as old as humanity.
Yet in the 1970s, their resurgent popularity, coincident with the rise of
various cults—from pyramid power to Scientology—and the decline of
student interest in science, alarmed many. In response, philosophy professor Paul Kurtz, a controversial figure within the American Humanist
Association, formed the Committee for the Scientific Investigation of
Claims of the Paranormal (CSICOP, pronounced "sci-cop"), with the
goal of challenging the intellectual merits of pseudoscientific and occult
notions.[23]

Sagan was a founding member of CSICOP. Certainly he was
attracted to the skeptics movement by his scorn for pseudoscience, and
by his desire to educate the public about real science. He might also,
however, have joined the skeptics movement partly to reassure his colleagues—the Donald Menzel types who questioned his loyalty to orthodox science—that he was really a loyal (if highly speculative) member of
the epistemological mainstream, and not a budding Lilly or Hynek about
to fly off to fairyland.

At the same time, Sagan would always feel ambivalence about certain elements of the skeptics movement. Some of its members were too lacking in "compassion" for those deluded by foolish ideas, he complained.[24] He refused to sign astronomer Bart Bok's anti-astrology petition because, in Sagan's view, its tone was too authoritarian;[25] in an age when the public increasingly distrusted "experts," astrology buffs would not be converted to reason by an elitist-sounding petition signed by a band of astronomers. More subtle means were required to combat pseudoscience. One must not talk to the people as if they are children babbling about Santa Claus; rather, they must be educated, patiently and respectfully so. And for that educational mission, Carl Sagan was ideally suited.

SAGAN'S FORTIETH BIRTHDAY found him in the lush jungle of Arecibo, Puerto Rico. There, standing beside the dish of the world's biggest radiotelescope, he and Frank Drake transmitted into space a radio message containing easily decoded information about Earth and its inhabitants.[26] The transmission was a publicity stunt, similar to Sagan's other space stunts, like the *Pioneer* plaques and the *Voyager* records. But it triggered a backlash from two noted scientists, English astronomer Sir Martin Ryle and Harvard biologist George Wald, who feared, respectively, that aliens might be hostile, or that the discovery of them would damage human self-confidence. Why advertise our position in the galaxy, they asked?[27]

Because, Sagan replied, it's too late—we've been inadvertently sending television and radio signals into space since about 1900. Writing in *TV Guide*, Sagan noted that the first massive, regular television transmissions were a quarter-century old. "That [electromagnetic] wave front is about 25 light-years from earth. There are probably no civilizations as close to us as 25 light-years. The nearest are probably a few hundred light-years away. So we have at least 175 years before they discover us," Sagan wrote. "I can imagine them routinely scanning the heavens, using large but primitive radio telescopes . . . and, stumbling upon our signals, gradually decoding Clarabell and Roy Cohn."

The cavalier manner in which he dismissed Ryle and Wald's concerns is typical of his optimistic belief—one totally unsupported by terrestrial history—that "advanced" civilizations will be morally superior to ours and hence benevolent. But to believe otherwise was, of course, to deny Progress, to deny the foundation faith of his optimism. Which he could not do. It is one of his starkest intellectual contradictions: he refused to recognize directionality in biological evolution but assumed it as a given in social and technological evolution. The New York World's

Fair had persuaded him, at an impressionable age, that intelligence and reason would make the world a better place. Humanity would get better and better with time; the future would be happier than the present. And with technological advance would come moral advance; our descendants will be more peaceful than we. Hence technically advanced aliens would also be morally refined; they would view our faint signals at worst with amusement, at best with compassion. They might even offer recipes (he assumed, like all technocrats, that all problems have technical or at least "rational" solutions, which are readily transferable from culture to culture) for escaping our present global woes (such as nuclearism or pollution). He did not see the contradiction between this cheerful outlook and his own politics—did not grasp that Earth might be exploited or conquered by technically advanced aliens as Vietnam was ravaged by the technically superior United States, or Poland by the technically superior Germany. He had no good reason, other than juvenile wishfulness, to believe that the galaxy would be any less of a jungle "red in tooth and claw" than Tennyson's.

When it came to understanding history, Sagan was as naive as a Dickensian industrialist, as teleological as a prophet. Not until the 1980s, shocked by revived U.S. militarism and shaken by his own near death and the deaths of his parents, would he appreciate how slippery is the tightrope upon which humanity walks, and how uncertain is the destination to which the rope leads.

The next year, Sagan participated in the only SETI experiment of his career. With occasional breaks for snorkeling and sailing, he and Drake stayed at Arecibo and listened for alien signals using the giant radiotelescope.

In those days, Arecibo felt more remote from the world than it does today. Observatory staffers had trouble getting news reports from the outside world. Cornell astronomer Jim Cordes recalls how he and his colleagues linked a radioastronomy spectrum analyzer to an antenna in order to pick up the Watergate hearings of 1973. He remembers Sagan in the summer of 1975, sitting in the control room and trying to detect alien signals using the same "old, clunky spectrum analyzer. It was a thing on wheels. It looked kind of like the old-fashioned TV, remember the little circular TV screens? You could see the signal strength plotted against frequency, showing up in real time. Just like an oscilloscope display."[28]

Sagan and Drake aimed the telescope at a large nearby galaxy. During the first half-hour alone, they scanned ten billion stars. "When a full hour passed and we still hadn't found anything, I could sense Carl's disappointment," Drake later wrote. "After a few days he was even a little bored by the sight of the green dots appearing uneventfully on the screen. And who could blame him?"[29] Sagan later confessed that he had been depressed by the failure to detect alien signals at Arecibo.[30]

He was not alone. A few other radioastronomers—notably Ben Zuckerman and Gerrit Verschuur—had attempted to detect alien signals and failed, becoming SETI skeptics as a result.[31] In the Soviet Union, even Sagan's coauthor on *Intelligent Life in the Universe*, I. S. Shklovskii, was entertaining doubts.[32] According to SETI scientist Michael Papagiannis, after 1975 SETI went through "a major crisis of identity and purpose."[33]

It is one thing to see childhood dreams sour; it is quite another thing for them to sour at age forty, Vidal's "shadow line." So far, Sagan was batting zero when it came to extraterrestrial life: there was no life on the Moon, it appeared to be unimaginable on Venus or Mercury, and he had heard no alien messages from the stars. An even bigger disappointment, however, lay ahead.

AFTER SAGAN'S FRUSTRATION at Arecibo, his attention returned to his first love: Mars. In 1971, the upbeat imagery from *Mariner 9* had revived hopes that life might have existed there in the past, if not today. Perhaps it had even survived to the present, eking out an existence in a dry, cold, radiation-baked environment more hostile than Antarctica. NASA was in the midst of planning two new missions to Mars—the *Viking 1* and *2* landers—and Sagan expressed wildly optimistic hopes about what the landers might discover. Though he no longer suggested that probes might uncover alien "artifacts" on the red planet, he refused to rule out the possibility that they might encounter various kinds of life. There is "no reason to exclude from Mars organisms ranging in size from ants to polar bears," he claimed in a *New York Times* op-ed piece in February 1975. In fact, he argued, large creatures might fare better than small ones: because large objects have a lower surface-area-to-volume ratio than small objects, large creatures would lose heat and moisture more slowly than small ones. "Organisms with an interest in the conservation of heat and water," he explained, "thus may select larger sizes." Sagan even insisted that the *Viking* include a camera capable of spotting an object moving past its lens in real time. To test the device during field experiments at Great Sand Dunes National Monument, he placed before it a snake, a chameleon, and two tortoises (rented from a local pet store).[34] The camera worked. Even so, Sagan complained about the *Viking*'s prime limitation: its inability to get up and move around, to stroll over the next hill and see what's on the other side. "I keep having this fantasy that there, twenty feet away, will be this tree or something, and we can't get to it," he said.[35] He tried unsuccessfully to have a lamp installed on the *Viking* to detect anything moving around at night, and he expressed concern (tongue in cheek?) that the camera might one morning observe tracks of creatures that had visited during the night. It might even spot footprints.

When Sagan received criticism for suggesting such things, he responded (as he had in the debate over the Venusian atmosphere) by questioning the psychological motivations of his critics. He was the visionary, they were the sticks in the mud. "Some ideas are considered 'far out' for reasons that involve a lack of imagination or nerve—rather than a lack of scientific plausibility," he declared rather pompously. "One such idea is the speculation that Mars is inhabited by largish beasts." These are remarkable words coming from someone who so clearly harbored his own psychological motivations, inspired by a childhood of reading science fiction.

Sagan's wild assertions alternately amused and exasperated his *Viking* team members. Some of the scientists on the team seemed to think that Sagan "was grabbing the limelight, that he was not a 'scientist's scientist,'" team member Gil Levin recalls. At the same time, "I never sensed any real hostility [toward him]. I felt people really liked him," Levin says. The head of the landing site certification team, Gentry Lee, recalls that during their meetings, Sagan "made tremendous contributions," but he would go off the topic and "could be counterproductive." Finally Lee decided to meet with Sagan before each meeting to brief him on what was going on. This seemed to forestall Sagan's tendency to make trouble during the meeting.[36]

Later in Sagan's life, conservatives would accuse him of being a doomsayer who saw apocalypse at every turn (an ironic view, given his normally cheerful outlook). Certainly Sagan displayed certain Chicken Little tendencies while serving on the *Viking* site selection team. The key goal of these teams was to figure out how to safely land the two *Vikings*, and then find life, if any. The trouble was, locales that looked like good candidates for life also tended to be dangerous places to land (for example, what looked like water-carved terrain might also be cluttered with flood-scattered boulders). Everywhere one looked on Mars, there were trade-offs, and each scientific group pushed to visit the places most interesting to its specialty. The geologists wanted to visit terrain that was geologically more rugged and, therefore, more interesting; but the biologists preferred the lowlands, which were the most likely to have water (and thus life). And *Viking* chief meteorologist Seymour Hess advocated landing on a flat plain, where he believed the onboard weather stations would function best.[37]

The biologists were especially excited about the possibility of landing at one of the poles. The pole might be wet and therefore more likely to be inhabited, they reasoned. Joshua Lederberg was upset when he sensed that the polar option was being given short shrift, and protested in person to NASA chief James C. Fletcher.[38] There was a good argument, however, against a polar landing: the low angle of the pole relative to Earth made it difficult to scan with Earth-based radar in order to detect hazards such as rocky terrain. No one wanted to have *Viking* land atop a boulder and fall over. Sagan wrote to project manager Jim Martin protesting "serious shortcomings in the landing site selection procedures," particularly based on what he viewed as misinterpretations of radar mappings of Mars. Certain areas with lower radar reflectivity, which others had interpreted as sand or dunes, might actually be deep basins of dust. He envisioned "a *Viking* lander sinking up to its eyebrows." This was the same scenario that Tommy Gold had proposed for the Moon, and some were amazed that Sagan would revive that flubbed scenario for the Mars mission.[39]

Sagan also fretted that high winds might topple the probe. At the time, this did not seem like a totally unreasonable fear. A Soviet lander had recently descended to Mars during a sandstorm and transmitted twenty seconds of illegible video noise, then shut down for good. Sagan warned that Martian winds might be extremely high, perhaps as fast as 200 meters per second (roughly 400 miles per hour, faster than the fastest radar-verified speed of a terrestrial tornado). True, the winds would be less damaging than terrestrial gales because the Martian air pressure is much lower; but it might not be low enough to spare the *Viking*, Sagan said. If he was right, and if a dust storm was under way on Mars as *Viking* approached it, that would seriously constrain the choice of final landing sites.[40]

The debate over *Viking* landing sites persisted for years, and one close observer would ultimately describe the process as "traumatic." Site selection had appeared so simple at first but "every time we thought we [had] it, we would find another problem."[41] Finally, on May 7, 1973, the tentative landing sites were announced. One site was in Chryse, where the first *Viking* would land in July 1976, and the other in Cydonia, where *Viking 2* would land two months later.[42]

On the one hand, Sagan's *Viking* colleagues could not deny his ability to promote public interest in their project. Sagan also served as a helpful media liaison, complaining to news media about their alleged lack of coverage of the *Viking* mission. On the other hand, his speculative leaps—his remark about polar bears on Mars, for example—raised questions about his judgment. He also threatened to set the public up for disappointment if the *Vikings* landed on Mars and discovered a lifeless wasteland. Sagan's continual talk about big creatures—"macrobes," he and Lederberg called them—so close to the landing date seemed reckless.[43]

ON A LATE AUGUST AFTERNOON in 1975, a Titan Centaur rocket hurled the *Viking 1* space probe into space and toward Mars. *Viking 2* followed it into space three weeks later. They were scheduled to arrive on Mars the following summer, in time for the celebration of the nation's two hundredth birthday. Each *Viking* probe consisted of two parts, a landing vehicle and an orbiter. The latter would orbit Mars, taking pictures, while the lander searched for life on the surface.[44]

On June 22, 1976, just before *Viking 1* was scheduled to land, its orbiter transmitted a high-altitude photo of the prospective landing site. "You would have believed that all the people in that room were ten years old," Gentry Lee later recalled, "because we all got up and forty of us ran over to the scope and watched it [the first photo] come in line by line." What they saw horrified them. They had expected the landing site to be fairly smooth and safe. Instead, the orbiter photo showed that the site was a geological nightmare—"a deeply incised river bed," according to the official NASA history.[45] The terrain looked much too dangerous for a landing. Very small craters, once believed to be rare, were visible all over the place. The landing site had to be changed; no one wanted to risk crashing a *Viking* on Mars on or about the Fourth of July, the nation's bicentennial. At stake was an extraordinary scientific mission, $1.1 billion in taxpayers' money.

Sagan and the site certification committee voted to abandon a July 4 landing as too risky.[46] Then, after working around the clock to find a safer site, they finally picked one west of the Chryse basin. The "Northwest Territory," they dubbed it.[47]

Before the landing, tensions were high. It was, Lee says, "as exhilarating as staying upside down on a rollercoaster."[48] At 5:12 P.M. Pacific daylight time on July 20, 1976, after descending through the atmosphere, firing its retrorockets, and deploying a parachute, *Viking 1* landed safely on Mars. To test the camera, it transmitted to Earth an image of its footpad. Later the camera looked upward toward the horizon. Surrounding it was an arid, orange-red terrain like parts of the desert in the southwestern United States. Even the sky was pink, apparently because of windblown dust.

The *Viking* began searching for life on July 28. It scooped its first samples of Martian dirt into onboard biology instruments. There were four basic experiments—the gas exchange experiment, the labeled release experiment, the pyrolitic release experiment, and the gas chromatograph/mass spectrometer experiment.

On July 31, mission official Harold Klein told reporters that the gas exchange experiment had indicated that the soil was "very active," due to "some chemical or physical entity." Could that entity be living organisms? Not necessarily, he cautioned; it could be some chemical event that impersonated biological activity. At the same time, the "fairly high level of radioactivity" measured by one experiment looked "very much like a biological signal." The instruments also detected extraordinary amounts of oxygen generated in the soil. Could the oxygen have been produced by living organisms? The scientists were trying to study their data while the entire world, or certainly the press corps, was looking over their shoulders. As one of the leading *Viking* biologists, Norm Horowitz, admitted, "Having to work in a fishbowl like this is an experience that none of us is used to."[49] Brazenly, Sagan continued to talk about large Martian creatures even after the first *Viking* landing. In an op-ed piece for the August 11, 1976, *New York Times*, he wrote: "The possibility of life, even large forms of life, is by no means out of the question."[50] But for most of the scientists, the instruments' decisive measurement came from the gas chromatograph–mass spectrometer. Its purpose was to detect any organic molecules on Mars. It failed to find any at all. Life without organic molecules? Impossible! Horowitz, a distinguished biologist, concluded that Mars was lifeless.[51]

Sagan wasn't so sure. He scrutinized the *Viking* images for any sign of life—lichen on a rock, a trail left by a slug, footprints, artifacts of an intelligent civilization. Levin claimed he could see lifelike colors on the pictures, a claim that briefly intrigued Sagan. But Sagan soon decided via a pixel-by-pixel statistical analysis of Levin's purported color anomalies that they could not unambiguously be distinguished from chance electronic noise in the camera.[52] "The greatest disappointment in Gil's life is that Carl didn't agree with him," says Horowitz, now white-haired and in his eighties. "If anyone, it would be Carl that would take up Gil's argument. But even Carl didn't go for it."[53] To this day, alone among his *Viking* colleagues, Levin argues that the unusual phenomena revealed the presence of life on Mars.[54]

With time, Sagan steeled himself to admit the inevitable. In a paper titled "Lander Imaging as a Detector of Life on Mars," Elliott C. Levinthal of Stanford, Kenneth L. Jones of Brown, and Paul Fox and Carl Sagan of Cornell reported (in words that sound very much like Sagan's):

> With one exception, nothing was observed which suggests an artifact of intelligent life. The exception is the rock exhibiting the letter 'B' shown in Figure 3. 'Lettered' rocks are sometimes found in the desert sculpted by eolian and other erosion in a manner visually indistinguishable from that sculpted by a chisel. It is clear that a single letter by itself is not sufficiently improbable to force the hypothesis of intelligent origin. This is in addition to the unlikely universality of the Roman alphabet.[55]

As a boy, Sagan had fantasized about Martians and hoped to visit their world. So it must have been hard for him to write, in the same article, that

> no evidence, direct or indirect, has been obtained for macroscopic biology on Mars.[56]

VIKING 2 LANDED SAFELY at 3:58 P.M. PDT on September 3, 1976, at a site designated as "B3," in Utopia Planitia west of the crater Mie.[57] It also checked for living organisms, with equally negative results.

After the landing, Sagan and Timothy Ferris met in Sagan's Pasadena apartment. Sagan unfurled a photographic panorama of Mars photographed by the *Viking* camera as it turned. Like little boys playing fort, they wrapped the photo partly around themselves, to sense what it was like to stand on the red planet. Gazing at the black-and-white image of a desert world littered with rocks, they had "this sense that you were there," Ferris recalls. "We looked around for quite a while in silence."

Then Ferris said, softly: "You know, I keep thinking that I see a little patch of coconut palms out there right on the horizon." Sagan chuckled. "You know," he replied, "I had precisely the same hallucination."[58]

Difficult as the *Viking* results were to accept, Sagan did accept them, and apparently in good humor. He even joked in an appearance on *The Tonight Show* about how absurd it would be to think that aliens might carve the letter *B* on a rock. Carson and the studio audience roared with laughter. If Sagan was aching inside, he concealed it well.

"IT'S THE SOLAR SYSTEM we want. . . . The solar system we can never have again." Isaac Asimov had written those words in the 1960s, after *Mariner 4* had flown by Mars and transmitted home to Earth its melancholy pictures.[59] For a time, the exciting pictures from *Mariner 9* had revived hopes of a habitable Mars, but the *Viking* imagery scotched such dreams, save for a few true believers like Levin. Especially astonishing was the *Vikings'* failure to find organic molecules on Mars. The planet's surface had some kind of chemical constituent (probably hydrogen peroxide) that readily destroyed organics. This was something that Sagan, headstrong with excitement over the Miller-Urey experiment, had failed to remember: nature might dismantle organics as readily as it manufactured them. The universe might be more hostile to life than he had assumed.

Might that explain why his and Drake's radiotelescope survey of the galaxies had failed to hear from a single alien radio transmitter? Incredible as it seemed, might Earth be the only world inhabited by intelligence in this sector of the universe?—perhaps in the entire cosmos? Had he dedicated much of his career to the subject of extraterrestrial life in vain? And if so, what could he, at age forty-two, do now?

Rose and Leib Gruber, Rachel Sagan's stepmother and father. According to one version of a family legend, Leib fled Austria for the United States in 1904 after murdering an anti-Semite. (*Courtesy of Cari Sagan Greene*)

Sam and Rachel Sagan, Carl Sagan's tender-hearted father and intense, emotionally erratic mother. (*Courtesy of Cari Sagan Greene*)

Carl Sagan with his mother, Rachel. In early photos, Sagan was an unusually serious-looking child. At age five, he asked what the stars were; his mother advised him to go to the library to find out. (*Courtesy of Nick Sagan*)

Carl, about age ten, with his sister, Carol (Cari), about age four; probably at Coney Island, near his childhood home in Bensonhurst, Brooklyn, where he lived from 1934 through World War II. (*Courtesy of Cari Sagan Greene*)

Sagan's teenage home at 576 Bryant Street in Rahway, New Jersey, where his family moved after World War II when Sam Sagan became the manager of his uncle George Sagan's garment factory. (*Courtesy of Cari Sagan Greene*)

Sagan's 1951 graduation photo from Rahway High School, where he was named the male Class Brain and the male Most Likely to Succeed. (*Courtesy of Nick Sagan*)

Sagan (standing, center) with the radiation biology class of the Tuskegee Institute in Alabama during the summer of 1963, when he was a guest lecturer there. (*Courtesy of J. H. M. Henderson*)

A 1991 photo of Sagan's first wife, Lynn Margulis, and Lynn and Carl's son Dorion Sagan. Margulis is now a renowned biologist and a member of the National Academy of Sciences, the elite organization to which Sagan was denied membership. (*Courtesy of the* Daily Hampshire Gazette, *Northampton, Massachusetts*)

Sagan's second wife, Linda Salzman Sagan, with the Sagan family in 1968—*left to right:* Rachel, Sam, Linda, Cari, and Carl. (*Courtesy of Nick Sagan*)

Carl, Nick, and Linda at a space launch at the John F. Kennedy Space Center in the early 1970s, just before Sagan's early fame turned incandescent with the publication of *The Cosmic Connection* and his first appearances on *The Tonight Show*. (*Courtesy of Nick Sagan*)

Sagan with Nick and his orange Porsche with its PHOBOS license plate, which alludes to a moon of his favorite planet: Mars. (*Courtesy of Nick Sagan*)

Carl and Nick, whose middle name is Julian in honor of the civil rights leader Julian Bond; father and son enjoyed a much closer relationship than Carl did with the two sons from his first marriage, to microbiologist Lynn Margulis. (*Courtesy of Nick Sagan*)

Left to right: Lester Grinspoon; Linda Salzman Sagan; Lester's wife, Betsy Grinspoon; and Sagan, with rarely worn mustache. Grinspoon was Sagan's best friend for three decades; he saved Sagan's life and shared his enthusiasm for marijuana. (*Courtesy of Lester Grinspoon*)

Sagan at a press conference discussing *Pioneer 10*'s encounter with Jupiter in 1973. (*Courtesy of NASA*)

Sagan with students at Cornell, with the Drake equation on the blackboard behind him. Next to Sagan's head is the ominous variable L, which represents the average lifespan of a technological civilization in the galaxy. (*Courtesy of Cornell University*)

Sagan and Immanuel Velikovsky debating at the April 1974 meeting of the American Association for the Advancement of Science in San Francisco. (*Courtesy of Dale P. Cruikshank*)

Timothy Ferris, mid-1970s,
the acclaimed *Rolling Stone*
writer turned science essayist,
who lost Ann Druyan to Sagan.
(*Courtesy of Timothy Ferris*)

Ann Druyan, mid-1970s, Sagan's third wife, a brilliant,
endearing leftist, who would transform Sagan intellectually,
emotionally, and politically, and reunite his three divided
families. (*Courtesy of Timothy Ferris*)

Sagan with Johnny Carson on *The Tonight Show*—two astronomy buffs, one a professional and the other an amateur, who conspired to get late-night TV viewers interested in the cosmos. (*Courtesy of Carson Productions*)

Sagan with a model of the *Viking* lander, in Death Valley, 1980. Despite his colleagues' scorn, Sagan placed a turtle and a snake in front of the lander to test its ability to detect any large, moving animals on Mars. (*Courtesy of The Planetary Society*)

Sagan in front of the Great Sphinx in Egypt, next to a replica of the Rosetta Stone, while filming *Cosmos*. (*Courtesy of Bill Ray*)

Sagan and Druyan on the set of *Cosmos*, standing next to a model of the *Viking* lander. (*Courtesy of The Planetary Society*)

To avoid being subpoenaed by the attorneys for his estranged wife, Linda Salzman, Sagan sent his secretary, Shirley Arden, to New York to accept the Peabody Award for *Cosmos* in his stead. Third from the left is a glum-looking Adrian Malone, the acclaimed director of the series, who warred so angrily with Sagan that they quit speaking to each other. (*Courtesy of George Lange*)

Ann Druyan and Sagan at their wedding at the Hotel Bel Air in Los Angeles in June 1981, just after the stunning success of the television series *Cosmos* and just before the bitter debates with Edward Teller, William Buckley, and Reagan Administration officials during the "nuclear winter" controversy. (*Courtesy of Ann Druyan*)

Jim Pollack in his office at NASA's Ames Research Center in California in 1986. A gay man, he began as Sagan's first graduate student, was his closest scientific colleague for three decades, and became one of the most revered planetary scientists of the space age. (*Courtesy of NASA*)

Sagan with the other founders of The Planetary Society, Bruce Murray (left) and Louis Friedman, in front of the society's home office in Pasadena; it became the most prominent grassroots lobbying group for space exploration. (*Courtesy of The Planetary Society*)

At the 1985 dedication for The Planetary Society's Project META, a privately funded effort to detect alien radio signals using a Harvard radiotelescope. Sagan stands with filmmaker Steven Spielberg (at left). (*Courtesy of The Planetary Society*)

Sagan with Chuck Berry, whose music Sagan was persuaded to send into the galaxy upon the *Voyager* record; at a Planetary Society celebration in Pasadena. (*Courtesy of The Planetary Society*)

Receiving the Public Welfare Medal from the National Academy of Sciences in 1994, two years after the same group battled over, then rejected, his bid for membership. (*Courtesy of the National Academy of Sciences*)

Sagan at his sixtieth-birthday extravaganza at Cornell in 1994, the year during which he, Ann Druyan, Lynda Obst, and other bright minds held "think tank" sessions to plan the film *Contact*. (*Courtesy of Cornell University*)

11

The Dragons of Eden

DESPITE THE DISAPPOINTMENT of the *Viking* missions, they enhanced Sagan's fame. He became a favorite guest of television talk-show hosts and news reporters, who sought his commentary during space missions and appreciated his enthusiasm and ability to explain technical details in understandable terms.

As a result of his growing celebrity, Sagan's life became dizzyingly complex. He juggled responsibilities with the space program with his responsibilities as an academic, while spending increasing amounts of time fielding calls from publishers, television producers, and reporters. His office records from this period, with notes from secretarial staff, indicate that he was developing a devoted—perhaps overly devoted—fan club; he was starting to become something of a cult figure. His office was flooded with inquiries, a fair percentage of which came from people Sagan and his staff privately referred to as "fissured ceramics" (crackpots), as a sampling of staff memos to Sagan will attest:

Young man named ———— called from Opelika, Alabama. Wanted to speak to you. I put him off since I suspect he may be on the edge of the fissured ceramics file. However, I suggested he write to you and assured him you would answer . . . he wants nothing more than to become involved in Astronomy in any capacity at all. Says he is studying independently . . . sad-sounding voice.[1]

Two young men . . . came in today [July 15] to try to make a date to play ping pong with you. (They've been in twice before and I found a letter in the chron file you wrote to one of them promising a match after six months of practice—that was written in April.)[2]

This young man came into the office looking for you today about 3 p.m. He will try to see you again the week of August 18th. As he left, he cautioned me not to discuss the above subject with anyone but you.

Said if the military or the oil companies got hold of the invention (because it will cause them to lose a lot of money) it would be disastrous. Maybe you should be wary—he seems a little bit wavy in retrospect.[3]

A fan with a neat southern accent . . . called from Dallas Texas—very enthusiastic about your appearance on the Carson show.[4]

A call from "Shirley ———" . . . wanting to know if you have a job in the laboratory for her shy boyfriend.[5]

Ms. ——— called from Washington. To make a long story short, she . . . was recently taken to the hospital by the police because she was hallucinating and getting radio-signals in Morse code. She wants to know if you can tell her how to answer the signals when/if they start again.[6]

A young man named ——— wants your permission to use the Pioneer 10 plaque illustration. He wants to paint it on his van![7]

——— called again wanting to talk with you about the impact of nuclear testing on the orbit of the Earth.[8]

UFOs have been sited [sic] in the area. ——— called at ———'s suggestion. She saw this thing from her trailer park home. Glows, moves, glows, sends shafts of light to the earth etc.[9]

Sagan's typical day in the mid-1970s also included numerous calls from magazine editors asking him to write for them. He also received a host of speaking invitations. He was assuming the role of a public guru, and devotees projected onto him all sorts of bizarre hopes, interests, and theories that he did not actually subscribe to.

His hectic career took its toll on his private life. One of secretary Shirley Arden's tasks was to remind him about personal matters that he sometimes forgot amid the swirl of celebrityhood. For example, at one point his friend Gentry Lee's southern California home was endangered by wildfire. A few days later Arden reminded Sagan to call Lee to check on the status of his house.[10] Another memo reminded him that his oldest son's eighteenth birthday would be coming up during a forthcoming business trip: "You also want to think about where you will sleep overnight and whether/ when you can see Dorion, whose birthday is the 17th."[11]

Arden's memos give a day-to-day view of the microstructure of fame—how it works, how it is cultivated and nourished, and how it affects the famous one and those around him. Decisions, decisions: If he handles the business deals, the calls from famous scientists, reporters, publishers, and TV hosts, will he have time to see his eldest son on his eighteenth birthday? If he talks to Francis Ford Coppola and Sir Fred

Hoyle and Murray Gell-Mann, will he remember to call his friend Gentry to see if his house burned down?

And sometimes Arden relayed word from the little world where Sagan was often absent—his home: "Linda called to say you are urgently wanted at home because [two guests] are there and they are hungry! (I promised I'd shoo you out the door as quickly as I can!)"[12]

While Sagan's fame soared, his marriage deteriorated. He and Linda fought over his absences, his refusal to do housework, his indifference to her wish to transcend housewifery. According to Lynda Obst, Sagan believed that Linda's role in life was to cook and clean for him so that he could focus on science.

Linda is affectionately depicted as the fictional character Nineveh in Paul West's 1999 novel *Life with Swan*, in which a central character is the Saganish Dr. Raoul Bunsen. (West and his wife, the poet Diane Ackerman, lived in Ithaca and were close to the Sagans.) The book is based heavily on characters from Sagan/Bunsen's life, all very thinly disguised (or not at all), ranging from secretary Shirley Arden ("Shirl Cornwall") to radioastronomer I. S. Shklovskii ("I. I. Shklovsky") to Isaac Asimov ("Isaac Asimov"). Astronomers "from all over the world showed up at Raoul's and Nineveh's soirees," West writes. "Sometimes Isaac Asimov was there, having stepped out of a cloud, exercising his favorite lines as if they were borzois." Sagan/Bunsen's parties "were almost a statement, a demonstration," West observes slyly, "revealing how many people he knew and, just perhaps, how many adored him."

Plagued by his esophageal problem, Bunsen/Sagan's face "often showed strain, or even pain. . . . I knew he was unable to swallow much solid food and went off to his office daily on a chocolate milk shake that only Nineveh knew how to mix. . . . One sympathized without saying anything; he liked some things to be known, but not saluted in public."

West makes clear how Linda/Nineveh—"a shorter Ingrid Bergman"—improved Sagan/Bunsen's sometimes offensive behavior. She "was a hugger and a kisser, the image of the wholly undemanding spouse, at least as far as we could see. She didn't seem to get much painting done, but much of her time she gave to their son Ptolemy . . . and to Raoul's intensive social life. . . . At first I had shrunk from Bunsen lest he regale me with hubris, but Nineveh kept him sweet and spent her time watering his courtly, civil side, so even when he tape-recorded in your face he seemed to be doing you a favor."

While Sagan repeated many of the mistakes he had made in his first marriage, he had, however, become a better father. He had missed out on seeing his first two sons, Dorion and Jeremy, grow up; he would not make the same mistake with Nick. This may explain why Nick, now a laid-back television writer in Studio City, California, seems to be the gentlest and most open-hearted of Sagan's three adult sons.

Dorion Sagan depicted his father in often sharply critical terms in an essay for *Whole Earth Review* the summer after Sagan's death. While growing up, Dorion had often been angry at his father, and at one point he wrote a harsh letter expressing many of his grievances. But he decided (with a friend's advice) not to send the letter; rather, he would "give up" on his father. Later, his father "mentioned that our relationship had improved and asked me if I knew why that was," Dorion wrote in the original draft of his *Whole Earth* article. "Basically, I gave up on you, I admitted. Is there anything he could do to improve our relationship, he asked me. I said no, not really, it's a Zen thing. There's nothing that can be done. Nothing. Just accept it. . . . In retrospect, a week after his death, I doubted the wisdom of such nonattachment. I loved him. I wanted to love him. I wanted him to love me."

During this writer's interview with Sagan's son Jeremy, he evaded almost all questions about his attitude toward his father. He did, at one point, complain about a television biography of his father that was "too positive. . . . He wasn't a perfect father . . . not by a long shot." He added: "I'm a determinist. His mother [Rachel] had a lot to do with it. . . . I think she just *drove* him . . . did everything for him, wiped his butt or whatever. . . . That's what [Sagan's novel] *Contact* is about—trying to get your parents back. . . . I could see a lot of him in [the novel]."

Lynn Margulis spoke more bluntly. She recalls a time when Jeremy was living in San Diego, and Sagan happened to pass through town. Yet Sagan "would not fit [Jeremy] onto the schedule." She remembers Jeremy's sad voice as he talked to his father on the phone and the boy—then close to adulthood—said sadly to Sagan: "Oh, you're too busy? Okay." Margulis then hugged her son and declared: "Jeremy, I don't care who's with me, what I'm doing, I don't care *who* I'm running away with—you can *always* come wherever I am, at any time." She adds: "That was the first time in Jeremy's young life that he stopped blaming himself and started blaming Carl—[or] not *blaming* Carl, [but] becoming aware that his godlike father was not this godlike father."

Sagan's relationship to his son Nick was much closer. "I remember him tossing me up in the air and catching me," Nick says. "I remember taking walks with him." Before long car trips, Sagan would dictate stories in advance into a tape recorder, so that Nick could listen to them en route. It was great to have a father whom he could ask, "Why is the sky blue?" and he could tell you. He didn't (Nick observes) say, "I don't know," or "Look it up!" or "Shut up!" Nick was precocious, too; he learned to read very early and amazed his parents with his ability to read road signs.[13] Supportive as Sagan was, however, he was alarmed when

Nick said he had two ambitions: to be a daddy and to be "a host," like his father's friend Johnny Carson.[14]

Much as he enjoyed time with his father, Nick also remembers his parents fighting a good deal. "My mother's feeling," he observes, "was and I think still is that she made a lot of sacrifices so that he could do the things that he did. She cooked and took care of the house and helped him in many, many, many, many different ways." The Adam-and-Eve graphic for the *Pioneer* plaque? She drew it. Sounds of Earth on the *Voyager* record? She collected them.[15]

"Intellectually and temperamentally, in many ways, they were so different in their interests," says Sagan's associate Steven Soter. As a young woman Linda Salzman had been a sixties-style free spirit, "a sweet person . . . a frustrated artist." Then she married Sagan and ended up "spending a lot of time keeping their home together," Soter observes. "And that didn't leave a lot of time for art."[16]

Salzman particularly resented what she saw as Sagan's tendency to discuss "rationally" issues that she felt required more emotional empathy, the kind of affectionate spousal understanding that transcends cold, abstract "reason" and silently forgives "illogic."

His parents' differences led to regular fights about "little things," Nick says. "My mother would make my father breakfast before he would go off to work. . . . He would drink shakes because it was easier [for the food] to go down. She would make the shake and then she would put the toast in the toaster.

"And he said one day, 'Well, if you put the toast in the toaster, *then* make the shake, they'd be ready at the same time.' She said, 'You're talking about twenty seconds.' He said, 'Yes, but twenty seconds *every day*'—and he did this calculation to point out how much time he was losing [over the years]."* Stunned by this display of husbandly hyper-rationalism, Linda exploded. "She just lost it—went berserk," Nick recalls.[17]

As his relations with Linda soured, Sagan went to a psychotherapist to try to understand why the marriage wasn't working out, but he "didn't seem to be getting much out of it," Lester Grinspoon recalls. He advised Sagan to see a psychiatrist he knew at Harvard. Sagan saw the man only once, and later told Lester: "You know what he told me? He told me I had to choose between my prick and my brain. I asked, 'Why can't I have both?' "[18]

---

*Simple calculation shows that twenty wasted seconds per day equals about one hundred wasted hours over a fifty-year span. Hence (to steal George Sanders's riposte to Marilyn Monroe in *All About Eve*), Sagan "had a point—an idiotic one, but a point nonetheless."

SAGAN'S LIFELONG QUEST was for intelligence in the universe. By the mid-1970s, this quest spurred him to try to understand intelligence closer to Earth—the kind between human ears. The psychological issues on Sagan's mind during the writing of his next book, *The Dragons of Eden*, also resembled those with which he wrestled during his increasingly troubled second marriage.

Sagan was baffled and dismayed by Linda's anger at him. He was so obsessed with his "logic" that he assumed his wife was simply illogical. But he sincerely wanted to understand the schisms forming in his marriage; that may be one reason (although certainly not the only one) why he wrote *The Dragons of Eden*.

Dragons represents Sagan's attempt to understand, at the neurological level, the grand dichotomies that had always haunted him—reason versus unreason, science versus faith, desire versus objectivity. These dichotomies wrestled within him, causing him much emotional and personal turmoil; in writing *Dragons*, he hoped to understand them in scientific, quantifiable terms to gain some control over them.

Dragons was obviously written under the inspiration of marijuana. Its kaleidoscopic complexity, undisciplined speculations, and *Yellow Submarine*-style cheerfulness made *The Cosmic Connection* seem like a sober monograph by comparison. Indeed, some of Sagan's speculations had an off-the-cuff quality, the kind of "Gee, what if . . ." science that one expects from a stoned high school student, not from a serious scientist. But his sly humor, even when enlisted in the purpose of education, makes for engaging reading: "A single female silkworm moth need release only a hundredth of a microgram of sex attractant per second to attract every male silkworm in a volume of about a cubic mile. That is why there are silkworms."[19]

Dragons also won the Pulitzer Prize, certifying Sagan's emerging status as a populist intellectual. Never again would he be simply "that astronomer on the Carson show." *Dragons* affirmed his talent for writing lucidly and entertainingly—if not always responsibly—about topics far outside his professional ken. It marked the last major step on his trek toward *Cosmos* and international celebrity.

To say that *Dragons* is about the brain is like saying that *Citizen Kane* is about the newspaper business. The nature of intelligence had long been an important issue to Sagan. It was, after all, what he hoped to discover in the stars. Since the early 1960s, he had been enthralled by neuroscientist John Lilly's investigations of dolphin brains and "intelligence."

Different generations harbor different fundamental concepts of the brain—the brain as bureaucracy, as computer, as hologram, as thermodynamic engine, as neural network, and so on. Each concept usually founders in some way and loses favor with scientists, but can survive in popular folklore as a metaphor, a mirror of an abandoned Zeitgeist. In *Dragons*, Sagan presented two different models for the nature of the brain. One model is neuroscientist Paul D. MacLean's concept of the "triune brain," a sort of neuroanatomical send-up of Freud. According to MacLean (then chief of the Laboratory of Brain Evolution and Behavior at the National Institutes of Mental Health), the brain has three basic layers—from youngest to oldest, the neocortex, the limbic system, and the reptilian. (Similarly, Freud posited the mental holy trinity of id, ego, and superego. The functions of MacLean's hypothetical triumvirate, however, do not directly correspond to those of Freud's.) Each of MacLean's layers "corresponds to a separate major evolutionary step." Put simplistically, the neocortex is the waking, rational, self-aware self, whereas the reptilian (or "R-complex") is the realm where UFOs, ghosts, religious impulses, lust, and aggression lurk.[20]

The other model is the "split brain" thesis of Caltech neuroscientist Roger Sperry (later a Nobel laureate), according to which our cerebral tissue compartmentalizes major perceptual and cognitive functions into the left and right halves of the brain. This left brain–right brain lateralization had a symmetry, a yin-yang quality, that appealed to many people. It was also popularized by commentators on the then-fledgling feminist movement, who hoped to determine whether male–female behavioral differences somehow resulted from the left-to-right "lateralization" of the brain.[21]

Dragons starts like a logical lion and ends like a New Age–style lamb. Sagan begins by asserting his commitment to the reductionist faith: his "fundamental premise" was that the brain and "its workings—what we sometimes call 'mind'—are a consequence of its anatomy and physiology, and nothing more."[22] Yet within a matter of pages he is speculating flamboyantly about topics that extreme neuro-reductionists treat as mere epiphenomena: dreams and myths. In *Dragons*, Ramón y Cajal and Charles Sherrington meet Sigmund Freud and Carl Jung.

Sagan discusses the old claim that brain mass correlates with intelligence. (Being a good feminist, he cautions: "When cultural and child-rearing biases are taken into account, there is no clear evidence of overall differences in intelligence between the sexes."[23]) He counters that "a better measure of intelligence than the absolute value of the mass of a brain is the *ratio* of the mass of the brain to the total mass of the organism. . . . Of all the organisms shown [in a chart on the same page], the beast with the largest brain mass for its body weight is a creature called *Homo sapiens*. Next in such a ranking are the dolphins."

Then he offers a somewhat scientistic calculation. First, assume that each brain synapse is capable of two vaguely defined "mental states" (like the "0" and "1" binary code of computers). The brain has 10 trillion (10^{13}) synapses. Assuming that the number of possible mental states rises exponentially with the number of synapses (2 synapses = 4 [2^2] states, 3 synapses = 8 [2^3] states, 4 synapses = 16 [2^4] states, and so on), then the number of possible mental states in one brain is 2 "multiplied by itself 10 trillion times. This is an unimaginably large number, far greater, for example, than the total number of elementary particles (electrons and protons) in the entire universe." Therefore "no two humans, even identical twins raised together, can ever be really very much alike. These enormous numbers may also explain something of the unpredictability of human behavior and those moments when we surprise even ourselves by what we do." His upbeat conclusion: "Each human being is truly rare and different and the sanctity of individual human lives is a plausible ethical consequence."[24]

As for rationalism and irrationalism, Sagan might have been thinking of his own marriage, or of his confrontations with pseudoscientists, when he wrote: "There are many people who are, in their conscious lives, almost entirely rational, and many who are almost entirely intuitive. Each group, with very little appreciation of the reciprocal value of these two kinds of cognitive ability, derides the other: 'muddled' and 'amoral' are typical adjectives used in the more polite of such exchanges. Why should we have two different, accurate and complementary modes of thinking which are so poorly integrated with each other?"

In *Dragons*, Sagan tried to show that despite his reductionistic stance, he could be open to nonreductionistic modes of thought and insight—particularly myths (his old love) and dreams (which had awakened him from childhood slumbers in cold sweats). He cautioned that by "myth" he meant not falsehood ("its present popular meaning") but, rather, "a metaphor of some subtlety on a subject difficult to describe in any other way."

To many, myths and dreams offer interesting metaphors or means of stimulating thinking (as do, say, Rorschach blots) but do not constitute meaningful scientific data *in themselves*. Sagan suspected otherwise. He believed that both might contain clues to our evolutionary past.

"That scientific myths make contact with more ancient myths may or may not be a coincidence," he wrote.[25] He cited the snake in the Garden of Eden: might this represent a primal fear of reptiles; in particular, of creatures like Komodo dragons? (Hence the title of the book—*The Dragons of Eden*.) Or even a fear of the "reptilian" part of ourselves? Just as Sagan was intrigued by the prevalence of swastika images in world culture (and later suggested, with Ann Druyan, that they stemmed from ancient observations of a cometary flyby), he was intrigued by the "pervasiveness of dragon myths in the folk legends of many cultures," which "is probably no accident." "Is it only an accident that the common human sounds commanding silence or attracting attention seem strangely imitative of the hissing of reptiles?"[26]

This evolutionary heritage, Sagan argues, is encoded in the anatomy and chemistry of our brains. It presumably still affects our waking lives, eons after we stopped routinely worrying about reptiles disturbing our slumbers on the moonlit veldt. Throughout the book he tosses out ideas that are pure speculation, nothing more. It was this tendency to speculate that got him most in trouble with his colleagues. Sometimes it is difficult to tell whether he is speculating or joking. For example:

> There are also as yet unconfirmed reports of brain damage that results only in the inability to understand the passive voice or prepositional phrases or possessive constructions. (Perhaps the locale of the subjunctive mood will one day be found. Will Latins turn out to be extravagantly endowed and English-speaking peoples significantly short-changed in this minor piece of brain anatomy?)[27]

And:

> The attachment of domestic animals to humans is, I think, beyond question. The apparently sorrowful behavior of many mammalian mothers when their young are removed is well-known. One wonders just how far such emotions go. Do horses on occasion have glimmerings of patriotic fervor? Do dogs feel for humans something akin to religious ecstasy?[28]

And:

> The gracile Australopithecines were erect, agile, fleet and three and a half feet tall: 'little people.' I sometimes wonder whether our myths about gnomes, trolls, giants and dwarfs could possibly be a genetic or cultural memory of those times.[29]

And in a passage reminiscent of Velikovsky's "collective amnesia," Sagan suggests that our distant ancestors' memories are transmitted to us over the eons by the DNA we share with them. What he was proposing, in effect, was an updated, more materialistic version of Jung's "collective unconscious." In Sagan's words:

> The fall from Eden seems to be an appropriate metaphor for some of the major biological events in recent human evolution. This may account for its popularity. It is not so remarkable as to require us to believe in a kind of biological memory of ancient historical events, but

it does seem to me close enough to risk at least raising the question. The only repository of such a biological memory is, of course, the genetic code.[30]

What is one to make of such speculation? Sagan offers it without the remotest attempt to provide supporting evidence. One imagines a hard-working neuroscientist who has toiled all day in the lab, perhaps pointing electrodes at synapses in the nervous system of a neurally dismantled lobster or sea hare, hoping to make an incremental advance in a topic such as the neurochemical basis of memory storage—and then curling up in the evening on the sofa at home, after dinner, with a copy of *The Dragons of Eden*. As she reads Sagan's words, she gets madder and madder. Who is this astronomer, this TV celebrity, this *upstart*, who vents such speculations with abandon? Who writes a moneymaking, best-selling, prize-winning book of neurological whimsies, while *she* must struggle to verify every little fact and face withering questions from colleagues who ensure that she does so? To her, Sagan may not seem like a serious scientist. He is simply having fun—and getting a lot of money and attention in the process, while she labors in obscurity at a modest salary. From this perspective, it is no wonder that Sagan made enemies.

He speculated wildly on the basis of almost trivial evidence. For example, "some children seem capable of remembering extremely early experiences," Sagan wrote. He cited only one piece of evidence for this sensational assertion: his son Nick, who, asked what the earliest thing he could recall was, "replied in a hushed tone while staring into middle distance, 'It was red, and I was very cold.' He was born by Caesarean section. It is probably very unlikely, but I wonder whether this could just possibly be a true birth memory."[31] "Very unlikely," yet he speculates about it anyway; no wonder some of Sagan's harder-boiled colleagues ground their teeth at the thought of him entertaining the ignorant masses with lurid speculations that were, upon investigation (like most far-out ideas), almost certain to disappoint. How could the public get interested in *real* brain science, in the adventures of numerous unknown Livingstones poking through the neural forests, while this sideshow popularizer and TV talk-show guest entertained them with "What if" questions? The sad truth is that for all its literary merits and inspirational power, *Dragons* does not offer a balanced diet of neuroscientific learning; it is all ice cream and Acapulco Gold.

At the same time, Sagan's appreciation for mythic murkiness is contradicted by his proposal of a straightforward, scientific solution to a moral controversy—the abortion debate. He suggests that the then-emerging debate over abortion could be resolved scientifically by using electroencephalography to determine when a fetus acquires "human" intelligence. In his words, "the ultimate key to the solution of the abortion debate would seem to be the investigation of prepartum neocortical activity."[32] In effect, Sagan was arguing that abortion of a fetus during the first trimester is okay because its brain is still in a MacLean-style reptilian state. Rarely had Sagan's political naïveté, his failure to grasp the complexity and fierce passion of great moral disputes, been so glaring.

Sagan discusses both the MacLean and the Sperry hypotheses at length, as if trying to choose between them. MacLean's triune hypothesis is, in a sense, more pessimistic than Sperry's hypothesis (although they are not necessarily incompatible). Like Freud's, MacLean's view of a triumvirate brain is a dark one, positing the existence of forces of irrationalism, desire, and violence lurking deep within the skull, within the R-complex. By contrast, Sperry treated the brain as a kind of dual (not triple) entity, a two-party democracy, as it were, where opposite sides grumble and bicker but basically get along.

On the one hand, Sagan wittily suggests (following MacLean) that the dark forces of the R-complex control "a great deal of modern human bureaucratic and political behavior. I do not mean that the neocortex is not functioning at all in an American political convention or a meeting of the Supreme Soviet; after all, a great deal of the communication at such rituals is verbal and therefore noncortical. But it is striking how much of our actual behavior—as distinguished from what we say and think about it—can be described in reptilian terms. We speak commonly of a 'cold-blooded' killer. Machiavelli's advice to his Prince was 'knowingly to adopt the beast.'"[33]

Which leads Sagan to a chilling question:

"If bureaucratic behavior is controlled at its core by the R-complex, does this mean there is no hope for the human future?"[34] In other words, is the value of L (the lifespan of an average civilization—see chapter 5) small? It might not be too much to say that MacLean's vision troubled him because it implied that civilization might be doomed and, therefore, that the value of L is low, perhaps too low to make the detection of extraterrestrial life likely.

On the other hand, since at least the late 1960s, Sagan had been concerned about the divide in society between the advocates of science and reason and the advocates of alternative worldviews. The latter were beginning to appear everywhere—the "counterculture," the New Age, various pseudoscientists, new religions, and trends in the arts that went against his aesthetically conservative grain (rock music irritated him, and he saw modern art in general as reflecting a very non-Saganish despair over the human condition).[35] Could these contradictory worldviews better understand each other? He was asking a question not unlike C. P. Snow's question about the Two Cultures almost two decades earlier. But unlike Snow, a scientist-novelist who dedicated the bulk of his thesis to an elegant attack on his literary colleagues' hostility to science, Sagan tried to be more conciliatory, to appreciate the merits of both the scientific and the artistic worldviews. Hence it is not surprising that by his book's end he seemed to prefer the split-brain thesis of Sperry and others. In this sense *Dragons* could be viewed as part of a grander popular-science tradition that uses scientific metaphors to deliver a profoundly optimistic message, one that says (as did the 1939 New York World's Fair) that social tensions can be resolved without resort to major societal upheaval or violence. That kind of message was immensely appealing to many Americans in the 1970s, a period that was still being shaken by post-sixties radical skirmishes such as kidnapping and robbery by the Symbionese Liberation Army.

This kind of writing has something in common, psychologically speaking, with Rev. William Paley's writings of the late eighteenth and early nineteenth centuries. Paley saw inherent design in a divinely ordained Nature that allotted each organism its just place and purpose.[36] His delightful writings (young Darwin loved them) were popular in class-conscious England partly because of their soothing, nonradical vision of society, a nice relaxant for the post-Robespierre, pre-1848 generation. Undoubtedly Sagan, as a no-nonsense neo-Darwinian, would be furious to be compared with the cheerful Reverend Paley. But their common commercial success is easier to understand if one keeps in mind what they also had in common: they delivered a "good news" view of the nature of life in general, and of humans in particular. Good news sells, especially in bad times.

"It is the verbal hemisphere that controls the right side. There may not in fact be more dexterity in the right side; but it certainly has a better press. The left hemisphere seems to feel quite defensive—in a strange way insecure—about the right hemisphere." In this quote from *Dragons* Sagan is obviously referring to scientists' growing sense in the 1970s of being embattled by those who viewed science as a tool of power, as a means of dominating the world. He is also obviously referring to many scientists' persistent feeling of cultural inferiority, as if somehow they are not true intellectuals. (In high school, scientifically bright kids are denounced as "nerds" and "geeks." But what slurs are hurled at youths who excel in music, art, or writing?) Also, many artists of the 1960s and 1970s saw themselves as morally superior to a scientific generation that had sold out its extraordinary powers to the nuclear weapons makers, the napalm makers, and the like. (Perhaps Sagan harbored guilt feelings along these lines; he had, after all, done a small amount of classified research.) And of course, scientists were viewed as depriving humans of a *why* for living.

Sagan calls for a truce in the culture war between the two super-powers of the brain, between the left and right hemispheres, for a recognition of the virtues of both; for a détente between the forces of reason and intuition, a peaceful coexistence between the analysts of the mind and the guardians of the heart. "I know of no significant advance in science that did not require major inputs from both cerebral hemispheres," he writes in *Dragons*. "I think the most significant creative activities of our or any other human culture—legal and ethical systems, art and music, science and technology—were made possible only through the collaborative work of the left and right cerebral hemispheres."[37] For example, the great Scottish physicist James Clerk Maxwell proposed the concept of the displacement current because it made his equations "aesthetically more appealing."[38] These equations led indirectly to the invention of radio. Sagan's assertion that the two halves of the brain need each other, like quarreling lovers, had a charming, middlebrow appeal to it, as did Paley's essays on how all parts of nature are interconnected in a harmonious whole.

The Dragons of Eden ultimately is a paradox. It begins by offering a reductionist vision—that the brain and "its workings . . . are a consequence of its anatomy and physiology, and nothing more"[39]—yet the book leaves us feeling that the brain is more mysterious than ever. Sagan tried, with some success, to restore to our understanding of the brain something it has lost in our age: its mythic aspect. The phenomenal success of pharmacological drugs such as lithium, and more recently Prozac, as well as a host of findings in neuroscience that seem to suggest that the brain is very much like a machine, have popularized the notion that there is nothing more than chemical and electrical activity going on in our brains. Artificial intelligence researchers even suggest that once they figure out the trick to the brain's "wiring," they will be able to create machines that think very much as we do. The rich mythology of the personality that Sigmund Freud developed—and that partly accounts for Freud's enormous appeal to many nonscientists, especially novelists, artists, and some historians— has been largely undermined by this mechanistic vision of what makes us who we are. Despite his reductionistic leanings, Sagan was too broadly cultivated to settle for a purely mechanistic concept of the mind.

In writing *Dragons*, Sagan tried to restore a sense of mythology to brain science. He did this not by returning to Freud's myths or those of his countless imitators but by finding new ones, myths connecting neuroses and psychoses and yearnings not to the foibles of one's parents but, rather, to the meanderings of evolution, millions of years ago, which remain encoded in our DNA and still inspire our dreams, fears, and behaviors. He wished to explain the brain scientifically while allowing it to retain its sense of mystery. This is exactly what he did in planetary science, of course: he disenchanted old dreams of Venus and Mars, yet offered new ones in their place.

In other words, Sagan wanted to conciliate between contradictory strands of the psychological thought of the 1970s, particularly within American Humanist circles, where B. F. Skinner's behaviorism was pitted against Abraham Maslow's humanism.[40] Sagan wanted to be both a reductionist and a mythologist, a disenchanter and an enchanter—a Skinner and a Maslow, a John Watson and a Jung. His dream was to establish a myth linking the human brain with its primordial ancestors—a myth grander, in ambition if not in execution, than Freud's *Totem and Taboo*, or all of Jung's archetypes.[41] Like a child, he wanted to have logic and wonder simultaneously—to have his chocolate cake and eat it too. Ultimately, the author of *Dragons* was not Carl Sagan, master reductionist, but a little Brooklyn boy who had once covered a school blackboard with legends of vanished gods.

Dragons also broached an issue that increasingly intrigued Sagan: the possibility of animal intelligence. As we have seen, he had been fascinated by Lilly's claim that dolphins are intelligent. This implied that the universe might favor the general emergence of intelligence in widely different environmental contexts, whereas many anthropologists had traditionally assumed it was a result of behaviors associated with land-based living, such as toolmaking. If so, then might ordinary animals on Earth possess qualities of intelligence or semi-intelligence?

This had possible implications for SETI. If evolution repeatedly generates intelligence as readily as (say) Miller-Urey processes generate organic molecules, then intelligence might be a routine phenomenon of the galaxy.

Humans have always wondered what animals are "thinking," if they "think" at all. Are they simply bundles of reflexes? (To some extreme behaviorists, that's all *we* are!) Or are there glimmers of consciousness and intelligence within the skulls of a panting dog, a purring cat, a grinning chimp, even a shivering laboratory mouse as the scalpel slices into its fur? Sagan said: "A typical chimpanzee brain volume is 400 cubic centimeters; a lowland gorilla's, 500 cc. This is the range of brain volumes among the tool-using gracile Australopithecines. . . . Are [primates] capable of abstract thought? If they're smart, why don't they talk?"

He discussed the work of Beatrice and Robert Gardner at the University of Nevada, who suspected that chimps might "have substantial language abilities which could not be expressed because of the limitations of their anatomy" (that is, their pharynx and larynx). They had the idea of trying to communicate with chimps via American Sign Language.[42] The chimp Washoe was supposedly able to sign in ways that suggested linguistic ability—for example, spotting a duck in a pond, it combined the words "water" and "duck" to yield "waterbird."[43]

Sagan speculated that chimps might be trained to talk via hand gestures, and "pass down the language to subsequent generations"; that a chimp might eventually produce his "memoirs"; and that future generations of primates might worship the legends of those who gave them the gift of communication—for example, the Gardners or other primate researchers—as *Homo sapiens* cultures have worshiped gods and folk heroes. He also offered early hints of his uneasiness about research on laboratory animals, an uneasiness he shared with a historical scientist he greatly admired, Alfred Russel Wallace, who pioneered evolution theory independently of Darwin and was a leader in the nineteenth-century antivivisection movement. If chimps have consciousness, Sagan wondered, do they deserve the equivalent of "human rights"? "How smart does a chimpanzee have to be before killing him constitutes murder?"[44] He entered a chimp lab, where one of the animals spat at the director. He compared the animals' rage to that depicted in old prison movies, where "the prisoners banged their eating utensils against the bars at the appearance of the tyrannical warden."[45] Why, Sagan asked, "are apes in prison?"

THE DRAGONS OF EDEN drew mostly favorable reviews, some almost giddy with enthusiasm. It confirmed Sagan's status as a new "voice" of the American scientific-intellectual establishment. It even drew an admiring letter from his old tormentor, Harold C. Urey. On June 21, 1977, Urey wrote to Sagan that he had not only read *The Dragons of Eden* but that "in fact, I have reread it to a considerable extent. I like it very much and am amazed that someone like you has such an intimate knowledge of the various features of the problem. . . . I congratulate you and wish you great success with this very interesting book. You are a man of many talents."[46] On July 23, Sagan responded gratefully, "There are few people whose praise of my book I value as much as yours."[47] Sagan was featured in a cover story in *Newsweek* on August 15.

The novelist John Updike reviewed *The Dragons of Eden* for the *New Yorker*. Updike was not an offbeat choice; he had, and has, a long-standing interest in things scientific, and has occasionally written fiction pieces and poetry with scientific allusions. (These include a delightful little poem, sometimes reprinted, on the nature of the neutrino.) Updike correctly complained that the book contained too little solid information and too much speculation (particularly that based on research by scientists other than Sagan himself), and added: "Mr. Sagan's speculations, where they are not cheerfully wild, seem tacked on and trivial." Updike contrasted Sagan with popular science writers such as Desmond Morris, who might speculate colorfully about something but whose speculation seemed like a not unreasonable extrapolation from known data. Likewise, Updike said, when psychology professor Julian Jaynes speculated that the ancients lacked "consciousness," this bizarre thesis was at least supported by a compelling collection of data. But when Sagan speculates about the prevalence of sleep "among highly evolved animals . . . we feel that his guess is no better than ours." Even so, Updike added, "it remains to say that there is much fascinating information here, amid the fluff of computer printouts, Escher lithographs, and vacuous editorializing on matters ranging from abortion law to government funding for scientific research."[48]

The *Atlantic Monthly*, after running mathematician Alfred Adler's slash-and-burn piece on Sagan in 1974, made up for it with Robert Manning's review of *Dragons* as a "rational, elegant, and witty book. . . . No doubt some scientists will quarrel or quibble over some of Sagan's speculations. Many others will surely squirm with envy that one of their number can combine such clarity and charm of prose with a considerable measure of humility."[49] (This may be one of the few times in history that anyone accused Carl Sagan of humility.)

Business Week said *The Dragons of Eden* indicated that Sagan was "one of the chief contenders" for the job of "finest scientific prose stylist," given the recent death of Loren Eiseley.[50] The *Village Voice* called the book a "shrewd, graceful, and captivating rumination on the human brain and how it got that way."[51]

The reactions of the scientific community were less consistently enthusiastic. Writing in the *New York Times Book Review*, the neurologist-author Richard Restak questioned the factual basis of some of Sagan's assertions and accused Sagan of overstating the importance of natural selection in the rise of intelligence. Wrote Restak: "In place of competing individuals striving for biological immortality by passing on only the 'best genes,' modern evolution stresses communities of common interest where organisms compete, cooperate, and in some cases are even altruistic." Restak's reaction was fairly mild, considering that Sagan was tap-dancing through a scientific minefield—namely, the time-old "nature vs. nurture" controversy.

Restak concluded: "While [the book] is often insightful and challenges several scientific paradigms, it is also sometimes embarrassingly naive and on occasion just plain fantastic. All in all, though, it is a thought-provoking, maddening, generally worthwhile performance that is unlikely ever to be precisely duplicated."[52]

Ralph L. Holloway of Columbia University, whose research Sagan had cited briefly in *The Dragons of Eden*, reviewed the book in the *American Journal of Physical Anthropology*. He suggested that Sagan was guilty of "an overdependence and too literal reliance on P. D. MacLean's valuable [theoretical] syntheses." The book "has presented this reviewer with an enormous dilemma: how to fairly review a book so delightfully written, provocative, speculative, yet in its anthropological content, weak and sometimes misinformed," Holloway wrote. "I think it would be impossible to find someone who read this book and did not enjoy it. Yet I feel somewhat intimidated at the thought of having to respond in the future years to the inevitable questions of students that will begin, 'What do you think about Carl Sagan's idea on _____ ?' To wit, 'I sometimes wonder whether our myths about gnomes, trolls, giants and dwarfs could possibly be a genetic or cultural memory of those times.'"[53]

The journal *Human Ecology* ran a somewhat hostile review of *The Dragons of Eden* by Joseph C. Pitt of the department of philosophy and religion at Virginia Polytechnic Institute and State University. "This book is crammed full of fascinating bits of information, intriguing theories, humor, vision, and some caustic observations about society as a whole," Pitt said. "What it does not contain is intellectual balance and rigor. . . . For [the] gullible soul Sagan has produced a rather bizarre theory about the reptilian ancestry of our brain, and he has developed the rest of his discussion around this idea without any indication of the status of the theory. He cites just enough people who have worked with these ideas to create an atmosphere of respectability, but he fails to indicate what objections there are, what alternative theories might have to offer, or the general degree of the theory's acceptance by physiologists, psychologists, or anthropologists. . . . We find the most absurd conclusions drawn from otherwise uncontroversial points. . . . What I find most distressing is that the volume is now available in paperback."[54]

The October 1977 issue of the journal *Human Behavior* called *The Dragons of Eden* "just a dazzling display of mishmash." But the reviewer added: "I don't mean to say that a dose of Sagan's mishmash isn't a lot of fun."[55]

SAGAN'S FASCINATION with Sperry's left brain–right brain dichotomy reflects a fascination with such dichotomies in everyday life—and within himself. It is an old myth that every person is a half of some severed being, struggling to reconnect with the lost half. For Sagan, that missing half would come in the form of a woman.

12

Annie

In the 1970s, Timothy Ferris worked for *Rolling Stone*, and one of his friends there was Jon Cott. After Ferris's astronomy book *The Red Limit* was published to great acclaim, Cott asked Ferris to have lunch with Cott's girlfriend, Ann Druyan. She was an aspiring writer and needed his advice. "We went to lunch, and here's this amazing creature, you know?" said Ferris. "Stone beautiful, unbelievably intelligent, incredible sense of humor."

"I remember every moment of that meeting, the light in the room and everything, because I had a very clear insight, which was: I must have absolutely nothing to do with this gal. . . . Jon Cott's in love with her, and Jon Cott's my friend."[1]

At that time, Ferris was, he recalled, "in the drug culture—in those days I used to walk around with forty or fifty hits of mescaline in my jacket pocket. I would just sort of chew on them all day." He suffered a "bad trip" during a breakfast with Cott and Druyan, who took him back to her place so he could calm down. He lay in the dark in her bedroom, sipping a beer she had given him, and his desire for her grew. Yet again, he did nothing about it.

Years later, Ferris said, "either Annie called me or I called her." After the call, a guest said, " 'Who was that?' I said, 'It's this girl Annie, who I think I'm going to marry.' And I went and met her for lunch, and proposed to her some months later." She said yes.

But lovers' minds surge with fears in the months between proposal and "I do." For whatever reason, Ferris seemed depressed; that dispirited her. "We were both getting increasingly uncomfortable. So we postponed the wedding."[2]

It was during this period in the mid-1970s that Ferris and Druyan were invited to a party at the New York home of writer-filmmaker Nora Ephron. (Because of his association with *Rolling Stone*, Ferris was frequently invited to parties with the literati.) Druyan believes the dinner party occurred about October 1974. Sometime earlier, when she was visiting Ephron's East Side apartment, Ephron told her: "I just met the most brilliant, attractive man. . . . Have you ever heard of Carl Sagan?" (Ephron, who was then married to star Watergate reporter Carl Bernstein of the *Washington Post*, explained that she had met Sagan at a luncheon of the newspaper's editorial board.) "I really want you to meet him," Ephron told Druyan. Druyan and Sagan finally met at Ephron's dinner party, a small but illustrious affair whose guests included Ann Druyan, Timothy Ferris, Carl and Linda Sagan, Lynda Obst and her then-husband David Obst, and the writers Taylor Branch and Frank Rich.

Two decades later, Druyan looks back on that "enchanted evening at Nora Ephron's." She and Sagan "talked about Communism, God, and baseball," Druyan recalls—three subjects not commonly associated. "And it was wonderful!" she says. "I remember Carl rolling on the rug, laughing uncontrollably at something I had said. This is three years before we ever were together in any nonsocial way. I thought, 'Gee, that guy has a great laugh. He really knows how to laugh.' . . . His sleeves were rolled up, he looked *so* handsome, laughing *so* hard. It was wonderful." What was he laughing about so merrily? "I don't know," she says, crinkling her nose. "For some reason, I think it had something to do with Leon Trotsky."[3]

SAGAN'S FRIENDS DISPUTE how comfortable he felt with women. Men tend to regard the grown-up Sagan as sexually naive, oblivious to the siren call of the hormones—he was not given to commenting, for example, when an attractive woman walked by. His friend Gentry Lee says, "I'm going to hazard a guess that Carl had probably not been to bed with more than two women other than the women he was married to. It simply never was a subject that he showed much interest in." Sagan never made sexual innuendos about women, or commented about their looks, or talked about sex at all. "Never! *Ever!*" says Lee.[4]

Despite his reticence about women when in the company of men, Sagan seems to have felt comfortable with women themselves. Women appreciated the quality of conversation they could have with him. They seem to have regarded him as the next best thing to a girlfriend. He eagerly discussed ideas with them as if they were men, patiently explained science to their children, and defended feminist stances with fervor. He was this way even as a teenager. Sagan's cousin Arlene Sagan remembers that when they were both young in the 1940s, she was amazed that he enthusiastically discussed with her their common interest, science fiction, although that was not generally viewed as a fit interest for a girl.[5] He took a sincere interest in the scientific careers of female colleagues (such as Carolyn Porco of the University of Arizona, now a leader on the *Cassini* mission to Saturn), and tried hard to boost their chances of making it in the male-dominated world of the physical sciences. This seems ironic, given his very traditional attitude toward his first two wives, to whom he left the responsibilities for housework and child-rearing. He was not the only middle-aged man of the 1970s torn between traditional family standards and emergent feminism. He was a man who would never cook a meal or make a bed, but he would write a *New York Times* article ridiculing the Miss Universe Contest and campaign to rename Venusian features after women. Under Druyan's tutelage, Sagan's feminism would become more consistent and fervent.

During their two decades together, Sagan also revealed an envy of something that many women have, something that many men of his generation lacked—a noncarnal intimacy with others, especially women. Ann Druyan recalls that Sagan envied her affectionate relationship with her friend Lynda Obst; the two women sometimes took off on adventures together, without Sagan. Druyan recalls him asking them plaintively: "Can I be a girlfriend, too?"[6]

Evidently, many women sensed this tenderness beneath the cool, imperturbable exterior of his public persona; they lusted for him. In his 1976 profile of Sagan for the *New Yorker*, Henry S. F. Cooper Jr. noted how Sagan spoke in Houston about Mars and ended by saying, smiling, "And if we go there we might have to listen to equally boring speeches," at which, Cooper said, "a tremendous, unladylike sigh filled the auditorium."[7] When Sagan was making *Cosmos* at KCET-TV in southern California, it was the duty of one of his assistants, Deane Rink, "to protect [Sagan] from women who somehow found out he was there, and wandered into the station and demanded to see him, convinced that he had been speaking to them personally and directly from his television set."[8] There was one especially sad case of a woman who tried to enter the set under a subterfuge, saying that she was a member of the *Cosmos* crew and that she had to see Sagan. As it turned out, she was a Pennsylvania resident who had had trouble applying to the Cornell graduate school, and she had written to Sagan to complain. He had responded thoughtfully, which she "had taken as a show of deep personal interest." And so here she was in southern California, far from home and trying to meet her fantasy man.[9]

Of all these admiring women, though, only one definitely caught Sagan's attention. Gentry Lee recalls being flabbergasted when Sagan, after a dinner where Druyan and Ferris were present, asked him "a somewhat elliptical question" about whether Lee thought Druyan had been attracted to him. "I was floored," Lee recalls. "It was the only time I ever thought he even understood a woman's flirtations."[10]

AT ABOUT THE SAME TIME, in 1977, Sagan began working on what might be called his grandest artistic project, the *Voyager* records. It is artistic in the sense that, like the *Pioneer* plaques, each record is a form of public art—launched into space with taxpayer dollars—and a symbolic grand statement (akin to statuary) of humanitarian values. The project is the ultimate time capsule, hurled into the galaxy where it will drift for millions of years, perhaps (although it is highly unlikely) to be recovered by aliens. If aliens do find it and decode its messages, they will see and hear (if they have eyes and ears) sounds, music, and images from the planet Earth of the 1970s: the hush of oceans, the cry of birds, the rock music of Chuck Berry, the image of a mother breast-feeding her baby.[11] The *Voyager* record's messages are very sweet, very soothing, akin to those heart-tugging television commercials by giant corporations eager to assert their humanity. The *Voyager* message gives no hint of humanity's potential for barbarity.

The project is also significant to Sagan's story because it brought him into regular contact with Ann Druyan, the woman who would change his life profoundly.

Sagan was a true liberal. The *Pioneer* plaque had triggered a minor wave of public criticism that it was pornographic, sexist, or ethnocentric. Sagan was troubled by these charges and decided to do better next time. A few years later, he organized a little group, mostly friends—his wife Linda Salzman, Timothy Ferris, Ann Druyan, Frank Drake, and the artist Jon Lomberg—to design a message for the *Voyager* probes, specifically, recordings of faces, voices, and music from representatives of a wide diversity of nations and ethnic groups. In retrospect, the record reflects the emerging egalitarian and multicultural spirit of late-twentieth-century America, during the dawn of modern feminism, the high noon of Third World assertiveness, and the afterglow of Martin Luther King Jr.'s civil rights activism.

The twin *Voyager* probes were scheduled for launch in 1977. Like the *Pioneers*, the *Voyagers* would pass by Jupiter and Saturn. Then, because of their great speed, the *Voyagers* would (also like the *Pioneers*) escape from the solar system into the galaxy.[12] What messages should be placed aboard them? Sagan expressed interest in sending selections of terrestrial music. The trouble was that a tape recording wouldn't last long enough. He and Frank Drake discussed the *Voyager* message further in January 1977, at the American Astronomical Society meeting in Honolulu, during which Drake and the Sagan family shared a cottage overlooking a dolphin pool at the Kahala Hilton Hotel.[13] Drake suggested that they send messages on the equivalent of a phonograph record. The grooves in the record could encode both images and music.[14] A company called Colorado Video "was willing to convert the pictures into sound on their equipment free of charge as a public service," Lomberg writes.[15] Some fifteen years earlier, Shklovskii had speculated that the Martian moons might contain "libraries and museums," relics of a vanished Martian civilization. Likewise, the *Voyager* record would be a sampling of terrestrial libraries and museums, launched into the Milky Way.

By this time, the mid-1970s, as Sagan entered his forties, he was becoming increasingly aware of his own feelings and those of others. *The Dragons of Eden* had been, in part, an attempt to grasp the nature of human emotion, previously as baffling to him as it was to *Star Trek*'s Mr. Spock. Sagan's marriage to Linda Salzman had helped loosen him up emotionally; so had marijuana. So when he began planning to send the *Voyager* record, he wanted it to include more than the usual scientific data, such as information about the location of Earth relative to neutron stars. He wanted it to say something about a facet of human culture far harder to express—feelings. As Lester Grinspoon told the journalist Roger Bingham a few years later, "I think Carl used to lead more with his intellect: now, he leads equally with his humanity. It's very impressive, the degree to which he's grown in this respect. . . . Carl is more and more comfortable with, more and more aware of human beings as other than carriers of cerebral cortices."[16]

In planning the *Voyager* record, Sagan wrote that "there is much more to human beings than perceiving and thinking. We are feeling creatures."[17] But human emotions would be difficult to explain to aliens. The best way to do so, he reasoned, would be through music.

But what kinds of music? Sagan had loved classical music since childhood. Its rational intricacy and structure appealed to the left side of his brain, while it nurtured the emotions lurking timorously within the right side. When young, his sister, Cari, had argued with her brother (she recalls) over a classical tune on the radio, which, she believes, he had identified as Rachmaninoff's Rhapsody on a Theme from Paganini and she as the same composer's Concerto in C Minor. It turned out that he was wrong and she was right, which thrilled her because "he was nearly always right about everything."[18] Sagan had studied the piano while young and, according to his friend Jon Lomberg, "loved the big, gooey piano concertos of Rachmaninoff, and his favorite piece of music of all time, he once told me, was the Russian Easter Overture by Rimsky-Korsakov."[19]

His colleagues on the *Voyager* record team, however, were more broad-minded. Of the many intellectual disputes they had in planning the record, their disagreements over music are the most characteristic of the 1960s and 1970s. The generation gap in music still yawned; parents still bellowed at their teens to "turn down that racket!" And Sagan made no bones about his distaste for pop music. In *Intelligent Life in the Universe*, he had referred to "the mindless outpourings of rock-and-roll stations."[20]

It was Druyan's idea to send Chuck Berry's music aboard the *Voyager*. She and Ferris played Berry's music for Sagan, who responded: "Sounds pretty awful."[21] But Druyan had a way of encouraging doubters to listen, really *listen* to what a musician was trying to say. Under Druyan's influence Sagan finally gave in—Chuck Berry would go to the stars. The decision paid off; it not only enriched the cultural diversity of the *Voyager* records, it also provided priceless publicity: *Saturday Night Live* ran a skit in which the aliens responded to Earth by saying, "Send more Chuck Berry!" Years later, at a Planetary Society celebration when Sagan was on stage, Berry showed up as the surprise guest, armed and ready with his guitar.[22] And in the long run, Sagan's own artistic sensibilities broadened. His sister, Cari, recalls him in his last years conversing with her daughter Sharon on the comparative merits of different rock groups.[23]

But other musical disputes loomed. Sagan was particularly concerned to avoid the charges of sexism and ethnocentrism that had clouded the launch of the *Pioneer* plaques. Different cultures have different musical traditions; which should be chosen to represent Earth? Recalls Ferris: "A lot of things were played that one or the other of us would say, 'Why are we listening to this crap?' and somebody else would say, 'Wait a minute. There's something here.' "[24]

Space was at a premium on the record; the more music they included, the lower the fidelity. To select pieces, they consulted with music experts and scoured music libraries and record stores. They were particularly helped in selecting music by Alan Lomax, who recorded and saved ethnic music.[25] They debated whether to send a Miles Davis version of Gershwin's "Summertime." "On the one hand," recalled Sagan (the civil rights activist who had been upset by accusations that the figures on the *Pioneer* plaque looked too "white"), "it was argued that this was a pleasing transcultural mixture of African and American musical motifs; but the position that carried the day was that the black tradition in America has been a major, if not the principal, source of important indigenous American music and should be presented without encumberment." One of the team's associates called the Smithsonian's jazz curator at 11 P.M. for advice; he responded: "Now, let's see if I got this straight. You're calling me up at home at eleven o'clock on a Sunday night to ask which jazz to send to the stars?"[26]

"At other times," Sagan recalled, "there were long debates on Gregorian chants, Charles Ives and Bob Dylan (would the music stand if the

words were incomprehensible?); whether we should include more than
one Bulgarian or Peruvian composition; . . . whether to include music
performed by alleged Nazi sympathizers," and so on. Should they send
Elvis Presley? Schoenberg? country-western music ("argued to be the
music most enjoyed by those who actually put together the nuts and
bolts of the spacecraft")?

NASA kept an eye on the development of the record, to ensure "that
no untoward sound or musical selection, no ditty that might embarrass
NASA, had been included."[27] Sagan recalled receiving "an agitated
phone call from a NASA associate administrator concerned that no Irish
music had been included. The Speaker of the House of
Representatives, it had suddenly been recalled, was of Irish descent, and
NASA was concerned not to give . . . offense. I had to explain that there
were many ethnic groups unfortunately unrepresented. There was, for
example, no Italian opera, or Jewish folk music."[28]

Even so, it was impossible to please everyone. The age of multicultural consciousness was dawning, and every major social group justly
refused to be passed over. If Captain Kirk could haul a multicultural
crew across the galaxy, then why couldn't the *Voyager*? Lomberg recalled
how, during dinner at a Cape Canaveral restaurant, after the team had
held a press conference to announce the contents of the *Voyager* record,
"an Italian-American NASA official . . . came to the table, intoxicated
enough to speak from the heart, and said, 'You put three German com-
posers on the Record and not one Italian one?' He gave us a gesture of
such forceful clarity that I wish we had put a photo of it on the Record as
an example of how humans communicate non-verbally."[29]

ANN DRUYAN WORKED TIRELESSLY on the record. Seeking a particular
piece of music from India, she looked all over New York City until she
hit the jackpot—in a carton under a card table in an Indian-owned appli-
ance store.[30] She and the group also tried to collect "sounds" of Earth,
in a manner so unsystematic it might have given an anthropologist fits.
Druyan recalled that she, Ferris, and a colleague, Wendy Gradison,
"joined the Sagans at their dining-room table for a vigorous round of
group onomatopoeia. We tried to think of every sound we'd ever heard,
and I wrote most of them down. On the following day I returned to New
York City and set about trying to locate the best examples of each." She
phoned "sound libraries and universities" across the continent, asking for
sounds of "the meanest hyenas" or "the most devastating earthquake,"
and going through a considerable ordeal each time to explain the purpose: "We're sending a record into interstellar space."[31] Some of the

people they contacted were enthusiastic, such as the whale researcher who offered the "most beautiful whale greeting," and the possessor of the recording of the "best rocket launch you ever heard."[32] Among other sounds: a wild dog's "lonely baying." Also: "We tested several roosters and crows, but they all sounded terribly stagy."[33]

Druyan also went to New York University Medical Center to have an electroencephalogram performed on herself, just in case "a highly advanced technology of several million years from now [could] decipher my thoughts."[34] The team tried a variety of different ways to mimic a kissing sound, and finally, reported Druyan, Ferris "kissed me softly on the cheek; it felt and sounded fine."

Linda Salzman Sagan described "sitting for hours, telephoning friends of friends who might know someone who could speak, let's say, the Chinese Wu dialect." Bishun Khare brought in Indian speakers.[35] The record supposedly represents more than 87 percent of Earth's languages.[36] Sagan brought his son Nick (then about six) to a studio to record the words "Hello from the children of planet Earth." Says Nick: "I had these weird fantasies about aliens coming [to Earth] and recognizing me by my voice."

Perhaps because of the cultural backlash against sending a picture of naked people aboard the *Pioneer*, NASA vetoed Sagan's plan to send an anatomically complete photo of a male and an obviously pregnant female on the *Voyager*. "There was no way," Sagan acknowledged, "that NASA was going to launch full frontal nudity to the stars."[37] So the picture was recorded in silhouette instead. (They did, however, include a photo of a Filipino mother breast-feeding her baby.) Druyan recalled that when the sound of the kiss was recorded, "we were under strict orders from NASA to keep it heterosexual."

To select the record's 118 pictures,[38] Lomberg recalled, "Wendy [Gradison] and I scoured the Cornell and local public libraries and amassed a stack of coffee-table and picture books that would have done credit to a major bookstore at Christmastime. *The History of Toys, Birds of North America, The Family of Man, Plant-Devouring Insects, The Age of Steam*, and a hundred others teetered in precarious racks alongside every issue of the *National Geographic* back to 1958." They also took their own photos of terrestrial life, sometimes with a whimsy reminiscent of the early Surrealists. Lomberg recalled how he and four others, seeking images of terrestrial food, descended on a supermarket: "With Frank in the lead, we began loading up carts with foods. . . . Predictably, the manager came over and politely asked what the hell we were doing. Frank did the talking, and while the rest of us tried to look appropriately serious, one of the world's great astronomers explained to a suspicious store manager that we wanted to send his supermarket to the stars."[39] Drake also took a picture of a plane taking off "on the runway of Syracuse airport, one jump ahead of the security guards."[40]

The team managed to assemble all this sound and imagery into the record, copies of which were placed aboard *Voyagers 1* and *2*. The records were made of copper and coated with gold.[41] "Each record contains 118 photographs of our planet, ourselves and our civilization" and "almost 90 minutes of the world's greatest music," Sagan and his colleagues wrote in *Murmurs of Earth*, their subsequent collection of essays about the making of the record.

In the rush to create what they hoped would be a record of lasting sociological and artistic merit, though, they made a nontrivial scientific goof. Harvard astronomer A. G. W. Cameron had suggested placing radioactive uranium and thorium, which decay over time at known rates (like little clocks), on the *Voyager* record. That way, anyone finding the probe would, by determining the ratios of isotopes and their decay products, be able to estimate how much time had passed since the probe's launch and gain valuable information about the history of our solar system. Unfortunately, they put on board samples that had been isotopically separated, which was costly and scientifically unnecessary for the first purpose and erased the necessary information for the second. As a result, Cameron lost some respect for Sagan as a scientist. "On the one hand, he was intellectually broad. But at the same time, he was scientifically shallow; he didn't really delve very deeply into things." The failure to handle the radioactive materials properly "was terribly stupid. That's what I mean about Carl being somewhat scientifically shallow."[42]

A far more serious question is whether the record grossly misrepresents the nature of human beings. "There were a few topics that we intentionally avoided," Lomberg later wrote. "We reached a consensus that we shouldn't present war, disease, crime, and poverty. . . . We decided that the worst in us needn't be sent across the galaxy."[43] Druyan did not agree; she did her best to convince the group to send tougher-minded imagery. In her effort to locate interesting sounds, she came across a particularly chilling example of the banality of human horror, of an Eichmann in the making: a World War I recording of a soldier, his voice "horribly cheerful and thoughtless," as he fired mustard-gas grenades.[44] But other group members feared that the aliens might misinterpret any ugly information, especially any with military connotations. Both Sagan and (at the time) Lomberg assumed that aliens would be not only technically but also morally superior; if we sent the "wrong" social messages, they might dismiss us as galactic riffraff and spurn further contact. Sagan recorded that the team debated this very subject "long and hard." Lomberg says, "We wanted to avoid any sort of political statement in this message, and a picture of Hiroshima or My Lai—

or of a noble or heroic warrior, for that matter—seemed more an ideological statement than an integral part of an image of Earth. Nor did we want any part of the message to seem threatening or hostile to recipients ('Look how tough *we* are'), which is why we didn't send a picture of a nuclear explosion."[45] The result is the cosmic equivalent of a Hallmark greeting card—all sweetness and light, but with no deep, dark truths.

The record's naïveté and pretensions to cultural universality deserve more scrutiny from critical theorists and cultural anthropologists. An important step toward a *Voyager* critique has been taken by the radical writer-artist Connie Samaras, an associate professor of studio art at the University of California at Irvine. In the 1997 anthology *Processed Lives: Gender and Technology in Everyday Life*, she complains that the Sagan team only pretended to be all-inclusive in representing world culture. In fact, she argues, the record is saturated with mainstream political prejudice. She writes:

> These two [*Voyager*] spacecraft, containing copper-etched images, writings and audio recordings as a salutary overview to "possible extraterrestrial civilizations," have currently reached our solar system's end and continue to purposefully travel on. Predictably erased are any vestiges of that era's social change movements e.g. civil rights, women's liberation, anti-war, lesbian/gay liberation, nuclear disarmament. The result is a privileging of elite white male American/Eurocentric culture where women's bodies are depicted as reproductive vessels, non-Western communities are timelessly portrayed as outside of technology and where whiteness and heterosexuality are naturalized because, once again, they are not commented upon. However, the Voyager selection team, headed by astronomer Carl Sagan, saw themselves as having made every attempt to be as rational and inclusive as possible.[46]

Ironists, rejoice: for all the team's efforts to present Earth's "best face to the cosmos," they blew it. The completed record includes a greeting to beings of space from the man who, at that time, was Secretary General of the United Nations. "I send greetings on behalf of the people of our planet. We step out of our solar system into the universe seeking only peace and friendship, to teach if we are called upon, to be taught if we are fortunate."[47] The man who uttered those words—whose voice now sails in recorded form into the galaxy—was Kurt Waldheim.

Afterward, press accounts revealed that Waldheim had been an officer during the war in a German unit guilty of war crimes (although he denied knowing anything of the crimes).[48] For all NASA's skittishness about sending "pornography" to the stars, for all the reluctance of Sagan and his colleagues to say anything unpleasant about Earth, they had just

unwittingly propelled into the heavens a greeting from a former agent of
Adolf Hitler.

AS THEY WORKED TOGETHER on the record, Sagan and Druyan grew
closer. She found herself thinking of him often. He was captivating—that
dark hair, those big dark eyes, that college grin, that good-humored
aplomb, that vision of boundless frontiers. She confided in her close
friend Lynda Obst, a *New York Times* editor for whom Tim Ferris had
written. "It was pure romance," recalls Obst, now a movie producer.[49]
Druyan felt guilty about falling in love with Sagan. After all, he was a
married man, his wife had become Druyan's friend, and Druyan was
committed to Ferris, who was Sagan's friend. The situation was reminiscent of a French sex comedy.

As Obst recalls, she "was Annie's confidante and I helped her through
the incredible guilt that she had in facing the fact that she was falling
in love with Carl, in terms of Linda [Salzman Sagan] and Nick, and in
terms of Tim [Ferris], all of whom she loved; she loved Linda as well.
She didn't see herself as the kind of person who was capable of hurting
people in this way." But Obst urged Druyan to pursue the relationship:
"I was the great enabler in that I just *believed* in love—I'd never seen love
like this before. . . . It's that classic argument: Is the great love worth
burning down the house for? [I argued to Annie that] the universe doesn't
give you this many opportunities; if you feel this way and you deny it,
it's toxic!"[50]

Sagan was thinking a lot about Druyan, too. Ann Druyan was a thin,
pretty brunette with long hair and smiling eyes. Her voice was soft and
alluring. Yet she was no plantation belle; she was a New York girl, a
would-be writer, and a strong and ambitious one. She was Jewish, born
to garment workers and raised in Queens, in a time and place that
encouraged dissidence rather than domesticity. Growing up in the 1950s
and 1960s, she saw the world tipped awry and decided to right it. She
was horrified at an early age by the prosecution of the Rosenbergs; later
she protested the war and surfed the early tides of feminism. As is true of
Gloria Steinem, Druyan's kindness, wit, and beauty made her feminist
convictions less offputting to men than they might have been.

Ann-Marcia Druyan (her legal name) is the granddaughter of Lat-
vian Orthodox Jews who emigrated to Stockholm, Sweden (via Den-
mark), at the turn of the century, then to the United States about 1916.
Druyan's father, Harry Druyan, is a New York University graduate who
at one time co-owned a New York knitware firm, Hercules-Carnation,
based at 1370 Broadway, that made women's sweaters. He and his wife,
Pearl (both still alive as of mid-1999), have two children: a boy, Les,

born in 1944, who is now a private investor living in Costa Rica; and Ann, born on June 13, 1949.

Druyan's politics grew out of her family life. Her childhood home could be characterized as "FDR liberal." (Druyan saw to it that the heroine of Sagan's novel, *Contact*, was named Eleanor after Eleanor Roosevelt, who was one of her personal heroes.)

"None of these people that I grew up with in Queens were rich people," Druyan recalls. "But they were all fanatical readers. My mother trained me to read the *New York Times* when I was five years old; she would expect me to be able to digest what I was reading there. . . . My father would read Shakespeare to me at night and tell me, 'That's the way you should learn to write.' " She and her father would put on little two-person Shakespeare plays, with her at the top of the stairs (as Juliet) and him at the bottom (as Romeo). Her mother "took me to museums every single week—to the Metropolitan, to the Frick Collection. . . . [E]very Thursday as I was growing up, I would get a penny for every painting I could identify. . . . It was a fantastic upbringing."

"When I was a very small child, my parents used to get *American Heritage*. . . . [One issue] contained an article on the Triangle Shirtwaist fire, which was a sweatshop in New York City [in 1911] . . . where 118 women were burned to death. *American Heritage* had these great photographs. And as a kid—I don't know why—I became obsessed with these images of these women, all in a row, burned up, lying beneath this twisted fire escape and there was a sign with a skull and crossbones saying, 'Killed for Greed.' "[51]

As she matured, she recalled, "I was much more attracted to more radical politics—to Leon Trotsky. To me, he's still one of the greatest historical writers of all time." She quoted a passage from his writings, one about how, despite all the misery he had been through (the murder of his children and grandchildren, and Stalin's efforts to kill him), the blue light still came through his window, and life was truly beautiful, and we should do all we can to ensure that every human being can live a full life. That's what politics is *for*.

Druyan backed up her political views with action. "I went to every major march on Washington. I was teargassed many times at Dupont Circle and various other places, over and over again. I completely thrived on that! I just loved getting in those buses and going to Washington . . . and I remember the community and the sense of exhilaration and the cute boys and the fun. Everything about it was sensational."[52]

Ann Druyan recalls her father and mother as being remarkably similar, personality-wise, to Carl Sagan's parents, Sam and Rachel. Like Sam Sagan, Harry Druyan was endearingly indulgent. "When I was fifteen," Ann Druyan says, "he came to me one day and [asked] me: Did I ever smoke marijuana? And I said 'Yes!' And he threw his hands up and said, 'Don't tell me about it until I'm older!' That was such a cool reaction." As for the mothers, "Rachel and Pearl were so bright and difficult to get along with and unbending—I don't think even [my mother] Pearl would argue with the notion of them being unbending," Ann Druyan says. She suspects that both women were "difficult" personalities because they were bright, well-read women (both superb writers) who, in those days, "had no acceptable means of expression because they were women. . . . They were born twenty to twenty-five years too early."

During those years, she was "in and out of NYU. I was not a good student. I was not a serious student at all." She was an English major, "but it wasn't until after I left school that I was really ready to *become* a student. . . . My attention span, I believe, was [previously] very limited. That was another thing that Carl gave me: a kind of discipline and rigor which I completely and totally lacked until I knew him. I was uncritical in my thinking; I believed whatever I wanted to believe, whatever felt good."

At the time Ann Druyan met Sagan, she was working on her first (and, to date, only) novel, under contract to a small publishing firm, Stonehill. (The book, a short fantasy titled *A Famous Broken Heart*, was published in 1977.) She also had a small inheritance from her mother's father that enabled her to live on her own. She was living at 10 West 74th Street, just off Central Park West, helping support herself with a variety of jobs. These included renting tape-recorded tours at the Metropolitan Museum of Art, clerking at Brentano's bookstore, and working at the State Department of Conservation, where she issued hunting and fishing licenses and "fielded calls from people in New Rochelle saying a deer was getting sick on their lawn."

Druyan was a vivacious, committed, and warm woman, and Sagan found her utterly charming. Immediately after the *Viking* landing, they met in the Russian Tea Room in New York City and chatted eagerly as always. As Druyan recalls, Sagan gazed into her eyes and confided that the best conversations he'd ever had with a woman were with her. "We always talked about ideas. He turned to me and said, 'You know, there's one thing that really bothers me about you. . . . I wish you were a man. . . . It would make life a lot easier for me." Her eyes widened in dismay. In retrospect, she says, "I realize that was the beginning of an overture, which I completely deflected."

On June 1, 1977—Druyan recalls the precise day—they confessed their love for each other. She was not quite twenty-eight; he was forty-two. At some point—the exact dates are hazy—Ferris learned what his friend Sagan was up to.

Sagan, Druyan, Ferris, and the others attended the launch of *Voyager 2* on August 20, 1977. "We kissed and embraced, and many of us cried," Sagan wrote.[53] Billions of years in the future, "our sun, then a distended red giant star, will have reduced Earth to a charred cinder. But the *Voyager* record will still be largely intact, in some other remote region of the Milky Way galaxy, preserving a murmur of an ancient civilization that once flourished—perhaps before moving on to greater deeds and other worlds—on the distant planet Earth."[54] Eventually, *Voyager 2* and *Voyager 1* will "orbit the massive center of the Milky Way galaxy once every quarter billion years, essentially forever."[55]

And after the team had achieved this great feat—had launched a greeting card where no greeting card had gone before—what would remain of their friendships, of their little Bloomsbury of the space age? Ferris's attitude toward Sagan was souring, and not just because of Sagan's involvement with Druyan. Though Ferris retained affection and respect for Sagan, he was tiring of what he viewed as Sagan's self-absorption, self-promotion, and pomposity.

During their years of close friendship, ever since Ferris had profiled Sagan for *Rolling Stone*, Ferris had watched Sagan's growing fame going to his head. Ferris began to see Sagan as an overly ambitious careerist. "I made a lot of jokes about his careerism," he recalls, "because he was the most energetic careerist I ever met, working full-time on enhancing his own fame every minute. I'm a careerist myself," Ferris admits, "but the dimensions of his [careerism] were so great." Ferris was also annoyed that Sagan refused to admit this about himself. "He thought of everything he did as for the good of science and humanity, and he thought of himself as self-effacing and not wanting to attract attention to himself."

Their relationship came to a head at the *Voyager* launch. Ferris and Sagan were walking and talking along the beach by the launch site; Sagan put his arm around Ferris's shoulder. Ferris decided then and there that he "wanted to get this guy out of my life. Something false had crept in." He raised his hand and removed Sagan's arm from his shoulder.[56]

"I learned Carl was involved with Annie long before Linda knew," Shirley Arden recalls. "I handled his personal bills and one day some telltale American Express bills crossed my desk that showed Carl paying for Annie's transportation. I quietly called it to his attention and suggested he be more careful if he was going to have a fling so that he would not hurt anyone unnecessarily.

"He told me he did not want to hurt anyone, but that he had fallen deeply in love with Annie. He said he was going to tell Linda when they went to Cape Cod and that Annie was going to tell Tim [Ferris] at the same time in New York City." He "asked me to be supportive of Linda and do what I could to help her during the difficult days ahead."

HAVING FALLEN IN LOVE with Ann Druyan, Sagan decided to end his marriage to Linda Salzman. But telling Linda wouldn't be easy. On a visit to Cambridge, he asked his close friend Lester Grinspoon to go for a walk. As they strolled through a local bird sanctuary, Sagan told Grinspoon about his relationship with Druyan. "Here I am, a married man," Sagan said, "and I've fallen in love with her." Grinspoon cautioned Sagan to be careful, for "romantic love was one of the two socially acceptable psychoses." (The other was adolescence.) "I urged him to let it sit for a bit," Grinspoon says. But Sagan was emphatic: Druyan was the woman for him. "Then he asked me to help break it to Linda."[57]

So fearful was Sagan of Salzman's reaction that he felt he needed allies. The Grinspoons had a place on Cape Cod, overlooking the ocean, and they let Sagan break the news to Linda there, in their presence, in August 1977. Lester's son David, then a teenager, was present. He recalls that during the Sagans' stay "the adults were always going off on these long, mysterious walks." Linda was upset; "Carl was Mr. Calm."[58]

After the initial shock, Linda calmed down enough to discuss a property settlement with Sagan. They wrote down their thoughts on a big yellow pad. According to Lester Grinspoon, Linda wanted to have another child with Sagan before they split, "and tried to make having a child with him part of the condition of the divorce. It sounded strange to us." Sagan didn't go along with that; otherwise, Grinspoon had the impression that Sagan "was agreeing to give her everything—to get the divorce so he could marry Annie."[59] (Linda Salzman declined to be interviewed for this book.)

That yellow pad caused legal troubles later. According to a slightly sarcastic report in the "People" column of the New York *Daily News* (January 25, 1979), Sagan and his wife Linda Salzman drafted the "separation settlement" in longhand in August 1977. "Then he and Linda signed it and separated when she went off to Ithaca with their son, Nicholas, . . . and [Sagan] moved into a bachelor's pad [in New York City]." But on January 24, 1979, the newspaper continued, "the expert on outer space had lawyers in Manhattan Supreme Court alleging that the agreement wasn't legal and he didn't have to abide by it. [He] asked Justice Irving Kirschenbaum to toss out a lawsuit by Linda, who charged that the astronomer failed to live up to the deal he penned. Linda's lawyers told our [reporter] Stewart Ain that it's a battle for the rights of women and wives."

According to Shirley Arden, "Linda was devastated when Carl told her that he was leaving her for Annie. She tried very hard in a number of ways to keep him from leaving. Carl felt so guilty. He was willing to do most anything to make Linda feel better except abandon Annie."

Sagan was very close to Nick, who was seven at this time, and Nick adored his dad. Now Sagan had to approach his third son, the child to whom he was closest, and announce that he was leaving Mommy for another woman. Carl and Linda "sat me down," Nick says, "and were very clear in telling me they loved me, and the fact they were splitting up didn't mean they didn't love me."

Nick was a bright little boy, and he responded with the solemnity of Solomon. He recalls: "I had been reading a children's book of Chinese parables. I proceeded to tell them two parables. . . . [One was a] story about a mother and father who are being bitten by mosquitoes every night. And the kid decides to sleep in the bed where they would normally sleep, so [he] sacrifices himself to be bitten by mosquitoes instead." Then Nick announced to them: "But I'm *not* going to do that, because we have mosquito netting and insect repellent." No doubt a long pause followed as his parents mulled this over.

Now in his late twenties, Nick reflects: "What a weird kid I was." As the divorce unfolded, he vowed to remain neutral. But beneath his Saganish imperturbability, he was obviously in torment. "I don't know if this is an actual memory or if it was just a dream: . . . [I] remember being downstairs and watching my mother upstairs and my dad downstairs by the door, and them yelling at each other. I don't know what they were yelling about.

"I either said, or just thought I said, 'What's wrong with you people?! Why can't you just *love* each other?'"

The fight—real or dreamed—ended with "my dad going out and slamming the door, and my mom slamming the door to the bedroom." Such was Nick's life as the marriage slowly expired, ending in long and costly litigation. "They were fighting a lot," Nick says. "I think that they both had fears of abandonment. I think that Dad feared abandonment because of Lynn [leaving him]; my mother fears abandonment because of her parents [dying early]. And at a certain point it became like a powder-keg and a match."[60]

BEHIND EVERY SUCCESSFUL MAN . . .

Linus Pauling worshiped his wife, Ava Helen. She had a profound social conscience and was politically more radical than he was. She helped guide him toward the overt antinuclear activism that won him the Nobel Peace Prize in 1962. Once in the early 1960s, he picketed the White House, then donned a tuxedo and strolled inside to have dinner with President Kennedy. Asked why he picketed, he replied: "To be worthy of the respect of my wife." Ava died in 1981, devastating him.

Five years later Sagan and Druyan dined with Pauling, whom Druyan recalls as "a grinning guy with this little hat askew." She mentioned Ava's name. Suddenly Pauling "started to weep. I felt like a total idiot." Through his sobs, he revealed the secret of his and Ava's six-decade happiness: "Nothing held back. No secrets. No lies."[61]

Sagan and Druyan had a love like that. Druyan became Sagan's Ava. She transformed him emotionally, intellectually, and politically.

"Annie is the best thing that ever happened to Carl," says Lynn Margulis. This is quite a tribute, coming from Sagan's first wife.[62] Her son Dorion, Sagan's oldest, concurs: "She's the best thing that ever happened to him. Even her nickname, I've seen in print, is Miss Bliss. And actually, when he was alive I felt much more comfortable talking to her than him. . . . Annie Druyan is like a celestial diplomat."[63]

How many women fall in love with a man and dream of transforming him into something better, only to be disappointed? Druyan was one of those who succeeded. "I think that it would be very difficult for most people to live with him," Dorion says. But Druyan had the "ability to see how he had been hurt, on an emotional or psychological level, and being able to be, you know, the Mother Teresa to his soul." Dorion suspects that Sagan and Druyan hit it off because they had a similar family history "of a very difficult mother and a very supportive, almost infinitely accepting, loving father. . . . I thought [Carl and Annie] were the same person, they were just different gender projections of a single multi-dimensional [being]."[64]

At least since his book *The Dragons of Eden*, with its speculations about the hostile twin superpowers of the cranium, Sagan had perhaps dreamed about finding his mythic missing part. In his marriage to Ann Druyan, he seems to have found that missing part.

DURING THEIR MARRIAGE, Druyan influenced Sagan's politics. She brought her more radical leftist perspective to his outlook. "My politics were always further left than Carl's," she recalls. One time they attended a talk at Cornell by a speaker who had recently written an article titled "The Triumph of Capitalism." Afterward, Druyan approached the speaker and asked if his next speech would be titled "The Triumph of Cocaine."[65] Sagan picked up on Druyan's ideas about economics, enough to irritate Dorion, who had come of age during the Reagan 1980s and regarded his wealthy father's criticisms of capitalism as hypocritical.[66]

As noted earlier, it is difficult to be both a political leftist and a space enthusiast. Druyan was fascinated by space, too, but her heart and political convictions kept tugging her earthward; and she tugged Sagan with her. She encouraged him to ponder more the fate of this little planet and its peoples—particularly his children, and especially Jeremy and Dorion, whom he often overlooked. "*Be* a father!'" she scolded him.

She was "a really strong influence on him to become a better father . . . to me and to all of his kids," Nick says. She also made him "very focused in reaching people around the world and in his family, and religious figures." Her credo was: "People over concepts."[67]

Druyan even charmed Sagan's mother, Rachel, that tough old bird who had pecked the first two wives half to death. Rachel was in her early seventies when Sagan told her the news: marriage number two was over. He loved Druyan and planned to marry her.

Rachel had met Druyan and knew what she was like. Rachel approached her and, almost humbly, offered her a family heirloom—a bonnet that Carl had worn as a baby. "I've been saving this all of Carl's life," she said, "because I was waiting for you."[68]

Evening was falling when Sagan gave the news to his father, Sam. Sam had been a heavy smoker and had spent much of his life in the fiber-filled atmosphere of the garment industry; now he had lung cancer, and his time was short. He was adjusting the venetian blinds as Sagan entered the room. "Dad," Sagan said, "I've got something to tell you. Linda and I are going to get a divorce—because I've fallen in love with someone else."

Sam didn't turn around; he continued to watch the gathering dusk. "Well," he said, "I hope it's Annie Druyan."[69]

13

Cosmos

THE *COSMOS* TELEVISION SERIES is the achievement that finally fixed Carl Sagan's place in the celebrity firmament. With assistance from Druyan and others, Sagan told the saga of our universe—"The Cosmos is all that is or ever was or ever will be."[1] The thirteen-part series was eventually seen by more than four hundred million people and became a spectacularly successful book (it is still in print as of this writing). It inspired countless teenagers to consider science careers. Most significantly for Sagan, *Cosmos* provided the celebrity status that later allowed him to challenge the revival of cold war militarism, which he and many others believed threatened terrestrial life. The series was the climax of his ascent to fame, even to iconic status in North American culture, making his face immediately recognizable to millions of viewers. Sagan's on-screen persona was compelling. He addressed the audience as a magician might in setting up a spectacular trick. With his strangely halting yet melodic voice, he came across as an entrancing visionary who could reveal the marvels of the universe, from the smallest grain of sand to the most distant stars. One journalist commented that Sagan's "face combines hauteur, sensuality, and a winning boyishness—a pleasing amalgam of Rudolph Nureyev and George Plimpton."[2]

The man who set Sagan on the road to *Cosmos* was Gentry Lee, his associate from the *Viking* missions. Like Sagan, he was flummoxed by the vacillating reaction of the public and the press to the missions. "I was concerned about the lack of scientific knowledge and curiosity in most of the press covering the *Viking* mission," he recalled. "But I was equally appalled by the scientists, most of whom made no effort whatsoever to communicate the excitement and wonder of *Viking* in accessible terms that could be appreciated by the average intelligent reader."[3]

So in October 1976, a month after the second *Viking* landing, Lee approached Sagan on the steps of Von Karman Auditorium at Caltech's

Jet Propulsion Laboratory in Pasadena. Lee told Sagan that they should set up a private company to make television shows and movies about science. Sagan demanded: "How are we going to do that?" Lee responded: "Leave the details of the business to me." Their firm would bear the name Carl Sagan Productions (the same name Sagan had planned to use, then decided not to, on his WUCB radio script a quarter of a century earlier). "I wanted Carl Sagan Productions to become the Walt Disney of science and technology," Lee says. Lee wanted to share "the excitement and wonder" of space with the public. Sagan, he said, "was very wary. Carl was not, and never could have been, associated with organizing large tasks. It's just not the way his mind works."[4]

Sagan's wariness is understandable for another reason. He had always been scornful of television. In speeches, he drew laughs by ruefully pointing out that humans had already unwittingly transmitted their first electromagnetic greetings to the stars—television images of Roy Cohn, the Beverly Hillbillies, and the like. Yet Sagan knew that television was essential to persuade the masses of the value of scientific exploration. By the time Lee approached him, Sagan had already appeared on television many times, including numerous appearances on the Carson show. He had narrated a 1969 BBC television show about science, tried to develop a space series with producer David Wolper (it never came to pass), and been asked to host at least one other series in 1975.[5] His office records of the mid-1970s are full of references to phone calls from television executives such as Joan Cooney (of the Children's Television Workshop). He also began working with Francis Ford Coppola to develop a TV movie about the discovery of extraterrestrial life.[6] The networks excitedly covered the astronaut missions of the 1960s but tended to downplay the robotic missions of the 1970s. This deeply upset Sagan. (He later blasted the networks' "tepid depiction" of the *Viking* missions of the mid-1970s to Mars.[7]) He was convinced that the average viewer would thrill to the *Vikings*' imagery if the media ballyhooed it as much as they ballyhooed, say, their latest sitcoms or police dramas. British journalist Roger Bingham identified Sagan's basic faith: that "the viewing public is simply not as dumb as the television network planners seem to believe."[8]

Sagan also believed that television coverage of science could lure the public away from its unhealthy fascination with pseudoscience and irrational belief systems. Pseudoscience promoted lazy thinking, unsuitable in a democracy where laypeople had to make decisions affecting their government's future actions. Yet by the late twentieth century, the most scientific epoch in history, television was like an anthropologist's fever dream: a cornucopia of inanity, including political campaigns that sold candidates like detergent, advertising that propagandized for often useless or dangerous products, fantasy and science-fiction shows that dismissed scientific accuracy as an elitist fetish, and news coverage that rarely questioned government edicts about foreign and military policy. Television was Freud's id writ large (and underwritten by giant advertisers). Whatever happened to the dream of television as an educational tool for the masses?

So Sagan and Lee formed Carl Sagan Productions. On October 25, 1976, Sagan received the following note from his secretary, regarding a call from KCET-TV in Los Angeles:

> Greg Andorfer, Manager of Program Development for KCET, would like to speak with you to see if you would be interested in acting as host-presenter to a series of 13 one-hour presentations entitled "The Heavens," along the lines of Bronowski's "Ascent of Man." This would be for PBS Network. The series would explore man's responsibility to explore the unknown.[9]

Sagan wrote back on October 31, expressing an interest in the project.[10] He and Lee reached an agreement with KCET to develop a thirteen-part series that would air in the autumn of 1980. The series would mimic Jacob Bronowski's series *The Ascent of Man* in trying to present its host's unitary vision of life, science, and society.

"On December 26, 1976," Gentry Lee recalls, "Carl and I outlined a thirteen-part series sitting around my swimming pool in La Canada one block from the Angeles National Forest."[11] It was originally called *Man and the Cosmos*. Sagan liked to have good friends working around him. So he called on old friends and associates, among them Steven Soter and Don Goldsmith. Another person hired for the *Cosmos* staff was Deane Rink, the former SDSer who had shared a joint with Sagan at his Ithaca home many years earlier.[12]

Sagan, Druyan, and his long-time secretary Shirley Arden moved to Los Angeles for the venture. They had no idea what a difficult journey they were undertaking.

SAGAN AND LEE SCOUTED for a director. After interviewing candidates, they selected the British director Adrian Malone. Malone's star then shone brightly: he had recently directed the fabulously successful Bronowski series, which Sagan had admired (he quoted Bronowski on both the opening and the closing pages of *The Dragons of Eden*).[13] *The Ascent of Man* won an Emmy award for best documentary program and the Screen Writers Guild Award for best television program, plus the

Silver Award for best documentary from the Royal Television Society in Britain.

Sagan's secretary Shirley Arden recalls how in her first meeting with Malone he expressed great ambitions for the show, and for Sagan. He took her aside at one point and "what sticks in my mind," she recalls, "is how he told me he intended to 'make Carl a star,' and his fierce intensity when he told me he would require my full cooperation to accomplish this mission. That was the beginning of a rocky ride for the four of us."[14]

Of Malone, Lee says: "I liked him. He was voluble, funny, full of energy—egotistical, yes, but I'd had all this experience dealing with software designers who were the most egotistical persons on the planet." Malone "would always tell me he was from the inner city of London. A striver." Malone seemed to be saying, "I'm smarter than anybody and I've got to do everything to prove it."[15] What Sagan did not sufficiently heed was that Malone had been not simply director of *The Ascent of Man* but also its coauthor and perhaps expected to play a similarly creative role on *Cosmos*. But Sagan was someone who liked to control *everything*. Trouble lay ahead.

Still, at the beginning, Malone and Sagan "got along very well," Soter recalls. Everyone was excited to be working with two such talented people on such a glamorous project (three really: David Morrison thinks that besides Jim Pollack, Gentry Lee was the smartest person Sagan ever worked with). How could it lose? "Later on," Soter adds, "there were difficulties I never imagined."[16]

THE MIDLIFE CRISIS is a mythic transition in the life of the American male. For years one has dedicated oneself to work, career, climbing the ladder of success. And suddenly, in one's forties, comes disillusionment, as reliably as wrinkles and abdominal bulge. One looks in the mirror one morning and sees a stranger, an aging man with hollowed-out eyes, and wonders: Is this my life? Is this what I dreamed about when I was young? Panic ensues. Then may come irrational purchases and pursuits—the sports car, the solo hike through the Yukon, the passionate affair. Carl Sagan had always been a devoted careerist. He had put his work and achievement ahead of everything, including family. Hence, to anyone who knew him well, it would have been inconceivable that as work began on the *Cosmos* project—the most important undertaking to date in his career—he would have risked the whole endeavor to run off on a romantic getaway. But that is precisely what he did.

The opening week of the *Cosmos* production, its star was absent. Sagan was on a trip to Paris with Ann Druyan.[17] Malone was furious. He had assembled the entire production team and had scheduled meetings to go over the content. Sagan's presence was vital; he was not only the star but the creative and intellectual core of *Cosmos*. But in classic midlife crisis fashion, Sagan, the consummate careerist, had thrown caution to the winds and was letting himself live a little. He was madly in love and he was letting it show. "This was the first time that Carl was really, thoroughly, and completely in love. This was the first time he really knew what love *was*," recalls Steven Soter. His past marriages "had not been an intense passion—he [later] told me that. [After meeting Annie,] he told me that he now understood what the intensity of love was about. This was a revelation to him. He was glowing. His life was transformed by it. It was the most intense thing I've ever seen."[18]

The torrid passion between Sagan and Druyan amazed their friends and family. Even a decade after they met, they were so passionately playful in the presence of Druyan's dad, Harry Druyan, that he commented: "It's too hot not to cool down."[19] Gentry Lee would later have serious differences with Druyan, but around her, he acknowledges, Sagan "seemed much happier." In terms of his personal happiness, "there is no question that Annie was the greatest thing that ever happened to him. She was his fantasy woman. He was totally blinded by her love and affection."[20] During the making of *Cosmos*, British journalist Roger Bingham observed that Sagan was "a paradoxically private individual." When Bingham pushed him to reveal something about himself personally, Sagan finally offered one observation: "I would be most happy if you would say that I am deeply in love with Annie."[21]

Sagan saw to it that Druyan, who had a small amount of published writing to her credit, was added to the *Cosmos* writing staff. Creative collaborations tend to be tense, because of both time pressures and the difficulties inherent in weaving competing individual visions into a seamless whole. Typically a love affair between two members of the team enhances both the tensions and the creative output. That was the case with *Cosmos*.

On the one hand, Druyan's presence and input seemed to bolster Sagan's confidence and energy. Gentry Lee recalls that "her contribution to his stamina, attitude, and overall dedication to the task was monumental. He liked having Annie as his window on the world.[22] With Annie by his side, Carl was more energetic, happier, and less difficult." By some accounts, Druyan made many significant contributions to the script of the series. She shrewdly suggested making one of the heroes of the series the ancient female scientist Hypatia.[23] Having been schooled in the classics at Chicago, Sagan was receptive, and the result was one of the most compelling historical figures of the series, a role model for young women interested in science and an anticipation of the heroine of Sagan's novel, *Contact*.

Partly because of Sagan's own hectic schedule, much of the script-writing was done at the last minute. For example, at one point the team was trying to produce the episode on the life of the seventeenth-century astronomer Johannes Kepler. Scriptwriting and filming were sometimes asynchronous because different teams did each. As it turned out, the footage for the show about Kepler had already been shot; now Steve Soter and Druyan, working together, had to write a script to fit the footage. Working with Druyan "was quite wonderful," Soter recalls. "She was very perceptive and just a very good judge of human nature, and very, very creative. She would find all kinds of neat solutions to things."[24] Druyan also pointed out to Sagan that the original working title for the series, *Man and the Cosmos*, was sexist, and it was changed to *Cosmos*.[25]

On the other hand, Druyan's influence on Sagan and the series also caused some resentment. Gentry Lee felt that Sagan relied too exclusively on Druyan's judgment. He describes Sagan's reliance on Druyan as "addictive dependence." And he says that "she became his interpreter of nonscientific things. I think he felt he was not as good at reading people as she was."[26]

Indeed, he was not, and on the *Cosmos* set, the off-putting qualities of Sagan's personality—perhaps due to the enormous pressure he felt—grew pronounced. Lee had long familiarity with Sagan's abrasiveness, which was often completely unwitting, a result of his insensitivity to social niceties. Lee notes, for example, how Sagan would offend KCET staffers by implying that they didn't know what they were doing—once, for example, he told the lighting staffer, "I don't think the lighting's right." "Carl found himself startled by other people's responses to him because he did not . . . tune into what other people were saying," Lee recalls. "When I would explain to him that he had irritated somebody on *Cosmos*—had said something that was demotivating rather than motivating—he would look astounded." Sagan "would go into what we called his 'Delphic oracle' mode," recalls Lee, "when he'd seem to be saying, 'O hear me, you of little ability.' When Carl was in his Delphic oracle mode, he knew everything about *everything*." Originally, Lee would kid Sagan about this—and Sagan would laugh. But as shooting progressed and strains built, Sagan seemed to lose his sense of humor and became increasingly brusque, even petulant at times. "When he [Carl] would become angry, he would use his command of the language to belittle people in the most logic-chopping way," Lee recalls. Sometimes he resorted to "nuance and sarcasm" to cast aspersions on others' ideas. But "it's important to relate in his defense," Lee adds, "that he did not belittle somebody ad hominem. He didn't call someone an asshole, for example. [Rather], he would belittle the work as 'inadequate.'"[27]

Sagan was not, however, the only member of the *Cosmos* team with a healthy ego. Adrian Malone was a highly successful television director, a winner of awards. He expected to exercise a great deal of control over the series, and it was inevitable that he and Sagan would rub each other the wrong way. For one thing, Malone never quite got over Sagan's initial display of unprofessionalism—his decision to cavort around Paris instead of showing up for the first production meeting. During the making of *Cosmos*, both Sagan and Malone complained about each other repeatedly to Lee, "and neither," Lee says, "was right. They both thought they knew everything." During the shooting of the opening scene on the idyllic, flower-dappled cliffs at Monterey, California, both Sagan and Malone became so angry that they wanted to fire each other. But they couldn't: Lee had presciently specified in their contracts that neither could fire the other. Both of them called Lee "in the middle of the night" to complain about the other. Why? "Insufficient obeisance," Lee says, laughing. "It was typical of the kinds of disputes that existed on the set. For the whole last part of shooting, they wouldn't speak to each other."[28]

As Soter recalls, "It got to the point where they were not on speaking terms. Necessary communications were written or [passed] between intermediaries." Adrian Malone did not hesitate to reveal his growing irritation with Sagan. Speaking to journalist Roger Bingham, he said: "[Sagan is] a very literal man, you know—he likes to see the wounds in the hands before he believes—I think he's someone who focuses the laser on a certain area and devours it, focuses on another area and devours it. That makes—probably at the age of 95—an extremely well-balanced, educated, grand-tour human being. In the process, however, it makes for a lot of imbalances."[29] The bad relations between Malone and Sagan continued when the show traveled around the world to shoot scenes in different locations—Greece, India, England. Druyan came along for the world tour and did what she could to smooth relations between Sagan and Malone. Despite her "warm human sensitivity . . . the one breach that she couldn't overcome was that between Adrian and Carl," Soter says.[30] Druyan now says: "Adrian was brilliant; he had so much to contribute. But you couldn't make friends with him."

This clash of personalities was fueled by anxiety. Sagan had everything at stake: it would be his face on the television screen, not Malone's. Sagan knew his reputation might stand or fall based on *Cosmos*. Bingham, who visited the set, reported on production stresses exemplified by "some of Sagan's more obvious displacement activities—extravagant throat-clearing before takes, fussiness about the placing of the cue-card light, the way he 'constantly delves into other people's jobs,' as one of the team puts it. Sagan is a man who likes to be in control."[31]

Sagan's desire for control, in fact, led to a *Cosmos* crisis halfway through the project. He was swamped by work—the show, writing projects, residual Cornell duties, editing *Icarus*, litigating the end of his second marriage. Yet, like a paranoid CEO, he was unwilling to delegate authority to others. Consider the following comments from a memo in which Shirley Arden reports on a call she received from Gentry Lee, dated February 27, 1979. It shows that the stresses on the production—then at its halfway point—were driving it close to collapse.

> Gentry says you told him you were going to prepare a list of issues you feel need to be discussed. He asks (strongly) that your list contain only generic issues, no personal ones. . . .
>
> [The staff] *all* want *Cosmos* to go forward. But the hangup is their belief that you are holding on to authority in areas where you have no *time* or *energy* to do it. (Note that they do not question your ability to do it, only time and energy.)
>
> . . . Gentry feels we can all work together—your help is badly needed to assure the team that you will give them authority where they need it and are qualified to carry it through. . . .
>
> Gentry feels a compromise can be brokered *IF* there is evidence on your part that you believe the people are competent and that you are willing to give them written/verbal—in any case, *clear*, authority in areas where you will not have time to participate.[32]

Arden, the loyal secretary, was an emotional Rock of Gibraltar. She talked Sagan and Druyan through the crisis period, at one point sending them this message (in uppercase to emphasize her point): "I MISS YOU BOTH VERY MUCH. KEEP UP YOUR COSMOS HEAD OF STEAM AND REMEMBER, IT IS FOR THE AGES—AND ESPECIALLY FOR THE CHILDREN."[33] (Arden's support meant so much to Sagan and Druyan that later, in 1985, they dedicated their book *Comet* to her.)

Not all of Sagan's imperiousness during the filming of *Cosmos* can be attributed to the stresses of the production. His friends and family tell plenty of stories that reveal he could be overbearing and witheringly arrogant in plenty of other, less stressful situations. One time, for example, when he, Ann Druyan, and Gentry Lee were having dinner at a Chinese restaurant, Lee recalls, "He was very particular about the way he wanted his iced tea served, among other things." Sagan was unhappy with the service, and "when he confronted the waitress about her mistakes, she was not apologetic, and became hostile when Carl felt compelled to badger her." Sagan decided the woman was an idiot. "The bill was $49.43," Lee recalls, "and he left her a 57-cent tip." When Lee asked why he didn't just leave her nothing, Sagan replied that by leaving only 57 cents, "then she'll *know* I think she's a fool."[34] Lester Grinspoon's son, David, to whom "Uncle Carl" had once told bedtime stories, recalls how at hotels Sagan "would throw temper tantrums if he didn't get the presidential suite. I saw him be very abusive to waiters in restaurants." Once, at the Beverly Hilton, David saw him address a waiter "in a stern, angry voice" because he had brought one container of salad dressing instead of two. "Everybody in the room was aware of the severity of it."[35]

This same imperiousness regularly appeared on the set of *Cosmos.* Fortunately, Donald Goldsmith recalls, "Someone discovered that Carl had a chocolate fixation, . . . and if you gave him a bowl of chocolate pudding, the whole situation became much better."[36]

Sagan's insistence on quality hotel rooms—even on receiving his favorite brand of chocolate milk—irritated some observers. "People that didn't know him may have thought he was just being a prima donna," acknowledges one of the show's creators, Geoff Haines-Stiles. In reality, he says, Sagan was right to insist on such perks, because they were clearly essential to his creativity. Haines-Stiles realized this after observing how excruciatingly hard Sagan worked: "I saw how hard he pushed himself. . . . he would worry away until he got the right word." Haines-Stiles watched in astonishment and excitement as Sagan and Steve Soter (himself a trained planetary scientist) interrupted a scriptwriting session to "calculate, literally on the back of an envelope, the amount of oxygen in a planetary moon's atmosphere. . . . [Sagan] was absolutely committed to getting the science right, an incredibly finicky editor." Haines-Stiles concluded that if, in order to help Sagan complete making the show, "it took the right ambience with the right hotel and the right chocolate milk, then that was it."[37]

THE ATMOSPHERE ON THE SET was at times magical. Among the show's notable effects was one showing Sagan "walking through" the famed library in ancient Alexandria, Egypt. The "library" was actually a miniature, intricately designed. Nowadays, digital technologies could readily overlap Sagan's image with that of the miniature. But in the late 1970s, special effects experts used a system called Magicam, in which two cameras, one photographing the library and the other photographing Sagan, were closely synchronized. Computers allowed the image of Sagan to be blended into the miniature of the library to create the illusion that Sagan was actually walking through it.[38]

Nick Sagan, then about nine years old, recalls going to KCET and seeing the models of planets that the camera was going to swoop down upon. He also watched his father do the voice-overs for the show. For

Nick, the sight of TV-making in action was "pivotal": eventually, he would establish a career for himself in television.[39]

For Deane Rink, working on *Cosmos* was an intellectual treat. Each of the thirteen episodes had to be thoroughly researched. Thanks to Sagan's international reputation, Rink had no trouble arranging interviews with experts to consult on issues ranging from astronomy to evolution to archeology.

The tight deadlines were a source of stress, though. "The demands of doing the series, writing the companion book, dealing with the media, and still keeping his hand in at Cornell's Laboratory for Planetary [Studies] took its toll on Carl," Rink says. "He was a gaunter, more somber individual at series' end. . . . He had come under fire for not meeting his deadlines," so he pushed himself and others to work, work, work. "He frayed some people's nerves in the process, including mine." Rink says Soter's and Druyan's "protean efforts" made all the difference between success and failure.

At one point, Sagan hired Rink for a particular task and promised to get the necessary material to him by a certain time. It didn't arrive, so Rink accepted an offer of a new job elsewhere. When Sagan learned that Rink was leaving, "he acted like a petulant child who was denied something he wanted and thought he deserved." That ended the friendship. "The fact that I had completed perhaps three-quarters of the required work meant nothing. I was drummed out of the Carl Sagan Productions camp and was stunned, when the book [version of *Cosmos*] was released, to find that my work was not credited, my efforts not acknowledged."[40]

Sagan never fully lost his temper, according to Steven Soter. "He was never out of control. Never. But sometimes he was clearly angry." Sagan was juggling an amazing number of responsibilities at the time that *Cosmos* was being made. "I never understood how he could do so many things," Soter comments. "He had an enormous library—thousands and thousands of books—and you could pull almost any one off the shelf, and it had been annotated by Carl!"[41]

The amount of responsibility that Sagan was trying to juggle at this time was, in fact, staggering. For example, NASA continued to face repeated assaults on its budget for robotic space missions, and the agency saw Sagan, the nation's best-known space scientist, as its savior. His office files show that while making *Cosmos* he received a number of requests from agency backers to lobby Congress on behalf of NASA's budget.[42] Meanwhile, at Cornell, his old colleagues struggled to get in touch with him, to get him to deal with student matters and to edit leftover articles for *Icarus*. They weren't even sure when he would return from the land of palm trees and beaches to the snow-ringed Finger Lakes. Some wondered if he would return at all. Rumors of wild Hollywood parties circulated through the planetary science community. (By the standards of your average college astronomy department, they probably *were* pretty wild.) At one point, when Sagan was working on the film *Contact*, producer Lynda Obst decided to introduce him to Hollywood by throwing him a party. Bianca Jagger was among the guests. Obst laughs to recall one particularly attractive—but uninformed—party girl who leafed through a collection of space photos taken by a *Voyager* probe and asked Sagan: "These are great—did you take these?"[43]

The old envies at Cornell turned to jealousy and resentment. Despite all the publicity that Sagan had brought to Cornell, some professors grumbled that he didn't fulfill anywhere near his just teaching load. An effort was made to move Sagan's laboratory—where Bishun Khare worked to simulate alien atmospheres—off campus, to a building at the Ithaca airport. (The lab stayed on campus.)[44] In later years, a campus newspaper played on Sagan's reputation for absenteeism by sponsoring a contest called "I Touched Carl Sagan." And an apocryphal story held that Sagan agreed to address a local fraternity if it paid him a whopping fee, to which the frat boys responded by erecting a banner that read: FUCK YOU CARL.[45]

SAGAN'S CAREER STRESSES made *Cosmos* grueling, and his personal crises made it worse. His divorce from Linda Salzman mutated from a sad squabble into expensive courtroom maneuverings. It was a "bitter, bitter divorce," Nick Sagan says. Linda felt abandoned by Sagan and "very hurt and betrayed" by Druyan, who had been a trusted friend. Linda fought tenaciously for recompense.[46]

For Sagan's part, he showed he had truly "gone Hollywood" by his choice of a lawyer—Marvin Mitchelson.[47] A flamboyant headline grabber who represented glitterati including Michelle Triola Marvin in her "palimony" suit against actor Lee Marvin, Mitchelson represented Sagan in the divorce proceedings, which dragged on for years and consumed small fortunes from both parties.

Nick Sagan recalls that "they fought over money a lot. My mother's attitude was that he was being very withholding and trying to starve her and me. And my father's attitude was that he was paying a lot of money and then she would take that money and spend it on lawyers instead of on me . . . [and that she was taking] a scorched-earth policy. . . . She did things to delay the divorce. . . . She had her abandonment issues and he had his abandonment issues. . . . There was a lot of blame to be passed around."

As in many divorces, these money battles became astonishingly petty. "I remember my Mom coaching me to ask my Dad for, like, an extra ten dollars a week for computer lessons," Nick recalls. His father agreed to do it, but he said he would deduct it if the money was passed on to Linda. "Just ten dollars! My mother thought that was incredibly cheap, a hurtful sort of thing to do."[48]

The other emotional stress in Sagan's life at this time involved his father Sam's battle with lung cancer. Sagan arranged for his parents to move out to southern California so that Sam could receive treatment at a Los Angeles hospital. During Sam's declining days, Sagan repeatedly interrupted his work on *Cosmos* to be with his father in the hospital. The stress was also painful for Rachel, who became increasingly unglued as her husband's end neared; at one point she was so distraught that she wildly threatened to "run away," and on another occasion she said she'd shoot the doctors if her husband died. Sam died in late 1979, when Carl Sagan was forty-five. Sam's passing had a lasting impact on Sagan, ending his access to the one person who had given him unreserved love without the accompanying wackiness and bile that were Rachel's stock in trade. Several years later, Sagan would memorialize the loss of his father in his novel, *Contact*, in which Sagan's fictional alter ego, Ellie Arroway, is stricken by the death of her father. And when Sagan and Druyan had a little boy, they would name him Samuel.

Shirley Arden recalls how sad Sagan was after his father died. Later, after Sagan received a medal, she told him that his father was "looking down and smiling" on Sagan because he was so proud of his boy. "Carl looked me squarely in the eye," Arden says, "and said, 'Shirl, I'd give anything if I could believe that.' There was a very human yearning to connect with a loved one after death."

The end of Sam's long suffering did not entirely ease the strain on Sagan, for now his mother, having lost a husband of almost a half-century, needed all the attention she could get. For all her tough-mindedness, she couldn't manage everyday life by herself; for example, she couldn't drive a car or balance a checkbook, her daughter, Cari, recalls. She stayed for a while in Ithaca, before returning to Florida. Shirley Arden did what she could to help Rachel cope. For example, Arden explained to Rachel how to read her credit-card bill.[49]

DESPITE ALL THE STRESSES on the production, *Cosmos* came together steadily, and in the end, Gentry Lee says, everyone involved was proud of it, "with the possible exception of Adrian Malone." (Malone did not respond to requests for an interview.) Toward the end, Malone, speaking to Gentry Lee, said over and over: "This is his [Sagan's] show. Not my show."[50]

The first episode of *Cosmos* was scheduled to broadcast on Sunday, September 28, 1980. A big media campaign (big by PBS standards) preceded it. The news media received a fat promotional package touting the show as "the culmination of almost two years of filming and videotaping at more than forty locations around the world and more than three years of planning and executing exciting and scrupulously accurate special effects." Wonders of the universe "will be seen through the window of the specially-designed 'spaceship of the imagination.' Free of hardware or gadgetry, the spaceship, with its translucent skin and control panel of colorful spectral crystals, travels near the speed of light as Dr. Sagan takes viewers to realms previously known only by telescopes and robot explorers."[51]

The show used clever and occasionally spectacular visual effects to make important points. For example, Sagan compared the brevity of human history to the age of the solar system by unfurling a "cosmic calendar." According to the "calendar," if the age of the cosmos equaled a year, then modern humanity's duration has been only a fraction of a second before the end of the last day of that year. Not all the show's "visuals" worked aesthetically, though. Sagan was repeatedly depicted cruising the universe in a vehicle that was supposed to be a starship, but the interior of the ship more closely resembled that of a modernistic cathedral. Occasionally, Sagan was shown waving his hands mysteriously over what appeared to be some kind of control panel on the ship while a New Age–style musical score played languidly in the background. The pace was occasionally sluggish, even boring. Yet in thirteen episodes, Sagan managed to cram in discussions on numerous scientific topics such as the evolution of terrestrial life, asteroid and cometary impacts, the history of theories of Martian life, the emergence of mathematics among the ancient Pythagoreans, the possibility of interstellar flight, the nature of the human brain, the hope of detecting alien radio signals, and the threat of global self-annihilation.

The publicity worked wonders, and the premiere of *Cosmos* was a media event. A few weeks after the first episode, Sagan appeared on the cover of *Time* magazine in a composite photograph showing him standing on the "shores" of the galaxy, next to the headline "Showman of Science." The *Time* article, by science writer Frederic Golden, called Sagan "the prince of popularizers, the nation's scientific mentor to the masses." To that majority of Americans who had never heard of Sagan before *Cosmos*, Golden made him sound refreshingly sexy for a scientist: "In the casualness of turtleneck jersey and chino pants, his butcher-boy haircut tousled by the wind, Sagan sends out an exuberant message: science is not only vital for humanity's future well-being, but it is rousing good fun as well."

But Golden also put his finger on why many scientists were less than enamored of Sagan. Even some of Sagan's scientific supporters had to admit that he didn't have the patience for serious experimental research,

Golden noted. "Nor has he come close," Golden wrote, "to the kind of breakthrough work that wins Nobel Prizes."

"Watching with wonder—and no doubt a little envy—the whirling star named Sagan," Golden commented, "some of his colleagues feel that he has stepped beyond the bounds of science. They complain that he is driven by ego. They also say he tends to overstate his case, often fails to give proper credit to other scientists for their work and blurs the line between fact and speculation."

The reception of *Cosmos* thus stirred up, in an unprecedently public way, all of the old scientific controversies over Sagan. On the one hand, the phenomenal commercial success of the series—reputedly the most successful PBS series to that time—was due largely to Sagan and his quirky yet compelling persona. On the other hand, some scientists perceived the series as a last straw. From that time on, they perceived him first and foremost as a showman. To them, he simply could no longer be regarded as a serious scientist. Yet—and this was their guilty conscience speaking—they owed him much, and they knew it. What little popularity science had in the 1980s was due substantially to Sagan. Other scientists had been so famous that they were household names—Albert Einstein, for example—but none in living memory had introduced so many inhabitants of Earth (thanks to television) to so rich a banquet *of the science itself.* As Golden wrote in *Time,* whether grudgingly or not, "Most scientists, increasingly sensitive to the need for public support and understanding of research, appreciate what Sagan has become: America's most effective salesman of science."[52]

ON SUNDAY EVENING, September 28, the creators of *Cosmos* gathered at a party in New York City to watch the premiere. Malone was absent.

"The first program had some problems," Soter says, looking back. "There was this long tour of the universe that was just too long and unbroken." But he loved a sequence showing the evolution of creatures over time—a visual delight and a powerful aesthetic argument for evolution and against creationism.[53]

A generation of young people got their first taste of science from watching *Cosmos.* Some are now space scientists—for example, Jeff Moersch, a former student of Sagan's at Cornell, who watched the show in early high school. Now he is a scientist at NASA-Ames who is working on a forthcoming planetary mission. He says that in his generation, "people that are just starting out with their Ph.D.'s right now, all of them were inspired by that show."[54]

Rachel, now a widow, had by this time returned to her home in Delray Beach, Florida. Once a week she and her friend, Ethel Kramer, "sat every Sunday night and watched *Cosmos*," Kramer recalls. "Carl's secretary sent her Xeroxed copies of all the fan letters."[55]

Of eight letters published by *Time* magazine in response to Golden's cover story on Sagan, four were friendly, four hostile. A Texas viewer said that Sagan is "a genius" and added, extravagantly, "He is to astronomy what Einstein is to physics and what Pythagoras is to mathematics." But an Indiana viewer griped that Sagan's "type of presentation imbues science with the razzle-dazzle of show biz and reduces it to bubble gum mentality."[56]

Also prompting viewer response were hints in the show of Sagan's nonreligious outlook, an outlook that would soon make him a target for the religious right. "Poor Carl Sagan," a Pennsylvania man wrote to *Time*. "He so desperately wants to find man's significance in the cosmos, but he simply cannot bear to speak the word that would give his grand search coherence and conclusion: God."[57] Ironically, *Christian Century* ran an article by A. P. Klausler that said: "Carl Sagan has been accused of being a showman and a popularizer—an accusation which may reflect jealousy on the part of some members of the scientific community. I for one am grateful for his ability to clarify some of the complexities of our universe."[58]

Sagan's scientific colleagues reacted diversely to *Cosmos*. His old associate from RAND, W. W. Kellogg, said that he never missed an episode of *Cosmos*. Sagan was "a source of great pride and joy to me."[59] But astronomer Jay Pasachoff, who had known Sagan at Harvard, thought *Cosmos* was "atrocious, embarrassing in terms of the treatment of some of the material—the space ship console, for example."[60]

Dale Cruikshank, who had been at Yerkes when Sagan was there, recalls how he and his colleagues watched the show, "and we'd sit there and just have a wonderful time making fun of Carl." He found Sagan's idiosyncratic manner of speaking—the punched consonants, the hand gestures, the beatific gazes toward the sky—off-putting. "The pace was so plodding and slow. Then there are these occasions when he's in a spaceship and he'd have this big panel of crystals that are glowing and he waves his hands over the crystals. We thought that was just really hokey. And of course, there's the laborious pronunciation of certain words, including 'bill-eee-yuns.'"

However, Cruikshank admired other aspects of the show: "We thought the techniques he used to explain complicated issues in science were great, because he had found new ways to demonstrate and explain very difficult concepts that other people hadn't found good ways to explain."[61]

Sagan's very persona also troubled some viewers. *Time* magazine perceived "more than a few milligrams of arrogance. . . . The camera lingers too often on the Sagan profile. His lyrical language sometimes lapses into flowery excess, and occasionally *Cosmos'* galloping pace straggles to a crawl."[62] John J. O'Connor wrote in the *New York Times:* "On several levels, obviously, 'Cosmos' could be subtitled 'The Selling of Carl Sagan.' . . . Some viewers may find Dr. Sagan's brand of exuberance irritating. He can sometimes sink in a sea of exclamations: 'How lovely are trees!,' or 'What a marvelous cooperative arrangement!'" In addition, "some of the details border on the ludicrous . . . a succession of decidedly goofy grins."[63]

Indeed, of all the things that people remember most vividly about the *Cosmos* series, the most annoying are the long, tedious close-ups of Sagan's face. "Most of the criticism of *Cosmos* centered on Carl's shit-eating grin in the spacecraft," says Don Goldsmith—a grin that he gleefully imitates. Stanley Miller claims that Sagan blamed the shots on Malone, who (Sagan told Miller) kept shooting Sagan in close-up "to screw him."[64] (Soter and Goldsmith doubt this.[65]) In Soter's view, the space ship shots were "the major flaw of the series. Those were all Adrian's idea. . . . Carl went along with Adrian's judgment and it turned out to be a bad call," Soter said.[66] But Sagan certainly deserves at least some of the blame: after all, he had driven the *Cosmos* staff half-crazy by trying to run everything.

Toward the end of the series, O'Connor of the *New York Times* declared that *Cosmos* "has established itself as a phenomenon demanding, in varying degrees, admiration, substantial reservations and serious objections." The show's ratings make it "among the most popular of domestic series" produced for PBS. O'Connor also complained that the rest of the series had continued to be overdominated by "Dr. Sagan's profile. . . . Dr. Sagan tends to play too forcefully the role of 'merchant of awe.' His favorite adjective is 'astonishing.'" O'Connor noted that even Sagan's fan Johnny Carson had recently done a spoof on *The Tonight Show* in which Carson portrayed a Saganish character who expected to earn "billions and billions of dollars" from *Cosmos.*[67] Carson's comic pronunciation of "billions" made Sagan an overnight pop reference.

Yet for all the criticisms, the show was a cultural triumph—the most ambitious science series ever aired on U.S. television, one that achieved a new high in textual clarity and visual dazzle. It was to television science documentaries what *2001: A Space Odyssey* had been to science-fiction cinema: a new standard to shoot for.

The show would win numerous national and international awards, including the Emmy and the highly prestigious Peabody, which was awarded jointly to KCET, Adrian Malone, and Sagan. Unfortunately, Sagan was unwilling, for legal reasons, to travel to New York to receive the Peabody. At the time, he was establishing residency in California, and he could not venture into New York without the risk of being presented with a subpoena by Linda's attorneys. So he found a replacement—one ready to hand—his secretary, Shirley Arden.

Arden seems to have been the kind of secretary Bogart had in *The Maltese Falcon*—the boss's all-purpose Girl Friday, the one who takes care of his personal, as well as professional, business. Arden was Sagan's full-time cheerleader, adviser, and gatekeeper. She moved to Los Angeles to work on *Cosmos* with him; then, returning to Ithaca, she fixed up his home for his return.[68]

Time eventually separated Sagan, Druyan, and Arden for complex personal reasons. Still, Arden has many warm memories of her years with Sagan, among them the time she accepted his Peabody award for him in New York. "I was given top-drawer treatment," Arden recalls with great pleasure. "[I] gave a brief proxy acceptance speech, and had the opportunity of meeting Marlo Thomas and Carroll O'Connor, who also received Peabody awards that year. They were warm and charming. Adrian [Malone] was accompanied by a couple of BBC colleagues and was quite cordial."[69]

SAGAN'S BOOK VERSION of *Cosmos* was published shortly after the series aired, and it became a best-seller, staying on the *New York Times* best-seller list for seventy weeks.

Overall, critics liked both the television show and the book, although the latter fared better in their estimation. In fact, some book critics used their otherwise enthusiastic review of the book to bash the show. Writing in the *Village Voice*, Eliott Fremont-Smith noted that the book was linked to the television show, "but don't be put off by that. Sagan on TV is an unctuous scene-stealer from the stars, but as a science writer he's OK, able for long stretches to dwell on cosmologies other than himself. The book—a scrapbook of astronomical history, discovery, and speculation (up-to-date on Jupiter, behind the times on Saturn)—is as munchable as buttered popcorn. Start anywhere and you're hooked (at least I am)."[70]

The *New Yorker* said that *Cosmos* "will come as an often charming, sometimes eloquent surprise to people who may have been put off by what they have seen of the [television] series. . . . Very few scientists would have had the nerve to write a book like this, with all its possibilities for disaster. Sagan has done a remarkably good job."[71]

However, the historian of science David H. DeVorkin, of the National Air and Space Museum, cited in *Sky and Telescope* what he called the book's "little blunders and frequent historical howlers." He charged that Sagan, like the nineteenth-century French astronomy popularizer Camille Flammarion, relied on "lurid romanticism."[72]

Some scientists protested Sagan's focus on the life of Johannes Kepler, the seventeenth-century mystic who corrected the basic flaw in Copernicus's cosmology—its circular planetary orbits—by replacing them with ellipses. Sagan's Cornell colleague Tommy Gold "quite liked" the show *Cosmos*, but disliked the focus on Kepler. In Gold's view, "Galileo and Newton were so far ahead [of Kepler] in general comprehension." Responding to an objection that Kepler had made Newton's work possible, Gold disagreed, arguing that Newton would have worked out Kepler's contribution—the elliptical nature of planetary orbits—in a month on his own. In private life, Kepler "was an absolute crackpot."[73] Likewise, the physicist-author Michael Riordan wrote in *Technology Review*: "I only wish Sagan had spent more time with Newton and less with Kepler. For me, the conceptional leap from a few phenomenological rules of elliptical orbits to a universal law of gravitation is by far the greater achievement, one that lies at the heart of modern science."[74]

In fact, by discussing Kepler at length, Sagan made a valuable point about the nature of scientific evolution. Kepler "has been strangely neglected and misunderstood," according to the noted science historian Gerald Holton.[75] Kepler was a contradictory character—an astronomer who practiced astrology, a rationalist who speculated about neo-Pythagorean mathematical mysticism and whose mother was persecuted as a witch.[76] By including Kepler, Sagan showed that scientific ideas occasionally emerge from a pseudoscientific context. Scientists have been reluctant to accept this fact, but it is now received wisdom among many historians of science. It doesn't mean that pseudoscience is "true," just that (as mentioned earlier) scientists are sometimes right for the wrong reasons.

Sagan may have concentrated on Kepler for another, more personal reason: he may have glimpsed aspects of himself in the astronomer-astrologer. Like Kepler, Sagan was a contradictory figure, a man with one foot in science and the other in imagination, one in logic and the other in Edgar Rice Burroughs. (While helping to pioneer astrophysics, Kepler wrote a fantasy story about a voyage to the Moon, which he speculated was inhabited.) Sagan's handling of Kepler constitutes part of a broader habit of Sagan's that might be called "covert autobiography." His books include many mini-biographies of great scientists. These superb biographical essays emphasize numerous minor aspects of the subject's life, perhaps because, although Sagan never says so, they reminded him of himself. Sagan's detractors might dismiss his taste for covert autobiography as an idiosyncrasy, like his love of epigraphs (with which he jammed his books). Others might attribute it to his egocentricity, to his purported inability to grasp anything external to himself except on his own terms. In reality, he may have been seeking support or consolation for his own eccentricities or failings by spotting them in the lives of scientists far greater than he.

For example, in his book *Comet* (coauthored with Druyan), Sagan profiles Edmond Halley. He notes how Halley wrote letters at age eighteen to a top astronomer (just as Sagan wrote early on to Donald Menzel and other astro-notables); used opium (and, as with Sagan's secret use of marijuana, "hardly seems to have suffered much from the so-called amotivational syndrome sometimes associated with opium and other euphoriants"); was denied a top professorship (just as Sagan was denied tenure at Harvard); and, in the most overt example of covert autobiography, wrote a paper about a meteor sighting that offers "a kind of naked enthusiasm which has been effectively eliminated from the literature of science today."[77]

SOME OF THE MOST INTERESTING CRITIQUES of *Cosmos* deal with Sagan's lack of faith in God and his overwhelming faith in the virtue and potential of science. Sagan made no bones about his lack of religiosity. How truly irreligious was he, though? As noted earlier, his speculations about "advanced" extraterrestrials resembled high-tech versions of religious mythology. Some people who were close to him, including Ann Druyan, maintain that Sagan was a religious agnostic.[78] But his views on religion lack the tentativeness characteristic of true agnosticism. *Cosmos* was certainly irreligious enough to upset one friend of Sagan's, the distinguished historian of science Owen Gingerich, who is religiously devout. Gingerich tried, unsuccessfully, to develop his own television series in response. Had he succeeded, he would have called it *Anti-Cosmos*.[79]

It is one thing to say that religion is *not* the royal road to salvation or understanding; it is another thing to say that science *is*. Contrary to popular misconception, atheists do not necessarily see science as potentially resolving all the mysteries of the cosmos. It is this question—science and its epistemological limits—that stirred some of the most valuable intellectual and literary reactions to *Cosmos*.

Writing in the journal *Social Science and Modern Society*, David Paul Rebovich praised much about *Cosmos* but said that the show's subtext was "an optimistic populism. . . . Sagan's claim that science, rather than religion, traditional philosophy, or politics, is the path to redemption seems, like those of many would-be reformers, an overly simplistic and unsubstantiated solution to the ills of the day."[80]

An offbeat literary response to *Cosmos* came from the famous Southern novelist Walker Percy. He wrote an eccentric book, titled *Lost in the Cosmos: The Last Self-Help Book*, which was a parody of both *Cosmos* and the self-help books flooding the market. At one point Percy proposed a long satirical subtitle for the book that would include the question "or, Why it is Carl Sagan can be so smart and so dumb." The book acknowledges the pleasures of Sagan's *Cosmos*, despite its "unmalicious, even innocent, scientism, the likes of which I have not encountered since the standard bull sessions of high school and college—up to but not past the sophomore year." It questions Sagan's quest for extraterrestrial life, notes his remark that humans seek to overcome their cosmic loneliness, and asks the unsettling question: "Why is Carl Sagan so lonely?" Percy replies:

> (a) Sagan is lonely because, as a true devotee of science, a noble and reliable method of attaining knowledge, he feels increasingly isolated in a world in which, as Bronowski has said, there is a failure of nerve and men seem willing to undertake anything other than the rigors of science and believe anything at all: in Velikovsky, von Daniken, even in Mr. and Mrs. Barney Hill, who reported being captured and taken aboard a spacecraft in Vermont.

> (b) Sagan is lonely because, after great expectations, he has not discovered ETIs in the Cosmos, because chimpanzees don't talk, dolphins don't talk, humpback whales sing only to other humpback whales, and he has heard nothing but random noise from the Cosmos, and because *Vikings 1* and *2* failed to discover evidence of even the most rudimentary organic life in the soil of Mars.

> (c) Sagan is lonely because, once everything in the Cosmos, including man, is reduced to the sphere of immanence, matter in interaction, there is no one left to talk to except other transcending intelligences from other worlds.[81]

Cosmos drew particular heat from political conservatives. Previously marginalized, these voices were gaining ground within the American intelligentsia in the 1980s, following the election of Ronald Reagan. In the journal *Commentary*, the editor, former leftist Norman Podhoretz, ran a long, well-written analysis of *Cosmos* by Jeffrey Marsh. Marsh criticized Sagan for promoting a naive belief in the power of a scientific perspective on the world to point the way to more rational relations between peoples and countries. Marsh wrote:

> We have already had over sixty years' experience with one society [the USSR] built according to notions of scientific materialism, where science is hailed as the foundation of a new order which will produce a new man. . . . Not only is this society one of the least free and most imperialistic in the history of mankind, . . . but it cannot even produce enough food for its own population. Clearly Carl Sagan does not

regard the Soviet Union as his model of a society based on scientific ideas, but it is a measure of his intellectual irresponsibility that he has not even approached the stage of thinking seriously about who would perform the redesign of society he calls for.

Marsh was especially critical of Sagan's advocacy in *Cosmos* of a push for universal disarmament, to be led by the United States.

Were he [Sagan] to come down to earth, he would be forced to recognize that this supposedly universalist message of surrender of national sovereignty must appear utterly bizarre to all that vast majority of mankind which does not share Sagan's own benign view of human nature and civilization.

Such criticism foreshadowed the angrier right-wing attacks on Sagan of the 1980s, when he would become active in the antinuclear movement and promote the concept of "nuclear winter."[82]

DESPITE THE CRITICISMS of the television series, the book *Cosmos* would endure. In October 1991, a decade after the book's publication, *Astronomy* magazine referred to it as "one of the best popular books on astronomy ever written." It remains in print to this day, in paperback (like most of Sagan's books from *Dragons* on).[83]

Two decades after *Cosmos*, Steve Soter has a mixed opinion of the show. "Every show—some more than others—has wonderful sequences, brilliant sequences that work wonderfully and some that just flop, that make me cringe to think about them." His favorite sequences include the discussion of the Heike crab, a marvel of evolution by artificial selection; the depiction of Mars; and a sequence that compares New York City to a living organism. A segment depicting the chemical basis of the origin of life "seemed like a good idea at the time, but it didn't work.

"There are some things that just soar, that just sing, that work beautifully—and others that just don't," Soter says. "Actually, I haven't watched the whole thing since the first broadcast. I may have seen one or two tapes [from the series] separately since then. It's almost painful." He admits that "parts of the programs were a pale reflection of what it could have been. . . . So for me it was this very strange mixed bag—elation and cringing."[84] (A few years later, PBS showed an edited, faster-paced version of *Cosmos*.)

The phrase "elation and cringing" might also describe Gentry Lee's summary of his years with Carl Sagan. During their five-year business relationship, they considered trying to become the Walt Disney Inc. of science popularization. They even discussed the possibility of opening a theme park where you could, as Lee recalls, "immerse yourself in science and technology—a geology spot, an astronomy spot, and so on." The theme park never got past the idea stage. However, they did start a company, The Cosmos Store, whose purpose was to publish science-related items such as astronomical charts. The company failed, though, and closed after a few years. Lee and Sagan also tried to develop a new television series, *Nucleus*, based in part on nuclear physics, but its backer, ABC-TV, pulled out after the Soviets shot down the KAL 007 airliner in 1983. (Druyan says ABC feared that with a television series hosted by Carl Sagan, a known antinuclear activist, the network risked being tarred as the Moscow Broadcasting Network.)

For various reasons, Lee eventually pulled out of Carl Sagan Productions, and his friendship with Sagan disintegrated. Their falling-out resulted from personal accusations and business disagreements, as well as Lee's discomfort with Druyan's powerful role in Sagan's life. Their disagreements are too intricate to detail here and lack clear-cut good guys or villains. The disputes that ended their relationship are of the kind that seem trivial to all save the combatants (at least in this writer's judgment).

Lee is now a highly successful science-fiction writer, who has coauthored a number of science-fiction books with Arthur C. Clarke. He looks back on his friendship with Sagan with mixed feelings. For almost two decades, he kept silent about the saga of his relationship with Sagan. Even when Sagan died in 1996 and reporters called Lee for comment, he declined to speak, feeling it was "inappropriate." The fact is, he says, "When I think about Carl, and the things that happened, the pain is very real."

On the one hand, Lee praises Sagan's gifts as a popularizer. "Carl probably touched more hearts and minds than any scientist in history. I would guess that more people decided to pursue scientific careers because of him than any person in history. For all these things the world should be eternally grateful."

On the other hand, Lee says that certain features of Sagan's personality undermined his respect for Sagan as a person. "As a thinker, writer, speaker, popularizer, and scientist, he . . . if you were to do some sort of metric he would probably reach up there, as a great. But as a person, his shortcomings were almost as great." Lee wanted to be close to Sagan, but found it hard to feel affection for him. "I am of the opinion that for one to feel affection for someone, it's important that they show a certain amount of vulnerability." Sagan never really did, although he'd talk about "disconnects with his sister or some minor contretemps with his parents." The personal relationship with Sagan never really gelled as Lee had hoped it would. When Ann Druyan arrived on the scene, Sagan and Druyan became an unbreakable team; Sagan had left Gentry's treehouse for a girl.

Sagan's emotional remoteness troubled Lee. "He was my partner; I might have called him my friend. But he never called me and said, 'Gentry, I'm having some emotional problems; would you listen to me?' And I dare say that probably never happened with anybody in his life—except Ann." Lee compares Sagan to a character in Lawrence Durrell's *Alexandria Quartet*. The character is Pursewarden, who "is reputedly a genius," Lee explains. "He definitely has difficulty making emotional connections with people. Another character in the novels, whose name is Balthazar, makes the comment, 'It's not enough simply to respect a man's genius; one must love him a little also.'"

Two or three years after their friendship ended, Lee ran into Sagan at a Lunar and Planetary Science Institute meeting in Houston. "We were cordial," Lee recalls. "He was tentative at first—he couldn't handle confrontations at all. He never asked me how I was. It was sad."

Lee still speaks of the series as a source of deep satisfaction. "It was a great product," he says. "Was it as good as we could have done? No." But he's proud that it conveyed "the sense of the excitement and wonder that existed in science. The richness of the context for science in society—how it is a part of society, how it relates to people. There were so many ideas in the show, and they came through. It was a tremendously ambitious gamble."

Lee is also glad that he knew Sagan, even for a while. "Do I forgive [Sagan]? I do," he says. "Because if I integrate the positives with him in my life, it outweighs the negatives."

Conveying a sense of just how special the *Cosmos* experience was to him, Lee recalls that in an elevator one time at a science-fiction convention, a young man and his wife, both about twenty-five, saw Lee's name tag. The man's eyes started welling up with tears. He had seen *Cosmos* at age fifteen and had read the "Rama" novels that Arthur C. Clarke and Lee had written. The young man gushed to Lee, "I have dreamed of meeting you all these years." He said his life had been unalterably changed. His wife kept saying, "Yes, that's true." Lee adds that when encounters like that happen, "It's sort of hard to get into anger and 'what might have been.'"[85]

14

Contact

C OSMOS GAVE SAGAN the muscle to do bold new things: to sell a multi-million-dollar novel to Hollywood, to single-handedly save NASA's SETI project from congressional budget-cutters, to launch a privately funded SETI program—and to try to save the world from nuclear war. The early-to-mid-1980s marked the peak of his fame. He was now a TV star and a target of considerable praise, gossip, criticism, and parody. He was no longer simply a well-known and controversial scientist; rather, he was known to hundreds of millions of people who normally couldn't care less about science.

He sometimes found his new fame difficult to manage. He was recognized at restaurants, where people felt free to come up to him and chat. Sagan was torn: sometimes he enjoyed being noticed, but at times it made him uncomfortable. One time in Cambridge, he and his friend radioastronomer Paul Horowitz went to an expensive restaurant. Horowitz recalls "the rather curious thing that we sat in the large dining room with tables around the edge, and he wanted to sit facing the wall, because when people recognized him they all went gaga and he couldn't get any work done."[1]

Creationists attacked him; military brass debated him; columnists reported on his costly divorce from Linda Salzman and (later) his dream marriage to Ann Druyan. Marlon Brando privately "did a wicked takeoff of Carl Sagan, whose *Cosmos* TV series he'd been watching on tape as a model for the American Indian series he still insisted he was going to make," according to Peter Manso's biography of the actor.[2]

Sagan's long absence from Cornell also stirred resentments among the faculty, even in one who was devoted to him: astronomy chair Yervant Terzian. In early 1981, right after *Cosmos*, Terzian vented his fury about Sagan's long sabbatical to Sagan's secretary Shirley Arden. Arden summarized Terzian's blast in a memo to Sagan. Terzian, Arden wrote, said the entire faculty has lost confidence in you ever returning to Cornell and that most would prefer you did not. He said you made your decision to go on half time and that everyone else would have preferred you to come back to Cornell and resume your teaching and research full time "just like the rest of us." He said it was "impossible" for you to have the kind of situation at Cornell you seem to want, that he was certain the faculty would not change their minds. . . . I asked him whether he had told you how he felt about all the above matters and he said absolutely; that he had been very frank with you on the phone and had told you exactly what he was telling me. I said I was happy to hear that because it has often been my experience that people here would talk about you in a certain vein or tone of voice and when they talked with you it would be in quite another manner.[3]

Still, if Sagan was crying about his colleagues' anger and his lost anonymity, he was crying all the way to the bank. His fame brought him a fortune. His colleagues' hearts ached when he received a $2 million advance from Simon & Schuster in early 1981 to write the novel *Contact*.[4] The contract caused "intense feelings" among some other astronomers who wrote popular accounts of their field, recalls astronomer Stephen P. Maran (now the spokesperson for the American Astronomical Society). The advance was the largest ever made for a book that had not yet been written.[5] A film version was expected in 1984.

Nick Sagan recalls that his father turned down many offers to do television commercials. He also turned down an offer to host *Saturday Night Live*, which Nick didn't understand. "I thought that would have been really cool. . . . Jesse Jackson was on, and do you think it hurt *his* career?"[6]

Characters based on the Sagan persona started showing up in films of this period. The 1984 film *Starman* depicted the aftermath of the *Voyager* mission, in which an alien visits Earth and encounters, among others, a vaguely Saganish scientist from Cornell;[7] and in 1985 the film *Real Genius* featured an evil scientist who had a *Cosmos*-like show called *Everything*.[8]

The phrase for which Sagan became most famous was "billions and billions." This upset him; not only did the phrase sound idiotic, but (as he testily reminded interviewers) he never actually said it. Johnny Carson had coined the term in a *Tonight* show sketch wherein he imitated his sometime guest. But an astronomy popularizer who cannot use the word "billions" without fear of being laughed at is in big trouble, for "billions" is the numerical workhorse of astronomy. When Sagan gave a speech and uttered a lone "billions," the audience tittered. Sagan felt that the notoriety of the phrase trivialized him. "For a while, out of childish pique, I wouldn't utter or write the phrase, even when asked to," he reflected many years later.[9]

Still, Sagan must have felt a special sense of vindication when, on a publicity tour, he lectured at his alma mater, the University of Chicago. A major dinner was held in his honor; the guests included Subrahman-yan Chandrasekhar, his Yerkes boss. More than two decades earlier, Chandra had scoffed at Sagan's initial proposal for a doctoral thesis and called his lecture series "Sagan's circus." But that was a different time, when an astrophysicist might still pursue his career as a monkish calling and view publicity as unseemly. No longer; now outer space was show business, with Sagan as its best-known ringmaster. So many people turned out to hear Sagan that two rooms had to be set aside for the audience, recalls Sagan's college chum Peter Vandervoort (later associate chair of the Chicago astronomy department). Chandra "told a typical Chandra story. He said, 'Carl, seeing you after all these years reminds me of a story about Stanley Baldwin when he was prime minister of England. He greeted his former tutor on campus and the tutor said: "Baldwin, Baldwin, how good to see you! What are you doing these days?"'"

Sagan "gave a wonderful talk and everybody was very enthusiastic," Vandervoort says. "He came to a little reception before our dinner. He 'worked' the room; he made a point to get around to every little group." After the crowd had melted away, Sagan and Vandervoort and a few others "sat down together and chatted for a few minutes. The twenty years had just melted away. We pretty much picked up things where we had left them off in 1960. I cannot speak for all of Carl's classmates and friends as to whether or not he remembered them," Vandervoort adds. "He always remembered *this* friend. It was very touching."[10]

Still, there was no escaping a fact: Sagan was no longer truly one of them. Now he was a national—no, global—figure. And for all his scientific work, most people knew him for a silly phrase that he had never uttered. He was learning about a contradictory property of limelight: it trivializes as much as it illumines. At a scientific dinner honoring Sagan, one particularly mischievous guest could not quite resist standing up and making the dreaded request: "Carl, you've *got* to say it: 'Billions and billions!'"[11]

AMID THE SWIRL of his many activities and the artillery barrages of all his critics, Sagan and Druyan formed a remarkable partnership. She made him more explicitly conscious of certain political issues, as well as of his own family. Sagan paid attention to Druyan in a way that he had never paid attention to anyone. He was constantly shuttling across the nation, from Cornell to KCET to the Jet Propulsion Laboratory, but he didn't want to let his careerism sour this third, most treasured relationship. In a note to his secretary in October 1978, he asked: "I wonder if you could remind me so that I can see to it that every week that Annie and I are in one place—Ithaca or Pasadena—that I bring her some fresh flowers. She likes it a lot and I'd like to be able to do that regularly. I think it's just a question of poking me on my way home to do that."[12]

Meanwhile, Linda Salzman Sagan tried to pick up the pieces of her life. She and Sagan had both been good friends of radioastronomer Frank Drake, and they asked him to act as witness to the division of property on the day that the moving van came to cart away Sagan's share of the furniture. "Carl was moving out of the house in Ithaca and they were squabbling over who got what, what pieces of furniture and stuff, and I was apparently the only mutual friend at that time," recalls Drake, who no doubt had better things to do but is a man with a heart of pure gold. "And they asked me to come and be the referee. I remember it was snowing; this big moving van came up. Carl wanted me to stand there and keep an inventory of everything that went out the door. . . . That was my job: I was taking inventory." Sagan and Linda were barely speaking—"only in very unpleasant voices. They were at each other's throats. Arguments as to who gets this painting or that chair."[13]

The divorce finally came through in May 1981. Druyan and Sagan were married almost immediately, at the Hotel Bel-Air in Los Angeles, on June 1, the fourth anniversary of their declaration of love for each other. Cari Sagan Greene recalls: "At the dinner the night before Carl and Annie got married, Annie's brother raised his glass as a toast and said something to the effect that, 'Annie has made Carl a human being.' And everybody knew, intuitively and instantly, exactly what he meant. And everybody agreed! . . . She made him a whole person; she made him aware of human beings, and not to be arrogant and aloof."[14] Druyan's recollection is more graphic: "The night before we were wed, there was a big party. . . . [Guests] would get up, [one] after the other, and say, 'You know Carl was [once] a real asshole before he met Annie; we couldn't stand Carl in those days. I remember the time Carl really hurt my feelings'. . . . And then my brother got up and he said, 'Well, all I want to say is, I'm really glad I didn't meet Carl before he met Annie.' It brought the house down. Everybody was laughing—Carl most of all."[15]

Even so, Druyan cheerfully refuses to believe that Sagan was ever that bad: "All of this potential, all of this goodness, all of this brilliance at love was residing in Carl all the time. There's no way you could turn a [mean] person into this man."[16]

Sagan's friend Paul West—who liked and missed wife No. 2, Linda—viewed the wedding more cynically, judging by his fictionalization of it in his novel *Life with Swan*. Therein, Ann Druyan is represented by the fictional Florinda Demetz. The luxurious, cuisine-packed wedding was "pagan chic, a crowd scene with hundreds of guests. . . . Raoul and Florinda circulated as if in some parody of Brownian motion. . . . All the people they had offended were there, patching things up. . . ." In one poignant moment, West notes how Florinda, as she circulated through the well-wishers, resembled "a freshly released frigate bird watching the sad ghost of Nineveh [Linda] beckon her from the shadows and then depart murmuring an ancient Hebrew curse."

The wedding caused some hurt to Druyan's close friend Lynda Obst because Sagan insisted that the matron of honor be his secretary Shirley Arden, not Obst. "He hurt my feelings very deeply," Obst recalls, "and I began to see how complex our relationship was going to become. . . . They all later apologized. . . . It showed the distance Annie had to travel in getting balance in that relationship. The good news is: You fall in love with the great alpha male. The bad news is that you fall in love with the great alpha male!"[17]

But with time, Druyan began to exercise more control in the relationship. She "helped [Carl] to try to make up to Dorion and Jeremy, to make up for not being quite as attentive as he might have been before that," Lester Grinspoon recalls. When Sagan married Druyan, it was "the first time that Betsy and I saw Carl really get into being a father. It was the first time Carl really knew what being a father was like." Druyan gave him two children, Sam and Alexandra (Sasha), and "it was obvious he was really enjoying being a father. It's an accomplishment that I thought Annie brought to him."[18]

Sagan also began making amends with his past. "He took me out twenty years after I had married him and divorced him," Lynn Margulis recalls, "and he told me that he apologized." He explained that he hadn't appreciated how much work she had to do around the house while he was off jetting around and becoming famous. "Which was completely true—he just didn't realize. And he apologized, formally apologized to me. But Annie made him, I'm sure. He wouldn't have realized unless she were aware [of what really happened]. Because she's aware. Annie's great."[19]

He had every reason in the world to be making his peace. He had found the love of his life; he was wealthy; he was famous and growing more so, while working on projects that had fascinated him since childhood. But his oldest dream was in growing danger.

TWO DECADES AFTER the Green Bank conference on SETI, the search for alien intelligence faced both glorious prospects and utter failure. On the one hand, NASA was close to starting an official search for alien signals using radiotelescope dishes. On the other hand, SETI faced growing criticism from critics who scorned it as a waste of time.

The backlash had partly political roots. Scientific disciplines tend to be fractious; they rarely present a united front as they clamor for funds before Congress, NASA, and the National Science Foundation. Planetary astronomers fight with galactic astronomers over their respective shares of the federal pie. So do cell biologists and those who map the human genome; so do geologists who map continental mineral resources and those who probe undersea subduction zones.

In astronomy, and especially in radioastronomy, SETI was long viewed as a not entirely welcome guest. Some distinguished astronomers—Otto Struve, for example—backed it early on. But inside the radio observatories, "the troops" grumbled about headline-grabbing colleagues who wasted valuable radiotelescope time listening for aliens. The skeptics scorned SETI in the same way that planetary scientists (including Sagan) scorned space-shuttle flights by astronauts—as public-pleasing show business that diverted funds from "real" science.

Thus the anti-SETI backlash of the late 1970s might have stemmed, in part, from the fear of some scientists that SETI would become an *Apollo*-like national project that would bleed the serious business of radioastronomy dry. Silly as this fear seems now, it seemed perfectly reasonable in the 1970s, when SETI guru Bernard Oliver of Hewlett-Packard proposed his Project Cyclops, a monstrous array of radiotelescopes that would act in concert as a single, supersensitive "ear" on the heavens. In theory, Cyclops might be able to "eavesdrop" on broadcasts from alien civilizations (their equivalent of our radio and television broadcasts).[20] Cyclops would also have cost billions of dollars. It won the support of no less a public figure than Norman Cousins, editor of *Saturday Review*, who seconded SETI scientists' claim that aliens might teach us how to solve our terrestrial problems.[21] Naturally, orthodox radioastronomers feared that Cyclops would, like its mythical man-eating namesake, devour their own comparatively unglamorous studies—such as mapping the distribution of carbon monoxide gas in the galaxy, for example.

The SETI backlash may be traced to a 1975 paper by the astronomer Michael Hart in the *Quarterly Journal of the Royal Astronomical Society*. Hart reiterated the old "Fermi paradox" (named for the great nuclear physicist Enrico Fermi, who stated it decades earlier): If alien civilizations exist, then enough of them must be old enough to have developed interstellar travel. Hence, given the great age of Earth and terrestrial civilization, we should have seen their spaceships by now. But we haven't. Why? Hart's skeptical answer was simple: aliens don't exist.[22] In coming years, more detailed arguments were developed by others, in particular physicist Frank Tipler of Tulane University.

Ironically, two major arguments against the existence of aliens had been implicit in Shklovskii and Sagan's *Intelligent Life in the Universe*, although they had not appreciated the fact at the time. In the book, Sagan had argued for the feasibility of travel between stars, even galaxies. And Shklovskii had argued that the moons of Mars might be giant space stations.

In the 1970s, picking up where Sagan left off, a number of scholars developed schemes for interstellar travel. For example, the British Interplanetary Society proposed a design for Project Daedalus, a thermonuclear-powered starship. The physicist Robert Forward described a way to use futuristic super-lasers to push low-density "light sails" to the stars (as the wind blows sailboats). Some of these schemes sounded eerily credible; that is, they involved no obvious fallacies. Hence the Fermi paradox began to seem more urgent than before. If interstellar travel is indeed feasible, and if aliens exist, then why haven't they visited us? (UFO sightings don't count; most good scientists rejected these as nonsense.)

As for Shklovskii's hypothesis of the Martian moons, it anticipated an idea that became popular in the 1970s, physicist Gerard O'Neill's proposal for giant orbital space colonies miles in length and housing thousands, even millions, of people.[23] (The same idea had been anticipated by visionaries such as Dandridge Cole and J. D. Bernal.) Advocates depicted "O'Neill colonies" in idyllic terms—they'd be big enough to have rivers, farmlands, even clouds and rainfall. Such schemes encouraged backers of interstellar travel to think that starflight might be not only feasible but also relatively comfortable. Some imagined titanic inhabited "arks" that drift slowly across the galaxy for millennia, occasionally docking at new worlds to look for intelligent residents. (Sagan had briefly backed O'Neill schemes, even commenting on them favorably during congressional testimony. He planned to devote the final episode of *Cosmos* to space colonization, but Steve Soter talked him out of it, arguing that humanity had more pressing needs than the construction of orbital Levittowns.)[24]

If O'Neill colonies were feasible, then the same question could be asked: Where were the aliens? There are about three hundred billion stars in the Milky Way, and Sagan estimated that it contains perhaps one million civilizations. If interstellar travel is feasible, then it was hard to believe that an alien race had not visited us even once during human history. Unless, of course, they don't exist.

In the early 1980s, the leading SETI opponent was Frank Tipler. He pushed the Fermi paradox to its logical absurdity, arguing that some of the aliens would (for reasons never made entirely clear) build self-replicating robots that would swarm across the galaxy, making copies of themselves out of disassembled asteroids, planets, and stars. Thus, if aliens exist, why don't we see self-replicating robots swarming through our solar system, reducing it to rubble, like so many biblical locusts? Tipler concluded that aliens don't exist.[25]

Tipler's arguments impressed Wisconsin senator William Proxmire, who cited them in attacking NASA's SETI project. Proxmire gave NASA his "Golden Fleece" award (a dubious tribute to projects that he thought wasted tax dollars). Proxmire persuaded Congress to kill SETI funding.[26]

Fortunately, Sagan knew Proxmire; they had been in contact (possibly about NASA or arms control issues) at least as early as 1979. Sagan (with Druyan) visited Proxmire in Washington and convinced him to drop opposition to NASA's future requests for SETI funding. Druyan was present and sat watching, quietly, as Sagan, with "total patience," explained to Proxmire Frank Drake's equation for estimating the number of civilizations in the galaxy now engaged in interstellar communication. Sagan emphasized the variable L, which represents the average survival time of a technically advanced civilization. Like Sagan, Proxmire was a well-known critic of militarism; suddenly he grasped the link between the search for alien intelligence and the survival of humanity. Druyan recalls how during the meeting the senator's attitude shifted from "I'm going to hear this egghead out and then get him out of my office" to "being slack-jawed with fascination and amazement. . . . And he admitted he was wrong, very gracefully. He said he would never do that again, never make that mistake again. He was wonderful. And he never did fight it again."[27] Others would, however.

SAGAN HAD SAVED SETI for the time being, but he learned a valuable lesson: Congress was not a reliable source of SETI funds. To guarantee SETI's survival, its backers needed to establish privately funded SETI searches as backups.

In 1979, Sagan, JPL's Bruce Murray (with whom he often fought over life on Mars, only to become a close friend), and Louis Friedman (former advanced programs manager at JPL) agreed to found The Planetary Society. Its goal: to serve as a grassroots movement supportive of robotic space missions, especially to the planets. With enough members, it might constitute a powerful lobby able to rally support for endangered space missions, especially as the space-shuttle program took bigger and bigger bites from robotic expeditions. (The first shuttle flight was in 1981.) They established the society with guidance from Harry Ashmore, a noted ex-Southern liberal journalist with the Center for the Study of Democratic Institutions in Santa Barbara, and prominent liberal political theorist John Gardner of Common Cause. Ashmore and Gardner saw the society as an experiment in democratic grassroots political organizing. The Planetary Society became the world's most visible pro-space organization, with more than a hundred thousand members and a slick magazine with high-quality photos and often excellent educational articles on developments in planetary exploration.[28]

On behalf of the society, Sagan persuaded filmmaker Steven Spielberg to contribute $100,000 in start-up funds for a private SETI search using an old radiotelescope at Harvard. The project director was (and is) Paul Horowitz. In 1985, during a ceremony at the radiotelescope, and in Sagan's presence, Spielberg held his infant son Max and pulled the switch to start the search. The moviemaker joked: "I just hope that there is more floating around up there than just old reruns of *The Jackie Gleason Show*."[29]

SAGAN'S MOST INTENSE EFFORT to defend SETI came in the form of a novel, which he titled *Contact*. (He had dreamed of writing science fiction for decades. In the 1950s, while a graduate student, he had shyly approached the noted science-fiction writer Judith Merril for advice. She was one of the few women writing science fiction at the time.[30]) In *Contact* he tells the story of Dr. Eleanor ("Ellie") Arroway, a Wisconsin girl who overcomes the roadblocks placed in her path by hostile teachers and sexist professors to become a radioastronomer. She leads an effort to discover radio signals from aliens. Ellie can be read as a thinly disguised version of Carl Sagan (but she also incorporates aspects of the lives of radioastronomer Jill Tarter and Ann Druyan, among others). In the novel, via his alter ego, Sagan grapples with issues close to his heart—sexism, militarism, and religion versus reason. He also struggles, hamhandedly but sincerely, to understand the new phenomenon in his life: true love.

The book's climax concerns the meaning of the universe itself. En route to this discovery, Ellie interacts with old-fashioned evangelicals fresh out of *Elmer Gantry*. These characters represent Sagan's concept of the Enemy: religious superstition. That Sagan viewed the Enemy so simplistically—as if William Jennings Bryan were still stumping the nation—is one reason some intellectuals involved in the modern "science and religion" debate felt they couldn't take Sagan seriously. He was beating a dead horse, not addressing the subtler, more philosophical issues that the modern dialogue encompasses. In fairness to Sagan, however, his view of the Enemy did not seem totally off base in the early 1980s. Jerry Falwell and Pat Robertson had just helped to elect a president, who addressed them with respect and himself talked vaguely about the coming End Times; and creationists were on the warpath, terrorizing school boards and textbook publishers. Even SETI was not immune to evangelical wrath. As the fundamentalist magazine *The Plain Truth* said in 1983:

"Men vainly scan the skies in an attempt to contact presumed physical life forms. . . . Better it is to spend time and effort communicating with God than listening to the empty crackling of static on 10 million microwave channels. With God there will be real and tangible results."[31]

As mentioned earlier, Ellie got her first name from Eleanor Roosevelt, and her last name is (according to Druyan) "an anglicized spelling of Voltaire's middle name."[32] (Voltaire is the pen name of François-Marie Arouet.) Ellie's surname might also, however, pay homage to Sinclair Lewis's famous novel of a noble doctor-scientist, *Arrowsmith*, whose character Max Gottlieb was based on a real-life biologist, the Jewish humanist and outspoken atheist Jacques Loeb (1859–1924). *Arrowsmith* is the kind of book that probably encouraged many young people to enter science (Nobel Prize–winning chemist Glenn Seaborg, who first synthesized plutonium, called it his favorite book).[33]

In *Contact*, the similarities between Sagan and Arroway are overt. Like him as a child, she suffers through unimaginative classroom instruction and enjoys cosmic reveries while watching the heavens; and like him as an adult, she is a religious nonbeliever who battles skeptics about SETI. After her radiotelescope detects an alien signal, it is decoded and proves to contain instructions for some kind of machine. This device, once assembled, allows her and several colleagues to travel through a network of interstellar "wormholes" to the galactic center, where she encounters a representative of the aliens (disguised as her long-dead father) in a dreamlike sequence on a beach. On her return to Earth, she discovers that all scientific evidence of her experience has mysteriously vanished. Ironically for a hard-boiled scientist, she has only one surviving reason to believe in the reality of her alien encounter—sheer faith.

Had Sagan ended the novel at that point, it would have raised fascinating philosophical questions about the limits of scientific knowledge (à la the philosopher David Hume). But Sagan did not end it there. By the novel's end, his scientistic, optimistic side reasserted itself, and he rescued Ellie from Humean ambiguity by having her discover proof (numerically encoded within the value of pi, the ratio of the circumference of a circle to its diameter) that a super-intelligence (God? aliens?) had designed the universe. Thus, with *Contact*, the ever-contradictory Carl Sagan—avowed nonbeliever—offered one of the most religious science-fiction tales ever written. (As we shall see, the film version of *Contact* would end more ambiguously, by omitting the pi plot twist.)

The publication of *Contact* in 1985 evoked the same kind of mixed reaction that had greeted *Cosmos*. Said *Time* magazine: "Despite dialogue like 'Holy Toledo. That's hundreds of janskys,' the book is an engaging pastiche of science and speculation. . . . The time is 1999, when, in Sagan's irrepressibly progressive vision, the President of the U.S. is a woman, and the world's smartest man is a Nigerian."[34] The *Antioch Review* called *Contact* "a good, though not great, adventure story," and complained that Sagan "spends time and effort frying theological and feminist fish."[35]

In the conservative journal *American Spectator*, Robert Royal wrote that Sagan's "real accomplishment has been to drape the prestige of science over less savory purposes."

> In the grand tradition of Bertrand Russell and Albert Einstein, the prototypes of twentieth-century scientific moralists, Sagan is breaking new ground as an *idiot savant*. Russell and Einstein were utter innocents in their understanding of history, but they were at least familiar with parts of our ethical and philosophical heritage. Sagan, on the other hand, is so enslaved by *l'esprit de géométrie* that he deliberately strives to eliminate from his work almost all nonscientific modes of thought—the very tools needed to understand history and apply its lessons to the present.

Royal accused Sagan of scientism, which views science alone as the royal road to truth.

Like Jeffrey Marsh in his *Commentary* assault on *Cosmos*, Royal had a political agenda. By the time *Contact* was published, Sagan had become an outspoken foe of the Reagan Administration's nuclear saber-rattling and push to build the "Star Wars" antimissile system. By contrast, Royal feared the USSR and supported Reagan's antimissile plan. His article went on:

> As is clear in all of Sagan's work, he opposes nuclear weapons and technical attempts to defend against them because he wishes to abolish the categories of politics and history *tout court*. He says in *Cosmos*, "astronomically, the United States and the Soviet Union are the same place." That's a neat formula. Since our quarrel with the Soviet Union would have no importance to an ETI, it should [Sagan implies] have no importance to us either.[36]

The first half of *Contact* is stronger than the rest. At its best, it is a scientific version of Aldous Huxley's *Point Counter Point*—a true novel of ideas, with long, fascinating conversations. *Contact*'s second half is an unfortunate muddle with a few bright spots. The worst failing of the novel is the ending, where Sagan implies that Ellie's drive to find aliens is fueled by an urge to fill the emotional void within her—her failure to find love. In a passage that sounds eerily like a self-description, Sagan writes:

> She had spent her career attempting to make contact with the most remote and alien of strangers, while in her own life she had made contact

with hardly anyone at all. She had been fierce in debunking the creation myths of others, and oblivious to the lie at the core of her own.
She had studied the universe all her life, but had overlooked its clearest
message: For small creatures such as we the vastness is bearable only
through love.[37]

Read unsympathetically, this passage implies that a woman's ambition
must be explained psychologically, as if it were unnatural, whereas a
man's is natural.

It is harder to read sexism into the ending, however, if one sees Ellie
as a stand-in for Sagan himself. The literary and cinematic cliché of the
male careerist who conquers worlds, then realizes he has lost everything
else that matters is no less true for being a cliché. Sagan's innovation was
that he realized that he had been such a man. As a man, of course, he had
too much pride to admit this openly; so he confessed it via the lamenta-
tions of his heroine and alter ego—Ellie.

Contact ends on a cheerful note: Ellie discovers alien intelligences,
who prove to be benevolent (albeit a bit aloof). They operate super-
civilizations even more grandiose than those whose hypothetical radio
signals Sagan had once tried, but failed, to detect from Arecibo. We are
children—no, fetuses—compared to Sagan's fictional aliens; but they are
patient, and will teach us. Thus Sagan placed his readers in the same
emotional state of mind he had enjoyed all his life: the state of feeling
childlike before unimaginable immensities.

But Sagan's fiction constituted a form of whistling in the dark. The
anti-SETI movement had done real damage. Whether right or wrong,
the Tiplerians had posed some important questions for which SETI
advocates had no reliable answers—yet.

THE BIGGEST SHOCK of the anti-SETI backlash came with the defec-
tion of Sagan's old associate I. S. Shklovskii, coauthor of *Intelligent Life in
the Universe*. Shklovskii was not the first SETI turncoat; before him, the
radioastronomers Gerrit Verschuur and Ben Zuckerman had given up
the ship. By the late 1970s, no alien civilizations had been detected;
Shklovskii concluded that they were probably extremely rare, perhaps
even nonexistent. SETI believers pointed out that we had searched only
an infinitesimal percentage of the available stars, and that our search
strategies might be radically flawed; perhaps we aren't listening at the
right frequencies, for example. A thorough search might take decades,
even centuries. But Shklovskii gave up anyway.

Perhaps his new pessimism was reinforced by personal despair. He
was approaching the age of seventy as Soviet society, once the presumed

harbinger of global socialism, its economy seeming to bound forward with every new five-year plan, stagnated in the late Brezhnev era. Meanwhile, both superpowers continued to arm themselves to the teeth. According to Frank Drake, Shklovskii decided that civilization was doomed. If our civilization is self-destructive, then perhaps all technically advanced societies are. The value of L is very, very small; the galaxy is full of dead societies, of radioactive ruins of civilizations that no "Pete" can fix.[38]

The physicist-author Freeman Dyson may have unwittingly put his finger on the real problem. In a profile of Shklovskii, he noted that he was publicly buoyant, but in private, "like many Soviet intellectuals, he is melancholic. He told me once that he has lived with a feeling of inner loneliness since he discovered, at the end of World War II, that he was the only one of his high school graduating class to have survived."[39]

Shklovskii's reasoning may not have been totally emotional, however. Space scientist Herbert Friedman, in his introduction to the English-language edition of Shklovskii's autobiography, said that Shklovskii pointed toward the Fermi paradox. Many other civilizations must be far more advanced than ours, so why don't we see their spaceships?[40] It was an important question, and he was not the only one demanding an answer.

In the late 1970s and early 1980s, then, Sagan began to wonder: Might Shklovskii's gloom be justified? Do intelligent civilizations tend to self-destruct? Is intelligence somehow an unnatural state of being—an inherently unstable phenomenon, like a needle standing upright, that nature hastens to correct? And if so, will our civilization be the next to topple?

15

The Value of *L*

ONLY ONE THING ever really shook Carl Sagan's confidence, even for a moment: the existence of nuclear weapons. Once a cautious liberal, he became a leading antinuclear activist who got arrested while protesting nukes in the desert, debated military brass before large crowds, confronted right-wing zealots and the archdeacons of American global hegemony on national television, detailed the potential horrors of nuclear war before the Pope, and refused dinner invitations from the man who joked about bombing the USSR, Ronald Reagan.

What caused Sagan's political transformation? The failure to detect SETI signals was one factor. Addressing the "Case for Mars" conference in Boulder in the late 1980s, he repeated one of his arguments for SETI—to learn whether other civilizations have survived a technological adolescence akin to ours. An alien message would imply (he said), that "We have *survived*." The audience exploded in applause.[1]

Sagan had begun to express interest in the nuclear weapons issue no later than the opening days of the Carter Administration. He was invited to White House conferences on arms issues[2] and was on friendly enough terms with Carter aides to be asked to contribute to the defeated president's farewell address in January 1981. Carter's speech included these words from Sagan:

> Nuclear weapons are an expression of one side of our human character. But there's another side. The same rocket technology that delivers nuclear warheads has also taken us peacefully into space. From that perspective, we see our Earth as it really is—a small and fragile and beautiful blue globe, the only home we have. We see no barriers of race or religion or country. We see the essential unity of our species and our planet, and with faith and common sense, that bright vision will ultimately prevail.[3]

Ever since his childhood reading of "Pete Can Fix It," Sagan had pondered humanity's potential for destroying itself. The age of nuclear weapons was a technological bottleneck through which humanity had to pass. If it survived, then it might endure for millions of years, exploring the galaxy, perhaps even encountering alien beings face-to-face. If not . . . then that might explain the radio silence of the stars: their "advanced" civilizations had self-destructed, as ours eventually might. In *The Dragons of Eden*, Sagan discussed for the first time at any length what he regarded as the dark side of human nature, the hypothetical reptilian complex within the brain. It is (he thought) the oldest part of our psyches, and its primal passions—ideal for survival on the Serengeti, but ill suited to survival in a world of nuclear weapons on hair-trigger alert—might yet oversee our bright, noisy end.

There was an existential factor, too. His father's death in 1979 was a huge emotional blow. Sam had set a high moral example for his children. He did not lecture them about morality, but he set an example of the right way to behave. In Sagan's novel, *Contact*, the most lovingly rendered character is the father of the ambitious, Sagan-like protagonist, Ellie Arroway. His death shatters her, and it inspires her to redouble her effort to achieve something that would make him proud.

After Sam's death, Rachel was terribly lonely. She dated a man named Marty, a former garment worker. Marty adored Rachel; they attended symphonies together.[4]

Time had softened Rachel. The approach of death makes the old seek the forgiveness of the young, seek reassurance that they will not go unlamented into that dark night. She praised her daughter, Cari, (who had always felt neglected) in a letter after she visited an Israeli kibbutz. Rachel was ecstatic at the birth of Cari's daughter, Sharon (although Rachel initially refused to believe it was not a boy). Cari—whose memories of her mother otherwise tend to be unhappy—glows to recall how the aged Rachel, enchanted by her granddaughter, did a delightful impression of Sharon singing "I'm a Little Teapot." A few years later, in 1982, Rachel died of pancreatic cancer.[5]

Now Sagan's only blood tie to the past was his sister, Cari. At Druyan's insistence, Sagan began to reconnect with Cari,[6] whom he had previously largely ignored, in part by remembering her birthday and by paying attention to Sharon, whom he adored. In November 1983, when Sharon was almost six, he wrote her a letter explaining what snowflakes were:

Dear Niece:
    Thank you so much for your very nice letter. It was so good to hear from you. I see you are growing up fast. Annie and I and Sasha

want to see you soon. It would be too bad if we have to wait years to see you. So let's try and get our families together in the next few months, or at least by the time spring comes. I know your mother and Annie think it's a good idea too.

Before spring comes, you know, it will be winter. In the winter it gets so cold that water freezes and the ground gets icy. Also, the water in the air freezes and comes floating down as snowflakes. Every snowflake is flat and spins as it falls through the air. Also, every snowflake has six sides. And did you know that if you looked at a snowflake under a microscope it shows a beautiful pattern? No two snowflakes are alike. Think of all those snowflakes in the wintertime and how many different pretty patterns there must be, if you could look closely at all of them.

All of us send you our love.

—Carl (Uncle)

P.S. Also thank your mother for the wonderful 1939 World's Fair memorabilia; they mean a great deal to me.[7]

In short, Druyan had begun to tug Sagan to earth, to make him feel more concern for his family and for political issues—in particular, terrestrial survival. After Rachel's death, Sagan began to look at himself and his family "in a different way," recalls his son Nick.[8] Sagan and Druyan had a child, Alexandra (Sasha), in 1982. Human beings were no longer simply "cortices" (to use Lester Grinspoon's term) to him; they were real people to whom he felt a new closeness and about whom he felt newly protective. Their planet was threatened. To save them, he had to save the planet.

His first big opportunity to do so came in the early 1980s, when he almost died himself.

HE WAS USED TO CLOSE CALLS, of course. In the late 1970s, when he and Druyan were first together, he went to Beth Israel Hospital in Boston and had his gallbladder removed. While he was there (she recalls), the doctors told him that he apparently had Hodgkin's disease. He replied, "Well, as long as I can be with Annie, I don't care what I have." Two days later, the doctors returned with better news: he didn't have Hodgkin's disease. Strangely, the false alarm had perturbed neither him nor Druyan, she says. "It actually hadn't made a single bit of difference to either of us because we were in such a euphoric state of being in love with each other. . . . We were so happy to be together."

Then in 1983, in another hospital, following complications from an operation, Sagan "came as close to dying as you can come and not die," she says. After the operation, she slept on the floor of his hospital room (just as he had slept on the floor of her hospital room months earlier when she gave birth to Sasha). One night Sagan sat straight up in his hospital bed. Druyan awoke and gasped to see him: he was white as a sheet, as he was bleeding internally from a surgical incision. He got out of bed, then collapsed on the floor. Druyan says a surgeon urged her to take Sagan to another hospital because, the doctor explained, "Your husband is going to die, and we just prefer he wouldn't die here. He's too famous to die in our little hospital."[9] At 2 A.M., frantic, Druyan phoned and awakened Shirley Arden, who was not only Sagan's secretary but one of the couple's closest friends. Arden got out of bed and drove through an upstate New York blizzard to reach the hospital. "There was obviously massive internal bleeding," Arden says. "When I got there they were pumping blood into Carl as fast as they could." As the storm raged, the hospital transferred Sagan by ambulance to Upstate Medical Center in Syracuse. Druyan rode in the ambulance with Sagan, while Arden "followed right behind them in my car." Arriving at Upstate, they were greeted in the parking lot by surgeon David Fromm who, Arden recalls, "was holding a steaming cup of coffee. . . . He talked with Carl and with Annie and me, and said apparently the varicose veins in [Carl's] esophagus had ruptured. [Fromm] laid out the [medical] options and the odds, and said he could do the [surgical] job. Carl told him, 'Let's do it!' "

While Sagan was in the hospital, it was flooded with flowers and telegrams from his well-wishers, "and fans began to besiege the place," Arden says. A woman who claimed (falsely) to be Sagan's niece managed to talk her way to the door of the intensive care unit until she was turned away. Lester Grinspoon flew from Boston to be by Sagan's side. Grinspoon was in the intensive care unit "almost constantly, telling Carl what was going on and reassuring him," Arden says. "Carl would write little notes on a pad for Lester since [Sagan] was on a respirator and could not talk." One of Sagan's shakily written notes read: "Unremitting pain . . . how long?"

Fortunately Sagan recovered. During his recovery Ronald Reagan went on television and delivered one of the most controversial speeches of the cold war. Unlike Sagan's admirer Jimmy Carter, who had real intellectual leanings, Reagan was a simple soul, unashamed of his ignorance and happy to quote from a deep box of newspaper clippings that supported his worldview. His revival of cold warriorism enraged many intellectuals and academics; Isaac Asimov, for example, in his diary, attacked Reagan's "mad panting for Nicaraguan blood."[10] Yet the old actor's charm and self-deprecating wit won him wide respect, even from people repelled by his policies. (Undergoing surgery after an assassination attempt, Reagan told his doctors: "I hope you're all Republicans.") So amiable a politician could, and did, sell the nation all brands of snake oil. The prime example is his proposal in his March 1983 television speech that American scientists develop a technology able to render nuclear weapons "impotent and obsolete." He gave no specifics on the proposal, which he had developed with little or no unbiased scientific advice; but Washington insiders immediately knew he was talking about an antimissile system that would shoot down ICBMs. (It sounded, in fact, something like the fantasy weapon of the 1940 film *Murder in the Air*, in which an exotic device shot down a spy plane. The star of that film had been the twenty-seven-year-old Ronald Reagan.[11]) Since the antiballistic missile debate of the 1960s, liberal and dovish scientists had opposed antimissile systems partly because they would increase the likelihood of a nuclear exchange, not lessen it, by threatening the Soviets' confidence in the deterrent value of their nuclear weapons; hence they might feel compelled to launch a first-strike attack before such a system became operational.

Besides, there were serious reasons for doubting that an impermeable antimissile system was technically feasible. Reagan's proposed shield was the Strategic Defense Initiative (SDI), or "Star Wars" in popular parlance. If only a small percentage of missiles got past the shield, they would be enough to kill tens of millions of Americans. Writing in *Parade* magazine, Sagan compared the Star Wars project to an ineffective form of birth control:

> A contraceptive shield that deters 90 percent of 200 million sperm cells is generally considered worthless—20 million sperm cells penetrating the shield are more than enough. Such a shield is not better than nothing; it is worse than nothing, because it might well engender a false sense of security, bringing on the very event it was designed to prevent. The same is true for the leaky shield of Star Wars.[12]

As Sagan lay in his hospital bed, still on life support, Druyan told him about Reagan's speech. He was weak, but he managed to ask her: "Do you have a pencil?" She found one, plus a sheet of paper. He then dictated to her the manifesto of an anti-SDI petition. He gave her a long list of noted scientists and other figures to contact, from atomic pioneer Glenn Seaborg to astronaut-senator John Glenn.

With Arden's help, Druyan began to contact the scientists, using the phone in the intensive care unit. "Hello," she began, "my name is Annie Druyan and my husband is Carl Sagan . . . " Everyone she called agreed to add their name to the petition. "It was amazing. Nobody wouldn't talk to me." Such was the power of the man who made *Cosmos*.

Proudly, she showed Sagan the completed petition, with every name affixed. Sagan scanned it. "Annie," he said, "you misspelled 'cislunar.'" Exasperated, she fired back, "I got the prime minister of Japan, for

Christ's sake! What do you want from me? I haven't slept in four nights. Give me a break!"[13]

Druyan notes the timing of Sagan's brush with death and his promotion of the anti-SDI petition. "He had almost died, and he was lucky to be alive, and in a way that [the antinuclear campaign] was [a way of paying] something back for his great good fortune to be alive. It was redemptive of science, because it distressed him bitterly that more than half the world's scientists were at work on weapons of mass destruction . . . that the science that he loved and saw as a great liberation was aimed at our children's heads."[14]

IRONICALLY, SAGAN CHOSE to mention his new goal in life at RAND Corporation in Santa Monica, his old stomping ground from the *Mariner 2* days. He had moved on to other subjects, but RAND theorists continued to play nuclear "war games" and to design U.S. nuclear targeting strategies as if Stalin still loomed over Berlin, as if Khrushchev were still sneaking missiles into Cuba. As David Morrison tells the story, in the early 1980s, many years before its launch, Sagan had been part of the image analysis team for the *Galileo* space probe, which was slated to fly to Jupiter. On one occasion the team met at RAND. Morrison recalls that post-*Cosmos* Sagan came to two days of meetings: "It was just like old times . . . really pleasant . . . like he was getting back into science."

At the end of it, a discussion leader asked everyone in the room what their plans were for the next year. Sagan said, "I've really enjoyed being at this meeting. But honestly, I have to tell you I'm not likely to do much of anything on *Galileo* for the next year or so, because I am concentrating most of my energies on saving the world from nuclear holocaust."

There was a pause. Afterward, Morrison recalls, a couple of them said, "Well, given the choice, that's probably more important than working on *Galileo*."[15]

THE LAST TWO great scientific debates of the cold war concerned, first, SDI, and second, "nuclear winter." Sagan figured in both debates, but more prominently in the second. The nuclear winter hypothesis directly challenged an old, albeit rarely acknowledged, assumption by U.S. strategists: that a nuclear war might be survivable, even "winnable." It is for this reason that the Reagan Administration, right-wingers and nuclear weaponeers and strategists (the "wizards of Armageddon," journalist Fred Kaplan once called the latter),[16] reacted so furiously to the nuclear winter hypothesis and its glamorous champion, Carl Sagan. In a subsequent book by Sagan and his colleague Rich Turco, they recall that an exasperated administration official asked Sagan: "You want me to be responsible for telling the President that his whole nuclear strategy is wrong?"[17] Terrified of repercussions from the Reagan Administration, NASA temporarily tried to suppress the research, but Sagan saved the day.

According to the theory, a nuclear exchange might trigger massive urban fires that could cloud the atmosphere for weeks or months, blocking sunlight and lowering Earth's temperature so severely as to cause freezing or near-freezing conditions. This, in turn, would prevent millions, even billions, of survivors from growing crops and rebuilding their lives. Nuclear winter might destroy civilization after a nuclear war, if the war itself did not.

Sagan did not invent the nuclear winter hypothesis (contrary to some erroneous press accounts, no fault of his). But his energetic advocacy and his face-to-face battles with right-wingers from William F. Buckley to Edward Teller gave the issue public attention it otherwise wouldn't have received. Along with the much larger "Nuclear Freeze" movement of the same era, it helped to put Reaganites and militarists on the defensive at a time when they were scheming to revive the cold war, forcing them to be more receptive to Soviet leader Mikhail Gorbachev's peace feelers. How great a role the nuclear winter hypothesis played in ending the cold war remains an interesting topic for exploration by future historians, especially as the U.S. and Russian governments throw open vast files of once-classified cold war archives. The memoirs of Reagan Administration officials generally say little or nothing about nuclear winter, but anecdotal reports suggest that the Soviets took the hypothesis more seriously.

The main scientific work was done by four other scientists—Rich Turco, Brian Toon, Thomas P. Ackerman, and Jim Pollack. (Toon and Pollack were former students of Sagan's.) Working in collaboration with Sagan, they formed the group known by their initials as TTAPS (the "S" is for "Sagan"). Some thought the label TTAPS was eerily appropriate, as if they were playing taps for humanity.

To the general public during the cold war, a "winnable" nuclear war was unthinkable. They had watched countless television shows and movies in which a single nuclear launch triggered an all-out atomic assault by both sides, leaving Earth a smoking, radioactive ruin. To the lay public, the idea of "waging" nuclear war battlefield by battlefield—as if it were simply a brighter, noisier replay of the Battle of the Bulge—was insane. That's one reason why most Americans didn't bother to build underground shelters; they doubted they would reemerge into a habitable world. And that's why audiences roared so loudly watching *Dr. Strangelove*, when a general (played by actor George C. Scott) urged the

President to complete another general's unauthorized nuclear assault on the USSR to "catch 'em with their pants down," while acknowledging that it wouldn't be an easy victory: "I'm not saying we wouldn't get our hair mussed!"

A substantial number of U.S. strategists, however, believed that nuclear victory was possible. In "Victory Is Possible," an article written in the early 1980s for the respected journal *Foreign Policy*, Colin S. Gray and Keith Payne of the Hudson Institute argued: "If American nuclear power is to support U.S. foreign policy objectives, the United States must possess the ability to wage nuclear war rationally. . . . The United States should plan to defeat the Soviet Union and to do so at a cost that would not prohibit U.S. recovery." In the most cold-blooded passage, Gray and Payne cautioned that "a U.S. president cannot credibly threaten and should not launch a strategic nuclear strike if expected U.S. casualties are likely to involve 100 million or more American citizens." This raised the question: Were Gray and Payne willing to sacrifice, say, 70 million or 50 million or 20 million Americans in return for toppling the Soviet regime?[18] One can imagine how Soviet leaders must have reacted to seeing such a document in print in a distinguished American publication. How might our leaders have reacted if the Soviets had published such a piece, contemplating the annihilation of America?

The strategists most prone to such nuclear "logic" were not, contrary to popular myth, the brass (with the vivid exception of cigar-chomping Gen. Curtis "Bomb 'Em Back to the Stone Age" LeMay, former chief of the Strategic Air Command). Too many generals had real fighting experience, knew what the face of war looked like—men dying horribly in combat, the best-laid battle tactics thrown into confusion by the "fog of war." (The decision to bomb Hiroshima was bitterly criticized by the former commander in chief of the Allied forces during World War II, Dwight D. Eisenhower.) No, the true deacons of nuclear "logic" were civilian strategists, particularly certain academic types, true-life Strangeloves, men who took macho pride in "thinking about the unthinkable" and talking about "megadeath," although some of them had no military record and probably couldn't distinguish a howitzer from a Huey. One of these was Herman Kahn of RAND Corporation (who did, however, serve in the army in World War II). A man of Falstaffian girth and Faustian imagination, he complained in his 1961 book *On Thermonuclear War* that popular writers routinely assumed that a nuclear exchange would mean the end of the world. In fact, he maintained, a "properly prepared country" would not be wiped out; "it is more likely to be set back a given number of years in its economic growth," he wrote.[19]

The TTAPS team challenged this whole way of thinking. If the nuclear winter hypothesis was correct, then a nuclear war could not be played like a game of chess. They argued that even a tiny percentage of the world's nuclear arsenal, detonated in a nuclear conflict, might trigger a global nuclear winter. In other words, nuclear war would backfire on whoever launched it. Hence a nation launching a first-strike attack might well be committing suicide, even if it managed to "ride out" its foe's counterattack (as the Strangelovians believed was possible).

NEWTON ONCE SAID that he stood on the shoulders of giants. Scientists often quote this remark yet fail to appreciate its full relevance. There is no such thing as a totally original idea; every scientific notion has deep roots. (Even specific aspects of Einstein's special theory of relativity were dimly anticipated by others,[20] and Darwin had predecessors galore.[21])

Likewise, we can glean threads leading to the fabric of nuclear winter in some of Sagan's earlier work. It is striking, in retrospect, how much of his work touched on one question: How do specific aerosols, gases, or other factors alter the temperature structure of a planetary atmosphere? Examples include his objection to Öpik and Kuiper's "dust cloud" theories of Venus, which would have blocked sunlight and prevented Sagan's greenhouse effect from generating the extreme temperatures of Venus; his study, based on *Mariner 9* data, of how a Martian dust storm cooled the planetary surface (a fact also explored in detail by his Soviet friend Georgi S. Golitsyn);[22] his and George Mullen's thesis that ammonia warmed the early atmosphere of Earth; and his 1979 paper with Jim Pollack and Brian Toon, which explored how human settlement of Earth had (by, say, replacing green forests with granite cities) altered its reflectivity (albedo) and, perhaps, its average temperature.[23] Pollack, Toon, and Sagan also wrote a series of papers studying climate changes caused by volcanic eruptions. Pollack and Toon took airplane flights to examine volcanic plumes in the atmosphere. "These studies were direct precursors of the nuclear winter work," Toon recalls.

A key trigger for the nuclear winter hypothesis, though, was a thesis that was almost unknown until 1980 but is now familiar to every schoolchild. This is the hypothesis that a falling asteroid or comet triggered a climate change sixty-five million years ago, wiping out the dinosaurs. This theory was published in 1980 by a father-son team at Berkeley, Luis and Walter Alvarez, along with Frank Asaro and Helen Michel.[24] Their key evidence was a geological layer rich in the element iridium, located in a layer of rock dating from sixty-five million years ago. Iridium is rare on Earth but common in meteorites and, presumably, asteroids. This offered persuasive evidence that an asteroid had struck Earth sixty-five million years ago. They suggested that the impact generated a massive cloud of dust that circled the globe, blocking out sunlight and triggering a major cooling. Result: the dinosaurian ecosystem was devastated, destroying the "thunder lizards."

JIM POLLACK WAS A QUIET MAN; like other quiet people, he heard things that others missed. Besides, he worked all the time; it was no surprise to find him in the office on a Sunday.[25] So it is also no surprise that in 1980 he heard about the Alvarez et al. paper prior to its publication and got his hands on a copy.[26]

By 1980 Pollack was ensconced at NASA's Ames Research Center in Mountain View, south of San Francisco. For a gay man, there was no better place to live; San Francisco was the nation's "gayest" city. Sagan knew that Pollack was gay, according to Sagan's secretary, Shirley Arden. She recalls that she "loved to be a matchmaker for my unmarried friends. Once I asked Carl how he thought Jim would get along with a [certain] woman. . . . Carl told me to relax, that Jim was not likely to want to marry, settle down, and have a family because he was gay. We had never discussed Jim's sexual preference because it was of no significance." Living in the Bay Area, Pollack loved the city's culture (he had season tickets to the San Francisco Opera) and shared its liberal sympathies. (According to his sister, he left much of his estate to the homeless and the fight against AIDS.[27]) Pollack's colleagues at Ames and elsewhere revered him: "a great man, a great scientist" (Dale Cruikshank).[28] "Probably the best planetary scientist I know" (David Morrison).[29] "Really astounding" (Rich Turco).[30] "Many people who worked in the space sciences division [at Ames] were absolutely devoted to Jim, and were absolutely crushed when he died." (Don Hunten).[31] Ironically, despite Pollack's workaholism, he professed to love California for its relaxed atmosphere.[32] Despite his wariness of publicity, among his colleagues he was "a real and forceful science leader," Morrison says. They trusted Pollack's scientific judgment; it was impeccable. And so Tom Ackerman and Brian Toon paid close attention when Pollack handed them an advance copy of the Alvarez paper and said, "Take a look at this."[33]

Pollack was nothing if not meticulous, and he suspected that the Alvarez team had made an important error. They based their estimates of the severity of an impact-induced "winter" on the radiative properties of aerosols expelled by volcanoes. But, Pollack pointed out, a falling asteroid or comet would not generate the same kinds of aerosols as volcanoes. A volcano generates enormous amounts of ash and SO_2, or sulfur dioxide; the latter gradually dissolves into water and forms sulfuric acid droplets, which reflect sunlight and cool the lower atmosphere. Since the sulfuric acid aerosols are extremely fine and descend extremely slowly, they can linger in the upper atmosphere for long periods. The ash is bulkier and falls faster from the sky.

But what kinds of aerosols would an asteroid impact generate? How big would the aerosols be? What would their shapes be? (Shape affects radiative properties.) And how long would they remain in the sky, blocking out the sun, before returning to Earth? Pollack and his colleagues began investigating the question.[34]

In October 1981, Toon traveled to Snowbird, Utah, for a conference called "Geological Implications of Impacts of Large Asteroids and Comets on the Earth." He delivered a paper titled "Evolution of an Impact-generated Dust Cloud and Its Effects on the Atmosphere." After the conference, a representative of the National Academy of Sciences approached Toon. Previously, an NAS panel had concluded that a nuclear war would not significantly affect the global climate and environment. But now (the NAS representative told Toon) the Alvarez hypothesis had raised questions about the 1970s study. Would Toon be interested in participating in an Academy meeting to reassess the 1970s finding?

Toon was. He and Turco had already studied volcanic clouds for many years, and Turco had contacts with the nuclear weapons community. Toon suggested to Turco that they both attend the Academy meeting. Before the conference, based on Turco's knowledge of how nuclear blasts spew dust into the atmosphere, they made preliminary calculations of the possible climatic impact. The impact, they concluded, might be significant. They also consulted Ackerman, who helped them with the extraordinarily complex calculations of radiative transfer.

Initially, Ackerman hesitated to get involved. He recalls: "My immediate response—I shall remember this forever because it shows how wrong you can be—was: 'I don't want anything to do with this, because all we'll do is show the weapons effects have very little effect.'" And he didn't want to publish such a conclusion, lest it imply that "it's okay to use nuclear weapons."[35]

Meanwhile, the researchers Paul Crutzen and John Birks studied the possible climatic effects of smoke generated by nuclear bomb–ignited forest fires.[36] Turco et al. had been thinking about nuclear bomb–generated dust, which has very different optical properties from smoke. They cogitated further after reading Crutzen and Birks's paper. It dawned on them that smoke from forest fires was trivial compared to the quantities and opaqueness of the smoke—thick, black soot—that would gush from burning cities. "If you're ever in the city and see a burning building, the smoke is black because you're burning plastics, treated materials like carpets, and stuff like that," Ackerman said. Soot—long, black, tangled chains of carbon molecules—is a superb barrier to sunlight: "The amount of solar radiation that gets through a soot cloud is orders of magnitude less than gets through a dirt cloud."[37] A lurid image began to form in their minds: hundreds of nuclear-fried cities, flickering orange and vomiting skyward Niagaras of pitch-black soot, blacking out the sky, transforming day into night. Hours pass; the surface temperature plunges. The next day, the sun rises but is barely visible through the aerial black pall. As sunlight cannot penetrate to the surface, the temperature keeps falling, perhaps to freezing—perhaps lower.

High-altitude winds blow the dark clouds around the planet. Soon, the black shroud envelops Earth. Snowflakes fall in the tropics. Millions who survived the nuclear war freeze to death. Others starve because crops and cattle have died from frost. Earth is locked in "the cold and the dark."[38] Civilization might disintegrate. A nuclear squabble between superpowers—two nations with about a half-billion people between them—ends up wrecking the global climate and endangering the planet's more than six billion other people. Meanwhile, many light years away, alien SETI scientists notice that our artificial electromagnetic emissions—our radio and television signals—have gone dead. Calmly, they scratch another candidate planet off their list.

"I started running climate simulations [on the computer], and when I started doing that, I started getting weird results," Ackerman recalls. With the soot clouds overhead during a nuclear crisis, no sunlight penetrates to the surface, so it doesn't warm up during the day. With every twenty-four-hour cycle, "it just continually cools, and after a week, it's really cold. It's below freezing all the time."[39]

Turco worked at the other end of California, in Santa Monica, at a firm called R & D Associates, a smaller think tank within RAND Corporation. Naturally he had access to Department of Defense information about nuclear weapons. That information greatly benefited the TTAPS team, allowing them to better estimate the atmospheric effects of nuclear weapons.[40] It "was a wonderful group," Ackerman says. "Four bright guys, all interested in different things, who had good relations with each other."

"We were convinced we were envisioning an extremely cold world," Ackerman says. "I, in my own mind, had moved from the position of 'This isn't a big deal' to 'This is as monstrous a climatic effect as I can imagine producing on our globe.'"

Then NASA-Ames management discovered what the four scientists were up to. At that moment, Ackerman recalls, "the shit hit the fan." [41]

Ames director Clarence A. Syvertson was an aeronautical engineer by training.[42] He was also evidently terrified of doing anything to antagonize the Reagan Administration. The Administration was still young and full of right-wing ideological fervor. It was not only calling for a new face-off with the Soviets, it was also making unpleasant noises about axing some parts of the space program (particularly robotic missions to the planets) and privatizing others. Syvertson didn't want to give the Administration any excuse to carve up the Ames budget.

So, Ackerman recalls, Syvertson summoned Pollack, Toon, and Ackerman "up to his office and told us we weren't supposed to work on this anymore." Toon and Pollack countered (Ackerman recalls) "that this was a scientific problem; that we had been asked to work on it by the Defense Department; that we didn't see any reason we shouldn't work on it; and that we didn't feel the NASA center had the right to tell us what we could work on." NASA still insisted that the research be dropped, and accused the TTAPS team of failing to subject it to the peer review process required by the space agency.

Syvertson "got very upset. We had a subsequent meeting with him, where he found out we were continuing merrily on our way [doing the nuclear winter research]. He got really upset and threatened to fire us. He said he could [order a] RIF [reduction in force] of our whole division. I was dumbfounded."[43]

Turco was planning to speak about their research at the annual American Geophysical Union meeting in San Francisco that December (1982). NASA forced cancellation of the speech. Those who think that Lysenkoism is a purely Soviet phenomenon—that American science exists in a cultural vacuum, immune from political pressures—should ponder this incident.

IT'S WHO YOU KNOW, as they say. Jim Pollack knew Carl Sagan, and apparently passed on word of their plight to him. "Carl had contacts and political presence, and that basically made the management at Ames back off. I have no idea how he did it," Ackerman says.[44] (It might have been easier than it seemed. Syvertson knew Sagan, having personally invited him to Ames a few years earlier for a conference on Venus.[45] One call from Sagan to Syvertson might have set things straight.) Thus the man who saved NASA's SETI project from Proxmire also saved nuclear winter research from NASA.

To get around NASA's peer review objection, Sagan quickly organized an unusal form of peer review—a meeting at which experts on climate and nuclear weapons read drafts of the TTAPS team's nuclear winter research. During its own subsequent review of the TTAPS team's work, NASA objected to their use of the phrase "nuclear war" in the title. Politically as jittery as ever, NASA didn't want its employees dabbling too obviously in a topic about which the White House and the Defense Department had strong views. During a phone conversation,

Turco and Toon hit on a less obvious, politically safer term—"nuclear winter." Eventually, the TTAPS paper was published in *Science*, and the term "nuclear winter" became a catchphrase in the media.

Sagan invited Toon and Turco to visit him in Ithaca. It was wintertime, and the roads were icy. Turco was impressed by the handsome home, located on a gorge near "a huge waterfall," overlooking Lake Cayuga. Inside were towering bookcases and trees growing within the house. "It's really a spectacular place."

"Then Carl appears," Turco continued, "and he's in a bathrobe and pajamas and slippers. He's pale white and gaunt and he comes kind of shuffling in his bathrobe. He sits down and he apologizes. He says that he's just had this serious operation where he was close to death and he's just recovering." During their discussion, an aide brought Sagan a bowl of soup. "And the amazing thing was that here's this guy that's just been close to death . . . but he really drove our discussion. . . . By the end of the evening I was, like, exhausted." Yet Sagan was still chugging along. Turco wondered: "How can this guy do this?"[46] Sagan's energy was especially remarkable considering his total disdain for regular physical exercise. (This disdain is noted by his close friend, Lester Grinspoon, who recalls an instance when Sagan bought a treadmill and tried it once, during which time, lost in thought, he fell off it. He never used it again.) Sagan's energy came from pure intellectual enthusiasm.

Ackerman recalls that the first time he met Sagan, there were more than fifty people in the room, all of them "revolving around Carl." Sagan had the remarkable ability to connect with people one-on-one, to make each listener feel that he or she was the most important person present. "And I don't think that was an act," Ackerman adds. "He liked interacting with people." Sagan also had a near-photographic memory for details about people, as well as about scientific articles. He was brilliant and charismatic, and seemed to know everybody. "I always said Carl would have been a successful politician."[47]

Sagan was also intensely imaginative. His tendency to fly from topic to topic irritated many colleagues, who perceived it as laziness or a lack of depth. But Pollack felt differently. "Jim loved to work with Carl," Toon says. "Jim definitely respected Carl's opinion, because otherwise he wouldn't have worked with him." Jim was like a farmer who will "grow something, and grow it again, and again and again, and make it better and better, whereas Carl was flitting from flower to flower." But Sagan, Toon said, "would come up and have some idea that was totally out in left field, that you hadn't thought about at all."[48]

Sagan was exceptionally valuable to the TTAPS team for another reason: he evidently still had access to what Ackerman delicately calls "special knowledge," that is, data from classified sources. "I never asked him specifically about it, but some of the information which trickled back to our group was clearly stuff that arose from Carl or Rich's 'special' knowledge."[49]

Sagan once impressed Frank Drake with a non-flashy display of his special knowledge. In the early 1970s, a Soviet radioastronomer had approached Sagan and Drake, stating that he was detecting a peculiar radio signal from space. Could it be aliens? Sagan discreetly checked with his sources—whoever they might be—and relayed back the sad news: the signals came not from aliens but from an American reconnaissance satellite.[50]

How deep was Sagan's acquaintance with U.S. intelligence services? His office records indicate that he was in contact with the CIA at least as late as the early 1980s. As Ackerman observes, Sagan "knew *everybody*." In 1972, he lectured (on an unknown topic) at what was then perhaps the most secretive of intelligence agencies, the National Security Agency (NSA) in Fort Meade, Maryland, which monitors foreign transmissions. (He was invited to speak by an official named Bond—Jack Bond.) The NSA invited Sagan to speak again several years later (again, on an unknown topic). It is unclear whether he spoke the second time. Interestingly, Sagan doesn't cite either NSA speech in his otherwise excruciatingly detailed résumé.[51]

In March 1977, Sagan's secretary sent him this cryptic note: "Jack Bond (National Security Agency) called to tell you that Lambros Callimahos has had 2 brain tumor surgeries. He is now back to work but is debilitated, although teaching his courses. No way to know for sure whether he will be there in the fall. Said you would understand his message."[52]

According to James Bamford's classic 1983 study of the NSA, *The Puzzle Palace*, Lambros D. Callimahos was a master cryptoanalyst, also "known as the Nameless One and His Cerebral Phosphorescence, the Guru and Caudillo . . . an NSA legend. For twenty-two years the white-haired Mr. C. with the gentle blue eyes and natty bow tie taught the Intensive Study course with a rare combination of wit and brilliance." He died in October 1977.[53] What relationship, if any, did he have with Sagan? The answer—perhaps exciting, perhaps mundane—may lie within massive cold war archives still waiting to be declassified.[54] The Callimahos memo is one of a few odd details from Sagan's career that hint that there was even more going on in his life than was listed on his résumé. His life was a jigsaw puzzle, and not all the pieces fit.

THE NUCLEAR WINTER THEORISTS' first big coming-out event occurred in late October 1983 in Washington, D.C., at a two-day conference

titled "The World after Nuclear War." Sagan and Stanford ecology professor Paul Ehrlich (author of *The Population Bomb*) were the two stars.
Sagan described the atmospheric effects of a nuclear war involving the
detonation of 5,000 megatons (five billion tons) of TNT: Aerial debris
would block out about 95 percent of sunlight in the temperate zone of
the Northern Hemisphere. The surface temperature could drop as low
as −23°C. Even a far smaller war (involving 100 megatons dropped on
100 cities) could trigger a subfreezing nuclear winter. During the Washington conference, Sagan and Ehrlich engaged in a conversation with
four prominent members of the Soviet Academy of Sciences via television satellite hookup. Covering the conference for *Science* magazine,
Constance Holden emphasized that the research raised fundamental
doubts about the nation's nuclear strategy: "A single nuclear counter-
force strike, even if unilateral, would be suicidal to the nation launching
it."[55] The magazine later ran an editorial by publisher William D. Carey,
who praised the nuclear winter scientists' research. "It has been a very
good thing for the integrity of science, and a sign of courage, that some
40 scientists of high standing have gone public with their considered
estimates of the global atmospheric effects and long-term biological consequences of nuclear war."[56]

How might nuclear winter be prevented? The most obvious way, of
course, was never to fight a nuclear war. The superpowers, however, had
built much of their national defense strategy around their nuclear arsenals. They were not about to announce, "Don't worry, we'll never actually launch those awful things!" So a second-best solution was for the
superpowers to reduce the size of their nuclear arsenals below a certain
number of nukes—below a "threshold" likely to trigger a nuclear winter.
Sagan didn't know what the threshold for triggering nuclear winter was,
but hinted that a thousand nuclear explosions might do the trick.

At that time, the two superpowers together possessed more than
sixty thousand nuclear warheads. Sagan called for a massive weapons cut-
back by both sides in a solo article for *Foreign Affairs*, which is read by
many world leaders.[57]

Nuclear winter theory gave peace activists something they had long
lacked: a scientific rationale for backing out of the nuclear age. Their
previous arguments had been largely moralistic, focusing on the inherently genocidal nature of nuclear weapons. But moralistic objections
drew yawns from the cold-eyed nuclear strategists, who preferred arguments that could be quantified. To the strategists, a moral argument was
no argument at all.

By contrast, the strategists could not afford to ignore the nuclear
winter hypothesis. It put the strategists in the same situation as a gun-
man who learns that his gun is faulty: if he fires it, it might explode,

killing him. Would he, then, risk firing it? If the nuclear winter hypothesis was correct, then a nuclear-triggered "winter" would at the very least radically alter the postwar environment in which U.S. citizens would have to survive and U.S. troops would have to maneuver. Nuclear winter offered a novel, selfish rationale for not launching a first-strike attack, even to preempt an expected attack by the Soviets. Even a moderate-sized nuclear attack could trigger environmental suicide; it was that simple. Suddenly, the "lessons" of thousands of nuclear "war games" played at RAND and elsewhere over the decades seemed moot. It appeared (to quote from *War Games*, a popular movie of the time) that "the only way to win a nuclear war is not to play it."[58]

To the famed science writer Lewis Thomas, the nuclear winter hypothesis was "the greatest piece of good news to emerge from science in the whole twentieth century. . . . Thermonuclear warfare is an impossibility, and the weapons can never be used for any kind of decisive military accomplishment."[59] The *Atlantic Monthly* ran a cover story on the topic, with the arresting title: "Is Nuclear War 'Impossible'?" The author, Thomas Powers, shared Lewis Thomas's point of view:

> In a sense, the bad news about nuclear winter is *so* bad that it might even be taken as grounds for a perverse optimism. If we finally admit that we can't fight a nuclear war without destroying ourselves—*really* destroying ourselves—then perhaps the time has come to quit preparing to fight one. . . . [The] recognition of the nuclear-winter problem, awful as it is, seems a piece of immense good fortune at the eleventh hour, and a sign that Providence hasn't given up on us yet.[60]

At that time a young analyst named Joseph Cirincione was working at the Center for Strategic and International Studies in Washington, D.C. To him, nuclear winter sounded "ridiculous—how could a few hundred nuclear weapons change the climate of the Earth?" But "the more I looked into it, the less confident I was that I was right." In retrospect, Cirincione, now director of the Non-Proliferation Project at the Carnegie Endowment for International Peace, believes the nuclear winter issue had "a very significant impact on arms control issues of the 1980s. Nuclear winter [was a] compelling vision or nightmare that motivated people." Nuclear holocaust did not require an exchange of tens of thousands of nuclear warheads; rather, the apocalypse might be triggered by a far smaller exchange, by a "so-called limited nuclear war. This is what got people off their couches and into the streets! And writing letters, and visiting Congressmen, and into the town hall meetings."[61] Along with the publication of Jonathan Schell's *The Fate of the Earth* in 1982, the nuclear winter hypothesis "revived nuclear fear in the early 1980s and probably made a substantial contribution to the growth of the peace movement in that period," in the opinion of sociologist Sheldon Ungar in his 1992 book *The Rise and Fall of Nuclearism.* The "idea of 'nuclear winter' entered the public vocabulary and provided final proof that nuclear war on any scale was intolerable."[62]

A "1985 Strategy Paper" from the Nuclear Weapons Freeze Campaign says, among other things,

> The other critical development of the past four years is the enormous surge of citizen awareness and activity in reaction to the nuclear threat. As a result of scientific studies like the "Nuclear Winter" report, popular dramatizations like "The Day After," dozens of physicians' conferences in major cities on the "Consequences of Nuclear War," and thousands of one-on-one and small group encounters on the part of Freeze advocates all over the country, people in unprecedented numbers are aware of the danger posed by the nuclear arms race.[63]

Foreign peace groups may have taken nuclear winter more seriously than did American activists. A February 18, 1984, memo from the records of Britain's Campaign for Nuclear Disarmament notes: "[A colleague] and I have been discussing what CND could be doing to use the recent discovery of the 'nuclear winter' effect to strengthen the antinuclear movement. We both believe that, if it is properly used, this could be a very powerful campaigning tool." But the campaign required a certain finesse, the memo adds; "the point was . . . made that this concept should always be presented with something positive, so as not to dispirit the listener completely."[64]

Because liberals, leftists, and antimilitarists welcomed the nuclear winter hypothesis, right-wingers frantically attacked it and its leading champion, Sagan. Nuclear winter theory was "a fraud from the start," charged an editorial by William F. Buckley Jr., the editor of the conservative journal *National Review.* The editorial was ominously titled "Reichstag Fire II"[65]—exactly what one might expect from Buckley, whose wit, arcane vocabulary, and strange facial expressions (the flickering eyes, the darting tongue) entertain viewers of his PBS-TV talk show.[66] Buckley can be mean and funny at the same time: he once attacked Sagan's congressional testimony on nuclear issues by declaring that Sagan was arrogant, so arrogant that people might have confused him with Buckley himself.

It wasn't so funny, however, when the November 15, 1985, issue ran the single most vitriolic attack on Sagan penned by a respected journal since Alfred Adler's feverish hit piece in the *Atlantic Monthly* in the early 1970s. *National Review*'s cover story on nuclear winter was titled "Flat-Earth Sagan Falls Off the End of the World." The subtitle was "Nuclear-Winter Fundamentalism Challenged by Responsible Scientists." The

cover showed a schematic of a frozen landscape with destroyed buildings and a human body (presumably Sagan's) falling off the "end of the
world." The article claimed that nuclear winter was scientific claptrap
designed to camouflage the political agenda of antinuclear scientists.[67] It
was written not by a distinguished scientist but by one Brad Sparks, an
enthusiastic UFO investigator who believes saucers are real (though
Buckley's magazine did not mention this fact).

Sparks wrote:

> The nuclear-winterists have persistently ignored, evaded, and even sup-
> pressed evidence that contradicts their theory. Moreover, they have
> tried to con the public into believing (falsely) that nuclear winter has
> widespread support. And the broader scientific community, on the
> whole, has been too meek or simply too naive and inexperienced to take
> effective action to counter the winterists.

Sparks quoted the famous Princeton physicist Freeman Dyson as
saying, "Frankly, I think [nuclear winter theory is] an absolutely atrocious piece of physics, but I quite despair of setting the public record
straight. . . . . Who wants to be accused of being in favor of nuclear
war?"[68] In fact, Dyson's opinion of nuclear winter was far more complex.
In his book *Infinite in All Directions*, which was published in 1988, Dyson
wrote:

> Carl Sagan deserves enormous credit for raising the nuclear winter
> question and forcing us to think about it. He is as much a hero of our
> times as Pauling was a hero of the fifties. . . .
>   When Carl Sagan and his colleagues began two years ago to bring
> the possibilities of nuclear winter dramatically to the attention of the
> public, they put professional scientists like me into an awkward posi-
> tion. . . . My instincts as a scientist come into sharp conflict with my
> instincts as a human being. As a scientist I want to rip the [nuclear win-
> ter] theory apart. But as a human being I want to believe it. This is one
> of the rare instances of a genuine conflict between the demands of sci-
> ence and the demands of humanity. As a scientist I judge the nuclear
> winter theory to be a sloppy piece of work, full of gaps and unjustified
> assumptions. As a human being I hope fervently that it is right. It is a
> real and uncomfortable dilemma.[69]

Initially skeptical of the theory, Dyson

> spent a few weeks in 1985 trying to make nuclear winter go away. . . .
> I found, after about two weeks of work, that I could not make nuclear
> winter go away. That is to say, I could not prove the theory wrong. As a
> result, I now understand the theory better and believe it much more

than I did when it was first announced. But I do not yet believe it a hundred percent.

Dyson wondered why he and Sagan could analyze the same data yet reach opposite conclusions. He suggested that the difference lay in their different personal experiences—Sagan had studied how dust storms cool Mars, whereas Dyson (a Britisher by birth) had seen how the temperature stayed warm beneath one London fog. Wet fog blocks rising heat, whereas Sagan's hypothetical dry dust or soot allows heat to escape into space while keeping out sunlight. So the climatic aftermath of a nuclear war would depend on whether the aerosols are wet or dry, "and the computers are not clever enough to tell who is right."[70]

Dyson also pointed out a possible flaw in Sagan's style of antinuclear activism: it raised technical objections to nuclear war, not moral objections to the evil of nuclear war itself. Dyson worried that the Pentagon might respond to the nuclear winter hypothesis not by rapidly shrinking the arsenal (as Sagan hoped) but by redesigning their nuclear weapons and tactics to minimize the risk of a nuclear winter. (They could, for example, use neutron bombs that would emit intense radiation, killing people but causing minimal property damage and, presumably, minimal fires. Or they could design missiles that would drill deep into the ground before exploding; this would muffle the explosion's great heat, also minimizing fires.)

Dyson concluded:

> With this possibility in mind, I give my blessing to Carl Sagan's campaign but continue to feel some anxiety about his tactics. The wave of moral outrage which Sagan has created must be directed against the evil of nuclear war itself and not merely against its consequences.[71]

Sagan made a number of television appearances on the subject of nuclear winter, including one on *Nightline* with Ted Koppel. The guests on that occasion included William F. Buckley, Elie Wiesel, Henry Kissinger, and Robert McNamara.

Ann Druyan angrily recalls that during a break, she, Sagan, and Wiesel were talking. Buckley "walked in, obviously drunk—very drunk—and said: 'Oh, who is this group, the Concerned Holocaust Survivors?' To Elie Wiesel!? It just took our breath away." Wiesel made a motion indicating that they should ignore the remark. "Carl was ready to take Buckley and just, like, nail him up against the wall.

"It's so funny," Druyan adds, "because I agree with [Buckley] about [the need to liberalize] drug policy very strongly. . . . I always wonder how could he be . . . such an asshole about other things.[72]

THE INITIAL SCIENTIFIC ATTACK on the nuclear winter hypothesis was led by Edward Teller, co-inventor of the U.S. hydrogen bomb. He was the same man who had fought "fallout" fears in the 1950s, debating Linus Pauling on San Francisco public television.[73] By the mid-1980s Teller was in his eighties, a gnomelike figure with a seemingly perpetual scowl. He spoke with a thick Hungarian accent, carried a fearsome-looking wooden cane, and alternately charmed reporters and verbally denounced them, pointing his gnarled finger at them for their alleged distortions and sensationalism.[74] He blamed them for much of the agony of his life—the agony of being widely regarded as the real-life incarnation of Dr. Strangelove.

Teller's problems had begun in the 1950s, when he failed to express overt support for his long-time associate J. Robert Oppenheimer's bid to renew his security clearance. Oppenheimer was widely respected, and many accused Teller of short-circuiting "Oppie"'s clearance in revenge for his opposition to development of the hydrogen bomb. After the 1954 hearing, Teller was snubbed at a Los Alamos meeting by an old college friend, who refused to shake his hand. Teller was so shaken that he returned to his room and wept.[75] Other old friends ostracized him, too. Thus abandoned, Teller soon fell into the grip of the hawks and right-wingers. He remained a prominent adviser to presidents through the George Bush era. (Bill Clinton sent Teller a fawning congratulations on his ninetieth birthday.) Teller is widely regarded as the godfather of Reagan's ill-fated Star Wars project to build a space-based array of antimissile weapons.[76]

Teller and Sagan debated nuclear winter before Congress on May 16, 1984. The press was not invited to the hearing, which was arranged by Representatives Newt Gingrich and Timothy E. Wirth. Teller's biographers later described the session as a free-for-all. At one point Teller said, "Now, ladies and gentlemen, I am not a meteorologist. I have talked more about meteorology than I should. Perhaps Dr. Sagan is a better meteorologist than I am. I am very sure that he knows less about the strategic defense than I do, and he knows less than [anti-SDI scientist Richard] Garwin does, and Garwin knows less than he could know if he were really diligent." Sagan interjected, "This is getting very close to ad hominem arguments which I had hoped we would be able to —" Teller cut in: "They cannot be avoided." Later Teller said, "I apologize to the extent I was personal."[77]

That August, Teller's critique of the nuclear winter hypothesis was published by *Nature* magazine. He wrote that meteorological processes important in nuclear winter are "inadequately understood"; the actual amount of smoke generated is "very uncertain." TTAPS argued that smoke might float for weeks in the atmosphere, but Teller thought it might fall in "a week or less." Given these and other uncertainties, he argued, "the concept of a severe climatic change must be considered dubious rather than robust." Still, "the *possibility* of nuclear winter has not been excluded." He admitted that even if the cooling effect was much less than TTAPS forecast—say, 5 to 6 degrees Centigrade rather than 50 to 60 degrees Centigrade—it "could still lead to widespread failure of harvests and famine."[78]

Freeman Dyson had worried that militarists would seek technical end runs around the nuclear winter hypothesis. And that is exactly what Teller proposed doing in his *Nature* article—using smaller, more precise nuclear weapons that would generate smaller fires and less smoke. Furthermore, such small weapons could be targeted against strictly military targets such as Soviet bomber bases or missile silos, producing far less soot and smoke than burning cities would. "If only purely military targets were attacked with relatively small bombs, the amount of smoke generated would be much lower than that required for a nuclear winter, and the argument for the unavoidability of a nuclear winter would lose all force."[79]

Teller and Sagan "really hated each other," David Morrison recalls. Yet their differences kept drawing them together. In later years Morrison discussed with Teller an issue of special interest to all three of them, the possible threat to Earth of falling asteroids. (Teller speculated on the possibility of repelling asteroids with nuclear weapons. But Sagan warned that "a Hitler or Stalin" might use future technology to hurl an asteroid *at* Earth!) Once Teller had breakfast with Sagan at an airport. While they were eating, three different people came up and asked Sagan for his autograph—and no one asked Teller for *his* autograph. Out-autographed, Teller, in a subsequent conversation with Morrison, glumly conceded that day's debate to Sagan: "He won."[80]

A LEADING FIGURE in the SDI project was one Pete Worden, an astrophysicist who publicly debated Sagan. "Pete told me once after a few drinks that one of his assignments in SDI was to neutralize the opposition to SDI—and Sagan and George Field [of Harvard] in particular," Morrison recalls. "He thought there was no question that his job was to destroy them, including character assassination or anything else." Morrison adds that Worden didn't use the term "character assassination," but he claims that that was the implication.[81]

But Sagan was too clever and quick a debater to be out-talked by Worden. So the Reagan Administration tried a slicker tactic, one harder to resist: it invited Sagan and Druyan to dinner at the White House.

Druyan says: "I remember Carl calling me from the office and saying, 'Well, the Reagans have invited us for dinner.' I said: 'Not me—I'm not going.' We talked about it quite a bit." True to her leftist convictions, she felt that if they attended the dinner, their presence would imply support for all of the Administration's actions, "and this is when [Central American] nuns were being decapitated and people were being butchered, and children." For her, it would be impossible to attend the dinner "and feel good about yourself." They received three separate invitations and turned down every one. On another occasion, Druyan adds, "We made the mistake of having dinner with Queen Elizabeth and Prince Phillip on the royal yacht *Britannia* when it came to Los Angeles, and we felt so scuzzy after that! . . . There we were with Frank Sinatra. . . . It was appalling, just appalling, really!" She began arguing about Central America with another guest, an industrialist of some sort, and "we almost got into a hitting-each-other fight. . . . I was almost screaming at the guy."

At another time, the First Couple of space science attended a big gala dinner at the National Air and Space Museum in Washington. They were approached by a man who claimed to be the helicopter pilot at the White House. He told them: "Do you know that these guys talk about you day and night? They hate you, they really hate you! . . . They are always talking about Sagan, Sagan, Sagan." Druyan admits, "We were thrilled!"[82]

In time, Sagan decided it wasn't enough (as Dyson had rightly warned) to oppose nuclear weapons on purely technical grounds. He had to express his opposition to their use *in general*, and in a dramatic way. So in 1986, he and other protesters went to the Nevada nuclear test site to demand a ban on nuclear tests. "The White House has been captured by extremists," he charged. Sagan and Druyan and more than 130 other protesters (including their friend Lester Grinspoon) were arrested and bused by local authorities to a holding area, then released on their own recognizance. "It was a big thing for him to do that, because he was a little worried that [afterwards] he might not be able to work on these spacecraft missions, which he loved, for NASA," says Druyan. Sagan told her, "It would be a shame if I couldn't go back to Mars."[83]

He knew that by being an overt activist he risked losing much of his credibility as a scientist; but he felt morally obligated to do so. He didn't want to be "standing by doing nothing when there was some moral challenge, some ethical challenge to him as a person," Druyan says. "Our parents were always saying to us, 'Don't be a "good German."'"[84]

IN THE FIGHT AGAINST NUCLEARISM, Sagan made a personal sacrifice by turning for help to the institution he had always spurned— religion. Ever since his youth, he had been a nonbeliever. In his novel, *Contact*, he portrayed religious leaders as buffoons.

Yet an odd thing happened to *Contact* between the publication of the novel in 1985 and the release of the film version in 1997. The film's leading religious figure (played soberly by Matthew McConnaughey) was sophisticated, educated, thoughtful, gentle. He was nothing like the Bible-slapping, revival-tent vulgarian of the novel. What had happened to Sagan's attitude toward religion in the twelve years between the book and the movie?

The answer is best understood by recalling a cynical old saying, which goes something like this: "Religion is anathema to the intellectuals, consolation to the masses, and useful to the politicians." What had happened is that Sagan discovered that organized religion could be a powerful ally in his effort to save the world from nuclear and environmental disaster. Exactly how he came to this realization is unclear. It may have stemmed from his meeting in 1984 with the most majestic religious leader of the Western world, Pope John Paul II.

John Paul is a different kind of Pope. While conservative in many ways (especially on reproductive and women's issues), he is more genuinely intellectual, and certainly more liberal and sophisticated on certain issues, than his predecessors. He has been a constant frustration and surprise to liberals and leftists: a foe of reproductive freedom, yet a scholar trained in philosophy who, late in life, raised a serious debate about the implications of postmodernist thinking for rationalism; a conservative on many social issues, yet one who has defended labor unions and attacked unbridled capitalism. This was the kind of Pope with whom Carl Sagan could talk. A group of about fifteen scientists, including Sagan and Stephen Jay Gould, the famous paleontologist and essayist, were invited by the Pontifical Academy to "brief the Pope about what the nuclear winter scenario was," Druyan recalls. "So we were ushered into his Vatican apartments." The papal household was spectacular. She thought: "I want this man's decorator!" John Paul "seemed to glow from within—he was wearing these exquisite ivory vestments." Sagan gave a talk in a "magnificent reception room" in the apartment. The talk lasted thirty to forty-five minutes, explaining the risks of nuclear winter. John Paul asked Sagan questions, and "it was clear he had been paying attention and he understood what Carl was saying."

Afterward, Druyan asked the Pope to bless a religious medal that she wished to give her housekeeper, a native of Peru. Druyan was startled by the skeptical look on John Paul's face. Surrounded by scientists, "he wanted to make it very clear to us that he didn't believe in this [superstition]! That it meant nothing to him! . . . I was shocked!" Nonetheless, he perfunctorily blessed the medal. Atheists aren't the only cynics.[85]

Gould later wrote: "The days I spent with Carl in Rome were the best of our friendship. We delighted in walking around the Eternal City, feasting on its history and architecture—and its food! Carl took special delight in the anonymity that he still enjoyed in a nation that had not yet aired *Cosmos*, the greatest media work in popular science of all time."[86]

The ultimate result was a papal statement warning of the danger of nuclear winter, and of nuclear weapons in general. The statement undoubtedly made the nuclear winter scientists' warning seem more credible to much of the world. After all, if the Pope was worried about nuclear winter, then it must be a serious issue! The Pope had unwittingly done a big favor for Carl Sagan, one of the century's more glamorous atheists. Perhaps for this reason, Sagan began to rethink his attitude toward religion. True, to him it was anathema; but it might also be useful.

IRONICALLY, SAGAN ALSO GAINED admirers in the citadel of world atheism—the Kremlin. The new Soviet leader, Mikhail Gorbachev, admired Sagan's proposal that the United States and the Soviet Union defuse cold war tensions by sponsoring a joint mission to Mars. The idea also won support from Gorbachev and the future U.S. vice president, then Senator Albert Gore, one of Sagan's friends in Congress.

Sagan's push for the joint Mars mission was an updated version of his old dream of using space exploration to end warfare. David Morrison observes: "Carl had unique access to the USSR science community. . . . [He] felt he was at a pivotal time in history, when he could help forge a solution that simultaneously addressed his two largest passions: the search for peace and the expansion of the human presence to Mars. . . . It was the ultimate vision of beating swords into plowshares." Sagan frequently traveled to the USSR, working with Soviet scientists to make their space program more open to the world. One result was live global television coverage of a Soviet space probe's close encounter with Halley's comet in 1986. Morrison recalls seeing Sagan "featured on the podium in Moscow at the *Sputnik* anniversary in October 1987, chatting and joking with cosmonaut Leonov and other dignitaries. He was great!"

During the Reagan-Gorbachev summit in Moscow in 1988, Gorbachev tried to interest Reagan in the possibility of a U.S.-Soviet Mars mission. Gorbachev science advisor Roald Sagdeev was present and later wrote:

> No doubt [Gorbachev] was still emotionally involved in the anti-SDI rhetoric and thought that Mars could divert the American military-industrial complex from SDI.
>
> Later that evening there was a state dinner honoring Reagan. . . . When it was my turn to be introduced to the guest of honor, Gorbachev seized my arm and said, "Mister President, this is the man who is

promoting the flight to Mars." I had the funny feeling that Gorbachev's words struck some chord of curiosity in Reagan. As if to underscore his apparently successful start to his Mars public relations campaign with the American president, Gorbachev added: "Academician Sagdeev has friends and colleagues in America who share the same vision of a joint flight."

Then Gorbachev turned to me, as if looking for help with a few names. But before I could react, he went on: "Carl Sagan."

In a fraction of a second I could tell that something had clicked the wrong way. The guest of honor appeared to lose interest in the subject immediately. Gorbachev apparently didn't understand that there was not a great deal of political compatibility between Ronald Reagan and Carl Sagan.[87]

THE FATE OF THE NUCLEAR WINTER hypothesis remains contested. In 1986, the atmospheric scientist Stephen Schneider and his colleagues concluded that the cooling effect would not be as severe as TTAPS had estimated, although it would still be substantial. Some news accounts implied that the result would be a nuclear "autumn," not a "winter."[88] Skeptics grumbled (and still do) that the hypothesis was largely bunk, a pseudoscientific camouflage for Sagan's political convictions. By contrast, the TTAPS team published in 1990 a follow-up study defending their original conclusions (with some modifications).[89]

Politically speaking, the nuclear winter hypothesis appears to have affected the Soviet government more than the American. "In the first half of the 1980s, the findings of U.S. and Soviet physicians on the aftermath of nuclear war and the 'nuclear winter' theory noticeably influenced the Soviet leadership," according to Andrei A. Kokoshin, former First Deputy Minister of Defense in Russia, in a 1998 historical study of the evolution of Soviet strategic thought. The realization that a post-nuclear environment would be even more horrible than previously imagined spurred a growing acknowledgment of "the irrelevance of nuclear war," so Soviet theorists began speculating about a shift to "large-scale conventional war."[90] Whether this influenced the Kremlin's willingness to make unilateral reductions in arms remains unknown. Perhaps Soviet officials would have made the reductions anyway, given the rapid decline of the Soviet economy in the 1980s. In any case, the nuclear winter hypothesis provided another debating point for those advocating cuts because the fantasy of "winnable" nuclear wars was just that—a fantasy.

As of this writing, two of the five TTAPS scientists, Carl Sagan and Jim Pollack, are dead. Ronald Reagan is retired and suffering from Alzheimer's disease. Mikhail Gorbachev is out of power. And the super-powers—or, rather, the last superpower and Russia—are rapidly slashing their nuclear arsenals. Soon, the total world nuclear stockpile will be a small fraction of its former might. Of course, the nuclear nations are not slashing their arsenals from fear of nuclear winter. Rather, they have long since realized that they have no need to fear each other. So Sagan's old dream—that the superpowers would radically cut their arsenals—has come true, although not for the reason he expected. Once again, he was prophetic for the wrong reason.[91]

ONE AGED TITAN still haunts the nuclear scene: Edward Teller. He turned ninety in early 1998, and he remains bitter about Carl Sagan. In June 1998 I visited him at his Stanford office. Before the interview, I asked him if we could begin by discussing Sagan. "Who was he?" he replied. So I started to remind him who Sagan was. Abruptly he cut me off, snapping: "He was a *nobody!*" He refused to discuss Sagan further. So I continued the interview. We discussed other topics. He relaxed, warmed up; recalled his childhood in Austria-Hungary (he recalls hearing about the shooting of Archduke Ferdinand), his affectionate memories of Truman, his half-defensive, half-regretful explanation for his testimony against Oppenheimer. Living history, addressing my tape recorder.

Toward the end of the interview, somewhat timidly, I again asked him for his reassessment of Sagan. He fired back: "I know nothing about him! What did he do? I know he criticized me—that is the only accomplishment of his that I know of. I think it's a great thing to criticize Dr. Teller but it is not quite enough for great fame. What did he do? . . . What did he discover?"

I cited the work of Sagan and his colleagues on the nuclear winter hypothesis, which suggested a remarkable (albeit controversial) new form of atmospheric thermal restructuring with (to say the least) practical implications. Teller, who showed America how to use the power of the Sun to obliterate the world, thundered on: "Idiot! Idiot! Don't you know? If cities burned, is the smoke the worst consequence? The cities that have burned are the worst consequence! . . . Whoever talks about [nuclear destruction] this way has no sense of proportion. . . . [Isn't it disgusting], a scientist saying how a war will be terrible because the winter will be hard afterwards? After so many cities have burned?"

He gripped his cane and glared at me. "He never did *anything* worthwhile. I shouldn't talk with you. You waste your time writing a book about a nobody."[92]

16

Look Back, Look Back

LESTER GRINSPOON HAS countless memories of his long friendship with Carl Sagan—"so many I don't know where to begin," he said. He and Sagan smoked pot together on an ocean cruiser surrounded by thunderheads, with "beautiful views of the islands going by." They vacationed together in Cape Cod, Trinidad, and Tobago.[1]

To Grinspoon's son, David, Sagan was "Uncle Carl." David was about six, in 1966, when he first met the man who was his father's best friend for three decades. "I can remember Carl showing up at our home in 1971, when I was eleven, with the latest pictures from *Mariner 9*." Sagan was always visiting, or phoning, or joining them on vacations. "He once said he felt like he was my co-father." He was "a great storyteller," too: as David, Jeremy, and Dorion lay in bed, Sagan would tell them "complex, swashbuckling stories about swordsmen."[2]

Sagan and Grinspoon "must have spoken on the phone a couple of times a week for decades," David says. "Carl would be calling for medical advice, political advice, advice about the kids. If he was going to debate General Abrahamson [about SDI], he'd call up my dad.

"It was as if my dad was not only a friend but a general adviser. I can't tell you how many times I'd call my dad and there'd be a beep on the line and he'd say, 'I'm on the phone with Carl.' I think Carl actually depended on my parents a lot for personal support and guidance."

David recalls that Sagan conversed respectfully with children, as if they were little adults. "He really paid attention to what kids said. He took you seriously," David says. When David was twelve, he and Sagan debated the merits of rock music versus classical music. Sagan "said rock music was like a cartoon compared to classical painting." Yet David didn't feel as if Sagan was lecturing him; it was an intelligent, mutually respectful argument. "When I began to study science, he helped me get cool summer jobs"; for example, with Sagan's research colleagues W. Reid

Thompson and Bishun Khare. Sagan also got David a job assisting the *Voyager* imaging team, an amazing opportunity for a college sophomore. In *Cosmos*, David appears momentarily on screen as "this really skinny, geeky-looking kid with what looks like an Afro—a 'Jewfro,' I called it." David Grinspoon is now on the cusp of forty, a noted planetary scientist at the University of Colorado, and the author and coauthor of two books on the planet Venus.[3]

So many years, so many memories. Sagan was able to relax with the Grinspoons, Lester and his wife, Betsy, and the kids; they grounded the young astronomer as he shot to fame. "I remember him being playful, and running and playing Frisbee at Cape Cod," David says. And other times, Sagan, in his swimming trunks, would take his microcassette recorder and disappear on long solo walks down Nauset Beach.[4]

People change.

AS SAGAN GREW FAMOUS, he sometimes behaved like a middle-rank movie star; or so some observers felt. He developed traits that Lester Grinspoon, a psychiatrist, identifies as narcissism and a sense of "entitlement," the belief that one is owed something. For example, Sagan acquired a taste for limousines. Perhaps this taste stemmed from years of riding in black limos provided by the television networks, as they ferried him from fancy hotels to talk shows. One evening (probably in the late 1980s, Grinspoon thinks) Sagan was staying at the Ritz in Boston and preparing to give the Roger Baldwin Lecture to the Massachusetts Civil Liberties Union. Grinspoon was present. Sagan decided he wanted a limo to transport him to the conference, although the meeting location was only about eight blocks away. He also wanted the limo to wait outside for him. Grinspoon was miffed; "it seemed to Betsy and me this sense of entitlement was becoming more and more prominent."[5]

One old acquaintance of Sagan's refused to put up with Sagan's limo-mania. At Berkeley in the early 1960s, Saul Landau and his then-wife, Nina, had known Sagan and Lynn Margulis; had dined and danced and toked with them. After the divorce, Landau had let Sagan cry on his shoulder (figuratively speaking) as he lamented his failed marriage and nibbled infinitesimal bits of food. By the 1980s, Landau was a prominent political leftist, author, and scholar connected with the left-wing think tank Institute for Policy Studies in Washington, D.C. Like most leftist institutions, IPS is not exactly rolling in cash. When it invited Sagan to speak, Landau remembers "him making what were, I thought, rather silly demands. He demanded that a limousine meet him at the airport.

"I remember talking to him and saying, 'What? Are you out of your mind?' Even celebrities don't get well treated at the IPS." Not only did

IPS staffers not provide the limo, they decided to "teach him a lesson": "We picked the rattiest car we could find, and we sent the lowest-level staff person we could find to pick him up.

"His head was a little swollen, I think. I thought, 'He's become a schmuck.' It's a sign of insecurity: If you need to have the outward trappings of importance in order to feel important, then you're insecure about your accomplishments. I'd always felt he was an insecure person. Otherwise, he would have been looser. I mean, what's he holding in?"[6]

Meanwhile, Shirley Arden worried that her colorful boss was stuffing his curriculum vitae with trivia "which really did not belong there. I told him so," she now recalls. "But Carl was no longer listening to my Dutch uncle advice on public relations. In my opinion he had become so full of himself that he really was not thinking clearly on certain issues. He was absolutely unbending." Indeed, his c.v. was becoming something of a joke among his colleagues. It listed almost every little speech he had made (to the College of Twin Falls, in Twin Falls, Idaho, for example, and to West Chester University in West Chester, Pennsylvania) and numerous minor news articles recovered by his clipping service (from the Claremore, Oklahoma, *Progress* and the Hobart, Indiana, *Gazette*, among others). When Arden appealed to Druyan, though, Mrs. Sagan was able to persuade her husband to quit making such a fool of himself, c.v.-wise. "I cannot stress too much what a strong influence Annie had on Carl," Arden says. Even so, at the time of his death, his 265-page résumé measured slightly more than an inch thick.

Sagan's growing awareness of his own mortality may have accounted for his imperiousness, says radioastronomer Jill Tarter (who is often identified as a model for the Ellie Arroway character in *Contact*). She says Sagan sometimes acted like "King Carl." After his recent close brush with death, "he had really faced his own mortality and decided that he just didn't have any time to waste for anyone or anything except what he was passionate about.

"He came out one time to be a part of our [SETI] review committee, and—stupid thing—he needed to eat special food because of his [health] experience. So he had [SETI leader] John Billingham and two of our administrative assistants working for an hour and a half or two to get exactly the right kind of corned beef sandwich from a deli—he couldn't eat this, he couldn't eat that. They got on the phone; 'No, that won't do.' The fact that Carl would take up the time of three people, to satisfy his requirements, just incensed me. But it came out of this fact that he really sensed that he had a lot to do, and there might not be an infinite amount of time to do it."[7]

Still, Sagan deserves some sympathy. He was, after all, not a well man; because of his achalasia, he had repeatedly come close to choking to death. He could hardly go hunting for the sandwich himself; he would have had to sign a dozen autographs simply to walk through the deli. "I think that this was the great curse and blessing of his existence," observes a distinguished popularizer of astronomy, Andrew Fraknoi of the Astronomical Society of the Pacific. "Einstein always complained that people would feel that they knew him and could walk up to him. . . . I think Sagan was hit by that same phenomenon; that he was both, I think, delighted by his fame, and also terribly put off by the liberties that people would take. People would just walk up to him and feel they owned him. Privacy was very difficult. He would eventually really take care how to travel. He had a whole set of regulations about if you hired him or asked him to do a talk. . . . People said that was kind of snooty, but I think it was just self-protective. I think it was what you have to do because of the American tendency for people to feel they own you."[8]

At times, though, Sagan apparently realized he was acting like King Carl. Once he and Grinspoon were visiting Moscow, and Sagan mentioned something that Grinspoon had written about how public figures' personalities change. Sagan said something like: "If I ever get too big for my britches, Lester, I'm counting on you to call it to my attention." Grinspoon agreed to do what he could.[9] It was an ominous exchange.

SOME YEARS LATER, Sagan invited the Grinspoons, along with their son, David, to a gala fortieth birthday party for Ann Druyan. It was a chic affair, held on a yacht on Block Island Sound off the coast of Long Island. There David met a charming and sexy woman, some years older than he, who was a friend of Sagan and Druyan's. The woman (who will not be identified here to protect her from further hurt) traveled in Hollywood circles. The woman and David started a pleasant romance. At that time, David was a rising figure in planetary science; he was excited as she introduced him to the glamorous world of Hollywood. After a couple of years, though, he came to resent the glamor; it struck him as shallow and deceptive. He ended their relationship. Tearfully, the woman lamented her loss to Sagan and Druyan.

Soon after, David and Sagan were on a car trip to San Francisco. According to David, Sagan "ambushed" him during the trip by arguing that the breakup was a big mistake. Sagan pulled out "a prepared list of eight points—a written list—[explaining] where he felt I had gone wrong in this relationship," David says. Among other things, Sagan accused David of being sexist because (Sagan assumed) David had split up with the woman just because she was older. David got madder and madder as Sagan—the veteran of three marriages—lectured him about love. "It took me completely by surprise. It struck me as so inappropriate."

Afterward, David wrote an angry letter to Sagan and Druyan. What right (David demanded) did Sagan have to interfere in his private life? "Carl did have some blind spots," David now observes. "He was brilliant at many things, but being aware of the subtleties in interpersonal relationships was not one of his strong points." To save a friendship, compromise is sometimes necessary. But "it basically became impossible to resolve conflicts with Carl. You were wrong and he was right."

Over their long friendship, David notes, Sagan had "changed a lot. I knew him over thirty years and I witnessed that. I think in the long run, it did go to his head . . . all the fame, all the people telling him he was great." To David (now "happily married" to another woman), his falling-out with Sagan "was very painful, because Carl had been a very important figure most of my life."

Lester Grinspoon sided with his son. Sagan and Druyan had only recently dedicated their best book, *Shadows of Forgotten Ancestors*, to the elder Grinspoon; even so, the psychiatry professor was furious over Sagan's treatment of his son. "I could no longer deal with [Sagan's] narcissism and sense of entitlement," Grinspoon now says. "It's like Lord Acton's comment: Power corrupts and absolute power corrupts absolutely.

"We drifted apart at the end. The whole thing just broke my heart. It's not something I'm comfortable talking about. It's a very distressing story. I think it's better not to talk about it. I don't want to diss a man whom I loved so much."

Druyan remembers the episode very differently. She insists that Sagan showed no disrespect for David in questioning his decision to end the relationship with the woman. Yet David later fired off a "vitriolic" letter to Sagan and her, she says. She and her husband traveled to Boston to meet with Lester, in hopes of salvaging the relationship with him. To anyone who has ever lost a friend, what happened next may look familiar—a series of misunderstandings and resentments that accumulate, one upon another. They look silly to outsiders, yet they are titanic grievances to the parties involved—for example, a dispute over whether the Sagans had failed to invite David to speak at Sagan's sixtieth birthday party.

Druyan also denies the accusation (by Lester Grinspoon and others) that Sagan had fallen in love with luxuries, such as limousines. "Carl drove a 1981 Volkswagen Rabbit," she says. "It's still in the garage. . . . Taking him shopping was one of the only things hard to do with him. . . . He didn't want to waste the time. He had one Seiko watch, I think [costing] $89. . . . It's a bum rap to say he was into luxury."

The split with Lester and David Grinspoon never healed—although it came close, in a manner that was simultaneously comic and poignant.

One day in the mid-1990s, Lester received a phone call from Sagan. At that moment Sagan was lying in his sickbed in Seattle, undergoing one of a number of treatments for the disease that was to kill him. He was in exquisite pain; doctors gave him morphine to ease his suffering. The drug caused Sagan to suffer an eerie hallucination: he imagined seeing a giant head floating outside his bedroom window. Oddly enough, it appeared to be the head of entertainer Dean Martin.

Frantic, Sagan seized the phone and called the person who had stood by so many of his sickbeds: Lester Grinspoon. On the other side of the continent, Grinspoon listened to the terrified voice of his former friend. He tried to console Sagan, to assure him that it was all a phantasm, one of the mind's mirages. Sagan was unconsoled: "I'm telling you, it's Dean Martin! As big as a building, looking in at me!"

Finally Grinspoon managed to calm Sagan down, to reassure him that the specter would disappear "once he was off those high doses. . . . It was probably the last time I was able to reassure him about anything."

IT SEEMS TO BE A RULE that when aging scientists (to quote Sagan) "get too big for their britches," they trust their intuition more than they should. They *sense* a theory is valid; therefore it *is* valid.[10]

The decline of Mikhail Gorbachev's Soviet Union had created a geopolitical power vacuum around the world. Had the Soviets continued to have strong influence over Iraq (which they had supported for years), they might have checked the desire of its leader, Saddam Hussein, to send troops to seize the adjacent oil kingdom of Kuwait. But the Soviets were too busy struggling to keep alive their bric-a-brac empire of sulking nationalities when, in August 1990, Hussein grabbed Kuwait. The United States assembled a coalition of nations that threatened military retaliation if Hussein did not withdraw his forces from Kuwait. Hussein refused. Sagan watched the growing preparations for the Gulf War with horror. Like most American liberals and doves, he had been relieved to see the cold war end and the world drift into an age of peace. Now it was drifting back toward war. Humanity's primal, bloody instincts—the dragons within Eden—were prowling again.

At this time, Random House was about to publish Sagan and Rich Turco's magnum opus on nuclear winter, the oddly titled *A Path Where No Man Thought*. It was by far Sagan's biggest book—five hundred pages—and one into which he had poured all his passion and intellect. It is a remarkable work, dense with insights and persuasive arguments. But it was written for a world fast disappearing.[11] To most people, the end of the cold war meant the end of nuclear weapons as an issue. The book sold poorly; it seemed irrelevant.

Or was it? Western observers, many of whom regarded Hussein as a psychopathic madman out of a James Bond movie, feared that if the U.S.-led coalition struck Iraq, the dictator would set the oil wells ablaze, destroying a major source of the world's petroleum. In a paper published in *Nature*, Sagan and Turco forecast that the resulting blazes might generate immense dark clouds that might mimic the radiative effects of nuclear winter. The result might be a significant local or regional cooling, a temperature drop across the Middle East or even farther, perhaps with longer-term meteorological impact (disruption of the Indian monsoon season, for example) and damage to Asian agriculture. In response, William Buckley's *National Review* accused Sagan of playing into Hussein's hands by telling "the Butcher of Baghdad on prime time that he has his hands on the throttle of a global doomsday machine."[12]

Sagan sent the Gulf War forecast to *Nature* although a majority of his TTAPS colleagues opposed it. According to Toon (now a professor of atmospheric science at the University of Colorado), both he and Pollack "looked at this Kuwaiti oil fire thing and decided basically that nothing was going to happen." Toon remembers thinking that there would be no more climatic impact than one gets from Amazon rainforest fires, which are burning all the time. "I didn't think anything was going to happen, and said so to numerous members of the press. Carl was off the deep end on this one. I told him I thought it was [risky to forecast climatic impact] when you're dealing with a madman like Saddam Hussein because it would encourage him to set everything on fire."[13]

When Sagan and Turco's paper arrived at *Nature*, it was sent to peer reviewers including Toon. Toon recommended rejecting the paper for publication. "I was pretty scathing in my review. I said I thought it was unethical [to make the forecast], because he [Carl] was just encouraging Saddam Hussein." Toon criticized Sagan's methodology; he accused his TTAPS colleague of making extreme-case assumptions in designing the forecast. "He had to really push [the data] to get an [atmospheric] effect." Toon said that for Sagan to make the forecast "was unwise and that he would be tested quickly and found wrong. Carl never discussed this problem with the rest of us. In this case, Carl kind of took off by himself."[14] Sagan's critics occasionally suspected him of theoretical "handwaving" (that is, making a fuss that obscured the weak empirical basis for his speculations), but in this case, Toon says, Sagan "wasn't even obeying his own rules for hand-waving."

Thomas Ackerman agreed with Toon and Pollack's view of the paper. "There were a lot of reasons not to think that anything was going to happen. I think [Sagan and Turco] did us a disservice by suggesting that something would happen, because when it didn't, it would raise doubts about the whole subject" of nuclear winter.[15]

In January 1991, the U.S.-led coalition launched a massive air, sea, and land assault on Hussein's forces. As many had feared, Hussein's troops ignited the oil wells, creating fireball-lit, smoke-gushing terrains. But the climatic impact was nil. In Sagan's last book published while he was alive, he took the unusual step of listing "a few" of the scientific mistakes of his career. Among them was this one:

> Just before Iraq torched the Kuwaiti oil wells in January 1991, I warned that so much smoke might get so high as to disrupt agriculture in much of South Asia; as events transpired, it *was* pitch black at noon and the temperatures dropped 4–6 degrees Centigrade over the Persian Gulf, but not much smoke reached stratospheric altitudes and Asia was spared. I did not sufficiently stress the uncertainty of the calculations.[16]

THE BAD NEWS started coming in batches. NASA's SETI project, for example, did not long survive the cold war. In early 1993, Senator Richard Bryan, a Democrat from Nevada, stood on the floor of the Senate and asked his colleagues to kill government support for SETI. Showing no ability to distinguish between SETI and UFO-chasing, he referred to SETI as a "great Martian hunt." The Senate went along; all SETI funding was ended.

After it all ended, SETI scientist Jill Tarter flew home, crushed. "I literally asked my husband to stay around over the weekend and not go into his office and not leave me alone with any sharp objects," she recalls with a laugh. "It was pretty grim. How could we have screwed up so badly? How could we have let this happen?"[17] Fortunately, the SETI program was privatized and has since survived with support from Silicon Valley industrialists and other sugar daddies. Based at the SETI Institute in a tree-shaded office park in Mountain View, California, the search is conducted under the name Project Phoenix, after the mythical bird that ascended from its own ashes.[18]

It was the same scenario that Sagan had envisioned in *Contact*, when Ellie Arroway, abandoned by a federal scientific agency, seeks support for her SETI project from a private donor. The whole episode illustrated one of Sagan's old fears—that poor science education would create a society unable to distinguish between scientific exploration and pseudo-scientific flummery.

"OLD AGE IS A SHIPWRECK," Charles de Gaulle said. As Sagan approached his sixtieth year, he might have understood the Frenchman's words. The embarrassment of the Gulf War forecast; the fall of his most powerful ally in the world, Mikhail Gorbachev; the death of NASA's SETI program; the explosion of a long-awaited space probe, *Mars Observer*; the dismal failure of *A Path Where No Man Thought*—these and other setbacks surely stung.

Then came the Big One. He had been criticized, parodied, attacked, even ridiculed. He had been denied admittance to the Cosmos Club for a while. But publicly rejected by a powerful scientific body—never. Not until 1992.

In the life of an American scientist, admission to the National Academy of Sciences is generally regarded as the peak of a career, the scientific equivalent of election, in politics, to the U.S. Senate. To Sagan's old friend Stanley Miller, an NAS member, Sagan was due for admission. "I think a person of his visibility and scientific accomplishment should have been in there," Miller says. "A lot of people felt that." Typically, individual sections of the Academy nominate their favorite candidates and then rank them by performance. Eventually the entire Academy membership votes on the entire list of about 120 candidates, of which the top 60 are voted in. The process is slightly more democratic than selection procedures in a college fraternity: Anyone can object to a specific choice. If someone does object, then the whole Academy votes, and two-thirds must back the candidate to override the lone blackballer.[19] Obviously, anyone controversial—anyone who dares to take radical stances on topics, or to transgress the largely unspoken rule against publicizing one's work, or to have an occasionally abrasive or imperious personality— might have more trouble being admitted. (The boys'-treehouse exclusiveness of NAS may partly explain why so many Academy members privately complain that their annual meetings are "dull.")[20]

Miller prepared to push Sagan's name through by drawing up a list of his accomplishments. Sagan had produced, Miller says, "a hundred genuine papers, and a number of them are really very substantial. Do you have a copy of his vitae? It's astounding. When did he sleep?"[21] For the edification of NAS members who might know Sagan mainly as a television star, Miller cautioned that Sagan's fame as a popularizer "must not be allowed to overshadow his scientific contributions." Miller cited Sagan's pioneering work on the Venusian greenhouse effect, his activities on planetary missions, and his study of dust storms on Mars, which demonstrated that brightness variations on the red planet "are caused by shifting sands, and not by any seasonal vegetation effects." His studies of the impact of aerosols (of ammonia on the early Earth and soot from nuclear blasts, among others) on the terrestrial climate "have become an important part of climatology," Miller claimed. Miller was the best-known living figure in the study of the origin of life, and his word should have carried great weight when he pointed out that Sagan had "worked vigorously" in that field, having operated the Cornell lab where researchers had synthesized pre-biological molecules, some of which were "good candidates" as explanations for Jovian colors. In short, Miller stressed, Sagan was an estimable scientist as well as a talented popularizer.[22]

However, Miller says, "several people objected" to the nomination. Debate ensued. In his presentation before the assembled Academy, with three hundred to four hundred people in the audience, Miller's lack of stage savvy stymied him. "I'm not like Carl—press a button and out comes a speech. . . . I'm not happy standing up doing this kind of stuff, making this kind of presentation."[23]

Some noted Academy members defended Sagan. One of them was John Bahcall of Princeton, a leading astronomer (he would win the National Medal of Science in 1990), co-pioneer of the Hubble Space Telescope, and a figure in solar-neutrino astrophysics. Bahcall later told Faye Flam of *Science* magazine: "In my view, Sagan has made as great a contribution to astronomy and the intellectual life of this country as anyone. I watched the 'Cosmos' series with all my three children." Sagan also won support from Paul Ehrlich of Stanford and Berkeley mathematician Steve Smale, who praised communication and research as the necessary twins of science: "For me it's hard to separate the two things. If you do one and not the other it's not worth anything."[24]

But there were opponents, too. One NAS member stood and said, "It's 'dangerous' to have these voluntary nominating groups [like Miller's]." Recalling this, Miller rolled his eyes in disbelief. " 'Dangerous!'? I don't see danger! Like being blown up by atom bombs?" He laughed almost maniacally at the absurdity of it. "I mean, what kind of self-importance is this?!"[25]

Lynn Margulis, an NAS member, sat in the meeting and fumed as the debate proceeded. Despite her personal anger at her former husband, she felt that he deserved entry to the Academy. She later wrote him a furious letter describing in detail the on-the-floor fight against his nomination. It is the most vitriolic—and perhaps the funniest—assault on the Academy by one of its own in long memory.

Margulis described the "miserable half hour" on April 28, 1992, when Sagan's nomination for NAS membership was debated. She sat there "squirming with disdain alternating with fury." Miller, she said, did a "creditable" job of championing Sagan's nomination, although Miller "is not the most eloquent and fervent orator." Chandrasekhar and other "luminaries" joined in nominating Sagan, at which point "it seemed that you could only win." Vera Rubin, a pioneering figure in modern cosmology, pointed out Sagan's accomplishments; Ralph Cicerone, a noted atmospheric scientist, praised Sagan's work on the faint early Sun paradox. But some scientists grumbled that Sagan had been nominated by a voluntary nominating group, rather than one that originated in the NAS astronomy group; to these critics (Margulis surmised), this implied that Sagan "had something to hide." Thomas Donahue, a leading authority on planetary atmospheres, "claimed that as an expert on Venus your accomplishments were not up to his professional standards," Margulis wrote. Her temper rose as she pointed out how another NAS member, Albert Cotton, "swayed that great body of self-inflated experts against you by forcefully railing against all your finest hours," for example by dismissing Sagan's popular science writing as "oversimplification" (Margulis's word).

"His objections, which to me bordered on the vomitous, resonated with every small mind, ugly body and verbal maladapt present and that means half the membership," Margulis continued. "They are jealous of your communication skills, charm, good looks and outspoken attitude especially on nuclear winter. With such a high proportion of henpecked conformists, I would guess that most probably don't like the three wives and five kids bit," she added wryly, alluding to Sagan's multiple families. "In neodarwinian terms you are simply too fit."

The vote "was very close to half and half," with a two-thirds majority needed for election. She tried to console Sagan by mentioning how she had recently asked another member why he never attended meetings, and he replied, "What? . . . that Old Boys Club?" She concluded amiably that "Everyone is very fine, especially your marvelous grandson [Dorion's son, Tonio], the origami whiz," and added: "In summary you deserved election to the National Academy years ago and still do; it is the worst of human frailties that keeps you out: jealousy."[26]

Agreement comes from another Cornell scientist, Nobel Prize–winning chemist Roald Hoffmann. "Carl Sagan's views on nuclear winter are controversial," Hoffmann wrote in a subsequent letter to the Academy, urging that Sagan receive the Academy's Public Welfare Medal. "His exposure to public view, the lingering presence of the Cosmos cinematographer's camera on his visage, all these have served to arouse the *worst*—petty jealousy—in some scientists' reaction to Carl."

Whether jealousy was a factor or not, Sagan's nomination "went down," Miller recalls. "I was humiliated . . . to put so much work into it and see it go down in that way."[27]

After Flam reported Sagan's rejection in *Science* magazine, Sagan wrote a short, typically stoic letter to Miller: "Of course I was disappointed. . . . But it was rewarding to know that you were among those who supported me."[28]

In retrospect, Miller insists that the main obstacle to Sagan's nomination—"the major thing"—was "jealousy. I can just see them saying it:

'Here's this little punk with all this publicity and Johnny Carson. I'm a ten times better scientist than that punk!' Nobody said this, but I can just see them saying it!"[29]

ANOTHER BIG DISAPPOINTMENT came with the critical reception to *Shadows of Forgotten Ancestors*, published in 1992, which Sagan co-authored with Druyan. Ironically, it was his best book. A peculiarity of Sagan's prose is that it varies from book to book, as if his books had been written by different people. Compare, for example, the youthful gushiness of *The Cosmic Connection* with the cool, unflashy prose of *The Demon-Haunted World* and the Bertrand-Russell-crossed-with-Noël-Coward elegance of *Shadows of Forgotten Ancestors*.[30] *Shadows* is a more sophisticated, grown-up grappling with issues Sagan had first broached in *The Dragons of Eden*: Why do human beings act and feel and think the way they do? No doubt the comparatively sober mood of *Shadows* also owed much to Sagan's personal experiences over the prior decade, especially his miserable health and his battles with powerful people over the use of nuclear weapons. But much of the wit and maturity of *Shadows* is due to its coauthor, Druyan. She reconciled contradictions by bringing to Sagan's prose a cheerful gravity, a lighthearted sobriety that it had previously lacked.

Subtitled *A Search for Who We Are*, the book (which took its title from a 1964 Russian film) was inspired by the nuclear tensions of the early 1980s, when apocalypse had seemed possible. How did humanity develop such self-destructive ways? In quest of answers, Sagan and Druyan explored social and biological evolution. Unlike many popular writers on the origin of human aggressiveness, they did not settle for pat answers of either the "nature" or "nurture" kind, refusing to put exclusive blame on our genes or our social conditioning. Like all great popularizers, they acknowledged (in a passage reminiscent of Schrödinger's *What Is Life?*) that to answer such titanic queries they were breaching walls into subjects in which they lacked expertise. "And yet such a search has no chance of succeeding unless those walls are breached." The rest of the book is, structurally, roughly like *Cosmos*, but deeper, more sophisticated, less sure of easy answers, and ultimately more somber, but with a silver lining of hope. The book's prose is simply elegant (Charles Darwin's father, Robert, was "a great big, fat man, a silhouette out of Dickens"), and its humor is abundant and sly (Druyan and the thrice-married Sagan, who knew something about lawyers, noted that famed nineteenth-century geologist Charles Lyell had originally "been a lawyer for as long as he could stand it").

Druyan's impact on Sagan's politics was never more fiercely evident than in a passage noting how racists and neo-racists apply paleoanthropology selectively to suit their political prejudices. Bigots emphasize "the primate connection to the veldt and the ghetto, but never, ever, perish the thought, to the boardroom or the military academy or, God forbid, to the Senate chamber or the House of Lords, to Buckingham Palace or Pennsylvania Avenue." Likewise, bigots argue that women's hormonal fluctuations render them unfit for public office, yet few right-wingers and anti-feminists invoke biology in discussing whether "raging hormonal imbalances . . . propel men to violence [and] make them less than optimal for leadership of a modern state." Sagan and Druyan's acidic commentary on the misuse of scientific research for political purposes has few literary peers.

Shadows sold well (it is still in print, seven years later). The *Washington Post* pronounced it "a tour de force of a book that begs to be seen as well as to be read," the *Financial Times* of London called it "an amazing story masterfully told," and the *New Orleans Times-Picayune* said that it "should be required reading." The *School Library Journal* picked it as one of the nine best books of the year.[31] But some heavy-hitting book critics, such as the distinguished British science writer Roger Lewin, were rather hostile.[32] It is hard to understand why *Dragons* received so many glorious plaudits and the Pulitzer Prize in 1978, whereas its far superior descendant, *Shadows*, received such a lukewarm reception in 1992. Perhaps it is for the same reason that in 1992, Sagan was rejected by the NAS: he had become too famous for his own good. To most people, he was known first and foremost as a creature of television. Hence the intelligentsia was less likely to take him seriously.

The *New York Times Book Review* didn't even bother to review *Shadows* (although a review in the New York Times Syndicate wire service praised it). Every Sunday, Druyan waded through the *Book Review*, looking for a report on the book into which she had poured so much of her talent and heart. It never appeared. She wept.[33]

WHEN ONE'S PUBLIC LIFE FALTERS, what remains? The private life. As the years passed, Sagan's compassion for others seemed to grow. He paid more attention to his three families, even as his third family grew in size. Annie had their daughter Alexandra (her nickname is Sasha) in 1982 and their son (Sagan's fourth), Samuel Democritus, in 1991. Sagan's old TTAPS colleague Thomas Ackerman recalls meeting him a few times after the nuclear brouhaha had settled down, and their encounters were always "friendly and fun, but not very serious. They mostly occurred in the context of other meetings. Carl as usual was holding center court, and I would have a few minutes of his time." Mainly they discussed their growing families. Ackerman's son was fifteen, and Sagan had just had a daughter (his first and only one). They talked "half the time not so much about science as about our kids."[34]

SAGAN'S PREVIOUS FAMILIES had gotten on with their lives. His first wife, Lynn, had remarried in the late 1960s, becoming Lynn Margulis, and had two more children, then divorced again. By the 1970s she was a well-recognized figure in microbiology, and in time one of the best-known (albeit still somewhat controversial) biologists in the world. In the 1980s, Sagan's second wife, Linda Salzman, and their son, Nick, left Ithaca for good and became permanent southern California residents. Both eventually became television writers. To date, Linda Salzman has not remarried.

Sagan's oldest "kid" was Dorion. He was a few years old when his parents divorced. Through the 1960s, 1970s, and 1980s, Dorion watched his biological dad ascend to scientific, then to national, then to international fame.

Dorion is now an articulate, impressive man—a successful science writer, author of many books (some coauthored with his mother, Lynn Margulis). After his father's death, he recalls, "I [went] to his memorials and I hear people talk, and people are so stupid. Some of them get up and say, 'He was a great scientist, he was a great human being and he was a great father.'"

In fact, Dorion says, "he was a *sucky* father. He didn't *know* how to be a father. Even in his most recent incarnation as a father, he had four or five people in the house helping him. He needed *attention*. He wasn't selfless enough to be a good father. I really don't think so."

Some children of celebrities self-destruct. "How did I not fuck up? . . . Well, it's my mother. Because she's so down-to-earth. . . . My father was a very difficult person in that if [he] was the only influence in your life, if you were insularly exposed only to his success and his need for attention, it would be very easy to become very fucked up. And I'm certainly not claiming to be free of the influence. I think I've been able to differentiate myself from him in part, strangely, by actually theatrically embodying Oedipal conflict in some of my prose."[35]

Dorion does, however, have some happy childhood memories of his father. As little boys, he and his brother, Jeremy, now a computer expert and musician living (like Dorion) in Massachusetts, loved to hear their father's stories about science. Sagan told them, for example, how a star collapses into a black hole. Dorion became a magic buff and performed his own boyhood shows; he recalls how his dad, sitting in the audience, laughed out loud with "childish delight."

Dinner-table conversation was more formal. "My father has a paragraphical sentence structure, and one of the problems I had with him all through my life is that I have always felt more comfortable in conversations that are open to witty repartee and give-and-take of barbs and quips and epigrams." At his father's house, "there's this weird ethic of oratory where you're not allowed to interrupt. It's very stifling.

"My other complaint about my dad is that I don't really think that he had much of a sense of humor. I know that Annie Druyan and other people will argue and say, oh, no, he had a great sense of humor, he laughed till the tears came out of his eyes. But the thing is, I always had the impression that he would belly laugh over a pun.

"I think that's part of the whole fame dynamic. . . . I think he basically took himself very seriously. He couldn't laugh. He's an authority figure for millions of people, the most recognized scientist in history maybe."[36]

They argued over economics. "He tended to assume he knew more about anything than anybody else, whether he did or not," Dorion said in late 1997. "His understanding of markets, which I had been studying, was simplistic. I remember being up at the Ritz Carlton . . . with his friends and his new wife [Annie]. Top floor of the Ritz Carlton, getting all kinds of perks—and they were going on about the virtues of communism. And that's classic champagne socialism, you know?"

Dorion wrote his dad a letter implying that his left-leaning economic views were hypocritical—a letter that was, Dorion admits, a pretext for his own inner hurts. "In the letter I said stuff like, 'You say that we should have an equal allotment of wealth. . . . Okay, why don't we cap [the maximum allowable wealth] at your earnings last year and we call the unit 'one sagan,' and nobody can make more than one sagan. While we're doing it, let's cap the number of books that anybody can write."[37]

Dorion feels that his father was usually critical of him. "An archetypal example of his criticism of me is he'd always say, 'Why do you just write these books with your mother? Why don't you go back to school and learn some other kinds of biology or strike out and do something on your own?' This kind of Oedipal criticism of me.

"Then when I finally did [write] a book with Eric Schneider on thermodynamics, he said, 'You don't know anything about thermodynamics.' "[38]

Sagan also criticized the television show *Star Trek*, which Dorion loved. "I thought *Star Trek* was great. I said, 'Just watch one episode with me.' And then he watched it and he would say, 'Oh, this is ridiculous. Is this supposed to be the future? It's all the same races, everybody speaks English.' Those were his kinds of comments."

Dorion acknowledges that with time, Sagan mellowed. Druyan made him open up to his children. "I remember when I was married in Florida, we went to visit him in his hotel room, . . . and he started touching my hair. . . . He started just kind of, like, massaging my head." Dorion grinned sheepishly at the memory. "And it felt so good. I mean, it felt great."[39]

Dorion's assessment of his father wavers back and forth. He explained how his son, Tonio, had recently faced a problem involving a potentially dangerous adult. The problem caused Dorion great anxiety; now *he* was the father, with a child of his own, whom he had to protect at all cost. Dorion nostalgically recalled one of his father's qualities: cool self-confidence in the face of evil.

Carl Sagan, Dorion recalled, had gone on television to combat the nuclear weaponeers and cold warriors—and made mincemeat of them. "My dad," Dorion declared with fierce pride, "wasn't afraid of *anybody*."[40]

SAGAN'S YOUNGEST ADULT SON is Nick. His childhood memories of his father seem warm—memories of trips to see the dolphins, for example. But his adolescence was also shadowed by his father's mega-fame on *Cosmos* and his parents' bitter, litigious divorce. Between the ages of eleven and fifteen, he went through a "dark time," he said, when he was "an angry, lost kid" who did "dangerous, risky things, . . . I hung out with friends who liked to drink and liked firearms—not a great combination!" He hated his prep schools in southern California. His grades were bad. Being the child of a famous person "is a blessing and a curse. There are definitely some good things to be said about it. But the negatives kind of stick more in your mind."[41]

Nick recalls, for example, the misery of dining publicly with his father while numerous people approached him for autographs. Nick was trying to explain to his father why he needed a bike, or why he didn't want to take a certain class in school; meanwhile, the autograph hounds lined up. And his dad was always happy to interrupt their father-son conversation to sign an autograph book. Another drawback, Nick says, is those people who assume that he somehow owes his adult accomplishments to his father's fame. He has to "fight to show that I belong. . . . I am not 'The Son of Carl Sagan.' . . . My identity is 'Nick Sagan,' who happens to be the son of Carl Sagan."[42]

Still, his father was "very loving and emotional. To me, he was never withholding." Yet Nick was sometimes bothered by his father's criticisms: "He used logic against everyone in my early childhood." It's one thing to use ruthless logic to deflate William Buckley in public debate and quite another thing to wield ruthless logic in family arguments, as when explaining to one's son, for example, why he should read Nietzsche's

Man and Superman instead of buying a "Superman" comic. Had Sagan—long celebrated for his childlike air—finally forgotten how he, too, had once drawn primal inspiration from tawdry comics and science-fiction pulps?

Fortunately, at least one adult in Nick's life was sensitive to his imaginative needs: his mom, Linda Salzman. She gave him three videotaped episodes of *The Prisoner*, a 1960s television show. A suave, surreal British import starring Patrick McGoohan, who played a spy imprisoned in a weird village at an unknown location, the show was Postmodern before Postmodernism was hip. "I went to my room, I locked my door, I watched them, and walked out with a nimbus of light surrounding me," Nick recalls. He then decided: "I know what I want to do."[43] He enrolled in Santa Monica Community College, made the dean's list, and transferred to UCLA film school, where he graduated summa cum laude. He now writes for television's *Star Trek: Voyager*, develops CD-ROMs and projects for film companies, and is working on a science-fiction novel.

Despite Carl Sagan's disdain for the *Star Trek* series, his son's success as a writer for the show "really cemented the last hurdle in my relationship with my dad," Nick says. "He was very impressed that I took my own path, that I dropped out and I did what I did without really anyone pushing or prompting me. I always felt: If people just leave me alone, I'll figure it out."

In 1994, NAS made up for repudiating Sagan's membership bid by awarding him its Public Welfare Medal, which recognized his popularization of science, not his scientific work. A number of other recipients were present at the award ceremony. Sagan's award was the last to be presented; with his "amazing virtuosity," Druyan recalls, he proceeded to explain to the NAS audience the importance of the other recipients' accomplishments.[44] "No one," the NAS citation states, "has ever succeeded in conveying the wonder, excitement and joy of science as widely as Carl Sagan and few as well. . . . His ability to capture the imagination of millions and to explain difficult concepts in understandable terms is a magnificent achievement."

That same year, Sagan's book *Pale Blue Dot* was published. It primarily concerned space exploration, and included gorgeous color art and Sagan's usual engaging prose. The book devoted considerable attention to research that he and Bishun Khare did on "tholins," a complex and puzzling substance that Sagan thought existed in space and on other worlds and might offer clues to the origin of life.[45]

Meanwhile, Sagan continued to do interesting work on the origin of life with bright young minds like Christopher Chyba and W. Reid

Thompson, whom he regarded as "absolutely first-rate."[46] By the time Sagan died, the old divide within origin-of-life research—between endogenous and exogenous theories—was as broad as ever. He tended to be an endogenist, although he perceived the virtues of exogeny. For example, he and Chyba published papers examining ways that comets might have delivered organic molecules to the surface of Earth.[47]

The origin of life had always intrigued Sagan, but as he matured he wondered as well about other types of origins—in particular, his own and humanity's. His close calls with death, and his heightened concern about our planetary fate, impressed on him the transience of life as his sixtieth birthday neared. "We are fleeting, transitional creatures, snowflakes fallen on the hearth fire,"[48] he and Druyan wrote in *Shadows*. In Sagan's last works, he began to open up a little about himself: who he was, where he came from—his childhood, his parents, even the "rumor" of his maternal grandfather's murder rap.[49] Sagan had once seemed so seamless, so imperturbable, like a man who was all on the surface; now he was hinting at vulnerabilities and secrets. Perhaps the refusal of the NAS to admit him had taken some of the wind out of his pride.

His last two books published before his death have something in common—their titles refer to Earth, not to space.[50] Sagan had once looked only forward, into the future; now he was looking back, to where he and his generation had been. Theirs was a unique generation, the first generation of the space age. Some fifteen years had passed since he and Ann Druyan, his new love, walked on the Florida shore and watched the *Voyager* space probe soar into the sky, into infinity, never to return. Now, in the last decade of the century, *Voyager* was nearing the edge of the solar system. He urged NASA to turn *Voyager* around so that its camera could snap one last look at our solar system.

The instincts of pure scientists said: No! Why mess with the instruments? Why risk pointing the sensitive camera directly at the Sun? And besides, why bother? A photograph of the solar system—that wasn't science, it was only a picture. But Sagan fought successfully. Druyan recalls: "He was like an Old Testament prophet pleading with NASA: Look back, look back toward this tiny planet and see it the way it is, not the frame-filling *Apollo* image of the Earth [viewed from the Moon] . . . but that little, tiny dot . . . "

She recalls "that brilliant passage of Carl's about every maximum leader, every thug, every dictator, everyone you ever loved, everyone is on that little tiny pale blue dot—the rivers of blood shed—over what? For momentary dominion over *a piece of a dot*."[51]

"Look back, look back . . . " The boy who had once hoped to fly to Mars now looked back, through his aging mind's eye, to Earth. It was the only world he would live on long enough to call home.

17

Hollywood

AND SO WE COME TO the Indian summer of Carl Sagan's career, to his last major creative project, the making of the film version of *Contact*. He had lived so many different lives—the scientist, the writer, the TV star, the political activist, the teacher, the novelist; now, the moviemaker. The making of *Contact* was the culmination of all his forays into show-biz—his performances in school plays; his radio and television appearances in high school and college; his gripping lectures at Yerkes and the University of Chicago; his star turn as *The Tonight Show*'s Mr. Science; and his creation of the television series *Cosmos*. "Showman of Science," *Time* magazine had christened him. But for the Brooklyn native whose father had once been a movie usher, the ultimate showmanship would be filmmaking. Sagan had flirted with the film business since the mid-1960s, when he consulted with Stanley Kubrick and Arthur C. Clarke on the making of *2001*. Thereafter, he and Francis Ford Coppola had discussed the possibility of making a film about alien contact, but the idea went nowhere (and ended up in court after Sagan's death[1]). Not until the last year of Sagan's life was his one movie, *Contact*, firmly on the road to completion.

Contact expressed all that was hopeful and generous in Carl Sagan: in its cosmic vision, in its feminism, in its commitment to reason over superstition, and in the determination and scientific passion of its heroine, who is a transgendered version of Sagan himself. The opening sequence is a technical triumph: a long journey through the cosmos—past galaxies, interstellar clouds, stars, and planets—into the eye of a little girl, scrutinizing the stars through her telescope. She is about the same age that Sagan was when he began to believe in extraterrestrials; and her father is about to die. On that discordant note—discovery and death—*Contact* ushers us one last time into the soul of Carl Sagan, who himself repeatedly skirted the shoals of death as the film was being made, and was dead before it opened.

Contact is not a great film, but it is a good and noble one. It is far superior to the usual special-effects-jammed blockbusters with microsecond editing, assembly-line dialogue, Dolby racket, and casual brutality that we now glumly know as "the movies." In *Contact*, Sagan comes closer than he ever did—even in *Cosmos*—to unifying the Two Cultures in his soul, to reconciling the left and right sides of his brain. The movie portrays cosmic exploration as a quest to discover meaning in the "cosmos" within us, as well as in the stars.

But the movie business is a tricky place for those who want to imprint a personal vision on a film. Film is the most collaborative of artistic media. Movie-making involves complex technology that requires the elite skills of representatives of numerous art forms (writers, painters, set designers, actors, musicians, and so on), many of them exquisitely egotistical and almost all of them sternly unionized. The industry's holy mandate is to appeal to the masses, to the largest potential market; hence artistic vision is often sacrificed on the altar of commercialism.

With all of the egos and pressures involved, every filmmaking enterprise is a ticking atomic bomb waiting to explode. If it does, then it destroys careers, even studios, plus whatever hapless investment group of Singaporean high rollers or Midwestern physicians has foolishly sunk their capital into the sorry business. The dread of empty seats at five thousand Bijous from Vancouver to Coral Gables spurs conservatism: Don't alienate the audience at any cost. Give them "what works," what is "safe," what is predictable (sex, car crashes, monosyllabic dialogue). Hence it is a miracle that any good film is ever completed—especially a film as intellectually ambitious, and with so unlikely a heroine, as *Contact*.

She was a scientist, an atheist, and a woman. "Strike three!" one imagines the studio head snapping during the pitch meeting. In the traditional Hollywood film, the hero is rarely a scientist (Gene Barry in *The War of the Worlds*[2]), almost never a smart, attractive woman (Faith Domergue in *It Came from Beneath the Sea*[3]), and never, ever an atheist! (Jodie Foster in *Contact*). In most films, scientists tend to be nerdy losers or sinister schemers whose prime role is to be blown up/vaporized/laser-fried/arrested/devoured or otherwise destroyed before the climax.

Thus the makers of *Contact* faced at least three key questions: First, if we make the film scientifically challenging and accurate, do we risk alienating the audience (especially the teenagers who despise nerds and who constitute the bulk of the audience)? Second, how can we make the lead, a female scientist—one who does not seem terribly interested in sex, marriage, or motherhood—appealing to a mass American audience, many of whom still fear and despise feminist values? And third, how can we make an atheist a sympathetic character to an audience that still clings to religious hopes, more than a century after Huxley humbled Wilberforce?

It would have been splendid to be a fly on the wall, listening to the filmmakers' deliberations. But that isn't necessary, because the filmmakers—Sagan, Druyan, and producer Lynda Obst—had professional transcriptionists record their hundreds of hours of conversations verbatim. Reading these transcripts, one gains new respect for that tiny percentage of idealistic moviemakers who struggle to turn difficult, unsettling ideas into popular entertainment, to defend their convictions without losing their shirts at the box office.

ONE WOULD NOT normally expect a film producer to be capable of debating the epistemological limits of science, much less to be interested in doing so. Someone once said that people who are smart and ambitious move to New York City, people who are just smart move to San Francisco, and people who are just ambitious move to Los Angeles. But Lynda Obst was no ordinary movie producer. Previously an editor with the *New York Times Sunday Magazine* who edited a book on American life in the 1960s, she left New York for southern California (following her then husband) in the 1970s, then rose through the ranks of the film industry. She is now one of the hotter players on the Hollywood scene; her autobiography, *Hello, He Lied*, published in 1995, is an occasionally insightful look at the film business and the challenges it poses to a young, ambitious woman.[4] We met one evening in a teahouse off Melrose Avenue. She has Hollywood style: being late for our appointment, and knowing men, she sent a smart, stunning blonde assistant to keep me company while I sipped an exotic tea in the southern California twilight.

Finally Obst sauntered in. She was petite, fast-talking, captivating, and tough—a sexy forty-eight-year-old. Do not cross this woman. During our interview, she excused herself, pulled out a cell phone, phoned a Hollywood player she found troublesome and delivered the coolest-tempered and calmest-voiced, yet most intimidating, tongue-lashing I have ever heard. A reporter once called and informed her, "You have been named one of the ten biggest bullies in Hollywood." (Obst denies being a bully.)

In fact, by Hollywood standards, Obst is an intellectual. She studied philosophy at Columbia University, where she had a special interest in the philosophy of science. She recalls graduate school fondly, but was frustrated by some of its intellectual constraints. She grew discouraged when a paper she wrote on the metaphysics of emotions received an unimpressive grade and the professor "said it was an unacceptable topic."

She eventually dropped out because, as she recalls, "[At Columbia] I was surrounded by Talmudic students so much more serious than me and I thought, 'You know what, Lynda? You're not really a philosopher—you're 'pop'!' "[5]

For Obst, the experience of working with Sagan and Druyan was an intellectual breath of fresh air, a relief from her earlier experiences in Hollywood and meetings "full of boys and men who were talking tits and ass and saying they couldn't have 'real' conversations in front of me."[6]

When she read *Contact*, she knew she wanted to produce the film version. Despite its dramatic flaws, the book is a rarity in that it is a novel of ideas, exploring the limits of science, the validity or invalidity of religion, the role of women in research, the impact of politics and superstition on the quest for truth. These are subjects rarely addressed in Hollywood movies, yet Obst hoped to confront them.

Especially in the early years of their relationship, Sagan felt terribly possessive of Druyan, and he was intensely jealous of her intimacy with Obst. As she looks back on the way Sagan behaved at that time, Obst credits his self-centered demands to a sense of "patriarchal entitlement" that he had developed because he had been a "childhood genius," the "privileged prince son" of Rachel, and because of the brilliance he showed at the University of Chicago. She also credits the "little chip on the shoulder" he carried from having been denied tenure at Harvard. She sometimes suspects he knew he would die relatively young, so "he had to do so much in a short period of time." And when one is driven to do so much—when one's life is all about science, truth, ambition, and success—then, Obst observes, other people's purpose is to serve one's career agenda; their own needs are less important.

She also thinks that Sagan had some abandonment anxieties that her friendship with Druyan exacerbated. "It was really hard for him to share her when I was there," she recalls, "to see her completely engrossed with someone else." Obst recalls that "he would be hurt [if she had] the desire to go to the movies alone or to go to a store [for] three hours. Obviously that bridled on her independence."

Yet, over time Druyan's influence on Sagan worked to good effect, and Obst and Sagan became close. "Annie had the task . . . of turning his mind from the heavens to the earth, of making him a humanist. When I say that, it sounds trite, but it was so profound to watch," Obst says. He was forty when he met Druyan. "People rarely change, particularly successful people who are constantly being reinforced in the world. [But after he married Annie] I watched him grow."[7]

In working on *Contact*, Sagan, Druyan, and Obst constituted a smaller version of the *Voyager* record team, although this team summoned into their midst outside experts. For example, Caltech physicist Kip Thorne came and explained how he had advised Sagan, while he was writing the novel, on the design of the "wormhole" through which Ellie travels to the center of the galaxy for her ultimate rendezvous with aliens.[8]

The filmmakers' passion is clear in the transcription of the making of *Contact*. These transcripts make enthralling reading; they show how seriously these bright, enthusiastic, middle-aged children of postwar America and the 1960s wanted to make a movie that would intellectually entice the viewers. By Hollywood standards, some of the discussions are so erudite that it is heartbreaking that more of their ideas did not make it into the final film.

Around Druyan and Obst, Sagan loosened up, confessed vulnerabilities that he didn't share with other people. It is a truism that many men feel more comfortable discussing personal feelings with women than with men. "The mistake I make in writing is forgetting what has been happening emotionally," he remarked during one of the script meetings.[9]

The little team talked for hours, day after day, debating how to depict controversial aspects of the story. One question was whether the film should have a visually spectacular ending. Earlier science-fiction epics, such as *Close Encounters of the Third Kind* and *2001: A Space Odyssey*, had had visually orgasmic climaxes. Following this pattern, *Contact* originally was to conclude with some kind of light show in the sky, triggered by the aliens, as heavenly evidence of their existence. Sagan, Druyan, Obst, and the original director George Miller (who was replaced part-way through by Robert Zemeckis) discussed how to stage this light show.

They considered showing various people witnessing the celestial wonders: a homeless person crawling out from his cardboard box; prostitutes on Eighth Avenue; miners emerging from mines in Zaire, "with their helmets with the little lanterns." Miller proposed showing a man on Death Row looking through the bars of his cell and seeing the light show. Yet none of this was used in the final film, and it is aesthetically the better for it. The movie's ending—which is veiled in ambivalence about the true nature of Ellie's experience—is brave precisely because it refuses to satisfy a mass audience's lust for the emotionally cathartic "big finish" of most Hollywood spectaculars. Its ambivalence reflects, perhaps, Sagan's realization that despite his scorn for religion, the scientific quest itself reflects a kind of faith—faith not only in one's dream (say, in aliens) but also in the ultimate rationality of the universe.

As the project made sluggish progress toward the screen, Obst arranged "think tank" sessions to which she invited leading scientists, religious divines, and others to swap ideas about the film's topics. She assigned to those attending the think tanks a reading list that included

Kip Thorne's *Black Holes and Time Warps*, theoretical physicist Michio Kaku's *Hyperspace*, Timothy Ferris's *The Red Limit*, David Swift's *SETI Pioneers*, and SETI radioastronomer Frank Drake and Dava Sobel's *Is Anyone Out There?*[10]

One important issue the think tank dealt with was how realistic the film should be. Hollywood science-fiction films normally play fast and loose with scientific accuracy (one hears explosions in the vacuum of space, for example). To some Hollywood filmmakers, an academic obsession with scientific or historical accuracy may get in the way of a film's message. Sagan, by contrast, Druyan says, was made physically ill by scientific mistakes in a movie. "Couldn't they afford to hire a graduate student?" he asked.[11]

One complaint about Hollywood depictions of scientists is that they are rarely depicted doing science. Filmmakers know well that their biggest audience is young people, who are fearful of being labeled "nerds"; thus most films eliminate detailed depictions of reasoning processes and experimental procedures that might tax the audience's short attention span. During one script meeting, Obst recalled, she received a note from studio executives warning her about "nerdifying" Ellie. But exasperating as this warning was, it is true that watching scientists at work does not often make for good drama—"Eureka!" moments are rare in real-life laboratories. Hence Obst and Miller taught Sagan and Druyan the merits of avoiding too much scientific detail. This, however, upset one of the scientists who read an early script for *Contact:* she complained that its "scientific" dialogue sounded nothing like the conversation of real scientists. Though Sagan fought furiously for scientific accuracy, he was willing to concede that rigid verisimilitude risked obscuring the film's deeper messages. His target audience was not the intelligentsia.

For all the sophistication that the team brought to their discussions, this fear of boring the masses weighed on them heavily, and ultimately the final film version of *Contact* omitted the novel's most enjoyable conceit, the concept of a cosmic secret embedded within the value of pi. (A real-life backwater of mathematical research is the calculation of the value of pi to an ever-more-remote decimal place. In *Contact*, Ellie learns that once pi's value is calculated to a certain decimal place, an intelligent code begins to emerge. Because the value of pi is an inherent property of the universe, the discovery proves that our universe was created by some kind of super-intelligence.) Why did they omit it? They went around and around on the issue of whether pi would be too difficult a concept to explain to a mass audience. One science adviser urged them to keep it in the script. Sagan certainly hoped to keep it. But in the end, for whatever reason, someone high up decided that pi, a concept taught in every high school, is too challenging for mass audiences.

This omission was the filmmakers' worst mistake. *Contact* is an admirable film, but with the connecting thread of pi, it might have been a great one. Pi's omission ensured that the film would lack the intellectual depth that might have inspired conversations akin to those about *2001* and its enigmatic ending.

THE MOST CONTENTIOUS ISSUE in *Contact* concerned how to portray the heroine, Ellie Arroway. A strong-minded female scientist is not a Hollywood staple, and the filmmakers struggled over how to make her both strong and appealing. Their task was especially difficult because of the mixed messages in Sagan's original novel. On the one hand, it was mostly an admirably feminist depiction of a female researcher's struggles in a male-dominated environment. On the other hand, its ending appeared sexist, selling Ellie short by implying that her quest for alien intelligence was really just a quest for love, a compensation for personal loss and failure—for a sense of inner emptiness following the death of her father (lovable, like Sam), for her inability to relate to her difficult mother (like Rachel, albeit not as noisy), for her failure to have a viable adult romantic relationship. The notion that female ambition such as Ellie's must be psychologically "explained," whereas male ambition is a given, certainly seems sexist.

In fact sexist interpretations of the book haunted the movie from its early days of pre-production, as far back as the early 1980s. In Hollywood, projects can kick around for years, bouncing from producer to producer and studio to studio. *Contact* was an example of such a waif-like script. Obst originally worked on the project, then lost control of it, then regained control of it, all over more than a decade. She initially worked on *Contact* when she was a young, up-and-coming producer under the controversial mogul Peter Guber. Guber found it hard to believe that Ellie would be seeking extraterrestrials for purely intellectual reasons; he assumed she was driven by neurotic motivations. As Obst recalls: "The first thing Peter Guber said to me was, 'This girl must be searching out there [for life] because she has given up a baby and she doesn't know how to pay attention to the issues on Earth." Obst fumed: "You don't think it's sympathetic for a woman to be searching for the [scientific] truth? That it has to be neurotic?"[12]

Did Carl Sagan, a professed feminist, in fact write a sexist ending? Lynda Obst, for one, doesn't think so. "He loved strong women because his mother was as strong as it gets," she observes. "He was appalled by the lack of women in science. . . . He attacked colleagues for being sexist. He put young female students on his papers, in a professional way. . . . I think he was a banner feminist, one of our champions. He would have laid his body on the ground for equal pay. He would have promoted a woman, in an affirmative-action way, over a man ten times out of ten." Druyan recalls how, in group conversations, Sagan grew furious when other men would ignore her or cut off her remarks with their own pontificating. The normally cool Sagan would snap: "I believe *Annie* was talking!"[13] He even wrote to a leading art museum in 1978, protesting sexism in their literature. An official wrote back, saying they'd take his advice.[14] So fiercely did Sagan adhere to feminist ideals that, as we have seen, this view contributed to the wrecking of one of his dearest, oldest friendships.

Why, then, did Sagan write what seemed like a blatantly sexist ending? Sagan's intentions might be clarified if we assume that Ellie Arroway *was* Carl Sagan. His creation of Ellie clearly afforded him the opportunity to express perhaps unacceptable or embarrassing feelings through a fictional character. When he wrote about Ellie's self-absorption and aloofness from love, he was actually writing about himself. Therefore the climax of *Contact* might not actually betray his feminist values.

In the end the film version of *Contact* is more clearly true to Sagan's feminist ideals. This may be partly because there were so many women involved in the making of the film who kept an eye on the contents. Druyan and Obst were both ambitious, nontraditional women, of course, but so were executive producers Lucy Fisher and Courtney Valenti, and, most famous of them all, the actress who was finally picked to play Ellie, Jodie Foster. "So Jodie protected this movie, and Lucy protected this movie, and Courtney—all the women protected this movie," said Obst.[15] Foster, a well-liked, Yale-educated actress with impeccable acting credentials (*Taxi Driver, Little Man Tate*), was enthralled by the film's plot. Her signing on to *Contact* was "money in the bank"; it ensured that the film was doable because it now had a star who could pull in audiences. Foster had devoted followings—among film critics, liberals, and lesbians, for example—that might help the film at the box office.[16]

Sagan, Druyan, and Obst were determined to depict Ellie as a woman who had struggled to be accepted as a scientist and radioastronomer. As part of the think tank sessions, they invited a middle-aged female scientist to meet with them, to read the script and assess the crises that faced a young woman rising through the scientific ranks during the period of Ellie's career in the novel (the 1950s and 1960s). To protect her identity because of the highly personal nature of her comments, the woman is herein referred to as "Hypatia." She is highly accomplished in her field (not radioastronomy) but is largely unknown to the public. Hypatia's account of her own career is a disturbing illustration of the obstacles that women of her generation faced in entering scientific careers.

The obstacles are first faced in childhood. During one script meeting, Hypatia recalled her own childhood, when her brothers beat her up and would "lock her in closets and chase her around the house with dead bugs. It was positively hostile. I spent a lot of time on my own." Her mother criticized her for studying physics, saying that she should study literature instead, and pressured her to get married. At one point her mother said to her—when she was thirty—"Let's face it, you're a spinster." Hypatia said: "I got so mad, I took the chair I was sitting on and I threw it across the room." Although her mother was proud of Hypatia's subsequent success in science, "she felt she failed because I wasn't married."

At her university, she said, "I was constantly fighting males, . . . competing with males." There, it was "both hell and heaven for me. [In one professor's class], I asked one too many questions. He turned to me and said, 'Now, now, don't get your tits in an uproar.' [I was] 21 years old . . . and I wanted to knock his fucking teeth out. . . . [Another professor] walked in to start teaching the class and kind of patted me, gave me a loving pat on the head, and the whole class burst out laughing. I was very embarrassed by that. . . . I had a Nobel laureate grab me and sit me on his lap, like I was some kind of little baby." She recalled her thesis adviser making remarks such as "Women can't think in the abstract."

Hypatia shared with the group how she would "put on my alpha-male persona" in order to command her scientific team. "I deliberately tried to do what a male would do, especially if he is going to go to the head of the table. He comes in and throws the book down and sits like this and [will] just be male-like, take up a lot of room, make noise. . . . I try to be very, very male-like. . . . You can't be too female and nurturing because they don't take you seriously."[17]

Hypatia, then, was the reality of that generation of scientific women. How much would that reality be transferred to the screen? Unfortunately, there is still a limit to how tough a female character can be made in films, at least films that hope to be commercial successes. Hypatia, for one, felt that the script sent a "punishment message," that Ellie's character was being punished for her strong-mindedness. "This woman is punished in the end for making the most colossally important discovery— not of the decade, not of the century, but in the history of humanity," she argued in one script meeting. She also objected to a crucial line in the film. When Ellie finally encounters the alien who symbolizes her father on the beach at the center of the galaxy, her father tells her, "Ellie, it is time to grow up." Hypatia observed that if Ellie had been a male character, it would be unimaginable for the scriptwriter to have the parent say, "Now, son, it is time to grow up."[18]

Obst, who had fought her own gender battles in Hollywood, de-fended the script, stating that sometimes "the patriarchy is punishing to women who try to bite off more than they were expected to bite off. . . . I think that is the point we're trying to get across, that there is a toll that is paid for shooting [for] the Moon, for going for the goals that men have gone for. Not that you are ultimately punished, but along the way, it is not easy for you. Men aren't throwing themselves at your feet. Men aren't saying 'You're the image of femininity that I always dreamt of.'"[19]

As part of the struggle over how to make Ellie a sympathetic charac-ter, the production team also debated over whether Ellie should have a baby at the film's end. Despite the advance of feminist consciousness, many filmmakers still feel obligated to pay homage to the marriage-and-reproduction rituals of the mainstream culture. Even the hyper-tough character played by Sigourney Weaver in *Alien* was softened in the sequel by having her take charge of a little girl; and Linda Hamilton's kick-ass revolutionary in *Terminator 2* was similarly burdened with an adolescent boy.[20] It is hard to believe that the feminist team on *Contact* would have seriously considered saddling their heroine not only with a SETI search, a congressional inquisition, and a trip to the center of the galaxy, but with a pregnancy as well; but consider it they did. They seem to have feared that many viewers might be put off by a woman who chooses a childless life.

Obst (the mother of a teenage boy) argued eloquently for the baby. While asserting that "my feminist credentials are somewhat [on] the table," she said she "burst into tears" in reading the novel, at the scene where Ellie, as she is about to board the galactic transport, says, "I wish I had a baby." "It is the first moment," Obst continued, "that Ellie recog-nizes the implications of the choices she has made to be single, and there is not a woman in the audience who is not going to wonder with her at that moment how different she would have been if she had been able to do that. . . . In the recognition that she missed something [by not having a baby], she's giving a gift to every woman in the world because she's connecting with them."[21]

Obst was making a point that has haunted the feminist movement—how to make one's way in a man's world without seeming to repudiate the values of traditional women. George Miller opposed the baby as "very Disney, Hollywood." Ann Druyan (mother of two) singled out for attack a scene in one draft of the script in which Ellie weeps after meeting a little girl named Ellie. The scene, Druyan charged, implied that Dr. Arroway deserved punishment for having chosen science over motherhood.[22]

The filmmakers also spent a comical amount of time trying to figure out how to hitch Ellie up romantically to someone—*anyone*—no matter how badly he suited her. The preacher (Palmer Joss) who fought her ideologically? The egomaniacal scientific politician (David Drumlin) who destroyed her SETI search? The Russian scientist who collected dirty playing cards? All were seriously discussed as possible romantic candidates. They finally settled on Joss—a bizarre choice, but given his basic decency and real intellect, the best one (he also was closest to her in age).

To their credit, though, the filmmakers resisted the temptation to make the romantic relationship credible; it might as well not have existed. Ellie and Palmer kiss, then he pays her a pointless last-minute visit before she jets off for the center of the galaxy—and that's it; having paid the ritual sacrifice to Hollywood mythology, the filmmakers can get on with the movie.

Striking the right balance of toughness and femininity was probably an impossible goal. To some tastes, Ellie wasn't strong enough, while to others she was too strong. When the film came out, for example, *New York Times* critic Stephen Holden complained that Ellie showed "little vulnerability."[23]

RELIGION WAS ANOTHER CONTENTIOUS ISSUE addressed by the film. Like his fictional character Ellie, Sagan was an atheist/agnostic, but not a simple one. His attitude toward religion (in public, anyway) mellowed somewhat as he entered the late 1980s and established "strange bedfellow" political alliances with religious leaders in an effort to fight nuclearism and environmental recklessness. His vacillating comments about religion during the making of *Contact* show how much his views had evolved since his youthful quarrels with Rachel.

In the novel *Contact*, Sagan had depicted American religion in one of its more primitive forms: tent-revival evangelism. It is hard to believe that a sophisticated thinker like Carl Sagan, even writing as a "pop" novelist, could depict modern religion so simplistically, as if the world had not turned since the Scopes trial of 1925. Sagan wasn't fighting modern religion, he was fighting Elmer Gantry; he was still waging the "warfare of science with theology" that Andrew Dickson White had fought a century earlier.[24] And this is why the novel *Contact*'s treatment of religion is of far less intellectual interest than its treatment of scientific issues. Religiously speaking, he was beating a dead horse.

The film's treatment of religion is subtler. The stereotype of screenwriters is that they are the ultimate pampered victims, creative types who sob all the way to the bank, lamenting how a heartless, vulgar producer has mangled their brainchild. In reality, films are sometimes better than the written material on which they are based. In some respects, *Contact* is such a film. On the one hand, the film lacks the frisson of the novel's intellectual conversations, notably the complex dialogue and the conceptual thrill of making pi a kind of cabalistic clue to the beyond. On the other hand, the film is leaner, less bogged down in dated depictions of evangelicals, and it does not betray Ellie at the end. At the same time, thanks to Sagan's new maturity on religious issues, and thanks partly to the good sense of his two female compatriots, the film's main representative of religion is an intelligent neo-yuppie played by Matthew McConnaughey. A religious man himself, McConnaughey refused to utter the one sentence that Ann Druyan had hoped would make the film: "My God was too small." The line was sacrilegious, McConnaughey told her. The more she talked to him about it, the more she realized the depth of his intelligent and sincere faith; in time they became good friends.[25]

Sagan worried that the final film would mute his underlying atheistic message. "The natural way for the Hollywood movie to go is to mitigate, moderate, lose the force of really vigorous anti-religious arguments, because it offends people in the audience," he complained at one script meeting. "I guess what I am worried about is that in the late stages of production and editing, there will be [decisions made] . . . [which] lose sight of the importance of the skeptical remarks."[26]

The religious discussions are among the most fascinating in the transcripts. They show that Sagan, far from being a knee-jerk atheist, had exceptional knowledge of the Bible and well-thought-out arguments against religion.

For example, in one script meeting the group began by discussing the origin of the concept of religion, which Sagan traced to dominance hierarchies in primates and to a child's attitude toward its seemingly "omnipotent parents." Obst countered that Sagan's ideas explained "monotheism and sort of Judeo-Christian, all-powerful God [ideas. But] there is a pagan tradition . . . [that is] a kind of spiritual instinct and impulse that's not necessarily looking for an all-powerful other." Sagan replied that in ancient Greece, Rome, and India, the polytheistic religions did have dominance hierarchies—"there is a king of the gods. That's the thing that counts." And so on, through the day.[27]

Sagan failed to fully grasp, however, a key aspect of religious belief: it is irrationalism that unashamedly knows it is irrational, that does not pretend to be scientific as Velikovsky or UFOlogists pretend to be scientific. Religion is "faith," after all. Not grasping the distinction between pseudoscientific irrationalism and religious irrationalism, Sagan seems to have believed that he could argue the religious out of their beliefs, as if their beliefs were in the same class as, say, believing that fragments of a flying saucer litter the New Mexico desert. Anthropologists and sociologists know better, of course; but social science was never one of Sagan's strong points.

Sagan saw no need for this kind of faith because he did not think the so-called miracles of life required miraculous explanation. The "argument from design" that theologians often used to defend the idea of God—life and the order of the universe are so perfect and miraculous that there must be a God—was utterly unconvincing to Sagan. He argued, by contrast, that evolution could explain the remarkable order and diversity of life. "Now we live in a time," he said in a *Contact* script session, "where we understand that order can be extracted out of chaos, the most beautiful order from the most random chaos, without any intelligence intervening."[28]

"There are no atheists in foxholes," goes an old saying. That is, the fear of death guarantees that religion will always be with us. Sagan's commitment to his atheism would shortly be tested in a frighteningly personal way.

18

The Night Freight

"SIX TIMES NOW have I looked Death in the face," Sagan wrote in his last book, *Billions and Billions*. "And six times Death has averted his gaze and let me pass. Eventually, of course, Death will claim me—as he does each of us. It's only a question of when. And how." By his shaving mirror, he kept a framed postcard from a passenger aboard the *Titanic*—as a reminder "that 'going grand' can be the most temporary and illusory state. So it was with us."[1]

In late 1994, Sagan wrote, Druyan noticed "an ugly black-and-blue mark on my arm that had been there for many weeks." She asked, "Why hasn't it gone away?" Sagan went to the doctor for blood tests. A few days later, when they were in Austin, Texas, the doctor called: "Please get retested right away," he said.[2]

Another test revealed the grim news: Sagan had a mysterious disease he knew nothing about called myelodysplasia. Myelodysplasia is a rare blood disorder that often leads to acute leukemia; the bone marrow manufactures a large number of immature and misshapen (dysplastic) blood cells. According to the National Institutes of Health, three thousand new cases of myelodysplasia appear in the United States every year. If he did nothing, he would be dead in six months. He needed a bone marrow transplant from a compatible donor. An obvious candidate was his sister, Cari. They called and asked her if she'd be the donor. She replied readily: "You got it. Whatever it is . . . liver . . . lung . . . it's yours."[3] He and the family (including Druyan's parents, Harry and Pearl) moved to Seattle, where Sagan entered a leading center for bone marrow transplants, the Fred Hutchinson Cancer Research Center. "Even with the perfect compatibility [of donor], my overall chances of a cure were something like 30 percent," Sagan later wrote. He was allowed to self-administer painkillers including morphine derivatives. In the middle of the night, he had to awaken and swallow seventy-two chemotherapeutic pills at a time—enough to kill him if the marrow transplant did not "take." He lost weight and looked "somewhat cadaverous." Almost all his hair fell out. His four-year-old, Sam, commented: "Nice haircut, Dad."[4]

Eventually Sagan's condition improved. The family returned to Ithaca. He continued to need "all sorts of medical attention, including drugs administered several times a day through a portal in my vena cava. Annie was my 'designated caregiver'—administering medication day and night, changing dressings, checking vital signs, and providing essential support."[5]

The near disaster complicated his already complex ruminations on an old issue: animal research. He had long argued for sparing animals from pain and stressed "how morally bankrupt it is to slaughter them to, say, manufacture lipstick."[6] He and Druyan received an award from People for the Ethical Treatment of Animals, and he served as Cornell faculty adviser to the campus chapter.[7] He also sent a letter to NASA chief Dan Goldin suggesting ever so subtly that it might be time to stop launching primates into space.[8] Yet he had survived death because of a marrow grafting made possible because of research on rodents and dogs. "I remain very conflicted on this issue," he wrote. "I would not be alive today if not for research on animals."[9]

NOW TIME WAS TRULY SHORT. Too much to do, not enough time to do it. In his final years, he churned out books faster than ever. Besides *Shadows of Forgotten Ancestors*, his books of the 1990s include *A Path Where No Man Thought* (with Rich Turco) in 1990, *Pale Blue Dot* in 1994, *The Demon-Haunted World: Science as a Candle in the Dark* in 1996, and the posthumously published *Billions and Billions* in 1997. Except for the book with Turco, all sold well and received generally good reviews, although they lacked the literary elegance and depth of *Shadows*. To write a book like *Shadows* takes a lot of time, time for reflection and study and intricate wordsmithing—more time than he had.

Cornell threw a gala party for Sagan to celebrate his sixtieth birthday; top scientific speakers came, such as Kip Thorne. But his seventh decade began bittersweetly: in California, Jim Pollack died of cancer of the spine.[10] In Ithaca, W. Reid Thompson, one of Sagan's younger associates in the study of extraterrestrial organic molecules, also died of cancer.[11] With Pollack's death, Sagan lost a vital link to the past; with Thompson's death, to the future.

During the final two years of his life, Sagan continued to play armchair scientist, advising generally younger colleagues. He remained deeply interested in SETI and was intrigued by the results of galactic observations by Paul Horowitz, the SETI astronomer supported by The Planetary Society, which Sagan had co-founded. Over the years, Horowitz's

META (Mega-channel Extraterrestrial Assay project) had detected dozens of brief, one-time signals from different points in the galaxy. They were probably flukes—radio noise from terrestrial sources, say, or perhaps from secret military projects or "dark" satellites.[12]

Or might they be beacons of alien civilizations? And if so, then why did they flash only once?

Radio sources in space tend to "twinkle" because of interference as they pass through ionized matter in the galaxy. This phenomenon is called scintillation. Sagan and his colleagues explored the possibility that scintillation causes transient increases in the intensity of SETI signals (just as varying ionization in Earth's atmosphere can reflect radio signals over unusually long distances. Hence, for example, a driver in the Rocky Mountains sometimes picks up a Miami radio station). Could scintillation cause us to momentarily detect transmissions from civilizations normally too distant to be "heard"? If so, then some of Horowitz's detections might have been real alien beacons, glimpsed only briefly, like fireflies that spark briefly then disappear into the night.[13]

As mentioned earlier, after Sagan's death Timothy Ferris wrote a brief, cryptic line in an otherwise positive obituary: "I knew Carl Sagan too well to regard him as a hero."[14] By the mid-1990s Ferris was one of the world's leading science essayists. In 1996, one of the last times he saw Sagan, he "looked shockingly like somebody who's nearly died," Ferris recalled. Druyan was there. Two decades had passed since they were young friends, since Druyan was Ferris's fiancée, since they had all worked to design a message to send aboard the *Voyagers* into the galaxy. "I don't think the three of us had ever really sat down like that . . . so it was a fairly strange dynamic," Ferris recalls.

Being intellectuals, they argued over ideas—in this case, an old and touchy question: Can different fields of thought be unified as one? Ferris mentioned a scholar who once told science historian Joseph Needham: "Joseph, to have a liberal arts education you must be familiar with five fields: science, philosophy, religion, art, and history. If you are familiar with those five fields, you'll have a good education and you can go on to many other things. But if you are missing any one of the five you will lack a proper liberal education." Needham himself added: "I see no need to unify them."

Instantly, Sagan replied: "Well, three of the five are reducible to science. And the other one"—meaning religion—"is a delusion."

"So we started into a very spirited and vulgar argument," Ferris recalls. "I felt that what he was doing was basically saying, 'Fuck you.' So

I took the argument to a kind of truck driver level very fast, just to let him know that I wasn't going to be pushed off the dime on this. . . . Being that it was Carl, it turned into a tough sort of argument." Sagan mentioned, among other things, how he had skeptically discussed religion with a Zen master.

"I remember at one point for some reason we touched on the old question of whether good art can serve an illegitimate purpose, and he brought up Leni Riefenstahl. I started to talk about that, and I said, 'Shit, Leni Riefenstahl is a tough case.' He said, 'That's why I mentioned her.'" Like two bulls fuming over old hurts, they crashed their way around C. P. Snow's china shop.

"I was trying to sever the concept of mysticism from the idea of an afterlife. I was saying that there is a context of mystical thought that has nothing to do with an afterlife. And he kept saying that most people believe mystical things because they're afraid to die. Every time I would come back to this he would say, 'Yes, but most people . . .'

"I finally said, 'Look. It is not true of people like this Zen master you're talking to, and it's a bit *infra dig* for you to keep bringing it up.'"

Then Sagan—the omniscient one, the man who always seemed to know everything—said: "I have a confession to make."

"What is that?"

"I have to confess that I have never known what *infra dig* meant." They laughed.[15]

SAGAN'S LAST BOOK published before his death was *The Demon-Haunted World* (1996). On the surface, it appears to be an entertaining, easily readable series of essays about pseudoscience and irrationalism. Its prose style is simple—closer to *Parade* magazine (to which Sagan frequently contributed) than to the *New Yorker*-ish broodings of *Shadows*. It also offers something that very few scientists have ever offered: a list of their mistakes.

"It might be useful for scientists now and again to list some of their mistakes," Sagan wrote. "It might play an instructive role in illuminating and demythologizing the process of science and in enlightening younger scientists." Besides the previously cited mistake (the forecast of a Gulf War–triggered climate change), he mentioned a few other

> cases where I've been wrong: At a time when no spacecraft had been to Venus, I thought at first that the atmospheric pressure was several times that on Earth, rather than many tens of times. I thought the clouds of Venus were made mainly of water, when they turn out to be only

25 percent water. I thought there might be plate tectonics on Mars, when close-up spacecraft observations now show hardly a hint of plate tectonics.* I thought the highish infrared temperatures of Titan might be due to a stable greenhouse effect there; instead, it turns out, it is caused by a stratospheric temperature inversion.[16]

However, the list does not include Sagan's most embarrassing goofs—his suggestion that creatures the size of polar bears might inhabit Mars, for example, or that the lunar surface might conceal organic molecules and microbes, or his suggestion that "near-death" experiences might actually be memories of birth (this suggestion was undermined in a statistical study by the British psychologist Susan Blackmore).[17]

Still, it was admirable and wonderfully rare for a man of Sagan's age and ego to offer *any* scientific apologies, much less several. In the face of death, he was growing up.

"ANYBODY THAT IS THAT BRILLIANT and that famous and that productive is a 'control' person," observes Andrea Barnett, Sagan's assistant during the time he was ill. "Control—you think you have control over things . . . 'I can *do* this.' . . . [But] his illness became such a constant opponent." He'd fly to Seattle for treatment, then return to Ithaca healthier, relieved: "I'm back. . . . I made it. Phew." And then, suddenly, "this bony hand would come out and grab him by the neck again—and back he'd be in Seattle."

In the office, "it was so sad for my co-worker and me, because we could feel the difference in him as it became obvious to him that this was a desperate attempt to come out even. It was no longer looking to the future. . . . It was a desperate attempt to come out even. To not leave things undone."[18]

Sagan's last book was *Billions and Billions*, published posthumously in 1997. It includes the following "Postscript":

> Since writing this chapter a year ago, much has happened. I was released from the Hutch [the Hutchinson Cancer Research Center], we returned to Ithaca, but after a few months the disease recurred. It was much more grueling this time—perhaps because my body was weakened by the previous therapies, but also because this time the pretransplant conditioning involved whole body X-irradiation. Again, my family accom-

---

*He spoke too soon. Recent spacecraft observations hint that Mars underwent plate tectonic activity, or something like it, billions of years ago.

panied me to Seattle. Again, I received the same expert and compassionate care at the Hutch. Again, Annie was magnificent in encouraging me and keeping my spirits up. Again, my sister, Cari, was unstintingly generous with her bone marrow. . . . People survive years even with a few percent of their host cells. But I won't be reasonably sure until a couple of years have passed. Until then, I can only hope.[19]

This writer last saw Sagan in late 1995, when he delivered a speech at the World Affairs Forum in San Francisco. Fallen leaders were there—Gorbachev, Margaret Thatcher, George Bush. Sagan looked haggard. His hair was thin, bristly, gray; his eyes were shadowy, his skin sagging. He had always looked so young; now, for the first time, he was an old and sick man. But he was charming, pleasant, his voice as resonant as ever. And he gave by far the best speech of the conference, an evening lecture based on *Pale Blue Dot*.[20] He will be remembered, if for nothing else, for his oratory—for his power to inspire a room of cynical world leaders and skeptical journalists, to remind them of their childhoods and the dreams that once stirred them. People were crying.

IN LATE 1996, the Reverends Joan Campbell and Albert Pennybacker (respectively, the general secretary and associate general secretary of the National Council of Churches) dined with Sagan, Druyan, and their daughter, Sasha, in Ithaca. "It was a rare evening," Campbell later recalled. "The conversation, as always, was intellectually challenging and emotionally rewarding. As we embraced to say goodbye, I held him close and said to him, 'I think you'll make it this time, Carl.'

"He winked at me and said, 'I pray so. I want so very much to live.' "[21]

Over the years, Sagan had made a number of appearances on Ted Koppel's late-night television show, *Nightline*. In October, he appeared on the show for the last time. Druyan later recalled: "Ted Koppel looked at Carl and realized he had clearly had been through a harrowing physical experience. His hair was gone and he was quite gaunt. He said, 'Carl, you've been through so much recently. Surely this terrible illness that you've been through must have elicited in you some personal thoughts that you might be willing to share with the audience.'

"I sat back and I thought, well, this is going to be about our family. And then I saw Carl break out into that radiant smile. He said: 'These are our true circumstances. We live on a tiny ball of rock and dust, in a cosmos vast beyond our imagining.' "[22]

Thanksgiving brought the whole family to Ithaca—Sagan's sister, Cari, his adult sons, Dorion, Jeremy, and Nicholas, and Dorion's son,

Tonio. "By unanimous acclaim," Druyan writes, "it had been the best Thanksgiving we'd ever had."[23]

In early December at home, Sagan sat down to dinner. Druyan watched anxiously as he gazed unenthusiastically at the dish, normally "a favorite meal." She argued that he was just suffering "a fleeting disinterest in food." He smiled slightly and said, "Maybe."[24]

A workaholic to the end, he insisted on flying to San Francisco to give two lectures, long promised. Afterward, at the hotel, "he was exhausted. We called Seattle," Druyan later wrote. They began their fourth trip to the cancer center—the last. Druyan informed Sasha and little Sam, "Yes, Hanukkah will have to be postponed. But once Daddy is better . . . "

A day later, an X-ray machine at Seattle scanned Sagan's frail body. He had pneumonia, its cause unknown.

Later, Sagan told Druyan: "This is a deathwatch. I'm going to die." No, no, she insisted, he was wrong. "He turned to me with that same look I had seen countless times in the debates and skirmishes of our twenty years of writing together and being wildly in love. With a mixture of knowing good humor and skepticism, but as ever, not a trace of self-pity, he said wryly, 'Well, we'll see who's right about this one.' "[25]

Almost twenty years earlier—on June 1, 1977—they had declared their mutual love. "June 1" was their private term of affection. Both were religious skeptics; both knew that Sagan's death would be the end, that they would never meet again.

Lynda Obst flew from Los Angeles to join them; she hugged and kissed Sagan on his deathbed. Druyan summoned the children to Seattle. She also called all the family members, and "placed the phone near Carl's ear so that he could hear, one by one, their good-byes."[26]

Sasha entered the hospital room. "Beautiful, beautiful, Sasha," Sagan told his slender, lovely teenage daughter. "You are not only beautiful, but you have enormous gorgeousness."

"For days and nights," Druyan later wrote, "Sasha and I had taken turns whispering into Carl's ear. Sasha told him how much she loved him and all the ways that she would find in her life to honor him.

" 'Brave man, wonderful man,' I said to him over and over. 'Well done.' With pride and joy in our love, I let you go. Without fear. June 1. June 1. For keeps . . . "[27]

Five-year-old Sam entered. Sagan was having trouble breathing and speaking. He gazed at his youngest child. Sam was the same age that Sagan had been when he first looked at the stars and wondered: What are they? Now Sagan's body was slowly, imperceptibly disintegrating into the starstuff from which it came. He composed himself and whispered to his boy: "I love you, Sam."

CARL SAGAN DIED at thirty-two minutes after midnight on December 20, 1996, at the Fred Hutchinson Cancer Research Center in Seattle. The immediate cause of death was pneumonia resulting from complications of myelodysplasia. Druyan says that his last words to her and Sasha were "I love you."

In an epilogue that Druyan wrote for Sagan's last book, *Billions and Billions*, she says:

> Contrary to the fantasies of the fundamentalists, there was no deathbed conversion, no last minute refuge taken in a comforting vision of a heaven or an afterlife. For Carl, what mattered most was what was true, not merely what would make us feel better. Even at this moment when anyone would be forgiven for turning away from the reality of our situation, Carl was unflinching. As we looked deeply into each other's eyes, it was with a shared conviction that our wondrous life together was ending forever.[28]

"He thought that was the end," Druyan said later. "He thought [to believe] anything else was spiritual narcissism. If you weren't going to think that chimpanzees were going to go on forever, then why would you think humans would? It made no sense."

And when he died, "I felt like I could hear the Furies calling in my ears. I felt I was participating in some Aztec ceremony in which my chest was being opened and my beating heart was being ripped out of my chest. And for weeks I could feel and hear this physiological thing, literally like the Furies 'calling'—I'm sure it was completely psychological or biological—this amazing sound I heard in my head. . . . Since June 1, 1977, from that very first moment that we told each other that we loved each other, I had been thinking about how the piper would have to be paid. I don't think you can be that lucky and that happy without paying a huge price for it."[29]

JOHNNY CARSON WAS THE FIRST to phone with condolences.[30] The *New York Times* ran Sagan's photo on the front page, with a long biography inside.[31] Some scientists were surprised by how much Sagan's passing upset them. Despite his repeated illnesses, he had always seemed so youthful; despite the lost hair and grizzled appearance of his last, sickly days, they couldn't believe that he wouldn't soon be his old self again, stimulating and exasperating them. And who would replace him? What scientists came anywhere close to gripping the popular imagination as he had?

To noted astronomer Alan Boss, the emotional impact of Sagan's death rivaled that of John F. Kennedy.[32] Stephen Jay Gould observed: "I could only recall Nehru's observation on Gandhi's death—that the light had gone out, and darkness reigned everywhere. . . . Carl . . . shared my personal suspicion of the nonexistence of souls—but I cannot think of a better reason for hoping we are wrong than the prospect of spending eternity roaming the cosmos in friendship and conversation with this wonderful soul."[33] Tributes flowed in from around the world, from writers and world leaders, from scientists and ordinary people. A rare disparaging comment appeared in an obituary in *Forbes*, the business magazine; its author was one of Sagan's more abrasive foes in the nuclear winter debate.[34]

Three memorial services were held—in Ithaca, Pasadena, and New York City. The last was at St. John the Divine Cathedral, where the dignitaries included the scientifically savvy vice president, Al Gore. Rev. Joan Campbell told those gathered: "Carl Sagan was one of religion's most severe critics and best friends. Carl demanded of religion clarity, honesty, and excellence—qualities we would do well to demand of ourselves. . . . He would say to me with a smile, 'You're so smart. Why do you believe in God?' and I would say to him, 'You're so smart. Why don't *you* believe in God?'"

The vice president recalled Sagan's last appearance on *Nightline*, and noted that it came a few months after David McKay and his colleagues reported finding possible evidence of fossil microbes in a rock from Mars (a claim now doubted by most scientists). Sagan, the victim of many extraterrestrial disappointments, had reacted cautiously to the McKay team's announcement, but added that if it was true, it would be a historic discovery. According to Gore, Sagan had been the first person invited to a White House gathering, scheduled for December 1996, to plan future space missions. He was too sick to come, but he sent a letter listing prime space objectives and added this plea: "There should be no backing off from these missions and their objectives."

"There will not be, Carl," Gore vowed.

> We won't back off from these missions. We will look for new ways to understand the cosmos. It is part of the legacy Carl Sagan leaves behind; the mandate to explore, to learn, to ask the right questions. . . .
>
> I'd like to close . . . with the image of an eight-year-old Carl Sagan lying on his back in a field, filled with wonder at the image he beheld of the cosmos. . . . This evening, if we go outside and look up and stare deeply into the sky and lose ourselves in the magnificent "starstuff" of Carl Sagan's youth, we'll see that his spirit shines on. It shines on Annie and his children, on his friends and colleagues and students, and on all those who are impassioned by the unending search for knowledge. Those of us who were privileged to bask in that light, however briefly,

will never, ever forget its brilliance. We will miss him, and today we celebrate Carl Sagan.[35]

Jeremy Sagan spoke, too. Those unfamiliar with him might have gasped at his face: he bore a stunning resemblance to his father. Jeremy was the quiet son, not a sardonic intellectual like Dorion or a wordsmith like Nick. In theory, Jeremy might have nursed legitimate grievances against his dad, who had been too often absent in both body and spirit. Yet Jeremy was no hand-wringing, accusatory victim. He had turned out fine—smart, handsome, successful (in the computer field), and able to forgive. He strode to the podium and, with an aplomb rivaling his old man's, said:

> I'd like to say a few words briefly about my father. He was a warrior for the world, a scientific explorer of the galaxy and the universe as well. His passionate opposition to nuclear testing, including his arrest for civil disobedience at the Nevada test site, and his calculations providing evidence for nuclear winter, made me extremely proud. Not just as a son, but as a member of the human race. His message that nuclear weapons should not be used is something we should remember always.
>
> He was an avid anti-racist. He abhorred prejudice and would not hesitate to speak up when presented with it. In the 1960s he traveled to Tuskegee, Alabama, to give a talk at an all-black school entitled, "Is There Intelligent Life on Earth?" At times it must have seemed like there wasn't. . . .
>
> He was an incredible debater. He was a critical thinker who would never resort to petty insults and would always be prepared, confident, in command of the material he was talking about. He was always sharp, even up until his inevitable demise in December.
>
> He was an extremely talented teacher who inspired intellectual curiosity in others. He was a liaison between the scientific community and the public. He had a unique ability to present very complex material in a way that was understandable to all. Many scientists resented this ability, possibly out of jealousy or perhaps because they were afraid that when others understood what they were doing they might be exposed to appropriate criticisms. Unlike other professors, he avoided using jargon to mask ignorance.
>
> It saddens me deeply that he died at only 62 years of age. But I think we should remember him as a noble truth-teller who lived an extremely full life. He had love, fame, wealth, family, and he had adoration from all corners of the earth. And from me.[36]

IN MY YEARS OF RESEARCH, I met not one person—not one—who knew Sagan closely and who strongly disliked him. I met people who had falling-outs with him, to be sure. Yet they seemed more regretful than bitter, more puzzled than accusatory; their good memories of Sagan far outweighed the bad. Both Gentry Lee and Lester Grinspoon urged me not to overstate their criticisms of Sagan. "My father and I are very happy to have had Carl in our lives," David Grinspoon asserts.[37]

David also sternly defends Sagan's scientific reputation against any detractors: "He was an *excellent* scientist. He had broad knowledge, was fast on his feet, knew the math, and did some groundbreaking work, especially in his early years." After Sagan's death, the American Astronomical Society's Division of Planetary Sciences (which Sagan helped to found) considered whether to award him posthumously its highest award, the Kuiper Prize (named for Sagan's old mentor). As with Sagan's nominations to the Cosmos Club and the National Academy of Sciences, the proposal triggered "a little bit of controversy." David and other scientists wrote letters to the nominating committee urging that Sagan receive the award. Receive it he did: Druyan accepted the award at a ceremony in Madison.[38]

There is an addendum to David Grinspoon's story about his decades with Sagan. After their falling-out, "we didn't speak for a couple of years." Then David published an article about Venus in the *Journal of Geophysical Research*. It touched on an old issue close to Sagan's heart, one he had first entertained as a young man—the possibility of terraforming Venus into a habitable world.

About this time, as his end neared, Sagan was making efforts to apologize to those he had wounded, to acknowledge that he might have critiqued them too harshly. Like crotchety old Harold Urey in his last, sickly years, Sagan regretted his former unkindnesses; he sought the forgiveness of the young. So he reopened connections with David—cautiously and indirectly, the way males do—by writing him a letter that expressed interest in the younger man's scientific ideas. David sent back a "collegial" letter. That was all; soon "Uncle" Carl was dead. But David is consoled by his memories of their final exchange.[39]

THE FILM *CONTACT* premiered in the early summer of 1997, a half-year after Sagan's death.[40] Lynda Obst had lived with the project so long— since the early 1980s, when she was a young studio staffer—that she held unreasonably high hopes for the movie. She had wanted to make a film of ideas, something that would do justice to the man she had hugged and kissed on his deathbed, do justice to his dreams and convictions. She hoped that audiences would flock to the film and be enchanted by its optimistic vision of contact with extraterrestrial life, of a young woman struggling to navigate a man's world as Obst had waded through the testosterone tides of La-La Land. That was her dream.

The audiences came, and they liked the film, and it made money. As usual, intellectual reaction was mixed, and (typically for Sagan's projects) sometimes divided along ideological lines. The shrewdest critics were quick to spot how *Contact* contradicted the image of Sagan as a scientistic technocrat and a naive rationalist. Writing in the liberal Jewish journal *Tikkun*, editor Michael Lerner praised *Contact* as "a meaning-oriented film that challenges a narrow empiricist scientific method and calls for an expanded conception of 'experience.' In the dominant materialistic worldview, that which is 'real' is that which can be subject to verification or falsification by some relevant sense data." The film twice mentioned William of Occam's "Razor," a philosophical principle according to which nothing should be explained in a more complex way than necessary. But, Lerner continued, "*Contact* sets out to challenge Occam's Razor and the entire empiricist philosophy on which it is based," by depicting Ellie—"a staunch advocate of a narrow empiricist scientism"—discovering alien life, although her discovery "is not registered by any of the devices that her earth-bound colleagues have available"; hence her amazing story is widely doubted. How ironic: "The narrow empiricism which had become her religion is shown to be inadequate to the complexity and mystery of the universe."

Linking modern-day scientism to corporate interests, the Defense Department, and other powerful agencies, Lerner added optimistically: "*Contact* dares to question the dominant scientism. It is not anti-science. Nor are we. Science has an important role to play. But the empiricist worldview that has come to be the dominant shaper of 'common sense' . . . is deeply distorting to our public and private lives." He traced the film's "box-office success" to "a deep spiritual revival" under way in modern life, as Americans challenge the scientistic values of the powerful.

But Sagan's old nemesis, the conservative Jewish journal *Commentary*, had a different take on *Contact*. In an article titled "God and Carl Sagan in Hollywood," the writer Daniel J. Silver complained about Ellie's "self-righteousness," which was a "reflection of Sagan's own personality." Her on-screen romantic relationship with Palmer Joss "seems fake . . . no doubt due to the incoherence of the roles they are asked to play." While some critics praised the film's even-handed treatment of issues of science and religion, Silver dismissed the praise as "nonsense," citing how a priest ineptly tries to console Ellie after her father's death; the implication is that religious solace "is a cheap and impotent thing." Also, a religious fanatic blows up the original model of the machine that was supposed to transport Ellie to the galactic center. In these and other ways, the film's representatives of faith are "trashed for their dishonesty, hypocrisy, bad faith, and fanaticism." Hence the film offers no hint of religion's "sources of truth or of its power."

Among scientists, the film was well-received. In a *New York Times* article on the making of the film, veteran science writer John Noble Wilford noted that astronomers "who have seen the movie are impressed by how, on a scientific level, it is remarkably faithful to the spirit, strategy and techniques of [SETI]." *Nature* magazine praised the general scientific accuracy of the film, "even though some artistic liberties are taken" (for example, Ellie's decision to literally listen for alien signals by wearing earphones, which no real SETI radioastronomer wastes time doing; computers are available to detect any intelligent-sounding signals). The magazine also praised Ellie's passionate speech in defense of SETI as "pure Sagan, right down to the turtleneck sweater and tweed jacket Arroway wears."

Still, Gore Vidal was probably thinking of Hollywood when he observed that it is not enough for one to succeed; others must fail. Open up any issue of the *Hollywood Reporter* and see the two-page ads that announce, in blaring headlines, the latest box-office take for the latest blockbuster: "$100,000,000," or whatever. The grim reality is that *Contact*'s earnings were far outranked by those of two other recent alien-contact films—*Men in Black* and *Independence Day*.[41] The first was a mean-spirited bloodbath, the second a genocide-fest. Both depicted extraterrestrials as the foe, not as potential friends. The universe is a scary place; let's hide from it. This was not Carl Sagan's universe. This was the cosmos of our medieval ancestors, who huddled, shuddering and superstitious, inside their walled towns.

The immense popularity of *MIB* and *ID4*, as they became known, shook Obst's Saganish optimism. Sagan believed that science influences our world, and that therefore the public must know something about science in order for democracy to work. "The saddest thing about *Contact* for me," Obst said—"apart, obviously, from losing Carl before it reached the finish line, which is inexpressibly sad—is that Carl had always told me that if you give them the real [scientific] stuff, they won't need the reptilian-brain stuff, they won't need the sex and the blood and the guts and the gore. And that inspired me though my career. I believed it. But now I'm not sure that it's true." When Sagan was sick in the Seattle hospital, Obst and Druyan "snuck out of the hospital when he was sleeping to see *ID4*. [Watching it], I almost became physically ill. I see this guy *punching an alien in the face* . . . and the audience roaring and cheering." As a young woman, she had been enthralled by Sagan's book *The Dragons of Eden*. Maybe, she reflects, that's what the audience really wants: "They need the R-complex stuff; they're trained and habituated to respond to a punch in the nose." If Sagan had to die, she added, then "I'm glad he didn't live to see that."

Sagan was an all-American optimist, a cultural democrat of the purest sort. He believed in the public's "best-case virtues, and he believed that if you told them what was really happening out there, they'd prefer to know that over believing in angels. . . . And he believed that if the people just got exposed more to the real stuff, the need for medieval thinking would go away. . . . And I bought it and I believed in it, and I wanted it to be true.

"And I don't know if *Men in Black* and *ID4* did five times the business of *Contact* because that's false, or not. But I fear that it is. And it really, really depresses me. . . . I just want what he believed to be true. And I'm no longer sure that it is."[42]

SINCE SAGAN'S DEATH, Ann Druyan has been writing, working on a film project, handling the estate, speaking at conferences, and accepting awards on Sagan's behalf. Given more time, she and Sagan might have become the Will and Ariel Durant of science. They had already written two superb books together, and more projects (including a television show) were in the offing when Sagan died. Druyan is also deeply engaged in the lives of her two children, Sasha and Sam. Sasha is a warm and chatty teenager who wants to be an actress, and Sam is an animated, ever-grinning grade-schooler, who talks a mile a second about his latest accomplishments. Druyan's parents also live nearby and visit often.

By the kitchen table, Druyan keeps the old photo of Sam and Rachel Sagan kissing passionately on the boardwalk. "How many people have a picture of their parents making out?" she observes. Reflecting on the passion between them, and on their lust to live life fully, she comments that their son also "wanted to live completely. He wanted to know as much about love as he knew about physics and astronomy, and everything else." Certainly in his fifteen-year marriage to Druyan, Sagan learned to be the kind of respectful, attentive, even symbiotic life partner that his parents had been for one another. So close did Sagan and Druyan's relationship become that, as she recalls, there was a powerful form of communication, often unspoken, between them. "It was like sea mammals," she recalls. "You watch them in the ocean and they're swimming along at fast speeds and then they peel off. . . . How do they both know to make a right at that moment? It's because something is passing between them, some communication that we're not smart enough to figure out. . . . We always called it 'sea mammaling'."

Sagan rarely helped out around the house, but to Druyan, this wasn't a particularly troubling issue. "Could he cook? No, absolutely not," she says. "Couldn't fold a towel. And after a couple of years, I realized that I didn't need him to fold towels. . . . Would he make a bed? Every once in a while he made the bed, because he knew how it made me happy. But it was such an alien thing for him to do. But I feel he would have absolutely died for me, and I would have died for him, in a second. One thing that Carl and I discovered together is that it is possible to stay in love forever."[43]

What is a visionary? Carl Sagan measured time in eons and space in light-years; he maintained an interplanetary perspective. To such a person, the petty bigotries and tyrannies of terrestrial life are provincialism in the extreme. That was the core theme of *Pale Blue Dot:* ours is one planet in a vast cosmos—who are we to subdivide it into the privileged and the oppressed? Says Druyan: "He took science so seriously, so deeply to heart. He understood the human species to be precisely what it is—part of the fabric of nature, obviously related to the non-human primates in ways that were very striking. And so for him racism was completely appalling. And sexism, too. Since there was no scientific basis for any sense of inferiority for women or non-white people, he couldn't bear it.

"That was true in our relationship, personally, in terms of arguments that we would have as a couple. The best argument *won.* [There were] no 'arguments from authority,' no 'because I say so' or 'because I want it this way.' . . . He was really concerned about the truth." His commitment to logic was such that when he believed he had been proven wrong, he readily admitted it, Druyan says. When she won one of their debates, he would smile "brilliantly," pretend to doff a hat, and say, "Hats off to you, Annie." So, Druyan recalls, "you had a sense that not only would every problem ultimately be solved—because it was a process of trying to get at the truth—but that this guy wanted to keep on growing for the rest of his life! He didn't want to settle for the boring rituals and repetitions that most people are happy with. . . . For him what matters is what is true, not the thing that will affirm his cherished belief." The "real dream of science" is to understand the universe not "as I want it to be, to make myself feel less afraid of the vastness, but the universe *as it really is.*"[44]

ON A WET, GLOOMY DAY, much of Ithaca braved the rain to get a feel for the solar system "as it really is." A remarkable memorial to Sagan's memory was dedicated: the Sagan Planet Walk, created and developed by the Ithaca Sciencenter. It's a series of monuments, located in the downtown area, that represent the planets of the solar system. The monuments are separated by distances that are proportional to the distances between the planets. Walk the Planet Walk, and you'll never again doubt the immensity of space, or the isolation that we face on our little home, this pale blue dot that we are so selfishly exploiting. Hundreds of children showed up for the dedication. They cheered wildly at the appearance of TV's "Bill Nye the Science Guy," one of Sagan's former students.

The children were generally very young, too young to be sure who Carl Sagan was. Yet all of them were, in a sense, his children. One day, some of them might grow crystals aboard the International Space Station; or tend crops in an underground farm on the Moon; or stand on the surface of Mars, buffeted by windblown dust that repeatedly paints the surface in shades of light and dark, as Sagan guessed a half-century earlier. Or perhaps one of them will remotely guide a robotic probe to a soft landing onto the icy crust of Europa, beneath which washes a dark and perhaps inhabited sea. Or perhaps they will travel farther . . .

THE DREAM OF FLIGHT to the stars is so alluring, yet so frightening—a flight into the vast blackness that terrified Pascal—that one must wonder: are there psychological reasons for its appeal? Contradictory as ever, Sagan had assured Timothy Leary that starflight was impractical. Yet soon afterward, Sagan wrote chapter 32 of *The Cosmic Connection*, titled "The Night Freight to the Stars."[45] This child of immigrants—people who crossed the choppy sea in search of a better life—begins by alluding to his own youthful wanderlust, his yearning to get out of Brooklyn and make his way in the world:

> For three generations of human beings there was—as an ever-present, but almost unperceived, part of their lives—a sound that beckoned, a call that pierced the night, carrying the news that there was a way, not so very difficult, to leave Twin Forks, North Dakota, or Apalachicola, Florida, or Brooklyn, New York. It was the wail of the night freight.[46]

Nowadays, he noted, few hear that train call. Passenger train travel is rare, the world is homogenizing into a "global civilization," and "there are no exotic places left on Earth to dream about." But there is always the sky. Someday, he wrote, we may build starships that propel us to "the great galactic cities. . . . And then there will once again be the whistle of the night freight."[47]

Two decades later, *Pale Blue Dot* included color paintings of possible starships. One is a hollowed-out asteroid within which teeming masses dwell; exotic engines propel it into the galaxy, where it enters a new planetary system and goes into orbit around an Earth-like planet.[48] That might be our future, Sagan wrote. Indeed, we might one day be forced to head starward. Each human enjoys only a short time in the sun, and by contrast, the solar system seems eternal; but in the great span of astronomical time, the Copernican realm is also transient, as transient as the many empires of earthly history. The Milky Way looks peaceful, but it is actually a wilderness, full of unknown dangers.

> In the long run, the Sun may generate stupendous X-ray and ultraviolet outbursts; the Solar System will enter one of the vast interstellar clouds lurking nearby and the planets will darken and cool; a shower of deadly comets will come roaring out of the Oort Cloud threatening civilizations on many adjacent worlds; we will recognize that a nearby star is about to become a supernova. In the *really* long run, the Sun—on its way to becoming a red giant star—will get bigger and brighter, the Earth will begin to lose its air and water to space, the soil will char, the oceans will evaporate and boil, the rocks will vaporize, and our planet may even be swallowed up into the interior of the Sun.[49]

In other words: in order to survive, humanity might one day have to travel to the stars.

To where? Sagan envisioned our descendants initially migrating toward the outer solar system, colonizing the hundreds of billions of water-rich comets of the "Oort Cloud," which swarms around the Sun like fruit flies around a fallen peach. And once you've gotten to New Rochelle, you might as well see New York. "The outer edge of the Sun's Oort Cloud is perhaps halfway to the nearest star," Sagan wrote. The Cloud might, he conjectured, be our springboard to the rest of the galaxy. "Perhaps . . . we will ultimately spread far from home, sailing through the starry archipelagos of the vast Milky Way galaxy."[50] Millions of years will pass; humans will evolve into new types of beings on countless new worlds. And to our galactic descendants, their terrestrial forebears will seem as mythological as our proto-human ancestor *Australopithecus* does to us.

Sagan's vision enchanted Daniel Goldin, the administrator of NASA. Goldin is a NASA chief for the Sagan generation, one who looks and acts more like a Broadway impresario than a bureaucrat. Goldin has a sense of theater, of Hollywood: he once opened a NASA-Ames "open house" show for the general public by declaring to a crowd of taxpayers and their children: "Let the force be with you," as a giant hangar door growled open and giant speakers blared *Thus Spake Zarathustra*.[51] While fighting ever-tighter budgets, he has brought a sense of vision and fun to an agency that, frankly, hasn't had much fun since the end of the Moon program.

Goldin was in fine form in July 1997, when the Mars *Pathfinder* landed on the red planet. It unleashed a little roving robot, Sojourner (named for the nineteenth-century civil rights activist Sojourner Truth), which rolled around, examining the terrain and transmitting haunting color pictures back to Earth. It bumped into rocks, then "sniffed" them (with an alpha proton X-ray spectrometer) for interesting materials; it was adorable. Kids loved it, and clamored for hard-to-find *Pathfinder* toys. On NASA's *Pathfinder* Web site, the number of "hits" exceeded 100 million—a world record to that date. At a Pasadena ceremony, Goldin announced that he was renaming the *Pathfinder* the "Carl Sagan Memorial Station." Later, NASA authorized sending to Mars a space probe fulfilling one of Sagan's old dreams: it would carry a microphone to hear the whistling of Martian winds, the crackle of creeping dust, and other eerie sounds.[52]

During a *Pathfinder* press conference at JPL, Goldin made an off-hand but startling remark, so startling that almost all the reporters ignored it. They probably dismissed it as just another Goldinism—a purely visionary remark, bordering on hot air, that represented no fundamental change in NASA policy. What Goldin said was that he was having his people look into the feasibility of interstellar robotic missions. I suspected that Goldin wasn't kidding. Shortly thereafter, I crossed the JPL campus to annoy JPL chief Ed Stone. I asked Stone if his people planned to assist Goldin's investigation of the feasibility of interstellar probes. Stone stared at me as if I had inquired about the feasibility of perpetual motion. There must (he assured me) be some mistake. Surely Goldin didn't mean *interstellar* travel. Was I sure he said *interstellar*?

As if on cue, Goldin strolled by in the hallway. I buttonholed him: Had he really meant to say interstellar travel using robotic probes? Like, to the stars? Yes, he assured me. Not anytime soon, of course, but paper studies would soon be under way. He emphasized that it was strictly visionary, blue-sky stuff. No promises, no commitments. And certainly no scheduled launches! Not for many decades to come, anyway—if ever.

Yet no NASA administrator had ever seriously discussed the possibility of interstellar flight. How did he get the idea? Simple, he explained—by reading Sagan's *Pale Blue Dot*. Sagan talked about traveling to the Oort Cloud. And (Goldin reasoned) if we can send robots to the Oort Cloud, why not continue to the next star? True, he emphasized, we have no idea whether interstellar flight is technically feasible, much less affordable. No one knows what futuristic engine designs if any, might do the trick. Unknown technical barriers may lie en route to the stars. Still . . . who knows? It doesn't hurt to think about it, right? This was the spirit of Carl Sagan at its purest: speculation for the fun of it.

Goldin was planning to speak shortly afterward at a ceremony honoring Sagan. I asked him to repeat what he had just told me, just in case no one believed me later. Sure, he said.

Some experts roll their eyes at Goldin's talk of interstellar flight. "Somebody should have shook him by the lapels," says SETI scientist

Paul Horowitz, "and said: 'Hey, watch out what you're saying, because this is nonsense! Which it is.' "[53]

But what if the visionaries are right? Then decades or centuries from now, the first robotic probes will embark for the stars, accelerated toward a fraction of the speed of light by energies we cannot imagine. Humans may follow. Their Odyssean journeys will be agonizingly long and risky. Generations may pass before the travelers transmit home the first close-up photos of extrasolar terrains. But the long wait will be worthwhile. And long after we are all dead, a future historian may mention, in his footnotes, how one "Dr. Carl Edward Sagan (1934–1996)" unwittingly planted the idea in the head of a long-forgotten government official.

Of course, it's anyone's guess whether Sagan will be remembered by 2050 or 2100 or 2200. Who would now recall Amerigo Vespucci, save for the name that he gave to the New World?

ON THE DAY of Goldin's press conference, the southern California weather was miserably hot. Later that day, a merciful breeze blew through the San Gabriel Mountains. A crowd gathered in the JPL court-yard for a ceremony to honor Sagan's memory. Thirty-plus years earlier, Carl Sagan had scurried around this campus proposing wild ideas about Venus and upsetting the orthodox; now the Laboratory was honoring his memory with a memorial the size of a Cadillac. Goldin was there, along with Druyan and a little flock of Sagans. The NASA chief spoke eloquently about Sagan's role in the space age (and briefly alluded to the starflight scheme). The large stone memorial was unveiled. Applause.

Then Druyan spoke. She looked smaller, somehow—sad, dignified, a little shy, dressed in pearl white, her hands behind her back. Her voice was almost inaudibly soft. She spoke of Sagan's life, his work, his dreams, his legacy, his humanity. Hardly anyone heard a word, though. Her eyes spoke volumes, but her voice was drowned out by the wind.

Notes

Abbreviations

Interviews (except where indicated, all were conducted by the author)

ABB	Andrea and Bill Barnett
AC	A. G. W. Cameron
AD	Ann Druyan
AF	Andrew Fraknoi
AS	Arlene Sagan
BK	Bishun Khare
BO	Brian O'Leary
BR	Beatrice Rubenstein
CC	Christopher Chyba
CG	Cari (Sagan) Greene
CS	Carl Sagan (interviewed by Ronald E. Doel in 1971; the six tapes are archived at the Niels Bohr Library, American Institute of Physics)
CSG	Carl Sagan (interviewed by Joseph Goodavage)
DC	Dale Cruikshank
DG	Donald Goldsmith
DGR	David Grinspoon
DJH	Donald J. Hunten
DL	David Layzer
DM	David Morrison
DMS	Deborah M. Shillaber
DO	Donald C. Osterbrock
DS	Dorion Sagan
EK	Ethel Kramer
FB	Flora Bernstein (interviewed by Lucille Nahemow)
FD	Frank Drake
FM	Fred Murphy
FW	Fred Whipple
GB	Geoffrey Burbidge
GEL	Gentry Lee
GHS	Geoff Haines-Stiles
GL	Gilbert Levin
GM	George Mullen
GRN	Gerald R. North
HT	Helene Thorson
JA	Jerome Agel
JC	Joseph Chamberlain
JCo	Jim Cornell

JCB	John C. Brandt
JCL	John C. Lilly
JH	James Henderson
JL	Joshua Lederberg
JLu	Jerome Luks
JM	Jeff Moersch
JNC	Joseph N. Cirincione
JP	Jay Pasachoff
JS	Jeremy Sagan
JT	Jill Tarter
LG	Lester Grinspoon
LM	Lynn Margulis
LO	Lynda Obst
MB	Rabbi Morrison Bial
MR	Marcus Raskin
NH	Norman Horowitz
NiS	Nina Serrano
NS	Nick Sagan
OBT	Owen Brian Toon
PH	Paul Horowitz
PM	Philip Morrison
PP	Peter Pesch
PV	Peter Vandervoort
RB	Ronald Blum
RG	Robert Gritz
RM	Ruth Mariner
RPB	Regina (Ginny) Pollack Breslauer
RPG	Rachel Patinkin Grainer
RT	Rich Turco
SA	Shirley Arden
SC	Stillman Chase
SG	Sharon Greene
SL	Saul Landau
SM	Stanley Miller
SPM	Stephen P. Maran
SS	Steven Soter
TF	Timothy Ferris
TG	Thomas Gold
TPA	Thomas P. Ackerman
VS	Valerie Sorenson
WG	Walter Glanze
WK	William W. Kellogg

Books by, or coauthored by, Carl Sagan

APW	*A Path Where No Man Thought* (1990)
BiBi	*Billions and Billions* (1997)
BrBr	*Broca's Brain* (1979)
CC	*The Cosmic Connection* (1973)
Cos	*Cosmos* (1980)
CM	*Comet* (1985)
CT	*Contact* (1985)

DHW	*The Demon-Haunted World: Science as a Candle in the Dark* (1996)
DOE	*The Dragons of Eden* (1977)
ILU	*Intelligent Life in the Universe* (1966)
MAMOM	*Mars and the Mind of Man* (1973)
MOE	*Murmurs of Earth* (1978)
PBD	*Pale Blue Dot* (1994)
"*PSP*"	"Physical Studies of the Planets" (doctoral dissertation, 1960)
SOFA	*Shadows of Forgotten Ancestors* (1992)

Books edited by, or co-edited by, Carl Sagan

| *CET* | *Communication with Extraterrestrial Intelligence* (1973) |
| *UFO* | *UFO's: A Scientific Debate* (1972) |

Books

| *SSA* | *Solar System Astronomy in America: Communities, Patronage, and Interdisciplinary Science, 1920–1960* (1996), by Ronald E. Doel |
| *WANA* | *We Are Not Alone*, by Walter Sullivan (1964 and 1993 editions) |

Journals

PASP	*Proceedings of the Astronomical Society of the Pacific*
PNAS	*Proceedings of the National Academy of Sciences*
QJRAS	*Quarterly Journal of the Royal Astronomical Society*

Papers

"Arden papers" refers to documents generously provided by Sagan's former secretary, Shirley Arden, who now lives in Cocoa Beach, Florida.

"*Contact* script conferences" refers to the script meetings and "think tanks" that were held for the planning of the film. The conferences were recorded by professional transcriptionists. The papers are the property of Linda Obst.

Copies of Donald Menzel's papers are stored at three different sites: Harvard University; the American Philosophical Society, Philadelphia; and CSICOP's Center for Inquiry at Amherst, N.Y.

Preface

1. See Alan Boss, *Looking for Earths: The Race to Find New Solar Systems* (1998), p. 172.
2. May 23, 1997, p. 1215.
3. Summer 1998, p. 161.

Chapter 1. Brooklyn

1. These quotes about Rachel are from individuals who appear in this book—in order, Cari (Sagan) Greene, Lynn Margulis, Beatrice Rubenstein, Nick Sagan, Lynda Obst, Ann Druyan, and Flora Bernstein.

2. A copy of Rachel's 1981 letter was supplied by Ethel Kramer, her close friend in Delray Beach, Florida. Rachel did not exaggerate about threats: according to information given to this writer by a highly knowledgeable source (who was then personally close to Carl Sagan), on Mar. 12, 1981, a young man carrying a golf club (an iron) came to Sagan's office at Cornell and asked to see him. The man stated he had had "dreams" about Sagan. The man had written Sagan three letters about these dreams and received no response.

He had also called Sagan's office the day before and spoken angrily to a staffer, and asked her to tell Sagan "to go fuck himself." Eventually the man left, and Sagan's office filed a complaint with Officer Randy P. Bowman of the campus department of public safety. Later the suspect was detained and placed in custody. He was released in May, and was scheduled to be picked up by his father at the Ithaca airport. Sagan was traveling extensively at that time (right after the airing of *Cosmos*) and an aide advised him: "Nothing more we can do about this now EXCEPT TO BE VERY VERY CAREFUL NOT TO RUN INTO HIM AT THE AIRPORT ON SATURDAY." On another occasion, sometime between 1978 and 1980, Sagan, his son Nick, and Ann Druyan received such a serious death threat that Ithaca police drove them in a van to a motel for safety. "This guy was going around saying he was going to chop Carl's head off," Druyan says. She recalls staying in the motel "playing cards with Nick for a day or two" until the man making the threats was apprehended.

3. The novel, *Confessions of Summer* by Philip Lopate (New York: Doubleday, 1979), is about a fitful romance with an irresistible, politically radical young woman; the character is loosely based on Ann Druyan, who was to become Sagan's third wife.

4. FB interview, early 1990s, conducted by her daughter, Prof. Lucille Nahemow. I am grateful to Ann Druyan for referring me to Nahemow.

5. CG interview, Apr. 1998.

6. *PBD*, p. xv.

7. NS interview; and *PBD*, p. xv.

8. CG interview.

9. FB interview.

10. Ibid.

11. Ibid.

12. Ibid.

13. Ibid.

14. BR phone interview, early 1998.

15. FB interview.

16. Ibid.

17. CG interview.

18. CS interview.

19. Beth S. Wenger, *New York Jews and the Great Depression* (1996), p. 1.

20. CG interview.

21. Ibid.

22. Moses Rischin, *The Promised City: New York's Jews, 1870–1914* (1962), chapter 2.

23. Stephen G. Brush, *A History of Modern Planetary Physics*, vol. 1., *Nebulous Earth* (1996), p. 133.

24. Peter Gay, *Freud* (1988), p. 807.

25. See Ronald W. Clark, *Einstein: The Life and Times* (1971).

26. See George Smoot and Keay Davidson, *Wrinkles in Time* (1993).

27. Rischin, p. 45.

28. Trotsky is quoted in Norman Geras, *The Contract of Mutual Indifference* (1998), p. 158.

29. George Sagan would have been about fourteen at the time. The year of his and Sam's arrival in America (1910) is cited in George Sagan's obituary on p. 30 of the Feb. 1, 1975, *New York Times*: "George Sagan, 79, Led Coat Company."

30. Rischin, p. 75.

. *New York Times*, Oct. 11, 1966. I wish to thank Arlene Sagan, former wife of ge Sagan's son Eugene, for showing me her photo album of the George Sagan family aaring her memories of Carl Sagan as a teenager (Oct. 1997). George Sagan's sons included Bruce Sagan, a publisher of neighborhood newspapers in the Chicago area; Eli Sagan of the Sagan Foundation in Englewood, N.J.; and Eugene Sagan, a University of California–Berkeley teacher, who committed suicide in the 1980s by jumping off the Golden Gate Bridge.

32. *CT*, p. 238.

33. CG interview.

34. *DHW*, p. xi.

35. CG pointed this out during an interview.

36. *PBD*, p. xv.

37. *SOFA*, p. 383.

38. PP phone interview, early 1998.

39. RG phone interview, early 1998.

40. TF interview, San Francisco, late 1997.

41. LM interview, Amherst, Mass., Oct. 1997.

42. *DHW*, p. 108.

43. *DHW*, p. xii.

44. LM interview.

45. CG interview.

46. NS interview, Studio City, Calif., Apr. 1998.

47. FB interview.

48. CG interview.

49. LO interview, Los Angeles, May 1998.

50. CS interview.

51. CG interview.

52. CS interview.

53. CG interview.

54. Ibid.

55. CS interview.

56. CG interview.

57. Rabbi Mordecai Kaplan, *Judaism as a Civilization* (1934).

58. An excellent study of tensions within the twentieth-century American Humanist movement, with special attention to leading personalities including Sagan, is Stephen Prugh Weldon's doctoral dissertation, "The Humanist Enterprise from John Dewey to Carl Sagan: A Study of Science and Religion in American Culture" (University of Wisconsin at Madison, 1997). In the mid-1970s, a group of Humanists including Sagan founded the Committee for the Scientific Investigation of Claims of the Paranormal (CSICOP), a group dedicated to combating pseudoscientific and occultist claims. I am grateful to Marcello Truzzi for bringing Weldon's dissertation to my attention.

59. RG interview.

60. CG interview.

61. CG interview. Also see *BiBi*, pp. 180–181.

62. *Contact* script conference, Aug. 29, 1994. Sagan told the anecdote during a meeting that included the Reverends Joan Campbell and Albert Pennybacker of the National Council of Churches; the group discussed at length religious issues related to *Contact*.

63. The Wolfe quote appears in Daniel J. Kevles, *The Physicists* (1977), p. 279.

64. Many scholarly books and articles have assessed past visions of the future of technology, such as Joseph J. Corn, ed., *Imagining Tomorrow: History, Technology, and the American Future* (1986), especially chapter 5 regarding the world's fairs of the 1930s. Chapter 6 is Howard P. Segal's study of "technological utopianism" in American history. For novelistic treatment, see E. L. Doctorow, *World's Fair* (1985), and David Hillel Gelernter, *1939:*

The Lost World of the Fair (1995). The latter is an offbeat hybrid of a novel and a historical account.

65. Such views have many critics, of course. See, for example, the highly readable works of Lewis Mumford, especially *The Myth of the Machine* (1970), and Theodor Adorno and Max Horkheimer's more difficult *Dialectic of Enlightenment* (1947).

66. CS interview. Also see Sagan's recollections of the fair in *MOE*, chapter 1, and *DHW*, pp. xiii and 403–404.

67. RG interview.

68. CS interview.

69. CG interview.

70. RG interview.

71. CG interview.

72. Irving Howe (with Kenneth Libo), *World of Our Fathers* (1976), 142.

73. CS interview.

74. *Contact* script conference, Sept. 19, 1994.

75. *DHW*, p. 347.

76. MB interview, early 1998.

77. A biography of the spy/baseball player is Nicholas Dawidoff, *The Catcher Was a Spy* (1994). In that regard, as an adult, Sagan told Shirley Arden how, as a boy, he was traumatized when a bully stole his prized Louisville Slugger baseball bat (Arden, personal communication).

78. *DHW*, p. xiii.

79. CS interview.

80. A famous study of the sociological impact of the Welles radio broadcast is Hadley Cantril, *The Invasion from Mars: A Study in the Psychology of Panic* (1940).

81. See, for example, Carl Jung, *Psychology and the Occult* (1977), regarding the psychoanalyst's exploration of the "paranormal" at the turn of the last century.

82. As of early 1999, the only full-length Lowell biography is William Graves Hoyt, *Lowell and Mars* (1976), although a major new one is reportedly in the works. Recent studies explore the cultural and psychological context of Lowell's work. See Caroline A. Jones and Peter Galison, eds. (with Amy Slaton), *Picturing Science Producing Art* (1998), pp. 329–332; William Sheehan, *Planets and Perception* (1988); and a short, psychoanalytically oriented interpretation by Jackson Lears, *No Place of Grace* (1981).

83. "The idea that there were canals on Mars—we were still caught up in that" as children in the early 1940s, Sagan's friend Robert Gritz recalls (RG interview). Also see *DHW*, p. 49.

84. This human tendency is analyzed in anthropologist Stewart Elliott Guthrie's theory of religion as a way of anthropomorphizing nature: *Faces in the Clouds: A New Theory of Religion* (1993).

85. While this "projection" suggestion is my own, it is inspired by Richard Hofstadter's *The Age of Reform: From Bryan to FDR* (1955), especially chapter 5.

86. Quoted in Hoyt, p. 86. Also see Percival Lowell, *Mars* (1895), p. 209.

87. Boss, p. 13.

88. The shift from belief in tidal hypotheses of solar system origin to the modified nebular hypothesis is described at length in Stephen G. Brush, *A History of Modern Planetary Physics*, vol. 3, *Fruitful Encounters* (1996). A "transitional" work in popular science, written just after the modified nebular hypothesis emerged, is George Gamow, *The Birth and Death of the Sun* (1945). Pre-twentieth-century hypotheses of nebular origins, and their impact on U.S. scholars, are reviewed in Ronald Numbers, *Creation by Natural Law: Laplace's Nebular Hypothesis in American Thought* (1977).

89. Olaf Stapledon, *Star Maker* (1937), p. 266.

90. Edgar Rice Burroughs, *A Princess of Mars* (1917). Biographical accounts of Burroughs include Erling B. Holtsmark, *Edgar Rice Burroughs* (1986), and the huge, definitive Irwin Porges, *Edgar Rice Burroughs: The Man Who Created Tarzan* (1975). Sagan tells his anecdote in *MAMOM*, p. 10.

91. Carl Sagan, "Growing Up with Science Fiction," *New York Times Sunday Magazine*, May 28, 1978, p. 24. A similar piece appears in *BrBr*.

92. MB interview; also information supplied by Rabbi Valerie Lieber of Temple Beth Ahavath Sholom.

93. Sagan's high school registration card. I am grateful to Rahway High School for supplying me with copies of this and other documents.

94. DMS phone interview, early 1998.

95. CG interview.

96. DMS interview.

97. CS interview.

98. Ibid.

99. This quote is from Henry S. F. Cooper Jr., "A Resonance with Something Alive," *New Yorker*, June 21, 1976, p. 73.

100. For extensive details on V-2 tests in the postwar United States, see Frederick I. Ordway III and Mitchell R. Sharpe, *The Rocket Team* (1979), and David H. DeVorkin, *Science with a Vengeance: How the Military Created the U.S. Space Sciences after World War II* (1992). DeVorkin includes valuable information on Gerard Kuiper's role in the tests. Also see Walter A. McDougall, *The Heavens and the Earth: A Political History of the Space Age* (1985), and William E. Burrows, *This New Ocean: The Story of the First Space Age* (1999).

101. Andrew J. Butrica, *To See the Unseen: A History of Planetary Radar Astronomy* (1996), p. 6.

102. *New York Times*, Jan. 26, 1946, 1.

103. H. G. Wells, *Mind at the End of Its Tether* (1945).

104. Sagan indicates that he discovered *Astounding Science Fiction* in 1946. Actually, he must have discovered it later, as "Pete Can Fix It" was published in the Feb. 1947 issue.

105. Raymond F. Jones, "Pete Can Fix It," *Astounding Science Fiction*, Feb. 1947, pp. 64–83.

Jones, then thirty-two years old, began writing for *Astounding* in 1941. He later penned the tale that inspired a camp classic of science-fiction filmdom, *This Island Earth* (Universal, 1955). A biographical sketch of Jones appears in John Clute and Peter Nicholls, *The Encyclopedia of Science Fiction*, 2d ed. (1995), p. 650.

This writer obtained a copy of "Pete Can Fix It" from Frank M. Robinson, a writer and science-fiction collector in San Francisco. On sending me the story, Robinson mentioned he had read it "out of curiosity . . . and was totally blown away. It's a cautionary tale and excessively preachy but must have left an indelible impression on the young, idealist Carl Sagan. He would have been about the same age as the youthful 'Jack' in the story and for most of his life . . . tried to carry out the same mission as the fictional 'Jack.' . . . I've always thought that science-fiction could influence people—particularly younger people—and this is a shining example of it."

106. RB phone interview, early 1998.

107. Sagan, "Growing Up with Science Fiction."

108. Lynn Margulis gave this writer a copy of Sagan's school notebook, which she found after their divorce. She estimates that it was written in 1950; if so, then Sagan was either fifteen or sixteen when he wrote the essay.

109. Sir Harold Spencer Jones, *Life on Other Worlds* (1940), pp. 36 and 96. The quote is from the Mentor paperback edition, first published in May 1949. The paperback stayed

in print for many years and is easy to find in the science sections of large used-paperback stores.

110. An excellent history of American science-fiction magazines is Paul A. Carter, *The Creation of Tomorrow: Fifty Years of Magazine Science Fiction* (1977). Radical perspectives on the history and cultural meanings of early "pulp" science-fiction writing include H. Bruce Franklin, *Robert A. Heinlein: America as Science Fiction* (1980).

111. See, for example, G. G. Simpson, *The Meaning of Evolution* (1949), especially chapter 4; Julian Huxley, *Evolution in Action* (1953), chapter 6; and a brief reference in Ernst Mayr, *Toward a New Philosophy of Biology: Observations of an Evolutionist* (1988), p. 154.

112. Arthur Lovejoy, *The Great Chain of Being* (1936). In this famous work, Lovejoy argued (among many other things) that the notion of extraterrestrial life emerged centuries ago mainly because of changes in philosophy and theology, not from scientific logic. Steven J. Dick has questioned Lovejoy's claim, though; see note 58, chapter 5.

113. LM interview.

114. Sagan's letters to Fairchild and RAND are cited within his 1952 radio script for WUCB. A copy of the script is in the H. J. Muller archive at Lilly Library, Indiana University, Bloomington. Sagan's interest in rocketry was strengthened by what he later called "a turning point in my scientific development"—his teenage reading of Arthur C. Clarke's *Interplanetary Flight* (1950). (Source: Arthur C. Clarke, *Greetings, Carbon-Based Bipeds!* [1999], p. 516.)

115. CS interview. Until a few decades ago, the scientific community regarded science fiction as déclassé. As a result, scientists such as Richardson and Menzel published their science fiction under pseudonyms. Richardson (1902–1981) wrote science fiction for *Astounding* under the name "Philip Latham"; in the 1950s he wrote scripts for the television show *Captain Video*. A short biography of Richardson (under "Latham, Philip") is in Clute and Nicholls.

On Oct. 1, 1968, two years after his formal retirement from Harvard, Menzel wrote Sagan a poignant letter in which he criticized Sagan for writing so much speculative work about UFOs. Menzel comments that he, by contrast, wrote under a pseudonym when he was writing science fiction. The letter suggests the extent of aesthetic and emotional repression among American scientists of the Depression–World War II–early cold war era. (Menzel's letter is part of the Menzel papers at the American Philosophical Society, Philadelphia.)

116. Sagan's high school yearbook, 1951.

117. CG interview.

118. Sagan's high school yearbook, 1951.

119. AD interview, Nov. 1997.

120. Ironically, as an adult Sagan assumed that technically "superior" aliens would also be morally superior to humans. He failed to project the lessons of terrestrial history onto the cosmos as a whole.

121. David A. Hollinger, *Science, Jews, and Secular Culture: Studies in Mid-Twentieth-Century American Intellectual History* (1996), 159, says: "In Columbia's English department, the appointment of Lionel Trilling as assistant professor in 1939 was a breakthrough so striking that its story is still told by aging English professors around the country, in tones that Civil War buffs reserve for describing the battle of Gettysburg." The changed fortune of Jews in American universities after World War II is discussed in Edward S. Shapiro, *A Time for Healing: American Jewry since World War II* (1992).

122. Hollinger, p. 18.

123. PP interview.

124. CS interview.

125. Cooper, "A Resonance," p. 73.

126. CS interview.

127. Richard Rhodes, *The Making of the Atomic Bomb* (1986), especially chapter 13. Also see Richard G. Hewlett and Oscar E. Anderson Jr., *The New World: A History of the United States Atomic Energy Commission*, vol. 1, *1939–1946*, pp. 112–113.

Chapter 2. Chicago

1. C. P. Snow, *The Two Cultures* (1959, 1993). Snow's thesis triggered bitter controversy. The 1993 edition, published by Cambridge University Press, includes a long introduction by Stefan Collini that cites Snow's "antipathy to 'literary intellectuals'" and his "apparent hankering for the rule of a scientific elite" (p. xxiii). But to an American reader circa A.D. 2000, Snow's thesis seems rather less menacing than this. This may be partly because of Americans' traditional reverence for science and invention (e.g., Thomas Edison) and partly (as Collini shrewdly observes) because of the "specifically British genealogy for the 'two cultures' anxiety," one that was "inextricably entangled with elusive but highly charged matters of institutional status and social class" (pp. xi, xvi). Such concerns seem more relevant to postwar Britain as it elected socialists and lowered the imperial flag than to what Martin Amis, in a totally different context, has called the "moronic inferno" of late-twentieth-century American culture.

2. "Athens of the Midwest" is used in F. J. Pettijohn, *Memoirs of an Unrepentant Field Geologist* (1984), chapter 7.

3. *DHW*, p. xiv. Also, a recent profile of Hutchins is in Howard Gardner (with Emma Laskin), *Leading Minds: An Anatomy of Leadership* (1995), chapter 6.

4. *DHW*, pp. xiv–xv. Also see Weldon dissertation, p. 123. When Sagan was a boy, the war over science's place in culture divided to some degree along religious and ideological lines. In the 1940s, Hollinger noted in *Science, Jews, and Secular Culture* (pp. 79 and 158), Catholic intellectuals "often identified the influence of science as a source of the nation's apparently deficient value system." Mortimer Adler of the University of Chicago claimed that John Dewey—the leading U.S. philosopher of the day, an icon for Humanists and defenders of science—was a bigger threat to democracy than the Nazis.

By contrast, sociologist Robert K. Merton (who was Jewish, born Meyer H. Schkolnick) maintained that a scientific outlook nurtures democracy (Hollinger, *Science*, chapter 5). One key ingredient of science, Merton explained, is "organized skepticism," whereas in "modern totalitarian society, anti-rationalism and centralization of institutional control both serve to limit the scope provided for scientific activity." In other words, reason, science, and democracy are inextricably linked. While there is no direct evidence that Sagan ever read Merton's writings, the sociologist's position anticipated, and to some degree explains, the astronomer's triple loyalty—to science, skepticism and liberal democracy.

5. Pettijohn, pp. 199–200.

6. PP interview.

7. Sagan's college addresses are indicated in his early 1950s correspondence with Muller. Lilly Library.

8. JLu phone interview, early 1998.

9. Willy Ley, *The Conquest of Space* (1949). The popular impact of this book, which led to a 1955 film of the same name, is cited in Howard E. McCurdy, *Space and the American Imagination* (1997), pp. 33, 46, 47, 193, and 223–224.

10. CS interview.

11. Sagan's notes in the observatory log book are recorded in the University of Chicago Ryerson Astronomical Society's online "Log Book," posted on the World Wide Web.

12. DM interview, Feb. 1998.

13. Frank Drake and Dava Sobel, *Is Anyone Out There?* (1992), 151.

14. CS interview.

15. Richard S. Westfall, *Never at Rest: A Biography of Isaac Newton* (1980).

16. RB interview.

17. LM interview.

18. PP interview.

19. Jerome Luks recalled that Sagan was a competent basketball player who "played at the same level as the rest of us."

20. PV interview, July 1998.

21. CS interview.

22. NS interview.

23. TF interview.

24. RB interview.

25. CS interview.

26. RB interview.

27. Ibid.

28. PP interview.

29. CS interview.

30. Muller to Sagan, Nov. 3, 1955.

31. LM interview.

32. AD interview.

33. The standard biography of Muller is Elof Axel Carlson, *Genes, Radiation, and Society: The Life and Work of H. J. Muller* (1981). It includes a brief reference to Sagan.

34. The date is given in Jerome Clark, *The UFO Book: Encyclopedia of the Extraterrestrial* (1998), p. 27. Incredibly, I am, to my knowledge, the first writer to point out the connection between this date—Nov. 17, 1896—and the peak of the Leonid shower. The Leonids are the granddaddies of great meteor showers. As Donald H. Menzel and Lyle G. Boyd note in *The World of Flying Saucers* (1963, p. 90), "the Leonids are notable for their brilliant fireballs, which have deposited some of the largest meteorites ever found on the earth." The object reported over northern California on Nov. 17, 1896, was said to resemble "an electric arc lamp," which sounds very much like a meteoric fireball. The miserable intellectual state of UFOlogy is revealed by its devotees' failure to spot this obvious explanation for the initial sighting in the first UFO "wave" of a recognizably modern sort. (Note: The term "UFO" was not popularized until a half-century later.)

35. David Michael Jacobs, *The UFO Controversy in America* (1975), p. 13.

36. In the early 1990s, the veteran UFO skeptic and distinguished aerospace writer Philip J. Klass privately suggested to this writer that Arnold might have seen a disintegrating meteoric fireball. Arnold's description of the objects—glistening, constantly changing shape—bears a striking resemblance to eyewitness descriptions of fireballs. I offered to check into his suggestion. Several years later, after on-again, off-again investigation, I published an article in the *San Francisco Examiner Sunday Magazine* (June 1, 1997, p. 12) proposing that Arnold had, indeed, been fooled by a meteor. One reason he was fooled is that fireballs are extremely rare and unfamiliar to lay observers. Another likely reason is that, in the excitement of the moment, he seriously overestimated the length of the sighting (fireballs are brief events).

Soon afterward, Brad Sparks, a private UFO investigator, uncovered strong indirect evidence for the meteor theory. Sparks located an old, obscure newspaper report that on June 24, 1947, at almost exactly the same time as Arnold's sighting, witnesses in Idaho (adjacent to Washington) saw a high-altitude, elongated, static object that lingered in the sky for a considerable time. They described an object that, in retrospect, sounds like a fireball contrail. One of the witnesses was the lieutenant governor of Idaho. If the Klass-

Davidson-Sparks meteoric hypothesis is correct, then the UFO craze—the biggest pseudoscientific brouhaha of our time—began because a private pilot failed to recognize a rock falling from the sky.

I am grateful to Klass for his inspiring example and good humor through the years. His many skeptical books on UFOs—for example, *UFOs Explained* (1974)—are vital reading for any savvy reader who is unsatisfied with the urban legends, hucksterism, and sloppy thinking that pollute this subject.

37. Oral history interview with Gen. Robert B. Landry, Truman Library, Independence, Mo. Landry added that after his meeting with the president on saucers, "all [UFO] reports were made orally [by me to Truman]. Nothing of substance considered credible or threatening to the country was ever received from intelligence."

38. *DHW,* p. 67.

39. E. J. Ruppelt, *Report on Unidentified Flying Objects* (1956), p. 188.

40. Sagan to Muller, Apr. 4, 1952. Lilly Library.

41. True, in the late 1940s the RAND Corp. investigated the feasibility of a space satellite. But the United States did not formally commit itself to launching space satellites until 1955. See Rip Bulkeley, *The Sputniks Crisis and Early United States Space Policy* (1991), especially part 4.

42. Sagan to Muller, Apr. 4, 1952. Muller papers.

43. *Contact* script conference, Aug. 24, 1994, p. 112.

44. CS interview.

45. I am grateful to Willard for sending me copies of Sagan's letter and the State Department's response (see note 48).

46. Ruppelt, pp. 208–209.

47. Ibid., p. 220.

48. Ruckh to Sagan, Aug. 25, 1952.

49. Paul West, *Life with Swan,* p. 97.

Chapter 3. The Dungeon

1. No comprehensive historical account of the study of the origin of life exists. A valuable guide to early theories is John Farley, *The Spontaneous Generation Controversy from Descartes to Oparin* (1977). David Deamer and Gail R. Fleischaker, eds., *Origins of Life: The Central Concepts* (1994), reprints historical and modern documents in the field, including two papers coauthored by Carl Sagan and Christopher Chyba on possible delivery of cometary organics to Earth.

Early hopes for discovering the cause of the origin of life faded in the 1970s; the problem proved knottier than expected. A skeptical backlash was represented by books such as Francis Crick, *Life Itself* (1981), which proposed a return to a form of panspermia, and the most thoroughgoing critique of the field to date, Robert Shapiro's *Origins: A Skeptic's Guide to the Creation of Life on Earth* (1986). In recent years, origin-of-life theorists have been fascinated by "RNA world" theories, according to which life began as a self-replicating form of RNA or ribonucleic acid, which is under development in the laboratory. A recent survey is John Maynard Smith and Eörs Szathmáry, *The Origins of Life* (1999). "Complexity" theorists have also entered the field. Some believe life may have emerged in forms similar to those of pseudo-"life" forms that exist only on computer screens, yet appear capable of replication, mutation, and evolution; see, for example, Stuart Kauffman, *The Origins of Order* (1993). All in all, as the millennium begins, the quest for life's origin remains one of the previous century's great matters of unfinished business.

2. "Religion," in Tom Bottomore, ed., *A Dictionary of Marxist Thought* (1983), pp. 413–416.

3. Richard Dawkins, *The Blind Watchmaker* (1986), explains lucidly why the "watchmaker" myth is a myth, at least in terms of biology.

4. "Unnecessary hypothesis" is the term sometimes credited to Laplace; according to Michael J. Crowe, *The Extraterrestrial Life Debate, 1750–1900: The Idea of a Plurality of Worlds from Kant to Lowell* (1986), the astronomer's actual words to Napoleon were: "Citizen First Consul, I have no need for that hypothesis" (p. 78). Also see Numbers, especially chapter 1.

5. Kant's role as a pioneering theorist of solar system origins is discussed in Crowe, chapter 2.

6. Astronomers debated the true nature of "fuzzy" objects in the heavens for more than a century. By the early twentieth century, some were recognized as distant galaxies with billions of stars of their own. Others proved to be interstellar clouds of dust and gas within our own galaxy. Some of the latter clouds are continually collapsing into new planetary systems. For details, see Boss, plus Ken Croswell, *Planet Quest: The Epic Discovery of Alien Solar Systems* (1997), and Donald Goldsmith, *Worlds Unnumbered: The Search for Extrasolar Planets* (1997). The history of the debate over the nature of the interstellar medium is discussed in detail in Gerrit L. Verschuur, *Interstellar Matters: Essays on Curiosity and Astronomical Discovery* (1989). The present state of the science is depicted in James B. Kaler's well-illustrated volume in the *Scientific American* series, *Cosmic Clouds: Birth, Death, and Recycling in the Galaxy* (1997).

7. Crowe, especially pp. 182–195.

8. Ibid., especially pp. 195–202.

9. One reviewer for the *Theological and Literary Journal* called Whewell's argument against aliens "cold, barren, senseless, and atheistic" (Crowe, p. 343). At the same time, Crowe concludes (based on his thorough study of the mid-nineteenth-century literature) that although a majority of religious writers opposed Whewell, they were "significantly less inclined" to do so than scientists (p. 353).

10. Charles Darwin, *Origin of Species* (1859). On Darwin's impact on theories of extraterrestrial life, see Steven J. Dick, *The Biological Universe: The Twentieth-Century Extraterrestrial Life Debate and the Limits of Science* (1996), p. 29.

11. L. E. Orgel, *The Origins of Life: Molecules and Natural Selection* (1973), p. 13.

12. Edward S. Shapiro, p. 1: "The Holocaust . . . led some American Jews to doubt the existence of God. . . . How could God have allowed the slaughter of nearly six million Jews, over a million of whom were children?" For American Jews, one way to deal with the ghastliness of the Holocaust was not to talk about it; witness Rachel Sagan's refusal to discuss it in her home. "For the first decade and a half after the end of World War II, Jews were reluctant to discuss the Holocaust," Shapiro notes (p. 213). This reluctance ended with the Eichmann trial and the beginning of publication of memoirs of survivors, such as Elie Weisel's *Night* (1960).

13. CS interview.

14. Sagan, "Growing Up."

15. Sagan's many awards are listed in his résumé. Remarks on Rachel are in CS interview.

16. For example, Jerome Alexander, *Life: Its Nature and Origin* (1948).

17. Erwin Schrödinger, *What Is Life?* (1946).

18. On this thorny issue, see chapter 3 of Loren R. Graham, *Science, Philosophy, and Human Behavior in the Soviet Union* (1987).

19. Quoted in Carl Sagan, "Radiation and the Origin of the Gene" (hereafter referred to as "RAOG"), *Evolution*, 1957, p. 53.

20. A scathing history of the Lysenko controversy is Zhores A. Medvedev, *The Rise and Fall of T. D. Lysenko* (1969). Medvedev says that after Muller quit the Soviet Academy of

Sciences to protest the mistreatment of Soviet geneticists, it issued this rebuke: "The U.S.S.R. Academy of Sciences parts without regret from its former member who betrayed the interests of authentic science and openly joined the camp of the enemies of progress and science, of peace and democracy" (p. 34).

21. Muller to Sagan, Apr. 16, 1952. Lilly Library.

22. Ibid.

23. Ibid.

24. CS interview.

25. Orgel, p. 14.

26. Quoted in Shapiro, *Origins*, p. 99.

27. Interview with Frank Drake, July 1998. Payne-Gaposchkin is also the subject of an autobiography: *Cecilia Payne-Gaposchkin*, edited by Katharine Haramundanis (2d ed., 1996). Stephen G. Brush says in *Fruitful Encounters* that Miller's experiment was "indirectly inspired by the revival of the Nebular Hypothesis with the help of the Payne-Gaposchkin discovery of the high cosmic abundance of hydrogen" (p. 16).

28. Dick, *Biological Universe*, p. 340.

29. No full-length biography of Urey has been published. Details of his life appear in two bound annual editions of *Current Biography*, for 1941 and 1960. Also see James R. Arnold, Jacob Bigeleisen, and Clyde A. Hutchinson Jr., "Harold Clayton Urey," in *Biographical Memoirs*, National Academy of Sciences (1995). A valuable account of Urey's planetary work and controversies appears in Ronald E. Doel, *Solar System Astronomy in America: Communities, Patronage, and Interdisciplinary Science, 1920–1960* (hereafter referred to as *SSA*), particularly chapters 3 and 4. Also see Brush, *Fruitful Encounters*, parts 3 and 4, regarding Urey's scientific work and quarrel with Kuiper; especially see p. 204 on Urey's theory that a terrestrial impact event splashed the "ancient oceans of the Earth" onto the Moon, and p. 206 on Urey's cantankerous personality. Regarding Urey's work on the origin of life, see Dick, *Biological Universe*, pp. 345–347, 352–353, 360, 375, 376, 388, and 474. Also see two obituaries: "Harold Clayton Urey," *QJRAS*, vol. 26, 1985, p. 574; and "Harold Urey," *QJRAS*, 1986, vol. 27, p. 503. Regarding Urey's wartime work on the atomic bomb, see numerous references in Rhodes and in Hewlett and Anderson. His lunar research is discussed in Don E. Wilhelms, *To a Rocky Moon: A Geologist's History of Lunar Exploration* (1993).

30. During World War II, Von Weizsacker's work was reported to scientists in the Allied nations by George Gamow and J. Allen Hynek, "A New Theory by C. F. Von Weizsacker of the Origin of the Planetary System," *Astrophysical Journal*, vol. 101, Jan.-May 1945, pp. 249–254.

31. Harold Urey, *The Planets: Their Origin and Development* (1952). A long analysis of Urey's work in geochemistry and the origins of the solar system appears in Brush, *Fruitful Encounters*, especially parts 3 and 4.

32. David E. Fisher, *The Birth of the Earth* (1987), especially p. 181.

33. Biographical details on Miller are in Emily J. McMurray, ed., *Notable 20th-Century Scientists* (Detroit, Mich.: Gale Research, 1995), s.v. "Stanley Lloyd Miller."

34. In an interview with the author in early 1998, Miller laughed heartily to recall Urey's caustic comment on Calvin's energy-intensive effort to generate building blocks of life: "If you have to use 40 [mega-electron-volt] helium ions from a 60-inch cyclotron to get some formaldehyde or whatever, perhaps a new idea is needed!"

35. SM interview.

36. CS interview. The interview also contains many reflections on Urey's personality and Sagan's relationship with him.

37. Stanley Miller, "Production of Some Organic Compounds under Possible Primitive Earth Conditions," *Journal of the American Chemical Society*, May 12, 1955.

38. An example of such skepticism is Pierre Lecomte du Nouy, *Human Destiny* (1947), which includes a statistical argument against the probability of complex organic molecules assembling by chance.

39. Quoted in Keay Davidson, "How Did All Life Begin?" *San Francisco Examiner* "Spectra" science section, Aug. 6, 1986.

40. CS interview.

41. SM interview. Also see Stanley Miller, "A Production of Amino Acids under Possible Primitive Earth Conditions," *Science*, May 15, 1953, p. 528. A far more detailed report is Miller, "Production," p. 2351.

42. Isaac Asimov, *A Short History of Biology* (1964), p. 122.

43. The most popular (albeit one-sided) account of Watson and Crick's discovery of the structure of DNA is James Watson, *The Double Helix* (1968). More scholarly studies on the history of molecular biology are Robert Olby, *The Path to the Double Helix: The Discovery of DNA* (1974), and Horace Freeland Judson's magnificent *The Eighth Day of Creation* (1979). A much slimmer but valuable corrective to Watson's sexist account is Anne Sayre, *Rosalind Franklin and DNA* (1975).

44. "Vitalists" believed that living creatures possess mysterious qualities that cannot be reduced to physics and chemistry. In American biology, vitalism was essentially dead by the early twentieth century.

45. CS interview.

46. Ibid.

47. Ibid.

48. Ibid.

49. Sagan to Muller, Jan. 27, 1954. Lilly Library.

50. Gardner's book was originally published in 1952 as *In the Name of Science*. In 1957 it was re-released, with additional material, as *Fads and Fallacies in the Name of Science*.

51. *DHW*, p. 69.

52. Dean B. McLaughlin, "Interpretation of Some Martian Features," *PASP*, Aug. 1954, p. 161. Also see his follow-up article in the same journal, "Further Notes on Martian Features," Oct. 1954, p. 221.

53. Barry E. DiGregorio, *Mars: The Living Planet* (1997), p. 74. This book should be consulted with great caution. It surveys, among other things, the history of Mars research in the 1950s, including William Sinton's work. Unfortunately, DiGregorio damages his book's credibility by presenting a quasi-conspiracy theory for NASA scientists' rejection of alleged evidence for Martian life.

54. Margulis (1998), p. 16; and LM interview.

55. PP interview.

56. RPG phone interview, early 1998.

57. A profile of Margulis (including brief details on her marriage to Carl Sagan) appears in *Current Biography* (1992), where she is quoted as saying that their marriage was "tumultuous" and "an imbroglio."

58. LM interview.

59. Watson got an A in Muller's course "Mutation and the Gene," according to Olby (p. 299), but also correctly sensed that the "better days" of *Drosophila* research were over and that the future of genetics lay with microbes.

60. Judson (p. 109) notes that Crick, a Britisher and atheist who had been inspired by Schrödinger's "little book," entered biology after World War II at least partly to eliminate any surviving traces of vitalism.

61. Sheldon L. Glashow and Ben Bova, *Interactions* (1988), p. 34.

62. One of Sagan's finer qualities was his willingness to hear out offbeat ideas, even those he rejected. He published an early "Gaia" paper by Lynn Margulis and James Love-

lock: "Biological Modulation of the Earth's Atmosphere," *Icarus*, vol. 21 (1974), p. 471. Personally, though, Sagan "had a grave suspicion of Gaia," Ann Druyan told me. "There are different versions of Gaia, to be fair. [Still], he felt there was mysticism lurking there. . . . There were parts [of the hypothesis] he rejected and thought were not well thought out, not good science."

63. Carl Sagan's final résumé. I am grateful to Ann Druyan for giving me a copy of this thick, valuable document.

64. CS interview.

65. Sagan to Kuiper, Apr. 24, 1956. Gerard P. Kuiper papers, University of Arizona library archives, Tucson.

66. CS interview.

67. Biographical details on Kuiper are in Dale P. Cruikshank, "Gerard Peter Kuiper," *Biographical Memoirs*, National Academy of Sciences (1993), pp. 258–295. Also see Carl Sagan's obituary for his mentor in *Icarus*, vol. 22 (1974), pp. 117–118; "Kuiper, Gerard P(eter)," *Current Biography* (1959); and "Gerard Peter Kuiper," McMurray, pp. 1143–1145. An important account of Kuiper's research and battles with Harold C. Urey appears in Doel, *SSA*, chapter 4. Kuiper's postwar research on V-2s is cited throughout DeVorkin, *Science with a Vengeance*. His pioneering role in robotic space exploration is discussed in Joseph N. Tatarewicz, *Space Technology and Planetary Astronomy* (1990), especially pp. 54–56. Kuiper's views on Martian vegetation are in Dick, *Biological Universe*, pp. 118–123.

68. CS interview.

69. Kuiper had mixed feelings about Sagan early on. As this book went to press, Ronald E. Doel brought to my attention a 1959 letter from the Kuiper archive at the University of Arizona, in which the astronomer complains about the young Sagan's indifference to observing and preference for talking about extraterrestrial life. As a result (Kuiper writes) Sagan's ostensible goal for the summer of 1956—to observe Mars—was a failure.

70. Struve memo dated Dec. 15, 1949. Otto Struve papers, Bancroft Library, University of California, Berkeley.

71. CS interview.

72. JCB interview.

73. DC interview.

74. JCB interview.

75. E-mail from Helene Thorson, 1998.

76. CS interview.

77. E-mail from Thorson, 1998.

78. Struve papers.

79. FD interview.

80. Keay Davidson, "In the Frozen South, 'People Get Crazy,'" *San Francisco Examiner*, Jan. 10, 1989, p. A-1.

81. Keay Davidson, "S. F. Team Takes Signs of Stress in Space," *San Francisco Examiner*, July 27, 1997, p. A-1.

82. DC interview, early 1998.

83. This depiction of Kuiper at Yerkes is drawn from interviews with Cruikshank and Pesch.

84. GB interview, 1998.

85. CS interview.

86. At Yerkes, Geoffrey Burbidge "seemed to me to be the leading putschist," Sagan told Doel in 1991. In that interview, Sagan also discussed the "primate dominance hierarchy" and struggle to be "the alpha male" at isolated observatories. Burbidge's tense relationship with Kuiper is described in Doel, *SSA*, pp. 218–220.

87. Doel, *SSA*, pp. 141–142.

88. CS interview.

89. Struve memo dated Jan. 5, 1949. Struve papers.

90. Kameshwar C. Wali, *Chandra: A Biography of S. Chandrasekhar* (1991), p. 6. I am grateful to Lynn Margulis for introducing me to Professor Wali, whom I interviewed in Nov. 1997 in Ithaca, N.Y.

91. Ibid.

92. LM interview.

93. DC interview.

94. Wali, p. 194.

95. CS interview.

96. Ibid. In 1998 I interviewed Joseph Chamberlain by phone. He recalled how he and Sagan encountered each other many years after Sagan left Yerkes. Sagan reminded him of the time when the older astronomer "was coming out of the front door of Yerkes and he was coming in, and I said, 'Hi, Carl, I've been following your career in *Time* magazine.'" Chamberlain says Sagan seemed to find the remark "amusing." However, in a taped conversation with Doel in 1991, Sagan (who recalled Chamberlain's words as "I've been following your career in the papers, Sagan") does not sound terribly amused by it. Sagan also repeated the remark to Ann Druyan, who gave me the impression that it bothered her late husband. "He thought people would appreciate all this [popularization] stuff" he was doing at Yerkes, she says. "It never occurred to him that it was considered bad form."

97. Sagan, "RAOG."

98. Ibid., p. 53.

99. The genes do not "call the shots" consciously, of course! For a well-known modern treatment of this idea, see Richard Dawkins, *The Selfish Gene* (1976).

100. DO interview, 1998. Osterbrock's book is *Yerkes Observatory 1892–1950* (1997).

101. DO interview.

102. DC interview.

103. CS interview.

104. PV interview.

105. PP interview.

106. Margulis remains a dedicated secularist. When this writer stayed at her Amherst, Mass., home for two days in Nov. 1997, she suddenly interrupted some chore to scamper to her back door and yell at two unwanted visitors (Jehovah's Witnesses), "Don't ever come back! I'm a professional evolutionist!"

107. Lynn Margulis and Dorion Sagan, *Slanted Truths: Essays on Gaia, Symbiosis, and Evolution* (1997), pp. 10–11.

108. LM interview.

109. PP interview.

110. CG interview.

111. LM's wedding photo album.

112. Biographical material on Gamow, especially his contributions to cosmology, are in Smoot and Davidson, chapter 3.

In later years Sagan said virtually nothing about his summer with Gamow. This seems odd, considering Gamow's great fame as a scientist and science popularizer. I contacted Gamow's son, Prof. Igor Gamow of the University of Colorado, who was a boy at the time, but he was unable to shed light on exactly what Sagan did that summer at the university. The elder Gamow routinely destroyed his correspondence, Igor Gamow noted.

It is conceivable (although there is no direct evidence) that Sagan worked on some form of classified research that summer. (Gamow had ties to the military, and his early theoretical work indirectly influenced the development of nuclear weaponry; see Rhodes, p. 370.) It is also possible that Gamow, who was a heavy drinker (Smoot and Davidson,

p. 61), was less patient with young Sagan's flighty interests than his previous summer mentors (Muller and Kuiper) had been. This is speculation, of course. In any case, Gamow did subsequently serve as a guest speaker at Sagan's 1957–1958 science lecture series at the University of Chicago.

113. Sagan to Muller, July 31, 1957.

Chapter 4. High Ground

1. CS interview.

2. Nevil Shute, *On the Beach* (1957). When I was a child, my mother encouraged me to watch a television showing of producer Stanley Kramer's film version of Shute's book. That childhood viewing probably accounts for my present stance on nuclear issues. I shall never forget the last scene, set in a lifeless San Francisco, where the wind whistles past a sign left over from an evangelical rally. The words on the banner are Kramer's closing message to his 1959 audience: "There Is Still Time, Brother." Fortunately, there was—and is.

3. A multivolume history of the modern peace and antinuclear movements is Lawrence S. Wittner, *One World or None* (1993) and *Resisting the Bomb* (1997). A third volume is pending. A thick history of nuclear weapons testing and radiation safety is Barton C. Hacker, *Elements of Controversy* (1994). The political and diplomatic context of the shift to underground testing of nuclear weapons is described in Glenn T. Seaborg (with Benjamin S. Loeb), *Kennedy, Khrushchev and the Test Ban* (1981).

4. Walter Sullivan, *Assault on the Unknown* (1961), especially chapter 8 on the 1958 "Argus" nuclear test on the edge of outer space.

Teller's moon-nuking proposal was made at a secret conference in February 1957 at the Lawrence Livermore nuclear weapons laboratory in Livermore, Calif. According to *The Firecracker Boys* (1994), Dan O'Neill's history of Project Plowshares (a federal project to use nuclear weapons for "peacetime" civil engineering purposes), Teller said: "One will probably not long resist the temptation to shoot at the moon. The device might be set off relatively close to the moon and one would then look for the fluorescence coming off the lunar surface, or one might actually shoot right at the moon, try to observe what kind of disturbance it might cause" (O'Neill, p. 25).

Some experts feared that the Soviets might try to test nuclear weapons remotely in space, and advocated developing satellites able to spot such "clandestine explosions." See "Space Blast Detection System Considered," *Aviation Week & Space Technology*, Aug. 5, 1963, pp. 26–27. The article quotes President John F. Kennedy: "There is at present a possibility that deep in outer space, that hundreds and thousands and millions of miles away from the earth, illegal tests might go undetected."

5. A biography of Haldane is Ronald Clark, *JBS: The Life and Work of J. B. S. Haldane* (1968). Lederberg's memories of his encounter with Haldane in India are drawn from an interview with the author in November 1997 and from Lederberg's short memoir on the dawn of exobiology, titled "Sputnik 1957–1987," *The Scientist*, Oct. 5, 1987, hereafter referred to as "Lederberg memoir." Biographical details on Lederberg are in *Current Biography* for 1959, and in *Notable 20th-Century Scientists*, p. 1203.

6. All quotes above from Lederberg memoir.

7. Quoted in Joseph N. Tatarewicz, *Space Technology and Planetary Astronomy* (1990), p. 12.

8. I. F. Stone, *The Haunted Fifties* (1963), pp. 254–257.

9. CS interview.

10. Ibid.

11. GB interview.

12. FD interview.

13. Details on Sinton's erroneous "discovery" are in Barry E. DiGregorio, *Mars: The Living Planet* (1997), chapter 2.

14. In the Aug. 12, 1960, issue of *Science*, Lederberg cited the importance of Sinton's observation.

15. Urey, p. 152.

16. See Sagan's two-page, undated (1957–58?) "Proposed Thesis Topic" in Kuiper papers, University of Arizona. The actual thesis is Carl Sagan, "Physical Studies of the Planets" (hereafter referred to as "PSP"), doctoral dissertation for department of astronomy and astrophysics, University of Chicago, 1960. Available from University Microfilms, Ann Arbor, Mich.

17. Kaler, *Cosmic Clouds: Birth, Death, and Recycling in the Galaxy* (1997), chapter 5. An excellent popular introduction to the subject of interstellar matter, including organics, is Time-Life, *Between the Stars* (1990), especially chapters 2 and 3.

18. LM interview.

19. PP interview.

20. DC interview.

21. The address appears in Sagan's 1959 application for a Miller Fellowship at the University of California at Berkeley. I am grateful to Prof. Raymond Jeanloz and Kathryn Day-Huh of the Miller Institute in Berkeley for granting me access to the application file.

22. JL interview.

23. Joshua Lederberg and Dean B. Cowie, "Moondust," *Science*, June 27, 1958, p. 1473.

24. Walter Sullivan, *We Are Not Alone: The Continuing Search for Extraterrestrial Intelligence*, 2d ed. (1993), p. 91. The original, somewhat different edition of this classic book was *We Are Not Alone: The Search for Intelligent Life on Other Worlds* (1964) (hereafter referred to as *WANA*).

25. The study of symbiosis (i.e., cooperation of two or more life forms for their mutual benefit) is a central theme of Lynn Margulis's work. For a short popular introduction to her career, see her *Symbiotic Planet: A New Look at Evolution* (1998).

26. CS interview.

27. Lederberg memoir.

28. Ibid.

29. Melvin Calvin recommendation letter, Miller Fellowship application file.

30. Interview with Sagan in David W. Swift, *SETI Pioneers* (1990), p. 213.

31. JL interview.

32. AD interview.

33. In the book's acknowledgments, Sagan credited Lederberg for suggesting a central notion of *Contact*—that the best place to look for aliens is at the star-packed center of the galaxy.

34. JL interview.

35. Fred Hoyle, *The Black Cloud* (1957).

36. Quoted in Tatarewicz, p. xi.

37. Crowe, pp. 210–215.

38. W. H. Pickering, "Life on the Moon," *Popular Astronomy*, vol. 45 (1937).

39. As late as 1946, a semi-technical journal discussed the possibility of non-negligible amounts of water and snow on the present-day lunar surface—see Fred M. Garland, "Snow on the Moon," *Popular Astronomy*, vol. 54 (1946), p. 176. However, Garland reached a negative conclusion.

40. Carl Sagan, "Indigenous Organic Matter on the Moon," *PNAS*, Apr. 15, 1960, p. 393. In that regard, Kuiper was apparently concerned about how Sagan's lunar work

would be received by other scientists, concerned enough to seek an opinion from H. J. Muller. Muller responded in a handwritten letter to Kuiper on May 28, 1960 (Kuiper papers), stating that Sagan's *PNAS* paper and a second, accompanying *PNAS* article on the Moon were "of exceptional merit and originality, especially for a person who has not yet received the doctorate. . . . I wish there were more Ph.D. candidates today as worthy of the degree as I believe Mr. Sagan to be."

41. Carl Sagan, "Biological Contamination of the Moon," *PNAS*, Apr. 15, 1960, p. 396.

42. Rachel Carson, *Silent Spring* (1962).

43. "Germ Peril Seen in Space Flights," *New York Times*, May 3, 1960, p. 18.

44. Sagan, "Indigenous Organic Matter."

45. Miller Fellowship application file.

46. For example, after the *Sputnik* launch in 1957, "[a]lmost immediately Kuiper received $61,000 from the Air Force for lunar studies, a tenfold increase over his average annual grants in this field," Doel says in *SSA*, p. 216. Also, "in 1959, Kuiper arranged a study of Soviet astronomy for the Central Intelligence Agency," p. 218. It is conceivable that Kuiper's CIA work introduced Carl Sagan to this intelligence agency, with which the younger astronomer would remain in sometimes unhappy contact at least through the early 1980s.

47. GB interview.

48. CS interview.

49. Ibid.

50. Miller Fellowship application.

51. CS interview.

52. As this book was going to press, Ronald E. Doel brought to my attention a previously unpublished memo that directly links Kuiper to the Armour project. In this 1958 memo, coauthored with Thornton Page, Kuiper proposes dropping nuclear weapons on the Moon to test how they affect the crust (among other things). He calculates that a crater created by a nuclear weapon would be visible through terrestrial telescopes, big enough to be distinguished from regular lunar craters. The proposal includes an accompanying note on Armour stationery.

Sagan's Armour papers are titled "Possible Contribution of Lunar Nuclear Weapons Detonations to the Solution of Some Problems in Planetary Astronomy" and "Radiological Contamination of the Moon by Nuclear Weapons Detonations," dated 1958 and 1959, respectively. Sagan apparently had his first contact with Armour in 1957, when he gave a lecture, "Astronomical Objectives in Space Flight," at a "popular symposium" there. (His first scientific lecture had been in 1955, when he addressed the Society for the Study of Evolution in a lecture titled "Radiation and Primitive Life" in East Lansing, Mich.) Miller Fellowship application file.

53. Burrows, p. 220.

54. Ibid.

55. Cited in J. D. Bernal, *Origin of Life* (London: Weidenfeld and Nicholson, 1967).

56. "PSP."

57. Sagan's science-fiction reading might have inspired his speculations about Jupiter. The glory days of Jupiter as a setting for Africa safari-style fantasies (e.g., J. J. Astor's 1894 *A Journey in Other Worlds*, in which explorers hunt big game on Jupiter) were long gone by the 1940s, when Sagan discovered science fiction. However, a small number of wartime and postwar writers continued to speculate about Jovian life. In the 1940s his hero, Edgar Rice Burroughs, wrote about the "Skeleton Men of Jupiter." Also, according to the invaluable *Encyclopedia of Science Fiction* (1995 edition, p. 653), Clifford D. Simak's

story "Clerical Error" (1944) tells of humans who are biologically altered so they can enjoy life on Jupiter.

58. Dorion was born on Mar. 17, 1959. Letter from Sagan to Muller, Mar. 18, 1959, in the Muller archives, Lilly Library.

59. LM interview.

60. SM interview.

61. Carl Sagan and Stanley Miller, "Molecular Synthesis in Simulated Reducing Planetary Atmospheres," *Astronomical Journal*, vol. 65, 1960, p. 499. Miller gave this writer copies of his correspondence with Sagan circa 1960, partly quoted here.

62. At 9:30 A.M. on Sept. 23, 1959 (nine days after *Lunik II* hit the Moon), Muller "telephoned Carl Sagan . . . inviting him to give a paper at the NAS meeting. Provisionally accepted," states a memo from that date in the Muller archive, Lilly Library.

63. Carl Sagan, "Biological Contamination of the Moon," *Science*, Nov. 20, 1959, p. 1424. The Venus document is cited in Sagan to Muller, Dec. 9, 1959. Lilly Library.

64. Sagan, "Indigenous Organic Matter" and Sagan, "Biological Contamination." Both papers are reprinted in Sagan's doctoral dissertation.

65. Muller to Sagan, Feb. 22, 1960. Lilly Library.

66. Urey to Sagan, Dec. 17, 1959. The Harold C. Urey papers are archived at Mandeville Special Collections, Central University Library, University of California at San Diego.

67. Daniel K. Kevles, *The Physicists: The History of a Scientific Community in Modern America* (1978), p. 225.

68. Urey's cautious philosophy of science is suggested by this passage from the last pages of his book *The Planets:* "The chronology of events [depicted herein] is a complicated one but the true one is certainly even more complicated. . . . We will never be able to reconstruct the complete course of events which led to the solar system. In this sense, this treatise as well as all others is surely incomplete and at most only partly true. And this is a field where judgments in regard to the true and the false may require long periods of time" (p. 223).

69. Davidson, "In the Frozen South."

70. Quoted in Michael Michaud, *Reaching for the High Frontier* (1986), p. 193.

71. The quote is from a statement by Sagan to the Smithsonian Astrophysical Observatory (SAO) newsletter in 1963. It is part of Sagan's file with the Harvard-Smithsonian public relations office. I am grateful to Jim Cornell of that office for sharing the documents with me (hereafter referred to as "Jim Cornell papers").

72. LM interview.

73. MR phone interview, Apr. 1998.

74. NiS phone interview, mid-1998.

75. Carl Sagan, *Planetary Exploration* (1970), p. 68. This slim book is drawn from Sagan's lectures at the University of Oregon and Oregon State University in 1967–1968.

76. MR interview.

77. Donald H. Menzel and Fred Whipple, "The Case for H_2O Clouds on Venus," *Astronomical Journal* (1954), pp. 329–330. A Menzel-Whipple article with the same title is in *PASP* (1955), pp. 161–168.

78. Clute and Nicholls, p. 57.

79. Cornell Mayer, "The Temperatures of the Planets," *Scientific American*, May 1961, p. 58.

80. CS interview.

81. Details on early debates over the true cause of the Venusian microwave emission appear in Mikhail Ya. Marov and David Grinspoon, *The Planet Venus* (1998).

82. CS interview.

83. "Revelle, Roger," *Biographical Encyclopedia of Scientists*, 2d ed. (J. Daintith et al, eds., 1994), pp. 748–749.

84. "PSP," p. 17.

85. CS interview.

86. "PSP," p. 28. Sagan notes wittily that this is "one of the few astronomical applications of boiler and furnace technology."

87. CS interview.

88. Carl Sagan, Jonathan Norton Leonard, and the editors of *Life*, *The Planets* (1966), p. 112. This book was published as part of the Time-Life series of popular science books.

89. The concept of scientific hypotheses as different gestalts (i.e., different observers interpret the same data differently) has become a familiar one in the study of the history of ideas. See N. R. Hanson, *Patterns of Discovery* (1958), chapter 1; Thomas S. Kuhn, *The Structure of Scientific Revolutions*, 2d ed. (1970), p. 113; and Kuhn, *The Essential Tension: Selected Studies in Scientific Tradition and Change* (1977), pp. 263 and 269. A famous example is the shift from the Ptolemaic to the Copernican cosmology in the sixteenth century: Copernicus utilized the same data as Ptolemy had, yet reached a radically different conclusion (the Earth orbits the Sun, not vice versa). In this regard, see Kuhn's *The Copernican Revolution: Planetary Astronomy in the Development of Western Thought* (1959). For an obituary of Kuhn and an insightful survey of his life and thought, see J. L. Heilbron, "Thomas Samuel Kuhn," *Isis*, Sept. 1998, pp. 505–515.

90. "Target: Venus—There May Be Life There," *Life*, Dec. 21, 1959, p. 67. Perhaps not coincidentally, this large, picture-filled article and related news coverage (see note 91 below) appeared about the same time that Sagan was developing his abortive paper "Venus as a Planet of Possible Biological Interest."

91. "Shivering Look at Venus," *Time*, Dec. 14, 1959, p. 52.

92. Sagan, *Planets*, p. 79.

93. Ibid., pp. 110 and 112.

94. Undated draft of "Corrections and Additions" for "Venus as a Planet of Possible Biological Interest" (circa 1959–1960), Urey papers. Sagan alludes to the article in a letter to Muller, Dec. 9, 1959. Muller papers, Lilly Library. Urey favorably discussed Sagan's Venus work in a Nov. 9, 1959, letter to Lederberg, a copy of which I obtained from a source at the NAS as this book was going to press.

Regarding the dating of the Venus biology papers, Sagan wrote a follow-up letter to Muller on Jan. 12, 1960, that states: "I've been spending quite a bit of time recently trying to cook up a Venus greenhouse effect efficient enough to give surface temperatures near 600 degrees K[elvin], the values derived from radio observations. It now appears that a [carbon dioxide]-[water] atmosphere with a surface pressure of a few atmospheres is sufficient. In this case, there seem to be no objections to the 600 degree K figure, and the prospects for life on Venus seem very dim indeed." Muller papers, Lilly Library. Hence Sagan apparently concluded by very early in 1960 that the Venusian surface is not a place of "biological interest."

95. The Boyer case is cited in *Sky & Telescope*, June 1999, pp. 56–60. CS interview.

96. Doel, *SSA*, pp. 219–220.

97. Kuiper to Sagan, Apr. 23, 1969. Kuiper papers.

98. Kuiper to Bruno Rossi, Mar. 9, 1967. Kuiper papers.

99. "PSP."

100. JC interview.

101. CS interview.

102. JC interview.

103. Ibid. Also see note 96, chapter 3.

Chapter 5. California

1. B. F. Skinner, *Walden Two* (1948).

2. The brilliant scientific atmosphere at Berkeley, from the 1930s on, is recaptured in books such as Luis W. Alvarez, *Alvarez: Adventures of a Physicist* (1987); Nuell Pharr Davis, *Lawrence & Oppenheimer* (1968); John L. Heilbron, *Lawrence and His Laboratory* (1989); and Glenn Seaborg, *The Plutonium Story: The Journals of Professor Glenn T. Seaborg 1939–1946* (1994).

3. Miller Fellowship application.

4. Lederberg recommendation letter, Miller Fellowship application.

5. Calvin recommendation letter, Miller Fellowship application.

6. Muller recommendation letter (dated Jan. 15, 1960) for Carl Sagan's Miller Fellowship application. Muller papers, Lilly Library. The archive also contains Sagan's Jan. 12, 1960, letter to Muller that solicits the recommendation.

7. Sagan's Miller Fellowship file.

8. Ibid.

9. RB interview.

10. Ibid.

11. Ibid.

12. SL phone interview, Apr. 1998. Landau and his then-wife, Nina Landau (now Serrano), are listed among William Appleman Williams's student devotees in Buhle and Rice-Maximin, p. 118.

13. NiS interview.

14. Sullivan, *WANA* (1964 edition), p. 256.

15. NiS interview.

16. LM interview.

17. Sagan's résumé lists numerous such activities in the 1960–1963 period.

18. *Citizen Kane* (1941), directed by Orson Welles. The line is uttered by Kane's business manager to the reporter.

19. While more impressionistic than scholarly, Tom Wolfe's *The Right Stuff* (1979) splendidly recaptures the cold war atmosphere of the early space age. An excellent history of the Soviet space program is James and Alcestis Oberg, *Pioneering Space* (1986).

20. Arthur C. Clarke, *Voices from the Sky* (1967, paperback edition), p. 34.

21. Quoted in Howard E. McCurdy, *Space and the American Imagination* (1997), p. 76.

22. CS interview.

23. Carl Sagan, "The Planet Venus," *Science*, Mar. 24, 1961, p. 849.

24. Ernst Öpik, "Aeolosphere and Atmosphere of Venus," *Journal of Geophysical Research*, Sept. 1961, p. 2818. For a short biography of Öpik, see Patrick Moore, "The Turbulent Life of E. J. Öpik," *Sky & Telescope*, Feb. 1986, p. 149.

25. See these entries in Clute and Nicholls: "Williamson, Jack" (p. 1328) and "Terraforming" (p. 1213).

26. Clute and Nicholls, "Terraforming" (p. 1213).

27. Keay Davidson, *Twister* (1996), pp. 84-89.

28. Dan O'Neill's book discusses these schemes in detail.

29. Philip D. Thompson and Robert O'Brien, *Weather* (1965), p. 179.

30. Ibid.

31. Sagan, "The Planet Venus," p. 857.

32. *New York Times*, Mar. 27, 1961, p. 33.

33. John F. Allen, "Can Humans Make Venus Habitable?" *San Francisco Examiner*, Mar. 30, 1961.

34. "Venus—Nice Place to Live?", *Newsweek*, Apr. 10, 1961, p. 67.

35. Arthur C. Clarke, *The Promise of Space* (1968), p. 262.

36. Doel, in *SSA*, questions the statement (often repeated by Sagan and others) that U.S. planetary astronomy almost disappeared during the first half of the twentieth century. In fact, it was "far from neglected. . . . American astronomers played leading roles in resolving some of the great challenges of solar system astronomy by the mid-1950s, including the origin of meteors, the origin and physical structures of comets, and the nature of craters on the Moon and Earth" (p. xi).

37. DM interview.

38. CS interview.

39. Richard A. Kerr, "The Solar System's New Diversity," *Science*, Sept. 2, 1994, pp. 1360–1362. Kerr quotes Australian astronomer Ross Taylor: "If you look at all the planets and the 60 or so satellites, it's very hard to find two that are the same." For an editorial commentary on Kerr's article, see Keay Davidson, "Scientists Deluged with Data on Planets," *San Francisco Examiner*, Sept. 9, 1994, p. A-2.

40. Nov. 25, 1964, letter from Sagan to Menzel. The letter is in the Donald H. Menzel papers, Harvard University archives, Cambridge, Mass.

41. Jet Propulsion Laboratory, "History of Knowledge about Planet Venus," *Mariner-Venus 1962—Final Project Report* (1965), p. 6.

42. Sagan and Shklovskii, *Intelligent Life in the Universe* (1966), pp. 461–462.

43. Carl Sagan, "Biological Exploration of Mars," in George W. Morgenthaler, ed., *Exploration of Mars*, vol. 15, *Advances in the Astronautical Sciences* (American Astronautical Society, 1963), p. 576. This volume is a compilation of speeches from the AAS Symposium on the Exploration of Mars in Denver, Colo., on June 6–7, 1963.

44. "Mariner Scans a Lifeless Venus," *National Geographic*, May 1963, p. 733.

45. SC phone interview, June 1998.

46. CS interview.

47. Details on the *Mariner 2* mission and its instruments are in J. N. James, "The Voyage of Mariner II," *Scientific American*, July 1963, p. 70. Also see this 118-page book on the mission: Jet Propulsion Laboratory, *Mariner Mission to Venus* (1963, compiled by Harold J. Wheelock).

48. In CS interview Sagan recalled the 1960s theory that Venus had experienced a "substantial nuclear war." In that regard, see reference to hypothesis of "a radioactive particle density below the Venus clouds several orders of magnitude larger than the corresponding values for Earth" in Russell G. Walker and Carl Sagan, "The Ionospheric Model of the Venus Microwave Emission: An Obituary," *Icarus*, vol. 5, p. 107.

49. NS interview. However, he did appear in a newspaper ad for *Scientific American* that ran in the *New York Times* (May 5, 1976, p. 42). The ad includes several photos of him, including one in which he is playing with his young son Nick. It is important to add that modern historians of science have found few instances, if any, where Popperian models adequately explain major scientific advances.

50. Wolfe, *The Right Stuff*.

51. Paul R. Weissman, Lucy-Ann McFadden, and Torrence V. Johnson, *Encyclopedia of the Solar System* (1999), p. 958.

52. Numerous accounts of the Cuban missile crisis have been written. An especially enjoyable one appears in Michael R. Beschloss, *The Crisis Years* (1991).

53. LM interview.

54. The "nonsense" remark is part of physics folklore. Biographical details on Pauli are in Robert P. Crease and Charles C. Mann, *The Second Creation: Makers of the Revolution in 20th-Century Physics* (1986).

55. TPA interview, May 1998.

56. CS interview.

57. Carl Sagan and Russell G. Walker, "The Infrared Detectability of Dyson Civilizations," *Astrophysical Journal*, vol. 144, no. 3, 1966. pp. 1216–1218. Also see Sullivan, *WANA* (1964 edition), pp. 222–223.

58. Several outstanding scholarly histories of the subject have been published in the last two decades. See Steven J. Dick, *Plurality of Worlds: The Origins of the Extraterrestrial Life Debate from Democritus to Kant* (1982), and his irreplaceable *The Biological Universe: The Twentieth-Century Extraterrestrial Life Debate and the Limits of Science* (1996). Also see Michael J. Crowe's huge, rich *The Extraterrestrial Life Debate, 1750–1900: The Idea of a Plurality of Worlds from Kant to Lowell* (1986). Karl S. Guthke's *The Last Frontier: Imagining Other Worlds from the Copernican Revolution to Modern Science Fiction* (1990) is valuable. The modern concept of a vast universe with countless worlds contrasts with the comparatively smaller, cozier, one-Earth cosmos of medieval times; see Pierre Duhem, *Medieval Cosmology: Theories of Infinity, Place, Time, Void, and the Plurality of Worlds* (1985), and Edward Grant, *Planets, Stars, & Orbs: The Medieval Cosmos 1200–1687* (1994). Also, the author has researched the history of the idea of extraterrestrial life since 1974; see Keay Davidson, "19th Century SETI," *Planetary Report*, Jan.–Feb. 1984, pp. 4–5.

59. Crowe, p. 108.

60. Sullivan, *WANA* (1964 edition), pp. 178–179. A recent biography of Tesla is Marc J. Seifer, *The Life and Times of Nikola Tesla* (1996).

61. *New York Times*, May 5, 1933, p. 1.

62. Gerrit L. Verschuur, *The Invisible Universe Revealed: The Story of Radio Astronomy* (1987), chapter 7.

63. However, some have speculated that human concepts of mathematics may be rooted in human biology or social context; hence we might have difficulty communicating mathematically with aliens. See George Johnson, "Useful Invention or Absolute Truth: What Is Math?" *New York Times*, Feb. 10, 1998, p. B-9. The concept of an alternate mathematics (independent of the SETI issue) has been proposed by a doyen of the "Edinburgh school" of the history and philosophy of science, David Bloor, in his *Knowledge and Social Imagery* (2d ed., 1991).

64. Drake and Sobel, p. 28.

65. Ibid., p. 18.

66. Sullivan, *WANA* (1964), p. 200.

67. Ibid., chapter 14.

68. Ibid., p. 47.

69. Quoted in Dick, *Biological Universe*, p. 431.

70. FD interview.

71. Sullivan, *WANA* (1964 edition), p. 1.

72. Ibid., p. 249. The "Drake equation" has been the subject of considerable comment and controversy since the early 1960s. For criticisms, see Dick, *Biological Universe*, p. 452.

73. Ibid., p. 251.

74. Sullivan, *WANA* (1994 ed.), pp. 33–39.

75. Drake and Sobel, p. 56.

76. Sagan, "Direct Contact," p. 489. Also see G. G. Simpson, "The Nonprevalence of Humanoids," *Science*, Feb. 21, 1964, p. 769. Also see Ernst Mayr, "The Probability of Extraterrestrial Intelligent Life," *Toward a New Philosophy of Biology* (1988). Mayr debated SETI with Sagan in the 1990s; their exchange was published in *Planetary Report*, May 1996.

77. FD interview.

78. See, for example, chapter 9 of Lilly's autobiography: Francis Jeffrey and John C. Lilly, M.D., *John Lilly, So Far . . .* (1990).

79. Lilly confirmed in a phone interview with the author that his lab in the Virgin Islands was built with Department of Defense money.

80. Sullivan, *WANA* (1964 edition), pp. 1–2.

81. JCL interview.

82. *CC*, chapter 24.

83. JCL interview.

84. FD interview.

85. JCL interview.

86. *DHW.*

87. NS interview.

88. Through the mid-twentieth century, some anthropologists—for example, Leslie A. White—argued that terrestrial civilizations tend to evolve in similar ways over time (see his *The Evolution of Culture*, [1959]). My impression is that many SETI scientists unconsciously projected White-type views onto the cosmos and assumed, optimistically, that alien societies would evolve in directions similar to terrestrial ones.

89. Sullivan, *WANA* (1964 edition), chapter 16.

90. Ibid.

91. Ibid., p. 234.

92. Shklovskii and Sagan, pp. 445–447.

93. Ibid., p. 444.

94. Sagan, "Direct Contact," pp. 493–497.

95. SM interview.

96. FD interview.

97. Sagan's Harvard colleague Donald H. Menzel was especially suspicious of Sagan's UFO views; see chapter 7 of this book.

98. Sagan's engaging account of the Schmidt trial is in Shklovskii and Sagan, chapter 1. I have used quotes from a similar, typewritten manuscript on file in the Menzel archive at American Philosophical Society (Sagan to Menzel, May 8, 1962).

99. *San Francisco Examiner,* Oct. 25, 1961.

100. *Oakland Tribune,* Oct. 25, 1961.

101. Ibid., Nov. 17, 1961. Records of the Schmidt case are now on microfilm at Alameda County Superior Court in Oakland. The case number is Superior Court case 32568. Schmidt's appeal was overturned and he was sent to state prison in Vacaville, Calif.

Chapter 6. Harvard

1. Patrick Moore, "The Turbulent Life of E. J. Öpik," *Sky & Telescope,* Feb. 1986, p. 149.

2. CS interview.

3. E. J. Öpik, "The Aeolosphere and Atmosphere of Venus," *Journal of Geophysical Research,* Sept. 1961, p. 2818.

4. Menzel and Whipple, "H_2O Clouds" (1954, 1955).

5. CS interview.

6. Menzel wrote to Sagan on Jan. 4, 1962, to inform him that Pusey approved his appointment; Menzel papers, Harvard University. Also see Whipple's letter to Pusey (Jan. 17, 1962, also in the Menzel papers) that thanks him for approving the appointment and that praises Sagan as "extraordinarily able."

7. Robert W. Smith, *The Space Telescope* (1989, 1993), especially the Introduction.

8. Wallace and Karen Tucker, *The Cosmic Inquirers* (1986), pp. 129, 130–131.

9. PV interview.

10. Tuckers, pp. 130–133.

11. PV interview.

12. Sagan to Kuiper, Apr. 16, 1963. Kuiper papers.

13. LM interview.

14. Ibid. Jeremy Sagan was born on Oct. 27, 1960.

15. Lynn Margulis, *Symbiotic Planet* (1998), p. 17.

16. LM interview.

17. AC phone interview, Apr. 1998.

18. FD interview.

19. LM interview.

20. LM's handwritten passages, inserted in early 1960s into Sagan's teenage notebook.

21. Margulis gave the author a copy of Sagan's self-critical memo, which she found after their divorce. CS interview.

22. RB interview.

23. SL interview.

24. *Dr. Strangelove* (1964), directed by Stanley Kubrick.

25. Details on the early days of RAND appear in Sylvia Nasar, *A Beautiful Mind* (1998), a biography of a Nobel Prize–winning mathematician. Histories and depictions of the nuclear strategy and targeting communities include Barry H. Steiner, *Bernard Brodie and the Foundations of American Nuclear Strategy* (1991); Fred Kaplan, *The Wizards of Armageddon* (1983); and Janne E. Nolan, *Guardians of the Arsenal* (1989). The most famous (or infamous, depending on one's attitude) examples of nuclear strategic thought include Herman Kahn, *On Thermonuclear War* (1960) and *Thinking About the Unthinkable* (1962), and Henry Kissinger, *Nuclear Weapons and Foreign Policy* (1957). For a psycho-ethical perspective, see Steven Kull, *Minds at War* (1988). William Poundstone's *Prisoner's Dilemma* (1992) portrays nuclear strategy in light of the career of John Von Neumann and his work on "game theory."

26. The astronomer Fred Whipple conducted such research in the 1940s. See Doel, *SSA*, chapter 2. Also see DeVorkin, *Science with a Vengeance*. Sagan also worked on unspecified "national security problems" at RAND, according to an undated (pre-1963?) curriculum vitae in his personal file at Harvard-Smithsonian (Jim Cornell papers).

27. Sagan's work at RAND might have adversely affected his ability to work with the people who hoped to improve relations with the Soviets. He told historian Ronald Doel about trouble dealing with Soviets regarding negotiations over spaceship sterilization: "They considered me an agent of the CIA," he told Doel in their 1991 interview. Doel also notes (personal communication with the author) that Kuiper was "a major (though not exclusive) point of contact between the American astronomical community and the intelligence community."

28. WK phone interview, late 1997. Kellogg's role as a pioneer of scientific space satellites is described in Helen Gavaghan, *Something New under the Sun: Satellites and the Beginning of the Space Age* (1998); also see references to RAND. Kellogg (now living in Boulder, Colo.) wrote to me on Oct. 19, 1997, to emphasize that Sagan "was an unforgettable personality—scientist, dreamer, poet, towering intellect. It was, quite simply, great fun to collaborate with him." Besides their *Atmospheres of Mars and Venus* monograph, they collaborated on a few other articles, including "The Terrestrial Planets," which appeared in the *Annual Review of Astronomy and Astrophysics*, vol. 1, pp. 235–266. This article was translated (by the Soviet scientist V. I. Moroz) into Russian and appeared in that language in *Problems in Astronomy and Astrophysics* (Moscow, 1962). Presumably by this means, Sagan's work on Venus came to the attention of I. S. Shklovskii, Sagan's future collaborator.

29. CS interview.

30. Sagan was impressed by Kopal and Wilson's decision to defend the journal's openness to offbeat ideas with a Karl Popperish quote from Arthur Stanley Eddington. The Eddington quotation (from his 1927 book *Stars and Atoms*) appears in vol. 1 (pp. ii-iii,

1962–1963) of *Icarus*, and cites the ancient legend of Daedalus: "Cautious Daedalus will apply his theories where he feels confident they will safely go; but by his excess of caution their hidden weaknesses remain undiscovered. Icarus will strain his theories to the breaking-point till the weak joints gape. For the mere adventure? Perhaps partly, that is human nature. But if he is destined not yet to reach the sun and solve finally the riddle of its constitution, we may at least hope to learn from his journey some hints to build a better machine." Cruikshank comments are from DC interview and documents.

31. CS interview.

32. Shklovskii's name is sometimes spelled in English as "Shklovsky," but according to Sagan, the preferred spelling has two "ii"'s on the end (Shirley Arden papers, Apr. 14, 1977). An English-language edition of Shklovskii's chatty autobiography is *Five Billion Vodka Bottles to the Moon* (1991), with an introduction by Herbert Friedman. An obituary of Shklovskii ran in the *New York Times* on Mar. 6, 1985, section 2, p. 10, and in the *Los Angeles Times*, Mar. 8, 1985, II-3. Details of Shklovskii's scientific career appear in another obituary, "Iosif Samuilovch Shklovskii," *QJRAS* (1968), p. 700. A brief personal reference to Shklovskii ("an outstanding and unusual character") is in Roald Sagdeev, *The Making of a Soviet Scientist* (1994); the book's foreword is by Sagan.

33. Shklovskii's groundbreaking paper "On the Nature of the Luminescence of the Crab Nebula" (1953) is reprinted in Kenneth R. Lang and Owen Gingerich, *A Source Book in Astronomy and Astrophysics, 1900–1975* (1979). Also see Shklovskii and Sagan, p. vii.

34. RB interview.

35. FM phone interview, Mar. 1998.

36. Ibid.

37. Shklovskii and Sagan, p. vii.

38. Ibid.

39. Ibid.

40. FM interview.

41. Sagan, *Biological Exploration*, pp. 576–577; and Shklovskii and Sagan, pp. 256–257.

42. Joshua Lederberg, "Exobiology: Approaches to Life beyond the Earth," *Science*, Aug. 12, 1960, p. 397.

43. SM interview.

44. Ibid.

45. Harvard-Smithsonian newsletter.

46. Joshua Lederberg and Carl Sagan, "Microenvironments for Life on Mars," *PNAS*, Sept. 15, 1962, p. 1473.

47. Keay Davidson, "Scientists Now Seek Remains of Life on Mars," *San Francisco Examiner-Chronicle*, June 23, 1996, p. A-1.

48. Hubertus Strughold, *The Green and Red Planet* (1953).

49. Sagan, *Biological Exploration*, p. 571.

50. JL interview.

51. Frank B. Salisbury, "Martian Biology," *Science*, Apr. 6, 1962, p. 17.

52. Ponnamperuma's career is detailed in "Ponnamperuma, Cyril (Andrew)," *Current Biography* (1984).

53. RM phone interview, June 1998.

54. Ibid.

55. Ibid.

56. Sullivan, *WANA* (1994 edition), p. 133.

57. Cyril Ponnamperuma, Carl Sagan, and Ruth Mariner, "Synthesis of Adenosine Triphosphate under Possible Primitive Earth Conditions," *Nature*, July 20, 1963, p. 223. Also see Ponnamperuma, Mariner, and Sagan, "Formation of adenosine by ultra-violet irradiation of a solution of adenine and ribose," *Nature*, June 22, 1963, p. 1199.

58. Shklovskii and Sagan, p. 235.

59. Cyril Ponnamperuma, "Life in the Universe," undated article from unidentified anthology (Government Printing Office code number 892–331), p. 69.

60. Ibid. The *Time* cover ran on Apr. 8, 1966.

61. RM interview.

62. Shklovskii and Sagan, p. 238.

63. William L. Laurence, "On Life Elsewhere," *New York Times,* June 23, 1963, p. E-7.

64. Ibid.

65. Shklovskii and Sagan, pp. 313–315.

66. Paul West, *Life with Swan* (1999), p. 85. West declined to be interviewed for this book.

67. RM interview.

68. SM interview.

69. Francis Crick and Leslie Orgel, "Directed Panspermia," *Icarus,* vol. 19, 1973, p. 341. A response by three scientists is in *Icarus,* vol. 21, 513–515, 1974.

70. RM interview.

71. Crosbie Smith and M. Norton Wise, *Energy and Empire: A Biographical Study of Lord Kelvin* (1989), pp. 639–643.

72. Svante Arrhenius, *Worlds in the Making* (1908), chapter 8, especially pp. 220, 226, and 229.

73. Julian Huxley, *Evolution: The Modern Synthesis* (1943). Also see Ernst Mayr, *The Growth of Biological Thought* (1982), chapters 12 and 13.

74. Fred Hoyle and N. C. Wickramasinghe, *Diseases from Space* (1980).

75. A review and critique of the McKay controversy is by Sagan friend and associate Donald Goldsmith, *The Hunt for Life on Mars* (1997).

76. Christopher F. Chyba and Carl Sagan, "Endogenous Production, Exogenous Delivery and Impact-Shock Synthesis of Organic Molecules: An Inventory for the Origins of Life," *Nature,* vol. 355 (1992), pp. 125–132; and Chyba, Paul J. Thomas, Leigh Brookshaw, and Carl Sagan, "Cometary Delivery of Organic Molecules to the Early Earth," vol. 249 (1990), pp. 366–373. Sagan's accomplishments in the study of the origin of life are cited by Stanley Miller in chapter 3, André Brack, ed., *The Molecular Origins of Life* (1998).

77. David Bergamini, "Wax and Wigglers: Life in Space?", *Life,* May 5, 1961, p. 57.

78. Sullivan, *WANA* (1964 edition), p. 121.

79. Sagan's memo on his meeting with Erdtman appears on p. 626 of Harold C. Urey, "Lifelike Forms in Meteorites," *Science,* Aug. 24, 1962, pp. 623–628. Urey responded in letters dated June 6 and July 11, 1962, Urey papers. Also see Sagan to Anders, June 4, 1962, Urey papers. Also see comments by Nagy and others in Edward Anders, "Meteoritic Hydrocarbons and Extraterrestrial Life," *Annals of the New York Academy of Sciences,* vol. 93, Aug. 29, 1962, pp. 649–664.

80. The Anders and Fitch article is cited in Sullivan, *WANA* (1994 edition), pp. 122 ff. Sagan's typewritten copy of his "Interstellar Panspermia" article is in the Muller papers, Lilly Library.

81. Urey to Sagan, Oct. 28, 1968. Urey papers.

82. Burgess proposed the idea for a *Pioneer* message, according to Richard O. Fimmel, William Swindell and Eric Burgess, *Pioneer Odyssey* (NASA, 1977), p. 183. Together, Burgess and freelance writer Richard Hoagland then suggested the idea to Sagan. However, Sagan does not credit Burgess in *CC,* noting only that "my attention was drawn to the possibility of placing a message in a space-age bottle" (p. 18). Frank Drake's essay in *MOE* (p. 56) recognizes Burgess and Hoagland's priority, though. Normally, Sagan was careful to credit others for their contributions; this case represents a puzzling lapse. (Bur-

gess is a respected veteran science writer. Hoagland is nowadays best known for arguing that a geological feature on Mars is a "face" carved by aliens.)

83. CC interview, Mar. 1998.

84. OBT phone interview, June 1998.

85. Carl Sagan and Rich Turco, *APW* (1990), dedication page.

86. Sagan to Menzel, Apr. 13, 1966. Menzel papers, American Philosophical Society, Philadelphia.

87. Phone interview not for attribution, 1998.

88. "PSP," p. 17.

89. CS interview.

90. SC interview.

91. Private communication from Gerry Neugebauer to author.

92. Sagan to L. H. Farinholt (of Alfred P. Sloan Foundation), Dec. 13, 1962. Menzel papers at Harvard University.

93. *National Geographic*, "Mariner . . . ," p. 734.

94. Gerry Neugebauer, Lewis Kaplan, and Stillman Chase, "Mariner II: Preliminary Reports on Measurements of Venus," *Science*, Mar. 8, 1963, p. 905.

95. "Venus says 'No,'" *New York Times*, Feb. 26, 1963, p. 8.

Chapter 7. Mars and Manna

1. Menzel to L. H. Farinholt (of Sloan Foundation), May 7, 1962. Menzel papers at Harvard University.

2. Sagan to Kuiper, Apr. 16, 1963. Kuiper papers.

3. DG Interview.

4. The black-and-white television segment where Sagan talked about Venus appeared in an A&E *Biography* of Sagan that aired shortly after his death. Sagan's first known television appearance to discuss spaceflight was on *CBS Reports*, hosted by Howard K. Smith, in 1961 (Jim Cornell papers).

5. Daniel J. Kevles has argued in *The Physicists* (1977) that cultural and political factors tended to diminish the identity of individual scientists during the cold war. In that sense, Sagan was going against a cold war trend.

6. William J. Broad, "Even in Death, Carl Sagan's Influence Is Still Cosmic," *New York Times*, Dec. 1, 1998, p. D-5.

7. Smithsonian Astrophysical Observatory newsletter, Apr. 1963.

8. Whipple to Sagan, Jan. 16, 1962. Menzel papers at Harvard University.

9. Menzel to Sagan, Feb. 8, 1963. Menzel papers at Harvard University.

10. CS interview.

11. JCo phone interview, June 1998.

12. JP phone interview, Apr. 1998.

13. VS phone interview, June 1998.

14. DL phone interview, Mar. 1998.

15. Carl Sagan and Sidney Coleman, "Spacecraft Sterilization Standards and Contamination of Mars," *Astronautics and Aeronautics*, vol. 3 (1965), pp. 22–27.

16. BK interview, 1998.

17. CS interview.

18. Menzel to Sagan, Jan. 13, 1965. Menzel papers at Harvard University.

19. DG interview.

20. Sagan, "Biological Exploration," p. 575.

21. Edward Clinton Ezell and Linda Neuman Ezell, *On Mars: Exploration of the Red Planet 1958–1978* (1984), p. 80.

22. Ibid.

23. See a short popular account by a famous science writer, Willy Ley, *Mariner IV to Mars* (1966). An official NASA history of Mars exploration, including the *Mariner 4* mission, is Ezell and Ezell (1984).

24. Ezell and Ezell, p. 379.

25. D. G. Rea, Brian O'Leary, and William Sinton, "Mars: The Origin of the 3.58- and 3.69-micron Minima in the Infrared Spectra," *Science*, Mar. 12, 1965, p. 1286.

26. SM interview.

27. Sagan to Urey, Apr. 23, 1964. Urey papers.

28. Urey to Sagan, Aug. 12, 1964, and Sagan to Urey, Sept. 8, 1964. Urey papers.

29. Carl Sagan, "Higher Organisms on Mars," in *Biology and the Exploration of Mars*, edited by Colin S. Pittendrigh et al. (National Academy of Sciences/National Research Council, 1966). This volume includes several articles authored or coauthored by Sagan.

30. Ezell and Ezell, pp. 59–62.

31. Sagan to Salisbury, Feb. 5, 1965. Menzel papers at American Philosophical Society, Philadelphia.

32. Clarke, *Voices from the Sky* (1967), p. 151.

33. Ibid., p. 105.

34. Jerome Agel, *The Making of Kubrick's 2001* (1970): see caption (no page number) in photo section that begins with the words, "Scenes not in 2001 . . ."

35. Vincent LoBrutto, *Stanley Kubrick: A Biography* (1997), p. 265.

36. Isaac Asimov, *Is Anyone There?* (1967 paperback edition), p. 319.

37. The *Times* editorial ran on July 30, 1965, p. 24. Sagan's comments are from CS interview.

38. Carl Sagan and David Wallace, "A Search for Life on Earth at 100 Meter Resolution," *Icarus* (1971), p. 515.

39. Sagan to Abelson, Nov. 30, 1965, Urey papers. In his 1991 interview with Doel, Sagan acknowledged that Abelson's skepticism about Mars life proved closer to the truth than Sagan had expected, so "you have to doff your hat to Phil Abelson."

40. McCurdy, p. 41.

41. GL phone interview, 1998.

42. CS interview.

43. Sagan, *The Planets*, p. 139. In his 1972 interview with Joseph Goodavage, Sagan complained that the editors for *The Planets* had pressured him to give his personal opinions on specific scientific issues rather than a survey of varying points of view. They told him (he recalled), "Don't confuse our readers with alternatives, just tell them what's right!" When Sagan replied that he didn't know which theory was right, they replied, "Well, just pick one!"

44. Carl Sagan, "Mars—A New World to Explore," *National Geographic*, Dec. 1967, p. 820.

45. William Plummer and John Strong, "An Answer to F. D. Drake," *Astrophysical Journal*, vol. 149, Aug. 1967, p. 463. This article is partly a response to Frank Drake, "Improbability of Non-thermal Radio Emission from Venus Water Clouds," *Astrophysical Journal*, vol. 149, Aug. 1967, p. 459.

46. Willard F. Libby, "Ice Caps on Venus," *Science*, Mar. 8, 1968, p. 1097.

47. V. A. Firsoff, *The Interior Planets* (1968), p. 65.

48. Harold J. Morowitz and Carl Sagan, "Life in the Clouds of Venus?", *Nature*, Sept. 16, 1967, p. 1259. Also see Sagan, "Life on the Surface of Venus?", *Nature*, Dec. 23, 1967, p. 1198.

49. Morowitz and Sagan, p. 1259.

50. Sagan, *The Planets*, p. 190.

51. Carl Sagan and E. Salpeter, "Particles, Environments, and Possible Ecologies in the Jovian Atmosphere," *Astrophysical Journal*, 1976, p. 737.

52. *Cosmos*, a thirteen-part television series starring Carl Sagan and produced by KCET-TV of Los Angeles, 1980.

53. Carl Sagan, Tobias C. Owen, and Harlan J. Smith, eds., *Planetary Atmospheres* (1971), p. 126.

54. An entertaining, albeit extreme, statement of this position—the scholarly polar opposite of Sagan's worldview—is the controversial Berkeley philosopher Paul Feyerabend's book *Against Method* (1975). Feyerabend, who died in 1994, questioned science's claims to being the superior route to knowledge. He also denied that its success is due to any consistent formula (e.g., the "falsification" process described by his former teacher, Karl Popper). "Anything goes" is Feyerabend's self-described anarchic philosophy. He writes so amusingly, though, that it is occasionally hard to tell when he is serious and when he is simply striking a pose. See his amiable memoir, *Killing Time* (1995). Feyerabend's work remains controversial: see Deborah A. Redman, *Economics and the Philosophy of Science* (1993), for an extended discussion.

55. Richard Feynman, *Surely You're Joking, Mr. Feynman* (1985).

56. Here Sagan and Pollack erred: Percival Lowell did claim to see linear features on Mercury (and Venus). (He did not claim they were artificial canals, however.) Lowell's observations of Mercury and Venus are described in Hoyt, chapter 8.

57. Carl Sagan and James Pollack, "On the Nature of the Canals of Mars," *Nature*, Oct. 8, 1966.

58. Sagan, *National Geographic*, p. 835.

59. Carl Sagan and Paul Fox, "The Canals of Mars: An Assessment after Mariner 9," *Icarus*, vol. 25, 1975, p. 602.

60. Sagan, "Mars: A New World to Explore," *National Geographic*, p. 835.

61. Rea's article was in *Icarus*, vol. 4 (1965), p. 108.

62. Sagan to Muller, Dec. 2? (date almost illegible), 1955. Muller papers.

63. RPB phone interview, June 1998.

64. Ibid.

65. DL interview.

66. CS interview.

67. RPB interview.

68. JP interview.

69. RPB interview.

70. Ibid.

71. Details of Sagan's grants and affiliations in the mid-1960s are from his Harvard-Smithsonian file, provided courtesy of Jim Cornell.

72. CS interview.

73. Ibid.

74. JH phone interview, Mar. 1998.

75. Kai Bird, *The Color of Truth—McGeorge Bundy and William Bundy: Brothers in Arms* (1998), p. 219. McGeorge Bundy called Raskin "that young menace."

76. LG phone interviews, Feb. 1999.

77. CS interview.

78. AD interview. An afterthought: In his 1991 interview with Doel, Sagan noted in passing that his supervisors offered to let him "recuse" himself on Vietnam War issues and "just worry about nuclear strategic issues." This hints that he might have continued to study nuclear-related issues well into the 1960s, as he had at the Armour Research

Foundation. It might also explain why he had a "Top Secret" Air Force security clearance at least as late as 1965, and possibly later (see Jim Cornell papers). Still, this is strictly speculation pending the declassification of more cold war records. See chapter 6, note 26.

79. VS interview.

80. NS interview.

81. Shklovskii and Sagan, p. 35.

82. Ibid., p. 130.

83. Ibid., p. 40.

84. Ibid., p. 441.

85. Ibid., p. 107.

86. Urey to Sagan, June 29, 1966. Urey papers.

87. Carl Sagan, "The Saucerian Cult," *Saturday Review*, Aug. 6, 1966, p. 50. This excerpt from *Intelligent Life in the Universe* is part of a cover story by John Lear that discusses (among other things) Sagan's ideas.

88. Carl Sagan, "Unidentified Flying Objects," *Bulletin of Atomic Scientists*, June 1967, p. 43. The article is an extract of his essay on UFOs for *Encyclopedia Americana*.

89. Dick, *Biological Universe*, p. 438. According to Dorion Sagan, his father was 6 feet 2 inches tall.

90. FM interview.

91. Cynthia Ozick, "If You Can Read This, You Are Too Far Out," *Esquire*, Jan. 1973, p. 74.

92. Drake and Sobel, p. 100.

93. *CT*, pp. 111–112.

94. Shklovskii (1991), p. 232.

95. FM interview.

96. RB interview.

97. FM interview.

98. DM interview.

99. Kuiper to Bruno Rossi, Mar. 3, 1967. Kuiper papers.

100. E. R. Lippincott, R. V. Eck, Margaret O. Dayhoff, and Carl Sagan, "Thermodynamic Equilibria in Planetary Atmospheres," *Astrophysical Journal*, vol. 147, no. 2, 1967, p. 753.

101. Urey to Bruno Rossi, Mar. 8, 1967. Urey papers.

102. FW phone interview, Mar. 1998.

103. LG interview.

104. Comment not for attribution.

105. CS interview.

106. Urey to Sagan, June 29, 1966. Urey papers.

107. CS interview.

108. Shklovskii and Sagan, p. 176. *On the Nature of the Universe* by Lucretius (d. 55 B.C.) is a famous poetic assertion of the ancient "atomist" philosophy, which maintained that nothing exists save atoms and the void, and that innumerable worlds fill the universe.

109. FW interview.

110. JC interview.

111. Sagan to Kuiper, May 1, 1968. Kuiper papers.

112. CS interview.

113. Ibid.

114. Redman, p. 31.

115. Isaac Asimov, *In Joy Still Felt* (1980), pp. 391 and 457.

116. NS interview.

Chapter 8. Mr. X

1. VS interview.

2. NS interview.

3. DM interview.

4. LG interview.

5. An enjoyable chronicle of current trends in pseudoscience and occultism, written from a skeptical stance, is the journal *Skeptical Inquirer*, published by CSICOP (see p. xix) of Amherst, N.Y. CSICOP activists critique intellectual flim-flams in Kendrick Frazier, ed., *Encounters with the Paranormal: Science, Knowledge, and Belief* (1998). An excellent journal that deserves a wider audience is the Caltech-based magazine *Skeptic* (Pasadena, Calif.). Its publisher is historian of science Michael Shermer, who critiques human gullibility in *Why People Believe Weird Things* (1997).

Sagan helped launch CSICOP in the mid-1970s, and was a patron saint to both journals. After his death, *Skeptical Inquirer* ran so many commentaries from celebrities praising his work that they had to appear in two separate issues. And *Skeptic* ran a dramatic cover painting of Sagan holding a candle to ward off the "demon-haunted darkness" (an allusion to the title of one of his last books). Sagan and CSICOP's war on pseudoscience and ocultism is placed in the larger context of the 20th-century Humanist movement in Weldon, especially chapter 6.

6. See note 55, chapter 7.

7. Carl Sagan, *Cos*, p. 127.

8. CS interview. Frank Drake, by then a radioastronomer at Cornell, also pushed to bring Sagan to Cornell: FD interview.

9. SS phone interviews, May and June 1998.

10. The authoritative history of the steady state vs. big bang debate is Helge Kragh, *Cosmology and Controversy* (1996). Hoyle's pivotal role in discussed in Smoot and Davidson, chapter 4.

11. Gold further expounds on his theories of "a vast subterranean [microbial] habitat and its significance for life's origins on our planet and the possibility of life elsewhere in the universe" in *The Deep Hot Biosphere* (1999). He discusses underground methane in detail, as well.

12. As paraphrased by Henry S. F. Cooper Jr., *The Search for Life on Mars* (1980), p. 60.

13. TG interview, Nov. 1998.

14. Ibid.

15. Ibid. For more details on Gold's theory and its larger scientific context, see Michael Ray Taylor, *Dark Life: Martian Nanobacteria, Rock-Eating Cave Bugs, and Other Extreme Organisms of Inner Earth and Outer Space* (1999), pp. 52–54.

16. TG interview.

17. CS interview.

18. Ibid.

19. Rink's reminiscences appeared in an essay on Sagan that Rink published on the World Wide Web in the 1990s. Grinspoon discussed Sagan's marijuana use in phone interviews with the author (hereafter referred to as LG interview).

20. Ibid.

21. Ibid.

22. Lester Grinspoon, *Marihuana Reconsidered*, p. 111.

23. Ibid.

24. Ibid., p. 113.

25. Ibid., p. 112.

26. Ibid., p. 115.

27. Ibid., p. 116.

28. Ibid., pp. 115–116.

29. SS interview.

30. Marov and Grinspoon, *The Planet Venus* (1998), p. 42.

31. CS interview.

32. *Biology and the Exploration of Mars*, p. 90.

33. Sagan, Tobias C. Owen, and Harlan J. Smith, eds., *Planetary Atmospheres* (1971), p. 126.

34. Ibid., p. 116.

35. Clark R. Chapman, *The Inner Planets* (1977).

36. Kuiper to Sagan, Apr. 23, 1969, Kuiper papers. For details on Cohen's thought, see David A. Hollinger, *Morris R. Cohen and the Scientific Ideal* (1975).

37. Sagan to Kuiper, May 5, 1969, Kuiper papers.

38. N. A. Kozyrev, "Observations of a Volcanic Process on the Moon," *Sky & Telescope*, Feb. 1959, p. 184. Kuiper's response is in the same journal, Apr. 1959, p. 307, and Kozyrev's reply is Aug. 1959, p. 561. See Ronald E. Doel, "The Lunar Volcanism Controversy," *Sky & Telescope*, Oct. 1996, pp. 26–30, and Doel's "Evaluating Soviet Lunar Science in Cold War America," *Osiris*, 2nd series, 1992, pp. 238–264. Sagan's quote is from Colin S. Pittendrigh et al., *Biology and the Exploration of Mars*, p. 93.

39. Don E. Wilhelms, *To a Rocky Moon: A Geologist's History of Lunar Exploration* (1993), pp. 64–65.

40. Isaac Asimov, "The Moon Could Answer the Riddle of Life," *New York Times Sunday Magazine*, July 13, 1969, p. 12.

41. "Is the Earth Safe from Lunar Contaminants?" *Time*, June 12, 1969, p. 78.

42. Ibid. Also, for the scientific controversy over the merits of interplanetary quarantines, see a critical (i.e., anti-Sagan) perspective from Norman Horowitz, R. P. Sharp, and R. W. Davies, "Planetary Contamination I: The Problem and the Agreements," *Science*, Mar. 24, 1967, p. 1501 ff. They argue that quarantine constraints should be eased because *Mariner 4* showed that "Mars is more hostile than had been supposed," and hence less likely to be inhabited. Also see "Report of the COSPAR Panel on Planetary Quarantine, Leningrad, May 1970," *Icarus*, vol. 14, p. 112 (1971).

43. Sagan résumé (dated June 1, 1997), p. 18, which also indicates that Sagan was a "Consultant, Manned Space Flight Center."

44. *Time*, June 12, 1969, p. 78.

45. LG interview.

46. Asimov, *Autobiography* (1980), pp. 493–494.

47. TF interview.

48. NS interview.

49. Quoted in David Nye, *The American Technological Sublime* (1994).

50. CS interview.

51. Henry S. F. Cooper Jr., "A Resonance with Something Alive—II," *New Yorker*, June 28, 1976, p. 47. Second installment of two-part profile of Sagan.

52. TG interview.

53. Brush, *Fruitful Encounters*, p. 216.

54. Urey to Cyril Ponnamperuma, Jan. 6, 1972, Urey papers.

55. Richard H. Hall, *The UFO Evidence* (National Investigations Committee on Aerial Phenomena, 1964).

56. John G. Fuller, *Incident at Exeter* (1966). Also see large photo story on UFOs in *Life* magazine, Apr. 1, 1966, especially p. 29.

57. Ibid.

58. Jerome Clark, *The UFO Book*, p. 476.

59. *U.S. News and World Report*, Apr. 11, 1966, p. 15.

60. A personal note: At age thirteen, I watched the Cronkite show. Cronkite showed incredible footage, filmed by an airline passenger, of a metallic-looking "UFO" outside her window. "That's it," I remember thinking, "UFOs are real!" Then, as Cronkite explained, investigators boarded the same plane and placed a camera by the same window. As it turned out, the "UFO" was a refraction of the airplane's metal wing caused by a warp in the glass. I was shattered, and have been a UFO skeptic ever since.

61. *Project UFO*, produced by Jack Webb (NBC-TV, 1978–79).

62. E. U. Condon, *The Scientific Study of Unidentified Flying Objects* (1969), especially pp. 49 and 542, with brief references to Sagan. A Condon Commission investigator's memoir is Roy Craig, *UFOs: An Insider's View of the Official Quest for Evidence* (University of North Texas Press, 1995), with critical remarks on Sagan on p. 262.

63. John G. Fuller, *The Interrupted Journey* (1966).

64. Joseph Jastrow, *Error and Eccentricity in Human Belief* (1935), p. 153.

65. Sagan to Walter N. Webb, Oct. 2, 1973. I am grateful to Mr. Webb, of Westwood, Mass., for sharing with me his correspondence with Sagan. Sagan's articles on the Hill case appeared in *Astronomy*, volume 3, Nos. 7 and 9 (1975).

66. John Mack, *Abduction: Human Encounters with Aliens* (1994). In the 1980s, Mack collaborated in the antinuclear movement with Sagan. Sagan discusses Mack's UFO views in *DHW*. In my interview with Ann Druyan, she recalled that Carl defended Mack's right to speak his mind although his UFO views were (in her words) "truly reprehensible."

67. Sagan to Webb.

68. PM interview, Apr. 1998.

69. For details on McDonald's suicide, see Philip J. Klass, *UFOs Explained* (1975), and J. Clark (1997). Sagan to Menzel, Apr. 13, 1966. Menzel papers at American Philosophical Society, Philadelphia.

70. Menzel to Sagan, May 2, 1967. Menzel papers at American Philosophical Society, Philadelphia.

71. Sagan to Menzel, May 5, 1967. Menzel papers at American Philosophical Society, Philadelphia.

72. Menzel to Sagan, June 16, 1967. Menzel papers at American Philosophical Society, Philadelphia. This exchange of correspondence occurred shortly after Menzel's public clash with McDonald at a Washington, D.C., convention of the American Society of Newspaper Editors, where they both spoke on Apr. 22, 1967. A United Press International dispatch dated Apr. 23 reported they "clashed sharply."

73. Menzel to Thornton Page, July 12, 1968. Menzel papers from Amherst, N.Y.

74. Sagan testimony, "Symposium on Unidentified Flying Objects," House of Representatives Committee on Science and Astronautics, chaired by Rep. J. Edward Roush, July 29, 1968, pp. 85–98.

75. C. Eugene Emery Jr., "*Dark Skies* Uses Pseudo-Sagan to Recast Astronomer's Motives," *Skeptical Inquirer*, Sept. 1997, p. 20.

76. Menzel to Sagan, Sept. 11, 1968. Menzel papers at American Philosophical Society, Philadelphia.

77. Several 1969 letters from Sagan and Page to Condon, and vice versa, are part of the Thornton Page papers filed at the Center for Inquiry in Amherst, N.Y. I am grateful to Timothy Binga for recovering these letters for me.

78. Clark, *UFO Book*, p. 40.

79. J. Allen Hynek and Jacques Vallee, *The Edge of Reality* (1975).

80. Jacques Vallee, *Forbidden Science* (1996). See pp. 146, 195, 233, 240, 306, and 339.

81. Carl Sagan and Thornton Page, eds., *UFO's: A Scientific Debate* (1972).

82. Ibid., pp. 272–273.

83. LG interview. Grinspoon told the author he no longer accepts this quasi-Freudian theory of UFOs, and in fact is embarrassed to have proposed it.

84. "Flying Saucers Deserve More Investigation, Scientists Say," *Houston Chronicle*, Dec. 28, 1969.

85. Page letters to E. U. Condon, William Liller, Donald Menzel, and Fred Whipple, Dec. 1, 1971, Menzel papers at Harvard University. Possible causes of Sagan's initial failure to win acceptance to the club are discussed in Arden papers, Sept. 16, 1975.

86. *The Air War in Indochina* (with R. Littauer and 17 others, including Sagan), Center for International Studies, Cornell University (1971); issued in a revised edition by Beacon Press of Boston in 1972. Also see R. Littauer et al., "The American Way of Bombing," *Harper's Magazine*, June 1972, pp. 55–58.

87. *CC*, p. 96.

88. Abram Chayes and Jerome B. Wiesner, eds., *ABM: An Evaluation of the Decision to Build an Antiballistic Missile System* (1969).

89. DC interview.

90. The case is discussed in the obituary for Long in *New York Times*, Feb. 11, 1999, p. C-32.

91. NS interview. Nick was born on Sept. 16, 1970.

92. Carl Sagan interview with Joseph Goodavage, late 1972. I am grateful to the late Mr. Goodavage's daughter, Maria Goodavage, for arranging with her mother to share with me this taped interview, which occurred just before Sagan became a full-fledged celebrity. The interview is particularly novel because Goodavage, whose writings appeared in pulp and semi-pulp magazines such as *Saga* and *Argosy*, was an enthusiast for fringe sciences, including astrology. Sagan clashed with Goodavage. A decade later, when Sagan's secretary sent him a memo asking if he wished to appear on a radio show with Goodavage, Sagan wrote with uncharacteristic force: "NO!!" Arden papers.

93. NS interview.

Chapter 9. Gods Like Men

1. Drake and Sobel, pp. 117–120.
2. DS interview, Nov. 1997.
3. CS interview.
4. See chapter 1, note 86.
5. Guthrie (1993).
6. Drake and Sobel, p. 108.
7. Carl Sagan, ed., *Communication with Extraterrestrial Intelligence* (1973), p. xii.
8. Ibid., p. 166.
9. Carl Sagan, *Broca's Brain* (1979), chapter 22. See skeptical reaction in Frank J. Tipler, "Additional Remarks on Extraterrestrial Intelligence," *QJRAS*, vol. 22 (1981), pp. 279–292.
10. Quoted in Frank Tipler, "Additional Remarks on Extraterrestrial Intelligence," *QJRAS* (1981). Sagan's hope for alien salvation had surprisingly deep cultural roots. In *Inventing American Broadcasting 1899–1922* (1987), Susan J. Douglas points out that in the early twentieth century, some viewed the new technological miracle of radio—voices, transmitted invisibly through space!—as putting them in touch with cosmic mysteries. Amusing as it seems now, radio sparked in some people a quasi-religious reaction (which major new technologies often do—for example, see Joseph Corn's *The Winged Gospel* (1983) regarding the cultural impact of early aviation). One rather religious hope was that we might contact aliens wiser than we. For example, in 1920, *Illustrated World* observed

that following such contact, "It is not unreasonable to believe that the whole trend of our thoughts and civilization might change for the better" (Apr. 1920, p. 242). Likewise, the March 13, 1960, *New York Times Magazine* ran an article about SETI by J. B. Edson, who said: "Could it be, perhaps, that our future is their history, that our most pressing problems have answers in the records of countless ancient libraries throughout the universe? If so, how can we make contact with them?" It seems somewhat incongruous, then, to read Edson's short biography at the bottom of the *Times* article: "J. B. Edson is chief missiles adviser to the Assistant Chief of Staff, Intelligence, Department of the Army."

Such indirect links between SETI and the military deserve further exploration by historians of astronomy. Like so much cutting-edge science of the postwar and cold war era, SETI is an indirect spinoff of military funding. Frank Drake—who is both the "father" of modern SETI and the former head of Cornell's Arecibo radiotelescope project in Puerto Rico—told the author how radiotelescope technology in the 1950s and 1960s benefited from hush-hush military concerns. For example, the giant Arecibo radiotelescope (later used as a backdrop in Sagan's film, *Contact*) was originally built with Navy funds to test the theory that the "dish" could track Soviet space satellites, which supposedly left ionized trails as they orbited Earth. After the "trails" proved to be nonexistent, the Navy lost interest and turned Arecibo over to the National Science Foundation and Cornell. Drake also told the author how radioastronomy benefited directly, and SETI indirectly, from technologies originally developed to monitor Soviet radio communications reflected off the Moon and to help submarines locate their positions at sea at all times of day by tracking astronomical radio sources. Further details are in FD interview.

11. Yet we continue to see unhistorical nonsense like this line from Douglas S. Robertson's *The New Renaissance: Computers and the Next Level of Civilization* (1998): "Ramses and Pericles failed to build telegraphs and phonographs only because they lacked the necessary information."

12. *CET*, p. 211.

13. Ibid., p. 355.

14. Ibid., p. 342.

15. Urey to Sagan, Sept. 17, 1973, Urey papers.

16. *CC*, chapter 3.

17. Ibid.

18. *CC*, pp. 25–27.

19. *CC*, pp. 26–27.

20. G. T. Sill, "The Composition of the Ultraviolet Dark Markings on Venus," *Journal of Atmospheric Sciences*, vol. 32 (1975), pp. 1201–1204. Also: Marov and Grinspoon, p. 250.

21. O. B. Toon, "Environments of Earth and Other Worlds," in Yervant Terzian and Elizabeth Bilson, eds., *Carl Sagan's Universe* (1997), p. 56.

22. OBT interview.

23. DM interview.

24. FW interview.

25. BO phone interviews, Apr. 1998.

26. Ibid.

27. DM interview.

28. DC interview.

29. OBT interview.

30. Ibid.

31. Carl Sagan and George Mullen, "Earth and Mars: Evolution of Atmospheres and Surface Temperatures," *Science*, July 7, 1972, pp. 52–56.

32. GM phone interview, May 1998.

33. Sagan and Mullen, p. 55.

34. GM interview.

35. A. Bar-Nun, N. Bar-Nun, S. H. Bauer, and Carl Sagan, "Shock Synthesis of Amino Acids in Simulated Primitive Environments," *Science*, Apr. 24, 1970, p. 470.

36. Carl Sagan and Bishun Khare, "Long-Wavelength UV Photoproduction of Amino Acids on the Primitive Earth," *Science*, July 30, 1971, p. 417.

37. Sagan to Noel Hinners, Jan. 17, 1973. Urey papers.

38. Paul D. Spudis, *The Once and Future Moon* (1996), p. 77.

39. CS interview.

40. Ibid.

41. Ibid.

42. Clark Chapman, James Pollack, and Carl Sagan, "An Analysis of the Mariner-4 Cratering Statistics," *Astronomical Journal*, Oct. 1969, p. 1047.

43. Carl Sagan, "The Long Winter Model of Martian Biology: A Speculation," *Icarus* (1971), p. 511. In a sense, the theory of the Martian "long winter" anticipated, very indirectly, the theory of "nuclear winter" in the 1980s. Each presumed life-threatening freezes triggered by atmospheric feedback effects that were related partly to the particulate composition of the air. A major difference, of course, is that one took millennia to transpire, and the other only days or weeks.

44. Ibid., p. 513.

45. *MAMOM*, p. 24.

46. Paul Raeburn, *Uncovering the Secrets of the Red Planet: Mars* (1998). Also see Ezell and Ezell.

47. *CC*, p. 114; and CSG interview.

48. Sagan and Paul Fox, "The Canals of Mars," *Icarus*, vol. 25, 1975, p. 602.

49. Gerard Kuiper, "Lunar and Planetary Laboratory Studies of Jupiter—II," *Sky & Telescope*, p. 76.

50. Sagan to Kuiper, Feb. 22, 1972. Kuiper papers.

51. For details of the Urey-Kuiper fight, see Doel, *SSA*. Over breakfast in a Mountain View, California, diner, Dale Cruikshank recalled his own troubles with his old mentor, Kuiper. "There was a little bit of a father-son relationship. . . . We had some very good times—years and years when he was very, very supportive and all that—and then toward the end there was a fairly serious breakdown in our relationship."

52. Kuiper quote is in *Time*, Jan. 21, 1974, p. 74. See Sagan's obituary for Kuiper in *Icarus*, vol. 22 (1974), pp. 117–118.

53. Theodore Roszak, *The Making of a Counter Culture* (1969).

54. Dennis Duggan, "A Man Always in Motion," *Newsday*, Mar. 9, 1997.

55. Author's correspondence and interviews with Jerome Agel, 1998. (Hereafter referred to as JA interviews.)

56. JA interviews.

57. Ibid.

58. Ibid.

59. Frederic Golden, "In Memoriam: Recollections of Carl Sagan," *Newsletter of the National Association of Science Writers*, Winter 1996–1997, p. 1.

60. See Roszak; also, Harvey Teres, *Renewing the Left: Politics, Imagination and the New York Intellectuals* (1996).

61. Amory Lovins, *Non-nuclear Futures: The Case for an Ethical Energy Strategy* (1975).

62. Timothy Leary, *Flashbacks: An Autobiography* (1990).

63. Stewart Brand, ed., *Space Colonies* (1977).

64. Robert M. Pirsig, *Zen and the Art of Motorcycle Maintenance* (1974).

65. *CC*, p. viii.

66. Isaac Asimov, *Yours, Isaac Asimov* (1995), edited by Stanley Asimov, p. 61. I am grateful to Nanette Asimov for bringing this collection of her uncle's letters to my attention.

67. *CC*, p. ix.

68. LG interview.

69. JA interviews.

70. *CC*, p. 51, and chapter 1 and pp. 45–46.

71. Quoted in promotional literature for *CC*.

72. "Spaced Out," *Time*, Jan. 21, 1974, p. 74.

73. Edward Edelson, "Star Struck," *Washington Post*, Nov. 25, 1973.

74. *Sky & Telescope*, Sept. 1974, p. 175.

75. Patrick Moore, *Journal of British Astronomical Association* (1974). Quoted in promotional literature for *CC*.

76. *Science*, May 10, 1974, p. 663.

77. *L. A. Free Press*. Quoted in promotional literature for *CC*.

78. *Denver Post*. Quoted in promotional literature for *CC*.

79. Alfred Adler, "Behold the Stars," *Atlantic Monthly*, Oct. 1974, p. 109. Reprinted in Donald Goldsmith, ed., *The Quest for Extraterrestrial Life: A Book of Readings* (1980), p. 224

80. Ibid.

81. *Atlantic Monthly*, Jan. 1975, p. 20.

82. Ian Ridpath, "A Man Whose Time Has Come," *New Scientist*, July 4, 1974, p. 36.

83. *CC*, p. 77.

84. WG phone interview, Mar. 1998.

Chapter 10. The Shadow Line

1. "Carson, Johnny," *Current Biography* (1964 and 1982). Also see detailed profiles of, and commentaries on, Carson in Edward Linn, "The Soft-Sell, Soft-Shell World of Johnny Carson," *Saturday Evening Post*, Dec. 22, 1962; "Johnny Carson, the Prince of Chitchat, Is a Loner," *Look*, Jan. 25, 1966, p. 98; Harriet Van Horne, "Johnny Carson: The Battle for TV's Midnight Millions," *Look*, July 11, 1967, p. 78; Joan Barthel, "Here's Johnny! Out There," *Life*, Jan. 23, 1970, p. 50; "Stranger in the Night," *Newsweek*, May 25, 1992; and "Notes and Comment," *New Yorker*, June 1, 1992, p. 23.

2. Biographical details on Jastrow are in *Current Biography* (1973). Phone interview with Robert Jastrow, Apr. 1998. Sagan's anti-Jastrow letter to the *Times* ran on Dec. 29, 1979, p. 20.

3. A list of all 26 programs on which Sagan appeared from 1973 to 1986 was provided by Helen Sanders of Carson Productions Inc. of Santa Monica, Calif. The database also records the contents of each program and the names of other guests. I am grateful to Ms. Sanders and her associates for sending the printout (plus a videotape of all Sagan's appearances) on behalf of Mr. Carson, who, however, declined to be interviewed for this book.

4. Boyce Rensberger, "Carl Sagan: Obliged to Explain," *New York Times Book Review*, May 29, 1977, p. 8.

5. TF interview.

6. Ibid.

7. Urey to Sagan, Sept. 17, 1973, Urey papers.

8. Sagan to Urey, Oct. 2, 1973, Urey papers.

9. Urey to Dianne Luhmann (University of Chicago Alumni Association), Oct. 7, 1976, Urey papers.

10. JA interview.

11. WG interview.

12. Donald Goldsmith, ed., *Scientists Confront Velikovsky* (1974), with an introduction by Isaac Asimov; especially see Sagan's attack on Velikovsky. (The book does not include the speeches by Velikovsky and his sole scientific backer on the AAAS panel, Irving Michelson. In an interview with the author, Goldsmith said that Velikovsky refused to allow his remarks at the AAAS symposium to appear in this book because he refused to abide by a length limit. When Velikovsky withdrew permission to publish his remarks, Michelson did the same. Also, Morrison did not speak at the symposium; his essay was written afterwards and included in the book, published by Cornell University Press.) Other books on the Velikovsky case include Henry Bauer, *Beyond Velikovsky: The History of a Public Controversy* (1984), which rejects Velikovskian theories but criticizes both sides in the debate. According to Bauer, Sagan "evidences few inhibitions in making sweeping, simplistic generalizations in areas where he is hardly expert." Bauer also notes that historians, philosophers, and sociologists of science "could well take exception" to Sagan's claim, without qualification, that science is "self-correcting." Pro-Velikovsky books include *Velikovsky Reconsidered* (1976), by the editors of the now-defunct journal *Pensée* and Charles Ginenthal's vitriolic *Carl Sagan & Immanuel Velikovsky* (1995). "It has been a deeply saddening experience to discover again and again the crassness of Sagan's work on Velikovsky. It has also been a deeply shocking experience to learn the political nature of the way science operates," Ginenthal says in his 448-page tome, which is published by a Tempe, Ariz., firm that also prints books on topics such as astrology, magic, and voodoo.

An early skeptical account (which Sagan read as a University of Chicago student) of Velikovsky's writings is Gardner (1952, 1957). Profiles of Velikovsky appeared in *Current Biography* (1957) and Gerard H. Wilk, "The Meteoric Velikovsky," *Commentary*, Apr. 1952, p. 380. His obituary ran in the *New York Times*, Nov. 18, 1979, p. 44. The psychoanalyst's access to high circles in Palestine during his pre–World War II stay there is suggested in Norman A. Rose, ed., *The Letters and Papers of Chaim Weizmann*, vol. 19, series A (1968), p. 24. He wrote a number of psychoanalytic papers in the 1930s for *Psychoanalytic Review* (for example, "The Dreams Freud Dreamed," Oct. 1941, p. 487). Also see Robert Jastrow's subsequent essay: "Velikovsky, A Star-Crossed Theoretician of the Cosmos," *New York Times*, Dec. 2, 1979, section IV, p. 22, which criticizes one of Sagan's statistical objections to Velikovskian theory; and Sagan's angry reply in the *New York Times*, Dec. 29, 1979, p. 20.

In my experience, the single richest source of information on the Velikovsky controversy is C. Leroy Ellenberger of St. Louis, Mo. A chemical engineering graduate of Washington University at St. Louis, Ellenberger is a former Velikovsky friend and devotee who eventually split with the Velikovskians (after the psychoanalyst's death) in the belief that his theories lacked scientific credibility. However, for the sake of a balanced record, it is important to note that Ellenberger also harshly criticizes Sagan's remarks at the AAAS symposium: "He never took [Velikovsky] seriously enough to state the [Velikovsky] thesis accurately," Ellenberger told me in a June 1998 phone interview. "Many of [Sagan's] strong arguments are against straw men." While I disagree with Ellenberger's assessment of Sagan, I am grateful to him for generously sharing his extensive personal knowledge of the case and personal reminiscences of Velikovsky, as well as many historical documents dating as far back as the 1940s (hereafter referred to as "Ellenberger papers"). Also, cultural historians interested in the Velikovsky dispute should be aware that Goldsmith, a resident of Berkeley, Calif., has a substantial collection of documents on the AAAS symposium that I lacked time to examine at length.

13. Lloyd Motz, "A Personal Reminiscence," in S. Fred Singer, ed., *The Universe and Its Origin* (1990), pp. 47–56.

14. Popper is discussed in Martin Curd and J. A. Cover, ed., *Philosophy of Science: The Central Issues* (1998), especially parts 1 and 4.

15. Gardner (1952, 1957).

16. James Gilbert, *Redeeming Culture: American Religion in an Age of Science* (1997), p. 197. This rich study of religion's durability and struggles in a scientific and secular age— as manifested by topics as diverse as UFOs, fundamentalism, Deweyan pragmatism, and science fiction—includes details on the AAAS symposia about UFOs and Velikovsky, and Sagan's roles in them.

17. DG interview.

18. Ibid.

19. Donald Goldsmith, *Scientists Confront Velikovsky*, p. 26.

20. DC interview.

21. Robert Gillette, "Velikovsky: AAAS Forum for a Mild Collision," *Science*, Mar. 15, 1974, p. 1059.

22. "Velikovsky and the AAAS: Worlds in Collision," *Science News*, Mar. 2, 1974, p. 132.

23. A useful short history of CSICOP, which also discusses some of the committee's critics, appears in Gordon Stein, *Encyclopedia of the Paranormal* (1996), pp. 168–181; Sagan served on this 859-page book's editorial advisory board. Weldon, chapter 6, situates the formation of CSICOP within the larger context of the twentieth-century Humanist movement "from John Dewey to Carl Sagan."

24. Sagan mainly praises CSICOP in *DHW*, pp. 298–301, arguing that it performs "an important social function." However, he warns that the "chief deficiency I see in the skeptical movement is in its polarization: Us vs. Them—the sense that we [skeptics] have a monopoly on the truth; that those other people who believe in all these stupid doctrines are morons; that if you're sensible, you'll listen to us; and if not, you're beyond redemption. This is unconstructive. It does not get the message across." By contrast, a "compassion" for those excited by pseudoscience "works to make science and the scientific method less off-putting, especially to the young" (p. 300). I am grateful to Timothy Binga of the Center for Inquiry in Amherst, N.Y. (which is connected with CSICOP), for gathering and sharing extensive archival records, including correspondence between Sagan, Thornton Page, Donald Menzel, E. U. Condon, Paul Kurtz, and others. Also, I obtained insights on the early history of CSICOP from phone interviews with Paul Kurtz and Marcello Truzzi.

Ann Druyan gave this writer a letter that Sagan wrote on Apr. 5, 1993, to a CSICOP official, in which Sagan said that there is "some degree of truth" to the "criticism that CSICOP fellows tend to be dismissive, close-mined [sic] and given to ad hominem arguments." Sagan called for a "little constructive soul searching" on the issue.

By way of full disclosure, the author wishes to add that he received CSICOP's Responsibility in Journalism award in 1991 and remains largely admiring of the organization, but is concerned about a small, unsophisticated, and noisy subculture within it that carelessly conflates banal pseudoscience and thought-provoking "Postmodernism" under the vague heading of "irrationalism."

25. "Objections to Astrology," the petition signed by 186 scientists, appears in *The Humanist*, Sept.-Oct. 1975, p. 4. See accompanying essay by Bart Bok, "A Critical Look at Astrology," p. 6. Bok's lifetime war against astrology is described in a biography of him by David H. Levy, *The Man Who Sold the Milky Way* (1993), chapter 15.

Sagan's letter explaining his refusal to sign Bok's petition ran in the Jan.-Feb. 1976 issue of *The Humanist*, p. 2. In it, he makes clear his disbelief in astrology, but says he objected to the petition partly on philosophical grounds. Its opposition to astrology because of the lack of an explanatory mechanism was irrelevant: "No mechanism was known, for example, for continental drift when it was proposed by Wegener. Nevertheless, we see that Wegener was right, and those who objected on the grounds of unavailable mechanism were wrong." This kind of observation hints that Sagan—whose foes often attacked him as scientistic—was, in fact, covertly more sympathetic to the emerging scholarly critique of science in the 1970s (e.g., Thomas Kuhn's) than is generally appreciated. Besides, Sagan continued, such anti-pseudoscience statements "that appear to have an authoritarian tone can do more damage than good. They never convince those who are flirting with pseudoscience but merely seem to confirm their impression that scientists are rigid and closed-minded." By contrast, symposia such as the AAAS debates on UFOs and Velikovsky "can play a useful role, particularly if published, in making alternative views available to youngsters and others who are interested in the subject. . . . What I would have signed is a statement describing and refuting the principal tenets of astrological belief. My belief is that such a statement would have been far more persuasive and would have produced vastly less controversy than the one that was actually circulated."

26. Drake and Sobel, pp. 180–185.

27. Wald's criticisms are discussed in "Panel Agrees That Life Beyond Earth Exists but Differs on Establishing Contact," *New York Times*, Nov. 20, 1972, p. 29. Wald, a Nobel laureate and early theorist on the origin of life, was often outspoken about what he saw as threats to terrestrial biology. See, for example, his letter to *Science* (Oct. 1, 1976, p. 6) about the hazards of research on recombinant DNA. Wald's widow, Prof. Ruth Hubbard of Woods Hole, Mass., reminded the author in a June 2, 1998, letter that Wald had not doubted the existence of aliens: "He took it for granted that such organisms exist if not in our solar system, then surely in some other one or more." However, he "was opposed to trying to locate and communicate with extraterrestrial organisms. . . . As I remember it, he felt that, if these beings were technologically or otherwise ahead of us, it would take the fun and joy out of our own quest if they chose to be generous and let us in on their knowledge." An outspoken political activist, Wald appeared on Richard Nixon's infamous "enemies list": see the *Los Angeles Times*, Dec. 21, 1973, p. 14. Obituaries of Wald are in the *New York Times*, Apr. 14, 1997, p. C-18, and *Nature*, May 22, 1997, p. 356.

Like Wald, Ryle was also a politically active Nobel laureate, especially in the antinuclear movement. For details on his opposition to SETI, see Drake and Sobel, p. 184. See Walter Sullivan, "Astronomer Fears Hostile Attack; Would Keep Life on Earth a Secret," *New York Times*, Nov. 4, 1976, reprinted (along with the *Times's* editorial reply) in Goldsmith (1980), pp. 267–269. An obituary for Ryle is in the *New York Times*, Oct. 17, 1984, p. D-27.

28. The *TV Guide* quote is from the June 1, 1974, issue. Interview with James Cordes, November 1997.

29. Drake and Sobel, pp. 150–151.

30. Interview with Jill Tarter, July 1998. After Sagan's death, when filmmaker Francis Ford Coppola sued the Sagan estate, Tarter was an expert witness for the estate. During my interview with her, she recalled how during the litigation she saw "a transcription of a phone conversation in which Carl said that he absolutely was very disappointed at the M-101 galaxy observation. . . . He said he was surprised to find out how let down he was."

31. Gerrit L. Verschuur, "A Search for Narrow Band 21-cm Wavelength Signals from Ten Nearby Stars," *Icarus* (1973), p. 329. Verschuur's SETI search and subsequent skepticism about SETI is discussed in Drake and Sobel, pp. 140–141. I wish to thank Verschuur for sharing with me a copy of his unpublished memoirs.

32. Shklovskii (1991), chapter 24, discusses SETI but offers little insight into his eventual turn toward skepticism about the topic. However, see p. 19 of Herbert Friedman's Introduction. Also see p. 253, where, in a critique of his younger protégé, the radioastronomer Nikolai Kardashev, Shklovskii accuses him of "adolescent optimism" about SETI, which is "based on faith in human society's unbounded progress and . . . exaggerated emphasis on the radio-technological prospects for extraterrestrial communication, while ignoring both the humanities and biological aspects. To my mind, this is inadmissible. In brief, from the beginning I have been convinced that the problem of extraterrestrial civilizations is in essence and effect complex" (p. 253). A similar criticism might be lodged against Sagan, at least against the SETI advocacy of his early years.

33. Quoted in Dick, *The Biological Universe*, p. 443.

34. Cooper, *Search for Life on Mars*, pp. 74–77.

35. Ibid., p. 66.

36. GEL phone interviews, Feb. 1999.

37. Ezell and Ezell, p. 278. Also see Keay Davidson, "Hess, Seymour Lester," *American National Biography* (1999).

38. Ezell and Ezell, p. 304.

39. Ibid., pp. 320–321.

40. Ibid., pp. 285–286.

41. Ibid., p. 313.

42. Ibid., p. 314.

43. Carl Sagan and Joshua Lederberg, "The Prospects for Life on Mars: A Pre-Viking Assessment," *Icarus*, vol. 28, 1976, p. 291. Sagan discussed the possibility of "largish beasts" on Mars in an op-ed for the *New York Times*, "Said the Martian Microbe . . . ," Feb. 22, 1975, p. 27. Also see his post-Viking essay "Going beyond Viking 1 . . . ," *New York Times*, Aug. 11, 1976, p. 35, where he says: "The possibility of life, even large forms of life, is by no means out of the question."

44. Ezell and Ezell, p. 259.

45. Ibid., p. 330.

46. Ibid., p. 334.

47. Ibid., p. 341. Also see Harold Masursky and Norman L. Crabill, *Viking Site Selection and Certification* (NASA, 1981), p. 15.

48. GEL interview.

49. Ezell and Ezell, p. 403.

50. Sagan, "Going beyond . . ."

51. Ezell and Ezell, p. 410.

52. GL interview.

53. Interview with Norman Horowitz, Apr. 1998.

54. GL interview. Also see his comments in chapter 9 of DiGregorio.

55. *Scientific Results of the Viking Project* (American Geophysical Union, 1977), p. 4472.

56. Ibid., p. 4468.

57. Ibid., p. 4430, and Masursky and Crabill, 29.

58. TF interview.

59. Asimov, *Is Anyone There?* (1967), p. 319.

Chapter 11. *The Dragons of Eden*

1. Arden papers, May 27, 1975.

2. Ibid., July 15, 1975.

3. Ibid., Aug. 5, 1975.

4. Ibid., Sept. 19, 1975.
5. Ibid., Sept. 22, 1975.
6. Ibid., Nov. 14, 1975.
7. Ibid., Dec. 14, 1976.
8. Ibid., Dec. 21, 1976.
9. Ibid., Feb. 9, 1977.
10. Ibid., Nov. 24, 1975.
11. Ibid., Mar. 9 and 17, 1977.
12. Ibid., Sept. 30, 1975.
13. NS interview.
14. Henry S. F. Cooper Jr., "A Resonance with Something Alive," a two-part profile of Sagan, *New Yorker*, June 21 and June 28, 1976 (hereafter referred to as, respectively, 1976a and 1976b).
15. NS interview; and Linda Salzman Sagan essay, chapter 4, in *MOE*, pp. 123-148.
16. SS interview.
17. NS interview.
18. LG interview.
19. *DOE*, p. 71.
20. *DOE*, chapter 3. MacLean's thesis is currently in doubt. Christopher Wills, in *The Runaway Brain* (1993), points out (p. 264) that Sagan, in *DOE*, "popularized [MacLean's] view of the brain as a progressively more sophisticated series of layers, each added on to the previous ones and with the forebrain making up the latest and most sophisticated addition. However . . . new molecular biological evidence indicates that the forebrain may in fact be the oldest part of our brain—and, although the forebrain has undergone enormous changes, the midbrain and the hindbrain have not stood still during our evolution." Even so, MacLean's idea continues to attract sympathetic attention from scholars interested in interactions between science and religion; see James B. Ashbrook and Carol Rausch Albright, *The Humanizing Brain: Where Religion and Neuroscience Meet* (1997).
21. *DOE*, p. 167 ff.
22. Ibid., p. 7.
23. Ibid., p. 35.
24. Ibid., p. 44.
25. Ibid., pp. 147 and 166.
26. Ibid., p. 150. The swastika theory is in *Comet*, chapter 10.
27. Ibid., p. 75.
28. Ibid., p. 68.
29. Ibid., p. 96.
30. Ibid., p. 99.
31. Ibid., p. 156.
32. Ibid., pp. 208–209.
33. Ibid., p. 63.
34. Ibid., p. 64.
35. For Sagan's early attitude toward rock music, see *ILU*, p. 394; and toward modern art, see CSG interview.
36. See critiques of Paley in *Dictionary of Scientific Biography* and in Peter Bowler, *Norton History of the Environmental Sciences*.
37. *DOE*, pp. 193–195.
38. Ibid., p. 245.
39. Ibid., p. 7.
40. Weldon, chapter 5.

41. Sigmund Freud, *Totem and Taboo*, The Standard Edition, James Strachey transl. and ed. (New York: W. W. Norton & Co., 1990). Carl Jung, *Four Archetypes*, G. Adler et al., eds. (Princeton: Princeton University Press, 1970).

42. *DOE*, p. 115.

43. Ibid., p. 127. Research on primate communication fell out of favor by the late 1970s, when researcher Herbert Terrace concluded that the creatures were responding to unconscious physical cues from their human trainers. See Eugene Linden, *Silent Partners: The Legacy of the Ape Language Experiments* (1986).

44. Ibid.

45. Ibid.

46. Urey to Sagan, June 21, 1977, Urey papers.

47. Sagan to Urey, July 23, 1977, Urey papers.

48. John Updike, "Who Wants to Know?" *New Yorker*, Aug. 22, 1977, p. 87.

49. Robert Manning, *Atlantic*, Aug. 1977, p. 91.

50. *Business Week*, Aug. 15, 1977, p. 18.

51. *Village Voice*, Dec. 26, 1977, p. 75.

52. Richard Restak, "The Brain Knew More Than the Genes," *New York Times Book Review*, May 29, 1977, p. 8. Includes a sidebar profiling Sagan by Boyce Rensberger.

53. *American Journal of Physical Anthropology* (1979, volume 50, page 137).

54. *Human Ecology*, Dec. 1978, p. 471.

55. *Human Behavior*, Oct. 1977, p. 80.

Chapter 12. Annie

1. TF interview.

2. Ibid.

3. AD interview.

4. GEL interview.

5. AS interview.

6. AD interview. In an interview with the author, Obst said she sensed that Sagan felt more comfortable with women: "That's why he wanted to become a girlfriend so much. . . . We all became 'girlfriends,' the three of us."

7. Cooper (1976a), p. 44.

8. Deane Rink, "Encounters with Authors: Carl Sagan—Deane Rink," personal essay about Sagan (dated Feb. 29, 1996, and published on World Wide Web). Hereafter referred to as Rink essay.

9. Arden papers, undated memo from July 1979 folder.

10. GEL interview.

11. The images aboard the *Voyager* disc are described and reproduced in *MOE*, pp. 78–121.

12. *MOE*, p. 11.

13. Ibid., p. 66.

14. Ibid., p. 67.

15. Ibid., p. 73.

16. Roger Bingham, "Carl Sagan," *New Scientist*, Jan. 17, 1980, p. 152.

17. *MOE*, p. 13.

18. CG interview.

19. Jon Lomberg, unpublished memoir, part 1, p. 3. I am grateful to Mr. Lomberg, a Hawaiian artist who illustrated many of Sagan's books, for sharing this document.

20. *ILU*, p. 394.

21. TF interview.

22. Interview with Louis Friedman (executive director, The Planetary Society), May 1998.

23. CG interview.

24. TF interview.

25. *MOE*, p. 16.

26. Ibid., p. 18.

27. Ibid., p. 32.

28. Ibid., p. 32.

29. Lomberg, part 1, p. 85.

30. *MOE*, p. 20.

31. Ibid., p. 150.

32. Ibid., p. 151.

33. Ibid., pp. 155–156.

34. Ibid., p. 157.

35. Ibid., p. 133.

36. Ibid., p. 146.

37. Ibid., pp. 32–35.

38. Ibid., p. 75.

39. Ibid., p. 108.

40. Ibid., p. 117.

41. Ibid., preface.

42. AC interview.

43. *MOE*, pp. 75–76.

44. *MOE*, p. 152.

45. Ibid., p. 76.

46. Ibid.

47. Jennifer Terry and Melodie Calvert, eds., *Processed Lives: Gender and Technology in Everyday Life* (1997), p. 208.

48. *MOE*, p. 26.

49. Lomberg, part 1, p. 88.

50. LO interview.

51. Ibid.

52. AD interview.

53. Ibid.

54. *MOE*, p. 41.

55. Ibid., p. 42.

56. Ibid., p. 9.

57. TF interview.

58. LG interview.

59. Phone interview with David Grinspoon, Feb. 1999.

60. LG interview.

61. NS interview.

62. AD interview.

63. LM interview.

64. DS interview.

65. Ibid. In this regard, one of the most fascinating chapters in *SOFA*, coauthored by Sagan and Druyan, is an examination of the ancient Greek myth of Caenis, a young woman whom a god transformed into a male warrior. Sagan and Druyan use the myth to explore the question of gender differences in behavior and how much they might result

from biology (versus social factors). The essay is intriguing primarily for its literary style and daring in linking an ancient myth with modern concerns. Reading it, and reflecting upon Dorion Sagan's remark, one wonders if Sagan and Druyan were also fascinated by the question of what underlying unity might lie beneath their sexual difference.

66. AD interview.

67. DS interview. In June 1999, when the author asked Ann Druyan if she is still a socialist, she replied: "I know I'm not a capitalist. I really don't believe in the long term that capitalism is going to provide the kind of sustainable, humane, democratic society for our planet that we need."

68. NS interview.

69. AD interview.

70. Ibid.

Chapter 13. *Cosmos*

1. *Cos*, p. 4.

2. Roger Bingham, "Carl Sagan," *New Scientist*, Jan. 17, 1980, p. 152.

3. GEL interview.

4. Ibid.

5. Arden papers, Oct. 14, 1975.

6. Various memos from Arden papers, such as Aug. 27, 1975, and Nov. 1976 folder. Also, Cooper (1976a), p. 44.

7. *Cosmos* promotional package sent to news media, developed by Ben Kubasik Inc. I wish to thank Andrew Fraknoi of the Astronomical Society of the Pacific in San Francisco for sharing with me his copy of the promotional package and the rest of his collection of Saganiana. The promotional package is hereafter referred to as "Promotional package," and the rest of the Fraknoi documents as "Fraknoi papers."

8. Bingham, p. 154.

9. Arden papers, Oct. 25, 1976.

10. Ibid., Oct. 31, 1976.

11. GEL interview.

12. Rink essay.

13. *DOE*, pp. 3 and 248.

14. Arden e-mail to author. Arden, now a resident of Cocoa Beach, Fla., declined to be interviewed by phone, but responded at length to my questions via numerous e-mails. I am grateful to her for also sharing copies of voluminous records related to her years with Sagan. She declined to discuss in extensive detail the cause of her ultimate parting from Sagan, which, she says, remains a source of great pain to her.

15. GEL interview.

16. SS interview.

17. Ibid.

18. Ibid.

19. AD interview.

20. GEL interview.

21. Roger Bingham, "Carl Sagan," *New Scientist*, Jan. 17, 1980.

22. GEL interview.

23. A biography of Hypatia is Maria Dzielska, *Hypatia of Alexandria* (Harvard, 1995).

24. SS interview.

25. GEL interview.

26. Ibid.

27. Ibid.

28. Ibid.

29. Bingham, p. 154. Such quotes by Malone could only have worsened his already tense relationship with Sagan. It is worth noting that Bingham was a friend of Malone, according to a Sagan office memo written before Bingham interviewed the astronomer (Arden papers, Oct. 30, 1979).

30. SS interview.

31. Bingham, p. 152. Bingham also observed of Sagan's speech: "His vocal delivery is idiosyncratic to a degree: words he wants to emphasise take on a glutinous quality and seem to emerge with the greatest reluctance. As if they seem to adhere to his vocal apparatus. As Adrian Malone describes it, 'Sagan f-o-o-r-r-m-m-s the w-o-o-r-r-d before you h-e-e-a-a-r it." Such descriptions make one wonder whether Sagan's "glutinous" speaking style was a nervous reaction to his achalasia—that is, whether he literally had as much trouble forcing words out as he had in swallowing food. This is pure speculation on the author's part, however.

32. Arden papers, Feb. 27, 1979.

33. Ibid., May 19, 1979.

34. GEL interview.

35. DGR interview.

36. DG interview. Frederic Golden later wrote in *Time* magazine: "Sagan, a novice at TV production, admits that he ruffled feelings among the TV staff with his constant questioning. . . . Inevitably, there were disagreements, some over scientific accuracy, others involving personality" (*Time*, Oct. 20, 1980, p. 69).

37. GHS phone interview, May 1999.

38. Undated article from 1981 issue of a technical journal, *Electro-Optical Systems Design*; Fraknoi papers. The article includes a photo of a very pleased-looking Sagan, with Ann Druyan and other *Cosmos* collaborators, standing beside the miniature of the library.

39. NS interview.

40. Rink essay.

41. SS interview.

42. Among many examples in the Arden papers, one is a memo urging Sagan to call Sen. Daniel P. Moynihan in hopes of deterring expected huge cuts in the NASA budget that "would cripple Galileo and Space Telescope": Arden papers, Mar. 30, 1979.

43. LO interview.

44. Departmental debates over available space and the future of Sagan's lab at Cornell are cited in Arden papers. Tommy Gold, who told this writer that he had little interest in Sagan and Khare's research on "tholins," was pushing in the late 1970s for more space for other researchers and hoped to take away some of Sagan's. See Arden papers of Jan. 4, June 1, July 16 and 20, and Sept. 7, 1979.

45. The fraternity anecdote was originally related to the author by a high-ranking Cornell official in the 1980s. Some years later, the official said he had since learned the anecdote was probably apocryphal. Still, the anecdote remains a campus "urban legend": during the writing of this book, from 1997 to 1999, more than one former Cornell student or area resident mentioned it to the author and asked if it was true.

Sociologists of urban legends have pointed out that while they are "false," many survive as folklore for decades, in part because they contain grains of truth. (A leading scholar of urban legends is Jan Harold Brunvand of the University of Utah, author of *The Choking Doberman* and related books.) The fraternity anecdote perhaps endured because it reflected some Ithaca residents' gripe that Sagan had "gone Hollywood" and begun cashing in on his fame. Indeed, according to the Arden papers, his usual speaking fee soared from about $2,000 in the mid-1970s to (in at least some cases) $12,000 by the early 1980s. The Arden papers also show how Sagan and a colleague tried to make money in the early

1970s by marketing belt buckles that bore the emblem of the *Pioneer* plaque. And in the early 1980s, The Cosmos Store was an unabashed effort to make money from Sagan's fame.

46. NS interview.

47. Golden (1980), p. 69. In 1993, a district judge sentenced Mitchelson to 30 months in prison for federal tax fraud: see *Los Angeles Times*, Apr. 13, 1993, p. B-5.

48. NS interview.

49. Arden papers, Oct. 27, 1979.

50. GEL interview.

51. Promotional package.

52. Golden (1980), p. 69.

53. SS interview.

54. JM interview, Mar. 1998.

55. EK phone interview, May 1998.

56. *Time* letters page, Nov. 10, 1980.

57. Ibid.

58. *Christian Century*, Jan. 7, 1981, p. 24.

59. WK interview.

60. JP interview. In a related matter, the staff of a leading popular astronomy journal, *Sky & Telescope*, debated whether to give *Cosmos* prominent advance coverage: Arden papers, June 4, 1980. (The magazine finally gave the show four pages of coverage.)

61. DC interview.

62. Golden (1980), p. 65.

63. John J. O'Connor, "*Cosmos:* A Trip into Outer Space," *New York Times*, Sept. 28, 1980, p. 39.

64. SM interview.

65. SS and DG interviews. Also see Glenn Collins, "The Sagans: Fiction and Fact Back to Back," *New York Times*, Sept. 30, 1985, p. B-11, according to which "Dr. Sagan spoke of criticism that he is egotistical and arrogant and said he believed that some of it derived 'from the interminable close-ups [in *Cosmos*] of me looking awed.' . . . He said he opposed the close-ups but that the spaceship notion 'was presented by the producers as a fait accompli.' "

66. SS interview.

67. John J. O'Connor, "Putting 'Cosmos' into Perspective," *New York Times*, Dec. 14, 1980. Also see discussion of Sagan and other science popularization on TV in Richard Zoglin, "Science on TV: How Sharp Is the Focus?" *New York Times*, Apr. 26, 1981, p. 31, section 2.

68. Shirley Arden was the secretary/assistant par excellence. She did not limit her responsibilities to Sagan's academic work. Examples of her nonacademic activities range from scheduling Sagan's haircuts (Arden papers, Dec. 18, 1979) to taking care of his home while he was away working on *Cosmos*; she even personally fixed his garbage disposal unit (June 21, 1979). In addition, she occasionally reminded him of family responsibilities (e.g., a child's birthday) and pushed him to take care of unfinished business, of which there was always a great deal, and one time snapped at him in a memo: "How shall I nag you to do whatever needs to be done for David Grinspoon's *Voyager* internship?" (Mar. 7, 1979). She also alerted Sagan to departmental developments of which he might be unaware while jet-setting around the country and the world—for example, of the need for "Cornell fence-mending" (Apr. 24, 1980), because some campus officials and/or faculty were upset by his long absence on *Cosmos*. During the latter project, Arden warned Sagan that rumors were sweeping the campus that he would delay his return to Ithaca, or perhaps not return at all (Aug. 2, 1979, and Apr. 28, 1980). See note 2, chapter 14.

69. SA interview. *Cosmos* co-creator Geoff Haines-Stiles of Summit, New Jersey, has several boxes of *Cosmos* documents and correspondence.

70. *New York Times*, May 15, 1983, p. 39; *Village Voice*, Dec. 3, 1980, p. 56.

71. Unsigned review, *New Yorker*, Nov. 24, 1980, p. 210.

72. *Sky & Telescope*, June 1981, pp. 536–537. Of Sagan's errors, DeVorkin says: "Would you believe that Harlow Shapley was engaged in his famous studies in galactic structure while a resident of Missouri? . . . Or that Immanuel Kant and Thomas Wright viewed spiral nebulae through telescopes in the 18th century?" (p. 537). Another semi-hostile review of the book was by John Gribbin in the British journal *New Scientist* (May 14, 1981, p. 434), who called it "conventional, worthy and dull, . . . breathless gee-whizzery, except notably in the chapter on Mars. . . . He is not, in fact, an outstanding writer, despite the plaudits he has received over the water." Gribbin also complained about technical errors and added: "It looks as if someone was in a hurry to finish the project, having dallied too long and self-indulgently over the historical material."

Sky & Telescope ran a four-page article on the making of *Cosmos* in Sept. 1980, pp. 191–194. *Cosmos* is still available in videotaped form (although difficult to obtain as of 1999 from the show's present owner, Turner Inc., reportedly because of disputes over royalties). The episodes are summarized briefly as follows:

"The Shores of the Cosmic Ocean" (aired Sept. 28, 1980). A tour of the cosmos; a visit to the library at Alexandria, "where Eratosthenes first measured the size of the Earth"; and a display of the "cosmic calendar" that shows how humanity occupies a tiny fraction of time compared to the age of the whole universe.

"One Voice in the Cosmic Fugue" (Oct. 5). The origin of life; the nature of evolution; possible life forms in the atmosphere of a Jovian planet.

"The Harmony of Worlds" (Oct. 12). The life of seventeenth-century astronomer Johannes Kepler, who "wrote the first science-fiction novel" and discovered how solar system objects move in elliptical orbits, thereby clarifying a crucial error in Copernicus's new cosmology.

"Heaven and Hell" (Oct. 19). A giant object (a large meteor or small comet or asteroid) hits remote Siberia in 1908. Sagan favors the comet hypothesis. He discusses the role of impact events in solar system history, and disproves the pseudoscientific claims of Immanuel Velikovsky. A visit to the planet Venus, which is hellishly hot and reminds us of the value of preserving our own planet's ecosystem.

"Blues for a Red Planet" (Oct. 26). A history of the human fascination with the planet Mars, including the career of Percival Lowell, champion of the Martian canals; H. G. Wells's novel *The War of the Worlds;* pioneer rocketeer Robert Goddard; and the *Viking* probes that landed on Mars in 1976.

"Travellers' Tales" (Nov. 2). How seventeenth-century Holland briefly dominated the seas; and Dutch scientist Christiaan Huygens studied Saturn, its rings and its largest moon, Titan. Life forms might inhabit Titan. A depiction of the *Voyager* spaceship as it exits the solar system and enters the Milky Way galaxy.

"The Backbone of Night" (Nov. 9). Sagan returns to his Brooklyn, New York, elementary school to discuss astronomy with its present pupils. How ancient thinkers discovered scientific reasoning and the true structure of the cosmos.

"Travels in Space and Time" (Nov. 16). Thanks to Einstein's "time dilation," future astronauts who travel at a significant fraction of the speed of light could "journey within a single lifetime to the center of the galaxy, and even to other galaxies. They will return, however, to an Earth millions of years older than the one they left," in the words of the *Cosmos* promotional package.

"The Lives of Stars" (Nov. 23). The evolution of stars, including supernovae, which "make cosmic rays which produce mutations in the genes of organisms on Earth. In the deepest sense, the origin, evolution, and fate of life on our planet is connected with the evolution of the cosmos."

"The Edge of Forever" (Nov. 30). The expanding universe; the Hindu theory of a cyclical cosmos; a visit to a black hole; and a tour of the Very Large Array in New Mexico, where 27 radiotelescopes survey the heavens and astronomers try to determine whether the cosmos will expand forever or eventually collapse back upon itself.

"The Persistence of Memory" (Dec. 7). The marvels of the human brain. Are other terrestrial creatures intelligent? Sagan tries to find out by examining the great whales.

"Encyclopaedia Galactica" (Dec.14). Do UFOs exist? Sagan explains why he sees no evidence that aliens have visited Earth. The possibility of communicating with aliens by radio.

"Who Speaks for Earth?" (Dec. 21). In the final episode, Sagan discusses the question of whether humanity will survive or destroy itself.

73. TG interview.

74. *Technology Review*, Aug. 1981, p. 19.

75. Gerald Holton, "Johannes Kepler's Universe: Its Physics and Metaphysics," in Robert M. Palter, ed., *Toward Modern Science* (1969), p. 460.

76. The best-known portrait of Kepler that respects, rather than scorns, his mystical leanings appears in Arthur Koestler's *The Sleepwalkers* (1963). Koestler, a fierce anti-reductionist who during his career migrated from Marxism to parapsychology, depicted Kepler as a scientist whose insights owed much to artistic or mystical inspiration, as well as to technical savvy. Koestler's book likely influenced Sagan's sympathetic portrait of Kepler in *Cosmos*. The bibliography of *Cosmos* recommends *Sleepwalkers* for further reading. Also, Steven Soter told me that he relied on *Sleepwalkers* in helping to script the television segment on Kepler.

77. Carl Sagan and Ann Druyan, *Comet* (1985), chapter 3. Another example of a Sagan "covert autobiography" appears in the couple's captivating portrait of Charles Darwin in *Shadows of Forgotten Ancestors*. Sagan was a fledgling animal rights theorist; not surprisingly, then, the book noted how young Darwin's sister "convinced him that it would be immoral to take a beetle's life merely for collecting." It also pointed out how Darwin's teacher Rev. John Steven Henslow (like Sagan dealing with questions about UFOs and Velikovsky) "exhibited an exceptional sensitivity to the feelings of his students. The novice's 'foolish' question was answered with respect"; and how Darwin (like young Sagan, the civil rights activist) was, by the standards of his day, a true liberal repelled by slavery, and said so.

78. AD interview. Timothy Ferris, by contrast, believes Sagan was an atheist, and adds this skeptical assessment of the astronomer's understanding of religion: "I felt that Carl, like most scientists that I know, did not adequately understand the religious issues that he sometimes addressed. Carl's reports of his encounters for instance with Buddhist thinkers struck me as kind of amusing, really. He told me twice the story about a Zen master who he had gotten to admit that if this master had a belief that was disproved by empirical proof [then] he would abandon it. This struck me as just so callow a way to spend your time with a Zen master, you know? It shows no understanding of what a Zen master does in the world or who he is."

79. AD interview.

80. David Paul Rebovich, "Sagan's Metaphysical Parable," *Social Science and Modern Society*, July 1981, pp. 91–95.

81. Walker Percy, *Lost in the Cosmos* (1983), pp. 173 and 201.

82. Jeffrey Marsh, "The Universe and Dr. Sagan," *Commentary*, May 1981, pp. 64–68.

83. *Astronomy*, Oct. 1991, p. 104.

84. SS interview.

85. GEL interview.

Chapter 14. *Contact*

1. PH interview.

2. Peter Manso, *Brando* (1996), p. 862.

3. Arden papers, Jan. 26, 1981. During a 1997 interview with the author, however, Terzian described Sagan in extremely glowing terms. Terzian also co-edited *Carl Sagan's Universe* (1997), a collection of speeches about Sagan's career.

4. Edwin McDowell, "Sagan Sells First Novel to Simon & Schuster," *New York Times*, Jan. 13, 1981, p. C-16. The "intense feelings" quote is from SPM interview, late 1997. The McDowell article offers valuable insights into how wealthy Sagan's writings had made him by the early 1980s, and how thoroughly entangled he was in deal-making of the most lucrative and complex sort. The article notes that Sagan negotiated the $2 million contract with Simon & Schuster "to the chagrin of his current publisher, Random House." The proposal for *Contact* was 115 pages long and "hand-delivered to officials of nine publishing houses Dec. 5, 1980," followed by an auction. Simon & Schuster won the auction after other publishers were told by Mr. Sagan's agent that the four-book contract the author signed with Random House in 1976 applied only to works of nonfiction. Sagan's agent was Scott Meredith, whose interpretation of the contract was seconded by his and Sagan's attorney, Charles Rembar. A Random House official was quoted as disagreeing with the interpretation of the contract "but we chose not to argue it." The *Times* article adds: "One well-placed publishing source said Random House probably felt that, even if it won in the courts, the fight could seriously erode relations with Mr. Sagan, a valuable literary resource."

The article also noted that by that time, *The Dragons of Eden*—the first book written under the $250,000, four-book deal—had "sold 200,000 copies in hard-cover and more than one million in paperback." As for *Cosmos*, Random House had 395,000 copies in print by that time, had ordered more printings, and "demand is so brisk that . . . it is trying to borrow copies from England and book clubs." In short, it is obvious, based on such evidence, why Sagan's rapidly accumulating wealth would stir "intense feelings"—i.e., intense jealousy—among his colleagues.

5. William J. Broad, "A Star Fades for Entrepreneur Sagan," *Science*, Jan. 8, 1982, p. 149.

6. NS interview.

7. *Starman*, directed by John Carpenter (1984). The "starman" was played by Jeff Bridges, and the Saganish scientist by Charles Martin Smith.

8. *Real Genius*, directed by Martha Coolidge (1985). The evil scientist was played by William Atherton.

9. Carl Sagan, *BiBi* (1997), p. 4.

10. PV interview.

11. Ibid.

12. Arden papers, Oct. 19, 1978.

13. FD interview.

14. CG interview.

15. AD interview.

16. Ibid.

17. LO interview.

18. LG interview. Alexandra ("Sasha") Rachel Druyan Sagan was born on Nov. 7, 1982, at Beth Israel Hospital in Boston.

19. LM interview.

20. *Project Cyclops: A Design Study of a System for Detecting Extraterrestrial Intelligent Life* (NASA, undated but probably 1972–73). A 243-page proposal for a novel SETI project; based on a 1971 summer study at Stanford co-directed by Bernard M. Oliver and John Billingham.

21. Norman Cousins, "The Ultimate in Communication," *Saturday Review*, Nov. 30, 1974, p. 4. To put this utopian article in the context of that gloomy time in American history (Watergate, oil crises, etc.), also see Cousins's article two weeks later in the same magazine: Norman Cousins, "Hope and Practical Realities," Dec. 14, 1974, p. 4. The same issue includes visionary articles on the future of space colonies, hydroponics, etc. Also see Cousins's article "Have We Anything to Learn from Other Planets?" (his answer is yes), *Saturday Review*, Jan. 11, 1975, p. 4.

22. Michael Hart, "An Explanation for the Absence of Extraterrestrials on Earth," *QJRAS*, vol. 16 (1975), p. 128. Reprinted in Goldsmith (1980), p. 228.

23. Gerard K. O'Neill, *The High Frontier* (1977), which should not be confused with a militaristic space book of the same name, written in the 1980s by retired U.S. general Daniel Graham. The inverse correlation between enthusiasm for SETI and enthusiasm for space colonies is revealed by Drake's remark that he and O'Neill "eventually parted company . . . when he predicted that in the future his colonies would expand into space until they literally infiltrated the Galaxy in a period of less than a million years" (Drake and Sobel, p. 128). If O'Neill was right, then why haven't aliens—if they exist—visited us in their own space colony–like ships? O'Neill's answer, of course, was that intelligent aliens probably don't exist: hence the galaxy is ours to settle on our own, uninhibited by "natives" on other worlds. It was the old "Fermi paradox" again, but in updated form.

A far more technical study of the feasibility of space colonies is Gerard K. O'Neill, ed., *Space Resources and Space Settlements* (1979, NASA publication SP-428). Space colonies and related extraterrestrial development are scrutinized from an environmentalist perspective in Eugene C. Hargrove, ed., *Beyond Spaceship Earth: Environmental Ethics and the Solar System* (Sierra Club Books, 1986). O'Neill died at age 65 in 1992.

24. SS interview.

25. Tipler's primary papers on SETI appeared in the *QJRAS* and include "Extraterrestrial Intelligent Beings Do Not Exist" (1980), p. 267; "A Brief History of the Extraterrestrial Life Concept," (1981), p. 133; and "Additional Remarks on Extraterrestrial Intelligence," (1981), p. 279. Sagan's response to Tipler (written with William I. Newman) is "The Solipsist Approach to Extraterrestrial Intelligence," *QJRAS* (1983), p. 113. Also see Tipler's article in the April 1981 *Physics Today*, with responses by Frank Drake (June 1982), p. 9 and general readers (Mar. 1982), p. 26. Since then, the *QJRAS* has run numerous articles examining different aspects of Tipler's argument or related views.

Since the 1980s, Tipler's speculations have branched into religion. In his book *The Physics of Immortality*, he argued that cosmological theory proves that God exists and that all humans who have ever existed will eventually be resurrected. The publication of this book may explain why SETI advocates no longer seem to regard Tipler as a major threat to their work.

26. Proxmire was anti-SETI before Tipler, however. The senator first attacked SETI in 1978, awarding it his "Golden Fleece," and succeeded in having NASA's $2 million

request for the project (with a projected cost of $15 million over seven years) stricken from the fiscal year 1979 appropriations bill. In July 1981, Proxmire learned that the project "has been continued at a subsistence level" in the exobiology division of the space agency, "despite our decision to delete these funds 3 years ago." Proxmire asked the Congress to pass an amendment specifically prohibiting "this ridiculous waste of the taxpayer's dollars"; he cited among his reasons Tipler's argument that if extraterrestrials exist, they would have visited our solar system by now. Proxmire's amendment passed. Details are in *Congressional Record*, July 30, 1981, p. 18635. Drake's memories of the fight with Proxmire are in Drake and Sobel, chapter 9, with references to Sagan's role in saving the SETI funding on pp. 195–196.

27. AD interview.

28. The Planetary Society is based in Pasadena, Calif. Its magazine, *Planetary Report*, is an excellent, well-illustrated guide to present and pending robotic planetary missions.

29. Joseph McBride, *Steven Spielberg: A Biography* (1997), p. 265. Also see Drake and Sobel, pp. 198 and 219.

30. Lomberg memoir, part 2, p. 21. A biographical sketch of Merril is in Clute and Nicholls, pp. 799–800.

31. *The Plain Truth*, Nov.–Dec., 1983.

32. AD interview.

33. Sinclair Lewis, *Arrowsmith* (1925). The novel received the 1926 Pulitzer Prize, but Lewis declined the honor. Seaborg (1912–1999) described his admiration for the book in an essay published on the World Wide Web by his employer, Lawrence Berkeley National Laboratory in Berkeley, Calif., at the time of his death.

Ellie Arroway is in "good part . . . based on Annie," who helped him plot *Contact*, Sagan told Glenn Collins for a *New York Times* article, Sept. 30, 1985, p. B-11. She is also arguably one of the most progressive heroines of modern science fiction, at least in books written by males. (Contrast her with, say, the Playboy bunny–types who populate the later writings of, say, Robert Heinlein, as in his 1970 novel *I Will Fear No Evil*.) Relevant studies include three articles from *Extrapolation*, a scholarly journal of science-fiction studies: Mary Kenny Badami, "A Feminist Critique of Science Fiction," Dec. 1976, pp. 6–19; George Fergus, "A Checklist of SF Novels with Female Protagonists," same issue, pp. 20–27; and Carolyn Wendell, "The Alien Species: A Study of Women Characters in the Nebula Award Winners, 1965–1973," Winter 1979, pp. 343–354. Also see Sarah Lefanu, *Feminism and Science Fiction* (1989); and Clute and Nicholls, "Women as Portrayed in Science Fiction," pp. 1342–1344, and "Feminism," pp. 424–425.

34. *Time*, Oct. 28, 1985.

35. *Antioch Review*, Spring 1986, p. 251.

36. Robert Royal, "Carl Sagan in Space," *American Spectator*, June 1986, p. 29.

37. *CT*, p. 430.

38. FD interview.

39. Freeman Dyson, *Weapons and Hope* (1984), p. 180.

40. Shklovskii, *Five Billion Vodka Bottles to the Moon: Tales of a Soviet Scientist* (1991), p. 19 (Friedman introduction).

Chapter 15. The Value of *L*

1. Observation by the author at the Case for Mars conference in Boulder, Colo., summer 1987.

2. See various Arden papers: for example, May 4, 1979, and memo detailing agenda for his June 5, 1979, visit to the White House for a meeting with President Carter and

his staff regarding the Strategic Arms Limitation Agreement (latter memo is inserted in folder for June 1979).

3. Douglas Brinkley, *The Unfinished Presidency* (1998), p. 32.

4. CG interview.

5. LG interview.

6. CG interview. Also, see Arden papers, Aug. 4, 1978, re Sagan and Druyan sending flowers to Sagan's sister, Cari Sagan Greene.

7. Phone interview with Sharon Greene, June 1998. I am grateful to Ms. Greene for sharing a copy of her uncle's letter.

8. NS interview.

9. AD interview.

10. Arden's reminiscences are from SA interview. Also: Asimov, *Yours, Isaac Asimov* (1995), p. 294.

11. H. Bruce Franklin, *War Stars: The Superweapon and the American Imagination* (1988), p. 202.

12. Allan M. Winkler, *Life under a Cloud* (1993), p. 205.

13. AD interview.

14. Ibid.

15. DM interview.

16. Kaplan, *The Wizards of Armageddon* (1983).

17. The statement was made to Sagan (RT interview).

18. Colin S. Gray and Keith Payne, "Victory Is Possible," *Foreign Policy*, Summer 1980, pp. 20–21.

19. Kahn, p. 23.

20. An authoritative discussion of the prehistory of Einstein's ideas (as well as his own life and brilliance) is Abraham Pais, *"Subtle is the Lord . . .": The Science and the Life of Albert Einstein* (1982), particularly pp. 60–69 and 119–129.

21. Of those who anticipated (with widely varying degrees of clarity) Charles Darwin's theory of evolution, Alfred Russel Wallace has received the lion's share of scholarly attention; but there were others, far less able and sometimes muddle-headed, who still deserve recognition as distant predecessors. See Janet Browne, *Charles Darwin* (1995), p. 52.

22. Golitsyn's work is discussed in detail in *APW*, pp. 38–39, 370, and 382. Sagan and Turco note that Golitsyn and colleagues were inspired partly by the discovery of "weather records that reveal [significant] temperature drops following the great Siberian forest fires of August 1915," when some regions turned as dark as night (*APW*, p. 38). Golitsyn visited the United States in the 1970s and was on friendly terms with Sagan: Arden papers, Sept. 1, 1978.

23. Carl Sagan, O. B. Toon, and James Pollack, "Anthropogenic Albedo Changes and the Earth's Climate," *Science*, Dec. 21, 1979, p. 1363.

24. Luis W. Alvarez, Walter Alvarez, Frank Asaro, and Helen V. Michel, "Extraterrestrial Cause for the Cretaceous-Tertiary Extinction," *Science*, June 6, 1980, pp. 1095–1108.

25. Phone interview with Gerald R. North, Mar. 1998.

26. TPA interview.

27. RPB interview.

28. DC interview.

29. DM interview.

30. RT interview.

31. Interview with Donald J. Hunten, early 1998.

32. RPB interview.

33. TPA interview.

34. Ibid.

35. TPA and OBT interviews.

36. See article by Paul Crutzen and John Birks, "Twilight at Noon: The Atmosphere after a Nuclear War," *Ambio* (Swedish Academy of Sciences), vol. 11 (1982), pp. 114–125.

37. TPA interview.

38. The phrase comes from the title of a book about a postnuclear ecological catastrophe: Paul R. Ehrlich, Carl Sagan, Donald Kennedy, and Walter Orr Roberts, eds., *The Cold and the Dark: The World after Nuclear War* (1984).

39. TPA interview.

40. RT interview.

41. TPA interview.

42. References to Syvertson's research appear throughout Edwin P. Hartman, *Adventures in Research: A History of Ames Research Center 1940–1965* (NASA, 1970). I am grateful to Ruth Mariner for lending me her copy of this book.

43. TPA interview.

44. Ibid.

45. Arden papers, Nov. 28, 1978.

46. RT and OBT interviews.

47. TPA interview.

48. OBT interview.

49. TPA interview.

50. FD interview. Also see Drake and Sobel, pp. 105–106, which describes how Soviet radioastronomer Yury Pariisky approached Drake and Sagan in 1973 while they were visiting Leningrad for a scientific meeting, and suggested "we take a walk together. . . . Pariisky said he'd detected extraterrestrial signals that seemed to be of intelligent origin. . . . Over the next several weeks, Carl was able to confirm the existence of a gigantic American reconnaissance satellite called Big Bird. Its orbital period exactly matched the pattern of signal appearance and disappearance Pariisky was describing." During our interview, Drake said "I really don't know" how Sagan was able to determine that Pariisky's signal came from the satellite. A history of the Big Bird or KH-9 (Keyhole) surveillance satellite program is in William E. Burrows, *Deep Black* (1986), chapter 10, and in Jeffrey Richelson, *American Espionage and the Soviet Target* (1987), pp. 228–232.

51. Sagan was visited by CIA representatives for unrecorded reasons in early 1980. A "Mr. Caffrey" who was "chief" of the "local bureau C.I.A." called on Feb. 27, 1980, to say that he and a Dr. Kit Green wanted to meet with Sagan the next morning "at your convenience" (Arden papers, Feb. 27, 1980). The meeting was scheduled for 9:30 A.M. and "I have notified security of their arrival," Arden alerted Sagan in a memo the same day.

Conspiracy buffs should not overinterpret such contacts between Sagan and U.S. intelligence services. Sagan frequently traveled abroad and had excellent scientific contacts within the Soviet Union, and it was not unusual during the cold war for scientists returning from foreign trips to share their observations with CIA representatives. Likewise, Gerard Kuiper, Sagan's doctoral mentor, had a well-established relationship with the CIA (Ronald E. Doel, private communication). It would not have been out of character for Sagan to chat with CIA representatives; despite his left-leaning politics and oft-expressed contempt for the United States' "national security" apparatus, he was by no means pro-Soviet (as Ann Druyan emphasized during an interview with the author). Such "human intelligence" (HUMINT, in espionage lingo) remains an invaluable source of information (often more valuable than surveillance satellites and other high-tech forms of espionage) about developments in other nations; see Jeffrey Richelson on HUMINT, in *American Espionage and the Soviet Target* (1987), pp. 42–72.

The NSA references appear in Arden papers of Feb. 16, Mar. 23, and Mar. 29, 1977. Sagan briefly mentioned having addressed the NSA in his confidential 1991 interview with Doel. Despite his attitude toward militarism, Sagan occasionally addressed military groups such as the U.S. Military Academy at West Point (1981) and the Air Force Academy at Colorado Springs (1983), according to his résumé.

52. Arden papers, Mar. 29, 1977.

53. James Bamford, *The Puzzle Palace* (1982), pp. 155–156.

54. The number of documents awaiting declassification is staggering. The U.S. government is struggling to develop computerized ways to hasten declassification, so far with less than satisfactory results: see Keay Davidson, "Race against Clock Imperils War Secrets," *San Francisco Examiner*, June 22, 1997, p. A-4.

55. Constance Holden, "Scientists Describe 'Nuclear Winter,'" *Science*, Nov. 18, 1983, p. 822.

56. William D. Carey, "A Run Worth Making," *Science*, Dec. 23, 1983, on editorial page.

57. Carl Sagan, "Nuclear War and Climatic Catastrophe: Some Policy Implications," *Foreign Affairs*, Winter 1983–84, p. 257. Also see "Editor's Note" at beginning of magazine. Readers' responses appear in the Fall 1986 issue.

To fully appreciate the courage and energy of Sagan's antinuclear activism, compare it with that of Albert Einstein. Sagan threw himself into the antinuclear movement with full strength, organizing conferences, writing articles, campaigning on television, and getting arrested in the desert. By contrast, Einstein's celebrated pacifism during World War I, while living in Germany, in reality "remained one more of creed than of deed. . . . In fact, from the available historiographical reports on the peace movement during World War I, Einstein emerges as a marginal figure, outstanding not for his activism but for his moral integrity," Hubert Goenner and Giuseppe Castagnetti assert in a reassessment of the great physicist's politics. See their article, "Albert Einstein as Pacifist and Democrat during World War I," *Science in Context*, vol. 9 (1996), pp. 325–386.

58. *War Games* (1983), directed by John Badham.

59. Lewis Thomas, "Nuclear Winter, Again," *Discover*, Oct. 1984, p. 57. Also see his previous article, "TTAPS for the Earth," *Discover*, Feb. 1984, p. 30.

60. Thomas Powers, "Nuclear Winter and Nuclear Strategy," *Atlantic Monthly*, Nov. 1984, pp. 53, 64.

61. Phone interview with Joseph N. Cirincione, Oct. 1997.

62. Sheldon Ungar, *The Rise and Fall of Nuclearism* (1992), pp. 28, 175.

63. I am grateful to Prof. Lawrence Wittner of Rutgers University, a leading authority on the history of the peace movement, for sharing this and other documents related to "nuclear winter" (hereafter referred to as Wittner papers). The strategy paper is filed in Box 17, Nuclear Weapons Freeze Campaign Records, Western Historical Manuscript Collection, Thomas Jefferson Library, University of Missouri at St. Louis.

64. Wittner papers. The "dispirit" comment is from the Mar. 3, 1984, minutes of the CND Executive Committee.

65. "Reichstag Fire II," *National Review*, Dec. 19, 1986, p. 19.

66. Sagan exacted a humorous revenge on Buckley in *DHW*, where Sagan referred to a particularly slow-witted limo driver of his acquaintance with the pseudonym of "William F. Buckley" (*DHW*, p. 3). Buckley's sometimes brutal prose reflected his political background in the 1950s, when he was a prominent defender of Red-baiter Sen. Joseph McCarthy; see William F. Buckley Jr. and L. Brent Bozell, *McCarthy and His Enemies* (1954, reprinted 1995). Buckley's importance in reviving the modern American right wing is discussed in Sara Diamond, *Roads to Dominion: Right-Wing Movements and Political Power in the United States* (1995).

67. Brad Sparks, "Flat-Earth Sagan Falls Off the End of the World," *National Review*, Nov. 15, 1985. For reader responses, see issue of Jan. 31, 1986, p. 4. By way of full disclosure, the author is personally friendly with Sparks, while strongly disagreeing with his views on Sagan and UFOs.

68. Ibid., p. 32. Also see Freeman Dyson, *Infinite in All Directions* (1988).

69. Quoted in Tony Rothman, "A Memoir of Nuclear Winter," chapter 5 in *Science à la Mode: Physical Fashions and Fictions* (1989), pp. 135–136.

70. Dyson, *Infinite in All Directions* (1988), pp. 262–264.

71. Ibid., pp. 258–263.

72. Buckley anecdote is from AD interview. Buckley did not respond to this writer's request for comment. A critique of a nuclear winter debate (including Sagan) on Ted Koppel's television show, *Nightline*, as an example of the poverty of modern public discourse is in Neil Postman, *Amusing Ourselves to Death—Public Discourse in the Age of Show Business* (1985), pp. 89–91, which depicts Sagan somewhat wryly as "the logical scientist speaking in behalf of the planet. It is to be doubted that Paul Newman could have done better in the role, although Leonard Nimoy might have." Postman says Sagan "made, in my opinion, the most coherent statement—a four-minute rationale for a nuclear [weapons] freeze—but it contained at least two questionable assumptions and was not carefully examined," apparently because the television network allotted so little time for serious scrutiny of this complex issue.

73. The Teller-Pauling debate was aired on KQED-TV in San Francisco, which retains a film of their confrontation.

74. Keay Davidson, "The Man behind the Bomb," *San Francisco Examiner Sunday Magazine*, Aug. 30, 1998, p. 6.

75. Stanley A. Blumberg and Louis G. Panos, *Edward Teller: Giant of the Golden Age of Physics* (1990), p. 162. Short biographies of Teller appeared in the 1954 and 1983 *Current Biography*.

76. See two books by William J. Broad that deal with nuclear weapons debates of the 1980s, and especially Teller's role: *Star Warriors* (1985) and *Teller's War* (1988). Clinton's birthday letter to Teller is in *Science and Technology Review* (Lawrence Livermore National Laboratory), July 1998, p. 3.

77. Blumberg and Panos, p. 177.

78. Edward Teller, "Widespread After-Effects of Nuclear War," *Nature*, Aug. 23, 1984, p. 621. Sagan responded to Teller in "On Minimizing the Consequences of Nuclear War," *Nature*, Oct. 10, 1985, p. 485. Another early scientific critique of the nuclear winter hypothesis (by a noted scientist who later became a prominent foe of "global warming" claims) is S. Fred Singer, "Is 'Nuclear Winter' Real?" p. 625 of the same issue. Meanwhile, the journal's editor, John Maddox, cautioned against jumping to conclusions about the nuclear winter hypothesis. See, for example, his essay "Nuclear Winter Not Yet Established," *Nature*, Mar. 1, 1984, p. 11. Sagan (in collaboration with Hans Bethe and other scientists) also attacked Robert Jastrow's support for the proposed antimissile "Star Wars" project. See "'Star Wars' & the Scientists: An Exchange," *Commentary*, Mar. 1985, pp. 6–11.

79. Teller, p. 624.

80. DM interview.

81. Ibid.

82. AD interview.

83. Ibid.

84. Ibid.

85. Ibid.

86. Stephen Jay Gould, "Nonoverlapping Magisteria," in James B. Miller, ed., *An Evolving Dialogue: Scientific, Historical, Philosophical and Theological Perspectives on Evolution* (AAAS, 1998), p. 327.

87. Sagdeev, p. 311.

88. See, for example, editorial by "TRB," titled "The Little Chill," *New Republic*, Feb. 16, 1987, p. 4. Also see Eliot Marshall, "Nuclear Winter Debate Heats Up," *Science*, Jan. 16, 1987, p. 271. A few years later, the cold war ended and funds for nuclear winter research dried up. The author has the impression, based on conversations with scientists over the years, that when the Soviet Union fell, researchers' attitudes (pro or con) toward the nuclear winter hypothesis froze in place and have not changed since. On the one hand, the most virulent Sagan-haters, who disregard the fact that Sagan himself played only a secondary role in the computer modeling of nuclear winter, insist that the theory was "disproven" by the "nuclear autumn" research of Schneider and others. The Sagan-bashers' hand was strengthened by Sagan's foolish suggestion that Gulf War oil fires might cause a significant cooling, a suggestion that was quickly disproven by events (see chapter 16).

On the other hand, some scientists (including Schneider himself) have complained that the media misrepresented nuclear "autumn" by portraying it as no worse than an autumn picnic in the country. On the contrary (Schneider said), a nuclear autumn could have serious environmental consequences for at least some parts of the globe. Of course, given the extreme complexity of climate modeling, only a real-life nuclear war would answer the question: how would a nuclear exchange affect climate? With any luck, we'll never find out.

89. Richard Turco, O. B. Toon, Thomas Ackerman, James Pollack, and Carl Sagan, "Climate and Smoke: An Appraisal of Nuclear Winter," *Science*, Jan. 12, 1990, p. 166.

90. Andrei A. Kokoshin, *Soviet Strategic Thought, 1917–91* (1998), p. 136. Also see Alvarez (1987): At the end of this memoir (pp. 282–283), the Nobel laureate—who had witnessed the atomic bombing of Japan in 1945 from an American military plane—speculates about the impact of nuclear winter theory, noting:

> There is as yet no agreement on the correctness of the nuclear-winter scenario, and the latest word is that it is seriously wrong. . . . But the fact that neither of the two superpowers' nuclear-weapons establishments had thought about the possibility of a nuclear winter has sobered everyone concerned with fighting a nuclear war. What else, they wonder, have they forgotten to think about? The most encouraging feature of the nuclear-winter scenario is that no one has been able to disprove it. It has had a very salutary effect on the thinking of military planners on both sides of the world. There is some indication that it is weakening the Soviet military's long-held belief that nuclear war is survivable.

91. Even in the late 1990s, the possibility of at least a mild nuclear winter persists as long as the superpowers maintain thousands of nuclear weapons in their arsenals. At the time of this writing, the United States and Russia are dismantling thousands of nuclear weapons per year in order to comply with arms control treaties. However, that still will leave thousands of weapons in their arsenals—perhaps more than enough to trigger a significant cooling should the global political picture darken. For this reason, former CIA director Stansfield Turner warns in his 1997 book *Caging the Nuclear Genie*: "Although the surface temperature change might not be as severe as suggested in early analyses of the potential for nuclear winter, there are enough effects associated with nuclear winter that it cannot be discounted entirely" (p. 31). Also see Carl Sagan and Richard P. Turco, "Nuclear Winter in the Post-Cold War Era," *Journal of Peace Research*, vol. 30 (1993), pp. 369–373.

92. Interview with Edward Teller, June 1998.

Chapter 16. Look Back, Look Back

1. LG interview.
2. DGR interview.
3. Ibid.
4. Ibid.
5. LG interview.
6. SL interview.
7. JT interview.
8. Interview with Andrew Fraknoi, Aug. 1998.
9. LG interview.
10. A recent example is the late Linus Pauling, winner of two Nobel Prizes, who in his nineties not only vehemently oversold the medical "benefits" of vitamin C but quixotically fought a rear-guard action against "quasicrystals," an important development in the study of crystal structures. See Keay Davidson, "The Nobel Pursuits of Linus Pauling," *California Magazine*, Feb. 1991, p. 61.
11. A very useful history of TTAPS and their work, including intellectual influences on their work, is in *APW*, Appendix C, pp. 455–467.
12. Also see "Nuclear Thaw," *National Review*, Feb. 19, 1990, p. 18, which suggests the nuclear winter theorists were driven more by antinuclear sentiments than scientific judgment, and which adds: "Real science is not where Barnums like Carl Sagan operate."
13. OBT interview.
14. Ibid.
15. TPA interview.
16. *DHW*, p. 257. Initially, however, Sagan viewed the Kuwaiti experience as vindicating at least some aspects of the nuclear winter hypothesis; see Sagan and Turco (1993), p. 370, which cites some analyses that "suggest that the soot injections may have altered the Indian monsoon circulation and caused torrential downpours in China." Also see articles in *Science:* "'Nuclear Winter' from Gulf War Discounted," Jan. 25, 1991, p. 372, and "Taking Stock of Saddam's Fiery Legacy in Kuwait" and "Rainy Forecast for Gulf Area?", both in Aug. 30, 1991, p. 971; Sagan's letter to the magazine, Dec. 6, 1991, p. 1434; and a response from a reader, Feb. 14, 1992, p. 783.
17. JT interview.
18. Interviews with FD, JT, and Kent Cullers of SETI Institute/Project Phoenix. Also see Keay Davidson, "Earth to E.T.: We'll Be Back in Touch One Day," *San Francisco Examiner*, Jan. 13, 1994, p. A-4; and "Unquenchable Search for Life Out There," Feb. 5, 1995, p. A-1.
19. Faye Flam, "What Sould It Take to Join Science's Most Exclusive Club?" *Science*, May 15, 1992, p. 960.
20. The scientific community remains divided on whether Sagan deserved to be admitted to NAS. In 1998, Sir Martin Rees, the British Astronomer Royal, told the author it was a "scandal" that Sagan had been denied the honor. Even if Sagan had not been an eminent popularizer, his scientific research would have justified his admission to the academy, Rees argued. "I was a great fan [of his]," said Rees, adding that NASA was very fortunate to have Sagan stumping for it, instead of "some zombie from NASA talking in acronyms." In contrast, Tommy Gold told the author that he warned Sagan's champions not to nominate him to NAS because it was "a hopeless case" and he would surely be rejected. Those who have won acceptance to NAS, Gold says, typically achieved "definite individual steps [in science] that nobody else had taken. . . . And [Sagan] would really not have anything like that to show." That is a harsh judgment, considering that it comes from the man who brought Sagan to Cornell.

The Academy has been attacked for its social exclusiveness on other occasions. Former *Science* editor Daniel Greenberg, now editor of the long-running science-gadfly newsletter *Science & Government Report*, has attacked NAS for having so few female members, noting that it is "carrying on a sexist tradition that would shame a redneck beer club" (Flam, p. 960). Also, for a skeptical look at the Academy's internal politics and role as a scientific adviser to the government, see Phillip M. Boffey, *The Brain Bank of America: An Inquiry into the Politics of Science* (1975), with an introduction by Ralph Nader.

21. SM interview.

22. Copies of Miller's documents proposing Sagan for NAS membership are filed in the Urey papers. They include Miller's selection of Sagan's top scientific papers, as follows:

1962. "Structure of the Lower Atmosphere of Venus" (*Icarus*)

1971. "Long Wavelength Ultraviolet Photoproduction of Amino Acids on the Primitive Earth" (*Science*; with Bishun N. Khare)

1972. "Earth and Mars: Evolution of Atmospheres and Surface Temperatures" (*Science*; with George Mullen)

1975. "Fluid transport on Earth and aeolian transport on Mars" (*Icarus*; with R. A. Bagnold)

1976. "The Surface of Mars: The View from the Viking 1 Lander" (*Science*; with T. A. Mutch et al.)

1976. "Volcanic Explosions and Climate Change" (*Journal of Geophysical Research*; with Jim Pollack et al.)

1979. "Tholins: Organic Chemistry of Interstellar Grains and Gases" (*Nature*; with Bishun N. Khare)

1979. "Evaporation of Ice in Planetary Atmospheres: Ice-covered Rivers on Mars" (*Icarus*; with David Wallace)

1981. "Encounter with Saturn: Voyager 1 Imaging Science Results" (*Science*; with Bradford Smith et al.)

1983. "Nuclear Winter: Global Consequences of Multiple Nuclear Explosions" (*Science*; with Richard P. Turco, O. B. Toon, T. P. Ackerman, and Jim B. Pollack)

1987. "Infrared Emission from Organic Grains in Comet Halley" (*Nature*; with Christopher Chyba)

1990. "Cometary Delivery of Organic Molecules to the Early Earth" (*Science*; with Christopher Chyba, P. J. Thomas, and L. Brookshaw)

23. SM interview.
24. Flam, p. 960.
25. SM interview.
26. I am grateful to Lynn Margulis for sharing a copy of this letter to Sagan. For Sagan, another personal upset came when he tangled publicly with Apple Corp. Staffers at the computer firm had assigned "Sagan" as a code name for a computer model under development. Sagan learned about it and had his lawyers write to Apple, charging that the use of his name illegally employed his name for commercial intent. Thereafter, Apple staffers purportedly changed the code name to "BHA," which Sagan was told stood for "Butt-Head Astronomer." In retaliation, he sued Apple in U.S. District Court in Los Angeles, charging that the use of "BHA" was "defamatory on its face" and exposed him to

"hatred, contempt, ridicule and obloquy." The tawdry episode (which, to some, suggested that Sagan was overly touchy about his image) resulted in a front-page feature in the *Wall Street Journal*, Apr. 11, 1994.

27. Hoffmann shared his letter with me. Also see SM interview.

28. In a subsequent letter, dated Feb. 10, 1994, Sagan stoically told Miller, "I've gotten more than my fair share of awards over the years and anyway I truly believe that the privilege of doing science is its own highest reward." I am grateful to Miller for providing copies of both letters.

29. SM interview.

30. *SOFA*'s literary excellence is head and shoulders above anything previously written by Sagan, which is saying a lot. Based on my conversations with Druyan, I believe she played a crucial part in molding the book in both a literary and an intellectual sense. It includes adventuresome passages—e.g., a harrowing description of power relationships among primates, as "told" through the observations of a female primate—and the only four-letter words in any of Sagan's or his many collaborators' works.

31. *SOFA* quotes are from pp. xiv, 38, 44, and 67. The book reviews are quoted on the cover, back cover, and inside page of the paperback edition of *SOFA*.

32. *New Scientist*, Jan. 16, 1993, p. 40.

33. AD interview.

34. TPA interview. Samuel Democritus Druyan Sagan was born on Jan. 15, 1991.

35. DS interview. His often critical written assessment of his father appeared in "Partial Closure: Dorion Sagan Reflects on Carl," *Whole Earth Review*, Summer 1997, pp. 34–37. I am grateful to Dorion for sharing an original, somewhat longer copy of his article upon which the *Whole Earth* essay was based. The *Whole Earth* article goes into considerable detail about their intellectual disagreements, particularly over postmodernist philosophies (which intrigue Dorion, an admirer of Jacques Derrida and Jacques Lacan) vs. his father's more traditional conceptions of logic and science. What seems clear, based on Dorion's recollections, is that his father actually knew very little about postmodernist philosophies. This might explain why he had so little to say about them publicly—even in his book *DHW*, ostensibly a defense of traditional reason and science—at a time, the 1990s, when they were beginning to stir major controversy among Western intellectuals and scientists who perceived them as a threat to the cultural hegemony of reason and science. (See, for example, Paul R. Gross and Norman Levitt, *Higher Superstition: The Academic Left and Its Quarrels with Science* (1994).) The word "postmodernist" appears only once, briefly, in *DHW*, on p. 257, and in a way that suggests Sagan has little grasp of its meaning (a not uncommon problem, even among intellectuals). Otherwise, Sagan remained silent on the postmodernism issue, probably because he realized he was not well grounded in the subject. This is in keeping with his lifelong habit: he shrewdly insisted on being well read in a topic before debating about it.

36. DS interview.

37. Ibid.

38. Ibid.

39. Ibid.

40. Ibid.

41. NS interview.

42. Ibid.

43. Ibid.

44. AD interview.

45. "Tholin" is Greek for "muddy." See *PBD*, p. 107. Sagan's long-time associate Tommy Gold was skeptical about tholins, however; he told the author they were just "brown gunk." But Chyba feels tholins show more promise: "With Bishun Khare and his

graduate student the late Reid Thompson, Carl showed that organic materials ('tholins') synthesized in simulation experiments of the nitrogen-methane atmosphere of Saturn's moon Titan provided an excellent match to spacecraft spectral data," Chyba writes in his obituary for Sagan in *Eos* (Apr. 22, 1997). In other words, tholin-like substances—which might be chemical links in the origin of life—could exist on that distant world. Thanks considerably to Sagan's efforts, planetary scientists—once wary of the notion of extraterrestrial organics—now view them as "simply another solar system material," Chyba observes. Indeed, he notes, up to 25 percent of the dust from Halley's comet appears to be organic.

46. CS interview.

47. See chapter 6, note 76.

48. *SOFA*, p. 31.

49. See, for example, *PBD*, p. xv, and the Preface to *DHW.*

50. These books were *DHW* and *PBD*.

51. AD interview. Sagan's actual quote appears in *PBD*, pp. 8–9.

Chapter 17. Hollywood

1. Shortly after Sagan's death, and a half-year before the premiere of *Contact*, Coppola filed suit in Los Angeles Superior Court to stop production of the film. Coppola claimed that the film was based on his plans, discussed in the 1970s with Sagan, for a TV movie about the search for alien life. Among those who gave depositions on behalf of the Sagan estate was noted astronomy popularizer Andrew Fraknoi, who explained how the idea of seeking aliens was an old one that long predated Coppola (AF interview). The suit was thrown out of court.

2. *War of the Worlds* (1953), directed by Byron Haskin.

3. *It Came from Beneath the Sea* (1955), directed by Robert Gordon.

4. Lynda Obst, *Hello, He Lied & Other Truths from the Hollywood Trenches* (1996). The book contains a number of references to Sagan, Druyan, and the making of *Contact*, then still under way.

5. LO interview.

6. Ibid.

7. Ibid.

8. Kip S. Thorne, *Black Holes & Time Warps: Einstein's Outrageous Legacy* (1994), chapter 14. Thorne describes how one day in 1985 he received a phone call from Sagan, a personal friend, who said: "Sorry to bother you, Kip. But I'm just finishing a novel about the human race's first contact with an extraterrestrial civilization, and I'm worried. I want the science to be as accurate as possible, and I'm afraid I may have got some of the gravitational physics wrong. Would you look at it and give me advice?" Thorne agreed, and a few weeks later received Sagan's manuscript. In this version of the book, Sagan had Ellie Arroway fly into a black hole and emerge an hour later at the star Vega, 26 light-years distant. The possibility of interstellar travel via black holes was a fairly old idea by that time, and it was impossible, as Thorne knew, because "tiny electromagnetic vacuum fluctuations" and radiation within the time–space tunnel would destroy the spaceship. Thorne began speculating about alternate means of travel and concluded that Ellie should fly through a "wormhole," not a black hole. Wormholes were theoretical concepts (implicit in Einstein's original calculations for general relativity) that would, if possible, allow travelers to move instantly from one point in the universe to another by moving, in effect, between two sides of a kind of "fold" in the space–time continuum (like a hole punched through a fold in a rug). Thorne suggested to Sagan that someone in the novel figure out

a way to create a wormhole for travel to Vega. And that is exactly what Sagan did in the final novel; for the technical details, see pp. 347–348 and 406 of *Contact*.

For a shorter version of Thorne's account of his work on Sagan's "wormhole," see Kip S. Thorne, "Do the Laws of Physics Permit Wormholes for Interstellar Travel and Machines for Time Travel?", pp. 121–134, in *Carl Sagan's Universe*, Yervant Terzian and Elizabeth Bilson, eds. (1997). This useful book, published by Cambridge University Press, is a compilation of speeches given at Sagan's sixtieth birthday celebration in 1994 at Cornell. The book includes extended comments by NASA official Wesley Huntress Jr., JPL chief Edward C. Stone, Gorbachev science adviser Roald Sagdeev, Bruce Murray, former National Academy of Sciences head Frank Press, and many other notables.

9. *Contact* script conference, Sept. 23, 1994.

10. Thorne (1994); Michio Kaku, *Hyperspace* (1994); Timothy Ferris, *The Red Limit* (1977); David Swift, *SETI Pioneers* (1990); Drake and Sobel (1992).

11. AD interview.

12. LO interview.

13. AD interview.

14. Arden papers, Dec. 15, 1978.

15. LO interview.

16. "Jodie Foster (Alicia Christian Foster)," in David Thomson, *Biographical Dictionary of Film* (Third Edition, 1994), p. 261. Also see "Foster, Jodie," in Ephraim Katz, *The Film Encyclopedia* (Second Edition, 1994), p. 476. Regarding Foster's popularity with lesbians, see the cover story on Foster in the lesbian periodical *Girlfriends* (San Francisco, Calif.), Nov. 1997, which describes her as "an icon for lesbians" (p. 3).

17. Obst comment is from *Contact* script conference, Sept. 21, 1994. "Hypatia's" remarks are from script conference of Aug. 26, 1994.

18. Ibid.

19. Ibid.

20. *Alien* (1979), directed by Ridley Scott; *Terminator 2* (1991), directed by James Cameron.

21. *Contact* script conference, Sept. 21, 1994.

22. Ibid.

23. Stephen Holden, "Which Way Upward, on a Wing or Prayer?", *New York Times*, July 11, 1997, pp. B-1 and B-20. Holden also called *Contact* a "technologically dazzling but intellectually strained and emotionally chilly science-fiction epic. . . . In its best moments, *Contact* becomes the most visually intoxicating 'trip' movie ever made." But Ellie's show of "little vulnerability" bothered Holden, who hardly concealed his sexism in complaining: "Even when shedding tears, Ellie is shown fighting them back, clenching her jaw, determined to solve the next problem. She never really lets go." Can one imagine a critic registering a similar complaint about a male character?

24. Andrew Dickson White, *A History of the Warfare of Science with Theology*, in two volumes (1896, reprinted by Dover in 1960).

25. AD interview.

26. *Contact* script conference, Aug. 24, 1994.

27. Ibid., Sept. 18, 1994.

28. Ibid., Aug. 29, 1994.

Chapter 18. The Night Freight

1. *BiBi*, p. 214.

2. Ibid., p. 216.

3. Ibid., p. 217.

4. Ibid., p. 218.

5. Ibid., p. 219.

6. Ibid.

7. One of Sagan's last assistants, Andrea Barnett, says his connection to the local PETA chapter "brought comment from a lot of people [who said,] 'I can't believe Carl's the faculty adviser for [PETA]!'" However, Barnett's husband, Bill, also an assistant to Sagan, pointed out that Sagan's support of the PETA discussions is "very emblematic" of his belief in the freest possible speech for all people, even those with whom (such as Velikovsky) he might vehemently disagree. In that regard, Mr. Barnett noted, Sagan, in his later years, "backed off a little bit on his involvement [with] CSICOP . . . because he felt that they were too confrontational. He felt that if you want to persuade the general public that pseudoscience is not intellectually worthy, you have to treat them [the pseudo-scientists] with respect and make your case, but don't ridicule them." From ABB interview, Nov. 1997.

8. Sagan to Goldin, Sept. 25, 1995. Sagan's letter to Goldin enclosed a copy of a Sept. 5, 1995, letter to him from Mary Beth Sweetland, a PETA official, seeking his help in ending the use of rhesus monkeys in space experiments to test the effects of weightless-ness on the creatures. Sagan's brief letter to Goldin states: "Enclosed is something that I think deserves your attention—if not for the justice of the complaint (I can't judge that), then at least for the potential bad publicity for NASA." Goldin responded (undated letter) to Sagan that the experiments were scientifically worthwhile and that the space agency "continues to remain committed to the humane and ethical treatment and use of animals." However, on Feb. 9, 1996, in response to a query from Goldin, presidential science adviser Jack Gibbons wrote the NASA chief: "I sympathize with your concern that the era of need for primates in NASA's research is now behind us, and that it may be time to retire those animals." I am grateful to a confidential source for providing me with copies of these documents. A skeptical view of the scientific merit of the monkey experiments is by science writer Daniel S. Greenberg, "Monkeys in Outer Space?", *Washington Post*, Apr. 20, 1997. Also see editorial, "Monkey Business," in *Space News*, May 20, 1996, p. 12.

9. *BiBi*, p. 219.

10. See obituary in the *New York Times*, June 15, 1994; also, Associated Press obituary, "James B. Pollack," which ran in the June 15, 1994, *San Francisco Examiner* (p. A-17) and in other newspapers. The space scientist Jeffrey N. Cuzzi wrote a detailed profile of Pol-lack that appeared in the July 24, 1994, "Astrogram" from NASA's Ames Research Center, Moffett Field, Calif. It notes that "Jim played key roles in nearly every NASA planetary mission since Apollo, including Mariner 9, Viking, Voyager, Pioneer Venus, Mars Observer and Galileo." Among other things, he "created the first detailed models of the early stages of formation of the giant gas planets" and, with other researchers, "developed the world's most complete model of Mars' atmospheric circulation." In addition, Pollack "laid the foundation for the study of evolutionary climate change on all the terrestrial planets including Earth."

Pollack's awards included the Gerard P. Kuiper Prize of the Division of Planetary Sci-ences of the American Astronomical Society "for excellent and enduring contributions to planetary science," and he co-won the Leo Szilard Award of the American Physical Soci-ety for research in the public interest. After Pollack's death, Sagan said: "Jim Pollack made fundamental contributions to our knowledge of . . . the origin of the solar system. His kindness was as impressive as his intellect. Planetary science is going to miss him very much" (Cuzzi, p. 3). Also see Pollack obituary in *Bulletin of the American Astronomical Soci-ety*, Vol. 26, No. 4 (1994), pp. 1607–1608. Pollack's posthumously published paper on ter-raforming other planets, written with Sagan, was "Planetary Engineering," *Eos* (American Geophysical Union), Nov. 1, 1994, pp. 98–99.

11. See Thompson obituary in Linda VanHoose, "High School Starts Scholarship in Memory of Space Scientist," *Lexington Herald-Leader* (Lexington, Ky.), June 25, 1997. I am grateful to Mr. Thompson's fiancée, Denise Weldon of Ithaca, N.Y., for sharing numerous documents related to Thompson's work with Carl Sagan, including correspondence with Sagan. Among other things, Thompson was closely involved with Sagan and Bishun Khare's study of "tholins," which may yet prove useful in understanding the possible cosmic origins of life.

12. In fact, the "signals" were probably computer glitches related to microchip flaws, a noted SETI expert told me after this book went to press. Horowitz described his observations in Paul Horowitz, "Extraterrestrial Intelligence: The Search Programs," in Terzian and Bilson, pp. 98–120.

13. Jim Cordes interview. See James M. Cordes, Joseph W. Lazio, and Carl Sagan, "Scintillation-Induced Intermittency in SETI," *Astrophysical Journal*, Oct. 1, 1997, pp. 782–808.

14. Timothy Ferris, "The Risks and Rewards of Popularizing Science," *Chronicle of Higher Education*, Apr. 4, 1997.

15. TF interview.

16. *DHW*, pp. 256–257. On pp. 258–259, after briefly alluding to "postmodernist" theories, Sagan comes as close as he ever did to confronting historians—specifically Joyce Appleby, Lynn Hunt, and Margaret Jacob—who analyze great scientific theories in light of the culture of the times in which they originated. However, Sagan never developed a detailed thesis on, or rebuttal to, modern trends in the study of the history and philosophy of science, and his views cannot easily be classified along the spectrum from old-fashioned scientism to Thomas Kuhn's "scientific revolutions" to "strong programme"-style thinking.

Alan Cromer makes the interesting suggestion that Sagan might be considered an "optimistic Kuhnian." Kuhn didn't seem to believe (although it is hard to tell, as his views vacillated over the years) that scientific knowledge accumulates over time (because "revolutions" in thought lead to reinterpretations of old data). By contrast, optimistic Kuhnians like to have their cake and eat it too; i.e., they enjoy watching the excitement of scientific revolutions, but they simultaneously wish to believe in "progress," that is, that the total sum of knowledge accumulates with time. See Cromer, *Connected Knowledge—Science, Philosophy, and Education* (1997), p. 8.

In that regard, a long analysis of *DHW* by Harvard evolutionary scientist Richard Lewontin appeared in the *New York Review of Books*, Jan. 9, 1997, p. 28. Lewontin's article is the most important criticism of Sagan's philosophy of science (such as it was) from a left-wing scholar, and it is unfortunate that it was published shortly after Sagan's death; Sagan's response would have been fascinating to read. Lewontin begins the article by recalling how as young men, he and Sagan had, at the bidding of H. J. Muller, both spoken in defense of evolution at Little Rock Auditorium in Arkansas in 1964; but "despite our absolutely compelling arguments, the audience unaccountably voted for the opposition. Carl and I then sneaked out the back door of the auditorium and beat it out of town, quite certain that at any moment hooded riders with ropes and flaming crosses would snatch up two atheistic New York Jews who had the chutzpah to engage in public blasphemy." Lewontin goes on to say that he and Sagan "drew different conclusions" from the experience: "For me the confrontation between creationism and the science of evolution was an example of historical, regional, and class differences in culture that could only be understood in the context of American social history. For Carl it was a struggle between ignorance and knowledge. . . . The struggle to bring scientific knowledge to the masses has been a preoccupation of Carl Sagan's ever since" (p. 28).

Lewontin, like many modern historians of science, regards "scientific method" as a myth. Scientific theories are, rather (at least to some degree), social constructions that reinforce the social power of intellectual elites. Sagan does not believe this, of course; he believes that theories largely reflect a physical reality that is external to social structures, that would be valid regardless of whether one lived in, say, 1990s America or 1930s Germany. Lewontin criticizes Sagan for championing, in *DHW*, "scientific method" as if it really exists. Sagan also believes that mere possession of knowledge will "free" the masses, but Lewontin counters that this is wrong: "It is not the truth that makes you free. It is your possession of the power to discover the truth. Our dilemma is that we do not know how to provide that power" (p. 32). For a reply to Lewontin, see Paul R. Gross, "Blockbuster Homiletics," *The New Criterion*, Oct. 1997, p. 69.

17. *BrBr*, chapter 25. Blackmore's falsification of the Sagan theory is cited in Schick and Vaughn, p. 275.

18. ABB interview.

19. *BiBi*, pp. 221–222.

20. Keay Davidson, "Future of World Topic of S.F. Meet," *San Francisco Examiner*, Sept. 25, 1995, p. A-1. Sagan's oratorical power was acknowledged by no less a conservative than William Safire, who included one of Sagan's speeches in *Lend Me Your Ears: Great Speeches in History* (1992, 1997). The speech, co-authored with Ann Druyan, concerned the need for nuclear disarmament and was delivered in 1988 at Gettysburg at the 125th anniversary of the Civil War battle.

21. Campbell comments at memorial service.

22. AD interview.

23. Ann Druyan, "Epilogue," pp. 223–228 in *BiBi*; quote is from p. 227.

24. Ibid., p. 223.

25. Ibid., p. 225.

26. Ibid., p. 227.

27. Ibid., p. 228; also AD interview.

28. *BiBi*, p. 225.

29. AD interview.

30. From Bill Barnett in ABB interview.

31. "Carl Sagan Dies," *New York Times*, Dec. 21, 1996, pp. 1 and 26. Also see Associated Press story by George Tibbits, "Science Popularizer Carl Sagan, Dead at 62," Dec. 20, 1966. After Sagan's death, NASA administrator Daniel Goldin issued this statement: "Carl Sagan brought astronomy home to millions of Americans. For the first time, people outside of the sciences learned and cared and understood about space and why it is important. It was not only the public in general Carl influenced; he helped me personally. Carl, along with others in the field, consulted with me, sharing his vision and insights for going to Mars and working with the Russians in space. Everything we learn about Mars will carry some of the seed of Carl Sagan's dreams." In this regard, see "The Future of Planetary Exploration: A Dialogue Between Daniel Goldin and Carl Sagan," *Planetary Report*, July 1993, pp. 18–23. For details on Sagan's scientific achievements, see *Eos* (American Geophysical Union), Apr. 22, 1997, p. 167.

Among the numerous commentaries on Sagan's death, see the unusually blunt editorial by Stephen Jay Gould in *Science*, Jan. 31, 1997, p. 299, titled "Bright Star among Billions," which says:

> As Saul despised David for receiving ten thousand cheers to his own mere thousand, we scientists often stigmatize, for the same reason of simple jealousy, the good work done by colleagues for our common benefit. Because we live in a Philistine nation filled with Goliaths, and because science feeds at a public trough, we all give lip service

to the need for clear and supportive popular presentation of our work. Why then do we downgrade the professional reputation of collegaues who can convey the power and beauty of science to the hearts and minds of a fascinated, if generally uninformed, public? . . . With the death of Carl Sagan we have lost both a fine scientist and the greatest popularizer of the 20th century, if not of all time.

Gould also assailed the "shameful incident" in which the NAS rejected Sagan for membership: "Too many of us never grasped his legendary service to science."

Nature magazine's obituary for Sagan (Jan. 30, 1997, p. 400) called him a "first-generation planetary explorer of the first rank." The American Geophysical Union, at its Spring meeting in 1997, held a special series of lectures titled "Carl Sagan: His Pioneering Science and Current Studies of Life in Extreme Environments," *Eos* (special meeting supplement), Apr. 29, 1997, pp. S45–S46.

The *Skeptical Inquirer* ran two long tributes to Sagan titled "The Darkened Cosmos," including comments from his many admirers (such as Arthur C. Clarke, Jill Tarter, Martin Gardner, Bill Nye, James Oberg, Neil deGrasse Tyson, and others) in its March and May 1997 issues. Details on the service at St. John the Divine Cathedral are in *Skeptical Inquirer*, July 1997, p. 5.

The journal *Skeptic*, published by the Skeptics Society of Altadena, Calif., ran a cover painting of Sagan showing him holding a candle to ward off the "demon-haunted darkness," plus a long commentary on his life (pp. 10–17). Paul H. Schuch, executive director of the SETI League of Little Ferry, N.J., which was organizing amateur scientists to seek SETI signals using small radiotelescope dishes, called Sagan's death "the darkest day of the year" (*SearchLites*, Spring 1997, p. 1).

Throughout his life, Sagan rarely spoke about his Jewish heritage. Writing in *New York Jewish Week* after Sagan's death, Eric J. Greenberg reported that the astronomer's "feelings about his own ethnicity were almost painfully private." The article quotes Rabbi David Sapperstein, director of the Religious Action Center in Washington, who knew Sagan for a decade, as saying he "was never comfortable talking about his own past."

32. Boss, pp. 209–210.

33. Gould (1998), p. 327.

34. Russell Seitz, "An Incomplete Obituary," *Forbes*, Feb. 10, 1997, p. 123. Seitz compares Sagan to the historical left-wing popularizers of science who worked in England during the first half of the twentieth century, such as J. B. S. Haldane.

35. Gore comments at memorial service. Note that Sagan and other scientists endorsed Bill Clinton and Al Gore for president and vice president in 1992: see press release from Clinton/Gore National Campaign Headquarters, Little Rock, Ark., Oct. 28, 1992, and related news stories in *Albuquerque Journal*, Oct. 29, 1992, and other newspapers. Sagan's influence on Gore is discussed in *Space News*, Nov. 16–22, 1992, pp. 4 and 28. Sagan appeared at a press conference with Gore in 1993 to announce the formation of the National Religious Partnership for the Environment: see "Gore Hails 'Greening' of America's Churches," *Washington Post*, Oct. 9, 1993. Regarding claims that the "Mars rock" is evidence of Martian life, see skeptical report in Richard A. Kerr, "Requiem for Life on Mars? Support for Microbes Fades," *Science*, Nov. 20, 1998, pp. 1398–1400.

36. Jeremy Sagan comments at memorial service.

37. DGR interview.

38. Ibid. Sagan's role in founding the DPS is described in Dale P. Cruikshank and Joseph W. Chamberlain, "The Beginnings of the Division for Planetary Sciences of the American Astronomical Society," in David H. DeVorkin, ed., *Centennial Volume of the AAS* (1998).

39. DGR interview.

40. LO interview.

41. *Men in Black* (1997), directed by Barry Sonnenfeld; and *Independence Day* (1996), directed by Roland Emmerich. Lerner's article, "'Contact': A Spiritual High," ran in *Tikkun*, Sept. 1997, p. 8. Silver's piece, "God and Carl Sagan in Hollywood," appeared in *Commentary*, Sept. 1997, p. 52. The article in *Nature* was Leslie Sage, "Film Review: Aliens, Lies and Videotape," *Nature*, Aug. 14, 1997, p. 637. Despite Holden's generally hostile review (see note 24, chapter 17), the *New York Times* ran two long, friendly features about the making of *Contact*. See Bernard Weinraub, "Using a Big Budget to Ask Big Questions," *New York Times*, July 6, 1997, Section II, pp. 1 and 9 (which calls the movie "sci-fi summer fare for, yes, grown-ups" and reports the movie cost $90 million to make); and the John Noble Wilford article in *New York Times*, July 20, 1997, Section II, p. 14. The film's sole egregious error is a mathematical miscalculation by Ellie (JT interview).

Some critics loved *Contact*. It was "the season's first superb major motion picture," said Gene Shalit of the *Today* show, and *Entertainment Weekly* called the film "as close to poetry as Hollywood gets" (quoted in *New York Times*, July 11, 1997, p. B-7). Further praise came from the CSICOP journal *Skeptical Inquirer* (Nov. 1997, pp. 47–51), where Edward Summer praised *Contact* as far superior to its summer box-office competitor, *Men in Black*. The latter is "empty-headed and entertaining," whereas *Contact* was a cinematic step forward on several fronts: "In an arena [Hollywood] where scientists are traditionally shown as bumbling idiots in white lab coats or Machiavellian misfits conniving to destroy us all in the service of their mad fixations, it is astonishing to find a hero who is not only an intelligent, dedicated, compassionate, and believable human being, but a female to boot." Also, "Never in my recollection has there been such an uncompromising motion picture portrayal of a moral, ethical, unswerving practitioner of the scientific method" (p. 49). For religious figures' reaction to *Contact*, see "Religiously Speaking, A Look at Films," *New York Times*, Mar. 14, 1998, A-15.

A critique of *Contact* and Sagan's views on extraterrestrials and religion is Peter Augustine Lawler, "Aliens in the Cosmos—Or, the Curious Affair of Carl Sagan and E.T.," *The American Enterprise*, Sept. 1998, p. 47. The film included scenes of President Bill Clinton that were digitally inserted into the movie to make it seem as if he was responding to Ellie's discovery of alien signals. The scenes were drawn from Clinton's public statement in Aug. 1997 following the McKay et al. team's reported finding of possible alien fossil microbes in the "Mars rock." The White House legal counsel issued a statement criticizing the film's use of the president's image, which naive moviegoers might have assumed meant that he acted in the film; see James Bennet, "Clinton's Not Moonlighting," *New York Times*, July 11, 1997, p. B-20.

In the final film, Obst was listed as executive producer along with Joan Bradshaw. Sagan and Druyan were listed as co-producers; the producers were Robert Zemeckis (who was also the director) and Steve Starkey. The final screenplay is credited to James V. Hart and Michael Goldenberg. The film studio was Warner Brothers.

42. LO interview.

43. AD interview.

44. Ibid.

45. *CC*, p. 227.

46. Ibid.

47. Ibid.

48. *PBD*, pp. 378 and 399; also see discussion of interstellar flight in chapter 22.

49. *PBD*, p. 385.

50. Ibid., pp. 391, 394.

51. The Goldin anecdote is in the *San Francisco Examiner*, Sept. 21, 1997, p. C-1.

52. Keay Davidson, "Mars, You're on the Air," *San Francisco Examiner*, Feb. 18, 1998, p. A-1.

53. PH interview. Among many serious discussions of the feasibility of interstellar flight, see Stephanie D. Leifer, "Reaching for the Stars," *Scientific American*, Feb. 1999, pp. 94–95; Saul J. Adelman and Benjamin Adelman, *Bound for the Stars* (1981), especially chapters 15–17; and Eugene Mallove and Gregory Matloff, *The Starflight Handbook* (1989). Also see a profile of a physicist (Robert Forward) who designs starships in Keay Davidson, "That Magnificent Man in His Flying Machine," *California Magazine*, Aug. 1987, pp. 84–87. Goldin's statement to the press is reported in the *San Francisco Examiner*, July 4, 1997, p. A-1; also see follow-up article on Aug. 11, 1997, p. A-1.

Bibliography

Abbreviations

PNAS   *Proceedings of the National Academy of Sciences*
QJRAS   *Quarterly Journal of the Royal Astronomical Society*

Adelman, Saul J., and Benjamin Adelman. *Bound for the Stars: An Enthusiastic Look at the Opportunities and Challenges Space Exploration Offers.* Englewood Cliffs, N.J.: Prentice-Hall, 1981.

Adler, Alfred. "Behold the Stars." *Atlantic Monthly,* October 1974, p. 109.

Adorno, Theodor, and Max Horkheimer. *Dialectic of Enlightenment.* London: Verso, 1947.

Agel, Jerome. *The Making of Kubrick's 2001.* New York: New American Library, 1970.

Alexander, Jerome. *Life: Its Nature and Origin.* New York: Rheingold, 1948.

Allen, John F. "Can Humans Make Venus Habitable?" *San Francisco Examiner,* Mar. 30, 1961, p. 55.

Alvarez, Luis W. *Alvarez: Adventures of a Physicist.* New York: Basic Books, 1987.

Alvarez, Luis W., and Walter Alvarez, Frank Asaro, and Helen V. Michel. "Extraterrestrial Cause for the Cretaceous-Tertiary Extinction." *Science,* June 6, 1980, pp. 1095-1108.

American Geophysical Union (AGU). *Scientific Results of the Viking Project.* Washington: American Geophysical Union, 1977.

Anders, Edward. "Meteoritic Hydrocarbons and Extraterrestrial Life." *Annals of the New York Academy of Sciences,* vol. 93, Aug. 29, 1962, pp. 649-664.

Arrhenius, Svante. *Worlds in the Making: The Evolution of the Universe.* New York: Harper, 1908.

Ashbrook, James B., and Carol Rausch Albright. *The Humanizing Brain: Where Religion and Neuroscience Meet.* Pasadena, Tex.: Pilgrim Press, 1997.

Asimov, Isaac. *In Joy Still Felt: The Autobiography of Isaac Asimov, 1954–78.* Garden City, N.Y.: Doubleday, 1980.

———. *Is Anyone There?* Garden City, N.Y.: Doubleday, 1967.

———. "The Moon Could Answer the Riddle of Life." *New York Times Sunday Magazine,* July 13, 1969, p. 12.

———. *A Short History of Biology.* Garden City, N.Y.: Natural History Press, 1964.

———. *Yours, Isaac Asimov: A Lifetime of Letters.* Edited by Stanley Asimov. New York: Doubleday, 1995.

Astor, J. J. *A Journey in Other Worlds: A Romance of the Future.* New York: Appleton and Co., 1894.

Badami, Mary Kenny. "A Feminist Critique of Science Fiction." *Extrapolation,* December 1976, pp. 6–19.

Bamford, James. *The Puzzle Palace: A Report on America's Most Secret Agency.* Boston: Houghton Mifflin, 1983.

Bar-Nun, A., N. Bar-Nun, S. H. Bauer, and Carl Sagan. "Shock Synthesis of Amino Acids in Simulated Primitive Environments." *Science*, Apr. 24, 1970, p. 470.

Barthel, Joan. "Here's Johnny! Out There." *Life*, Jan. 23, 1970, p. 50.

Bauer, Henry. *Beyond Velikovsky: The History of a Public Controversy*. Urbana: University of Illinois Press, 1984.

Bennet, James. "Clinton's Not Moonlighting." *New York Times*, July 11, 1997, p. B-20.

Bergamini, David. "Wax and Wigglers: Life in Space?" *Life*, May 5, 1961, p. 57.

Beschloss, Michael R. *The Crisis Years: Kennedy and Khrushchev, 1960–1963*. New York: Edward Burlingame Books, 1991.

Bingham, Roger. "Carl Sagan." *New Scientist*, Jan. 17, 1980, p. 152.

Bird, Kai. *The Color of Truth: McGeorge Bundy and William Bundy: Brothers in Arms*. New York: Simon & Schuster, 1998.

Bloor, David. *Knowledge and Social Imagery* 2d ed. Chicago: University of Chicago Press, 1991.

Blumberg, Stanley A., and Louis G. Panos. *Edward Teller: Giant of the Golden Age of Physics: A Biography*. New York: Scribner's, 1990.

Boffey, Phillip M. *The Brain Bank of America: An Inquiry into the Politics of Science*. New York: McGraw-Hill, 1975.

Bok, Bart. "A Critical Look at Astrology." *The Humanist*, Sept.-Oct. 1975, p. 6.

Boss, Alan. *Looking for Earths: The Race to Find New Solar Systems*. New York: Wiley, 1998.

Bottomore, Tom, ed. *A Dictionary of Marxist Thought*. Cambridge, Mass.: Harvard University Press, 1983.

Bowler, Peter. *Norton History of the Environmental Sciences*. New York: W. W. Norton, 1993.

Bradbury, Ray, Arthur C. Clarke, Bruce Murray, Carl Sagan, and Walter Sullivan. *Mars and the Mind of Man*. New York: Harper & Row, 1973.

Brand, Stewart, ed. *Space Colonies*. Sausalito, Calif.: Whole Earth Catalog, 1977.

Brinkley, Douglas. *The Unfinished Presidency: Jimmy Carter's Journey beyond the White House*. New York: Viking, 1998.

Broad, William J. "Even in Death, Carl Sagan's Influence Is Still Cosmic," *New York Times*, Dec. 1, 1998, p. D-5.

———. "A Star Fades for Entrepreneur Sagan." *Science*, Jan. 8, 1982, p. 149.

———. *Star Warriors: A Penetrating Look into the Lives of Young Scientists behind Our Space Age Weapons*. New York: Simon & Schuster, 1985.

———. *Teller's War: The Top-Secret Story behind the Star Wars Deception*. New York: Simon & Schuster, 1988.

Browne, Janet. *Charles Darwin: A Biography*. New York: Knopf, 1995.

Brunvand, Jan Harold. *The Choking Doberman and Other "New" Urban Legends*. New York: W. W. Norton, 1984.

Brush, Stephen G. *A History of Modern Planetary Physics*. 3 vols. New York: Cambridge University Press, 1996. Vol. 1, *Nebulous Earth: The Origin of the Solar System and of the Core of the Earth from Laplace to Jeffreys*. Vol. 2, *Transmuted Past: The Age of the Earth and the Evolution of the Elements from Lyell to Patterson*. Vol. 3, *Fruitful Encounters: The Origin of the Solar System and of the Moon from Chamberlin to Apollo*.

Buckley, William F., Jr., and L. Brent Bozell. *McCarthy and His Enemies: The Record and Its Meaning*. Chicago: H. Regnery Co., 1954.

Buhle, Paul M., and Edward Rice-Maximin. *William Appleman Williams: The Tragedy of Empire*. New York: Routledge, 1995.

Bulkeley, Rip. *The Sputniks Crisis and Early United States Space Policy: A Critique of the Historiography of Space*. Bloomington: Indiana University Press, 1991.

Burroughs, Edgar Rice. *A Princess of Mars*. Chicago: A. C. McClurg, 1917.

Burrows, William E. *Deep Black: Space Espionage and National Security*. New York: Random House, 1986.

———— . *This New Ocean: The Story of the First Space Age.* New York: Random House, 1999.

Butrica, Andrew J. *To See the Unseen: A History of Planetary Radar Astronomy.* Washington, D.C.: NASA, 1996.

Cantril, Hadley. *The Invasion from Mars: A Study in the Psychology of Panic.* Princeton, N.J.: Princeton University Press, 1940.

Carey, William D. "A Run Worth Making." *Science*, Dec. 23, 1983, on editorial page.

"Carl Sagan: His Pioneering Science and Current Studies of Life in Extreme Environments." *Eos* (special meeting supplement), Apr. 29, 1997, pp. S45–S46.

"Carl Sagan Dies." *New York Times*, Dec. 21, 1996, pp. 1 and 26.

Carlson, Elof Axel. *Genes, Radiation, and Society: The Life and Work of H. J. Muller.* Ithaca, N.Y.: Cornell University Press, 1981.

Carson, Rachel. *Silent Spring.* Boston: Houghton Mifflin, 1962.

Carter, Paul A. *The Creation of Tomorrow: Fifty Years of Magazine Science Fiction.* New York: Columbia University Press, 1977.

Chapman, Clark R. *The Inner Planets: New Light on the Rocky Worlds of Mercury, Venus, Earth, the Moon, Mars, and the Asteroids.* New York: Scribner's, 1977.

Chapman, Clark R., James Pollack, and Carl Sagan. "An Analysis of the Mariner-4 Cratering Statistics." *Astronomical Journal*, Oct. 1969, p. 1047.

Chayes, Abram, and Jerome B. Wiesner, eds. *ABM: An Evaluation of the Decision to Build an Antiballistic Missile System.* New York: Harper & Row, 1969.

Chyba, Christopher. "Carl Sagan (1934–1996)," *Eos* (American Geophysical Union), Apr. 22, 1997, p. 167.

Chyba, Christopher F., and Carl Sagan. "Endogenous Production, Exogenous Delivery and Impact-Shock Synthesis of Organic Molecules: An Inventory for the Origins of Life." *Nature*, vol. 355 (1992), pp. 125–132.

Chyba, Christopher, Paul J. Thomas, Leigh Brookshaw, and Carl Sagan. "Cometary Delivery of Organic Molecules to the Early Earth." *Science*, vol. 249 (1990), pp. 366–373.

Clark, Jerome. *The UFO Book: Encyclopedia of the Extraterrestrial.* Farmington Hills, Mich.: Visible Ink Press, 1997.

Clark, Ronald W. *Einstein: The Life and Times.* New York: World Publishing Co., 1971.

———— . *JBS: The Life and Work of J. B. S. Haldane.* London: Hodder & Stoughton, 1968.

Clarke, Arthur C. *Greetings, Carbon-Based Bipeds!* New York: St. Martins, 1999 (in press).

———— . *The Promise of Space.* New York: Harper & Row, 1968.

———— . *Voices from the Sky: Previews of the Coming Space Age.* New York: Harper & Row, 1967.

Clute, John, and Peter Nicholls. *The Encyclopedia of Science Fiction* 2d ed. New York: St. Martin's, 1995.

Collins, Glenn. "The Sagans: Fiction and Fact Back to Back." *New York Times*, Sept. 30, 1985, p. B-11.

Condon, E. U. *Final Report of the Scientific Study of Unidentified Flying Objects.* New York: Bantam Books, 1969.

Cooper, Henry S. F., Jr., "A Resonance with Something Alive." *New Yorker*, June 21, 1976, p. 73.

———— . "A Resonance with Something Alive—II." *New Yorker*, June 28, 1976, p. 47.

———— . *The Search for Life on Mars: Evolution of an Idea.* New York: Holt, Rinehart & Winston, 1980.

Corn, Joseph. *The Winged Gospel: America's Romance with Aviation.* New York: Oxford University Press, 1983.

Corn, Joseph, ed. *Imagining Tomorrow: History, Technology, and the American Future.* Cambridge, Mass.: MIT Press, 1986.

Cousins, Norman. "Have We Anything to Learn from Other Planets?" *Saturday Review*, Jan. 11, 1975, p. 4.

Craig, Roy. *UFOs: An Insider's View of the Official Quest for Evidence*. Denton: University of North Texas Press, 1995.

Crease, Robert P., and Charles C. Mann. *The Second Creation: Makers of the Revolution in 20th-Century Physics*. New York: Macmillan, 1986.

Crick, Francis. *Life Itself: Its Origin and Nature*. New York: Simon & Schuster, 1981.

Crick, Francis, and Leslie Orgel. "Directed Panspermia." *Icarus*, vol. 19, 1973, p. 341.

Cromer, Dean. *Connected Knowledge: Science, Philosophy, and Education*. New York: Oxford University Press, 1997.

Croswell, Ken. *Planet Quest: The Epic Discovery of Alien Solar Systems*. New York: Free Press, 1997.

Crowe, Michael J. *The Extraterrestrial Life Debate, 1750–1900: The Idea of a Plurality of Worlds from Kant to Lowell*. New York: Cambridge University Press, 1986.

Cruikshank, Dale P. "Gerard Peter Kuiper." *Biographical Memoirs*. National Academy of Sciences, 1993.

Cruikshank, Dale P., and Joseph W. Chamberlain. "The Beginnings of the Division for Planetary Sciences of the American Astronomical Society," in David H. DeVorkin, ed., *Centennial Volume of the AAS* (1998).

Crutzen, Paul, and John Birks. "Twilight at Noon: The Atmosphere after a Nuclear War." *Ambio* (Swedish Academy of Sciences), vol. 11 (1982), pp. 114–125.

Curd, Martin, and J. A. Cover, eds. *Philosophy of Science: The Central Issues*. New York: W. W. Norton, 1998.

"The Darkened Cosmos." *Skeptical Inquirer*, March 1997 and May 1997.

Darwin, Charles. *On the Origin of Species*. Cambridge, Mass.: Harvard University Press, 1964.

Davidson, Keay. "Comet: It Could Happen to Earth." *San Francisco Examiner*, July 17, 1994, p. A-1.

———. "Earth to E.T.: We'll Be Back in Touch One Day." *San Francisco Examiner*, Jan. 13, 1994, p. A-4.

———. "Flying Saucer Sagas." *San Francisco Examiner Sunday Magazine*, June 1, 1997, p. 12.

———. "For New Age Dowsers, Water Has Become Passé." *San Francisco Examiner*, Apr. 14, 1996, p. A-1.

———. "Future of World Topic of S.F. Meet." *San Francisco Examiner*, Sept. 25, 1995, p. A-1.

———. "Hess, Seymour Lester." *American National Biography*, Vol. 10. New York: Oxford University Press, 1999.

———. "How Did All Life Begin?" *San Francisco Examiner*, "Spectra" science section, Aug. 6, 1986.

———. "In the Frozen South, 'People Get Crazy.'" *San Francisco Examiner*, Jan. 10, 1989, P. A-1.

———. "The Man behind the Bomb." *San Francisco Examiner Sunday Magazine*, Aug. 30, 1998, p. 6.

———. "Mars, You're On the Air: NASA Sending Mike to Red Planet in '99." *San Francisco Examiner*, Feb. 18, 1998, p. A-1.

———. "19th Century SETI." *Planetary Report*, Jan.-Feb. 1984, pp. 4–5.

———. "The Nobel Pursuits of Linus Pauling." *California Magazine*, Feb. 1991, p. 61.

———. "Race against Clock Imperils War Secrets." *San Francisco Examiner*, June 22, 1997, p. A-4.

———. Review of "Contact." *San Francisco Examiner*, June 11, 1997, p. C-1.

———. "S. F. Team Takes Signs of Stress in Space." *San Francisco Examiner*, July 27, 1997, p. A-1.

———. "Saganville: A Nuclear Free Zone." *San Francisco Examiner*, Dec. 24, 1996, p. A-14.

———. "Salk, Jonas." *American National Biography*, Vol. 19. New York: Oxford University Press, 1999.

———. "Scientists Deluged with Data on Planets." *San Francisco Examiner*, Sept. 9, 1994, p. A-2.

———. "Scientists Now Seek Remains of Life on Mars." *San Francisco Examiner-Chronicle*, June 23, 1996, p. A-1.

———. "Space Odyssey." *San Francisco Examiner Sunday Magazine*, June 1, 1997, p. 8.

———. "Tales from the Dark Side of Flying Saucer Research." *San Francisco Examiner*, Mar. 30, 1997, p. A-11.

———. "That Magnificent Man in His Flying Machine." *California Magazine*, Aug. 1987, pp. 84–87.

———. *Twister*. New York: Simon & Schuster/Pocket Books, 1996.

———. "UFO Fan: Roswell Saucer Story Is Bunk," *San Francisco Examiner*, June 23, 1997, p. A-1.

———. "Unquenchable Search for Life Out There." *San Francisco Examiner*, Feb. 5, 1995, p. A-1.

———. "When Worlds Collide." *San Francisco Examiner*, Aug. 29, 1990, p. B-1.

Davies, Paul. *The Fifth Miracle: The Search for the Origin and Meaning of Life*. New York: Simon & Schuster, 1999.

Davis, Nuell Pharr. *Lawrence & Oppenheimer*. New York: Simon & Schuster, 1968.

Dawidoff, Nicholas. *The Catcher Was a Spy: The Mysterious Life of Moe Berg*. New York: Pantheon Books, 1994.

Dawkins, Richard. *The Blind Watchmaker: Why the Evidence of Evolution Reveals a Universe without Design*. New York: Norton, 1986.

———. *The Selfish Gene*. New York: Oxford University Press, 1976.

Deamer, David, and Gail R. Fleischaker, eds. *Origins of Life: The Central Concepts*. Boston: Jones & Bartlett Publishers, 1994.

Delitsky, Mona, ed. "Carl Sagan and the DPS: Stories About Carl Sagan and His Interactions with Fellow Scientists," Division for Planetary Sciences, American Astronomical Society, 1997. Privately published.

DeVorkin, David H. Review of Sagan's *Cosmos*. *Sky & Telescope*, June 1981, pp. 536–537.

———. *Science with a Vengeance: How the Military Created the U.S. Space Sciences after World War II*. New York: Springer-Verlag, 1992.

Diamond, Sara. *Roads to Dominion: Right-Wing Movements and Political Power in the United States*. New York: Guilford Press, 1995.

Dick, Steven J. *The Biological Universe: The Twentieth-Century Extraterrestrial Life Debate and the Limits of Science*. New York: Cambridge University Press, 1996.

———. *Plurality of Worlds: The Origins of the Extraterrestrial Life Debate from Democritus to Kant*. New York: Cambridge University Press, 1982.

DiGregorio, Barry E. *Mars: The Living Planet*. Berkeley, Calif.: Frog, 1997.

Doctorow, E. L. *World's Fair*. New York: Random House, 1985.

Doel, Ronald E. "Evaluating Soviet Lunar Science in Cold War America," *Osiris*, 2nd series, 1992, pp. 238–264.

———. "The Lunar Volcanism Controversy." *Sky & Telescope*, Oct. 1996, pp. 26–30.

———. *Solar System Astronomy in America: Communities, Patronage, and Interdisciplinary Science, 1920–1960*. New York: Cambridge University Press, 1996.

Douglas, Susan J. *Inventing American Broadcasting 1899–1922*. Baltimore: Johns Hopkins University Press, 1987.

Drake, Frank. "Improbability of Non-thermal Radio Emission from Venus Water Clouds." *Astrophysical Journal*, vol. 149, Aug. 1967, p. 459.

Drake, Frank, and Dava Sobel. *Is Anyone Out There?: The Search for Extraterrestrial Intelligence*. New York: Delacorte Press, 1992.

Druyan, Ann. *A Famous Broken Heart: A Fantasy Novel*. New York: Stonehill Publishing Co., 1977.

Duggan, Dennis. "A Man Always in Motion." *Newsday*, Mar. 9, 1997.

Duhem, Pierre. *Medieval Cosmology: Theories of Infinity, Place, Time, Void, and the Plurality of Worlds*. Chicago: University of Chicago Press, 1985.

du Nuoy, Pierre Lecomte. *Human Destiny*. New York: Longmans, Green & Co., 1947.

Dyson, Freeman. *Infinite in All Directions*. New York: Harper & Row, 1988.

——— . *Weapons and Hope*. New York: Harper & Row, 1984.

Dzielska, Maria. *Hypatia of Alexandria*. Cambridge, Mass.: Harvard University Press, 1995.

Eddington, Arthur Stanley. *Stars and Atoms*. New Haven: Yale University Press, 1927.

Edelson, Edward. "Star Struck." *Washington Post*, Nov. 25, 1973.

Ehrlich, Paul R., Carl Sagan, Donald Kennedy, and Walter Orr Roberts, eds. *The Cold and the Dark: The World after Nuclear War*. New York: Norton, 1984.

Einstein, Albert. *The World As I See It*. New York: Philosophical Library, 1949.

Emery, C. Eugene, Jr. "*Dark Skies* Uses Pseudo-Sagan to Recast Astronomer's Motives." *Skeptical Inquirer*, Sept. 1997, p. 20.

Ezell, Edward Clinton, and Linda Neuman Ezell. *On Mars: Exploration of the Red Planet 1958–1978*. Washington, D.C.: NASA, 1984.

Farley, John. *The Spontaneous Generation Controversy from Descartes to Oparin*. Baltimore: Johns Hopkins University Press, 1977.

Fergus, George. "A Checklist of SF Novels with Female Protagonists," Extrapolation, Dec. 1976, 20–27.

Ferris, Timothy. *The Red Limit: The Search for the Edge of the Universe*. New York: Morrow, 1977.

——— . "The Risks and Rewards of Popularizing Science," *Chronicle of Higher Education*, Apr. 4, 1997.

Feyerabend, Paul. *Against Method*. Atlantic Highlands, N.J.: Humanities Press, 1975.

——— . *Killing Time: The Autobiography of Paul Feyerabend*. Chicago: University of Chicago Press, 1995.

Feynman, Richard. "*Surely You're Joking, Mr. Feynman!*": Adventures of a Curious Character. New York: W.W. Norton, 1985.

Fimmel, Richard O., William Swindell, and Eric Burgess. *Pioneer Odyssey*. Washington, D.C.: NASA, 1977.

Firsoff, V. A. *The Interior Planets*. London: Oliver and Boyd, 1968.

Fisher, David E. *The Birth of the Earth: A Wanderlied Through Space, Time, and the Human Imagination*. New York: Columbia University Press, 1987.

Fisher, David E., and Marshall Jon Fisher. *Strangers in the Night: A Brief History of Life on Other Worlds*. Washington, D.C.: Counterpoint Press, 1998.

"Flying Saucers Deserve More Investigation, Scientists Say." *Houston Chronicle*, Dec. 28, 1969.

Franklin, H. Bruce. *Robert A. Heinlein: America as Science Fiction*. New York: Oxford University Press, 1980.

——— . *War Stars: The Superweapon and the American Imagination*. New York: Oxford University Press, 1988.

Frazier, Kendrick, ed. *Encounters with the Paranormal: Science, Knowledge, and Belief*. Amherst, N.Y.: Prometheus Books, 1998.

Friedan, Betty. *The Feminine Mystique*. New York: Norton, 1963.

Frisch, Otto. *What Little I Remember.* New York: Cambridge University Press, 1979.

Fuller, John G. *Incident at Exeter: The Story of Unidentified Flying Objects over America Today.* New York: Putnam, 1966.

———. *The Interrupted Journey: Two Lost Hours aboard a "Flying Saucer."* New York: Dial Press, 1966.

"The Future of Planetary Exploration: A Dialogue between Daniel Goldin and Carl Sagan." *Planetary Report,* July 1993, pp. 18–23.

Gamow, George. *The Birth and Death of the Sun: Stellar Evolution and Solar Atomic Energy.* New York: New American Library, 1952.

Gamow, George, and J. Allen Hynek. "A New Theory by C. F. Von Weizsacker of the Origin of the Planetary System." *Astrophysical Journal,* vol. 101, Jan.-May 1945, pp. 249–254.

Gardner, Howard (with Emma Laskin). *Leading Minds: An Anatomy of Leadership.* New York: Basic Books, 1995.

Gardner, Martin. *Fads and Fallacies in the Name of Science.* New York: Dover, 1952.

Garland, Fred M. "Snow on the Moon." *Popular Astronomy,* vol. 54 (1946), p. 176.

Gavaghan, Helen. *Something New under the Sun: Satellites and the Beginning of the Space Age.* New York: Copernicus, 1998.

Gay, Peter G. *Freud: A Life for Our Time.* New York: Norton, 1988.

Gelernter, David Hillel. *1939: The Lost World of the Fair.* New York: Free Press, 1995.

"George Sagan, 79, Led Coat Company," *New York Times,* Feb. 1, 1975.

Geras, Norman. *The Contract of Mutual Indifference: Political Philosophy after the Holocaust.* New York: Verso, 1998.

Gilbert, James. *Redeeming Culture: American Religion in an Age of Science.* Chicago: University of Chicago Press, 1997.

Gillette, Robert. "Velikovsky: AAAS Forum for a Mild Collision." *Science,* Mar. 15, 1974, p. 1059.

Ginenthal, Charles. *Carl Sagan & Immanuel Velikovsky.* Tempe, Ariz.: New Falcon Publications, 1995.

Glashow, Sheldon L., and Ben Bova. *Interactions: A Journey through the Mind of a Particle Physicist and the Matter of This World.* New York: Warner Books, 1988.

Gleick, James. *Genius: The Life and Science of Richard Feynman.* New York: Pantheon, 1992.

Goenner, Hubert, and Giuseppe Castagnetti. "Albert Einstein as Pacifist and Democrat during World War I." *Science in Context,* vol. 9 (1996), pp. 325–386.

Gold, Thomas. *The Deep Hot Biosphere.* New York: Copernicus, 1999.

Golden, Frederic. "In Memoriam: Recollections of Carl Sagan." *Newsletter of the National Association of Science Writers,* Winter 1996-7, p. 1.

———. "Showman of Science," *Time,* Oct. 20, 1980, pp. 2, 62–69.

Goldsmith, Donald. *The Hunt for Life on Mars.* New York: Dutton, 1997.

———. *Worlds Unnumbered: The Search for Extrasolar Planets.* Sausalito, Calif.: University Science Books, 1997.

———, ed. *The Quest for Extraterrestrial Life: A Book of Readings.* Mill Valley, Calif.: University Science Books, 1980.

———, ed. *Scientists Confront Velikovsky.* Ithaca, N.Y.: Cornell University Press, 1977.

Goodell, Rae. *The Visible Scientists.* Boston: Little, Brown, 1977.

"Gore Hails 'Greening' of America's Churches." *Washington Post,* Oct. 9, 1993.

Gould, Stephen Jay. "Bright Star among Billions," *Science,* Jan. 31, 1997, p. 299.

Graham, Loren R. *Science, Philosophy, and Human Behavior in the Soviet Union.* New York: Columbia University Press, 1987.

Grant, Edward. *Planets, Stars, & Orbs: The Medieval Cosmos 1200–1687.* New York: Cambridge University Press, 1994.

Gray, Colin S., and Keith Payne. "Victory Is Possible." *Foreign Policy*, Summer 1980, pp. 20–21.

Greenberg, Daniel S. "Monkeys in Outer Space?" *Washington Post*, Apr. 20, 1997, C-7.

Griffin, Nancy, and Kim Masters. *Hit & Run: How Jon Peters and Peter Guber Took Sony for a Ride in Hollywood*. New York: Simon & Schuster, 1996.

Grinspoon, Lester. *Marihuana Reconsidered*. Cambridge, Mass.: Harvard University Press, 1971.

Gross, Paul R. "Blockbuster Homiletics." *The New Criterion*, Oct. 1997, p. 69.

Gross, Paul R., and Norman Levitt. *Higher Superstition: The Academic Left and Its Quarrels with Science*. Baltimore: Johns Hopkins University Press, 1994.

Guthke, Karl S. *The Last Frontier: Imagining Other Worlds from the Copernican Revolution to Modern Science Fiction*. Ithaca, N.Y.: Cornell University Press, 1990.

Guthrie, Stewart Elliott. *Faces in the Clouds: A New Theory of Religion*. New York: Oxford University Press, 1993.

Hacker, Barton C. *Elements of Controversy: The Atomic Energy Commission and Radiation Safety in Nuclear Weapons*. Berkeley: University of California Press, 1994.

Hall, Richard H. *The UFO Evidence*. Washington, D.C.: National Investigations Committee on Aerial Phenomena, 1964.

Hanson, N. R. *Patterns of Discovery: An Inquiry into the Conceptual Foundations of Science*. Cambridge, Eng.: Cambridge University Press, 1958.

Haramundanis, Katharine, ed. *Cecilia Payne-Gaposchkin: An Autobiography and Other Recollections*. 2nd ed. New York: Cambridge University Press, 1996.

Hargrove, Eugene C., ed. *Beyond Spaceship Earth: Environmental Ethics and the Solar System*. San Francisco: Sierra Club Books, 1986.

Hart, Michael. "An Explanation for the Absence of Extraterrestrials on Earth." *QJRAS*, vol. 16 (1975), p. 128.

Hartman, Edwin P. *Adventures in Research: A History of Ames Research Center 1940–1965*. Washington, D.C.: NASA, 1970.

Heilbron, John L. *Lawrence and His Laboratory: A History of the Lawrence Berkeley Laboratory*. Berkeley: University of California Press, 1989.

——— . "Thomas Samuel Kuhn," *Isis*, Sept. 1998, pp. 505–515.

Heinlein, Robert. *I Will Fear No Evil*. New York: Putnam, 1970.

Hewlett, Richard G., and Oscar E. Anderson Jr. *The New World: A History of the United States Atomic Energy Commission*. vol. 1, 1939–1946. Berkeley: University of California Press, 1991.

Hofstadter, Richard. *The Age of Reform: From Bryan to FDR*. New York: Vintage, 1955.

Holden, Constance. "Scientists Describe 'Nuclear Winter.'" *Science*, Nov. 18, 1983, p. 822.

Holden, Stephen. "Which Way Upward, on a Wing or Prayer?" *New York Times*, July 11, 1997, pp. B-1 and B-20.

Hollinger, David A. *Science, Jews, and Secular Culture: Studies in Mid-Twentieth-Century American Intellectual History*. Princeton, N.J.: Princeton University Press, 1996.

——— . *Morris R. Cohen and the Scientific Ideal*. Cambridge, Mass.: MIT Press, 1975.

Holton, Gerald. "Johannes Kepler's Universe: Its Physics and Metaphysics." In Robert M. Palter, ed., *Toward Modern Science* (1969), p. 460.

Holtsmark, Erling B. *Edgar Rice Burroughs*. Boston: Twayne Publishers, 1986.

Horowitz, Norman, R. P. Sharp, and R. W. Davies. "Planetary Contamination I: The Problem and the Agreements." *Science*, Mar. 24, 1967, p. 1501.

Howe, Irving (with Kenneth Libo). *World of Our Fathers*. New York: Harcourt Brace Jovanovich, 1976.

Hoyle, Fred. *The Black Cloud*. New York: Harper, 1957.

Hoyle, Fred, and N. C. Wickramasinghe. *Diseases from Space*. New York: Harper & Row, 1980.

Hoyt, William Graves. *Lowell and Mars*. Tucson: University of Arizona Press, 1976.

Huxley, Julian. *Evolution: The Modern Synthesis*. New York: Harper & Brothers, 1943.

——. *Evolution in Action*. New York: Harper, 1953.

Hynek, J. Allen, and Jacques Vallee. *The Edge of Reality: A Progress Report on Unidentified Flying Objects*. Chicago: Regnery, 1975.

Illustrated World, April 1920, p. 242.

"Iosif Samuilovch Shklovskii," *QJRAS* (1968), p. 700.

"Is the Earth Safe from Lunar Contaminants?" *Time*, June 12, 1969, p. 78.

Jacobs, David Michael. *The UFO Controversy in America*. Bloomington: Indiana University Press, 1975.

James, J. N. "The Voyage of Mariner II." *Scientific American*, July 1963, p. 70.

Jastrow, Joseph. *Error and Eccentricity in Human Belief*. New York: Dover, 1962.

Jastrow, Robert. "Velikovsky, A Star-Crossed Theoretician of the Cosmos." *New York Times*, Dec. 2, 1979, section IV, p. 22.

Jeffrey, Francis, and John C. Lilly, M.D. *John Lilly, So Far . . .* Los Angeles: J. P. Tarcher, 1990.

Jet Propulsion Laboratory. *Mariner Mission to Venus*. Compiled by Harold J. Wheelock. New York: McGraw-Hill, 1963.

——. *Mariner-Venus 1962: Final Project Report*. Washington, D.C.: NASA, 1965.

"Johnny Carson, the Prince of Chitchat, Is a Loner," *Look*, Jan. 25, 1966, p. 98.

Johnson, George. "Useful Invention or Absolute Truth: What Is Math?", *New York Times*, Feb. 10, 1998, p. B-9.

Jones, Caroline A., and Galison, Peter, eds. (with Amy Slaton). *Picturing Science Producing Art*. New York: Routledge, 1998.

Jones, Raymond F. "Pete Can Fix It." *Astounding Science Fiction*, Feb. 1947, pp. 64-83.

Jones, Sir Harold Spencer. *Life on Other Worlds*. New York: Macmillan, 1940.

Judson, Horace Freeland. *The Eighth Day of Creation*. New York: Simon & Schuster, 1979.

Jung, Carl. *Psychology and the Occult*. Princeton, N.J.: Princeton University Press, 1977.

Kahn, Herman. *On Thermonuclear War*. Princeton, N.J.: Princeton University Press, 1961.

——. *Thinking About the Unthinkable*. New York: Horizon Press, 1962.

Kaku, Michio. *Hyperspace: A Scientific Odyssey through Parallel Universes, Time Warps, and the 10th Dimension*. New York: Oxford University Press, 1994.

Kaler, James B. *Cosmic Clouds: Birth, Death, and Recycling in the Galaxy*. New York: Scientific American Library, 1997.

Kaplan, Fred. *The Wizards of Armageddon*. New York: Simon & Schuster, 1983.

Kaplan, Rabbi Mordecai. *Judaism as a Civilization: Toward a Reconstruction of American Jewish Life*. New York: Macmillan, 1934.

Katz, Ephraim. *The Film Encyclopedia*. 2d ed. New York: HarperCollins, 1994.

Kauffman, Stuart. *The Origins of Order: Self-Organization and Selection in Evolution*. New York: Oxford University Press, 1993.

Kellogg, W. W. and Carl Sagan. "The Terrestrial Planets." *Annual Review of Astronomy and Astrophysics*, vol. 1, pp. 235–266.

Kerr, Richard A. "Requiem for Life on Mars? Support for Microbes Fades." *Science*, Nov. 20, 1998, pp. 1398–1400.

Kerr, Richard A. "The Solar System's New Diversity." *Science*, Sept. 2, 1994, pp. 1360–1362.

Kevles, Daniel J. *The Physicists: The History of a Scientific Community in Modern America*. New York: Knopf, 1978.

Kissinger, Henry. *Nuclear Weapons and Foreign Policy*. New York: Harper, 1957.

Klass, Philip J. *UFOs Explained*. New York: Random House, 1974.

Koestler, Arthur. *The Sleepwalkers*. New York: Macmillan, 1963.

Kokoshin, Andrei A. *Soviet Strategic Thought, 1917–91*. Cambridge, Mass.: MIT Press, 1998.

Kozyrev, N. A. "Observations of a Volcanic Process on the Moon." *Sky & Telescope*, Feb. 1959, p. 184.

Kragh, Helge. *Cosmology and Controversy: The Historical Development of Two Theories of the Universe*. Princeton, N.J.: Princeton University Press, 1996.

Kuhn, Thomas S. *The Copernican Revolution: Planetary Astronomy in the Development of Western Thought*. New York: Random House, 1959.

———. *The Essential Tension: Selected Studies in Scientific Tradition and Change*. Chicago: University of Chicago Press, 1977.

———. *The Structure of Scientific Revolutions*. Chicago: University of Chicago Press, 1962.

Kuiper, Gerard. "Lunar and Planetary Laboratory Studies of Jupiter—II." *Sky & Telescope*, Feb. 1972, p. 76.

Kull, Steven. *Minds at War: Nuclear Reality and the Inner Conflicts of Defense Policymakers*. New York: Basic Books, 1988.

Lang, Kenneth R., and Owen Gingerich. *A Source Book in Astronomy and Astrophysics, 1900–1975*. Cambridge, Mass.: Harvard University Press, 1979.

Laurence, William L. "On Life Elsewhere." *New York Times*, June 23, 1963, p. E-7.

Lawler, Peter Augustine. "Aliens in the Cosmos—Or, the Curious Affair of Carl Sagan and E.T." *The American Enterprise*, Sept. 1998, p. 47.

Lears, Jackson. *No Place of Grace: Antimodernism and the Transformation of American Culture 1880–1920*. New York: Pantheon, 1981.

Leary, Timothy. *Flashbacks: A Personal and Cultural History of an Era: An Autobiography*. Los Angeles: J. P. Tarcher, 1990.

Lederberg, Joshua. "Exobiology: Approaches to Life beyond the Earth." *Science*, Aug. 12, 1960, p. 393.

———. "Sputnik 1957–1987," *The Scientist*, Oct. 5, 1987.

Lederberg, Joshua, and Dean B. Cowie. "Moondust." *Science*, June 27, 1958, p. 1473.

Lederberg, Joshua, and Carl Sagan. "Microenvironments for Life on Mars." *PNAS*, Sept. 15, 1962, p. 1473.

Lefanu, Sarah. *Feminism and Science Fiction*. Bloomington: Indiana University Press, 1989.

Leifer, Stephanie D. "Reaching for the Stars." *Scientific American*, Feb. 1999, pp. 94–95.

Lerner, Michael. " 'Contact'—A Spiritual High." *Tikkun*, Sept. 1997, p. 8.

Levy, David H. *The Man Who Sold the Milky Way: A Biography of Bart Bok*. Tucson: University of Arizona Press, 1993.

Lewis, Sinclair. *Arrowsmith*. New York: Harcourt, Brace & Co,, 1925.

Lewontin, Richard. Review of *The Demon-Haunted World* by Carl Sagan. *New York Review of Books*, Jan. 9, 1997, p. 28.

Ley, Willy. *The Conquest of Space*. New York: Viking Press, 1949.

———. *Mariner IV to Mars*. New York: Signet, 1966.

Libby, Willard F. "Ice Caps on Venus." *Science*, Mar. 8, 1968, p. 1097.

Lilly, John C. *Man and Dolphin*. Garden City, N.Y.: Doubleday, 1961.

Linden, Eugene. *Silent Partners: The Legacy of the Ape Language Experiments*. New York: Times Books, 1986.

Linn, Edward. "The Soft-Sell, Soft-Shell World of Johnny Carson." *Saturday Evening Post*, Dec. 22, 1962.

Littauer, Raphael, et al. "The American Way of Bombing." *Harper's Magazine*, June 1972, pp. 55–58.

Littauer, Raphael, and Norman Uphoff, eds., with Carl Sagan and others. *The Air War in Indochina*. Boston: Beacon Press, 1971.

LoBrutto, Vincent. *Stanley Kubrick: A Biography*. New York: D. I. Fine Books, 1997.

Lovejoy, Arthur. *The Great Chain of Being: A Study of the History of an Idea*. Cambridge, Mass.: Harvard University Press, 1936.

Lovins, Amory. *Non-nuclear Futures: The Case for An Ethical Energy Strategy*. San Francisco: Friends of the Earth International, 1975.

Lowell, Percival. *Mars*. New York: Houghton Mifflin, 1895.

Mack, John. *Abduction: Human Encounters with Aliens*. New York: Scribner's, 1994.

Maddox, John. "Nuclear Winter Not Yet Established." *Nature*, Mar. 1, 1984, p. 11.

Mallove, Eugene, and Gregory Matloff. *The Starflight Handbook: A Pioneer's Guide to Interstellar Travel*. New York: Wiley, 1989.

Manso, Peter. *Brando: The Biography*. New York: Hyperion, 1994.

Margulis, Lynn. *Symbiotic Planet: A New Look at Evolution*. New York: Basic Books, 1998.

Margulis, Lynn, and James Lovelock. "Biological Modulation of the Earth's Atmosphere." *Icarus*, vol. 21 (1974), p. 471.

Margulis, Lynn, and Dorion Sagan. *Slanted Truths: Essays on Gaia, Symbiosis, and Evolution*. New York: Copernicus, 1997.

"Mariner Scans a Lifeless Venus." *National Geographic*, May 1963, p. 733.

Marov, Mikhail Ya., and David Grinspoon. *The Planet Venus*. New Haven: Yale University Press, 1998.

Marsh, Jeffrey. "The Universe and Dr. Sagan." *Commentary*, May 1981, pp. 64–68.

Marshall, Eliot. "Nuclear Winter Debate Heats Up." *Science*, Jan. 16, 1987, p. 271.

Marx, Karl, and Friedrich Engels. *The Communist Manifesto*. New York: Monthly Review Press, 1964.

Mayer, Cornell. "The Temperatures of the Planets." *Scientific American*, May 1961, p. 58.

Mayr, Ernst. *The Growth of Biological Thought: Diversity, Evolution and Inheritance*. Cambridge, Mass.: Belknap Press, 1982.

——— . *Toward a New Philosophy of Biology: Observations of an Evolutionist*. Cambridge, Mass.: Belknap Press of Harvard University Press, 1988.

McBride, Joseph. *Steven Spielberg: A Biography*. New York: Simon & Schuster, 1997.

McCurdy, Howard E. *Space and the American Imagination*. Washington: Smithsonian Institution Press, 1997.

McDougall, Walter A. *The Heavens and the Earth: A Political History of the Space Age*. New York: Basic Books, 1985.

McDowell, Edwin. "Sagan Sells First Novel to Simon & Schuster." *New York Times*, Jan. 13, 1981, p. C-16.

McLaughlin, Dean B. "Further Notes on Martian Features." *PASP*, Oct. 1954, p. 221.

——— . "Interpretation of Some Martian Features." *PASP*, Aug. 1954, p. 161.

McMurray, Emily J., ed. *Notable 20th-Century Scientists*. Detroit, Mich.: Gale Research, 1995.

Medvedev, Zhores A. *The Rise and Fall of T. D. Lysenko*. Garden City, N.Y.: Doubleday, 1969.

Menzel, Donald H., and Fred Whipple, "The Case for H$_2$O Clouds on Venus." *Astronomical Journal* (1954), pp. 329-330.

——— . "The Case for H$_2$O Clouds on Venus." *PASP* (1955), pp. 161-168.

Menzel, Donald H., and Lyle G. Boyd. *The World of Flying Saucers: A Scientific Examination of a Major Myth of the Space Age*. New York: Doubleday, 1963.

Michaud, Michael. *Reaching for the High Frontier: The American Pro-Space Movement*. New York: Praeger, 1986.

Miller, James B., ed. *An Evolving Dialogue: Scientific, Historical, Philosophical and Theological Perspectives on Evolution*. Washington, D.C.: AAAS, 1998.

Miller, Stanley. "The Endogenous Synthesis of Organic Compounds," in André Brack, *The Molecular Origins of Life: Assembling Pieces of the Puzzle*, chapter 3. New York: Cambridge University Press (1998).

———. "A Production of Amino Acids under Possible Primitive Earth Conditions." *Science*, May 15, 1953.

———. "Production of Some Organic Compounds under Possible Primitive Earth Conditions." *Journal of the American Chemical Society*, May 12, 1955, p. 2351.

Miller, Stanley, and Carl Sagan, "Molecular Synthesis in Simulated Reducing Planetary Atmospheres." *Astronomical Journal*, vol. 65, 1960, p. 499.

"Monkey Business." *Space News*, May 20, 1996, p. 12.

Moore, Patrick. "The Turbulent Life of E. J. Öpik." *Sky & Telescope*, February 1986, p. 149.

Morgenthaler, George W., ed. *Exploration of Mars*. Vol. 15, *Advances in the Astronautical Sciences*. North Hollywood, Calif.: American Astronautical Society, 1963.

Morowitz, Harold J., and Carl Sagan. "Life in the Clouds of Venus?" *Nature*, Sept. 16, 1967, p. 1259.

Motz, Lloyd. "A Personal Reminiscence," in S. Fred Singer, ed., *The Universe and its Origin*. New York: Paragon House, 1990, pp. 47–56.

Mumford, Lewis. *The Myth of the Machine: The Pentagon of Power*. New York: Harcourt Brace Jovanovich, 1970.

NASA. *Project Cyclops: A Design Study of a System for Detecting Extraterrestrial Intelligent Life*. NASA and Stanford University, 1972.

Nasar, Sylvia. *A Beautiful Mind: A Biography of John Forbes Nash Jr., Winner of the Nobel Prize in Economics*. New York: Simon & Schuster, 1998.

Neugebauer, Gerry, Lewis Kaplan, and Stillman Chase. "Mariner II: Preliminary Reports on Measurements of Venus." *Science*, Mar. 8, 1963, p. 905.

Nolan, Janne E. *Guardians of the Arsenal: The Politics of Nuclear Strategy*. New York: Basic Books, 1989.

"Notes and Comment." *New Yorker*, June 1, 1992, p. 23.

"Nuclear Thaw." *National Review*, Feb. 19, 1990, p. 18.

"'Nuclear Winter' from Gulf War Discounted." *Science*, Jan. 25, 1991, p. 372.

Numbers, Ronald. *Creation by Natural Law: Laplace's Nebular Hypothesis in American Thought*. Seattle: University of Washington Press, 1977.

Nye, David. *The American Technological Sublime*. Cambridge, Mass.: MIT Press, 1994.

Oberg, James, and Alcestis Oberg. *Pioneering Space: Living on the Next Frontier*. New York: McGraw-Hill, 1986.

"Objections to Astrology." *The Humanist*, Sept.-Oct. 1975, p. 4.

Obst, Lynda. *Hello, He Lied: And Other Truths from the Hollywood Trenches*. Boston: Little, Brown, 1996.

O'Connor, John J. "'Cosmos': A Trip into Outer Space." *New York Times*, Sept. 28, 1980, p. 39.

———. "Putting 'Cosmos' into Perspective." *New York Times*, Dec. 14, 1980.

Olby, Robert. *The Path to the Double Helix: The Discovery of DNA*. New York: Dover, 1974.

O'Neill, Dan. *The Firecracker Boys*. New York: St. Martin's, 1994.

O'Neill, Gerard K. *The High Frontier: Human Colonies in Space*. New York: Morrow, 1977.

O'Neill, Gerard K., ed. *Space Resources and Space Settlements*. Washington, D.C.: NASA (Publication SP-428), 1979.

Öpik, E. J. "The Aeolosphere and Atmosphere of Venus." *Journal of Geophysical Research*, Sept. 1961, p. 2818.

Ordway, Frederick I. III, and Mitchell R. Sharpe. *The Rocket Team*. New York: Crowell, 1979.

Orgel, L. E. *The Origins of Life: Molecules and Natural Selection.* New York: Wiley, 1973.

Osterbrock, Donald C. *Yerkes Observatory 1892–1950: The Birth, Near Death, and Resurrection of a Scientific Research Institution.* Chicago: University of Chicago Press, 1997.

Ozick, Cynthia. "If You Can Read This, You Are Too Far Out." *Esquire,* Jan. 1973, p. 74.

Pais, Abraham. *"Subtle Is the Lord . . .": The Science and the Life of Albert Einstein.* New York: Oxford University Press, 1982.

Palter, Robert M., ed. *Toward Modern Science: Studies in Ancient and Medieval Science.* New York: Noonday Press, 1961.

"Panel Agrees That Life beyond Earth Exists but Differs on Establishing Contact." *New York Times,* Nov. 20, 1972, p. 29.

Pensée, the editors of. *Velikovsky Reconsidered.* Garden City, N.Y.: Doubleday, 1976.

Percy, Walker. *Lost in the Cosmos: The Last Self-Help Book.* New York: Farrar, Straus, and Giroux, 1983.

Pettijohn, F. J. *Memoirs of an Unrepentant Field Geologist: A Candid Profile of Some Geologists and Their Science.* Chicago: University of Chicago Press, 1984.

Pickering, W. H. "Life on the Moon." *Popular Astronomy,* vol. 45 (1937).

Pirsig, Robert M. *Zen and the Art of Motorcycle Maintenance.* New York: Morrow, 1974.

Pittendrigh, Colin S., et al., eds. *Biology and the Exploration of Mars.* Washington, D.C.: National Academy of Sciences/National Research Council, 1966.

Plummer, William, and John Strong. "An Answer to F. D. Drake." *Astrophysical Journal,* vol. 149, Aug. 1967, p. 463.

Ponnamperuma, Cyril. "Life in the Universe." Undated article from unidentified anthology (Government Printing Office code number 892-331), p. 69.

Ponnamperuma, Cyril, Carl Sagan, and Ruth Mariner. "Synthesis of Adenosine Triphosphate under Possible Primitive Earth Conditions." *Nature,* July 20, 1963, p. 223.

Ponnamperuma, Cyril, Ruth Mariner, and Carl Sagan. "Formation of Adenosine by Ultra-violet Irradiation of a Solution of Adenine and Ribose." *Nature,* June 22, 1963, p. 1199.

Porges, Irwin. *Edgar Rice Burroughs: The Man Who Created Tarzan.* Provo, Utah: Brigham Young University Press, 1976.

Postman, Neil. *Amusing Ourselves to Death: Public Discourse in the Age of Show Business.* New York: Viking, 1985.

Poundstone, William. *Prisoner's Dilemma.* New York: Doubleday, 1992.

Power, Gen. Thomas S. (with Albert A. Arnhym). *Design for Survival.* New York: Coward-McCann, 1965.

Powers, Thomas. "Nuclear Winter and Nuclear Strategy." *Atlantic Monthly,* Nov. 1984, pp. 53, 64.

Raeburn, Paul. *Uncovering the Secrets of the Red Planet: Mars.* Washington, D.C.: National Geographic Society, 1998.

"Rainy Forecast for Gulf Area?" *Science,* Aug. 30, 1991, p. 971.

Rea, D. G., Brian O'Leary, and William Sinton. "Mars: The Origin of the 3.58- and 3.69-Micron Minima in the Infrared Spectra." *Science,* Mar. 12, 1965, p. 1286.

Rebovich, David Paul. "Sagan's Metaphysical Parable." *Social Science and Modern Society,* July 1981, pp. 91–95.

Redman, Deborah A. *Economics and the Philosophy of Science.* New York: Oxford University Press, 1993.

"Reichstag Fire II." *National Review,* Dec. 19, 1986, p. 19.

"Religiously Speaking, A Look at Films," *New York Times,* Mar. 14, 1998, A-15.

Rensberger, Boyce. "Carl Sagan: Obliged to Explain." *New York Times Book Review,* May 29, 1977, p. 8.

"Report of the COSPAR Panel on Planetary Quarantine, Leningrad, May 1970." *Icarus*, vol. 14, p. 112 (1971).

Restak, Richard. "The Brain Knew More Than the Genes." *New York Times Book Review*, May 29, 1977, p. 8.

Rhodes, Richard. *The Making of the Atomic Bomb*. New York: Simon & Schuster, 1986.

Richelson, Jeffrey. *American Espionage and the Soviet Target*. New York: William Morrow, 1987.

Ridpath, Ian. "A Man Whose Time Has Come." *New Scientist*, July 4, 1974, p. 36.

Rischin, Moses. *The Promised City: New York's Jews, 1870–1914*. Cambridge, Mass.: Harvard University, Press, 1962.

Ritchie, Michael. *Please Stand By: A Prehistory of Television*. Woodstock, N.Y.: Overlook Press, 1994.

Robertson, Douglas S. *The New Renaissance: Computers and the Next Level of Civilization*. New York: Oxford University Press, 1998.

Rose, Norman A., ed. *The Letters and Papers of Chaim Weizmann*. Vol. 19, series A. London: Oxford University Press, 1968.

Roszak, Theodore. *The Making of a Counter Culture: Reflections on the Technocratic Society and Its Youthful Opposition*. Garden City, N.Y.: Doubleday, 1969.

Rothman, Tony. *Science à la Mode: Physical Fashions and Fictions*. Princeton, N.J.: Princeton University Press. 1989.

Royal, Robert. "Carl Sagan in Space." *American Spectator*, June 1986, p. 29.

Ruppelt, E. J. *Report on Unidentified Flying Objects*. Garden City, N.Y.: Doubleday, 1956.

Safire, William. *Lend Me Your Ears: Great Speeches in History*. New York: W. W. Norton, 1992 and 1997.

Sagan, Carl. *Billions and Billions: Thoughts on Life and Death at the Brink of the Millennium*. New York: Random House, 1997.

———. "Biological Contamination of the Moon." *Science*, Nov. 20, 1959, p. 1424.

———. "Biological Contamination of the Moon." *PNAS*, Apr. 15, 1960, p. 396.

———. "Biological Exploration of Mars." In George W. Morgenthaler, ed., *Exploration of Mars*, Vol. 15, *Advances in the Astronautical Sciences* (American Astronautical Society, 1963), p. 576.

———. *Broca's Brain: Reflections on the Romance of Science*. New York: Random House, 1979.

———. *Contact*. New York: Simon & Schuster, 1985.

———. *The Cosmic Connection*. Garden City, N.Y.: Anchor Press, 1973.

———. *Cosmos*. New York: Random House, 1980.

———. *The Demon-Haunted World: Science as a Candle in the Dark*. New York: Random House, 1996.

———. "Direct Contact Among Galactic Civilizations by Relativistic Interstellar Spaceflight," *Planetary and Space Science*, May 1963, pp. 485–498.

———. *The Dragons of Eden: Speculations on the Evolution of Human Intelligence*. New York: Random House, 1977.

———. "Going beyond Viking 1. . . ." *New York Times*, Aug. 11, 1976, p. 35.

———. "Growing Up with Science Fiction." *New York Times Sunday Magazine*, May 28, 1978, p. 24.

———. "Higher Organisms on Mars." In *Biology and the Exploration of Mars*, ed. by Colin S. Pittendrigh et al. National Academy of Sciences/National Research Council, 1966.

———. "Indigenous Organic Matter on the Moon." *PNAS*, Apr. 15, 1960, p. 393.

———. "Kuiper, Gerard P(eter)." *Icarus*, vol. 22, (1974), pp. 117–118.

———. Letter on anti-astrology petition to *The Humanist*, Jan.-Feb. 1976.

———. "Life on the Surface of Venus?" *Nature*, Dec. 23, 1967, p. 1198.

———. "The Long Winter Model of Martian Biology: A Speculation." *Icarus* (1971), p. 511.

———. "Mars: A New World to Explore." *National Geographic*, Dec. 1967, p. 820.

———. "Nuclear War and Climatic Catastrophe: Some Policy Implications." *Foreign Affairs*, Winter 1983–4, p. 257.

———. "On Minimizing the Consequences of Nuclear War." *Nature*, Oct. 10, 1985, p. 485.

———. *Other Worlds*. New York: Bantam Books, 1975.

———. *Pale Blue Dot: A Vision of the Human Future in Space*. New York: Random House, 1994.

———. "Physical Studies of the Planets." Ph.D. dissertation. Chicago: University of Chicago, 1960.

———. "The Planet Venus." *Science*, Mar. 24, 1961, p. 849.

———. *Planetary Exploration*. Eugene, Ore.: State System of Higher Education, 1970.

———. "Radiation and the Origin of the Gene." *Evolution*, 1957, p. 53.

———. "Said the Martian Microbe. . . ." *New York Times*, Feb. 22, 1975, p. 27.

———. "The Saucerian Cult." *Saturday Review*, Aug. 6, 1966, p. 50.

———. Testimony, "Symposium on Unidentified Flying Objects." House of Representatives Committee on Science and Astronautics, chaired by Rep. J. Edward Roush, July 29, 1968, p. 85–98.

———. "Unidentified Flying Objects." *Bulletin of Atomic Scientists*, June 1967, p. 43.

Sagan, Carl, and Sidney Coleman. "Spacecraft Sterilization Standards and Contamination of Mars." *Astronautics and Aeronautics*, vol. 3 (1965), pp. 22–27.

Sagan, Carl, Frank Drake, Ann Druyan, Timothy Ferris, Jon Lomberg, and Linda Salzman Sagan. *Murmurs of Earth: The Voyager Interstellar Record*. New York: Random House, 1978.

Sagan, Carl, and Ann Druyan. *Comet*. New York: Random House, 1985.

———. *Shadows of Forgotten Ancestors: A Search for Who We Are*. New York: Random House, 1992.

Sagan, Carl, and Paul Fox. "The Canals of Mars: An Assessment after Mariner 9." *Icarus*, vol. 25, 1975, p. 602.

Sagan, Carl, and Bishun Khare. "Long-Wavelength UV Photoproduction of Amino Acids on the Primitive Earth." *Science*, July 30, 1971, p. 417.

Sagan, Carl, and Joshua Lederberg. "The Prospects for Life on Mars: A Pre-Viking Assessment." *Icarus*, vol. 28, 1976, p. 291.

Sagan, Carl, Jonathan Norton Leonard, and the editors of *Life. The Planets*. New York: Time Inc., 1966.

Sagan, Carl, E. R. Lippincott, R. Eck, and Margaret O. Dayhoff. "Thermodynamic Equilibria in Planetary Atmospheres." *Astrophysical Journal*, vol. 147, no. 2, 1967, p. 753.

Sagan, Carl, and Stanley Miller, "Molecular Synthesis in Simulated Reducing Planetary Atmospheres."*Astronomical Journal*, vol. 65, 1960, p. 499.

Sagan, Carl, and George Mullen. "Earth and Mars: Evolution of Atmospheres and Surface Temperatures." *Science*, July 7, 1972, pp. 52–56.

Sagan, Carl, and William I. Newman. "The Solipsist Approach to Extraterrestrial Intelligence." *QJRAS*, 1983, p. 113.

Sagan, Carl, and James Pollack. "On the Nature of the Canals of Mars." *Nature*, Oct. 8, 1966.

———. "Planetary Engineering." *Eos* (American Geophysical Union), Nov. 1, 1994, pp. 98–99.

Sagan, Carl, and E. Salpeter. "Particles, Environments, and Possible Ecologies in the Jovian Atmosphere." *Astrophysical Journal*, 1976, p. 737.

Sagan, Carl, and Steven Soter. "Pattern Recognition and Zeti Reticuli," *Astronomy*, vol. 3, no. 7, pp. 39–40.

———. "The Zeti Reticuli Affair," *Astronomy*, vol. 3, no. 9, pp. 16–17.

Sagan, Carl, O. B. Toon, and James Pollack. "Anthropogenic Albedo Changes and the Earth's Climate." *Science*, Dec. 21, 1979, p. 1363.

Sagan, Carl, and Richard Turco. *A Path Where No Man Thought: Nuclear Winter and the End of the Arms Race*. New York: Random House, 1990.

Sagan, Carl, Richard Turco, O. B. Toon, Thomas Ackerman, and James Pollack. "Climate and Smoke: An Appraisal of Nuclear Winter." *Science*, Jan. 12, 1990, p. 166.

Sagan, Carl, and Russell G. Walker. "The Infrared Detectability of Dyson Civilizations." *Astrophysical Journal*, vol. 144, No. 3, 1966, pp. 1216–1218.

Sagan, Carl, and David Wallace. "A Search for Life on Earth at 100 Meter Resolution." *Icarus* (1971), p. 515.

Sagan, Carl, ed. *Communication with Extraterrestrial Intelligence*. Cambridge, Mass.: MIT Press, 1973.

Sagan, Carl, Tobias C. Owen, and Harlan J. Smith, eds. *Planetary Atmospheres*. New York: Springer-Verlag, 1971.

Sagan, Carl, and Thornton Page, eds. *UFO's: A Scientific Debate*. Ithaca, N.Y.: Cornell University Press, 1972.

Sagan, Dorion. "Partial Closure: Dorion Sagan Reflects on Carl." *Whole Earth Review*, Summer 1997, pp. 34-37.

Sagdeev, Roald. *The Making of a Soviet Scientist: My Adventures in Nuclear Fusion and Space from Stalin to Star Wars*. New York: Wiley, 1994.

Sage, Leslie. "Film Review: Aliens, Lies and Videotape." *Nature*, Aug. 14, 1997, p. 637.

Salisbury, Frank B., "Martian Biology." *Science*, Apr. 6, 1962, p. 17.

Sayre, Anne. *Rosalind Franklin and DNA*. New York: Norton, 1975.

Schick, Theodore, Jr., and Lewis Vaughn. *How to Think About Weird Things*. Mountain View, Calif.: Mayfield Publishing Co., 1995, 1999.

Schrödinger, Erwin. *What Is Life?: The Physical Aspect of the Living Cell*. New York: Macmillan, 1945.

Seaborg, Glenn. *The Plutonium Story: The Journals of Professor Glenn T. Seaborg 1939–1946*. Columbus, Ohio: Battelle Press, 1994.

Seaborg, Glenn T. (with Benjamin S. Loeb). *Kennedy, Khrushchev and the Test Ban*. Berkeley: University of California Press, 1981.

Seifer, Marc J. *The Life and Times of Nikola Tesla: Biography of a Genius*. Secaucus, N.J.: Carol Publishing, 1996.

Seitz, Russell. "An Incomplete Obituary." *Forbes*, Feb. 10, 1997, p. 123.

Shapiro, Edward S. *A Time for Healing: American Jewry since World War II*. Baltimore: Johns Hopkins University Press, 1992.

Shapiro, Robert. *Origins: A Skeptic's Guide to the Creation of Life on Earth*. New York: Summit Books, 1986.

———. *Planetary Dreams*. New York: Wiley, 1999.

Sheehan, William. *Planets and Perception: Telescopic Views and Interpretations*. Tucson: University of Arizona Press, 1988.

Sheehan, William, and Thomas Dobbins. "Charles Boyer and the Clouds of Venus," *Sky & Telescope*, June 1994, pp. 56–60.

Shermer, Michael. *Why People Believe Weird Things: Pseudoscience, Superstition, and Other Confusions of Our Time*. New York: W. H. Freeman, 1997.

"Shivering Look at Venus." *Time*, Dec. 14, 1959, p. 52.

Shklovskii, I. S. *Five Billion Vodka Bottles to the Moon: Tales of a Soviet Scientist*. New York: W. W. Norton, 1991.

———— . "On the Nature of the Luminescence of the Crab Nebula" (1953). In Kenneth R. Lang and Owen Gingerich, *A Source Book in Astronomy and Astrophysics, 1900–1975*. Cambridge, Mass.: Harvard University Press, 1979.

Shklovskii, I. S., and Carl Sagan. *Intelligent Life in the Universe*. San Francisco: Holden-Day, 1966.

Shute, Nevil. *On the Beach*. New York: William Morrow, 1957.

Sill, G. T. "The Composition of the Ultraviolet Dark Markings on Venus." *Journal of Atmospheric Sciences*, vol. 32 (1975), pp. 1201–1204.

Silver, Daniel J. "God and Carl Sagan in Hollywood." *Commentary*, Sept. 1997, p. 52.

Simpson, G. G. *The Meaning of Evolution*. New Haven: Yale University Press, 1949.

———— . "The Nonprevalence of Humanoids." *Science*, Feb. 21, 1964, p. 769.

Singer, S. Fred. "Is 'Nuclear Winter' Real?" *Nature*, Oct. 10, 1985, p. 625.

Skinner, B. F. *Walden Two*. New York: Macmillan, 1948.

Smith, Crosbie, and M. Norton Wise. *Energy and Empire: A Biographical Study of Lord Kelvin*. New York: Cambridge University Press, 1989.

Smith, John Maynard, and Eörs Szathmáry. *The Origins of Life: From the Birth of Life to the Origin of Language*. New York: Oxford University Press, 1999.

Smith, Robert W. *The Space Telescope: A Study of NASA, Science, Technology, and Politics*. New York: Cambridge University Press, 1989.

Smoot, George, and Keay Davidson. *Wrinkles in Time*. New York: William Morrow, 1993.

Snow, C. P. *The Two Cultures*. New York: Cambridge University Press, 1993.

"Spaced Out." *Time*, Jan. 21, 1974, p. 74.

Sparks, Brad. "Flat-Earth Sagan Falls Off the End of the World." *National Review*, Nov. 15, 1985.

Spudis, Paul D. *The Once and Future Moon*. Washington, D.C.: Smithsonian Institution Press, 1996.

Stapledon, Olaf. *Last and First Men, and Star Maker*. New York: Dover, 1968.

" 'Star Wars' & the Scientists: An Exchange." *Commentary*, Mar. 1985, pp. 6–11.

Stein, Gordon. *Encyclopedia of the Paranormal*. Amherst, N.Y.: Prometheus Books, 1996.

Steiner, Barry H. *Bernard Brodie and the Foundations of American Nuclear Strategy*. Lawrence: University Press of Kansas, 1991.

Stone, I. F. *The Haunted Fifties: 1953–1963*. New York: Random House, 1963.

Strughold, Hubertus. *The Green and Red Planet: A Physiological Study of the Possibility of Life on Mars*. Albuquerque: University of New Mexico Press, 1953.

Sullivan, Walter. *Assault on the Unknown: The International Geophysical Year*. New York: McGraw-Hill, 1961.

———— . "Astronomer Fears Hostile Attack; Would Keep Life on Earth a Secret." *New York Times*, Nov. 4, 1976.

———— . *We Are Not Alone: The Continuing Search for Extraterrestrial Intelligence*. New York: Dutton, 1993.

———— . *We Are Not Alone: The Search for Intelligent Life on Other Worlds*. New York: McGraw-Hill, 1964.

Swift, David W. *SETI Pioneers: Scientists Talk About Their Search for Extraterrestrial Intelligence*. Tucson: University of Arizona Press, 1990.

"Target Venus—There May Be Life There." *Life*, Dec. 21, 1959, p. 67.

"Taking Stock of Saddam's Fiery Legacy in Kuwait." *Science*, Aug. 30, 1991, p. 971.

Tatarewicz, Joseph N. *Space Technology and Planetary Astronomy*. Bloomington: Indiana University Press, 1990.

Taylor, Michael Ray. *Dark Life: Martian Nanobacteria, Rock-Eating Cave Bugs, and Other Extreme Organisms of Inner Earth and Outer Space*. New York: Scribner, 1999.

Teller, Edward. "Widespread After-Effects of Nuclear War." *Nature*, Aug. 23, 1984, p. 621.

Teres, Harvey. *Renewing the Left: Politics, Imagination and the New York Intellectuals*. New York: Oxford University Press, 1996.

Terry, Jennifer, and Melodie Calvert, eds. *Processed Lives: Gender and Technology in Everyday Life*. New York: Routledge, 1997.

Terzian, Yervant, and Elizabeth Bilson, eds. *Carl Sagan's Universe*. New York: Cambridge University Press, 1997.

Thomas, Lewis. "Nuclear Winter, Again." *Discover*, Oct. 1984, p. 57.

———. "TTAPS for the Earth." *Discover*, Feb. 1984, p. 30.

Thompson, Philip D., and Robert O'Brien, *Weather*. New York: Time Inc., 1965.

Thomson, David. *Biographical Dictionary of Film*. 3d ed. New York: Knopf, 1994.

Thorne, Kip S. *Black Holes & Time Warps: Einstein's Outrageous Legacy*. New York: W. W. Norton, 1994.

Tibbits, George. "Science Popularizer Carl Sagan, Dead at 62." Associated Press story, Dec. 20, 1966.

Time-Life Books. *Between the Stars*. New York: Time-Life Inc., 1990.

Tipler, Frank. "Additional Remarks on Extraterrestrial Intelligence." *QJRAS*, 1981, pp. 279–292.

———. "A Brief History of the Extraterrestrial Life Concept." *QJRAS*, 1981, pp. 133–145.

———. "Extraterrestrial Intelligent Beings Do Not Exist" *QJRAS*, 1980, pp. 267–281.

———. *The Physics of Immortality: Modern Cosmology, God and the Resurrection of the Dead*. New York: Doubleday, 1994.

Toon, O. B. "Environments of Earth and Other Worlds." In Yervant Terzian and Elizabeth Bilson, eds., *Carl Sagan's Universe* (1997), p. 56.

Tucker, Wallace and Karen. *The Cosmic Inquirers: Modern Telescopes and Their Makers*. Cambridge, Mass.: Harvard University Press, 1986.

Turner, Stansfield. *Caging the Nuclear Genie: An American Challenge for Global Security*. Boulder, Colo.: Westview Press, 1997.

Ungar, Sheldon. *The Rise and Fall of Nuclearism: Fear and Faith as Determinants of the Arms Race*. University Park: Pennsylvania State University Press, 1992.

Updike, John. "Who Wants to Know?" *New Yorker*, Aug. 22, 1977, p. 87.

Urey, Harold. "Lifelike Forms in Meteorites." *Science*, Aug. 24, 1962, p. 623.

———. *The Planets: Their Origin and Development*. New Haven: Yale University Press, 1952.

Vallee, Jacques. *Forbidden Science: Journals 1957–1969*. New York: Marlowe and Co., 1996.

Van Horne, Harriet. "Johnny Carson: The Battle for TV's Midnight Millions." *Look*, July 11, 1967, p. 78.

VanHoose, Linda. "High School Starts Scholarship in Memory of Space Scientist." *Lexington Herald-Leader* (Lexington, Ky.), June 25, 1997.

Velikovsky, Immanuel. "The Dreams Freud Dreamed." *Psychoanalytic Review*, October 1941, p. 487.

———. *Worlds in Collision*. New York: Doubleday, 1950.

"Velikovsky and the AAAS: Worlds in Collision." *Science News*, Mar. 2, 1974, p. 132.

"Venus: Nice Place to Live?" *Newsweek*, Apr. 10, 1961, p. 67.

"Venus Says 'No.'" *New York Times*, Feb. 26, 1963, p. 8.

Verschuur, Gerrit L. *Interstellar Matters: Essays on Curiosity and Astronomical Discovery*. New York: Springer-Verlag, 1989.

———. *The Invisible Universe Revealed: The Story of Radio Astronomy*. New York: Springer-Verlag, 1987.

———— . "A Search for Narrow Band 21-cm Wavelength Signals from Ten Nearby Stars." *Icarus* (1973), p. 329.

Wali, Kameshwar C. *Chandra: A Biography of S. Chandrasekhar.* Chicago: University of Chicago Press, 1991.

Walker, Russell G., and Carl Sagan. "The Ionospheric Model of the Venus Microwave Emission: An Obituary." *Icarus*, 1966, vol. 5, p. 107.

Watson, James. *The Double Helix: A Personal Account of the Discovery of the Structure of DNA.* New York: Atheneum, 1968.

Weinraub, Bernard. "Using a Big Budget to Ask Big Questions." *New York Times*, July 6, 1997, section II, pp. 1 and 9.

Weissman, Paul R., Lucy-Ann McFadden, and Torrence V. Johnson. *Encyclopedia of the Solar System.* San Diego: Academic Press, 1999.

Weldon, Stephen Prugh. "The Humanist Enterprise from John Dewey to Carl Sagan: A Study of Science and Religion in American Culture." Ph.D. diss., University of Wisconsin, 1997.

Wells, H. G. *Mind at the End of Its Tether.* London: William Heinemann Ltd., 1945.

Wendell, Carolyn. "The Alien Species: A Study of Women Characters in the Nebula Award Winners, 1965–1973." *Extrapolation*, Winter 1979, pp. 343–354.

Wenger, Beth S. *New York Jews and the Great Depression.* New Haven: Yale University Press, 1996.

West, Paul. *Life with Swan: A Novel.* New York: Scribner, 1999.

Westfall, Richard S. *Never at Rest: A Biography of Isaac Newton.* New York: Cambridge University Press, 1980.

White, Andrew Dickson. *A History of the Warfare of Science with Theology.* 2 vols. New York: Dover, 1960.

White, Leslie A. *The Evolution of Culture: The Development of Civilization to the Fall of Rome.* New York: McGraw-Hill, 1959.

Wiesel, Elie. *Night.* New York: Hill & Wang, 1960.

Wilford, John Noble. "In 'Contact,' Science and Fiction Nudge Closer Together." *New York Times*, July 20, 1997, section II, p. 14.

Wilhelms, Don E. *To a Rocky Moon: A Geologist's History of Lunar Exploration.* Tucson: University of Arizona Press, 1993.

Wilk, Gerard H. "The Meteoric Velikovsky." *Commentary*, Apr. 1952, p. 380.

Wills, Christopher. *The Runaway Brain: The Evolution of Human Uniqueness.* New York: Basic Books, 1993.

Winkler, Allan M. *Life under a Cloud: American Anxiety about the Atom.* New York: Oxford University Press, 1993.

Wittner, Lawrence S. *One World or None.* Stanford, Calif., Stanford University Press, 1993.

———— . *Resisting the Bomb.* Stanford, Calif., Stanford University Press, 1997.

Wolfe, Tom. *The Right Stuff.* New York: Farrar, Straus, & Giroux, 1979.

Zoglin, Richard. "Science on TV: How Sharp Is the Focus?" *New York Times*, Apr. 26, 1981, section 2, p. 31.

Index

521